Dear Students,

Welcome to what might be a new area of study for you. We hope you find it as fascinating as we did when we were first introduced to young adult literature at the University of Iowa two generations ago. Among the things we like about it is the fact that it is a relatively new field of scholarly study and so newcomers are welcome to the field. While we were still graduate students, we were reviewing books and writing articles and helping to decide which books should be purchased by libraries and brought into English and reading classrooms.

Another positive aspect is that most of the writers are contemporary and so even when authors are writing historical fiction, fantasy, poetry, and science fiction, their books treat issues and concerns that are important to today's young readers. We love getting to know YA authors both as writers and as interesting speakers and friends.

We have taken the following steps to prepare this book so that you will want to keep it as a reference and a resource for your future work.

- We have made it comprehensive to give you guidelines for judging books across a wide spectrum ranging from the serious problem novel (even those written as graphic novels or poems) to humorous writings including parodies, satires, and exaggerations, and to nonfiction books including biographies, memoirs, and information books. While in the future many of the individual titles will change, the principles of evaluation will stay the same.

- And even with individual titles, we have been conscious of the need to write mainly about books that will last. This is why we rely not only on our own preferences, but also on the judgments of respected book reviewers, editors, and awards committees. The books on the Honor List: The Best of the Best, 1980–2007 (see Chapter 1) will be around long after we are gone.

- As you read the chapters and discuss them with classmates, we hope you will highlight sentences and the titles of books that resonate with you and that you will make margin notes about books that your classmates enjoyed, but that you did not yet have time to read. Of course, we have written about many more books than any one person can read in a semester and so we hope you will keep this textbook as a guide to your future reading—a wish list for continuing pleasure.

- We have supplemented the Title Index with the names of the authors and the original publishers and dates of publication. Such information is invaluable in helping you "place" books in the era in which they were written, but it is not information easily available because marketers, who wish to appear up to date, highlight the most recent year in which a book was reprinted.

In conclusion, please do not let what we—or other reviewers—say about various books substitute for your own reading. Our goal is to guide you to make good use of whatever time you have for reading. However, to speak knowledgeably about young adult literature, you need to have an extensive background of your own reading. We hope our book nudges you in that direction both for now and for the future.

Sincerely,

Alleen P. Nilsen

Ken Donelson

Literature for Today's Young Adults

EIGHTH EDITION

Alleen Pace Nilsen

Arizona State University

Kenneth L. Donelson

Arizona State University

Boston • New York • San Francisco
Mexico City • Montreal • Toronto • London • Madrid • Munich • Paris
Hong Kong • Singapore • Tokyo • Cape Town • Sydney

Executive Editor: *Aurora Martínez Ramos*
Series Editorial Assistant: *Kara Kikel*
Executive Marketing Manager: *Krista Clark*
Production Editor: *Annette Joseph*
Editorial Production Service: *Publishers' Design and Production Services, Inc.*
Composition Buyer: *Linda Cox*
Manufacturing Buyer: *Megan Cochran*
Electronic Composition: *Publishers' Design and Production Services, Inc.*
Interior Design: *Denise Hoffman*
Cover Administrator: *Kristina Mose-Libon*

For related titles and support materials, visit our online catalog at
www.pearsonhighered.com.

Between the time website information is gathered and then published, it is not unusual for
some sites to have closed. Also, the transcription of URLs can result in typographical errors.
The publisher would appreciate notification where these errors occur so that they may be
corrected in subsequent editions.

Library of Congress Cataloging-in-Publication Data
Nilsen, Aleen Pace.
    Literature for today's young adults / Aleen Pace Nilsen, Kenneth L. Donelson. — 8th ed.
        p.   cm.
    Authors' names appear in reverse order in 7th ed.
    Includes bibliographical references and index.
    ISBN-13: 978-0-205-59323-1 (alk. paper)
    ISBN-10: 0-205-59323-2
    1. Teenagers—Books and reading—United States.   2. Young adult literature—History
and criticism.   3. Young adult fiction—History and criticism.   4. Young adult
literature—Bibliography.   5. Young adult fiction—Bibliography.   I. Donelson, Kenneth L.
II. Title.

Z1037.A1D578 2008
028.5'5—dc22   2008002625

Printed in the United States of America

10 9 8 7 6 5 4 3 2 1 RRD-MO 12 11 10 09 08

Photo credits and acknowledgments appear on pages 453–454, which constitute an
extension of the copyright page.

**Allyn & Bacon
is an imprint of**

www.pearsonhighered.com

To the memory of
Our dear friend and teacher,

G. Robert Carlson,

1917–2003

*And to our grandchildren
and great-grandchildren,*
Who are happily finding many of these books:

From Alleen

to

Taryn, Britton, Kami, Erich, David, Lauren,

Michael, Jenna, Avery,

Jim, and Luke

From Ken

to

Kayden, Haylee, Emiley, and Dylann

Ken Donelson and Alleen Nilsen, professors of English at Arizona State University, became friends and colleagues before they met each other. They both earned their Ph.D. degrees at the University of Iowa from G. Robert Carlsen, a pioneer in the field of young adult literature. Ken was Carlsen's first Ph.D. student, with Alleen coming along a decade later. When Alleen and her husband moved to Arizona State in 1973, one of the first people she visited was Ken because Professor Carlsen had talked about him in class and had recruited Alleen as a writer for the *Arizona English Bulletin*, which Ken was editing.

Nevertheless, Professor Carlsen was surprised when his two former students, who happened to find themselves in the same part of the country, started working together because he thought they were so different. Ken writes like a historian, focusing on what's old, while Alleen writes like a journalist, focusing on what's new. And while Ken was a leader in fighting censorship, Alleen was a leader in fighting sexist language, which some people interpret as a form of censorship. She is the one who suggested they take turns with whose name goes first on each edition.

In spite of their differences, what they learned from Professor Carlsen brought them together in support of the academic study of young adult literature. In 1973, they helped found ALAN (Assembly on Literature for Adolescents of NCTE); both have received ALAN's Award for "Outstanding Contributions to the Field of Young Adult Literature," and both served as presidents of ALAN. In 1974, they were the founding editors of *The ALAN Newsletter*, the forerunner of what is now *The ALAN Review*.

After proving that they respected each other and could work together, they applied to be coeditors of the *English Journal*, a job they held from 1980 to 1987 when they wrote the first edition of *Literature for Today's Young Adults*. Thanks to Ken's knowledge of history and his interest in censorship, the book was more complete than other textbooks of the time which mostly focused on realistic problem novels—books sometimes identified as *bildungsroman* or *apprenticeship* novels—which are still the books most obviously identified as YA. But what Ken and Alleen demonstrated was that every genre, from adventure and biography to mysteries, fantasy, poetry, and the supernatural, were being written for teenagers and deserved a place in schools and libraries. And because Alleen's first job at Arizona State University was teaching in the Department of Library Science in the College of Education, it seemed natural for them to bring in the work of librarians and reading teachers as well as of English teachers.

What has kept *Literature for Today's Young Adults* the leading textbook in the field is the authors' continuing love and enthusiasm for their chosen field of study. For each edition they have highlighted new and interesting trends and illustrated them with lively discussions of well-written books. It has helped that they are well-rounded scholars and have remained active in education as a whole.

Ken has published over five hundred articles, mostly on censorship, YA books, and problems in teaching secondary English reflecting his thirteen years of teaching high school English in Iowa. His articles, as well as others related to college teaching, have appeared in such journals as *Clearing House, English Journal, High School Journal*, and *School Library Journal*. Ken collected YA books published from 1850 through 1950 and when he retired from ASU he donated some eight hundred historical YA books and a nearly complete run of *The Dime Novel Round-Up* to ASU's Hayden Library. The collection is strong in books by Kirk Munroe, Ralph Henry Barbour, and John Tunis, and in two Stratemeyer Literary Syndicate heroes, Tom Swift and Nancy Drew.

Alleen has worked with her husband, linguistics Professor Don L. F. Nilsen, to promote a new approach to the teaching of vocabulary, as explained in *Vocabulary Plus: High School and Up: A Source-Based Approach* and *Vocabulary Plus K–8: A Source-Based Approach* (Pearson, 2004). Their *Encyclopedia of 20th-Century American Humor* (Oryx/Greenwood) was chosen by the American Library Association as one of the twenty best reference books published in 2000. In 2007, they published *Names and Naming in Young Adult Literature* as part of the Scarecrow Series in Young Adult Literature, edited by Patty Campbell. Alleen is also the author of *Joan Bauer*, the first book in Greenwood Press's series Teen Reads: Student Companions to Young Adult Literature (2007), edited by James Blasingame.

Brief Contents

Contents

part two
Modern Young Adult Reading   111

chapter 7   Fantasy, Science Fiction, Utopias, and Dystopias   215

chapter 8   History and History Makers: Of People and Places   243

chapter 9   Nonfiction: Information, Literary Nonfiction, Biographies, and Self-Help Books   277

Special Features

Honor List

Young Adult Authors Speak Out

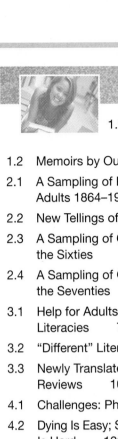

Focus Boxes

Film Boxes

We began our first preface back in 1980 with these words: "We had many reasons for writing this book, but chief among them was our belief that it was needed and worth doing." We believed in those words then and we believe in them now. We hope that our eighth edition will continue to answer the needs of teachers and librarians, neophytes and old-hands alike.

One of the saddest parts of growing old—other than watching the Cubs blow their race over and over—is watching literary tastes change and once-favored books slowly go out of fashion and drop off recommended reading lists. Today, for example, we have writers as fine as these being avidly read and recommended: David Almond, Laurie Halse Anderson, M. T. Anderson, Kimberly Willis Holt, John Green, David Klass, Stephenie Myers, Nancy Werlin, Ellen Wittinger, and Markus Zusak. And some writers continue to write books that win praise and readers: Avi, Joan Bauer, Aidan Chambers, Chris Crutcher, Nancy Farmer, Nancy Garden, Diana Wynne Jones, Ursula K. Le Guin, Robert Lipsyte, Walter Dean Myers, Gary Paulsen, Richard Peck, and Vivian Vande Velde.

All that's to the good. It's great to have new authors hit new notes and standard authors continue to produce provocative books. But what of the once-reliable writers who were constantly on the lists of worthwhile young adult books? What of the writers who, once hot, are increasingly forgotten? What of the Norma Kleins or the M. E. Kerrs? And what of writers as fine as: Alice Childress, James Forman, Bette Green, Rosa Guy, Isabelle Holland, Mildred Lee, Margaret Mahy, Zibby Oneal, Todd Strasser, Julian F. Thompson, and John Rowe Townsend?

Ten of Ken's favorites whom we rarely see mentioned today are Nancy Bond, Bruce Clements, John Donovan, Jane Gardam, Monica Hughes, Irene Hunt, Sandra Scoppettone, Walter Wangerin, Barbara Wersba, and Robert Westall. And he is more than a trifle irritated about the fact that Harry Mazer's *The Island Keeper* is out of print. The way young adult literature is marketed is a major concern for all of us.

In a preface, it's customary to mention lots of names—graduate assistants, members of the department who have contributed this or that, graduate students who are doing wondrous things. We'll do that in a few moments.

First, we'd like to list some names that rarely get mentioned, unless it's as footnotes. We're referring to critics and historians and commentators of all sorts, people who have written about young adult (YA) literature and who have taught us to be critical and to recognize what is worth knowing about YA literature and what is ephemeral, what is new and flashy and what is sound and worth knowing. We say this knowing that individual critics may not recognize what Nilsen and Donelson learn from them, but we say sincerely that we have read and learned from all of them, and we truly believe that our writing—not necessarily this book but whatever we have under way—is the better for having read these good people. In alphabetical order, we salute them: Gillian Avery, Dorothy Broderick, Mary Cadogan, Michael Cart, Aidan Chambers, Mary K. Chelton, Sheila Egoff, Jerry Griswold, Peter Hunt, Fred Inglis, Deidre Johnson, Monica Kiefer, Teri S. Lesesne, Anne Scott MacLeod, Cathi Dunn MacRae, Maria Nikolajeva, Bob Probst, David Rees, Hazel Rochman, William Sloane, Bob Small, Mary F. Thwaite, and John Rowe Townsend.

We saved one name for special commendation for all she's contributed to young adult literature. Patty Campbell has done so much for so many people it is difficult to mention specifics, but here are a few of her accomplishments. Her columns in the *Wilson Library Bulletin* and the *Horn Book Magazine* have made her one of the most quoted writers in our field. Her editing of the Twayne Young Adult Writers series and the Scarecrow Studies in Young Adult Literature has provided work on authors and topics valuable to us and to our students. We are sure there are things she cannot do, but we have no idea what they are.

Anyone who has read in the history of English education will recognize how much we owe the spirits of four great master teachers and writers, four people who were devoted to young students and their literature—Samuel Thurber, Dora V. Smith, Lou LaBrant, and Dwight Burton. Without them and their words there would never have been a reason for a book like this.

Another group, one even closer to heart and home, is made up of friends and colleagues we have known over the years from our work at the University of Iowa, Arizona State University, and in the National Council of Teachers of English, the Conference on English Education, ALAN, the International Reading Association, and assorted other groups. Here are a few people, some now gone, a coterie who meant much to us. We worked with them and argued with them and learned from them—and maybe they even learned from us: Dick Abrahamson, Bruce Appleby, Jackie Cronin, Chris Crowe, Hazel Davis, Bryant Fillion, Don Gallo, Beverly Haley, Bob Harvey, Ted Hipple, Terry Ley, Ben and Beth Nelms, Maia Pank Mertz, Bill Ojala, Linda Shadiow, John Simmons, David Sohn, Diane Tuccillo, Anne Webb, Jerry and Helen Weiss, and Carol Williams.

And now to thank the people here at ASU who helped with this eighth edition, we need to mention our Department Chair Neal Lester and our colleague James Blasingame. Erika L. Watt served as an amazing editorial assistant, doing everything from tallying the results of our survey, to gathering photos and permissions and even posing for pictures herself (see p. 425). The teachers and student teachers who administered our survey include Nicole Ainsworth, Bekka Besich, Jeri Brimhall, Kate Copic, Cynthia Kiefer, Frank Machado, and Jessica Zellner. We also thank Nichole Gilbert from the Young Adult Library Services Association of ALA for helping us obtain author photos.

And again we thank Aurora Martínez, the executive editor at Allyn and Bacon, who supported us on this edition, along with the reviewers that she arranged for. We are grateful for the guidance of Beverly J. Hearn, University of Tennessee at Martin; Raymond P. Kettel, University of Michigan–Dearborn; Carol B. Tanksley, University West Florida; and Joy L. Wiggins, University of Texas at Arlington. Thanks to their suggestions, we made the following changes:

- We devoted one page to the winners of the Margaret A. Edwards Award, which is given annually to an author in honor of a significant contribution to young adult literature. The award is sponsored by the *School Library Journal* and the Young Adult Library Services Association of the American Library Association. We were happy to do this as a reflection of how much growth has taken place in our field over the last two decades.

- Because of devoting these twenty pages to the Edwards Award winners, we invited fewer other authors to contribute statements, but we are pleased at the variety and the content of those who allowed us to use some of their words: Our thanks to Laurie Halse Anderson, Michael Cart, Stefanie Craig, James Cross Giblin, Kimberly Willis Holt, Cynthia Leitich Smith, Aaron Levy, Pat Mora, Naomi Shihab Nye, and Vivian Vande Velde.

- Again we tried to cut down on the length of transitional material by moving more books out of paragraphs and into focus boxes or time lines.

- Over Ken's objections, we moved even more of his material on films to our website, not because we disagree that film can be a wonderful teaching tool but because teachers tell us that in today's schools the study of full-length films has virtually disappeared.

- And also to save space, we cut down on the printing of the kinds of things that change rapidly and that can easily be found through Internet searches; for example, the addresses and prices of popular magazines and other URLs that are likely to change.

- In hopes of gaining some insights into just what people mean when they talk about "new literacies," we conducted a fairly extensive survey with 266 students attending various high schools and one junior high school in the metropolitan Phoenix area. We also launched a Media Watch during the first four months of 2007. See Chapters 3 and 10 for what we learned.

- And of course we have tried to find and include information on worthy new books, but we will be the first to admit that just because we haven't included a particular book in our discussions or focus boxes, you should not dismiss it from consideration. The field is so lively, with so many good books coming out, that we could not possibly have found them all.

We've often told our friends that while writing this textbook is a labor of love, it hangs over our heads sort of like the Golden Gate Bridge, which we've been told is constantly being repainted because as soon as the painters get to the end, it's time for them to go back and start scraping the rust from the other end. If we've missed some spots here and there, please forgive us, but also know that we will be happy to hear from readers so that we can make additions and corrections.

As a good-luck talisman, we will end by repeating the quote from Edward Salmon, which we started out with when it was only 90 years old. We agree with its sentiments even more now that it is closer to 120 years old.

It is no uncommon thing to hear children's literature condemned as wholly bad, and some people are good enough to commiserate with me on having waded through so much ephemeral matter. It may be my fault or my misfortune not to be able to see my loss. I have spent many pleasant and I may say not unprofitable hours in company with the printed thoughts of Mr. Kingston, Mr. Ballantye, Mr. Henry, Jules Verne, Miss Alcott, Miss Meade, Mrs. Molesworth, Miss Doudney, Miss Yonge, and a dozen others, and hope to spend as many more in the time to come as a busy life will permit. ("Should Children Have a Special Literature?" *The Parents' Review* 1 [June 1890]: 339)

And that, really, is why we are happy to have been given the privilege of writing—and rewriting—this textbook.

Alleen Pace Nilsen
Kenneth L. Donelson

Young Adults and Their Reading

chapter

1

"Of all passages, coming of age, or reaching adolescence is the purest, in that it is the loneliest. In birth one is not truly conscious; in marriage one has a partner, even death is faced with a life's experience by one's side," wrote David Van Biema for a special issue of *Life* magazine devoted to *The Journey of Our Lives*.

He went on to explain that going from boy or girl to man or woman is "a huge leap on the slimmest of information." The person who fails grows older without growing wiser and faces ostracism, insanity, or profound sorrow. Because such a debilitated or warped individual is a "drag on the community," the community bands together with the young person to see that the journey is accomplished.[1]

Life would go more smoothly if young people's aspirations were simply to step into the roles of their parents. The job of growing up, however, is more demanding because, at the same time that young people are trying to become adults, they are also trying to show that they are different from their parents. This leaves each generation scrambling to find its own way to be unique, which is one of the reasons that literature for young adults tends to be a contemporary medium. Each generation wants its own stories. See Film Box 1.1 on page 2 for some of these stories told on the screen.

What Is Young Adult Literature?

We have heard *young adults* defined as those who think they're too old to be children but who others think are too young to be adults. In this book, we

The World of Young Adults

American Graffiti (1973, color, 112 min., PG; Director: George Lucas; with Richard Dreyfus, Ron Howard, and Cindy Williams) Here is high school graduation in 1962 and what a few students learn about the real world.

Bend It Like Beckham (2003, color, 112 min., PG-13; Director: Gurindor Chadha; with Parminder Nagra) In this British film, Jess is an Anglo-Indian teenager who has grown up in London and loves soccer, but her traditional Sikh parents don't want her to play.

The Breakfast Club (1985, color, 97 min., R; Director: John Hughes; with Emilio Estevez, Judd Nelson, Molly Ringwald, Anthony Michael Hall, and Ally Sheedy) Some critics credit Hughes with creating the genre of YA movies in this story about five rebellious teenagers assigned Saturday morning detention.

Fast Times at Ridgemont High (1982, color, 92 min., R; Director: Amy Heckerling; with Sean Penn, Jennifer Jason Leigh, and Judge Reinholdt) California high school students spend most of their time in the mall thinking about drugs and sex.

Finding Forrester (2001, color, 135 min., PG-13; Director: Gus Van Sant; with Sean Connery and Rob Brown) A reclusive writer serves as a friend and mentor to a basketball player on scholarship at an exclusive New York prep school.

Juno (2007, color, 92 min., PG-13; Director: Jason Reitman; with Ellen Page, Michael Cera, Jennifer Garner, Jason Bateman, Allison Janney, and J. K. Simmons) It wasn't the situation (a teen pregnancy) but the characterization that made Roger Ebert nominate *Juno* as the best film of 2007.

The Last Picture Show (1971, black and white, 114 min., R; Director: Peter Bogdanovich; with Jeff Bridges, Timothy Bottoms, Cybill Shepherd, Ben Johnson, and Cloris Leachman) From Larry McMurtry's novel, the death of a movie theater is a symbol of the dying of a small Texas town.

My Life as a Dog (1985, color, 101 min., NR; Director: Lasse Hallström; with Anton Glanzelius, Tomass von Brömssen, and Anki Liden) A twelve-year-old boy is sent to live with relatives in 1950s Sweden.

Napoleon Dynamite (2004, color, 90 min., PG-13; Director: Jared Hess; with Jon Heder, Jon Gries, and Elfren Ramirez) Part of the unexpected popularity of this indie film is its rural Idaho setting and the earnestness with which a geeky high school boy with the ironic name of Napoleon sets out to find success.

October Sky (1999, color, 107 min., PG; Director: Jake Gyllenhall; with Chris Cooper and Laura Dern) In this film from Homer Hickam's *Rocket Boy*, a boy growing up in a West Virginia coal-mining town sees *Sputnik* streaking in the skies and determines to build his own rocket.

The Outsiders (1983, color, 91 min., PG; Director: Francis Ford Coppola; with Matt Dillon, Rob Lowe, and Thomas Howell) S. E. Hinton's novel is about two teenage groups in 1960s Oklahoma—the social superiors and the greasers.

Real Women Have Curves (2002, color, 86 min., PG-13; Director: Patricia Cardoso; with America Ferrera and Lupe Ontiveros) A bright young Hispanic girl in Los Angeles wants to go to college, but her mother wants her to work in a dress factory, lose some weight, and get married.

Rushmore (1998, color, 97 min., R; Director: Wes Anderson; with Jason Schwartzmann, Bill Murray, and Olivia Williams) A schoolboy is near expulsion because he is in almost every possible school activity and has no time for his studies. He falls in love with a first-grade teacher.

Slums of Beverly Hills (1998, color, 93 min., R; Director: Tamara Jenkins; with Alan Arkin and Natasha Lyonne) A father moves his motherless family first to this place and then that in Beverly Hills to give them a chance at a good education.

Whale Rider (2002, color, 101 min., PG-13; Director: Niki Caro; with Keisha Castle-Hughes) Filmed in Whangara and Auckland, New Zealand, this is a classic story of a young girl proving her worthiness to be a leader in modern Maori culture.

In addition to having young adult rooms and YA librarians, most libraries make an effort through programming and other services to show teenagers that they are no longer considered to be children, as with this invitation to join the Phoenix Public Library Teen Council.

Library Teen Council

Did you hear the news?

Library Teen Council
will be having 2 meetings
a month!
2nd Saturday monthly @ 2pm
4th Thursday monthly @ 4pm

Teen Central
Burton Barr Central Library
1221 N. Central Avenue, 4th Floor
Phoenix, AZ 85004

For details contact:
602.495.5114

www.phxteencentral.org

use the term to include students in junior high as well as those graduating from high school and still finding their way into adult life. By *young adult literature*, we mean anything that readers between the approximate ages of twelve and eighteen choose to read either for leisure reading or to fill school assignments. When we talk about *children's literature*, we refer to books released by the juvenile or junior division of a publisher and intended for children from prekindergarten to about sixth grade.

While our definition of *children's literature* is fairly standard, we should caution that not all educators define young adults the same as we do. The Educational Resources Information Clearinghouse (ERIC), for example, defines young adults as those between the ages of eighteen and twenty-two, whereas the National Assessment of Educational Progress (NAEP), administered by the Educational Testing Service, refers to "young adults, ages 21 through 25."

We confess to feeling pretentious when referring to a twelve- or thirteen-year-old as a *young adult*, but we shy away from using the term *adolescent literature* because as one librarian told us, "It has the ugly ring of pimples and puberty," and "it suggests *immature* in a derogatory sense." Still, many college courses in English departments are entitled Adolescent Literature, and because of our English teaching backgrounds, we find ourselves using the term for variety, along with *teenage books*, *teen fiction*, and *YA* or *young adult literature*. The terms *juvenile literature*, *junior novel*, *teen novel*, and *juvie* have been used in the past, but they became so weighed down with negative connotations that they are seldom heard today. Even with the newer terms of *young adult* and *YA*, some teenagers feel condescended to, so librarians and teachers are looking for alternatives. David Spritz, writing in *Time* magazine in 1999, used the term *teen fiction* for the genre that he said "used to be called" *young adult novels*.[2] While some librarians and bookstores have experimented with the term *popular literature*, at least in academic circles chances are that *young adult* is so firmly established that it will continue to be used for the near future. Anyone well acquainted with teenagers realizes that there is a tremendous difference between twelve-year-olds and seventeen-year-olds, or even between fourteen-year-olds and sixteen-year-olds. As teenagers are buying more books and publishers have become more interested in developing this market, a subcategory of young adult literature has developed. These are the books aimed primarily at students in junior high or middle school. Most Newbery Medal and Honor Book winners are written for the age level described as *tweeners*; see several examples in Focus Box 5.5, Books to Make Readers Smile (pp. 170–171).

Patty Campbell has described tweener books as fiction "hanging on to the literary coattails" of young adult fiction.[3] Tweener books sell better than "true" young adult fiction because in nearly every geographical area there are more middle school and junior high libraries than high school libraries. Also, this is an age in which adults (parents, grandparents, teachers, and librarians) are still purchasing books for young readers or at least having an influence on what they read. The books are, of course, shorter and simpler, and because they are about younger protagonists, the love relationships—and the language—are fairly innocent. This means the books are less likely to be censored.

Tweener books also are better fitted to series books because at least in the old-fashioned kind of series books, the protagonists resemble those in sitcoms. The story starts with the protagonist in a particular situation, then a complication occurs, which is solved as much through luck or help from outside as through the efforts of the protagonist. By the end, the situation is back to normal so that the protagonist is ready to be picked up and put into a similar, but slightly different story. This differs from "true" YA fiction because, as Patty Campbell explains,

> The central theme of most YA fiction is becoming an adult, finding the answer to the question "Who am I and what am I going to do about it?" No matter what events are going on in the book, accomplishing that task is really what the book is about, and in the climactic moment the resolution of the external conflict is linked to a realization for the protagonist that helps shape an adult identity.[4]

She then cited a Richard Peck statement that "the last page of every YA novel should say not, 'The End' but 'The Beginning.'"

As you will learn in Chapter 2, young adult literature has a relatively brief and unsettled heritage, and there are many disagreements about its quality and the role that it should play in modern schools, but on the positive side, such a changing field (see Michael Cart's statement) makes for a lively and interesting

Young Adult Authors Speak Out

Michael Cart on the Importance of Young Adult Literature

I was a teenager in the 1950s, a decade before what we regard as modern young adult fiction came into being with the 1967 publication of S. E. Hinton's *The Outsiders* and Robert Lipsyte's *The Contender*. For that reason I looked in vain for *my* face in the pages of books for young readers and, as a result, spent too many years thinking I was the only one of my kind and wondering what on earth was wrong with me. I was hardly unique in that, as I would discover years later when I would also realize there had been nothing whatsoever wrong with me. But how much easier my adolescent life would have been if only I could have read about me when I most urgently needed to. As a result, I have devoted my own career as a writer, reviewer, editor, and anthologist to creating and promoting books that give faces and fully realized lives to all young people but especially to those who have been invisible, overlooked, and neglected because of their sexual orientation, countries of national origin, religious beliefs, physical appearance, or personal idiosyncrasies—all of those, in short, who have been regarded as the outsiders, the other, and who, therefore, have been relegated to the darkest margins of society.

Teenagers urgently need books that speak with relevance and immediacy to their real lives and to their unique emotional, intellectual, and developmental needs and that provide a place of commonality of experience and mutual understanding, for in so doing, they bring the outsiders out of the darkness and into the light of community. But books can't do that unless their authors trust young readers with the truth, as the best writers—people like Robert Cormier, M. E. Kerr, Nancy Garden, Francesca Lia Block, Jacqueline Woodson, Adam Rapp, David Levithan, and others— have done and continue to do.

Since the mid-1990s something wonderful has happened to young adult literature. Not only has there been an explosion in the sheer quantity of new books being made available every year but also their quality has improved exponentially. For the first time, the term *young adult literature* can no longer be dismissed by its detractors as an oxymoron. Young adult literature has come of age, *as literature*. One has to look no further than to the establishment of the Michael L. Printz Award for evidence of that, for this is the first young adult book prize to be based solely on literary merit. Its recipients since its inception in 2000—Walter Dean Myers, David Almond, Angela Johnson, An Na, Aidan Chambers, Meg Rosoff, John Green, and Gene Yang—represent a "who's who" of contemporary YA authors. Like all of the best writers for young adults, their work offers a detailed map of the minds and hearts of young people everywhere. To say this reminds us that young readers need to see not only their own faces but also those of people who are different from them, for it's in this way that books show them not only the differences but also the commonalities that comprise their humanity.

By acquainting readers with the glorious varieties of the human experience, young adult literature invests young hearts and minds with tolerance, understanding, empathy, acceptance, compassion, kindness, and more. It civilizes them, in short, and for that reason I believe no other genre or literary form is as important. And that's why I am so deeply honored to be part of its world.

- Michael Cart is the author of *From Romance to Realism: 50 Years of Growth and Change in Young Adult Literature* (HarperCollins, 1996) and *My Father's Scar* (Simon & Schuster, 1996). He edits short-story collections including *Love and Sex: Ten Stories of Truth* (Simon & Schuster, 2001) and *Rush Hour: A Journal of Contemporary Voices* (Delacorte Press, 2004–2007).

It is a new level of sophistication for YA books to explore how different groups are crossing boundaries and learning about each other as shown in this cartoon illustration taken from Sherman Alexie's The Absolutely True Diary of a Part-Time Indian, *which won the 2007 National Book Award for young readers and the 2008 American Indian Youth Literature Award in young adult literature.*

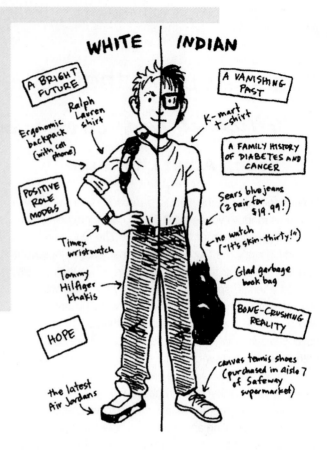

career for those of us working with books and young people. One thing that most people agree on is that those of us working in young adult literature should know and feel comfortable using the same literary terms that are used to talk about adult literature. We have, therefore, defined the main terms used throughout this textbook in Appendix A. Before going on to the other chapters, you might benefit from reviewing these terms to ensure that your understanding of them matches the way they are used throughout this textbook. Being comfortable using literary terms will:

- Give you terminology and techniques to use in sharing your insights with young readers.
- Help you gain insights into authors' working methods so that you get more out of your reading.
- Enable you to evaluate books and assist readers to move forward in developing the skills needed to further appreciate literature.
- Help you read reviews, articles, and critical analyses with greater understanding.

So many new books are published for young readers each year (nearly 5,000, with about one-fourth of them aimed at teenagers) that people who have preconceived ideas about what constitutes young adult literature can undoubtedly find examples to support whatever opinion they already hold. One illustration of the mixed feelings that people have is the argument that was waged in the Young Adult Library Services Association (YALSA), which is part of the American Library Association, before the 1998 establishment of the Alex Award, which each year honors ten titles published for a general adult audience but judged to have special appeal to young adults. The purpose is to help librarians encourage readers between the ages of twelve and eighteen "by introducing them to high-quality books written for adults." The award is named for Margaret Alexander Edwards, who, for her work during the 1940s and 1950s at the Enoch Pratt Free Library in Baltimore, is generally credited with being the first YA librarian.

A decade earlier, the Margaret A. Edwards Award had been established as a way to bring attention to an author who has made a lifetime contribution to literature for teenagers. The authors who have been so honored are each given their own page in this textbook. See S. E. Hinton's and Madeleine L'Engle's on pages 8 and 15, respectively. The winners are listed here in the order in which they received the award. (No award was given in 1989 when the ground rules were still being established.) Their pages are placed mostly in chapters related to the kind of writing they do.

- S. E. Hinton, 1988, see Ch. 1, page 8
- Richard Peck, 1990, see Ch. 8, page 275
- Robert Cormier, 1991, see Ch. 2, page 72
- Lois Duncan, 1992, see Ch. 6, page 207
- M. E. Kerr, 1993, see Ch. 10, page 331
- Walter Dean Myers, 1994, see Ch. 8, page 257
- Cynthia Voigt, 1995, see Ch. 4, page 137
- Judy Blume, 1996, see Ch. 2, page 74
- Gary Paulsen, 1997, see Ch. 6, page 187
- Madeleine L'Engle, 1998, see Ch. 1, page 15
- Anne McCaffrey, 1999, see Ch. 7, page 225
- Chris Crutcher, 2000, see Ch. 6, page 195
- Robert Lipsyte, 2001, see Ch. 6, page 197
- Paul Zindel, 2002, see Ch. 5, page 164
- Nancy Garden, 2003, see Ch. 12, page 414
- Ursula K. Le Guin, 2004, see Ch. 7, page 222
- Francesca Lia Block, 2005, Ch. 3, see page 82
- Jacqueline Woodson, 2006, see Ch. 11, page 371
- Lois Lowry, 2007, see Ch. 7, page 239
- Orson Scott Card, 2008, see Ch. 4, page 144

Margaret A. Edwards Award
Winner (1988)

S. E. Hinton, **The One Who Changed It All**

The Outsiders; *Rumblefish*; *Tex*; and *That Was Then, This Is Now* are the books that earned the very first Margaret A. Edwards Award for S. E. Hinton. Admittedly, our title is an exaggeration because no one person could have brought about all the changes that came to young adult literature in the late 1960s and early 1970s, but S. E. Hinton was at the right place at the right time to give the whole field a nudge that changed "the rules" about what was expected and what was possible in books published for teenagers.

After *The Outsiders* proved to be such a success, Hinton, who by the time it was published was nineteen, wrote in an August 27, 1967, article in the *New York Times Book Review*:

> The teenage years are a bad time. You're idealistic. You can see what should be. Unfortunately, you can see what is, too. You're disillusioned, but only a few take it as a personal attack. . . .
>
> Teen-agers know a lot today. Not just things out of a textbook, but about living. They know their parents aren't superhuman, they know that justice doesn't always win out, and that sometimes the bad guys win. They know that persons in high places aren't safe from corruption, . . . and that some people sell out. Writers needn't be afraid that they will shock their teen-age audience. But give them something to hang onto. Show that some people don't sell out, and that everyone can't be bought. Do it realistically. Earn respect by giving it.

The Outsiders spoke with such resonance to teenagers that in the spring of 1980, Jo Ellen Misakian, a librarian at the Lone Star K–8 School library in Fresno, California, mailed a copy of the book, a cover letter asking that the book be turned into a movie, and a petition signed by seventh- and eighth-grade students to film director Francis Ford Coppola. Coppola turned the letter over to his producer, Fred Roos, with instructions to "check it out." Three years later, on March 17, 1983, Roos and five of the young stars—Darren Dalton, Leif Garrett, Patrick Swayze, C. Thomas Howell, and Ralph Macchio—paid an official visit to the Lone Star School library to thank the students for suggesting the book. Star Matt Dillon arrived that night for the premier showing. Seventy-five of those who signed the petition and were now sophomores at Sanger High School came back for the celebration and to cheer their own credit line given at the end of the movie.

Hinton says that she has been lucky with the films of her books. She was invited to work with the producers on three of them. In 1983, when *Tex* was released, Gene Siskel and Roger Ebert did a special TV program about movies with young male protagonists. They cited *Tex* for being what the others only pretend to be—stories of growing up to be a man. They criticized the falseness of the male/female relationships shown in such movies as *Porky's*, *The Last American Virgin*, *Going All the Way*, *Spring Break*, *Homework*, *Class*, and *Private School*. In what they described as an epidemic of horny teenage movies, they pointed out how the boys never risk a real relationship. There is always a wall—either real or figurative—between them and the women they lust after. What is missing in these "lust/hate" relationships is affection, friendship, and honesty. They praised the line in *Tex* where big brother Mace confesses to fifteen-year-old Tex that he's never had sexual intercourse. The implication is that probably most of his friends haven't either and that it's generally unwise to believe everything one hears in locker rooms. Siskel and Ebert thought this bit of honesty was worth all the other movies put together.

On September 29, 2007, the Associated Press carried a long feature story written about Susan Eloise Hinton (who since 1970 has also been Mrs. David Inhofe) in celebration of the publication of a 40th anniversary edition of *The Outsiders*. Reporter Hillel Italie toured Tulsa with Hinton, who gladly pointed out landmarks from both the book and the 1983 film. At Will Rogers High School they visited the library where Hinton had sat while writing parts of the book and where her picture now sits in a glass case. Librarian Carrie Fleharty laughingly explained that she knows the book is still popular because so many students "forget" to bring it back. Hinton said it would "be a piece of cake" to write another book about Ponyboy, but not with the same passion she felt as a teenager so she doesn't want to interfere with the place he holds in the high school canon. She's now trying to write a "paranormal suspense" story for adults. She despises the newly fashionable "chick lit" because "It's just another version of 'Mary Jane Goes to the Prom.' . . . It's all about the boys." ●

Librarians, who voted against the idea of the additional Alex awards, were questioning the wisdom of moving teenagers out of YA books and into adult literature as fast as possible. Fans of YA literature point out that once students start reading adult books, they are unlikely to return to YA books. The situation is similar to that of parents who take pride in sending their fifth and sixth graders to Saturday morning "Great Books" programs where they struggle through some of the greatest and longest classics in the English language. In our university classes in children's literature, we sometimes meet students who have had such an experience, and they are amazed—and often resentful—at how much pleasure they missed by being forced into struggling through books that they did not have the life experience to understand and appreciate when they could have been reading wonderful "classics" written for children.

As shown by the fact that throughout the chapters in this book, and even on the Honor List, we include some books that were published for general adult audiences but "adopted" by teen readers, we do not believe in limiting high school students to YA books. But we do believe in letting young people know that some wonderful authors have written books across many different genres that focus on the kinds of experiences and emotions they are likely to relate to. This is why when we assign our college students to choose books for individual reading related to the chapters of this textbook (except for Chapter 2 which includes many books published before there were official young adult divisions in publishing houses) we ask them to read books that the publishers have marketed as YA. When students argue that they know teenagers who are reading whatever "adult" book they want to count, we assure them that we do, too, but since this is probably the only class they will ever take where the focus is on books specifically directed to young adults, we want them to read those books.

A Word about Spoilers

Another complaint we occasionally get is from people saying that we have broken a cardinal rule by giving away the ending of a book and have therefore *spoiled* their desire to read the book. Of course we do not want to go around "spoiling" people's pleasure as they read some of the books we recommend. But on the other hand, there is a difference between our goals in writing a textbook for professionals and the goals of teachers and librarians who give booktalks and newspaper and magazine writers who write reviews. Such people are probably communicating about only five or six books in hopes of inspiring their listeners or readers to pick up one of the books and begin reading. We, on the other hand, are writing about more than a thousand books, many more than even the most ambitious of you will be able to read within the next year or so. One of the benefits of taking a class in young adult literature is that both from what we write in our textbook and from what you hear from your instructor and from your fellow students, you will be able to give honest information to students about many more books than you have "personally" read. And to do this, you sometimes need to know the ending.

We are not saying that you should *spoil* a book by telling a potential reader everything you know about the story, but that as a responsible adult making recommendations to individual students, there are often things you need to know and so, yes, we do sometimes give away the endings. But in our own defense, we also want to say that the more you read, the more your pleasure will come not so much from being surprised at how a book ends but from your recognition of all the things the author did to bring you as the reader to the end of the story. As discussed in the following section, "Stages of Literary Appreciation," reading is similar to a journey where what you experience along the way is often as important as what you experience at your final destination.

A July 2007 *Time* magazine article entitled "Harry Potter and the Sinister Spoilers," by Lev Grossman and Andrea Sachs, hinted that the "Azkaban-level security" measures that were being taken to keep the plot of *Harry Potter and the Deathly Hallows* secret was more of a marketing ploy than an understanding of what reading is all about. If all readers care about is the ending, then "why would they turn out in such numbers to see the movie versions of the book?" They went on to explain:

> People read books for any number of reasons; finding out how the story ends is one among many and not even the most important. If it were otherwise, nobody would ever bother to read a book twice. Reading is about spending time with characters and entering a fictional world and playing with words and living through a story page by page. The idea that someone could ruin a novel by revealing its ending is like saying you could ruin the *Mona Lisa* by revealing that it's a picture of a woman with a center part. Spoilers are a myth; they don't spoil. No elaborate secrecy campaign is going to make *Harry Potter and the Deathly Hallows* any better than it already is, and no website could possibly make it useless and boring.[5]

Stages of Literary Appreciation

The development of literary appreciation begins long before children learn to read. Table 1.1, Stages of Literary Appreciation, presents an approximation of how individuals develop the personal attitudes and the reading, watching, and listening skills that are a necessary part of literary appreciation. The table should be read from the bottom up because each level is built on the one below it. We used to draw it as a wedding cake, but this cut down on how much information we could put on the page. Our reason for the wedding cake shape was to illustrate that the levels get increasingly smaller. There are dropouts all the way along, with many people never rising to even the level of losing themselves in a good story, much less coming to appreciate the aesthetics of particularly well-done presentations of drama, film, or writing. People do not go through these stages of development; instead they add on so that at each level they have all that they had before plus a new way to gain pleasure and understanding (see also the discussion of teaching literature in Chapter 11).

TABLE 1.1 Stages of Literary Appreciation

Read this chart from the bottom up to trace the stages of development most commonly found in reading the autobiographies of adults who love to read.

Level	Optimal Age	Stage	Sample Literary Materials	Sample Actions
7	Adulthood to death	Aesthetic appreciation	• Classics • Significant contemporary books • Drama • Film	• Reads constantly • Dreams of writing the great American novel • Enjoys literary and film criticism • Reads many books a year • Sees plays • Revisits favorites
6	College	Reading widely	• Best-sellers • Acclaimed novels, poems, plays, films, magazines	• Talks about books and films with friends • Joins a book club • Gathers books to take on vacation
5	High school	Venturing beyond self	• Science fiction • Social issues fiction • Forbidden material • "Different" stories	• Begins buying own books • Sees movies with friends • Gets reading suggestions from friends • Reads beyond school assignments
4	Junior high	Finding oneself in literature	• Realistic fiction • Contemporary problem novels • Wish-fulfilling stories	• Hides novels inside textbooks to read during classes • Stays up at night reading • Uses reading as an escape from social pressures
3	Late elementary	Losing oneself in literature	• Series books • Fantasies • Animal stories • Anything one can disappear into • Comic books	• Reads while doing chores • Reads while traveling • Makes friends with a librarian • Checks books out regularly • Gets "into" reading a particular genre or author
2	Primary grades	Learning to decode Developing an attention span	• School reading texts • Easy-to-read books • Signs and other real-world messages	• Takes pride in reading to parents or others • Enjoys reading alone • Has favorite stories
1	Birth to kindergarten	Understanding of pleasure and profit from printed words and from visual and oral presentations	• Nursery rhymes • Folktales • Picture books • Television programs • Songs	• "Reads" signs for certain restaurants and food • Memorizes favorite stories and pretends to read • Enjoys singing and listening to stories

Level 1: Understanding That Pleasure and Profit Come from Literature

Children are fortunate if they have loving adults who share songs and nursery rhymes and who talk with them about the television and the movies they see together. They are also lucky if they get to go to bookstores and libraries for buying and borrowing books and for participating in group story hours. Researchers in reading education are discovering the social nature of reading. Children who seem to get the most from their reading are those who have had opportunities for "talking story" and for having what Ralph Peterson and Maryann Eeds call "grand conversations" both with other children and with adults.[6]

If children are to put forth the intellectual energy required in learning to read, they need to be convinced that it is worthwhile—that pleasure awaits them—or that there are concrete benefits to be gained. In U.S. metropolitan areas, there's hardly a four-year-old who doesn't recognize the golden arches of a McDonald's restaurant. Toddlers too young to walk around grocery stores reach out from their seats in grocery carts to grab favorite brands of cereal. We know one child who by the time he entered first grade had taught himself to read from *TV Guide*. While its format breaks almost every rule any good textbook writer would follow in designing a primer for clear and easy reading, it had one overpowering advantage. The child could get immediate feedback. If he made a correct guess, he was rewarded by getting to watch the program he wanted. If he made a mistake, he knew immediately that he had to return to the printed page to try again. Today's equivalent is children who learn to read from the tiny screens on computerized games or from going online to find information, advertisements, or cartoons.

One of our students, Marlinda White-Kaulaity, who has now graduated with a Ph.D. (see her photo on p. 309) grew up on the Navajo Reservation in northern Arizona, and when she looked at our stages of literary appreciation, she thought our examples were too specific and too limited. See the article she wrote, "Reflections on Native American Reading: A Seed, a Tool, and a Weapon," published in the April 2007 *Journal of Adult and Adolescent Literacy.*[7] As you look at the chart, it might be a good idea for you to do what Marlinda did in questioning the different levels, as well as the examples, and thinking about how you developed your own interests in literacy. For her culture, she thought we focused too heavily on print literacies, while as we will show in Chapter 3, people living in today's world make use of many other kinds of literacy. Her earliest memories were of sitting on her grandfather's knee and being told stories and of participating in games and dances. She doesn't remember her parents ever reading a bedtime story to her, yet she grew up with a strong interest in stories and later in reading.

Level 2: Learning to Read

Learning the principles of phonics (i.e., to turn the squiggles on a page into meaningful sounds) is the second stage of development. It gets maximum attention during the primary grades, where as much as 70 percent of the school day is devoted to language arts. Developing literacy, however, is more than just decoding; it is a never-ending task for anyone who is intellectually active. Even at a mundane level, adults continue working to develop their reading skills. People tackling new computer programs or rereading tax guides in preparation for an audit exhibit the same symptoms of concentrated effort as do children first learning to read. They point with their fingers, move their lips, return to reread difficult parts, and in frustration slam the offending booklet to the floor. In each case, however, they are motivated by a vision of some benefit to be gained, so they increase their efforts.

Those of us who learned to read with ease may forget to help children who are struggling to find pleasure and enjoyment. Children who learn to read easily—the girl who sits in the backseat of the car and reads all through the family vacation and the boy who reads a book while delivering the neighborhood newspapers—find their own rewards for reading. For these children, the years between seven and twelve are golden. They can read the great body of literature that the world has saved for them: *Charlotte's Web*, the Little House books, *The Borrowers*, *The Chronicles of Narnia*, *The Wizard of Oz*, *Where the Red Fern Grows*, and books by Beverly Cleary, William Steig, Dr. Seuss, and hundreds of other good writers.

At this stage, children are undemanding. They are in what Margaret Early has described as a stage of unconscious enjoyment.[8] With help, they may enjoy such classics as *Alice in Wonderland*, *The Wind in the Willows*, *Treasure Island*, and *Little Women*, but by themselves they are far more likely to turn to less-challenging material. Parents worry that their children are wasting time, but nearly 100 percent of our college students who say they love to read went through childhood stages of being addicted for months to one particular kind of book. Apparently, readers find comfort in knowing the characters in a book and what to expect, and this comfort helps them develop speed and skill.

Level 3: Losing Oneself in a Story

Children who read only during the time set aside in school and children who live in homes where the television set is constantly switched from channel to channel and where the exigencies of daily life leave little time for uninterrupted conversations and stories probably have a hard time losing themselves in a good story. There are exceptions, of course, who are like Worm (short for bookworm), the eleven-year-old character in Rod Philbrick's *Max the Mighty* who escapes the horrors of her everyday life by reading. She even uses a miner's helmet and headlight to read in the dark.

Because of life's complications, many children do not lose themselves in a good story until much later than the third or fourth grades, which is typical of good readers, or it may not happen at all. In this segment quoted from *The Car Thief*, by Theodore Weesner, Alex Housman, who is being kept in a detention home, is seventeen years old when he first experiences losing himself in a story (i.e., finding what we refer to as "a good read"). Someone has donated a box of books to the detention home, and, because there's nothing else to do, Alex starts to read. He is intimidated by the words because he had never read anything before except school assignments, but because the book is straightforward and written in a style he can understand,

> [he] sat on the floor reading until he grew sleepy. When his eyelids began to slide
> down and his head began to cloud, he lay over on his side on the floor to sleep

awhile, pulling up his knees, resting his head on his arm. When he woke he got up and carried the book with him to the bathroom . . . reading the book again, he became so involved in the story that his legs fell asleep. He kept reading, intending to get up at the end of this page, then at the end of this page, if only because he would feel more comfortable with his pants up and buttoned, but he read on. . . . Something was happening to him, something as pleasantly strange as the feeling he had had for Irene Sheaffer. By now, if he knew a way, he would prolong the book the distance his mind could see, and he rose again, quietly, to sustain the pleasant sensation, the escape he seemed already to have made from the scarred and unlighted corridor. Within this shadowed space there were now other things: war and food and worry over cigarettes and rations, leaving and returning, dying and escaping. The corridor itself, and his own life, was less present.[9]

Level 4: Finding Oneself in a Story

The more experience children have with literature, whether through words or pictures, the more discriminating they become. To receive pleasure they have to respect the story. In reminiscing about his childhood fondness for both the Hardy Boys and motorcycles, the late John Gardner remarked that his development as a literary critic took a step forward when he lost patience with the leisurely conversations that the Hardy boys were supposed to have as they roared down country roads side by side on their motorcycles.

Good readers begin developing this critical sense in literature at about the same time they develop it in real life at the end of childhood and the beginning of their teen years. They move away from a simple interest in what happened in a story to ask why. They want logical development and are no longer satisfied with stereotypes. They want characters controlled by believable human motives because now their reading has a real purpose to it. They are reading to find out about themselves, not simply to escape into someone else's experiences for a few pleasurable hours. They may read dozens of contemporary teenage novels, looking for lives as much like their own as possible. They read about real people in biographies, personal essays, and journalistic stories. They are also curious about other sides of life, and so they seek out books that present lives totally different from their own. They look for anything bizarre, unbelievable, weird, or grotesque: stories of occult happenings, trivia books, and horror stories. And, of course, for their leisure-time reading and viewing they may revert to level 3, escaping into a good story. When they are working at the highest level of their capability, however, their purpose is largely one of finding themselves and their places in society. Parents and teachers sometimes worry when children seem stuck at a particular level or with a particular kind of book. In most instances, as long as there are other choices available as well as time for reading, students sooner or later venture onward in a natural kind of progression.

Level 5: Venturing beyond Themselves

The next stage in literary appreciation comes when people go beyond their egocentrism and look at the larger circle of society. Senior high school English teachers have some of their best teaching experiences with books and stories by such writers as Ernest Hemingway, John Steinbeck, Harper Lee, F. Scott Fitzgerald,

Margaret A. Edwards Award
Winner (1998)

Madeleine L'Engle, A Writer Who Asks the Hard Questions

Madeleine L'Engle, who died on September 6, 2007, was honored by the Edwards committee for two books from her series about the Austin family (*Meet the Austins* and *Ring of Endless Light*) and for two books from her Time Quintet about the Murray family (*A Wrinkle in Time* and *A Swiftly Tilting Planet*). While both sets were originally published as books for children, they have achieved a crossover audience partly because of the way L'Engle brings in philosophical and "other-world" considerations. The Time Quintet is about the intellectual Murray family and the disappearance of their physicist father, who is engaged in secret work for the government.

The introduction to the series, *A Wrinkle in Time*, which won the 1963 Newbery Medal, is still the most popular and as far as we know is the earliest of all the Edwards Award books. The next most popular one is *A Swiftly Tilting Planet*, which won the American Book Award. In it, the "baby" of the family, Charles Wallace, is now a fourteen-year-old who, with help from his sister Meg, inherits the task of rescuing their father.

In May 2007, the Time Quintet was reissued with two different covers for each book. Peter Sis drew the illustrations for the set designed to be marketed to children, while the well-known science fiction illustrator Cliff Nielsen drew the designs for the mass-market editions. Anna Quindlen wrote a new introduction to *A Wrinkle in Time*; also included as extras are a new interview with L'Engle and the text for her 1963 Newbery acceptance speech. In this speech, L'Engle noted that because of when she was born (1918) she belongs to the first generation who grew up benefiting from the wisdom of the librarians who chose to bring attention to particularly good books.

I learned about mankind from Hendrik Willem van Loon; I traveled with Dr. Dolittle, created by a man I called Hug Lofting; Will James taught me about the West with Smoky; in boarding school I grabbed Invincible Louisa the moment it came into the library because Louisa May Alcott had the same birthday that I have, and the same ambitions.

L'Engle grew up in New York City surrounded by artists of one kind or another; her father was a writer and her mother a pianist. In 1930, the family moved to Europe where they lived mostly in France and Switzerland, but Madeleine came home for college, first in South Carolina and then at Smith in Massachusetts. After college she lived in Greenwich Village with three college friends. Here she met and later married actor Hugh Franklin. In 1952, he retired from the theater and they moved to an old white farmhouse in northwestern Connecticut where they raised three children and supported themselves by resurrecting a defunct general store—a life *not* conducive to writing, L'Engle laughingly admits. Nevertheless, she plugged away at her writing, with her own children being her first audience. It took two years of rejection letters before she had a book accepted.

L'Engle frequently explores questions of science, philosophy, and religious faith, sometimes in the same book. When *A Wrinkle in Time* won the 1963 Newbery Medal, critics in the field argued that the book was a poor excuse for sci-fi. A colleague at a university where we previously taught conjectured that the women on the Newbery Committee had never read any "real" science fiction and were so bowled over by just a whiff of the genre that they gave it the prize. When, thirty-five years later, L'Engle won the Margaret A. Edwards Award, in her acceptance speech she said that she knew when she wrote *Wrinkle* that she was breaking taboos. One was that sci-fi protagonists had to be male and her protagonist was female: "I'm a female. Why would I give all the best ideas to a male?"

Another "rule" was that fantasy and science fiction don't mix. "Why not?" she asks. "We live in a fantastic universe, and subatomic particles and quantum mechanics are even more fantastic than the macrocosm. Often the only way to look clearly at this extraordinary universe" is through imagination. In her defense, she cited Erich Fromm's book *The Forgotten Language* (Rinehart, 1951), which makes the point that "fairy tales, fantasy, myths, and parables are the only universal language which crosses over barriers of race, culture, and time." ●

Carson McCullers, William Faulkner, Arthur Miller, and Flannery O'Connor. Students respond to the way these books raise questions about conformity, social pressures, justice, and other aspects of human frailties and strengths. Book discussions at this level can have real meat to them because readers make different interpretations as they bring their own experiences into play against those in the books.

Obviously, getting to this level of literary appreciation is more than a matter of developing an advanced set of decoding skills. It is closely tied to intellectual, physical, and emotional development. Teenagers face the tremendous responsibility of assessing the world around them and deciding where they fit in. Reading at this level allows teenagers to focus on their own psychological needs in relation to society. The more directly they can do this, the more efficient they feel, which probably explains the popularity of contemporary problem novels featuring young protagonists, as in the books by Will Hobbs, Brock Cole, M. E. Kerr, Robert Cormier, Jacqueline Woodson, Virginia Euwer Wolff, and Nancy Garden.

Although many people read fantasy and science fiction at the level of losing themselves in a good story, others may read such books as Nancy Farmer's *The House of the Scorpion*, Neal Shusterman's *The Dark Side of Nowhere*, Ursula K. Le Guin's *Tehanu*, and Philip Pullman's *The Golden Compass* and *The Subtle Knife* at a higher level of reflection. Such readers come back from spending a few hours in the imagined society with new ideas about their own society.

Levels 6 and 7: Aesthetic Appreciation

When people have developed the skills and attitudes necessary to enjoy imaginative literary experiences at all the levels described so far, they are ready to embark on a lifetime of aesthetic appreciation. This is the level at which producers, playwrights, authors, critics, talented performers, and literary scholars concentrate their efforts. Even they don't work at this level all the time, however, because it is as demanding as it is rewarding. The professor who teaches Shakespeare goes home at night and relaxes by watching *The Simpsons* or *The Office* or by scanning the Internet to see what might turn up on someone's blog or on YouTube. The author who writes for hours in the morning might put herself to sleep at night by listening to a CD of Ayn Rand's *The Fountainhead*, while the producer of a new play may flip through magazines as a way of relaxing. Teenagers are much the same. Top students take a break from the seriousness of homework by watching *CSI*, skimming the sports page, listening to music, or playing video games.

In summary, the important points to learn from this discussion of stages of literary appreciation are that teachers, librarians, and parents should meet young people where they are and help them feel comfortable at that stage before trying to move them on. We also need to continue to provide for all the levels below the one on which we are focusing; for example, people at any stage need to experience pleasure and profit from their reading, viewing, and listening. This is especially true with reading, which requires an extra measure of intellectual effort. People who feel they are not being appropriately rewarded for their efforts may grow discouraged and join the millions of adults who no longer read, view, or listen to materials for personal fulfillment and pleasure. Their literary efforts focus entirely on acquiring the factual information that is needed to manage the daily requirements of modern living.

A University of Exeter Study on the Qualities of Good YA Books

"The Good, the Bad and the Ugly: Teachers' Perception of Quality in Fiction for Adolescent Readers" is the way Rosemary Hopper, a lecturer in English Education at the University of Exeter, entitled her 2006 article published in the British journal *English in Education*.[10] The article reported on the first part of a study designed to assess the attitudes and the knowledge of educators in relation to how they view quality in young adult literature and how this affects their view of its place in schools.

The Exeter University researchers suspected that educators, who work mostly under the philosophy of a *cultural literary heritage*, do not make as much use of young adult literature as they could or should, now that the quality and the availability of YA books (including fiction, poetry, nonfiction, and drama) has increased over the past decade. Their underlying assumption was that the literary canon as it is usually interpreted marginalizes many students and does not provide opportunities for students to continue their development of literary appreciation in a smooth, upward line. The goal of the researchers was to see whether it is feasible for teachers to use young adult literature to teach principles of literary judgment and discernment. Teachers want to help teenagers learn to deconstruct stories and to apply criteria showing that they understand such literary conventions as story structure, narrative perspective, and genre conventions. The question being asked by the study was whether or not teachers and librarians think that young adult literature is rich enough to support such pedagogical uses.

The researchers conducted twenty-five in-depth interviews with twenty-one English teachers, three librarians, and one teaching assistant. The interviewees came from eleven different schools and were all volunteers, which the researchers cautioned may mean that they are not typical because they at least knew enough about young adult literature to want to be involved in the study.

One of the first questions asked in the semistructured interviews was how young adult literature should be defined. Some of the interviewees gave basically negative definitions that used such terms as "commercial," "stuff silly girls might read," "lacks weight," and "books set in schools." More positive interviewees focused on the content and used such terms as "issues teenagers would identify with," "explicitly informing," "technically aimed at teenagers," "relevant, accessible . . . and entertaining," "opportunities to explore other things/cultures," "allowing children to work out problems," and "having teenagers as the main characters."

The researchers suggested that those teachers who had the most negative views toward the concept of young adult literature probably "miss an opportunity to move their pupils forward in their reading." While the majority of the interviewees held more positive feelings toward YA books, they did not think they could accomplish their goals with just any book written for teenagers. They wanted to work with "well-written" young adult books, and expressed a shared assumption that books either were well written or poorly written. However, the researchers felt challenged to understand what the interviewees considered "good" books because they all found it easier to describe what made books "bad."

Nevertheless, while not managing to list "absolute criteria," the Exeter University researchers did find consistent patterns in what the teachers judged to be qualities that would help readers develop. Condensed here are the qualities that the interviewees judged to be important because of the way they allow young readers and their teachers to operate at several levels.

1. Imaginative and well-structured plots going beyond simple chronologies to include time shifts and differing perspectives.
2. Exciting plots that include secrecy, surprise, and tension brought about through narrative hooks and a fast pace.
3. Characters who reflect experiences of teen readers, something that is not found in much of the literary canon, especially when it comes to strong female protagonists.
4. Characters who go beyond typical experiences so that readers can use the fictional experiences to learn and develop in their own lives.
5. Lively, varied, and imaginative language that is grammatically correct while being neither patronizing and simplistic nor unnecessarily confusing through lexical density or complexity.
6. Themes that inform truthfully about the wider world so as to allow readers to engage with difficult and challenging issues relating to immediate interests and global concerns.
7. Themes that allow the possibility of emotional and intellectual growth through engagement with personal issues.
8. Varied levels of sophistication that will lead to the continual development of reading skills.

A challenge for the teachers and librarians who were being interviewed was to think of examples of books that would demonstrate these qualities. Ones they mentioned included Louis Sachar's *Holes*, David Almond's *Skellig*, and Philip Pullman's *The Golden Compass*, *The Subtle Knife*, and *The Amber Spyglass*. We were pleased to note that most of these books are included on our United States Honor List (pp. 21 to 26) even though the majority are from England. This gave us the idea of seeing how closely the eight characteristics of "quality" young adult literature developed in the Exeter study fit with the seven "characteristics" of the best young adult literature that we have been using in this textbook.

An important difference is in the methodology. The Exeter study set out to find the characteristics of "good" YA literature, while we started with YA literature judged by many people to be "good" (the books on our Honor List) and then examined the literature to see what characteristics it has. As we describe these characteristics, we will keep the Exeter ones in mind and note places where there are especially good matches. By doing this, we hope to fill in one of the needs noted in the Exeter study, which is the shortage of teachers' acquaintance with books containing the desired qualities. The teachers being interviewed assumed there were many such books, but they lacked knowledge of them.

Looking for the Exeter Qualities in the Books on the Honor List

Since 1980 we have been compiling a yearly Honor List in hopes of finding a manageable list of "best" YA books as judged by fellow critics, teachers, and librarians. We devise our yearly lists by examining those YA books that make it to the editors' choice lists of *School Library Journal* and *Booklist* and onto such prize lists as that of the National Book Awards, which now includes a youth section. As soon as the American Library Association meets in January, we receive news releases announcing more "best" books than we can hope to read. The Michael L. Printz Award, established in 2000, goes to the best YA book of the year, while the Newbery Medal winner and Honor Books are sometimes of interest to teen readers, as are the winners of the Coretta Scott King Awards for best African American books, the Pura Belpré Awards for best Latino/Latina books, the Robert F. Silbert Award for most distinguished informational book, and the Margaret A. Edwards Award, given to an author for a lifetime contribution to young adult books. On the YALSA (Young Adult Library Services Association) best-book list of some seventy books, we pay the most attention to the eight or ten that receive unanimous votes. We also look at their list of Quick Picks (designed for reluctant YA readers), and, as general interest has increased in books for young adults and the new category of tweeners, we look for the annual recommendations in such newspapers as the *New York Times* and the *Los Angeles Times* and the *Horn Book* magazine, with its *Horn Book Fanfare* and the *Horn Book/Boston Globe* Awards.

Over the past thirty years we have seen a tremendous increase in the number of awards and best-book lists, but deciding on the final selection for our Honor List is as hard as ever because readers' and critics' tastes are increasingly diverse and books are selected as "the best" on the basis of many different criteria. We hope that you will read many books so that you can recommend them not because you saw them on a list, but because you enjoyed them and believe they will appeal to a particular student.

When we made our first Honor List, we started with 1967 because this seemed to be a milestone year, when writers and publishers turned in new directions, but as the years have gone by, the number of books has made the list so unwieldy that for this edition we moved the books from the 1960s and 1970s to Focus Boxes in Chapter 2. We also deleted a few books that are out of print and we stayed with our earlier decision to move the biographies, nonfiction, and collections of poetry and short stories to Focus Boxes in appropriate chapters. Occasionally, we add a book to the Honor List when it appears to be growing in respect and popularity, as has happened with Sandra Cisneros's *The House on Mango Street*, Orson Scott Card's *Ender's Game*, Laurie Halse Anderson's *Speak*, Ursula K. Le Guin's *Tehanu*, and Yann Martel's *Life of Pi*.

We used to identify books as coming from either the juvenile division or the adult division of a publishing house, but this no longer seems like crucial information because within the last fifteen years nearly all the Honor books have been published by juvenile divisions. This is partly because the reviewing sources from which we take our lists are slanted toward juvenile books, and partly because today's publishers have a kind of freedom they did not have in 1975 when, for example, Bradbury felt it necessary to create an "adult" division to publish Judy Blume's *Forever* in hopes of softening the controversy over its sexual content.

Starting here with the Honor List, and continuing through this textbook, we have tried to be consistent in listing the original hardback publisher because this is the company who found the author and did the original editorial and publicity work. Readers interested in finding paperback editions or sound recordings, and so on, can easily check online with such marketers as amazon.com or Barnes and Noble or look in an online version of Bowker's *Books in Print*. However, there is still a challenge in recognizing which subdivisions or imprints belong to which companies because companies often merge and within the larger companies subdivisions are constantly being formed.

If a book is included on this Honor List, obviously it is outstanding in some way, but one book may be here because of its originality, another for its popularity, and another for its literary quality. We should also warn that many excellent books did not happen to find their way to this list and should not be dismissed as mediocre. The chart format was chosen for the convenience of those who want an efficient list of high-quality books to carry with them to a bookstore, a library, or to a computer for online research and buying.

Since 2000, Professor James Blasingame, Jr., who joined our English department faculty, has helped us make the decisions and write the Honor List reviews. These reviews have been published in the *English Journal*—usually the September or November issues—for the past decade or so. Here we use fairly recent books from the Honor List to illustrate the different qualities that over the last several editions of this textbook we have identified as characterizing high-quality young adult literature. And when a book seems to us to be a good illustration of one of the eight qualities outlined by the Exeter University researchers, we make a note. Other books on the Honor List are described in connection with the subjects of particular chapters.

Characteristic 1: Young Adult Authors Write from the Viewpoint of Young People

A prerequisite to attracting young readers is to write through the eyes of a young person. One of the ways authors do this is to write in first person, as with this beginning paragraph of Norma Fox Mazer's 1997 *When She Was Good*:

> I didn't believe Pamela would ever die. She was too big, too mad, too furious for anything so shabby and easy as death. And for a few moments as she lay on the floor that day, I thought it was one of her jokes. The playing-dead joke. I thought that at any moment she would spring up, seize me by the hair, and drag me around the room. It wouldn't be the first time. . . .

(text continues on page 26)

Honor List The Best of the Best, 1980–2007

Year	Title	Author	Publisher	Genre	Protagonist Sex	Protagonist Age	No. of Pages
2007	The Absolutely True Diary of a Part-Time Indian	Sherman Alexie	Little, Brown	Memoir	M	14	240
	Dreamquake: Book Two of the Dreamhunter Duet	Elizabeth Knox	FSG	Fantasy	F	Older teen	449
	Harry Potter and the Deathly Hallows	J. K. Rowling	Scholastic	Fantasy	M	19	759
	Tamar: A Novel of Espionage, Passion, and Betrayal	Mal Peet	Candlewick	Adventure Mystery/War	F	15	432
	Twisted	Laurie Halse Anderson	Penguin Viking	Realistic	M	16	272
	What They Found: Love on 45th Street	Walter Dean Myers	Random House	Short Stories	M/F	Mixed	256
	The White Darkness	Geraldine McCaughrean	HarperCollins	Adventure Mystery	F	14	384
2006	American Born Chinese	Gene Luen Yang	First Second Books	Graphic Novel	M	Young teen	233
	An Abundance of Katherines	John Green	Dutton/Penguin	Realistic	M	18	230
	Sold	Patricia McCormick	Hyperion	Realistic	F	13	263
	Surrender	Sonya Hartnett	Candlewick	Psychological Mystery	M	20	248
	The Astonishing Life of Octavian Nothing, Traitor to the Nation: Volume 1: The Pox Party	M. T. Anderson	Candlewick	Historical 1700s	M	Teens	351
	The Book Thief	Markus Zusak	Knopf	Young Teen	F	Childhood	550
	The Rules of Survival	Nancy Werlin	Dial/Penguin	Realistic Problem	M	13–18	260
2005	Criss Cross	Lynne Rae Perkins	Greenwillow Books	Realistic	F	14	337
	Elsewhere	Gabrielle Zevin	Farrar, Straus & Giroux	Fantasy	F	16	277
	Inexcusable	Chris Lynch	Atheneum	Realistic Problem	M	17	165
	Looking for Alaska	John Green	Dutton	Realistic Problem	M	17	227
	Peeps	Scott Westerfeld	Pengiun/Razorbill	Vampire Science Fiction	M	19	320
	Twilight	Stephenie Meyer	Little, Brown	Vampire Fantasy	F	16	498
2004	Airborn	Kenneth Oppel	Harper	Adventure/ Fantasy	M	15	368
	Chanda's Secrets	Allan Stratton	Annick Press	Realistic Problem	F	16	193
	Godless	Pete Hautman	Simon & Schuster	Realistic Problem	M	16	208
	How I Live Now	Meg Rosoff	Wendy Lamb	Realistic Dystopia	F	16	208
	Lizzie Bright and the Buckminster Boy	Gary D. Schmidt	Clarion	Historical Early 1900s	M/F	Early teens	224
	Private Peaceful	Michael Morpurgo	Scholastic	Historical War	M	18	195
2003	The Canning Season	Polly Horvath	Farrar	Realistic Humorous	F	13	208
	Fat Kid Rules the World	K. L. Going	Putnam	Realistic	M	Older teens	177
	The First Part Last	Angela Johnson	Simon & Schuster	Realistic	M	16	144
	A Northern Light	Jennifer Donnelly	Harcourt	Realistic Historical	F	16	396

(continued)

| Year | Title | Author | Publisher | Genre | Protagonist | | No. of Pages |
					Sex	Age	
	The River Between Us	Richard Peck	Dial	Realistic Historical	F	Older teens	164
	True Confessions of a Heartless Girl	Martha Brooks	Kroupa/Farrar	Realistic Problem	F	17	192
2002	Big Mouth and Ugly Girl	Joyce Carol Oates	HarperCollins	Realistic Problem Romance	F	17	226
	Feed	M. T. Anderson	Candlewick	Science Fiction Dystopia	M/F	Older teens	236
	The House of the Scorpion	Nancy Farmer	Atheneum	Science Fiction Dystopia	M	Young teens	380
	The Kite Rider	Geraldine McCaughrean	HarperCollins	Historical Adventure	M	Young teens	272
	My Heartbeat	Garret Freymann-Weyr	Houghton Mifflin	Romance Problem	F	14	154
	Postcards from No Man's Land	Aidan Chambers	Dutton	Problem Historical	M	17	312
2001	Damage	A. M. Jenkins	HarperCollins	Realistic Sports	M/F	17	186
	The Land	Mildred D. Taylor	Phyllis Fogelman	Historical	M	YA+	375
	Life of Pi: A Novel	Yann Martel	Harcourt	Magical Realism	M	16	319
	Lord of the Deep	Graham Salisbury	Delacorte	Realistic Romance	M	13	184
	The Rag and Bone Shop	Robert Cormier	Delacorte	Realistic Mystery	M	12	154
	Seek	Paul Fleischman	Marcato/Cricket	Realistic Quest	M	17	167
	The Sisterhood of the Traveling Pants	Ann Brashares	Delacorte	Realistic Romance	F	16	304
	A Step from Heaven	An Na	Front Street	Realistic Romance	F	17	156
	True Believer	Virginia Euwer Wolff	Atheneum	Realistic Romance	F	15	264
	Zazoo	Richard Moser	Houghton Mifflin	Realistic	F	13	248
2000	The Amber Spyglass	Philip Pullman	Knopf	Fantasy/Myth	M/F	Young teens	518
	The Beet Fields: Memories of a 16th Summer	Gary Paulsen	Delacorte	Realistic Memoir	M	16	158
	Homeless Bird	Gloria Whelan	HarperCollins	Realistic Quest	F	13	216
	Hope Was Here	Joan Bauer	Putnam's	Realistic Quest	F	16	190
	Kit's Wilderness	David Almond	Delacorte	Historical Supernatural	M	13	229
	Many Stones	Carolyn Coman	Front Street	Realistic Quest	F	Mid-teens	158
	Stuck in Neutral	Terry Trueman	HarperCollins	Realistic Problem	M	14	114
	The Wanderer	Sharon Creech	HarperCollins	Realistic Quest	M/F	Young teens	305
	A Year Down Yonder	Richard Peck	Dial	Historical Realism	F	16	130
1999	Anna of Byzantium	Tracy Barrett	Delacorte	Historical Fiction	F	Older teens	209
	Frenchtown Summer	Robert Cormier	Delacorte	Realistic Poetry	M	12	113
	Hard Love	Ellen Wittlinger	Simon & Schuster	Realistic Quest	M/F	16	224
	Monster	Walter Dean Myers	HarperCollins	Realistic Problem	M	16	240

| Year | Title | Author | Publisher | Genre | Protagonist | | No. of Pages |
					Sex	Age	
	Never Trust a Dead Man	Vivian Vande Velde	Harcourt	Mystery Supernatural	M	17	194
	Safe at Second	Scott Johnson	Philomel	Sports Problem	M	17	224
	The Smugglers	Iain Lawrence	Delacorte	Adventure	M	16	183
	Speak	Laurie Halse Anderson	Farrar, Straus & Giroux	Realistic Problem	F	13	197
	When Zachary Beaver Came to Town	Kimberly Willis Holt	Henry Holt	Realistic	M	13	231
1998	Clockwork: Or All Wound Up	Philip Pullman	Scholastic	Fantasy/Sci-Fi	M/F	Teens	112
	Go and Come Back	Joan Abelove	DK Ink	Realistic Historical	F	13	177
	Holes	Louis Sachar	Farrar, Straus & Giroux	Fanciful Adventure	M	14	233
	The Killer's Cousin	Nancy Werlin	Delacorte	Psychological Mystery	M	17	228
	Rules of the Road	Joan Bauer	Putnam's	Realistic Quest	F	16	201
	Soldier's Heart	Gary Paulsen	Delacorte	Historical	M	15	106
	Whirligig	Paul Fleischman	Holt	Realistic Quest	M	17	133
	The Wreckers	Iain Lawrence	Delacorte	Historical Adventure	M	14	191
1997	Blood and Chocolate	Annette Curtis Klause	Delacorte	Supernatural	F	18	288
	Buried Onions	Gary Soto	Harcourt Brace	Realistic	M	18	149
	Dancing on the Edge	Han Nolan	Harcourt Brace	Realistic	F	12	244
	Ella Enchanted	Gail Carson Levine	HarperCollins	Cinderella Retelling	F	12	232
	The Facts Speak for Themselves	Brock Cole	Front Street	Realistic Abuse	F	13	184
	Out of the Dust	Karen Hesse	Scholastic	Narrative Poetry	F	13	227
	When She Was Good	Norma Fox Mazer	Scholastic	Realistic Mental Health	F	Early 20s	240
	Whistle Me Home	Barbara Wersba	Holt	Realistic Homophobia	M/F	17	108
1996	After the War	Carol Matas	Simon & Schuster	Historical Realistic	F	15	116
	A Girl Named Disaster	Nancy Farmer	Orchard	Realistic Quest	F	14	306
	The Golden Compass	Philip Pullman	Knopf	Fantasy/Sci-Fi	F	14	396
	Jip: His Story	Katherine Paterson	Lodestar	Realistic Historical	M	11	181
	Rats Saw God	Rob Thomas	Simon & Schuster	Realistic	M	17	219
1995	The Eagle Kite	Paula Fox	Orchard	Realistic Death	M	13	127
	Ironman	Chris Crutcher	Greenwillow	Realistic Sports	M	16	181
	Like Sisters on the Homefront	Rita Williams-Garcia	Lodestar/Dutton	Realistic	F	14	165
	The Midwife's Apprentice	Karen Cushman	Clarion	Historical	F	13	122
	The War of Jenkins' Ear	Michael Morpurgo	Philomel	Realistic/ Religious	M	14	171
1994	Deliver Us from Evie	M. E. Kerr	HarperCollins	Realistic Homophobia	F	17	177
	Driver's Ed.	Caroline Cooney	Delacorte	Suspense	M/F	Teens	184

(continued)

| Year | Title | Author | Publisher | Genre | Protagonist | | No. of Pages |
					Sex	Age	
	Iceman	Chris Lynch	HarperCollins	Realistic Sports	M	14	181
	Letters from the Inside	John Marsden	Houghton Mifflin	Realistic	F	Teens	146
	When She Hollers	Cynthia Voigt	Scholastic	Realistic Abuse	F	17	177
1993	*The Giver*	Lois Lowry	Houghton Mifflin	Science Fiction Dystopia	M	Mixed	180
	Harris and Me	Gary Paulsen	Harcourt Brace	Realistic Humorous	M	Young teens	157
	Make Lemonade	Virginia Euwer Wolff	Holt	Realistic Single parent	F	14/17	200
	Missing Angel Juan	Francesca Lia Block	HarperCollins	Problem Occult	F	Teens	138
	Shadow Boxer	Chris Lynch	HarperCollins	Realistic Sports	M	Young teens	215
1992	*Dear Nobody*	Berlie Doherty	Orchard	Realistic Pregnancy	M/F	Older teens	192
	The Harmony Arms	Ron Koertge	Flare	Realistic Humorous	M	14	182
	Missing May	Cynthia Rylant	Orchard	Realistic Death	M/F	Mixed	89
	Somewhere in the Darkness	Walter Dean Myers	Scholastic	Realistic Family	M	14	224
1991	*The Brave*	Robert Lipsyte	HarperCollins	Realistic Sports	M	18	195
	Castle in the Air	Diana Wynne Jones	Greenwillow	Fantasy	M/F	Teens	199
	Lyddie	Katherine Paterson	Lodestar	Historical mid-1800s	F	13	183
	The Man from the Other Side	Uri Orlev	Houghton Mifflin	Historical, War	M	14	186
	Nothing but the Truth	Avi	Orchard	Realistic	M	14	177
1990	*The Shining Company*	Rosemary Sutcliff	Farrar	Historical	M	Mixed	296
	The Silver Kiss	Annette Curtis Klause	Bradbury	Occult Romance	F	Teens	198
	Tehanu: The Last Book of Earthsea	Ursula K. Le Guin	Atheneum	Fantasy	F	Childhood	226
	The True Confessions of Charlotte Doyle	Avi	Orchard	Historical Adventure	F	13	215
	White Peak Farm	Berlie Doherty	Orchard	Realistic Family	F	Older teens	86
1989	*Blitzcat*	Robert Westall	Scholastic	Animal	M	–	230
	Celine	Brock Cole	Farrar	Realistic	F	16	216
	Eva	Peter Dickinson	Delacorte	Science Fiction	F	13	219
	No Kidding	Bruce Brooks	HarperCollins	Science Fiction	M	14	207
	Shabanu: Daughter of the Wind	Suzanne Fisher Staples	Knopf	Realistic Problem	F	12	140
	Weetzie Bat	Francesca Lia Block	HarperCollins	Realistic Spoof	M/F	Teens	88
1988	*Fade*	Robert Cormier	Delacorte	Occult	M/F	Mixed	320
	Fallen Angels	Walter Dean Myers	Scholastic	Realistic War	M	Older teens	309
	A Kindness	Cynthia Rylant	Orchard	Realistic Family	M	15	117
	Memory	Margaret Mahy	Macmillan	Realistic Disability	M/F	19 80+	240
	Probably Still Nick Swanson	Virginia Euwer Wolff	Holt	Realistic Disability	M	Teens	144

Year	Title	Author	Publisher	Genre	Protagonist Sex	Protagonist Age	No. of Pages
	Scorpions	Walter Dean Myers	HarperCollins	Realistic Crime	M	Teens	167
	Sex Education	Jenny Davis	Orchard	Realistic Death	F	Teens	150
1987	*After the Rain*	Norma Fox Mazer	Morrow	Realistic Death	F	Mid-teens	290
	The Crazy Horse Electric Game	Chris Crutcher	Greenwillow	Realistic Sports Disability	M	Teens	224
	The Goats	Brock Cole	Farrar	Realistic	M/F	Teens	184
	Hatchet	Gary Paulsen	Bradbury	Adventure Survival	M	12	195
	Permanent Connections	Sue Ellen Bridgers	HarperCollins	Realistic Family	M/F	Teens	164
	Sons from Afar	Cynthia Voigt	Atheneum	Realistic	M	Mid-teens	224
	The Tricksters	Margaret Mahy	Macmillan	Occult	F	17	266
1986	*The Catalogue of the Universe*	Margaret Mahy	Macmillan	Realistic	F	17	185
	Izzy, Willy-Nilly	Cynthia Voigt	Atheneum	Realistic Disability	F	15	288
	Midnight Hour Encores	Bruce Brooks	HarperCollins	Realistic	F	16	288
1985	*Beyond the Chocolate War*	Robert Cormier	Knopf	Realistic	M	17	234
	Dogsong	Gary Paulsen	Bradbury	Adventure Occult	M	13	177
	Ender's Game	Orson Scott Card	Tor	Science Fiction	M	Young boy	357
	In Country	Bobbie Ann Mason	HarperCollins	Realistic	F	Teens	247
	The Moonlight Man	Paula Fox	Bradbury	Realistic Alcoholism	F	Teens	192
	Remembering the Good Times	Richard Peck	Delacorte	Realistic Suicide	M/F	Teens	192
1984	*The Changeover: A Supernatural Romance*	Margaret Mahy	Macmillan	Fantasy	M/F	Teens	214
	Cold Sassy Tree	Olive Ann Burns	Ticknor & Fields	Realistic Historical	M/F	Mixed	391
	Downtown	Norma Fox Mazer	Morrow	Realistic	M/F	Young teens	216
	Interstellar Pig	William Sleator	Dutton	Science Fiction	M	16	197
	The Moves Make the Man	Bruce Brooks	HarperCollins	Realistic	M	Young teens	280
	One-Eyed Cat	Paula Fox	Bradbury	Realistic	M	Young teens	216
1983	*Beyond the Divide*	Kathryn Lasky	Macmillan	Historical Fiction	F	Teens	254
	The Bumblebee Flies Anyway	Robert Cormier	Pantheon	Futuristic	M	Teens	211
	The House on Mango Street	Sandra Cisneros	Arte Publico	Realistic	F	Young teens	134
	A Solitary Blue	Cynthia Voigt	Atheneum	Realistic Family	M	Early teens	182
1982	*Annie on My Mind*	Nancy Garden	Farrar	Realistic Homophobia	F	Teens	233
	The Blue Sword	Robin McKinley	Greenwillow	Fantasy	F	Late teens	272
	A Formal Feeling	Zibby Oneal	Viking	Realistic Death	F	Teens	162
	A Midnight Clear	William Wharton	Knopf	Realistic War	M	Early 20s	241
	Sweet Whispers, Brother Rush	Virginia Hamilton	Philomel	Occult	F	Teens	224

Year	Title	Author	Publisher	Genre	Protagonist Sex	Protagonist Age	No. of Pages
1981	*Let the Circle Be Unbroken*	Mildred D. Taylor	Dial	Historical U.S. South	F	Early teens	166
	Notes for Another Life	Sue Ellen Bridgers	Knopf	Realistic Family	M/F	Teens	252
	Rainbow Jordan	Alice Childress	Coward McCann	Realistic	F	14	142
	Stranger with My Face	Lois Duncan	Laurel Leaf	Occult	F	17	250
	Tiger Eyes	Judy Blume	Bradbury	Realistic	F	15	206
	Westmark	Lloyd Alexander	Dutton	Historical Fantasy	M	16	184
1980	*The Beginning Place*	Ursula K. Le Guin	HarperCollins	Fantasy	M/F	Early 20s	183
	The Hitchhiker's Guide to the Galaxy	Douglas Adams	Crown	Fantasy	M	Adults	224
	Jacob Have I Loved	Katherine Paterson	Crowell	Realistic	F	Teens	216

This kind of immediacy serves as a narrative hook to grab and hold readers. First-person narration is so common that we have heard people discuss it as a prerequisite for YA fiction. It isn't really, but because when authors are writing from an omniscient viewpoint, they are careful to tell what the young protagonist thinks and says, readers come away with the impression that most, if not all, YA literature is told in first person.

Nancy Werlin's 2006 *The Rules of Survival* exemplifies the common practice of telling a story through the voice of the main character. Matthew, the oldest brother in a severely troubled family, is the narrator who starts his story after the dedication page, which reads: "This book is for all the survivors. Always remember: The survivor gets to tell the story." Matthew begins with a letter written to his youngest sister:

Dear Emmy,

As I write this, you are nine years old, too young to be told the full and true story of our family's past, let alone be exposed to my philosophizing about what it all meant. I don't know how old you'll be when you do read this. Maybe you'll be seventeen, like I am now. Or maybe much older than that—in your twenties or even thirties. . . .

After the boy finishes his two-page letter, he begins the story of his family life starting when he was thirteen, his sister Callie was eleven, and Emmy was five. His father is separated from Nikki, Matthew's extraordinarily beautiful mother, who about a third of the way through the story invites the "demons into her soul" and asks them to help her get whatever she wants.

What she wants is to win back the love and dependence of her children, which she thinks someone has stolen from her, but which, in fact, she forced away. The children's father and an aunt live nearby, but they find Nikki hard to deal with and so they mostly look the other way. The children accept their "fate," with the two older ones trying to protect their young half-sister. Their fear of being separated keeps them from going to authorities and asking to be placed in foster care, but when they witness an act of true bravery by a man who, in their neighborhood convenience store, comes between an angry father and his young son, they go looking for this stranger with the unrealistic idea that he can save them.

The harrowing story ends four years later when Matthew is getting ready to go away on a college scholarship. And thanks at least partially to the stranger in the convenience store and to Matthew's aunt and his father, he thinks his sister and his half-sister will be taken care of, but he has learned enough by now to know there are no guarantees. The real mark of how far Matthew has come is that the book ends with his writing another letter to Emmy, in which he confides, "You're never going to read this, are you? I'm never going to give it to you. I didn't write it for you. I wrote it for me."

Matthew's change of heart illustrates something that YA editor Stephen Roxburgh talked about at the 2004 NCTE/ALAN workshop. He said that the defining literary characteristic of young adult books is that the first-person narrator starts out as unreliable and then by the end of the book evolves into a reliable narrator. Werlin's book is a perfect example. Readers travel with the protagonist through a series of harsh but believable events that allow them to develop not only a literary knowledge about reliable versus unreliable narrators, but also to learn some hard lessons in life without having to undergo the dangers of Matthew's atypical life (Exeter Quality number 4) and to undergo emotional and intellectual growth (Exeter Quality number 7) through engaging with personal issues.

M. T. Anderson's *The Astonishing Life of Octavian Nothing, Traitor to the Nation: Volume 1: The Pox Party* provides another example of a protagonist who changes from being a narrator who does not understand his role in life to being so knowledgeable about how other people view him, that he rebels. See Chapter 8 p. 248 for a fuller discussion of this amazing book, which exemplifies nearly every one of the Exeter qualities.

Another technique related to point of view is for authors to have a young narrator even when the story belongs to someone else. For example, Joan Abelove's 1998 *Go and Come Back* is the story of two anthropologists who are in their late twenties when they go for a two-year study visit to a mountain tribe in Peru. What readers learn about the anthropologists comes through the eyes of a young Peruvian girl, Alicia, who refers to the anthropologists as "old women." The tribe is fictionally named the Isabos, and Alicia's first-person observations are supplemented by the conversations she has with her friends, with the two "old women," and with her observant and sarcastic mother.

In his 1988 *Fade*, Robert Cormier uses the technique of having the story told by the protagonist, Paul Moreaux, as long as he is in his youth. When the story gets to his adult years, however, Cormier changes the narrator to Moreaux's young female cousin, who aspires to follow in Moreaux's footsteps as a writer.

The most consistent characteristic of the books on the Honor List is the age of the protagonists. Teenagers like to read about other teenagers as shown by such books as Yann Martel's 2001 *Life of Pi: A Novel*, Orson Scott Card's 1985 *Ender's Game*, Bobbie Ann Mason's 1985 *In Country*, and Sandra Cisneros's 1983 *The House on Mango Street*. In spite of being published and marketed to general adult audiences, these books found their way to teen readers at least partly because the protagonists were young.

With other Honor List books published for adults, young people play important roles even if they aren't the main characters, as with the grandson in Olive Ann Burns's 1984 *Cold Sassy Tree*. General adult books that do not include teenagers—for example, William Wharton's 1982 *A Midnight Clear* and Douglas Adams's 1980 *The Hitchhiker's Guide to the Galaxy*—have protagonists who are only slightly older than teen readers and who are involved in activities with which young people can identify.

The big dividing line—the final rite of passage—between childhood and adulthood used to be having children of one's own so that stories about parenting seldom, if ever, appeared in young adult fiction. With the public acknowledgment of a soaring birthrate to teenaged mothers, however, this is no longer true, as shown by the success of Virginia Euwer Wolff's 1993 *Make Lemonade*, the story of fourteen-year-old LaVaughn, who answers a babysitting ad and is surprised to find that it was put up by Jolly, the teenaged mother of two-year-old Jeremy and a younger "gooey baby" named Jilly. Rita Williams-Garcia's 1995 *Like Sisters on the Homefront* is the story of fourteen-year-old Gayle, whose mother forces her to have an abortion after she gets pregnant a second time and then sends Gayle and her seven-month-old baby boy from New York to rural Georgia to live "with family."

Angela Johnson's 2003 *The First Part Last* is the most unusual of the books about teen parenting. Nia and Bobby are two middle-class, African American teenagers in Brooklyn who find themselves expecting a baby. They plan to give the baby up for adoption, but a medical aberration causes Nia to go into a permanent coma and so Bobby decides to "be a man," and raise their daughter. Bobby was not really ready for such a responsibility and the chapters alternate between telling about his old life and his new one. This is a fast-moving story that fits well with the Exeter Quality number 3 in presenting a story about a character not often found in the literary canon, Quality number 4 in taking readers beyond typical experiences, and Quality number 7 encouraging readers to develop their own emotional and intellectual growth through engagement with personal issues.

Characteristic 2: "Please, Mother, I Want the Credit!"

With formula fiction for young readers, one of the first things an author does is to figure out how to get rid of the parents so that the young person is free to take credit for his or her own accomplishments. Although the Honor List is not made up of formula fiction, authors have devised a multitude of ways for the young character to be the one who solves the problem or who in some other way becomes the hero of the story. This ties in with the Exeter qualities number 3 and 4 because when the focus is on a young protagonist, readers are encouraged to identify with the characters and to see what is relevant to them.

Markus Zusak's *The Book Thief* won the 2003 best children's book award in Australia and received high acclaim when it was published in the United States in 2006. It especially exemplifies Exeter Quality number 1, which asks for a plot that goes beyond simple chronologies and includes time shifts and differing perspectives; Quality number 3, which asks for strong female characters; and Quality number 5, which calls for lively, varied, and imaginative language. The story is narrated off and on by Death, who comes to pick up the soul of anyone who dies. The book is set in Nazi Germany during World War II and so, of course, Death is busy, especially in 1942 when the human race was cranking things up a little and increasing production "from Poland to Russia to Africa to Hawaii." See a fuller discussion in Chapter 8, pp. 248–249.

Paul Fleischman's 1998 *Whirligig* is more typical in having a male protagonist. Brent Bishop needs to atone for causing a fatal traffic accident, so author Paul Fleischman contrives to have him travel on a Greyhound bus to the four corners of the United States where he constructs a memorial in remembrance of the girl who was killed in the accident. Brent's wealthy father had brought his checkbook to the meeting with the grieving family and is surprised when they refuse his money and ask Brent to make amends by himself.

Other Honor books in which young people are forced to come to terms with their problems without the help of their parents include Iain Lawrence's 1998 *The Wreckers*, Gary Soto's 1997 *Buried Onions*, Carol Matas's 1996 *After the War*, Nancy Farmer's 1996 *A Girl Named Disaster*, Francesca Lia Block's 1989 *Weetzie Bat*, and Chris Crutcher's 1987 *The Crazy Horse Electric Game*.

Perhaps because they are on the edge of—close but not central to—the mainstream of power, young people seem able to relate more comfortably with elderly than with middle-aged adults. In Joan Bauer's 1998 *Rules of the Road*, sixteen-year-old Jenna Louise Boller is happy to leave behind her troublesome father when she is offered the summer job of driving the "supremely aged" Mrs. Gladstone cross-country to inspect each of the 172 shoe stores that her company owns. In Han Nolan's 1997 *Dancing on the Edge*, Miracle McCloy is at the mercy of some truly bad adults, but at least she knows that her grandfather is there for her. In Nancy Farmer's 1996 *A Girl Named Disaster*, it is the maternal grandmother and the paternal great-grandfather who save the girl, even though they come from different sides of an alienated family.

In keeping with the variety that exists in the Honor List, other books lead young readers to look more realistically at themselves and at parent-child relationships. Among the books that feature at least one capable parent playing a strong, supportive role for a young protagonist are Louis Sachar's 1998 *Holes*, Berlie Doherty's 1990 *White Peak Farm*, Peter Dickinson's 1998 *Eva*, Virginia Euwer Wolff's 1998 *Probably Still Nick Swanson*, Virginia Hamilton's 1982 *Sweet Whispers, Brother Rush*, and Alice Childress's 1981 *Rainbow Jordan*. In Bobbie Ann Mason's 1985 *In Country* and Bruce Brooks's 1986 *Midnight Hour Encores*, the young protagonists place great importance on learning about an unknown parent.

Characteristic 3: Young Adult Literature Is Fast Paced

In July 1999, *Time* reporter David Spritz wrote that, "Teen fiction may, in fact, be the first literary genre born of the Internet. Its fast-paced narratives draw upon the target demographic's kinship with MTV . . . and with the Internet and kids' ease in processing information in unconventional formats."[11] In reality, teen fiction, which Spitz calls "edgy" was around long before the Internet, but his point is well taken that many of the most popular books tell their stories at almost the same frantic pace and with the same emphasis on powerful images that viewers have come to expect from MTV. This concept will be further discussed in Chapter 3.

Postindustrial countries have become hurry-up societies, and people want their stories to be presented in the same fashion. Books from the Honor List that come close to being MTV stories because of their pace and their exaggerated and powerful images include Louis Sachar's 1998 *Holes*, Annette Curtis Klause's 1990 *The Silver Kiss* and 1997 *Blood and Chocolate*, and Francesca Lia Block's 1993 *Missing Angel Juan* and 1989 *Weetzie Bat*. The latter is only eighty-eight pages long. When it was published, it was a shocking book because people were so accustomed to reading realistic problem novels providing role models for teenagers that they weren't ready for a fairy-tale spoof of Hollywood and for a writer who was less interested in presenting role models than in presenting vivid images and unforgettable characters. See more about how Block's books resemble MTV in Chapter 3, p. 82, where we write about Block as a winner of the 2005 Margaret A. Edwards Award.

Not all young adult books are going to have the disjointed punch of music videos or the randomness of the Internet, but there is a relationship because modern mass-media entertainers appeal to the same powerful emotions of adolescence—love, romance, sex, horror, and fear—as do young adult authors. These strong emotions are best shown through a limited number of characters and narrative events and language that flows naturally while still presenting dramatic images. The shorter and more powerful books are among those that have been made into impressive movies.

The assumption that publishers start with is that teenagers have shorter attention spans than adults and less ability to hold one strand of a plot in mind while reading about another strand. However, there is a tremendous difference in the reading abilities of young people between the ages of twelve and eighteen. As students mature and become better readers, they are able to stick with longer, more complex books, and as proven by the Harry Potter books, even young readers can stick with long books if they are interested. Zusak's *The Book Thief*, discussed earlier, is 551 pages, and the first book in Philip Pullman's Dark Materials trilogy, *The Golden Compass*, is 351 pages long and, as with the other books in the set, exemplifies Exeter Quality number 1 in having an imaginative and well-structured plot that goes beyond simple chronologies as it includes time shifts and differing perspectives, and also Quality number 2 in having an exciting plot, secrecy, surprise, and tension brought about through narrative hooks and a fast pace. One of our college readers characterized the conflicts in *The Golden Compass* as a "*Da Vinci Code* for kids," citing such terms as the *Consistorial Court of Discipline, the Magisterium*, the *Oblation Board*, the *Papacy*, and the *absolute power of the Church*. While Pullman includes many plots and subplots, what impressed us was how quickly he draws readers into the story. On page 1, they are introduced to Lyra and the fact that she has a soul mate—a daemon who has the ability to change his shape as he serves as her guardian, conscience, companion, and pet—and that together the two of them are involved in something mysterious, secretive, and serious. Within a few pages readers figure out that the story takes place somewhere in the past, but not too far back because the 1898 Tokay wine is considered to be "old" and precious and the scholars prefer the softer Naphtha lighting to the newer anbaric (electric?) lights. There's also some edginess to the story as Lyra smells and watches the Master cut open half a dozen poppy heads to prepare for serving after the feast to clear "the mind and stimulate the tongue" of the scholars.

Characteristic 4: Young Adult Literature Includes a Variety of Genres and Subjects

Because moving from being a child to being an adult is at the core of most young adult fiction, the "genre" is commonly thought of as featuring a troubled teenager in some kind of rebellion. It is true that young adult writers have created thousands of variations on this theme, but the reason we put *genre* in quotation marks is that there is a tremendous crossover with what are traditionally defined as genres. Young protagonists might take important steps toward growing up while in outer space or while challenging nature by climbing a mountain or finding their way home after being lost. It could occur in a courtroom when a young person is either a witness or is on trial; it could occur as part of a love relationship or as part of facing up to a disaster in one's family or one's own life. The taking of such steps is a favorite theme for film producers as shown by the movies listed in Film Box 1.1, The World of Young Adults (p. 2). The world's great myths often feature young people accepting and overcoming challenges, and, as will be shown in the rest of this textbook, the story is an intrinsic part of the archetypal images that reside in the human psyche. This is why we not only have chapters about modern realistic, problem novels, but also about all the other genres including poetry, drama, humor, adventure, sports, the supernatural, mystery, fantasy, science fiction, historical fiction, and both literary and informative nonfiction.

Although we have moved such nonfiction books as poetry, biographies, memoirs, and information books to the appropriate chapters, in keeping with the Exeter Quality number 8 about varied levels of sophistication and Quality number 4 about going beyond typical experiences, the books on the Honor List reflect a tremendous variety of subjects, themes, and genres. Historical fiction includes Gary Paulsen's 1998 *Soldier's Heart*, Katherine Paterson's pre–Civil War *Jip: His Story* (1996), Olive Ann Burns's 1984 romantic *Cold Sassy Tree*, Kathryn Lasky's 1983 pioneer story *Beyond the Divide*, and Rosemary Sutcliff's 1990 *The Shining Company*, set in England in 600 AD. Elements of fantasy and science fiction are as old as the oldest folktale, as in Gail Carson Levine's 1997 *Ella Enchanted*, and as new as the latest board game in William Sleator's 1984 *Interstellar Pig*. Occult fiction is filled with romance as shown by Annette Curtis Klause's 1990 *The Silver Kiss* and Stephenie Meyer's 2005 *Twilight*, while futuristic stories thrive on high-tech intrigue as shown in Peter Dickinson's 1989 *Eva* and Robert Cormier's 1983 *The Bumblebee Flies Anyway*.

Although about half the books are contemporary, realistic fiction, they range from tightly plotted suspense stories as in Nancy Werlin's 1998 *The Killer's Cousin* and John Marsden's 1994 *Letters from the Inside* to serious introspection as in Paula Fox's 1984 *One-Eyed Cat*. Threats to the social order are explored in William Sleator's 1984 *Interstellar Pig* and in Lois Lowry's 1993 *The Giver*. A search for values is shown in Chris Crutcher's 1987 *The Crazy Horse Electric Game*. What it means to care for others is examined in Kimberly Holt's 1999 *When Zachary Beaver Came to Town*, Norma Fox Mazer's 1984 *Downtown*, Francesca Lia Block's 1993 *Missing Angel Juan*, and Gary Paulsen's 1993 *Harris and Me*.

Characteristic 5: The Body of Work Includes Stories about Characters from Many Different Ethnic and Cultural Groups

Characteristic 5 fits with Exeter Quality number 6, which asks for themes that truthfully inform about the wide world and allow readers to engage with difficult and challenging issues from both local and global perspectives. Forty years ago, the novels written specifically for teenagers and sold to schools and public libraries presented the same kind of middle-class, white-picket-fence neighborhoods as the one featured in the Dick and Jane readers from which most U.S. children were taught to read. But the mid-1960s witnessed a striking change in attitudes. One by one, taboos on profanity, divorce, sexuality, drinking, racial unrest, abortion, pregnancy, and drugs disappeared. With this change, writers were freed to set their stories in realistic rather than romanticized neighborhoods and to explore the experiences of characters whose stories had not been told before.

This freedom was a primary factor in the coming of age of adolescent literature. Probably because there was such a lack of good books about non-middle-class protagonists, and because this was where interesting things were happening, many writers during the late 1960s and the 1970s focused on minorities and on the kinds of kids that S. E. Hinton called *The Outsiders*. With the conservative swing that the United States took in the 1980s, not as much attention was paid to minority experiences; but with more globalization and instant communication, the trend is reversing so that there are many appealing new books that will be read by large numbers of teenagers of all races. It is also encouraging that we are seeing less segregation of characters. People are relating across ethnic boundaries, and in many of the books, the characters' ethnicity is downplayed. For example, in Virginia Euwer Wolff's 1993 *Make Lemonade*, there is no overt mention of skin color, but as one reviewer stated, Jolly and LaVaughn are held together by "the race of poverty."

In Chapter 3, we are going to discuss some of the reasons that today's teenagers are more interested in global concerns than they were a decade ago, but for now we will just mention a few books that demonstrate these expanded interests. Allan Stratton's 2004 *Chanda's Secrets* is about a sixteen-year-old girl who lives in sub-Saharan Africa, and is faced with arranging for the burial of her baby brother and eventually for her mother, both of whom succumb to AIDS. Patricia McCormick's 2006 *Sold* is a terrible—but beautifully told—story about Lakshmi, a girl in Nepal, who is sold to Auntie Bimla at the village store. She thinks she is going to work as a maid in a rich family, and that the money she earns will be sent home to provide her family with the new tin roof that their house needs. But actually Auntie Bimla sells her to "Uncle Husband." The reason for his name is that Lakshmi must pretend to be married to him when they cross the border into India. At the store where the arrangements are made, the store owner allows her stepfather to fill her mother's basket with goods. He chooses mostly things for himself, but Lakshmi bravely adds two things to the basket: "a sweater for Ana [her mother] and a coat for the baby." Then on this "rich and happy day for our family, an 800-rupee day, a festive and auspicious day" she adds "a bottle of Coca-Cola, the sweet drink that people say is like having tiny fireworks in your mouth."

My stepfather scowls, but he does not say anything. On any other day, he would not tolerate such defiance, especially from a mere girl.

But today I am no mere girl. (55)

Michael Morpurgo in his 2004 *Private Peaceful* tells a story from World War I, which is based on the British Army's practice at that time of summarily executing soldiers for relatively minor infractions. Today, the soldiers' actions would more likely have been recognized as a result of shock and fatigue. Other Honor List books that present a worldview include Joan Abelove's 1998 *Go and Come Back*, set in 1970s Peru; Carol Matas's 1996 *After the War*, set in 1940s Poland and Palestine; Nancy Farmer's 1996 *A Girl Named Disaster*, set in 1980s Mozambique and Zimbabwe; and Suzanne Fisher Staples's 1989 *Shabanu: Daughter of the Wind*, set in present-day Pakistan. Staples was a UPI news correspondent, who uses the story of a young woman's betrothal to introduce English readers to a culture very different from their own. Gary Paulsen's 1985 *Dogsong* is about a young Inuit; John Marsden's 1994 *Letters from the Inside* is set in Australia; Margaret Mahy's 1988 *Memory* is set in New Zealand; while Berlie Doherty's 1990 *White Peak Farm* grew out of her work preparing a BBC documentary in Sheffield, England.

Although most schools and libraries are making a concerted effort to stock and teach books reflecting many different cultures, educators worry that as publishers look more to marketing directly to teenagers, they may be less likely to publish "serious" stories about protagonists from minority groups because less-affluent kids, many of whom are from minorities, are not as likely to spend money on books as are white, middle-class teenagers. Also, as publishers try to attract readers by filling their books with wishful thinking, they tend to return to the romanticized beautiful-people view that was characteristic of the old adolescent literature.

Another fear is that, as with most television programming, everything will be watered down to suit mass tastes. But there are some crucial differences, because one person at a time reads a book, while television is usually viewed by a group.

Even with cable television, the number of channels from which a viewer can choose is limited, but books offer a vast choice. Moreover, advertisers pay for most television programs, while readers pay the production costs of books.

Characteristic 6: Young Adult Books Are Basically Optimistic, with Characters Making Worthy Accomplishments

The Exeter Quality number 6 mentions *truthfulness*, which relates closely to *credibility* and *believability*. It is emotionally satisfying to teenage readers to have the young protagonists portrayed as smart as, or even smarter than, their parents or teachers. Of course this isn't usually the situation, but good authors know that they have to write about their protagonists in such a way that they will be respected by the readers. The difference between short stories written for adults and those written for teenagers is often the attitude of the author. An author who views a teenager with either condescension or nostalgia will turn young adults away from the story. In young adult books, the protagonists must be involved in accomplishments that are believable but still challenging enough to earn the reader's respect. In the 1970s, when realism became the vogue and books were written with painful honesty about the frequently cruel world that teenagers face, some critics worried that YA books had become too pessimistic and cynical. However, even in so-called *downer* books, authors created characters that readers could admire for the way they faced up to their challenges.

A comparison of E. B. White's beloved *Charlotte's Web* and Robert Newton Peck's *A Day No Pigs Would Die* illustrates one of the differences between children's and adolescent literature. In White's classic children's book, a beloved but useless pig wins a ribbon at the County Fair and is allowed to live a long and happy life, whereas in Peck's young adult book a beloved but useless pig wins a ribbon at the County Fair but must be slaughtered anyway. Nevertheless, rather than being devastated by the death of the pig, readers identify with the boy and take pride in his ability to do what had to be done.

This kind of change and growth is the most common theme appearing in young adult literature, regardless of format. It suggests, either directly or symbolically, the gaining of maturity (i.e., the loss of innocence as part of the passage from childhood to adulthood). Such stories communicate a sense of time and change, a sense of becoming and catching glimpses of possibilities—some that are fearful and others that are awesome, odd, funny, perplexing, or wondrous.

One of the most popular ways to show change and growth is through a quest story (see Chapter 4 for a discussion and Focus Box 4.6, p. 138, for examples). Avi's 1990 *The True Confessions of Charlotte Doyle* is an almost pure example of a quest story camouflaged as a rollicking historical adventure. The intrepid narrator explains on page 1:

> . . . before I begin relating what happened, you must know something about me as I was in the year 1832 when these events transpired. At the time my name was Charlotte Doyle. And though I have kept the name, I am not for reasons you will soon discover the same Charlotte Doyle.

This captures the psychologically satisfying essence of quest stories, which is that the events in the story serve as a catalyst for the Exeter Quality number 7, which asks for emotional and intellectual growth through engagement with personal issues. This idea goes back to Stephen Roxburgh's observation (see p. 27) that by the end of most good books the young protagonist will have gained enough wisdom and understanding to become a reliable narrator.

Characteristic 7: Successful Young Adult Novels Deal with Emotions That Are Important to Young Adults

This characteristic overlaps with the Exeter Quality number 7 about emotional and intellectual growth. Often the difference in the life span between two books that are equally well written from a literary standpoint is that the ephemeral book fails to touch kids where they live, whereas the long-lasting book treats experiences that are psychologically important to young people. Of course, good authors do not peruse psychology books searching for case histories or symptoms of teenage problems that they can envision making into good stories. This would be as unlikely and as unproductive as it would be for a writer to study a book on literary devices and make a list: "First, I will use a metaphor and then a bit of alliteration and some imagery, followed by personification." In the best books, both the literary devices and the psychological insights must emerge from the honest telling of a story.

Pete Hautman's 2004 *Godless* is one of the Honor List books that does a good job of probing sixteen-year-old Jason Bock's psyche. As our colleague Jim Blasingame wrote when we reviewed the Honor List books for the *English Journal* (September 2005), Jason is "bullied, threatened, coerced, degraded, ridiculed, manipulated, and generally pinballed through life." The local tough guy "scares the crap" out of him, while his mother keeps scheduling him for doctors' appointments to see what's wrong with him, and his father, who is an attorney accustomed to getting problems solved, enrolls Jason in a church youth group called TPO (Teen Power Outreach).

In a moment of rebellion, Jason mockingly tells the TPO group that instead of being a practicing Catholic he is founding a new religion, one that will worship the town water tower and will be called *Chutengodianism*. To Jason's surprise, several of the teens join his new religion. They find it fun to be doing something so different, but Shin, a younger boy who, when the story starts, was Jason's only friend, takes the whole thing seriously.

A playful night spent "worshipping" the water tower (which really means climbing up and accidentally going swimming in the "holy water") ends badly and Jason is branded as a lost soul, a weirdo, a troublemaker, and a bad influence. Readers know differently and so does Jason, but still the book leaves readers, as well as Jason, pondering several questions of the kind that are often on kids' minds but not very often brought out for open discussion.

Psychological aspects of well-written novels are a natural part of the story as protagonists face the same kinds of challenges readers are experiencing, such as the developmental tasks outlined two generations ago by Robert J. Havighurst.

Adolescents at School: Perspectives on Youth, Identity, and Education, edited by Michael Sadowski. Harvard Education, 2003. In giving this 182-page book, written by sixteen educators, a positive review in *School Library Journal*, Mary Hofman wrote, "You will have an interesting and well-documented read that will support much of what it is hoped you are already doing."

The Culture of Adolescent Risk-Taking by Cynthia Lightfoot. Guilford Press, 1999. Lightfoot helps adults understand and deal with the pressures that contribute to teen attitudes of invincibility and daring.

Millennials Rising: The Next Great Generation by Neil Howe and William Strauss. Vintage, 2000. The authors claim that the Millennial Generation (those born between 1980 and 2000) are the grown-up kids of *Barney* rather than *Sesame Street*, of soccer moms rather than working moms, and of such bumper stickers as "Have you hugged your child today?" These "wanted" and loved children are having a different kind of adolescence than did the last generation.

Queen Bees and Wannabes: Helping Your Daughter Survive Cliques, Gossip, Boyfriends, and Other Realities of Adolescents by Rosalind Wiseman. Crown, 2002. Although the intended audience is adults, the writing is accessible to young women who might want to skim or read parts of it.

"Real Boys": Rescuing Our Sons from the Myths of Boyhood by William S. Pollack. Random House, 1998. Pollack is a clinical psychologist with the Harvard Medical Center and is asking people to take a second look at "the boy code," which describes boys as tough, cool, rambunctious, and obsessed with sports, cars, and sex. He thinks our major job is to help boys develop empathy and explore their sensitive sides so as to increase their ability to cope with frustrations.

When We're in Public, Pretend You Don't Know Me: Surviving Your Daughter's Adolescence So You Don't Look Like an Idiot and She Still Talks to You by Susan Borowitz and Ava L. Siegler. Warner Books, 2003. Siegler is a child psychologist and Borowitz is a Hollywood writer and producer, as well as a mother. The book is filled with sensible advice aimed mostly at mothers, but teachers and librarians can learn some things too.

1. Acquiring more mature social skills
2. Achieving a masculine or feminine sex role
3. Accepting the changes in one's body, using the body effectively, and accepting one's physique
4. Achieving emotional independence from parents and other adults
5. Preparing for sex, marriage, and parenthood
6. Selecting and preparing for an occupation
7. Developing a personal ideology and ethical standards
8. Assuming membership in the larger community[12]

Some psychologists gather all developmental tasks under the umbrella heading of "achieving an identity," which they describe as the task of adolescence. Some aspect of this is in practically any piece of fiction, poetry, drama, informative nonfiction, biographies, and self-help books that are written and published specifically for teenagers.

Close connections exist between adolescent literature and adolescent psychology, with psychology providing the overall picture and literature providing individual portraits. Because space in this text is too limited to include more than a hint of what you need to know about adolescent psychology, we suggest that professionals working with young people, read one or more of the books listed in Focus Box 1.1, Books to Help Adults Understand Teenagers. And as a reminder of the fact that teenagers face many different problems from those of adults, you might also want to view some of the films recommended in Film Box 1.1, The World of Young Adults. The more that you know, not only about the individual

Focus Box 1.2

Memoirs by Outstanding YA Authors

The Abracadabra Kid: A Writer's Life by Sid Fleischman. Greenwillow, 1996. Fleischman's story of his teenage years as a traveling magician is so interesting it was chosen for the Honor List.

All God's Children Need Traveling Shoes and *I Know Why the Caged Bird Sings* by Maya Angelou. Random House, 1986 and 1970. These lyrical and powerful autobiographies remain favorites of both adults and young readers.

Anonymously Yours by Richard Peck. Julian Messner, 1991. Readers can make interesting comparisons between the real-life events in *Anonymously Yours* and the fictional events that Peck writes about in his Newbery Medal–winning books: *A Long Way from Chicago* and *A Year Down Yonder.*

Bad Boy: A Memoir by Walter Dean Myers. Amistad Press, 2001. The two strengths of this book are the vivid details that Myers presents about Harlem in the 1940s and the documentation of his development from a street kid into a writer.

Counting Stars by David Almond. Delacorte, 2002. These eighteen stories about Almond's growing up in a large Roman Catholic family are told in the same magical and poetic tones that he has used in *Skellig, Heaven Eyes,* and *Kit's Wilderness.*

Frenchtown Summer by Robert Cormier. Delacorte, 1999. Although Cormier doesn't say this is an autobiography, the thirty narrative poems, all in first person, are told with such feeling that readers feel they are Cormier's own stories.

Hole in My Life by Jack Gantos. Farrar, 2002. Gantos spent a year in jail between high school and college because he helped sail a boatload of hashish from the Caribbean to New York City.

King of the Mild Frontier: An Ill-Advised Autobiography by Chris Crutcher. Greenwillow, 2003. Because Crutcher

works as a family counselor, many of us thought his plots came from the kids he counsels, but this forthright memoir shows that he has personally "lived" many of the emotions he writes about.

Knots in My Yo-Yo String by Jerry Spinelli. Knopf, 1998. Spinelli uses the lively style of his fiction to tell about the events he remembers from his first sixteen years.

Looking Back: A Book of Memories by Lois Lowry. Walter Lorraine, 1998. Lowry comments on and explains photos from four generations of her family. One reviewer shuddered at the thought of less-skilled writers following suit.

ME, ME, ME, ME, ME, Not a Novel by M. E. Kerr. Harper-Collins, 1983. Although these eleven short stories are just as much fun to read as are Kerr's novels, she says they are true accounts of the young life of Marijane Meaker, which is Kerr's real name.

My Life in Dog Years by Gary Paulsen. Delacorte, 1997. Paulsen recounts his experiences with ten different dogs—not the ones that went with him on the Iditarod race, which he writes about in his 1990 *Woodsong.*

Oddballs by William Sleator. Dutton, 1993. Kids who dream of getting even with family members by telling the world how strange they are can use Sleator's nine funny stories as a model.

The Pigman and Me by Paul Zindel. HarperCollins, 1992. Readers will both laugh and cry at this true account of a year in the teenage life of Paul Zindel when he was lucky enough to have Nonno Frankie (the model for Zindel's fictional Pigman) as a neighbor and friend.

A Way Out of No Way: Writing about Growing Up Black in America, edited by Jacqueline Woodson. Holt, 1996. Woodson writes about the hope and inspiration that she received from reading books by James Baldwin, Ernest J. Gaines, Rosa Guy, and Ntozake Shange.

teen readers that you work with but also about the emotional challenges and the interests that are common to most—if not all—young adults, the better able you will be to:

- Judge the soundness of the books they read.
- Decide which ones are worthy of promotion.
- Predict which ones will last and which will be transitory.
- Make better recommendations to individuals.
- Discuss books with students from their viewpoints.
- Gain more understanding and pleasure from personal reading.

Also included in this chapter is Focus Box 1.2, Memoirs by Outstanding YA Authors (p. 37). Because the authors are good writers and know what young adults are interested in, they have written their biographies with a focus on their own coming-of-age, a subject dear to the hearts of both adult and teenage writers. Besides introducing teen readers to some wonderful authors, these biographies illustrate new techniques and new attitudes, which can serve as models for teens' own creative writing and, in some cases, for their own artistic endeavors as with the drawings in Gene Luen Yang's graphic novel, *American Born Chinese*, and the illustrations in Sherman Alexie's *The Absolutely True Diary of a Part-Time Indian* (see p. 6). Students can get lots of inspiration and insight from looking at authors' websites, but they will get even more from reading such Honor List books as Yang's and Alexie's or one of the memoirs listed in Focus Box 1.2.

Notes

1. David Van Biema, "The Loneliest—and Purest—Rite of Passage: Adolescence and Initiation," *The Journey of Our Lives*, *Life* magazine (October 1991): 31.
2. David Spitz, "Reads Like Teen Spirit," *Time* magazine, July 19, 1999, p. 79.
3. Patty Campbell, "The Sand in the Oyster: Middle Muddle," *Horn Book* 76 (July–August 2000): 483–485.
4. Campbell, 485.
5. Lev Grossman and Andrea Sachs, "Harry Potter and the Sinister Spoilers," *Time* magazine, July 9, 2007, p. 52.
6. Ralph Peterson and Maryann Eeds, *Grand Conversations: Literature Groups in Action* (Scholastic, 1990).
7. Marlinda White-Kaulaity, "Reflections on Native American Reading: A Seed, a Tool, and a Weapon," *Journal of Adult and Adolescent Literacy* 50:7 (April 2007): 560–569.
8. Margaret Early, "Stages of Growth in Literary Appreciation," *English Journal* 49 (March 1960): 163–166.
9. First cited by G. Robert Carlsen in an article exploring stages of reading development, "Literature Is," *English Journal* 63 (February 1974): 23–27.
10. Rosemary Hopper, "The Good, the Bad and the Ugly: Teachers' Perception of Quality in Fiction for Adolescent Readers," *English in Education* 40 (Summer 2006): 55–70.
11. David Sptiz, "Reads Like Teen Spirit," *Time* magazine, July 19, 1999, p. 79.
12. Robert J. Havighurst, *Developmental Tasks and Education* (Longman Group United Kingdom, 1972).

A Brief History of Young Adult Literature

Of course, the best way to learn about young adult literature is to read widely in current books, but you will get more from that reading if you also know something about the history and the background of these new books. Knowing our common background gives us a sense of the past and insights into the values that our society wants to pass on to its young people. It also helps us realize why certain kinds of books have consistently proven popular while giving us a deeper understanding of current events and trends in the world of books and modern entertainment.

For example, when we went to our local theater to see Judd Apatow's 2007 *Knocked Up* comedy starring Katherine Heigl and Seth Rogen, we smiled at the poster featuring an enlarged quote from reviewer Joe Leydon because it reminded us of the differences between domestic and dime novels of the 1800s. Leydon praised the film as a balance of "the madcap swagger and uninhibited bawdiness of a high testosterone farce" (that is, a dime novel) with "the unabashed sweetness and romantic yearning of a chick flick" (that is, a domestic novel).

And in May, 2006 we thought of the Stratemeyer Syndicate when we read about Little, Brown recalling thousands of copies of a hot new book, *How Opal Mehta Got Kissed, Got Wild, and Got a Life*. The nineteen-year-old author, Kaavya Viswanathan, a sophomore at Harvard, was found to have plagiarized dozens of passages from two young-adult novels by Megan McCafferty.

Little, Brown editors shifted some of the blame by saying that the book had been prepared by a "book packager." According to a May 8, 2006, article in *Time* magazine entitled "An F for Originality" (p. 184), the book came to

Little, Brown through Alloy Entertainment, a company, "which develops book ideas, hires writers, then delivers a finished product to publishers." Such packagers usually work with nonfiction cookbooks or joke books, but Alloy, which owns a teen shopping website, delias.com, "has turned itself into a giant of young-women's fiction." Sara Nelson, the editor of *Publishers Weekly*, was quoted as explaining that book packagers do "the market researching of books, and every publisher is desperate for the teen market." Earlier, Alloy Entertainment had better luck in shepherding such books as Ann Brashares's *The Sisterhood of the Traveling Pants* and Lisi Harrison's *The Pretty Committee Strikes Back* (Book 5 of the Clique Series) to number one positions on the *New York Times* children's best-seller lists.

When we read an article in the *Arizona Republic* (April 13, 2007) under the title, "Whodunit? Your Favorite Author May Be Just a Brand Name," we again thought of the Stratemeyer Syndicate, which pretended to have such writers as Carolyn Keene for the Nancy Drew books and Victor Appleton for the Tom Swift books. *Arizona Republic* reporter Kerry Lengel started his article with the trick question, "Who wrote Tom Clancy's *Splinter Cell*?" and then went on to say that it certainly wasn't Tom Clancy. While Clancy's name is the biggest on the cover, David Michaels is identified as the writer, but there is really no David Michaels. It is a pseudonym created by ghostwriter Raymond Benson.

Lengel observed that in this age of high-power marketing, a new "common denominator is the centrality of an author's name as brand," as opposed to characters' names, as with James Bond or Nancy Drew. While "ghost writing is probably as old as Homer," today even the names of the "collaborators" are accruing value. James Patterson is supposedly the author of eight of the hundred most-popular books of 2006, but the majority of his books are written by coauthors who take a detailed outline and flesh it out. Clive Cussler's NUMA Files series is being written by Paul Kemprecos, and Dirk Cussler (Clive's son) is now doing the writing about the Dirk Pitt character. This is similar to the way that Christopher Tolkien is carrying on his father's Middle-earth universe and Brian Herbert is keeping Dune in the public eye.

In another example, when we read such highly acclaimed books as Patricia McCormick's 2006 *Sold*, about the sex trade in Nepal and India, and Allan Stratton's 2004 *Chanda's Secrets*, about the AIDS epidemic in Africa, we saw them as part of a continuing—but ever-changing—desire on the part of adults to use books as a way of instilling values and attitudes, and perhaps even inspiring social action, in the young.

Another reason to get acquainted with the history of young adult literature is that teachers and librarians may profit from discovering that books as different as John Bennett's *Master Skylark* (1847), Mabel Robinson's *Bright Island* (1937), and John Tunis's *Go Team, Go!* (1954) are fun to read or that Susan Coolidge's *What Katy Did* (1872), Ralph Henry Barbour's *The Crimson Sweater* (1906), and Mary Stolz's *Pray Love, Remember* (1954) are not without their charm.

See Focus Box 2.1, A Sampling of Books Appreciated by Young Adults 1864–1959 (p. 42) and also Focus Box 2.2, New Tellings of Old Stories (p. 44), which illustrates an interesting kind of recycling in which authors adapt and retell with contemporary sensibilities some of the same stories that young readers have appreciated over the last few centuries.

For the convenience of readers, this chapter is divided into four parts: 1800–1900, 1900–1940, 1940–1960, and 1960–1980.

1800–1900: A Century of Purity with a Few Passions

Before 1800, literature read by children and young adults alike was largely religious. Such books as John Bunyan's *The Pilgrim's Progress* (1678) reminded young people that they were merely small adults who soon must face the wrath of God. In the 1800s, the attitude of adults toward the young gradually changed. The country expanded, we moved inevitably toward an urban society, medical knowledge rapidly developed, and young people no longer began working so early in their lives. The literature that emerged for young adults remained pious and sober, but it hinted at the possibility of humanity's experiencing a satisfying life here on earth. Books reflected adult values and fashions, but of this world, not merely the next.

The American Sunday School Union

Largely forgotten, a spiritual and practical movement that began in 1817 in Philadelphia under the title of the Sunday and Adult School Union changed its title to the American Sunday School Union in 1824. By 1830, it had determined to change the course of U.S. education by offering Sunday School lessons that taught religion at the same time they educated young people in mathematics and grammar and history and all sorts of practical, job-related skills.

For the next forty years, the Union produced millions of books for use in Sunday Schools, which were open from 8:00 AM to 10:00 AM and from 4:00 PM to 6:00 PM. All titles were approved by a board representing six major religions. Titles varied from *History of Patriarchs*; *Wild Flowers: or the May Day Walk*; *The Early Saxons*; and *Curiosities of Egypt*; to *Delaware and Iroquois Indians*; and *Kindness to Animals, or the Sin of Cruelty Exposed and Rebuked*.

The Union was best known, however, for its heavily moralistic fiction, rarely deviating from two basic formulas. First, a young child near death would remind readers of all his or her virtues, all that they must remember and practice, and then the child would die, to the relief of readers. On page 1 of E. P. Grey's *My Teacher's Present: A Select Biography of the Young*, the author wrote:

> You have in this little volume the biography of six Sunday school pupils, who were early called from this world. They were happy and beloved whilst they lived, and deeply lamented when they died.

Another formula portrayed good children who had temporarily forgotten duties to parents and siblings and who would soon get their come-uppance. Most of the books were little more than sugar-coated sermons; the titles usually gave away the plot, and the writing was unbelievably mawkish. By the 1870s and 1880s, the Union books lost most of their readership to the almost equally badly written work of Horatio Alger, to the often brilliant prose of Louisa May Alcott, and to various writers of dime novels or domestic novels. At a time when few

A Sampling of Books Appreciated by Young Adults 1864–1959

1864: Frank the Young Naturalist by Harry Castlemon (really Charles Austin Fosdick) is close to unreadable today, but Castlemon's series books were popular well into the twentieth century.

1868: Little Women: Meg, Jo, Beth, and Amy. The Story of Their Lives. A Girl's Book by Louisa May Alcott is so honest that it is still loved today.

1870: The Story of a Bad Boy by Thomas Bailey Aldrich launched a new kind of literature about boys who were imperfect and tough—a refreshing counterbalance to the good-little-boy figures prevalent in too many unrealistic books of the time.

1872: What Katy Did by Susan Coolidge (really Sarah Chauncey Woolsey), featured a prankish and fun-loving tomboy and for a time rivaled *Little Women* in popularity.

1876: The Boy Emigrants by Noah Brooks is a romanticized but fascinating tale of boys traveling across the plains.

1883: Treasure Island by Robert Louis Stevenson is filled with the kind of adventure and derring-do that still appeals to boys.

1888: Derrick Sterling by Kirk Munroe. When Derrick's father dies, Derrick must leave school and work eleven-hour shifts in the mines. In this early, realistic picture of the mines and child labor, he becomes a hero when disaster strikes.

1897: Master Skylark: A Story of Shakespeare's Time by John Bennett is the witty account of young Nick Attwood, a golden-voiced boy singer involved in more than his share of adventure.

1899: The Half-Back by Ralph Henry Barbour was the first of many popular sports books, including *The Crimson Sweater* (1906), in which boys at school learn who and what they might become through sports.

1899: Peggy by Laura Elizabeth Richards is about a poor girl going to school and becoming a basketball hero.

1904: Rebecca of Sunnybrook Farm by Kate Douglas Wiggin sold more than 1.25 million copies and launched a formula in which a young child (usually a girl) makes life happy for apathetic or depressed adults.

1908: Anne of Green Gables by Lucy Maud Montgomery continued the Wiggin formula when an orphan girl is sent by mistake to a childless couple who wanted a boy to help on the farm.

1913: Pollyanna by Eleanor Porter, the climax (or the finishing blow) to the child-as-savior formula, was a popular adult novel, eighth among best sellers in 1913 and second in 1914.

1919: High Benton by William Heyliger. Steve Benson's parents want him to go to high school, but his friends are getting jobs. Heyliger shows Steve's next four years as he struggles between his ambitions and education. *High Benton, Worker* is the sequel.

1936: Tangled Waters, about a Navajo girl on an Arizona reservation, *Shuttered Windows* (1938) about an African American girl who leaves Minneapolis to live with her grandmother in South Carolina, and *The Moved Outers* (1945) about Japanese Americans forced into a relocation camp during World War II, all by Florence Crannell Means,

---

children had any chance of a formal education in schools, however, the American Sunday School Union books were widely read and did much to advance the cause of literacy in America.

Alcott and Alger

Louisa May Alcott and Horatio Alger, Jr., were the first writers for young adults to gain national attention, but the similarity between the two ends almost as it begins. Alcott wrote of happy family life. Alger wrote about broken homes. Alcott's novels were sometimes harsh but always honest. Alger's novels were

were the first sympathetic and rich portraits of young protagonists from minority cultures.

1936: *Peggy Covers the News* by Emma Bugbee, a reporter for the *New York Times*, launched a deluge of career books for girls that included Helen Boylston's books about nurse Sue Barton and Helen Wells's books about nurse Cherry Ames and flight attendant Vicki Barr.

1937: *The Great Tradition* by Marjorie Hill Allee intrigued young adults with its mixture of romance, college life, and the spirit of research among five graduate students at the University of Chicago.

1937: *Bright Island* by Mabel Robinson is the story of spunky Thankful Curtis, who was raised on a small island off the coast of Maine and later attends school on the mainland.

1938: *Iron Duke* by John Tunis was the first of several popular books written by an amateur athlete and sports reporter. Other Tunis titles, some of which have been recently reprinted, include *All American* (1942), *Yea Wildcats* (1944), and *Go, Team, Go!* (1954).

1942: *Seventeenth Summer* by Maureen Daly is the story of shy and innocent Angie Morrow and her love for Jack Duluth during the summer between high school and college.

1942: *Adam of the Road* by Elizabeth Janet Gray reveals the color and music of the Middle Ages as young Adam Quartermain becomes a minstrel.

1943: *The Innocent Wayfaring* by Marchette Chute covers four days in June 1370 when Anne runs away from her convent school to join a band of strolling players.

1945: *Pray Love, Remember* by Mary Stolz is one of the earliest and one of the best of Stolz's many quiet, introspective books; it is a remarkable story of Dody Jenks, a popular but cold young woman who likes neither her family nor herself.

1947: *The Divided Heart* and *A Cup of Courage* (1948) by Mina Lewiton were pioneering problem novels in being, respectively, an honest and groundbreaking study of the effects of divorce on a young woman and of alcoholism and its destruction of a family.

1950: *Swiftwater* by Paul Annixter (really Howard A. Sturzel) mixes animals, ecology, symbolism, and some stereotyped characters into a rousing tale that remains a better than respectable book.

1952: *Two and the Town* by Henry Gregor Felsen. A young girl is pregnant and a marriage is forced on two teenagers, something that at the time was taboo for YA books. Felsen is better known for *Hot Rod* (1950) and *Crash Club* (1958).

1957: *Ring Around Her Finger* and *The Limit of Love* (1959) by James Summers, were effective delineations of young people's sexual feelings and actions told from the boys' points of view. Critics feared readers were too young to handle such emotional intricacies.

1958: *The 23rd Street Crusaders* by John F. Carson. When Ed Sorrell's son dies in a reformatory, Sorrell gives up his job coaching basketball. Later, he finds some boys on probation and talks them into becoming a basketball team.

1959: *Jennifer* by Zoa Sherburne is an enduring portrait of the effects of alcoholism, but it is not as good as Sherburne's *Too Bad about the Haines Girl* (1967), a superb novel about teenage pregnancy that is honest and straightforward without being preachy.

romantic fantasies. Alcott's novels are still read, for good reason. Alger's novels are rarely read save by the historian or the specialist.

The second daughter of visionary Amos Bronson Alcott, Louisa May Alcott lived her youth near Concord and Boston with a practical mother and a father who was brilliant, generous, improvident, and impractical. The reigning young adult writer of the time was Oliver Optic (the pen name of William T. Adams), and Boston publisher Roberts Brothers was eager to find a story for young adults that would compete with Optic. Thomas Niles, Roberts's representative, suggested in September 1866 that Louisa May Alcott write a girls' book, and in May 1868 he gently reminded her that she had agreed to try.

The Amazing Maurice and His Educated Rodents by Terry Pratchett. HarperCollins, 2001. Loosely based on the old story of the Pied Piper, Pratchett's book makes readers laugh out loud. The rats will remind readers of those in Robert C. O'Brien's *Mrs. Frisby and the Rats of NIMH* (Atheneum, 1971).

The Ballad of Sir Dinadan by Gerald Morris. Houghton, 2003. Students who have enjoyed this lighthearted Arthurian tale about the younger brother of the famous Sir Tristram will have a head start when they get to college and read *The Faerie Queene*.

Beowulf: A Hero's Tale Retold by James Rumford. Houghton, 2007. Rumford's skilled retelling and his beautiful illustrations help to make this complex story accessible to students in middle school.

Book of a Thousand Days by Shannon Hale. Bloomsbury, 2007. In giving this retelling of the Grimm Brothers' fairy tale "Maid Maleen" a star, the *School Library Journal* reviewer praised it "as quite an improvement" over the original, especially in the way that Hale created its medieval and magical setting. Earlier Shannon Hale retellings that have been praised are *River Secrets* (2006), *The Goose Girl* (2003), and *Enna Burning* (2004), all from Bloomsbury.

Bound by Donna Jo Napoli. Simon & Schuster, 2004. This retelling of Cinderella is set in China where Xing Xing's stepmother's only concern is a good marriage for her daughter. Other Napoli retellings in which she creates fully developed characters include *Zel*, based on "Rapunzel"; *The Magic Circle*, which tells "Hansel and Gretel" from the witch's viewpoint; and *Sirena*, about a siren who falls in love with a mortal.

Fairest by Gail Carson Levine. HarperCollins, 2006. The fairy-tale setting allows readers to come with fresh eyes to this exploration of inner versus outer beauty. Levine's earlier retellings of fairy tales include *Ella Enchanted* and *Cinderellis and the Glass Hill*.

Golden by Cameron Dokey. S & S/Pulse, 2006. Two beautiful girls, Rapunzel and Rue, have their lives irrevocably changed at birth, one because she's bald and one because a wizard wants to teach her mother a lesson. Through a series of ins and outs worthy of the most complicated fairy tale, there is a happy ending.

The Lightning Thief by Rick Riordan. Hyperion/Miramax, 2005. The hero of this contemporary story, teenaged Perseus Jackson, is surprised to learn that he is the son of Poseidon and a mortal woman. He (along with readers)

She sent a manuscript to Niles, who thought parts of it dull, but other readers at the publisher's office disagreed, and the first part of *Little Women: Meg, Jo, Beth, and Amy. The Story of Their Lives. A Girl's Book* was published September 30, 1868. With three illustrations and a frontispiece for $1.50 a copy, *Little Women* was favorably reviewed, and sales were good, here and in England. By early November 1868, Alcott had begun work on the second part, which was published on April 14, 1869.

Little Women has vitality and joy and real life devoid of the sentimentality common at the time, a wistful portrait of the life and world Alcott must have wished she could have lived. The Civil War background is subtle, expressing the loneliness and never-ending war far better than many adult war novels. *Little Women* has maintained steady popularity both with new readers and with adults who reread it (sometimes repeatedly) to gain a sense of where they were when they were children.

Horatio Alger, Jr., son of an unctuous Unitarian clergyman, graduated from Harvard at 18, and, in 1864, was ordained a Unitarian minister. He served a Brewster, Massachusetts, church, only to leave it two years later under a cloud of

is also surprised to learn how active the Greek gods are and that they have a job for him in Hades's underworld, which he has to enter through Los Angeles.

Not the End of the World by Geraldine McCaughrean. HarperTempest, 2005. Both humans and animals get to offer their views in this 244-page retelling of Noah and his ark. Daughter Timna, who went against her father's instructions and helped save a young boy and his baby sister from drowning, has the most to say. The book won the Whitbread Children's Book Award in England. In her 1997 *The Silver Treasure: Myths and Legends of the World*, McCaughrean gives new life to Rip Van Winkle, King Arthur, and Sir Patrick Spens.

Robin of Sherwood by Michael Morpurgo, illustrated by Michael Foreman. Harcourt, 1996. The characters have the same names as in the classic tale, but they have distinguishing characteristics that make them quite different. The story starts with a contemporary boy's finding Robin's skull, fainting, and dreaming of Robin. The team also created *Arthur: High King of Britain* (Harcourt, 1995).

Shadow Spinner by Susan Fletcher. Simon & Schuster/ Atheneum, 1998. A young crippled storyteller, Marjan, brings a new story to Queen Shaharazad, who has already been spinning stories for nearly 1,000 nights. Complications ensue when Marjan can't remember the ending.

Spider's Voice by Gloria Skurzynski. Simon & Schuster/ Atheneum, 1999. Skurzynski retells the story of the twelfth-century French lovers Abelard and (H)Eloise through the voice of a fictional servant nicknamed Spider. The plot is as tangled as a spider's web and the characters' lives as easily dismantled.

Undercover by Beth Kephart. HarperFestival, 2007. In this beautifully written story, when Elisa's English class reads *Cyrano d'Bergerac,* the self-effacing girl, who has been writing notes for boys to give to their girlfriends, realizes that she has fallen into playing a role she does not want.

William Shakespeare's Hamlet retold by Bruce Coville, illustrated by Leonid Gore. Dial, 2004. Coville has kept a richness of language, along with all the "ghosts, murder, madness, and revenge," of the original story, but at the same time has made the story accessible to young teens.

The Witch's Boy by Michael Gruber. HarperTempest, 2005. Nearly four hundred pages long, Gruber's well-told story will make readers think a little differently about such old classics as "Hansel and Gretel," "Rumplestiltskin," and "Little Red Riding Hood."

scandal and claims of sodomy, all hushed up at the time. He moved to New York City and began writing full time.

He sent a manuscript, *Ragged Dick; or, Street Life in New York*, to Oliver Optic's magazine, *Student and Schoolmate*, a popular goody-goody magazine. Optic recognized salable pap when he spotted it, and he bought Alger's book for the January 1867 issue. Published in hardcover in 1867 or 1868, *Ragged Dick* was the first of many successes for Alger, and it is still his most readable work, probably because it was the first from a mold that soon became predictably moldy.

The plot, as in most Alger books, consisted of semiconnected episodes illustrating a boy's first steps toward maturity, respectability, and affluence. Ragged Dick, a young bootblack, is grubby but not dirty, he smokes and gambles occasionally, but even the most casual reader recognizes his essential goodness. Through a series of increasingly difficult-to-believe chapters, Ragged Dick is transformed by the model of a young man and the trust of an older one into respectability. While this sequence of events is hard to believe, Alger soon makes events impossible to believe as he introduces the note that typified his later books. What pluck and hard work had brought to Dick is now cast aside as luck enters

One teacher brought in pomegranates so her students could eat a few of the seeds when she told the Greek story of Pluto's kidnapping of Persephone from Demeter (c.f. the Latin story of Proserpine being taken from Ceres) to begin a discussion of the symbolic role that food plays in both old and new stories.

in—a little boy falls overboard from a ferry, Dick saves the child, and a grateful father rewards Dick with new clothes and a better job. Some readers label Alger's books "rags to riches" stories, but the hero rarely achieves riches, although at the close of the book he is a rung or two higher on the ladder of success than he has any reason to deserve. "Rags to respectability" is a more accurate statement about Alger's work.

The Two Most Popular Types of Novels: Domestic and Dime Novels

In 1855, Nathaniel Hawthorne wrote his publisher, bitterly lamenting the state of American literature:

> America is now wholly given over to a d—d mob of scribbling women, and I should have no chance of success while the public taste is occupied with their trash—and should be ashamed of myself if I did succeed. What is the mystery of these innumerable editions of *The Lamplighter*, and other books neither better nor worse?—worse they could not be, and better they need not be, when they sell by the 10,000?[1]

The trash was the domestic novel. Born out of the belief that humanity was redeemable, the domestic novel preached morality; woman's submission to man; the value of cultural, social, and political conservatism; a religion of the heart and the Bible; and the glories of suffering.

Most domestic novels concerned a young girl, orphaned and placed in the home of a relative or some benefactor, who meets a darkly handsome young man with shadows from his past, a man not to be trusted but worth redeeming and converting. Domestic novels promised some adventure amid many moral lessons. The heroines differed more in names than characteristics. Uniformly submissive to—yet distrustful of—their betters and men generally, they were self-sacrificing and self-denying beyond belief or common sense and interested in the primacy of the family and marriage as the goal of all decent women. Domestic novels were products of the religious sentiment of the time, the espousal of traditional virtues, and the anxieties and frustrations of women trying to find a role in a changing society.

Writing under the pen name of Elizabeth Wetherell, Susan Warner wrote more than twenty novels and the first domestic novel, *The Wide, Wide World* (1850). As much as forty years later, the novel was said to be one of the four most widely read books in the United States, along with the Bible, *The Pilgrim's Progress*, and *Uncle Tom's Cabin*. An abridged edition was published in England in 1950 by the University of London Press, and the Feminist Press republished Warner's book in 1987.

The novel was rejected by several New York publishers. George Putnam was ready to return it but decided to ask his mother to read it. She did, she loved it, she urged her son to publish it, and the book was out in time for the Christmas trade. Sales slowly picked up, and the first edition sold out in four months. Translations into French, German, Swedish, and Italian followed, and by 1852, *The Wide, Wide World* was in its fourteenth printing.

The author's life paralleled that of her heroine, Ellen Montgomery. Warner's father was pathetically and persistently broke, and although the fictional world is not quite so ugly, Ellen's mother died early, and her father was so consumed with family business that he asked Aunt Fortune Emerson to take over Ellen's life. Ellen, to her aunt's irritation, formed a firm friendship with the aunt's intended. Ellen's closest friend—the daughter of the local minister—was doomed to die soon and succeeded in doing just that. In the midst of life, tears flowed. When Ellen and her friends were not crying, they were cooking. Warner's novel taught submission, the dangers of self-righteousness, and the virtues of a steadfast religion. Despite all the weeping, or maybe because of it, the book seemed to have been read by everyone of its time. E. Douglas Branch called it, "The greatest achievement of any of the lady novelists."[2]

Warner's popularity was exceeded only by Augusta Jane Evans Wilson for her *St. Elmo* (1867). Probably no other novel so literally touched the American landscape—thirteen towns were named, or renamed, St. Elmo, as were hotels, railroad coaches, steamboats, one kind of punch, and a brand of cigars. The popularity of Wilson's book may be gauged by a notice in a special edition of *St. Elmo* "limited to 100,000 copies." Only *Uncle Tom's Cabin* had greater sales, and Wilson was more than once called by her admirers the American Brontë.

Ridiculously melodramatic as the plot of *St. Elmo* is, it was so beloved that men and women publicly testified that their lives had been permanently changed for the better by reading it. The plot concerns an orphaned girl befriended by a wealthy woman whose dissolute son is immediately enamored of the young woman, is rejected by her, leaves home for several years, returns to plead for her love, is again rejected, and eventually becomes a minister to win the young woman's hand. They marry, another wicked man reformed by the power of a good woman.

While domestic novels took women by storm, dime novels performed almost the same miracle for men. They began when two brothers, Erastus and Irwin

These two half-dime novels illustrate the promised action, the purple prose, and the erudite vocabulary of their day.

Beadle, republished Ann S. Stephens's *Malaeksa: The Indian Wife of the White Hunter* in June 1860. The story of a hunter and his Indian wife in the Revolutionary War days in upper New York state may be as melodramatic as any domestic novel, but its emphasis is more on thrills and chills than tears, and it apparently satisfied and intrigued male readers. Indeed, 65,000 copies of the six- by four-inch book of 128 pages sold in almost record time. The most popular of the early dime novels, also set in the Revolutionary period, appeared in October 1860. *Seth Jones: or, The Captives of the Frontier* sold 60,000 copies the first day; at least 500,000 copies were sold in the United States alone, and it was translated into ten languages.

For several years, dime novels cost ten cents, ran about 100 pages in a seven- by five-inch format, and were aimed at adults. Some early genius of publishing discovered that many readers were boys who could hardly afford the dime cost. Thereafter, the novels dropped to a nickel, although the genre continued to be called the *dime novel*. The most popular dime novels were set in the West—the West of dime novels increasingly meant Colorado and points west—with wondrous he-men like Deadwood Dick and Diamond Dick. Dime novels developed other forms, such as mysteries and even early forms of science fiction, but none were so popular or so typical as the westerns.

Writers of dime novels never pretended to be writing great literature, but they did write satisfying thrills and chills for the masses. The books were filled with stock characters. Early issues of the *Library Journal*, from 1876 onward for another thirty years, illustrate how many librarians hated dime novels for their immorality; but in truth dime novels were moral. The Beadles sincerely believed that their books should represent sound moral values, and what the librarians objected to in dime novels was nothing more than the unrealistic melodramatic plots and the stereotyped characters, more typical of the time than of just the dime novel.

Development of the American Public Library

The development of the public library was as rocky and slow as it was inevitable. In 1731, Benjamin Franklin suggested that members of the Junto, a middle-class social and literary club in Philadelphia, share their books with other members. That led to the founding of the Philadelphia Library Company, America's first subscription library. Other such libraries followed, most of them dedicated to moral purposes, as the constitution of the Salisbury, Connecticut, Social Library announced: "The promotion of Virtue, Education, and Learning, and . . . the discouragement of Vice and Immorality."[3]

In 1826, the governor of New York urged that school district libraries be established, in effect using school buildings for public libraries. Similar libraries were established in New England by the 1840s and in the Midwest shortly thereafter. Eventually, mayors and governors saw the wisdom of levying state taxes to support public libraries in their own buildings, not the schools, and by 1863, there were 1,000 public libraries spread across the United States. In 1876, Melvil Dewey, then assistant librarian in the Amherst College Library, was largely responsible for an October 4, 1876, conference of librarians that formed the American Library Association and created the first professional journal for librarians. *The American Library Journal* appeared that same year, but soon changed its name to the *Library Journal*. While there had been an abortive meeting in 1853, the 1876 meeting promised continuity that the earlier meeting had lacked.[4]

In 1884, Columbia College established the first school of Library Economy (later to be called Library Science) under Melvil Dewey's leadership. These early public libraries grew immeasurably under the philanthropy of Andrew Carnegie, a Scottish immigrant who donated millions of dollars for the creation of public libraries across the United States.

Fiction and Libraries

The growth of public libraries presented opportunities for pleasure and education of the masses, but arguments about the purposes of the public library arose almost as fast as the buildings. William Poole listed three common objections to the public library in the October 1876 *American Library Journal*: the normal dread of taxes; the more philosophical belief that government had no rights except to protect people and property—that is, no right to tax anyone to build and stock a public library; and concern over the kinds of books libraries might buy and circulate.[5] The controversy of whether a public library is established for scholars or for the pleasure of the masses raged for years. Poole believed that a library existed for the entire community, or else there was no justification for a general tax. Others argued that the library's sole *raison d'être* was educational. Waving the banner of American purity, W. M. Stevenson maintained:

> If the public library is not first and foremost an educational institution, it has no right to exist. If it exists for mere pleasure, and for a low order of entertainment at that, it is simply a socialistic institution.[6]

Many librarians of the time agreed. Probably, a few agree even today.

The problem lay almost entirely with fiction. Indeed, the second session of the 1876 American Library Association meeting was devoted to "Novel Reading," especially by young people. A librarian announced that he permitted no fiction in his library. His factory-patrons might ask for novels, but he recommended other books and was able to keep patrons without supplying novels. To laughter, he said that he had never read novels so he "could not say what their effect really was."[7]

Teachers worried almost as much as librarians. A principal of a large endowed academy was approvingly quoted by a librarian for having said,

> The voracious devouring of fiction commonly indulged in by patrons of the public library, especially the young, is extremely pernicious and mentally unwholesome.[8]

That attitude persisted for years and is occasionally heard even today among teachers and librarians.

1900–1940: From the Safety of Romance to the Beginning of Realism

During the first forty years of the twentieth century, the western frontier disappeared, and the United States changed from an agrarian society to an urban one. World War I brought the certainty that it would end all wars. The labor movement grew along with Ford's production lines of cars, cars, cars. President Hoover came along, then the Wall Street crash of 1929 and the Great Depression. By 1938, three million young people from age 16 through 25 were out of school and unemployed, and a quarter of a million boys were on the road. Nazi Germany rose in Eastern Europe, and in the United States, Roosevelt introduced the "New Deal." When the end of the Depression seemed almost in sight, the New York World's Fair of 1939 became an optimistic metaphor for the coming of a newer, better, happier, and more secure life. But World War II lay just over the horizon, apparent to some, ignored by most.

Reading Interests versus Reading Needs

In the high schools, which enrolled only a tiny fraction of eligible students in the United States, teachers faced pressure from colleges to prepare the young for advanced study, which influenced many adults to be more intent on telling young people what to read than in finding out what they wanted to read. Recreational reading seemed vaguely time-wasting, if not downright wicked. Young people nevertheless found and read books, mainly fiction, for recreation. Popular choices were series books from Stratemeyer's Literary Syndicate, including Tom Swift, Nancy Drew, the Hardy Boys, Baseball Joe, and Ruth Fielding. Non-Stratemeyer series books were also popular, as were individual books written specifically for young adults, along with some classics and best sellers selected by the Book-of-the-Month Club when it began in 1926 and the Literary Guild when it began a year later.

Arguments over what students choose to read have raged for years, and the end is unlikely to come soon. In 1926, when Carleton Washburne and Mabel Vogel put together the lengthy *Winnetka Graded Book List*, they explained, "Books that were definitely trashy or unsuitable for children, even though widely read, have not been included in this list."[9] Apparently enough people were curious about the trashy or unsuitable to lead the authors to add two supplements.[10] *Elsie Dinsmore* was among the damned, and so were Edgar Rice Burroughs's *Tarzan of the Apes*, Eleanor Porter's *Pollyanna*, Zane Grey's westerns, books from the Ruth Fielding and Tom Swift series, Mark Twain's *Tom Sawyer Abroad*, and Arthur Conan Doyle's *The Hound of the Baskervilles*. *The Adventures of Sherlock Holmes*, however, was considered worthy of inclusion.

Representative of the other side of the argument is this statement by English professor William Lyon Phelps:

> I do not believe the majority of these very school teachers and other cultivated mature readers began in early youth by reading great books exclusively; I think they read *Jack Harkaway, an Old Sleuth*, and the works of Oliver Optic and Horatio Alger. From these enchanters they learned a thing of tremendous importance— the delight of reading. Once a taste for reading is formed, it can be improved. But it is improbable that boys and girls who have never cared to read a good story will later enjoy stories by good artists.[11]

Girls' Books and Boys' Books

Up to the mid-1930s, teachers and librarians frequently commented that girls' books were inferior to boys' books. Franklin T. Baker wrote that with the obvious exception of Alcott, girls' books of 1908 were "painfully weak" and lacking "invention, action, humor."[12] Two years later, Clara Whitehill Hunt agreed that many girls' books were empty, insipid, and mediocre.[13] In 1935, Julia Carter broke into a review of boys' nonfiction with what appeared to be an exasperated *obiter dictum*:

> Will someone please tell me why we expect the boys to know these things and still plan for the girls to be mid-Victorian, and consider them hoydens beyond reclaiming, when instead of shrieking and running like true daughters of Eve, they are interested in snakes and can light a fire with two matches?[14]

Such writers as Caroline Dale Snedeker, Cornelia Meigs, Jeanette Eaton, Mabel Robinson, and Elizabeth Forman Lewis responded to these kinds of criticism by writing enough good girls' books that in 1937 Alice M. Jordan wrote as if the difference in quality was a thing of the past:

> There was a time not long ago when the boys had the lion's share in the yearly production of books intended for young people. So writers were urged to give us more

stories in which girls could see themselves in recognizable relationship to the world of their own time, forgetting perhaps that human nature does not change and the vital things are universal. Yet, nonetheless, the girls had a real cause to plead and right valiantly the writers have responded.[15]

Critics believed then, as they continued to insist for years, that girls would read boys' books, but boys would never read girls' books. At least part of the problem lay with stereotypes of boys' and girls' roles as expressed by two writers. Clara Vostrovsky, author of the first significant reading interest study, went back to ancient times for her stereotypes, suggesting that it was "probable" that the differences in reading interests between boys and girls lay "in the history of the race."[16] Psychologist G. Stanley Hall predicted reading interests of girls and boys on psychological differences:

> Boys love adventure, girls sentiment. . . . Girls love to read stories about girls which boys eschew, girls, however, caring much more to read about boys than boys to read about girls. Books dealing with domestic life and with young children in them, girls have almost entirely to themselves. Boys, on the other hand, excel in love of humor, rollicking fun, abandon, rough horse-play, and tales of wild escapades. Girls are less averse to reading what boys like than boys are to reading what girls like. A book popular with boys would attract some girls, while one read by most girls would repel a boy in the middle teens. The reading interests of high-school girls are far more humanistic, cultural and general, and that of boys is more practical, vocational, and even special.[17]

The simple truth, perhaps too obvious and discomforting to be palatable to some parents, English teachers, and librarians, was that boys' books were generally far superior to girls' books. That had nothing to do with the sexual or psychological nature of boys or girls but rather with the way authors treated their audience.

The Changing English Classroom

By 1900, some librarians were helping young adults find a variety of materials they liked; however, this was rarely true of English teachers saddled as they were with responsibility for preparing young adults for college entrance examinations. At first, these examinations simply required some proof of writing proficiency, but in 1860 and 1870, Harvard began using Milton's *Comus* and Shakespeare's *Julius Caesar* as alternative books for the examination. Four years later, Harvard required a short composition based on a question about one of the following: Shakespeare's *The Tempest*, *Julius Caesar*, and *The Merchant of Venice*, Goldsmith's *The Vicar of Wakefield*, or Scott's *Ivanhoe* and *The Lay of the Last Minstrel*.

In 1894, the prestigious Committee of Ten on Secondary School Studies presented its report making English an accepted discipline in the schools, although not yet as respectable as Latin. The committee had been appointed by the National Education Association and was chaired by the controversial Harvard president Charles W. Eliot. It was charged with determining the nature, limits, and

In the decades before the 1929 stock market crash, U.S. high schools developed in their present form, including the establishment of athletic teams as a way of "bribing" boys into reading and writing. Shown here is the 1917 Tempe Public Schools baseball team.

(Photo courtesy of the Tempe Historical Museum)

methods appropriate to many subject matters in secondary school. Samuel Thurber of the Boston Girls' High School tried unsuccessfully to promote his belief that a high school curriculum should consist almost entirely of elective courses. However, two adopted recommendations liberalized and dignified the study of English by saying that English should be studied for five hours a week during all four years of high school and that uniform college entrance examinations should be established throughout the United States.

The result was the publication of book lists dictating such classics as Shakespeare's *Twelfth Night* and *As You Like It*, Milton's Books I and II from *Paradise Lost*, Scott's *The Abbot* and *Marmion*, and Irving's *Bracebridge Hall* be used as the basis for college entrance exams. Teachers, inevitably concerned with their students' entry into college, increasingly adapted their classroom reading to fit the list.

National Council of Teachers of English Begins

Out of the growing protest about college entrance examinations, a group of English teachers attending a national Education Association meeting formed a Committee on College Entrance Requirements in English to assess the problem through a national survey of English teachers. The committee uncovered hostility to colleges presumptuous enough to try to control the secondary English curriculum through the guise of entrance examinations. John M. Coulter, a professor at the University of Chicago, tried to sound that alarm to college professors but without much success:

> The high school exists primarily for its own sake; and secondarily as a preparatory school for college. This means that when the high school interest and the college interest comes into conflict, the college interest must yield. It also means that the function of a preparatory school must be performed only in so far as it does not interfere with the more fundamental purpose of the high school itself.[18]

Some irate teachers recognized that the problem of college control would hardly be the last issue to face English teachers and formed the nucleus of the National Council of Teachers of English. The First Annual Meeting in Chicago on December 1 and 2, 1911, was largely devoted to expressing resentment about actions of the National Conference on Uniform Entrance Requirements, particularly because that body had representatives from twelve colleges, two academies, and only two public high schools (principals, not English teachers). Wilbur W. Hatfield, then at Farragut High School in Chicago and soon to edit the *English Journal*, relayed instructions from the Illinois Association of Teachers of English that the new organization should compile a list of comparatively recent books suitable for home reading by students and that they should also recommend some books of the last ten years for study because the "present custom of using only old books in the classroom leaves the pupil with no acquaintance with the literature of the present day," from which students would choose their reading after graduation.[19]

James Fleming Hosic's 1917 report on the Reorganization of English in Secondary Schools, part of a larger report published under the aegis of the U.S. Bureau of Education, looked at books and teaching in ways that must have seemed muddle-headed or perverse to traditionalists. Hosic chose works that pleased many, puzzled others, and alienated some. He explained that English teachers should lead students to read works in which they would "find their own lives imaged in this larger life," and would gradually attain from the author's "clearer appreciation of human nature, a deeper and truer understanding. . . . It should be the aim of the English teacher to make [reading] an unfailing resource and joy in the lives of all."[20] Hosic's list included classics as well as modern works, such as Helen Hunt Jackson's *Ramona* and Owen Wister's *The Virginian* for the tenth grade, Rudyard Kipling's *The Light That Failed* and Mary Johnston's *To Have and To Hold* for the eleventh grade, and John Synge's *Riders to the Sea* and Margaret Deland's *The Awakening of Helena Richie* for the twelfth grade. Teachers terrified by the contemporary reality reflected in these books—and perhaps equally terrified by the possibility of throwing out age-old lesson plans and tests on classics—had little to fear. In many schools, nothing changed. *Silas Marner*, *Julius Caesar*, *Idylls of the King*, *A Tale of Two Cities*, and *Lady of the Lake* remained the most widely studied books. Most books were taught at interminable length in what was known as the "intensive" method with four to six weeks—sometimes even more—of detailed examination, while horrified or bored students vowed never to read anything once they escaped high school.

A 1927 study by Nancy Coryell offered proof that the "intensive" method produced no better test results and considerably more apathy toward literature than the "extensive" method in which students read assigned works faster.[21] Again, however, little changed. But fortunately the work of two college professors influenced more English teachers. A 1936 study by Lou LaBrant on the value of free reading at the Ohio State University Laboratory School revealed that students with easy access to different kinds of books and some guidance read more, enjoyed what they read, and moved upward in literary sophistication and taste.[22]

Earlier, University of Minnesota professor Dora V. Smith discovered that English teachers knew next to nothing about books written for adolescents. She began the long process of correcting that situation by establishing the first course in adolescent literature. She argued that it was unfair to both young people and their teachers "to send out from our colleges and universities men and women trained alone in Chaucer and Milton and Browning to compete with Zane Grey, Robert W. Chambers, and Ethel M. Dell."[23]

School Libraries

The development of the school library was almost as slow and convoluted as the development of the public library. In 1823, Brooklyn's Apprentice Library Association established a Youth Library where boys and girls over twelve were allowed . . . but with their access limited to one hour an afternoon, once a week. In 1853, Milwaukee School Commissioner Increase A. Lapham provided for a library open Saturday afternoons and recommended that schools spend $10 a year for books. Rules for the Milwaukee library were clear and more than a bit reminiscent of rules in some school and public libraries until the 1940s:

> (1) Only children over ten years old, their parents, teachers, and school commissioner could withdraw books; (2) books might be withdrawn between 2:00 PM and sunset on Saturdays and kept for one week; (3) withdrawals were limited to one book per person; and (4) fines were to be assessed for overdue or damaged books.[24]

Writers in the early years of the *Library Journal* encouraged the cultivation of friendly relations between "co-educators."[25] The National Education Association formed a Committee on Relations of Public Libraries to Public Schools, and its 1899 report announced that "The teachers of a town should know the public library, what it contains, and what use the pupils can make of it. The librarian must know the school, its work, its needs, and what he can do to meet them."[26]

A persistent question was whether schools should depend on the public library or establish their own libraries. In 1896, Melvil Dewey recommended to the National Education Association that it form a library department (as it had for other subject disciplines) because the library was as much a part of the educational system as the classroom. In 1912, Mary E. Hall, librarian at Girls' High School in Brooklyn, argued the need for many more professionally trained librarians in high school libraries. She wrote that it was a pretense to organize high schools around the idea of preparing students for college, when "for the great majority of pupils it must be a preparation for life." Her other point was that school librarians were in the best position to offer not only reading guidance for students but also to provide teachers with "magazines, daily papers, pictures, and lantern slides to supplement the textbook."27

In 1916, C. C. Certain, as head of National Education Association committee, began standardizing high school libraries across the United States. He discovered conditions so mixed, from deplorable (mostly) to good (rarely) that his committee set to work to establish minimum essentials for high schools of various sizes. A 1923 study by the U.S. Office of Education found only 947 school libraries with more than 3,000 volumes, and these were mostly in the northeastern part of the United States. Six years later, 1,982 school libraries had holdings of more than 3,000 volumes, and the libraries were more equally spread over the country with New York having 211 such libraries and California having 191. However, the steady growth of high school libraries slowed drastically during the Depression.

Edward Stratemeyer's Literary Syndicate

The Boston publishing firm of Lee and Shepard established the format for young adult series, and to the distress of teachers, librarians, and parents, series books became the method of publishing for many young adult novels. If sales were any index, readers delighted in Lee and Shepard's 440 authors and 900 books published in 1887 alone. However, the format became far more sophisticated a few years later when Edward Stratemeyer became the king of series books.

Whatever disagreements librarians and English teachers may have had about books suitable for young adults, they bonded together, although ineffectively, to oppose the books produced by Edward Stratemeyer and his numerous writers. Stratemeyer founded the most successful industry ever built around adolescent reading. In 1866, he took time off from working for his stepbrother and wrote on brown wrapping paper an 18,000-word serial, *Victor Horton's Idea*, and mailed it to a Philadelphia weekly boys' magazine. A check for $75 arrived shortly, and Stratemeyer's success story was under way. By 1893, Stratemeyer was editing *Good News*, Street and Smith's boys' weekly, building circulation to more than 200,000. This brought his name in front of the public, particularly young adults. Even more important, he came to know staff writers such as William T. Adams, Edward S. Ellis, and Horatio Alger, Jr. When Optic and Alger died, leaving some uncompleted manuscripts, Stratemeyer was asked to finish the last three Optic novels, and he completed (or possibly wrote from scratch) at least eleven and perhaps as many as eighteen novels published under Horatio Alger's name.

His first hardback book published under his own name was *Richard Dare's Venture; or, Striking Out for Himself* (1894), first in a series he titled Bound to Succeed. By the close of 1897, Stratemeyer had six series and sixteen hardcover books in print. A major breakthrough came in 1898. After Stratemeyer sent a manuscript about two boys on a battleship to Lothrop and Shepard, one of the most successful publishers of young adult fiction, Admiral Dewey won his great victory in Manila Bay. A Lothrop editor asked Stratemeyer to place the boys at the scene of Dewey's victory. He rewrote and returned the book, and *Under*

Dewey at Manila; or, The War Fortunes of a Castaway hit the streets in time to capitalize on all the publicity. Not one to miss an opportunity, Stratemeyer used the same characters in his next books, all published from 1898 to 1901 under the series title Old Glory. Using the same characters in contemporary battles in the Orient, Stratemeyer created another series called Soldiers of Fortune, published from 1900 through 1906.

By this time, Stratemeyer had turned to full-time writing and was being wooed by the major publishers, notably Grossett and Dunlap and Cupples and Leon. For a time he turned to stories of school life and sports, the Lakeport series (1904–1912), the Dave Porter series (1905–1919), and the most successful of his early series, the Rover Boys (thirty books published between 1899 and 1926). These books were so popular that somewhere between five or six million copies were sold worldwide, including translations into German and Czechoslovakian.

Stratemeyer aspired to greater things, however. Between 1906 and 1910, he approached both his publishers, suggesting they reduce the price of his books to fifty cents. The publishers may have been shocked to find an author willing to sell his books for less money, but, as they soon realized, mass production of fifty-centers increased their revenue and Stratemeyer's royalties almost exponentially. An even greater breakthrough came at roughly the same time, when he evolved the idea of his Literary Syndicate. Stratemeyer was aware that he could create plots and series faster than he could possibly write them. He advertised for writers who needed money and sent them sketches of settings and characters along with a chapter-by-chapter outline of the plot. Writers had a few weeks to fill in the outlines, and when the copy arrived, Stratemeyer tightened the prose and checked for discrepancies with earlier volumes of the series. Then the manuscript was off to the publisher and checks went out to the authors, from $50 to $100, depending on the writer and the importance of the series.

Attacks on Stratemeyer were soon in coming. Librarian Caroline M. Hewins criticized both Stratemeyer's book and the journals that praised his output:

> Stratemeyer is an author who misuses "would" and "should," has the phraseology of a country newspaper, as when he calls a supper "an elegant affair" and a girl "a fashionable miss," and follows Oliver Optic closely in his plots and conversations.[28]

Most librarians supported Hewins, but their attacks hardly affected Stratemeyer's sales. A far more stinging and effective attack came in 1913 from the Boy Scouts of America. Chief executive James E. West was disturbed by the deluge of inferior books and urged the organization's Library Commission to establish a carefully selected and recommended library to protect young men. Not long afterward, Chief Scout Librarian Franklin K. Mathiews urged Grosset and Dunlap to make better books available in fifty-cent editions—to compete with Stratemeyer—and on November 1, 1913, the first list appeared in a Boy Scout publication, "*Safety First Week.*"

But that was not enough to satisfy Mathiews, who in 1914 wrote his most famous article under the sensational title "Blowing Out the Boy's Brains,"[29] a loud and vituperative attack, sometimes accurate but often unfair. Mathiews's attack was mildly successful for the moment, although how much harm it did to

Stratemeyer's sales is open to question. Stratemeyer went on to sell more millions of books. When he died in 1930, his two daughters ran the syndicate.

Series books were inevitably moral. Whatever parents, teachers, or librarians might have objected to about the unrealistic elements of the books or the poor literary quality, they would have agreed that the books were clearly on the side of good and right, if simplistically so. Series books—and many adult books as well—repeatedly underlined the same themes. Sports produced truly manly men. Foreigners were not to be trusted. School, education, and life should be taken seriously. The outdoor life was healthy, physically and psychologically. Good manners and courtesy were essential for moving ahead. Work in and of itself was a positive good and would advance one in life. Anyone could defeat adversity, any adversity, if that person had a good heart and soul. The good side (ours and God's) always won in war. Evil and good were clearly and easily distinguishable. And good always triumphed over evil (at least by the final chapter).

The Coming of the "Junior" or "Juvenile" Novel

Although for years countless books had been published and widely read by young adults, the term *junior* or *juvenile* was first applied in 1933 to *Let the Hurricane Roar* by Rose Wilder Lane. Lane was a journalist and the daughter of Laura Ingalls Wilder. She is now known to have given her mother considerable help in the writing of the *Little House on the Prairie* books published between 1932 and 1965. Her novel *Let the Hurricane Roar* had been marketed by Longmans, Green, and Company as an adult novel. A full-page blurb on the front cover of the February 11, 1933, *Publishers Weekly* bannered THE BOOK THAT MAKES YOU PROUD TO BE AN AMERICAN! and quoted an unnamed reader, presumably an adult, saying, "Honestly, it makes me ashamed of cussing about hard times and taxes." The tenor of the ad and ones to follow suggest an adult novel likely to be popular with young adults as well. It had been the same with the earlier serialization of the novel in the *Saturday Evening Post* and also with many favorable reviews. Sometime later in 1933, Longmans, Green began to push the novel as the first of their series of "Junior Books," as they termed them.

That the company wanted to attract young adults to Lane's novel is not difficult to understand. Lane wrote of a threatening frontier world in a compelling manner certain to win readers and admirers among young adults. *Let the Hurricane Roar* tells of newly married David and Molly and their life on the hard Dakota plains. David works as a railroad hand for a time, Molly waits for her baby to arrive, and both strive for independence and the security of owning their own fifty-acre homestead. When they realize that dream and the baby is born, all looks well, but David overextends his credit, grasshoppers destroy the wheat crop, and no nearby employment can be found. David heads east to find work and later breaks his leg, leaving Molly isolated on the Dakota plains for a winter. Neighbors flee the area, and Molly battles loneliness, blizzards, and wolves before David returns. In summary, *Let the Hurricane Roar* sounds melodramatic, but it is not. In a short, quiet, and loving work, Lane made readers care about two likable young adults living a tough life in a hostile environment. The book's popularity is attested to by its twenty-six printings between 1933 and 1958 and a recent television production and reissue in paperback under the title *Young Pioneers*.

The development of publishing house divisions to handle books lying in limbo between children's and adults' books grew after *Let the Hurricane Roar*, although authors of the time were sometimes unaware of the "junior" or "juvenile" branches as was John T. Tunis when he tried to market *Iron Duke* in 1934 and 1935. After sending the manuscript to Harcourt, Tunis was invited into the president's office. Mr. Harcourt clearly did not want to talk about the book but instead took the startled author directly to the head of the Juvenile Department. He explained that Harcourt wanted to publish the book as a juvenile, much to Tunis's bewilderment and dismay, since he had no idea what a "juvenile" book was. Thirty years later, he still had no respect for the term, which he called the "odious product of a merchandising age."[30]

1940–1960: From Certainty to Uncertainty

During the 1940s, the United States moved from the Depression into a wartime and then a postwar economy. World War II caused us to move from hatred of Communism to a temporary brotherhood, followed by Yalta, the Iron Curtain, blacklisting, and Senator McCarthy. We went from "Li'l Abner" to "Pogo" and from Bob Hope to Mort Sahl. Problems of the time included school integration, racial unrest, civil rights, and riots in the streets. We were united about World War II, unsure about the Korean War, and divided about Vietnam. The twenty years between 1940 and 1960 revealed a country separated by gaps of all kinds: generational, racial, technological, cultural, and economic.

Educators were as divided as anyone else. Reading interest studies had become fixtures in educational journals, but there was little agreement about the results. In 1946, George W. Norvell wrote, "Our data shows clearly that much literary material being used in our schools is too mature, too subtle, too erudite to permit its enjoyment by the majority of secondary-school pupils." Norvell offered the advice that teachers should give priority to the reading interests of young adults in assigning materials that students would enjoy and in letting students select a portion of their own materials based on their individual interests. He thought that three-fourths of the selections currently in use were uninteresting, especially to boys, and that "to increase reading skill, promote the reading habit, and produce a generation of book-lovers, there is no factor so powerful as interest."[31]

Other researchers supported Norvell's contention that young adults' choices of voluntary reading rarely overlapped books widely respected by more traditional English teachers. In 1947, Marie Rankin surveyed eight public libraries in Illinois, Ohio, and New York and discovered that Helen Boylston's *Sue Barton, Student Nurse* was the most consistently popular book.[32] Twelve years later, Stephen Dunning surveyed fourteen school and public libraries and concluded that the ten most popular books were Maureen Daly's *Seventeenth Summer*, Henry Gregor Felsen's *Hot Rod*, Betty Cavanna's *Going on Sixteen*, Rosamund Du Jardin's *Double Date*, Walter Farley's *Black Stallion*, Sally Benson's *Junior*

Miss, Mary Stolz's *The Sea Gulls Woke Me*, Rosamund Du Jardin's *Wait for Marcy*, James Summers's *Prom Trouble*, and John Tunis's *All American*.[33]

Near the height of the outpouring of published studies, Jacob W. Getzels assessed the value of reading interest surveys and found most of them wanting in "precision of definition, rigor of theory, and depth of analysis."[34] He was, of course, right. Most reports were limited to a small sample from a few schools, and little was done except to ask students what they liked to read. The studies at least gave librarians and teachers insight into books young adults liked and brought hope that somewhere out there somebody was reading—a hope that for librarians and teachers needs constant rekindling.

In the mid-1950s, G. Robert Carlsen summarized the findings of published reading interest surveys as showing that young people select their reading first to reassure themselves about their normality and their status as human beings and then for role playing:

> With the developing of their personality through adolescence, they come to a partially integrated picture of themselves as human beings. They want to test this picture of themselves in the many kinds of roles that it is possible for a human being to play and through testing to see what roles they may fit into and what roles are uncongenial.[35]

Carlsen's observations tied in with those of University of Chicago psychologist Robert J. Havighurst, who outlined the developmental tasks necessary for the healthy growth of individuals. (See Chapter 1, p. 36, for the tasks that Havighurst thought crucial to adolescence.)

An outgrowth of the tying together of reading interests and psychology was an interest in *bibliotherapy*, a term coined in 1929 by Dr. G. O. Ireland, who wrote about using books as part of his treatment for psychiatric patients.[36] By the late 1930s and early 1940s, articles about bibliotherapy became almost commonplace in education journals, and by the 1950s, the idea of using books to help readers come to terms with their psychological problems was firmly entrenched. Philosophically, it was justified by Aristotle's *Poetics* and the theory of emotional release through catharsis, a theory with little support except for unverifiable personal testimonials.

One clear and easy application of bibliotherapy was the free reading program (sometimes too clear and too easy for the inept psychologist/English teacher who, finding a new book in which the protagonist had acne, sought the acne-ridden kid in class and handed over the book saying, "You must read this—it's about you!"). Lou LaBrant, popularizer of free reading, sounded both a recommendation and a warning when she wrote:

> Certainly I can make a much wiser selection of offerings if I understand the potential reader . . . [but] [t]his does not mean, as some have interpreted, that a young reader will enjoy only literature which answers his questions, tells him what is to be done. It is true, however, that young and old tend to choose literature, whether they seek solutions or escape, which offers characters or situations with which they can find a degree of identification.[37]

Rise of Paperbacks

Young adult readers might assume paperbound books have always been with us. Despite the success of dime novels and libraries of paperbacks in the late 1800s, paperbacks as we know them entered the mass market in 1938 when Pocket Books offered Pearl Buck's *The Good Earth* as a sample volume in mail-order tests. In the spring of 1939, a staff artist created the first sketch of Gertrude the Kangaroo with a book in her paws and another in her pouch. It became Pocket Books' trademark. A few months later, the company issued ten titles in 10,000-copy editions, most of them remaining best sellers for years. Avon began publishing in 1941; Penguin entered the U.S. market in 1942; and Bantam, New American Library, Ballantine, Dell, and Popular Library began publishing in 1943. By 1951, sales had reached 230 million paperbacks annually. Phenomenal as the growth was, paperbacks were slow to appear in schools despite an incredible number of titles on appropriate subjects. Librarians complained that paperbacks did not belong in libraries because they were difficult to catalog and easy to steal. School officials maintained that the covers were lurid and the contents little more than pornography. As late as 1969, a New York City high school junior explained, "I'd rather be caught with *Lady Chatterley* in hardcover than *Hot Rod* in paperback. Hard covers get you one detention, but paperbacks get you two or three."[38]

Regardless of "official" attitudes, by the mid-1960s paperbacks had become a part of young adults' lives. They are easily available, comfortably sized, and inexpensive. Fortunately, not all school personnel were resistant. The creation of Scholastic Book Clubs and widespread distribution of Reader's Choice Catalogs helped paperbacks get accepted in schools and libraries. Eventually, Bantam and Dell's Yearling books became the major suppliers of books written specifically for young adults.

Changes and Growth in Young Adult Literature

Through the 1940s and 1950s, the quality of young adult literature rose steadily, if at times hesitatingly and uncertainly. Series books, so popular from 1900 to the 1940s, died out—except for Stratemeyer Syndicate stalwarts Nancy Drew, the Hardy Boys, and the new Tom Swift, Jr., series. They were killed by increasing reader sophistication combined with the wartime scarcity of paper. Many of the books that replaced the series celebrated those wonderful high school years by focusing on dating, parties, class rings, senior year, the popular crowd, and teen romances devoid of realities such as sex. The books often sounded alike and read alike, but they were unquestionably popular.

Plots were usually simple, with only one or two characters being developed, while others were stock figures or stereotypes. Books dealt almost exclusively with white, middle-class values and morality. The endings were almost uniformly happy and bright, and readers could be certain that neither their morality nor their intelligence would be challenged.

Taboos may never have been written down, but they were clear to readers and writers. Certain things were not to be mentioned—obscenity, profanity, suicide, sexuality, sensuality, homosexuality, protests against anything significant, social or racial injustice, or the ambivalent feelings of cruelty and compassion inherent in young adults and all people. Pregnancy, early marriage, drugs, smoking, alcohol, school dropouts, divorce, and alienation could be introduced only by implication and only as bad examples for thoughtful, decent young adults. Consequently, young adult books were often innocuous and pervaded by a saccharine didacticism.

Despite these unwritten rules, some writers transcended the taboos and limitations and made it possible for Stanley B. Kegler and Stephen Dunning to write in 1961, "Books of acceptable quality have largely replaced poorly written and mediocre books."[39]

Adult Books That Set the Stage for Contemporary YA Novels

Perhaps as a reaction to the realities of war, the most popular series of books for both adults and teenagers during the 1950s and on into the 1960s centered around the fascinating James Bond, Agent 007. Ian Fleming caught the mood of the time with escapist excitement tinted with what appeared to be realities. Kathleen Winsor was also one of a kind, although what one and what kind was widely debated. When her *Forever Amber* (1944) appeared, parents worried, censors paled, and young adults smiled as they ignored the fuss and read the book. The uproar was much the same as that awaiting Grace Metalious and *Peyton Place* when it appeared in 1956. Well-written romances include Margaret E. Bell's Alaskan story *Love Is Forever* (1954), Vivian Breck's superior study of young marriage in *Maggie* (1954), and Benedict and Nancy Freedom's *Mrs. Mike*, set in the northern Canadian wilderness. Elizabeth Goudge's *Green Dolphin Street* (1944) had everything working for it—a young handsome man in love with one of two sisters. When he leaves and writes home expressing his wishes, the wrong sister accepts. The true love, apparently overwhelmed by his unfaithfulness, becomes a nun. Passion, love, and adventure are all handled well by a first-rate writer.

Young readers, especially in the last year or two of high school, have often been receptive to books about human dilemmas. Between 1940 and 1960, society changed rapidly and drastically with deeply disturbing consequences. There was a growing awareness that the democracy described in our Constitution was more preached than practiced. As the censorship applied to John Steinbeck's *The Grapes of Wrath* (1939) and *Of Mice and Men* (1937) lessened—although it never entirely disappeared—young people read of the plight of migrant workers and learned that all was not well. Many were deeply disturbed by Alan Paton's stories of racial struggles in South Africa, *Cry the Beloved Country* (1948) and *Too Late the Phalarope* (1953). Still more were touched by Harper Lee's *To Kill a Mockingbird* (1960) set in the U.S. South.

Richard Wright and his books *Native Son* (1940) and *Black Boy* (1945) served as bitter prototypes for much African American literature. One of the greatest novels of any kind in the last fifty years is Ralph Ellison's *Invisible Man* (1952). Existential in tone, it is at different times bawdy (the incest scenes remind readers of Faulkner without being derivative), moving, and frightening, but always stunning and breathtaking.

The development from this period that has had the most direct effect on young adult literature was the popularization of the *bildungsroman*, a novel about the initiation, maturation, and education of a young adult. Most bildungsroman were originally published for adults but soon read by teenagers. Dan Wickenden's *Walk Like a Mortal* (1940) and Betty Smith's *A Tree Grows in Brooklyn* (1943) were among the first. William Golding's *Lord of the Flies* (1955) is better known, but none of these books won young adult favor or adult opposition as did J. D. Salinger's *The Catcher in the Rye* (1951). It is still the most widely censored book in U.S. schools and still hated by people who assume that a disliked word (that word) corrupts an entire book. Holden Caulfield may indeed be vulgar and cynical and capable of seeing only the phonies around him, but he is also loyal and loving to those he sees as good or innocent. For many young adults, it is the most honest and human story they know about someone they recognize (even in themselves)—a young man caught between childhood and maturity and unsure which way to go. Whether *Catcher* is a masterpiece similar to James Joyce's *A Portrait of the Artist as a Young Man* depends on subjective judgment, but there is no question that Salinger's book captured—and continues to capture—the hearts and minds of countless young adults as has no other book.

Nonfiction was not yet as popular as it would become, but Jim Piersall's *Fear Strikes Out* (1955) and Roy Campanella's *It's Good to Be Alive* (1959) attracted young readers. Popular true stories about battles and survivors included Richard Tregaskis's *Guadalcanal Diary* (1943), Ernie Pyle's *Here Is Your War* (1943) and *Brave Men* (1944), Robert Trumbull's *The Raft* (1942), and Quentin Reynold's *70,000 to One* (1946).

Rise of Criticism of Young Adult Literature

Today we take criticism of young adult literature as discussed in Chapter 10 for granted, but it developed slowly. In the 1940s, journals provided little information on, and less criticism of, young adult literature except for book lists, book reviews, and occasional references in articles on reading interests or improving young people's literary taste. The comments that did appear were often more appreciative than critical, but given the times and the attitude of many teachers and librarians, appreciation or even recognition may have been more important than criticism.

In 1951, Dwight L. Burton wrote the first criticism of young adult novels, injecting judgments along with appreciation as he commented on works by Dan Wickenden, Maureen Daly, Paul Annixter, Betty Cavanna, and Madeleine L'Engle. Concluding his article, Burton identified the qualities of the good young adult novel and prophesied its potential and future:

> The good novel for the adolescent reader has attributes no different from any good novel. It must be technically masterful, and it must present a significant synthesis of human experience. Because of the nature of adolescence itself, the good novel for the adolescent should be full in true invention and imagination. It must free itself of Pollyannaism or the Tarkington–Henry Aldrich–Corliss Archer tradition and

These "good girls" of the 1950s, waiting here to shake President Eisenhower's hand at Girls' Nation, were more likely to be reading fiction published in women's magazines and such books as Mrs. Mike, Forever Amber, *and* Peyton Place *than books published specifically for teenagers.*

maintain a clear vision of the adolescent as a person of complexity, individuality, and dignity. The novel for the adolescent presents a ready field for the mature artist.[40]

In 1955, Richard S. Alm provided greater critical coverage of the young adult novel.[41] He agreed with critics that many writers presented a "sugar-puff story of what adolescents should do and should believe rather than what adolescents may or will do and believe." He cited specific authors and titles he found good and painted their strengths and weaknesses in clear strokes. He concluded by offering teachers some questions that might be useful in analyzing the merits of young adult novels.

A year later, Emma L. Patterson began her fine study of the origin of young adult novels showing that "The junior novel has become an established institution."[42] But despite the leadership of Burton, Alm, and Patterson, helpful criticism of young adult literature was slow in arriving, yet biting criticism was soon forthcoming. Only a few months after Patterson's article, Frank G. Jennings's "Literature for Adolescents—Pap or Protein?"[43] appeared. The title was ambiguous, but if any reader had doubts about where Jennings stood, the doubt was removed with the first sentence: "The stuff of adolescent literature, for the most part, is mealy-mouthed, gutless, and pointless." The remainder of the article added little to that point, and although Jennings overstated his case, Burton, Alm, Patterson, and other sensible supporters would have agreed that much young adult literature, similar to much adult literature, was second-rate or worse. Jennings's article was not the first broadside attack, and it certainly would not be the last.[44]

1960–1980 Uncertainty Becomes Turbulence

In the 1960s, civil rights marches were almost a commonplace, and the war in Vietnam was increasingly controversial. President John F. Kennedy was assassinated, and so were Malcolm X, Martin Luther King, Jr., and Robert Kennedy. Tidings were a little better in 1969 when Neil Armstrong walked on the moon, but then the 1970s brought the National Guard's killing of four Kent State University students and the Mississippi police's killing of two black students at Jackson State University. Scandals forced the resignation of Spiro Agnew as vice president, and then Watergate did the same for President Richard Nixon.

It was not a great twenty years for our country, but at least some people feel that positive changes came from the 1966 founding of the National Organization of Women (NOW); the 1969 Stonewall rebellion in a New York City bar, which started the modern gay rights movement; the 1970 passing of the Environmental Protection Act (EPA), the 1971 lowering of the voting age from twenty-one to eighteen, and the 1973 U. S. Supreme Court decision in *Roe v. Wade*, which protected women's freedom to have a legal abortion. Some of these events were controversial when they took place and some remain so controversial that even today they are rallying cries for political actions.

Changes Related to Young Adult Literature

This twenty-year period was especially exciting to those of us who were already working with young adult books. The changes came from so many directions and were so interrelated that we decided the best way to show them would be through a timeline, more or less adapted from the "Two Hundred Years of Young Adult Library Services History" that is posted on *VOYA's* (*Voice of Youth Advocates*) website and the timeline included in a February 2007 *School Library Journal* article, "John, Paul, George, and YALSA." The article was published as part of the fifty-year anniversary of the founding of the American Library Association's Young Adult Library Services Association (YALSA), which happened to coincide with the founding of the Beatles singing group. We are adding perspectives from English teachers and other educators. See Focus Box 2.3, A Sampling of Good Books from the Sixties and Focus Box 2.4, A Sampling of Good Books from the Seventies. These are the books that set the stage for the success of such revolutionary authors as Robert Cormier and Judy Blume, both winners of the Margaret A. Edwards Award (see pages 72 and 74).

One of the things that made the 1960s such a pivotal time in education is that Russia's 1957 launching of *Sputnik* struck fear into the hearts of Americans. We were afraid that we could not compete against the Soviet Union and so the general public, along with government agencies and educators, scrambled to focus attention on education in high tech fields. Funds were first set aside for science and math, but very soon, people realized that students could not learn math and science if they did not know how to read, and so the educational focus was broadened to include the language arts and to advance the education of all young people.

A Sampling of Good Books from the Sixties (in addition to those written by Edwards Award winners)

Across Five Aprils by Irene Hunt. Follett, 1965. In this historical novel, the Civil War comes to a farm family.

A Blues I Can Whistle by A. E. Johnson. Four Winds, 1969. A boy who failed at suicide explains how he got there.

The Book of Three by Lloyd Alexander. Holt, 1964. This was the first of the Prydain series that came to include *The Black Cauldron* (1965), *The Castle of the Llyr* (1966), *Taran Wanderer* (1967), and *The High King* (1968).

The Chosen by Chaim Potok. Simon & Schuster, 1967. Through *The Chosen* and *My Name Is Asher Lev* (1972), Potok introduced a whole generation of high school students to a young man's life in a Hasidic Jewish community.

The Face of Abraham Candle by Bruce Clements. Farrar, Straus and Giroux, 1969. In silver-mining-era Colorado, a boy helps plunder treasures from Mesa Verde.

Jamie by Jack Bennett. Little, Brown, 1963. A young boy has one mission, to avenge his father's death by one of Africa's most dangerous animals, a water buffalo. See also Bennett's *The Hawk Alone* (1965).

Jazz Country by Nat Hentoff. HarperCollins, 1965. In this superb story, a white boy tries to break into the African American world of jazz.

The King's Fifth by Scott O'Dell. Houghton Mifflin, 1966. Conquistadors plunder and ravage the New World in search of gold.

A Love or a Season by Mary Stolz. HarperCollins, 1964. Stolz treated young love and sexual tension with both affection and dignity.

Mr. and Mrs. Bo Jo Jones by Ann Head. Putnam, 1967. Head was one of the first to treat a premarital pregnancy with respect and understanding.

The Owl Service by Alan Garner. Walck, 1968. Three young people replay a Welsh myth from the *Mabinogion*.

The Pushcart War by Jean Merrill. Scott, 1964. In this wonderful satire, war erupts between New York City pushcart owners and the drivers of those mammoth trucks that hog city streets.

Red Sky at Morning by Richard Bradford. Lippincott, 1968. A boy and his mother go to live in New Mexico while their father is at war and the experience brings the boy to examine his values.

A Separate Peace by John Knowles. Macmillan, 1961. The story of two boys whose friendship ends in tragedy, was predicted to be a story that would be taught in high school English classes for generations.

A Single Light by Maia Wojciechowska. Harper and Row, 1968. An unloved Spanish girl finds someone to love, a white marble statue of the Christ Child.

Sounder by William Armstrong. HarperCollins, 1969. An Academy Award–winning film brought even more readers to this sad story of a 1920s African American family that loses both its father and its dog.

1960: The American Library Association begins giving more attention to teenagers as shown by the Young Adult Services Division establishing a committee on Standards for Work with Young Adults and sending delegates, along with copies of the newly published *Youth in a Changing World in Fiction and Fact*, to the Golden Anniversary White House Conference on Children and Youth.

1960: Questions related to civil rights for African Americans come to the forefront. In Danville, Virginia, thirteen African American high school students entered the main library and refused to leave. During the 1960s, books by three African American nonfiction writers were appreciated by many young adults. They include Claude Brown's stark picture of African American ghetto life in *Manchild in the Promised Land* (1965), Malcolm X and Alex Haley's

Focus Box 2.4

A Sampling of Good Books from the Seventies (in addition to those written by Edwards Award winners)

Beauty: A Retelling of the Story of Beauty and the Beast by Robin McKinley. HarperCollins, 1978. Funny and surrealistic, McKinley's excellent writing undoubtedly inspired many of the more recent retellings of old stories.

The Bell Jar by Sylvia Plath. HarperCollins, 1971. Although not published as a YA book, Plath's own story of her emotional problems still attracts mature young adult readers.

Bless the Beasts and Children by Glendon Swarthout. Doubleday, 1970. Boys at a summer camp are appalled to see a government-sponsored slaughter of penned-up buffalo. Swarthout presented the first copy of his book to the governor of Arizona, where the slaughter was held.

The Book of the Dun Cow by Walter Wangerin, Jr. HarperCollins, 1978. Wangerin told his story as a beast fable, in which one of the beasts plays the role of the biblical Job.

A Day No Pigs Would Die by Robert Newton Peck. Knopf, 1972. On this Depression-era farm, Rob has to become the man of the family after the death of his father, whose job was slaughtering pigs.

Dragonwings by Laurence Yep. HarperCollins, 1975. When Yep found a historical allusion to a Chinese kite maker who succeeded in flying years before the Wright Brothers, he wrote a story of how it might have happened.

Happy Endings Are All Alike by Sandra Scoppettone. HarperCollins, 1978. Two lesbian girls are stalked by a dangerous young man interested only in rape.

A Hero Ain't Nothin' but a Sandwich by Alice Childress. Coward, McCann, and Geoghegan, 1973. A family tries to save a young drug user from himself.

Home Before Dark by Sue Ellen Bridgers. Knopf, 1976. A girl in a family of migrant workers manages to come to terms with a new life. In Bridger's 1979 *All Together Now*, a young girl comes to a small Southern town during the Korean War and becomes friends with the retarded but delightful Dwayne.

House of Stairs by William Sleator. Dutton, 1974. Six young people are placed in a strange house with stairs going everywhere and nowhere at all.

The Last Mission by Harry Mazer. Delacorte, 1979. Mazer tells at least part of his own story in this book about a young Jewish boy who enlists during World War II to destroy Hitler.

The Man without a Face by Isabelle Holland. Lippincott, 1972. A boy learns some hard lessons from the disfigured man who agrees to tutor him for a summer.

Ordinary People by Judith Guest. Viking, 1976. When two brothers are boating and one of them drowns, the surviving brother and his parents have a hard time moving on.

Run Softly, Go Fast by Barbara Wersba. Atheneum, 1970. In this haunting novel of the 1960s, a boy's father dies and his angry son is left trying to figure out why he hates the man he used to love.

The Slave Dancer by Paula Fox. Bradbury, 1973. A fife-playing boy is kidnapped and brought to a ship where he is to play exercise music to help keep the cargo (slaves) in good health until they can be sold.

The Strange Affair of Adalaide Harris by Leon Garfield. Pantheon, 1971. A comedy of errors begins when two schoolboys leave a baby sister outdoors to see if wild animals will rescue her.

A String in the Harp by Nancy Bond. Atheneum, 1976. A dysfunctional family, transplanted to Wales, learns how to become a family again when one of the children finds an ancient harp-tuning key that opens the door to the sixth century.

A Wild Thing by Jean Renvoize. Little, Brown, 1971. In this tragedy, a fifteen-year-old outcast and runaway girl is living in a cave and wanting one thing—a baby.

Z for Zachariah by Robert C. O'Brien. Atheneum, 1975. A girl in an isolated valley that had been protected from a nuclear blast, thinks she is the last person on earth—but then she discovers another survivor who makes it worse than being alone.

(the latter better known for *Roots*) *The Autobiography of Malcolm X* (1965), and Eldridge Cleaver's *Soul on Ice* (1968), an impassioned plea by an African American man in prison who wrote to save himself. In 1974, James Baldwin's novel, *If Beale Street Could Talk*, resonated with many young readers.

VOYA's *timeline poster prepared for the 2007 American Library Association conference celebrated fifty years of young adult librarianship and two hundred years of libraries.*

1962: In what is almost a repeat of the kinds of arguments that resulted in the founding of the National Council of Teachers of English in 1912, the Modern Language Association criticizes how high school students are, or are not, being prepared for college. High school English teachers are not amused, but they nevertheless participate in a series of Basic Issues conferences and in twenty Project English summer institutes held in 1962. Many of these institutes focused on what should be included in the high school English curriculum. Nearly everyone agreed on the holy tripod of literature, language, and composition, but from there opinions varied widely. Marjorie Smiley's center at Hunter College was exceptional in the way the participants focused on student involvement and interest and on finding personal and social significance in literature.[45]

1963: The Knapp Foundation sponsors a School Libraries Project to set up model media centers throughout the country. This new focus on media contributed to the alternative name of media centers for school libraries.

1963: Alfred E. Bestor publishes the first edition of *Educational Wastelands: The Retreat from Learning in Our Public Schools* (Univ. of Illinois Press), which sang what would become a national anthem of complaints about how U. S. schools were not preparing our country to compete against the Soviet Union.

1964: The International Reading Association, which was founded in 1956 as a professional organization for those involved in teaching reading, begins publishing the *Journal of Reading*, renamed in 1985 to the *Journal of Adolescent and Adult Literacy (JAAL)*. It presently goes to 15,000 subscribers and represents the interests of reading teachers at the secondary level. In all, IRA has 85,000 members in over one hundred countries, and nearly forty Special

Interest Groups (SIGs) including a Network on Adolescent Literature. Especially in recent years, *JAAL* has devoted several pages to articles and to reviews of new YA books. And at both national and regional conferences, awards are given and sessions are devoted to authors and scholars working with young adult literature.

1965: Congress passes the Elementary and Secondary Education Act (ESEA), which provides money for the purchase of library materials and textbooks. Many schools established their first libraries in order to qualify for these funds, which were available for almost a decade. The National Defense Education Act (NDEA) also provided funding for teachers' institutes throughout the country. Out of these came new ideas for teaching English and working with nonprint media (especially film); multicultural literature; adolescent literature, as it was then called; team teaching, linguistics, and performing rather than just reading Shakespeare.

1965: The College Entrance Examination Board turns its attention to the teaching of literature in its widely read *Freedom and Discipline in English.* It rejected the idea that "so-called junior books" might ease young readers into a frame of mind in which they will be ready "to tackle something stronger, harder and more adult," by writing:

> The Commission has serious doubts that it does anything of the sort. For classes in remedial reading a resort to such books may be necessary, but to make them a considerable part of the curriculum for most students is to subvert the purposes for which literature is included in the first place. In the high school years, the aim should be not to find the students' level so much as to raise it, and such books rarely elevate. For college-bound students, particularly, no such concessions as they imply are justified. Maturity of thought, vocabulary, syntax, and construction is the criterion of excellence in literature, and that criterion must not be abandoned for apparent expediency. The competent teacher can bridge the distances between good books and the immaturity of his students; that is, in fact his primary duty as teacher of literature. (49–50)

High school teachers resented such criticism coming from college professors who had clearly not read such good books as Marjorie Hill Allee's 1937 *The Great Tradition,* Esther Forbes's 1943 *Johnny Tremain,* Paul Annixter's 1950 *Swiftwater,* Mary Stolz's 1954 *Pray Love, Remember,* Rosemary Sutcliff's 1954 *The Eagle of the Ninth,* and Nat Hentoff's 1965 *Jazz Country.* Such negative criticism galvanized the resolve of knowledgeable teachers to change the public opinion.

1966: Daniel Fader publishes *Hooked on Books: Program and Proof* (Berkley). The book grew out of one of the 1962 Project English Centers in Michigan where participants worked with the W. J. Maxey Boys' Training School (a euphemism for reform school). Each boy was allowed to choose and keep two paperback books from the library, a paperback dictionary, and a spiral notebook (a journal) in which he was to write at least two pages a week. While railing against current practices in the teaching of reading, Fader used paperbacks of all sorts to get the boys to read—and read they did. His techniques were so successful that his book was revised and republished several times and quoted almost as if it were holy writ.

1967: The Young Adult Services Division of the American Library Association combines forces with ALA's Intellectual Freedom Committee to cosponsor a conference on "Intellectual Freedom and the Teenager." Five years later, ALA adopts "Free Access to Minors: An Interpretation of the Library Bill of Rights."

1967: G. Robert Carlsen publishes *Books and the Teenage Reader* (Harper and Row). While bringing national attention and a degree of respect to adolescent literature, his work also attracts several doctoral students to his English Education program at the University of Iowa, including the authors of this textbook, and such scholars as Ben Nelms, Terry C. Ley, Richard Abrahamson, and Ruth Cline, all of whom have gone on to train other doctoral students now working in the field. Carlsen earned his own Ph.D. at the University of Minnesota where he studied with Dora V. Smith, who is usually cited as doing for adolescent literature in English Education what Margaret A. Edwards did for it in libraries.[46]

1967: S. E. Hinton publishes *The Outsiders* and Robert Lipsyte publishes *The Contender*. See pp. 8 and 197 for statements about them as winners of the Margaret A. Edwards award. Other authors who published outstanding books in the 1960s and 1970s and were subsequently chosen as winners of the Margaret A. Edwards award include Paul Zindel (see p. 164), M. E. Kerr (p. 331), Robert Cormier (p. 72), Judy Blume (p. 74), Richard Peck (p. 275), Anne McCaffrey (p. 225), Lois Duncan (p. 207), and Ursula K. Le Guin (p. 222).

1969: Margaret A. Edwards publishes *The Fair Garden and the Swarm of Beasts* (Hawthorne). The title comes from an essay in *The Old Librarian's Almanac*, in which Jared Bean advised his fellow librarians that the Treasure House of Literature "is no more to be thrown open to the ravages of the unreasoning mob [the general public, especially the young] than is a Fair Garden to be laid unprotected at the Mercy of a Swarm of Beasts." Six years later, at the ALAN breakfast in San Diego, two hundred English teachers applaud the choice of Margaret A. Edwards as the recipient of the second ALAN Award for her contribution to the promotion of books for young readers. Thirteen years later, YALSA, in cooperation with the *School Library Journal*, establishes the Margaret A. Edwards Award to honor a living author whose books have spoken to young adults over a period of time. Winners of that award are featured on special pages throughout this text.

1969: Neil Postman and Charles Weingartner publish *Teaching as a Subversive Activity* (Delacorte), which begins with a metaphor borrowed from Ernest Hemingway: "We have in mind a new education that would set out to cultivate . . . experts at crap detecting." It may have been Hemingway's metaphor, but Charlie Weingartner made it his own, and its influence is still felt as shown in Chapter 3 on the "New Literacies." Neil Postman went on to work with media and language and is perhaps best known for his *Amusing*

Ourselves to Death: Public Discourse in the Age of Show Business (Viking, 1985).[47]

1972: Francelia Butler, a faculty member in the English department at the University of Connecticut, establishes the Children's Literature Association as a Division of The Modern Language Association. In these early years, she referred to children's literature as "the great excluded," because of the low status that most academics gave it. As the years have gone by, ChLA members no longer use the phrase and they have also begun to interpret "Children's Literature" as including books for young adults. For example, of the eight feature articles in the 2007 annual *Children's Literature* (Volume 35), four of them could have been in a journal focusing on young adult literature. One was an interview with M. E. Kerr, one an explication of David Almond's *Skellig*, one an investigation of Gothic elements in prep school literature, and one an exploration of the legacy of Jane Austen in the Harry Potter books.

1973: A group of about a dozen English teachers gather at the National Council of Teachers of English annual conference and form an Assembly on Literature for Adolescents of NCTE (ALAN). In keeping with their goal to promote the reading and teaching of young adult literature, they write their constitution to allow people to belong to the Assembly without having to pay dues to the National Council because they want to encourage membership from authors, publishers, reading teachers, and librarians, as well as English teachers. They planned a preconference workshop to be held at the 1974 convention in New Orleans. These workshops have been held every year since and have now been expanded to two full days. At the 2006 conference in Nashville, over sixty authors and over seventy members had parts on the two-day program attended by nearly four hundred participants, all of whom went home with boxes of books provided by the authors' publishers.

1974: The Young Adult Services Division (YASD) of the American Library Association tactfully changed the name of its annual listing of recommended books that were of high interest but with a low reading level from "Books for Slow High School Readers" to the more positive sounding "Quick Picks." This was only one of many changes reflecting an increased respect for the viewpoints of young readers and a desire to involve teenagers as members of library advisory boards and "Best Book" selection committees.

1975: What was to become *The ALAN Review*, now a glossy, refereed and professional journal of nearly one hundred pages coming out three times a year, has its beginning as a photocopied newsletter with eight pages of text, plus a couple of pull-out clip-and-file reviews. Alleen Nilsen and Ken Donelson were the founding editors, but in 1979, they passed the editorship on to Guy Ellis at the University of Georgia, who in 1984 passed it on to Arthea (Charlie) Reed at the University of North Carolina. In 1990, Leila Christenbury at Virginia Commonwealth and Robert Small at Radford University became coeditors, while in 1993, Patricia Kelly at Virginia Tech became a coeditor along with Robert Small. Pamela Sissi Carrol became editor in 1998, while in 2003 James Blasingame at Arizona State and Lori Atkins Goodson at Wamego

Margaret A. Edwards Award
Winner (1991)
Robert Cormier, **Who Took It to the Top**

The Chocolate War, *I Am the Cheese*, and *After the First Death* are the books that in 1991 Robert Cormier was honored for. Other exceptionally good books include *The Bumblebee Flies Anyway*, *Beyond the Chocolate War*, *Fade*, *We All Fall Down*, and *Heroes*.

In 1967, when S. E. Hinton's *The Outsiders* was published, critics rejoiced because Hinton's novel was a giant step forward for the young adult novel. Its gritty realism and its willingness to take on a hitherto topic like class differences in the teenagers' world made *The Outsiders* a hit with critics and young readers. YA books had reached the top.

That euphoria lasted until 1974 when YA books reached an even higher top. Robert Cormier's *The Chocolate War* was published to critical acclaim, and readers soon followed the critics. Censors, never willing to let a fine novel pass unnoticed and uncensored, took note. *The Chocolate War* was attacked from almost every imaginable viewpoint and for almost every imaginable sin. When Cormier's next two novels, *I Am the Cheese* and *After the First Death*, were published to the approval of critics and readers, censors trailed not far behind.

What were Cormier's sins? The fact that Archie in *The Chocolate War* had taken a picture of Emile in a restroom stall with his "pants dropping on the floor, one hand furiously at work between his legs." Masturbation, as decent people knew, was not to be mentioned. Crude language was everywhere in Cormier's books, and the books were filled with pessimism and, as one censor told the authors of this text, the books were "unnecessarily realistic." Immorality prevailed, terror and evil abounded, corruption was everywhere, and worse yet, *I Am the Cheese* and *After the First Death* were unpatriotic, implying that the Witness Relocation Program was dishonest and that our government could not be trusted.

What were Cormier's virtues? He was honest, and he told readers what they already knew but were often afraid to admit—that corruption existed around them, not in some far-off place, and that bad guys and evil sometimes won and good guys and innocence could lose even at the end of a book.

Patty Campbell remembers in her *Horn Book Magazine* column for March/April 2003 what it was like in the seventies to hope for real maturity in the YA novel and then to read Cormier's first YA book.

Finally in 1974, all of this excitement and rich promise came to fulfillment with The Chocolate War. *Oh, there had already been other YA books of lasting excellence. . . . But* The Chocolate War *was something else again—a book that shook us profoundly, a book that nobody could ignore. The critics went wild, some of them foaming at the mouth, others singing the book's praises extravagantly.*

From that first simple sentence in *The Chocolate War*, "They murdered him," readers knew Cormier was different. And from the first inklings of the plot, readers had the essentials before them. Jerry Renault was not superhuman, Archie and the Vigils were in charge of Trinity High School, and Brother Leon, who was nominally the assistant headmaster of the school but who "served as a flunky for the Head," was corrupt and enjoyed manipulating and corrupting others.

Sylvia Patterson Iskander nicely summed up the matter for the 1999 *St. James Guide to Young Adult Writers* when she wrote, "The novels of Robert Cormier have added a new dimension to young adult literature. Dealing with evil, abuse of power, and corruption, they present a dark view of humanity, but one tempered by an underlying morality."

Robert Cormier had never thought of himself as a writer for young people, but when his agent submitted *The Chocolate War* to Pantheon, the editor convinced Cormier that, as good as the book was, it would be simply one more in a catalogue of adult books. If it were published for teenagers, however, it might sell well, and it certainly would not be just one more in a long string of available adolescent novels. The editor's predictions came true and Cormier later acknowledged that although his initial reaction to becoming a *young adult* author was one of shock followed by a monthlong writer's block, he was grateful for the editorial help, which led to considerable attention from reviewers as well as his first financial success as an author. ●

Middle School in Kansas became coeditors. Editing the journal is a labor of love and each editing team has brought to it a new level of professionalism.

1975: *School Library Journal* begins publication separate from *Library Journal.* While *SLJ* started out with the idea of reviewing all books published for young readers, the burgeoning of the publishing business has forced it to modify such an ambitious goal, but still, in its twelve issues per year it manages to review over 4,000 books. It also publishes four or five feature articles and a half-dozen regular columns in each monthly issue. Readers especially await the December issue in which the editors list their choices of sixty to seventy books identified as the year's best.

1975: In "Reason, Not Emotion," published in the April 1975 *Top of the News,* Elaine Simpson expresses the frustration that many of us are feeling about the way new YA books are being received. She wrote:

> "For years librarians and others have criticized junior novels saying they are written to a formula: they all have pat, sweetness and light resolutions that instill false conceptions of life; they fail to deal with fundamental problems of personal and societal adjustments that are of immediate concern to young adults, etc. etc. etc. . . .
>
> Then juvenile authors and editors began giving us such books as *Go Ask Alice*; *Run Softly, Go Fast*; *Admission to the Feast*; *Run, Shelley, Run*; *The Chocolate War* . . . And what happened? All too many of those same people who had been asking for an honest story about teenage problems began protesting: language like that in a book for young people? Are rape, abortion, homosexuality, unwed mothers, suicide, drugs, unsympathetic portrayal of parents, and violence appropriate for junior novels? Are young people ready for such explicit realism?"[48]

1975: Prior to the American Library Association's annual meeting, the Young Adult Services Division holds a preconference in which participants go through the previous fifteen years of selections of "Best Books for Young Adults" and creates a consolidated list of two hundred books called "Still Alive in '75."

1978: *VOYA* (*Voice of Youth Advocates*) is established by Dorothy Broderick and Mary K. Chelton as a library publication focusing on young adult, as separate from children's, literature. The bimonthly journal has become a major force in reviewing and promoting young adult books and media. It is now published by Scarecrow Press in Lanham, Maryland, with Stacy L. Creel serving as editor. Although it is directed toward librarians, reading and English teachers have learned to rely on its feature articles, its help in drawing together thematically related units, and its columns to keep up with websites, computer games, and graphic novels.

1978: Patty Campbell, former YA librarian for the Los Angeles Public Library, begins writing "The Young Adult Perplex" column in *Wilson Library Bulletin.* She brought a refreshing level of aesthetic as well as pedagogical criticism to the field. When the *Wilson Library Bulletin* ceased publication, she

Margaret A. Edwards Award
Winner (1996)
Judy Blume, **Who Endures**

The Edwards committee honored Blume for her 1975 *Forever,* but other excellent books that young teens love include *Are You There God? It's Me, Margaret* (1970); *Then Again, Maybe I Won't* (1971); *Deenie* (1973); and our favorite, which is *Tiger Eyes* (1981), all published by Bradbury.

When in December of 2004, Judy Blume was the first author of young people's literature to be honored by the National Book Foundation, for her "distinguished contribution to American letters," readers all over the country—in fact all over the world—cheered because they owned one or more of the 75 million Judy Blume books purchased by readers within the past thirty-five years. Blume was a young housewife and mother living in a New Jersey suburb when she began writing. On the morning after she received the award, she explained in a PBS interview with Jeffrey Brown that she wrote her first book about Margaret at age twelve because she had such vivid memories and warm feelings toward the thoughts and emotions she remembers from that time in her life. She loves the optimism and the faith that young readers have as reflected in a letter she quoted in her acceptance speech: "Please send me the facts of life, in number order." She was still pondering on just how to answer that letter, but in general she says that her approach to writing is to go from deep inside herself and to be as truthful and honest as possible.

From the beginning, young readers loved the books and loved talking to Blume, either in person or by mail. Increasingly, college teachers of YA lit began recommending Blume's books and assigning them for class reading and Blume became a welcome speaker at meetings of teachers and librarians. But the more successful Blume's books became, the more censors paid attention to them. Her book about Margaret was described as being negative or flippant toward religion, while one principal would not allow *Deenie* in his school because the female protagonist masturbates. The principal told the librarian that it would have been different if she had been a boy.

Another librarian came up with the idea of blacking out unsuitable words and inserting proper words. Some attacks focused on Blume's lack of moral teachings. Our favorite censorial story came when a mother, upset by two pages about wet dreams in *Then Again, Maybe I Won't,* accosted Blume and said that she had ripped them out of her son's copy. When Blume asked, "What if they had been about a girl's menstruation? Would you still have torn the pages out?" "Oh no," the mother replied, "that's normal." Everyone knows that sexuality sometimes comes into Blume's books, but as Faith McNulty writing in the *New Yorker* (December 5, 1983) observed "only to the degree that it enters most young minds."

Sex isn't Blume's sole topic. In *Are You There God? It's Me, Margaret,* twelve-year-old Margaret is perplexed about what religion she should belong to. In *Then Again, Maybe I Won't,* Blume draws a devastating portrait of a family moving up in social class only to discover that the move may not have been a good thing. In *Tiger Eyes,* Davey has to accept the death of her father in a senseless act of violence. And in the most feared of all of Blume's books, *Forever,* Katherine struggles through the excitement of first sex only to learn that a first love may not endure. For the last edition of this textbook, Blume wrote that:

> *Fear has always made people anxious, and we are living in fearful times. . . . Book banning satisfies a need for parents to feel in control of their children's lives. This fear is often disguised as moral outrage. They want to believe that if their children don't read about something, their children won't know about it. And if they don't know about it, it won't happen.*

Blume is encouraged, though, by how many children and their parents and teachers are speaking out and defending children's right to read. Her message is that parents have "every right to decide what their child should read, but not what all children should read." ●

moved as a columnist to the *Horn Book Magazine*, where she writes her "Sand in the Oyster" columns. She also served as series editor for Twayne's Young Adult Authors series and later for the Scarecrow Studies in Young Adult Literature.

1980: Scott Foresman publishes the first edition of this textbook, *Literature for Today's Young Adults*, by Ken Donelson and Alleen Nilsen. It was the first comprehensive textbook to treat young adult literature as more than the problem novel and as an appropriate area of study in English departments as well as in colleges of education and schools of library science.

We will end this history of the 1960s and 1970s by agreeing with those who say that it was a turning point in establishing new ground rules for young adult literature. But it was also a period valuable for the literature itself. Many of the books from this period were written by authors who went on to win the Margaret A. Edwards Award for their overall contribution to young adult literature. Those books are written about in the individual write-ups for these twenty outstanding authors. Refer back to Focus Boxes 2.3 and 2.4 (pages 66 and 67) for a sampling of other books from the 1960s and 1970s that have proven their lasting power.

Notes

1. Caroline Ticknor, *Hawthorne and His Publisher* (Houghton Mifflin, 1913), p. 141.
2. E. Douglas Branch, *The Sentimental Years*, 1836–1860 (Appleton, 1934), p. 131.
3. Jesse H. Shera, *Foundations of the Public Library: The Origins of the Public Library Movement in New England*, 1629–1885 (The University of Chicago Press, 1949), p. 238.
4. A brief summary of the 1853 and 1876 library conventions can be found in Sister Gabriella Margeath, "Library Conventions of 1853, 1876, and 1877," *Journal of Library History* 8 (April 1973): 52–69.
5. William F. Poole, "Some Popular Objections to Public Libraries," *American Library Journal* 1 (October 1876): 48–49.
6. W. M. Stevenson, "Weeding Out Fiction in the Carnegie Free Library of Allegheny, Pa.," *Library Journal* 22 (March 1897): 135.
7. "Novel Reading," *American Library Journal* 1 (October 1876): 98.
8. "Monthly Reports from Public Librarians upon the Reading of Minors: A Suggestion," *Library Journal* 24 (August 1899): 479.
9. Carleton Washburne and Mabel Vogel, *Winnetka Graded Book List* (American Library Association, 1926), p. 5.
10. Carleton Washburne and Mabel Vogel, "Supplement to the Winnetka Graded Book List," *Elementary English Review* 4 (February 1927): 47–52; and 4 (March 1927): 66–73.
11. William Lyon Phelps, "The Virtues of the Second-Rate," *English Journal* 16 (January 1927): 13–14.
12. Franklin T. Baker, *A Bibliography of Children's Reading* (Teachers College, Columbia University, 1908), pp. 6–7.
13. Clara Whitehill Hunt, "Good and Bad Taste in Girls' Reading," *Ladies Home Journal* 27 (April 1910): 52.
14. Julia Carter, "Let's Talk About Boys and Books," *Wilson Bulletin for Librarians* 9 (April 1935): 418.
15. Alice M. Jordan, "A Gallery of Girls," *Horn Book Magazine* 13 (September 1937): 276.
16. Clara Vostrovsky, "A Study of Children's Reading Tastes," *Pedagogical Seminary* 6 (December 1899): 535.
17. G. Stanley Hall, "Children's Reading: As a Factor in Their Education," *Library Journal* 33 (April 1908): 124–125.
18. J. M. Coulter, "What the University Expects of the Secondary School," *School Review* 17 (February 1909): 73.
19. Wilbur W. Hatfield, "Modern Literature for High School Use," *English Journal* 1 (January 1912): 52.
20. *Reorganization of English in Secondary Schools*, Department of the Interior, Bureau of Education, Bulletin 1917, No. 2. (Government Printing Office, 1917), p. 63.
21. Nancy Gillmore Coryell, *An Evaluation of Extensive and Intensive Teaching of Literature: A Year's Experiment in the Eleventh Grade*, Teachers College, Columbia University, Contributions to Education, No. 275 (Teachers College, Columbia University, 1927).
22. Lou LaBrant, *An Evaluation of the Free Reading Program in Grades Ten, Eleven, and Twelve for the Class of*

1935. The Ohio State University School, Contributions to Education No. 2 (Ohio State University, 1936). See also Lou LaBrant, "The Content of a Free Reading Program," *Educational Research Bulletin* 16 (February 17, 1937): 29–34.

23. Dora V. Smith, "American Youth and English," *English Journal* 26 (February 1937): 111.

24. Graham P. Hawks, "A Nineteenth-Century School Library: Early Years in Milwaukee," *Journal of Library History* 12 (Fall 1977): 361.

25. S. Swett Green, "Libraries and School," *Library Journal* 16 (December 1891): 22. Other representative articles concerned with the relationship include Mellen Chamberlain's "Public Libraries and Public School," *Library Journal* 5 (November–December 1880): 299–302; W. E. Foster's "The School and the Library: Their Mutual Relations," *Library Journal* 4 (September–October 1879): 319–341; and Mrs. J. H. Resor's "The Boy and the Book, or The Public Library a Necessity," *Public Libraries* 2 (June 1897): 282–285.

26. "The Report of the Committee on Relations of Public Libraries to Public Schools," *NEA Journal of Proceedings and Addresses of the 38th Annual Meeting* (The University of Chicago, Press, 1899), p. 455.

27. Mary E. Hall, "The Possibilities of the High School Library," *ALA Bulletin* 6 (July 1912): 261–263.

28. Caroline M. Hewins, "Book Reviews, Book Lists, and Articles on Children's Reading: Are They of Practical Value to the Children's Librarians?" *Library Journal* 26 (August 1901): 58. Attacks on series books, especially Stratemeyer's books, persisted thereafter in library literature. Mary E. S. Root prepared a list of series books not to be circulated by public librarians, "Not to Be Circulated," *Wilson Bulletin for Librarians* 3 (January 1929): 446, including books by Alger, Finley, Castlemon, Ellis, Optic, and others, the others being heavily Stratemeyer. Two months later, Ernest F. Ayers responded, "Not to Be Circulated?" *Wilson Bulletin for Librarians* 3 (March 1929): 528–529, objecting to the cavalier treatment accorded old favorites and sarcastically adding, "Why worry about censorship so long as we have librarians?" Attacks continue today. Some librarians and English teachers to the contrary, the Syndicate clearly is winning, and students seem to be pleased.

29. Franklin K. Mathiews, "Blowing Out the Boy's Brains," *Outlook* 108 (November 18, 1914): 653.

30. John Tunis, "What Is a Juvenile Book?" *Horn Book Magazine* 44 (June 1968): 307.

31. George W. Norvell, "Some Results of a Twelve-Year Study of Children's Reading Interests," *English Journal* 35 (December 1946): 532, 536.

32. Marie Rankin, *Children's Interests in Library Books of Fiction*, Teachers College, Columbia University, Contributions to Education, No. 906 (Teachers College, Columbia University, 1947).

33. Stephen Dunning, "The Most Popular Junior Novels," *Junior Libraries* 5 (December 15, 1959): 7–9.

34. Jacob W. Getzels, "The Nature of Reading Interests: Psychological Aspects" in *Developing Permanent Interests in Reading*, ed. Helen M. Robinson, Supplementary Education Monographs, No. 84, December 1956 (University of Chicago Press, 1956), p. 5.

35. G. Robert Carlsen, "Behind Reading Interests," *English Journal* 43 (January 1954): 7–10.

36. G. O. Ireland, "Bibliotherapy: The Use of Books as a Form of Treatment in a Neuropsychiatric Hospital," *Library Journal* 54 (December 1, 1929): 972–974.

37. Lou LaBrant, "Diversifying the Matter," *English Journal* 40 (March 1951): 135.

38. S. Alan Cohen, "Paperbacks in the Classroom," *Journal of Reading* 12 (January 1969): 295.

39. Stanley B. Kegler and Stephen Dunning, "Junior Book Roundup—Literature for the Adolescent," *English Journal* 50 (May 1961): 369.

40. Dwight L. Burton, "The Novel for the Adolescent," *English Journal* 40 (September 1951): 363–369.

41. Richard S. Alm, "The Glitter and the Gold," *English Journal* 44 (September 1955): 315.

42. Emma L. Patterson, "The Junior Novels and How They Grew," *English Journal* 45 (October 1956): 381.

43. Frank G. Jennings, "Literature for Adolescents—Pap or Protein?" *English Journal* 45 (December 1956): 226–231.

44. See, for example, Alice Krahn, "Case Against the Junior Novel," *Top of the News* 17 (May 1961): 19–22; Esther Millett, "We Don't Even Call Those Books!" *Top of the News* 20 (October 1963): 45–47; and Harvey R. Granite, "The Uses and Abuses of Junior Literature," *Clearing House* 42 (February 1968): 337–340.

45. Arthur Applebee's *Tradition and Reform in the Teaching of English: A History* (NCTE, 1974) provides succinct comments on the Basics Conferences and Project English in Chapters 7 and 8.

46. Chris Crowe's "Starting with Dora V: A Genealogy of YA Literature Specialists" in the January 2000 *English Journal*, pp. 129–132, gives good insights regarding the growth of young adult literature as an academic field of study.

47. A good article on Neil Postman and Charles Weingartner is Herb Karl's "Of Questioning Assumptions, Crap Detecting and Splinters of Ice in the Heart," *English Journal* 94 (November 2004) 20–24.

48. *Top of the News* 31 (April 1975): 302.

New Technology, New Attitudes, and New Literacies

It is almost impossible to pick up an education journal or a publisher's catalog without running across the terms *literacy*, *literacy studies*, or *new literacies*. For example, five of the six books advertised on the opening pages of a spring/summer 2007 brochure from Teachers College Press were entitled:

> *Bridging the Literacy Achievement Gap, Grades 4–12*
> *Critical Literacy/Critical Teaching*
> *Culture, Literacy, and Learning*
> *The Effective Literacy Coach*
> *Literacy Leadership in Early Childhood*

Phrases in either the titles or subtitles of other new books in the same brochure tied the idea of literacy into the roles that adults can play as active partners in the lives of urban children, immigrant students, and Latino families and communities. A search under "Adolescent/YA Literacy" of the National Council of Teachers of English preliminary program for the November 2007 annual convention yielded the names of fifty-two different presenters who would speak about the subject, while the titles of various articles in the April/May 2007 *Reading TODAY*, which is distributed to all members of the International Reading Association, included:

> "Adolescent Literacy by the Numbers"
> "Adolescent Literacy Gains Support"
> "Adolescent Literacy 'Wish List' Poses Questions for Further Inquiry"
> "Conference Explores 21st Century Literacies"
> "Lessons in the Ethics of Literacy"

Focus Box 3.1

Help for Adults in Developing New Literacies

Anime Explosion: The What? Why? and Wow! of Japanese Animation by Patrick Drazen. Stone Bridge Press, 2002. Check the publisher's website, www.stonebridge.com, for other books on anime and manga. The author does a good job of explaining the different attitudes that Japanese and Americans have toward nudity and what constitutes sexuality in drawings.

Building Literary Connections with Graphic Novels: Page by Page, Panel by Panel edited by James Bucky Carter. NCTE, 2007. Contributors who wrote the chapters each take a traditional text and pair it with one or more graphic novels; for example, Dante's *Inferno* is taught alongside an *X-Men* story, while Dickens's *Oliver Twist* is taught alongside Will Eisner's *Fagin the Jew*.

"Don't Bother Me Mom—I'm Learning!" by Marc Prensky. Paragon House, 2006. The title of Prensky's Chapter 4, "Our Kids Are Not Like Us: They're Natives, We're Immigrants," spells out the idea that a generation that has grown up "surrounded by and using computers, videogames, DVD players, videocams, eBay, cell phones, iPods, and all the other tools of a digital age" has different thinking patterns and approaches to life than do those of us coming to the digital world as immigrants and still wait-

ing for someone to explain and "teach us" about each new device.

Everything Bad Is Good for You: How Today's Popular Culture Is Actually Making Us Smarter by Steven Johnson. Penguin/Riverside, 2005. Johnson makes a persuasive case for the idea that popular culture entertainment ranging from *The Simpsons* to *The Lord of the Rings* and to video games is growing more sophisticated and posing cognitive challenges that make us better thinkers.

Fame Junkies: The Hidden Truths behind America's Favorite Addiction by Jake Halpern. Houghton Mifflin, 2007. Halpern speaks out for moderation and for guiding teens into areas where they can feel fulfilled from developing skills and interests rather than longing for instant fame, which is something dependent on many factors outside of any young person's control.

Graphic Novels: A Genre Guide to Comic Books, Manga, and More by Michael Pawuk (Genreflecting Advisory Series). Libraries Unlimited, 2006. Written for both adults and young adults, this 663-page book is a good source for both skimming and answering specific questions.

Lesson Plans for Creating Media-Rich Classrooms edited by Mary Christel and Scott Sullivan. NCTE, 2007. Chapter

"Lieutenant Governor of Ontario an Advocate for Literacy, Mental Health, Racial Tolerance"

"Literacy Promotion Award Seeks Applicants"

"No Greater Pool of Expertise in Literacy"

"Verizon Foundation Spotlights Literacy"

In the United Kingdom, the Reading Association has changed its name to the Literacy Association because of wanting to get away from the idea that literacy means reading and that reading means decoding. The concept of literacy is changing not only because of digital technologies, but also because of all the ways that people's social identities are changing as the world moves closer toward economic and cultural globalization. See Focus Box 3.1, Help for Adults in Developing New Literacies; also see Focus Box 3.2, "Different" Literacies in YA Books for illustrations of how these concepts are finding their way into both fiction and nonfiction for teen readers.

topics range from how to manipulate photos for special effects to how to create video games and how to detect bias in print and broadcast news.

ReadWriteThink is an online partnership between the National Council of Teachers of English and the International Reading Association, along with the MarcoPolo Education Foundation. It was established in 2002 and is open and free to users, who can access it through either of the organizations or just by typing the name into any search engine. It provides classroom lessons and background material relating to many aspects of literacy.

Religious Literacy: What Every American Needs to Know and Doesn't by Stephen Prothero. HarperSanFrancisco, 2007. Prothero is the chair of the department of religion at Boston University. He chides Americans for operating under the assumption that religious ignorance is bliss. His thesis is that religious illiteracy is dangerous because religion is one of the greatest forces the human race has ever seen for not only good but also evil.

Secondary School Literacy: What Research Reveals for Classroom Practice edited by Leslie S. Rush, A. Jonathan Eakle, and Allen Berger. NCTE, 2007. Reviewers are praising this research book for the way the different chapters come together to show similar trends across different kinds of literacy education.

un.Spun: Finding Facts in a World of Disinformation by Brooks Jackson and Kathleen Hall Jamieson. Random House Trade Paperback Original, 2007. The authors' website, FactCheck.org, was listed by *Time* as one of the "25 websites you can't live without." The premise of their book is that "*Spin* is a polite word for deception," and that being able to recognize deception is a necessary literacy for our time.

What Video Games Have to Teach Us about Learning and Literacy by James Paul Gee. Palgrave, Macmillan, 2003. Gee is a well-known educator who explains thirty-six principles of learning and shows how computer games do a better job of building on these principles than do many standard teaching techniques.

Words That Work: It's Not What You Say, It's What People Hear by Frank Luntz. Hyperion, 2007. Luntz writes about the power of framing and how much more successful politicians are if they can learn to use phrases that will make them sound active and on task. For example, it is less effective for a politician to go on "a listening tour," than on a "getting it done" tour.

The World Is Flat: A Brief History of the Twenty-First Century, Updated and Expanded, Release 2.0 by Thomas L. Friedman. Farrar, Straus and Giroux, 2006. *School Library Journal* recommended Friedman's book not only to adults but also to sophisticated teenagers who are interested in the many ways that people from different countries are interacting with each other.

When any field develops, new terms are created and old terms are given new meanings. *Metalanguage* is a term from linguistics referring to language that is used to talk about language. For example, such grammatical terms as *noun*, *verb*, and *adjective* and such literary terms as *plot*, *denouement*, and *onomatopoeia* are metalanguage used by teachers as they communicate about writing and about literature with their students. Some of the metalanguage that refers to new literacy concepts is fairly simple, as with *indie* to refer to films, comics, and magazines that have been independently produced, and *squeeze text* to refer to compressing English by something like 30 percent to 40 percent to accommodate *SMs* (*Short Messages* or text messaging) as well as the *balloon speech* in comics. Squeezing is done mostly by replacing words with symbols, as when using + to stand for "more," ++ for "most" and 4 for "for"; leaving out vowels; and using single letters to stand for words as in the title of William Steig's famous picture book *CDB!* ("See the Bee"), which is made up mostly of letters and numbers "4 U 2 figure out." That Steig's picture book was published in 1968, and that for at least three decades Americans have been amusing themselves by looking for underlying

The Astonishing Adventures of Fanboy and Goth Girl by Barry Lyga. Houghton, 2006. Fanboy loves comics and dreams of being "discovered" at a comic-book convention because of his in-progress *Schemata* graphic novel, but his real life was far from such success. Then Goth Girl Kyra, herself a loner, reaches out to him through an Instant Message that shows him being beaten up. At first he thinks she is making fun of him, but her friendship is the beginning of better things.

Black Duck by Janet Taylor. Philomel/Sleuth, May 2006. Fourteen-year-old David is the hero of this exciting mystery story that gets told because David, an aspiring journalist, dares to knock on the door of his elderly neighbor and ask about his mysterious past. The Black Duck was a rum-running ship that back in the 1920s played a mysterious role in the posh town of Newport, Rhode Island.

The Braid by Helen Frost. Farrar/Frances Foster Books, 2006. Told through different poems in different voices, this is the unusual story of Scottish teenage sisters whose family is torn from their Highlands home in the 1850s. One stays with her grandmother in Scotland, while one moves with the rest of the family to Cape Breton, Nova Scotia. The girls stay connected only through pieces of a braid they intertwine in their hair.

Evil Genius by Catherine Jinks. Harcourt, 2007. A boy who hacked into computers when he was only seven and then more or less tests out of high school launches himself into a grown-up career at age fourteen by enrolling in the Axis Institute and taking classes in Misinformation, Disguise, Basic Lying, Embezzlement, and Explosives.

Harlem Hustle by Janet McDonald. Farrar/Frances Foster Books, 2006. *Harlem Hustle* tells the story of seventeen-year-old Eric "Hustle" Samson, who dreams of making his way out of the projects by becoming a rapper. McDonald, who grew up in the projects and went on to become an international lawyer, was praised for exactly nailing the hip-hop lingo and the street slang, while also throwing in a cultural-history lesson.

The Invention of Hugo Cabret by Brian Selznick. Scholastic, 2007. In this original novel, which was a finalist for the National Book Award, Selznick created 272 full-page drawings plus over 250 pages of text, all deliciously fitted onto black bordered pages that give readers the feeling of stepping into an old fashioned film or more mysteriously

into the back rooms of a museum that once housed the predecessors of today's robots, known as *automata*. Interwoven is the story of Frenchman Georges Méliès, the inventor of modern day movies.

The Last Days by Scott Westerfeld. Penguin/Razorbill, 2006. *The Last Days* is a continuation of Westerfeld's *Peeps*, but rock music plays a big part in this story, and in fact is the medium that calls up and helps to defeat the mysterious forces that almost destroy New York City.

Lugalbanda: The Boy Who Got Caught Up in a War by Kathy Henderson, illustrated by Jane Ray. Candlewick, 2006. Excavators in the 1800s found the cuneiform tablets on which this Sumerian legend was recorded, but the tablets were not transcribed until in the 1970s. And now readers can enjoy what is perhaps the oldest written story in the world. It is about a boy left behind by a marching army, but who becomes a hero anyway.

Memories of Survival illustrated by Esther Nisenthal Krinitz and told by Bernice Steinhardt. Hyperion, 2005. Thirty-four hand-stitched, embroidered, fabric panels tell in great detail the story of Esther's early childhood in a Polish village, then the Nazi invasion followed by a labor camp and death.

The Princess Academy by Shannon Hale. Bloomsbury, 2005. Petite fourteen-year-old Miri feels left out because she does not get to work in the quarry with the other girls. Hoping to prove her worth, she goes away to a special school—far different from a typical "princess" school—but while there she discovers her special talent for "quarry speech," which is a silent way of communicating.

The Road of the Dead by Kevin Brooks. Scholastic/The Chicken House, 2006. Two brothers are trying to solve the murder of their sister on the English moors. It is a grisly and violent story, and the most interesting part is how fourteen-year-old Ruben has the psychic power to see what his older, more impetuous brother, Cole, is doing and thinking even when they are miles apart.

Voices by Ursula K. Le Guin. Harcourt, 2006. Seventeen-year-old Memer and her mentor, the Waylord, are protectors of a secret library in a country where the written word has been declared demonic and books are outlawed. But then the stage is set for change when Orrec, a poet and storyteller, and his wife, Gry, come for a visit.

meanings on license plates, illustrates that many of the "new literacies" are not as new as most people think.

Ethnography relates to such words as *ethnic* and *ethos* and to *graphic* and *graphology.* It refers to the systematic studying and recording of human culture. *Framing* is a term used to talk about how contexts and situations provide a backdrop for messages and influence how they are interpreted. Frank Luntz's *Words That Work: It's Not What You Say, It's What People Hear* is about how politicians, for example, try to frame their words to appeal to the largest number of voters. We recently heard a good discussion of framing when one of our graduate students, Kathy Grismore, wrote her master's thesis on how the mass media framed news stories about Hurricane Katrina and the city of New Orleans.

Multimodalities refers to differences in the ways that material is presented. The *modality* part of the word comes from the Latin root *modus,* which gave us such English words as *modem, model, mood,* and *module,* all referring in some way to patterns or shapes. An obvious example of multimodalities is how in comic strips readers are required to interpret more than words. Because the words usually represent only what characters say to each other, the reader must also look at the drawings to get the full picture. Almost everyone knows that a balloon shape indicates that someone is saying the words, that a light bulb over someone's head means that the character has a "bright" idea, and that a cloud with jagged edges and such onomatopoeic words as *Zap! Ka-platz!, Smak! Boinggg! Pow! Klank!* and *Kazaam!* indicate something unusual has happened. Readers also recognize that a series of random typewriter symbols (*%#$+&) means that someone is swearing, but it is not so easy for readers to interpret facial expressions or to know what is symbolized by different colors and shadings.

Semiotics comes from the Greek word *séma,* which means "sign." It is related to such English words as *signature, signal, design, signify, significant, semantics,* and *semiology.* Before electronic communication, *semaphore* flags were used to send signals from boats, lighthouses, runways, and watchtowers. Today's semioticians are not communicating so directly; instead they are looking at what are sometimes called "signs of the times," which reveal underlying messages and attitudes that people may communicate without being aware of what they are doing. For example, semioticians have pointed out that when mainstream listeners "praise" a speaker from a minority group as "articulate," they may really be revealing that they had such low expectations that the person's communication skills come as a surprise worthy of comment. A semiotician might also point out that people are actually communicating the opposite of what the words say when they make such comments as, "Not that there's anything wrong with that, but . . . ," "Now, I'm not saying he's guilty, but . . . ," or "I don't mean to interrupt, but . . . ."

In April 2007, Professor Brian V. Street from King's College in London came to Arizona State University to speak on "New Literacies: New Times: Ethnographic Perspectives." One of the points he made is that Western culture has overemphasized writing and the written language as a means of communication. He also argued that some of the practices that we currently view as "new" literacies are very old. Going back to prehistory, cultures have had religious ceremonies and customs and have communicated not only through speech but

Margaret A. Edwards Award
Winner (2005)

Francesca Lia Block, The Bringer of Magical Realism

The five Weetzie books published between 1989 and 1995 (*Weetzie Bat*; *Witch Baby*; *Cherokee Bat and the Goat Guys*; *Missing Angel Juan*; and *Baby Be-Bop*) are the ones that the Edwards Committee cited when they chose to honor Francesca Lia Block. Her selection was a surprise because the Margaret A. Edwards Award is for lifetime accomplishment and Block is the youngest person to have been so honored. Everyone expects her to continue writing for many more years.

A second reason for the surprise is that her books are so controversial. Block says that she writes urban fairy tales, but critics point out that her fairy tales start where the traditional ones end, and rather than implying that as soon as young people step into adulthood they can walk off into the sunset and live happily ever after, Block encourages her characters to seek happiness and fulfillment wherever in life's journey they happen to be.

Having grown up in Hollywood and lived all her life in California, Block makes her Los Angeles setting as important as any of her characters. Actual names taken from the Los Angeles area include Hollywood Boulevard, Tick Tock Tea Room, Fredericks of Hollywood, Loves, Shangri-la, Shangri Los Angeles, Shangri-L.A., and Hollywood. She also uses the way Weetzie's father, Charlie Bat, describes Hollywood as an illusion and an imitation and a mirage, to help prepare her readers for the magical realism that she incorporates into the plots of her books.

Most readers think of the stories as lighthearted and fun, even while her characters take in stride such heavy issues as drug overdoses, broken families, sexual experimentation, and abandoned children left on their own. We remember reading *The Hanged Man* when it came out in 1994 and conjecturing with our students on whether Block had studied the *Newsletter on Intellectual Freedom* and made a list of all the reasons censors give for wanting to keep particular books away from kids and then concocted a story to include 90 percent of the actions and words that fundamentalist critics abhor.

When Block won the Margaret A. Edwards Award, even she was surprised. She told David Levithan, who interviewed her for the June 2005 issue of *School Library Journal*, that she suspected in this conservative political climate, the committee members said something like "In defiance of what's happening now, we're going to do this."

Block's books appeal to older teens and to what Michael Cart describes as a "crossover" audience of readers between the ages of sixteen and twenty-five. In 2005, HarperCollins published a follow-up adult book about Weetzie Bat entitled *Necklace of Kisses.* In this book, written almost twenty years after the first one, Weetzie's relationship with My Secret Agent Lover Man has withered and so Weetzie leaves the man who now goes by the more ordinary name of Max. Even though HarperCollins published the book in its adult division, a bookseller who brought the Weetzie Bat books to the 2006 convention of the Children's Literature Association in Mission Beach, California, laughingly assured customers that teen readers were going right through the original Weetzie books, now published in a single volume entitled *Dangerous Angels: The Weetzie Bat Books*, and then happily buying *Necklace of Kisses* to see what happens to the adult Weetzie and her uniquely named pals and children.

When Block was in college she started writing "short, odd, little punk-influenced stories." She remembers one about a girl who was mad at her boyfriend and so she got a Ken doll and practiced voodoo on him. She told Levithan how she came up with the concept of Weetzie. She was driving on the freeway in the Valley when she saw a Pinto:

> this weird box of a cartoon-looking car. It was light bubblegum pink, and at that time you never saw a pink car—ever, ever. On the license plate it said WEETZIE. And I just remember the moment—the time of day, the way the sky looked kind of smoggy—everything. And there's this bleach-blond head of this girl in this car. (47)

That was all it took—one name and one flashing image—for a character now loved worldwide to move into Block's creative mind and to make herself at home for at least the next twenty-five years. Only the future will tell if she's going to stay through middle and old age. Many readers hope she does. ●

through gestures and drawings and have had means of trading goods and of establishing respect and consideration for people besides oneself. Even in the modern world, people who are described as "illiterate" often understand such concepts as tickets, taxes, and maps. They are also skilled in trading and in interpreting such symbols as the internationally agreed-upon highway markers and such commercial logos as the golden arches for a McDonald's restaurant and the classic red and white design of Campbell's soup cans. We chose to put the page on Francesca Lia Block as a Margaret A. Edwards Award winner in this chapter because of the way she has her characters create symbols and meaning out of places and objects that go unnoticed by the majority of people who live in Hollywood.

Professor Street's speech reminded us of some of the new books we've recently seen in which authors are exploring alternative kinds of communication strategies. See Focus Box 3.2, "Different" Literacies in YA Books. Some of the literacies are as old as the hills, while others are so new that we considered putting the books in the science fiction and fantasy chapter. But with communication tools there is a shrinking line between fantasy and reality. Ten years ago who would have thought that today we would be picking up our cell phones, punching in a location, and waiting for a voice to guide us to our destination, or that we could go into YouTube and be like the proverbial fly on the wall watching total strangers "do their thing."

To describe a group's literacy practices, one must know a great deal about the social world of the group, which is where *ethnography* comes into the picture as a point of departure. Professor Street talked about how literacy is part of an array of modes including visual literacy, computer literacy, and political literacy. *Lowrider literacy* involves "reading" the stories told in the artwork drawn by Hispanic American youths. He has even heard of *palpatory literacy* to refer to the knowledge of masseuses about the feelings associated with particular kinds of touching. And today many people use the term *literacy* as a metaphor or a code to refer to "general competence" or awareness. For himself, he restricts literacy to ideas that somehow relate to communicating through visible or auditory symbols, but this is not as simple as it sounds because of all the different ways people either send or receive messages. He left his audience to ponder:

- How do genres and modes vary across disciplines, subjects, and fields?
- How do academic literacy practices vary from informal literacy practices?
- How can an understanding of New Literacy Studies, Multimodality, and "Literacy as Artefact" help in the development of literacies for "new times"?

When students in our spring 2007 young adult literature classes were discussing Trudy Krisher's *Fallout*, a book set in Florida during the 1950s cold war and Senator McCarthy's anti-communist crusade, they were especially interested in the futuristic predictions of the 1950s. Not a single prediction touched on the importance of communication or on what changes might occur. No one foresaw computers and how the digital age would change daily life.

The conversation made us aware of the fact that we are all experiencing some surprising changes, and so in preparation for writing this chapter we undertook two projects. One was to survey 266 local high school students about their literacy activities. We asked them about their favorite books, authors, magazines, games, and other online activities. We also gave them a chance to offer advice to teachers and librarians, most of which we are saving to report on in other chapters. We also conducted a Media Watch over the first four months of 2007. We clipped or downloaded news stories or took notes when we happened to hear of events related to or reflecting different kinds of literacy.

A New Kind of Democracy with an Emphasis on Youth

The first thing we noticed in our Media Watch is a new kind of digital democracy with an emphasis on youth and the valuing of individual opinions. The year of 2007 started with *Time* magazine's selection of "*You. Yes, You* as Person of the Year" (*Time*, December 13, 2006). A computer was pictured on the cover with a mylar screen that would reflect the viewer's face. Managing Editor Richard Stengel explained that individuals are changing the nature of the information age because as creators and consumers they are generating their own content and in doing so are transforming art and politics.

Time editors devoted practically the whole issue to exploring the ways that we have all become "Citizens of the New Digital Democracy." Lev Grossman observed that Thomas Carlyle's philosophy of the world's history being "but the biography of great men" has taken a beating because of the way the Internet allows the many to wrest power from the few. We counted over thirty individuals whose photos and stories were shown and were surprised that only a half-dozen were over thirty; the others were young people still in their twenties. Some were there simply as representatives of the 65,000 people who every day post new videos to YouTube, while others were there for specific contributions they had made; for example, the three young men who founded YouTube (Chad Hurley, Steve Chen, and Jawed Karim); a twenty-two-year-old Pakistani photographer (Ali Khurshid) who has loaded two hundred beautiful pictures to Flickr and brought the world an "alternative" image of his home country; the twenty-one-year-old news photographer (S. R. Sidarth), who Senator George Allen insultingly referred to as *macaca* and lost his re-election bid perhaps because of publicity surrounding the incident. There was also serious political fallout when Lane Hudson, the former Congressional page who is now twenty-nine, posted online the suggestive emails that he received in 1995 from now-deposed Congressman Mark Foley. Twenty-five-year-old Simon Pulsifer was featured because of having authored somewhere between 2,000 and 3,000 Wikipedia articles, while fifty-four-year-old Harriet Klausner, a former librarian, was featured for having posted nearly 13,000 reviews on amazon.com.

While many people decry this new democratization of information as "amateur," *Time* editor Stengel wrote that America was founded by amateurs. The framers of the Constitution may have been professional lawyers and military men and bankers, "but they were amateur politicians, and that's the way they thought it should be. Thomas Paine was in effect the first blogger, and Ben Franklin was essentially loading his persona into the MySpace of the eighteenth century, *Poor Richard's Almanack*."

The article that resonated the most with us was the concluding page, written by NBC news anchor Brian Williams, who under the headline "Enough About You," asked some interesting questions about "the celebration of self," and whether we've raised a generation of young people who are so focused on their own successes that they will miss out on some great things. "It is now possible," he wrote, "even common—to go about your day in America and consume only what you wish to see and hear." We can tune into a television network that we know will agree with what we already think, and just as we can program our iPods to play music we already know we like, we can filter our reading of news on the Internet.

But Williams argued, "there's a lot of information out there that citizens in an informed democracy *need* to know" especially in a world as complicated as ours is today. He is worried that:

> Millions of Americans have come to regard the act of reading a daily newspaper— on *paper*—as something akin to being dragged by their parents to Colonial Williamsburg. It's a tactile visit to another time . . . flat, one-dimensional, unexciting, emitting a slight whiff of decay. It doesn't refresh. It offers no choice. Hell, it doesn't even move. Worse yet: nowhere does it greet us by name. It's for *everyone*. (78)

Unexpected Complications Revealed through Our Media Watch

Here is a sampling of the kinds of technology-inspired complications that made it into the news between January and May 2007.

• "MySpace Sued, Blamed in Abuse of Kids" was the headline on an Associated Press story about four families suing News Corp. and its MySpace social-networking site in relation to underage daughters being sexually abused by adults they met online. The families from New York, Texas, Pennsylvania, and South Carolina filed suits in Los Angeles Superior Court, alleging negligence, recklessness, fraud, and misrepresentation. Attorney Jason A. Itkin said that he hopes the lawsuits, which are seeking monetary damages "in the millions of dollars" will spur MySpace into action and will prevent such events from happening to other children. Actions already taken by MySpace have included educational efforts and partnerships with law enforcement. "The company has also placed restrictions on how adults may contact younger users on MySpace, while developing technologies such as one announced [January 17] to let parents see some aspects of their child's online profile, including the stated age." (January 19, 2007)

• Sean Stevens, twenty-eight, and Peter Berdovsky, twenty-seven, were pictured in an Associated Press photo as they left Charlestown District Court in Boston after posting $2,500 bonds. The accompanying story said that on January 31 they had attached thirty-eight blinking electronic devices to poles, bridges, overpasses, a hospital, and other high-profile spots, including Fenway Park. The

Headlines make it clear that many changes are taking place in the way people communicate, but just how educators should prepare their students for such changes is not so clear.

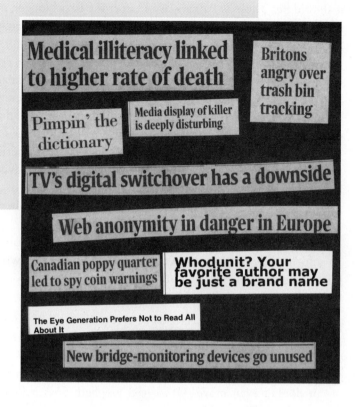

blinking circuit boards, with dangling wires, showed a cartoon character giving the finger. They were planted in ten cities as part of a guerrilla marketing campaign to promote the cartoon *Agua Teen Hunger Force* appearing on The Cartoon Network owned by Turner Broadcasting. Only in Boston, probably because of where they were placed, did a bomb scare ensue with highways, bridges, and part of the Charles River being closed to traffic. Within ten days, the general manager of The Cartoon Network resigned over the event and Turner Broadcasting and an advertising agency agreed to pay $2 million in compensation to the city of Boston. (February 2, 2007)

• A different kind of complication was discussed in an Associated Press story from London under the headline, "Terrrorists Using YouTube for Propaganda." It told how "Anyone with an Internet connection can watch videos of bombings and sniper attacks against U.S. forces—shot and edited by Islamic militants and broadcast on YouTube, the world's largest video-sharing Web site." German Chancellor Angela Merkel's chief of staff, Thomas de Maiziere, said authorities are struggling to glean information from cyberspace, but "Trying to uncover Internet meetings of terrorists is like searching for a needle in a haystack." The problem is even more complicated when looking for propaganda because 65,000 new clips are loaded onto YouTube every day and viewers tune into 100 million videos daily. Google, Inc., the owner of YouTube, reserves the right to remove videos that users flag as unsuitable, but nothing is done until someone complains. And even when a video is removed, someone else can post it under a different account where it will remain available until another complaint is received. (February 20, 2007)

● According to the Associated Press, Governor Phil Bredesen of Tennessee suspended four executions because the 100-page manual of instructions was so jumbled that it no longer made sense. It was designed to give prison officials minute-by-minute directions on how to conduct an execution. The state now uses lethal injections in place of electrocution, but apparently because of the ease of cutting and pasting when doing revisions on a computer, the manual still contained paragraphs left over from when prisoners were electrocuted. For example, officials were told to shave the prisoner's head and to engage the automatic rheostat and have a fire extinguisher on hand. They were also cautioned to disconnect the electrical cables in the rear of the chair before a doctor checks to see if the injection was successful. (February 20, 2007)

● "Egypt Blogger Gets 4 Years in Prison" read the headline on an Associated Press story about Abdel Kareem Nabil, a twenty-two-year-old former student at Egypt's Al-Azhar University. He was "sentenced to four years in prison for insulting Islam and Egypt's president." On his blog, he often lashed out at Al-Azhar, the most prominent religious center in Sunni Islam, calling it "the university of terrorism" and accusing it of encouraging extremism. The Committee to Protect Journalists, a New York–based media rights group, said "Internet writers and editors are the fastest-growing segment of imprisoned journalists." As of December 2006, forty-nine were behind bars. (February 23, 2007)

● "Web Anonymity in Danger in Europe," began an Associated Press story from Frankfurt, Germany, about how the German and Dutch governments are taking the lead in crafting legislation that will make it illegal to provide false information to Internet service providers and will require phone companies to save detailed records on customer usage. Graham Cluley, a tech consultant, said that Europeans have a long history of fighting for personal freedoms and are "unlikely to accept such regulations." He added that "No one disagrees with the need to take decisive action against terrorism and organized crime, but to introduce such restrictive surveillance . . . without proper safeguards in place, seems positively Orwellian." (February 25, 2007)

● About this time, our College of Education at Arizona State University had to devise new guidelines for its student teachers, one of whom was in trouble at the middle school where he was teaching because of the disruption caused when students in his class passed around a cell-phone picture of him downloaded from MySpace. He was dressed in nothing but a miniature Christmas stocking and was holding something that looked like an assault rifle—really a large water gun. He said it was all a joke for his college-age friends. The FBI searched his computer messages both because of the gun and the fact that he was working with children.

● Shortly after this, educators in the Phoenix area were even more surprised to read in the *Arizona Republic*, "Kids are finding new, technological ways to hurt or embarrass each other, and school officials have few answers for it." A twelve-year-old girl in Cave Creek (a suburb of Phoenix) "borrowed" a cell phone from an eleven-year-old classmate and then took a photo of herself "below the waist." She sent the image to other students giving the impression that the picture was of the owner of the telephone. The enterprising photographer was suspended from her middle school and may face criminal charges. The official reason given for her dismissal was that district rules say that cell phones must be turned off and concealed during school hours. (March 10, 2007)

- *Publishers Weekly* proudly began a story with "In case you needed proof that books can save lives—Michael Auberry, the twelve-year-old who disappeared from his Boy Scout troop on Saturday in North Carolina, was found alive Tuesday morning in a remote mountain area, and a children's book may have helped him survive." The boy had been missing for four days and near the beginning of the ordeal, Michael's father expressed hope that his son would manage to come out alive because together they had read Gary Paulsen's *Hatchet*, a powerful survival story of a lone boy lost in the Canadian woods after a plane crash. The father's comment was widely reported, and CNN newscaster Anderson Cooper managed to contact Gary Paulsen, who was in Alaska with his Iditarod dogs, and conduct a long-distance interview. Paulsen was gracious in not claiming to have provided a survival manual, and after the boy was found he told Fox News that he was just glad if remembering the book had helped Michael stay calm.

During the four days that the story was in the news, *Hatchet*, which over its twenty-year lifespan had already sold 131,000 copies, suddenly climbed to number 182 on the amazon.com sales list, but soon after Michael was found the story began losing some of its luster because it was learned that Michael had not wanted to go on the Scout trip and had purposely snuck away in hopes of finding the highway and hitchhiking home. His first comment to rescuers was that he wanted a helicopter ride out. (He was brought home in an ambulance.) When we talked about the event in our YA literature class, everyone was happy that Paulsen's book was gaining a new set of readers, but a couple of students suggested that it was just as likely that *Hatchet* inspired Michael to run off into the woods as it was that *Hatchet* saved his life. (March 20, 2007)

- The April 16, 2007, shootings on the campus at Virginia Tech in Blacksburg occurred eight years to the week after the shootings at Columbine High School in Colorado. Differences in communication strategies vividly demonstrate the kinds of changes occurring in less than a decade. The twenty-three-year-old shooter was an immigrant whose name variously appeared in news stories as Cho Seung-Hui, Seung-Hui Cho, and Cho Seung Hui. He bought one of his guns and several rounds of ammunition on eBay. He had been dismissed from Nikki Giovanni's creative writing class because of using his cell phone to take under-the-desk pictures of women students' legs and knees. The women felt intimidated and stopped coming to class, choosing instead to send their work in online. Email was used to warn students that a gunman was shooting on campus, and while the incident was still in progress, action photos from students' cell phones were broadcast. Within twenty-four hours, over 100,000 messages had been posted on the university's social network, which the university closed because of racist and hateful messages. A new site, which would be monitored, was opened. And most amazing of all, the shooter prepared his own press packet, which, between shootings, he took to the post office and sent by express mail to NBC in New York. It arrived a day late because he wrote the wrong zip code. When the video was broadcast, critics feared the publicity would inspire copycat crimes, while other critics said they did not want media officials deciding to withhold news.

- A happier story printed in the *Arizona Republic* began with "OMG!" It was about thirteen-year-old Pennsylvania teenager Morgan Pozgar's winning $25,000 by defeating nearly two hundred competitors to become first the East Coast text-messaging champion and then going on to beat the twenty-one-year-old West Coast champion, Eli Tirosh, by spelling Mary Poppins' famous "Supercalifrag-ilisticexpialidocious" in fifteen seconds. The contest was sponsored by LG electronics company. Morgan estimated that she probably sends out more than 8,000 text messages a month. (April 23, 2007)

- "Schools Banning iPods to Beat Cheaters" read the headline on an Associated Press story about how some schools are banning digital media players because it is so easy for students to download formulas and other material onto their players and then to thread the ear bud up a sleeve. They can listen to a recording in such a way that it appears that they are simply resting their head on their elbow. A spokeswoman for the National Association of Secondary School Principals said that "Trying to fight the technology without a dialogue on values and expectations is a losing battle," but there may be "a backdoor benefit" because as teachers think about how technology has corrupted some school practices, they might also think about ways it can be used productively. (April 27, 2007)

- We had a lesson in *T-shirt literacy* while observing a student teacher at a middle school. All the teachers were wearing bright new T-shirts emblazoned with the message "ONE SIZE DOES NOT FIT ALL." The screened-on picture showed three sneakers of different colors and different sizes. We thought the teachers were frustrated by the standardized tests they had been giving all spring and were protesting the heavily prescribed lessons that are now the rage. Then we noticed a few students also wearing the shirts and so took a second look at the fine print and read "Unity through Diversity: April 27, 2007." The shirts were a fund-raiser for a unity celebration to be held that evening. The mistake reminded us of our own ASU English Department T-shirts that say in large letters "English," and then underneath in the style of a dictionary definition "(n): Define Yourself." Our intended message relates to the idea that students who major in English will experience personal growth, but when we wear the shirts off campus we get comments and thumbs-up from people who think we are making a statement in favor of the "English Only" laws that frequently make their way to Arizona ballots.

- According to the numbers column in *Time* magazine, the Pew Research Center for the People and the Press found that 21 percent of people ages eighteen to twenty-nine cite *The Daily Show* and *Saturday Night Live* as regular sources of their election news. (April 30, 2007)

"Everyone Will Be World Famous for Fifteen Minutes."

The incidents cited, especially the *Time* magazine feature, are a vivid illustration of Andy Warhol's best-known observation made in 1966 when he looked into the future and declared that "everyone will be world famous for fifteen minutes." Other people had made similar observations, but art critic Harold Rosenberg has said that it is perfectly fitting that Warhol gets the credit because he devoted his life to getting credit.

Googling the phrase "fifteen minutes of fame" turns up three-and-a-half-million citations, with the most popular ones being associated with YouTube, which in March 2006 changed its offer of providing customers with fifteen minutes of fame to ten minutes of fame because they found that when people had fifteen minutes to fill, they were more likely to bring in bits of copyrighted materials from television shows and movies; hence the new time limit.

The same week that *Time* honored "everyone" as Person of the Year, Jake Halpern's book *Fame Junkies: The Hidden Truths Behind America's Favorite Addiction* was released by Houghton Mifflin. The author, who as a kid was hooked on Robin Leach's *Lifestyles of the Rich and Famous*, empathizes with people's desire to become famous, but still he views it as an addiction, which in today's media-saturated world has "metastasized." He cites Roman stories about Zeus and his sexual exploits to point out that people have always enjoyed hearing about bad behavior among the powerful, but while celebrity gossip used to be "contained," today it is everywhere, particularly among young people who have grown up to view the mass media as a kind of fairy godmother who at any moment is likely to tap the next "winner" with her magic wand.

Halpern thinks that young people are mostly responsible for the popularity of the *American Idol* television show, and he thinks it is teenage girls who are mainly responsible for making Paris Hilton's name the one "most Googled" in 2006. When he surveyed 653 middle-school students in the Rochester, New York, area he found that:

- Given a choice of becoming the CEO of a major corporation, the president of Yale or Harvard, a Navy SEAL, a U.S. senator or "the personal assistant to a very famous singer or movie star," almost half of the girls—43.4 percent—chose the assistant role.
- When given an option to become stronger, smarter, famous, or beautiful, boys in the survey chose fame almost as often as intelligence, and girls chose it more often.
- The teens who regularly watch certain celebrity-oriented TV shows were more likely than others to believe that they themselves will be famous someday.

While Halpern is not setting himself up as an ayatollah calling for a *fatwa* on shows such as *Access Hollywood*, he does think there's something to be said for moderation.[1]

Those of us who work with young people can probably tell stories of our own to illustrate the changing times and changing attitudes. During spring break, we were surprised to hear from the neighborhood boy who, when he was in middle school, used to come over and feed the Nilsens' cat when they were out of town. Now a freshman in college and home for a few days, he dropped off a fat envelope with the explanation that he wanted help in getting a book published. He had saved his emails from the last three years, and having heard that J. K. Rowling is now richer than the Queen of England, he decided that he too wanted to become a published author. Some of his emails were interesting, but for being

It's a new trend for parents to help their children become published authors. Here a father and daughter display their jointly produced book at the 2006 NCTE convention in Nashville. Penda Diakité wrote the story I Lost My Tooth in Africa *(Scholastic, 2006) and her father, Baba Wagué Diakité, illustrated it on ceramic tile plaques.*

such a bright young man, he was terribly naïve about what goes into writing a truly "publishable" book.

The incident reminded us of what Joan Bauer told us in an interview. She is always impressed when, after she makes a presentation, earnest young teenagers come up and tell her they have written a book. She congratulates them and tells them that she was in her thirties before she wrote a book. Then she braces herself for their next question: "How do I get it published?"

She struggles with her answer because she does not want to discourage young writers, but at the same time she knows that very few books written by teenagers—with some notable exceptions—really get published. What has surprised her over the last few years is that students come to her not only with their manuscript but with publicity packages they have designed for themselves. One girl even included a letter of endorsement from the mayor of her town.

Bauer wonders whether "our success-oriented culture is causing some young people to miss the joy of learning to love writing by focusing too much on publishing as the ultimate goal."[2] We wonder if perhaps we English teachers are a contributing factor because of our emphasis on praising and "publishing" our students' work.

We also began wondering whether our attempts to make school "fun" have led students to unreasonable expectations. A colleague who prides himself on making attractive and entertaining PowerPoint presentations was shocked when teaching evaluations came out and a boy complained that when the professor doesn't have time to finish a PowerPoint in class he "sends it to us through email and expects us to take our own time to look at it." His attitude was similar to that of a student who responded to our survey question asking whether he had listened to a sound recording of a book—with, "Just in school—never for my own benefit."

Critical Literacy

At least until fairly recently, the most common kind of literacy talked about in educational circles was *critical literacy*, whose advocates believe in questioning the social, political, and economic conditions that underlie the creation of stories, novels, books, films, essays, and other kinds of communication. Some advocates of critical literacy have as their first goal simply training people to look beyond the obvious and to become aware of the conditions under which they live and how these conditions are reflected in daily communications. Other advocates want to inspire people to transform the world in humane ways to make it a more just place to live. None of us could argue with such lofty goals, nor with asking thoughtful questions, but we need to strive for balance lest we raise a generation of students who will be as pessimistic and gloomy as Eeyore, the doleful donkey in *Winnie the Pooh*.

Cynicism can be dangerous to one's health. We overheard part of a discussion on National Public Radio about people who have become so critical of modern medicine and health care that they shell out millions of dollars to pay for alternative medicines that are often little better than snake oil. And in our own field of young adult literature, we have met some English teachers who are so cynical about books that are written and published specifically for teenagers that they choose the easy path of simply ignoring the whole field.

Educators are divided on the matter of critical literacy, with some complaining that it is a "bumper sticker" approach to life because teachers naturally tend to ask questions about issues of particular interest to themselves. It might balance out if students have teachers with different viewpoints, but still, it is sad when the joy of relaxing and losing yourself in a good story is replaced with feelings of angst and suspicion.

If we really believe that readers are going to bring their own experiences to a book, we cannot expect that they will all come away with the exact same "lesson." For the sixth edition of this textbook, Louis Sachar told how, when he won the Newbery Medal for *Holes*, he was besieged with interviewers asking him what he wanted "kids to learn from the book." He was so surprised that it took him a while to come up with an answer, but finally he told the *Houston Chronicle*:

> The best moral kids get from any book is just the capacity to empathize with other people, to care about the characters and their feelings. So you don't have to write a preachy book to do that. You just make it a fun book with characters they care about, and they will become better people as a result.[3]

He went on to say that people do not ask authors of adult novels, what morals or lessons they are trying to teach the reader, "but there is a perception that if you write for young people, then the book should be a lesson of some sort, a learning experience, a step toward something else." He sees this attitude not just with reporters but also with teachers, whose influence pervades some of the letters he receives, such as one in which a boy wrote, "Your book taught me that the acts of your great-great-grandfather can affect your life."

This boy was so involved in looking for a lesson that he missed the joke about the family curse. Sachar said he included the part about the curse to trigger smiles of recognition because most teenagers have at least occasionally thought they were cursed by family connections. The only lesson he was hoping to teach was that reading is fun.

Don Gallo is the editor of a regular column in the *English Journal* entitled "Bold Books for Teenagers." The underlying philosophy of the column is one of critical literacy, and in the September 2004 issue, he interviewed his wife, C. J. Bott, with the focus being on books about homosexuality. He used the subtitle of "The Boldest Books," and in January 2005, the *English Journal* editor printed three well-developed letters, each illustrating a different reaction to the column. One was from a gay man who appreciated the "open and honest article" and was going to distribute copies and buy some of the books for his community's Rainbow Club, "an accepting and nonthreatening place for gay and lesbian teenagers to gather once a week." The second letter was from a teacher who began by citing Sara Lawrence-Lightfoot's *The Essential Conversation: What Parents and Teachers Can Learn from Each Other* (Random House, 2003). She quoted the statement that "Schools have always been the arena where the cultural and historical dramas of our society get played out." She agreed with the idea that educators must help students "frame philosophical stances without animosity," but "the column did not offer validation for opposing groups" and implied that "religious groups are serving as 'a major obstacle' to achieving real equality in American education." She does not want "religious belief categorized as illogical or unenlightened." She concluded with the fact that she teaches to a captive audience and does not have a right to elevate one ideology over another:

> As a teacher, I am the permeable skin between politics and the classroom—a place where all students, including those of religious identity, are welcome. I cannot draw lines. The students make those decisions for themselves. My intent is to arm with objectivity so that when a proverbial bullet does fly, it hits an idea, not a person.

The third letter was from a man who appreciated the article because "There can be no denying that the avoidance in our schoolrooms of literature that focuses on lesbian and gay lives amounts to silent censorship." But Gallo's postscript, in which he said that the woman he was interviewing was his wife, made the man "grit his teeth."

> I'm sure that Gallo was sincere when he stated that "full disclosure" was the motive for inserting this fact, but I don't believe that's the only reason heterosexuals find it necessary to underline their heterosexuality when they find themselves defending (or even acknowledging the existence of) gay and lesbian people. How much more courageous it would have been to let some readers infer, even erroneously,

that C. J. Bott had been an organizer of the Gay/Straight Alliance in her former school because she was a lesbian. . . . True solidarity with gay and lesbian colleagues and students means being willing to experience some of the onus that falls on us when we are visible.[4]

We quoted these letters to illustrate that when real issues are being talked about, it is not easy to get agreement. In the typical high school class, teachers are keeping so many balls in the air that it is hard to predict what might happen in a conversation where, in an attempt to "get closure," teachers might lead students to oversimplify complex issues. When Robert Cormier was criticized for not providing a happy ending to *The Chocolate War*, he argued that he was simply providing a balance. He wanted his young readers who had been raised on television programs where every problem was solved within an hour—including time out for commercials—to recognize that the world is filled with problems that even with the best people putting forth their best efforts cannot be solved so quickly or easily.

In Christopher Paolini's 2003 *Eragon*, it is left to Saphira, the dragon, to try to explain this to Eragon. He and his traveling companion, Murtagh, are attacked by a group of slavers when they are on their way to take Arya, the drugged elf, back to her own people for healing. Eragon and Murtagh defend themselves with magic as well as with their highly cultivated warrior skills. As the finishing touch Eragon calls Saphira from the sky and the men race frantically away. Their leader, Torkenbrand, is accidentally knocked down by one of his own men's javelins and Murtagh rushes over and beheads the man.

Eragon is horrified and accuses Murtagh of being a murderer, of killing a defenseless man who could have just been left behind. Murtagh argues that he was only trying to stay alive; "No stranger's life is more important than my own." The next day Eragon flies on Saphira's back instead of riding with Murtagh because he wants to be away from his former friend. As they communicate back and forth in their thoughts (which Paolini puts in italics), Eragon argues,

> *That was murder yesterday. I've no other word for it.*
> Saphira banked to the left. *It was a hasty deed and ill-considered, but Murtagh tried to do the right thing. The men who buy and sell other humans deserve every misfortune that befalls them. If we weren't committed to helping Arya, I would hunt down every slaver and tear them apart.*
> Yes, said Eragon miserably, *but Torkenbrand was helpless. He couldn't shield himself or run. A moment more and he probably would have surrendered. Murtagh didn't give him that chance. If Tornkenbrand had at least been able to fight, it wouldn't have been so bad.*

Saphira "tells" Eragon that the results would have been the same because he and Murtagh are skilled swordsman, plus there were two of them. How would a mismatched duel have been more fair?

> *I don't know what's right!* admitted Eragon, distressed. *There aren't any answers that make sense.*
> *Sometimes,* said Saphira gently, *there are no answers.*

Visual Literacy for the Eye Generation

When *Washington Post* reporter Linton Weeks went out to do a story about young adults in a three-week summer movie production workshop, he described the participants not so much as members of the *Me Generation* as members of the *Eye Generation.*[5] His clever pun may catch on because it truly describes a generation who has grown up surrounded by the kinds of eye candy that makes not only television and movies fun to watch, but also influences consumers in making decisions of what to buy and where to go. For example, owners of athletic stadiums are now expected to put up giant screens to provide close-up views so that spectators who have chosen to come to the stadium can have the same advantages of the close-ups that people get when they stay home and watch on television. Manufactures are eager to beat the competition by putting more and more technology into smaller and smaller items even though few buyers are computer literate enough to take full advantage of their digital cameras, global positioning systems, and even their cell phones.

Back in 1970, when the National Council of Teachers of English passed a Resolution on Media Literacy and endorsed a "Summary Statement on Multimodal Literacies," few members realized the responsibility they would soon have in teaching their students to think critically about still images, photos, movies, animations, drama, art, alphabetic and nonalphabetic text, music, speech, sound, physical movement, gaming, and whatever else might come down the road or over the airwaves. We will write about film, television, and the Internet in Chapter 11 on the teaching of English, and about comic books, graphic novels, anime, and video games as interactive literature in Chapter 5, which used to be restricted to poetry, humor, and drama.

Religious and Ethnic Literacy

We are writing about religious and ethnic literacies not because they are the same thing, but because as some of the stories we collected in our Media Watch show, they are often related. For example, an Associated Press story under the headline "Hawaii Park Rangers Urge Folks Not to Trash Volcano," told about an ongoing conflict at the summit of Mount Kilauea, an active volcano in the Hawaii Volcanoes National Park. A Native Hawaiian belief is that lava is the physical representation of the goddess Pele, and so it is the custom to bring food and other offerings to be left at the summit. Rangers are trying to balance the kind of religious literacy that inspires people to leave ornately packaged and flower-bedecked food offerings against a new kind of literacy about caring for the earth and protecting its resources. The park superintendent explains that "the accumulation of rotting food and foliage attracts rats, flies, ants and cockroaches," and that officials are looking to the leaders of local communities to assist in communicating the message while still being sensitive to local customs (April 22, 2007).

In January of 2007, a long-festering debate at the University of Illinois about the school's use of Chief Illiniwek as an "honored symbol," moved a step closer to a resolution when the Oglala Sioux Tribe presented a demand for the return of the Lakota regalia worn by the school's mascot. According to a story written by Michelle Keller for the *Chicago Tribune*, the immediate impetus for the demand was racially insensitive comments posted on a social networking site, but for more than a decade, various groups had been pointing out that the Chief Illiniwek tradition begun in 1926 by the university marching band was insulting to peoples of the Kaskaskia, Peoria, Piankeshuw, and Wea nations because the gymnastic performance of whoever was "playing" the role of Chief Illiniwek perpetuated degrading racial stereotypes. The dances and other actions were a mishmash of nonauthentic customs and although the ceremonial dress was authentic to one of the tribes, its original purpose was religious and tied to serious ceremony rather than "play."

A February 16, 2007, University News release posted at www.uillinois.edu/chief was headlined "Chief Illiniwek Will No Longer Perform: NCAA to Lift Sanctions on Illini Athletics." The last appearance would be at the season-ending men's home basketball game on February 21, at which time the NCAA (National Collegiate Athletic Association) would lift the sanctions it had leveled against the university in August of 2005 when it ruled that teams using Native American logos would not be allowed to host tournament events.

A story more specifically related to religion ran under the heading, "The Bible Makes a Comeback" in *Education Week*.[6] It featured Harriet Kisilinsky, a veteran English teacher on Florida's northeast coast, who had successfully lobbied for a course to be added to the humanities curriculum for the 125,000-student Duval County public school district. She wanted the course because when the district began pushing to get more students into Advanced Placement classes, she noticed that many of them were unprepared to understand biblical allusions. "How can you expect them to read Dante's *Inferno*," she asked, "and write about it if they don't understand his nine circles of hell?" In another example, she told about teaching Andrew Marvell's "To His Coy Mistress," and when they came to the line, "I would love you ten years before the Flood," a boy asked, "What flood?"

Kisilinsky says she does not aspire to give students the same knowledge of the Bible that ministers have, "But they have to know the basics." Melissa Rogers, who teaches in the Divinity School at Wake Forest University cautioned that we are not likely to get agreement on how classes in the Bible as Literature should be taught because on one side are people who fear that such classes will be "equivalent to Sunday school," while on the other side are devout believers who "think it's really not sound to teach the 'holy book' in a neutral way." Other concerns are *whose* Bible will be taught. Students need to know that there are different versions and they also need to know something about religions of the world that go beyond the Judeo-Christian beliefs. Stephen Prothero from Boston University knows that problems will occur resulting in court cases, but thinks that eventually teachers and students will be able to "get it right." In an opinion piece quoted from the *Los Angeles Times*, Prothero had explained that biblical illiteracy is not just a religious problem; it is a civic problem. "How can citizens participate in biblically inflected debates on abortion, capital punishment, or the environment without knowing something about the Bible?"

Time magazine devoted seven pages to a cover story, "The Case for Teaching the Bible," in its April 2, 2007, issue. Writer David Van Biema started with a description of a "Bible-literacy class" being taught at New Braunfels High School in Texas, where the curriculum was designed to teach the Bible "as an object of study, not God's received word." It is now used in over 450 districts in at least thirty-seven states. Van Biema pointed out that "Not only is the Bible the best-selling book of all time, it is the best-selling book of the year every year." Shakespeare is said to have alluded to scripture some 1,300 times. A sidebar story, "The Bible in Pop Culture," showed how "Even our superficial pleasures are enhanced by a background in the Good Book." Cited films include *Babel*, *Superman*, *The Matrix*, and *Pulp Fiction*. Books made into films included C. S. Lewis's *The Chronicles of Narnia*, and Dan Brown's *The Da Vinci Code*. The televised teen drama *One Tree Hill* was described as echoing the birthright struggle of Cain and Abel, while the hit Broadway musical *Spamalot* is based on the 1975 film *Monty Python and the Holy Grail*. Van Biema's most persuasive example centered around seventh graders reading Hemingway's *Old Man and the Sea*. He observed that most teachers would be able to "tick off the references to Christ's Passion," which include the way the old man's palms bleed, the way he stumbles while carrying the boat's mast over his shoulder, and the way his hat cuts into his head, but then Van Biema asks, "wouldn't the thrill of recognition have been more satisfying" if students knew enough to ask for it on their own?

Global Literacy

Thomas L. Friedman's *The World Is Flat: A Brief History of the Twenty-First Century*, is a book that *School Library Journal* recommended to teens as well as adults. Friedman is not using "flat" in a negative sense as we might talk about a "flat drink" or a "flat tire." He is talking about the lowering of borders and dividers between countries, and how it is now possible to "innovate without having to emigrate." He makes a persuasive argument that today more people than ever before from all parts of the world can collaborate and compete in real time on a huge variety of tasks. He focuses on three contributing factors: the collapse of Communism, the worldwide Y2K gearing up for adjusting the world's computers to the new century, and the dot-com bubble, which resulted in heavy investments in fiber-optic telecommunications. When the bubble burst, the fiber optics were still in place and available below cost, which is what enabled Delta airlines, for example, to hire reservation clerks who are living in India and Jet Blue airlines to hire retirees and housewives to take its reservations from their homes in Utah.

The Friedman anecdote that is most likely to interest teenagers is the one about an owner of several McDonald's restaurants in Colorado who decided to consolidate the way his customers order their hamburgers at the drive-through window. In fast-food restaurants, nothing slows things down more than for a

Young Adult Authors Speak Out

Cynthia Leitich Smith on

Hosting 1.6 Million Visitors in Cyberspace

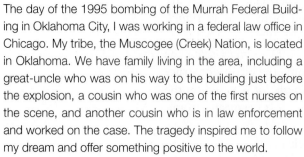

The day of the 1995 bombing of the Murrah Federal Building in Oklahoma City, I was working in a federal law office in Chicago. My tribe, the Muscogee (Creek) Nation, is located in Oklahoma. We have family living in the area, including a great-uncle who was on his way to the building just before the explosion, a cousin who was one of the first nurses on the scene, and another cousin who is in law enforcement and worked on the case. The tragedy inspired me to follow my dream and offer something positive to the world.

I took a long walk along Lake Michigan and came home to my husband, Greg. At the time, we still owed tens of thousands of dollars from student loans that had helped us to earn our law degrees. With little prior discussion, I announced, "I want to quit my day job and write full-time for kids." He paused before asking, "Are you any good at it?" I shrugged. He said, "Let's find out."

We did. The manuscript for my first children's book, *Jingle Dancer*, sold in 1998. Four years later, Greg joined me in the author ranks with the sale of *Ninjas, Piranhas, and Galileo* for preteens. Along the way, we decided the Internet would be a perfect way to raise awareness of quality books. At a time when library budgets were being cut, independent bookstores were closing, and celebrities were crowding literary voices off shelves, it wasn't enough to light a candle. We wanted to light a torch.

I have a background in journalism, while Greg has a technology background, and so we joined forces to create what might be the largest youth books website on the Internet: *Cynthia Leitich Smith's Children & YA Literature Resources* at www.cynthialeitichsmith.com. The site launched in 1998. Early on, I did the design work myself. I started small, with two author interviews and a few new

customer to get to the window and have the wrong order so that the whole line of cars has to wait while the new order is prepared. This owner managed to cut his restaurants' average wait time significantly by having all orders taken by someone in a sound-proof room trained to "get it right" and to send the correct order via computer to the kitchens in the originating restaurant. Although he set up his order system in his home state of Colorado, he could have as easily set it up in a different country or a different part of the United States.

We thought about Friedman's observations when we recently visited with Shannon Hale, author of the Newbery Honor Book *Princess Academy*. She is a young mother living in Utah, who flew into Phoenix to make a presentation and do a book signing at Changing Hands Bookstore. She was coming to promote her new book *Austenland: A Novel*, which is officially an adult book but which we are sure teen lovers of Jane Austen will be reading. Hale had brought her four-month-old baby with her and right after eating with us, then being interviewed by a newspaper reporter, making her presentation, and autographing books, she

links each month. I added book recommendations as I read or rediscovered each title. Greg contributed his share, too, especially those reflecting Asian American characters.

The site features a section about me and my work, which may be characterized as Native fiction, comedic picture books, and young adult Gothic fantasy. The largest section, though, is on the body of literary children's and young adult trade books as a whole. Articles, bibliographies, and links abound. But it's best known for interviews with authors, illustrators, editors, and other industry professionals. Multicultural, nonfiction, and genre titles are featured along with mainstream fiction. New and quality mid-list voices are highlighted alongside national award winners and *New York Times* best sellers. Put another way, the site contains some 1,000 files, 275 pages, 700 images, and more than 12,000 links to related Web pages. Those links include hundreds to my blog, Cynsations (cynthia leitichsmith.blogspot.com). The main site is easy to navigate with a guide bar and a search engine. In 2006, 1.6 million unique visitors surfed by.

Our family is European-Asian-Native American. Greg is the son of an immigrant. I'm descended from Native peoples who originally settled what's now the southeastern United States. Our family backgrounds offer us a certain insight into the need for multicultural literature—historical and contemporary—done well.

With regard to my Native fiction, I was one of the first writers to craft modern-day stories about young Indian characters. My books were cheered for bursting inaccurate and dated stereotypes. My debut tween novel, *Rain Is Not My Indian Name*, was one of the first to feature the Internet in an integrated way. An extension on my site was a natural tie in.

More globally, the site is important to us in that it offers a way to hear from and about young readers. I've gotten letters from kids who've lost a friend like Rain, and from black Indians who appreciate that my works reflect diversity within Native America. And since the publication of *Tantalize*, I am hearing from Gothic fantasy fanatics who want their sequel—now!

The Web is all about information and connections. With Greg's support, the site personalizes it to our work and that of our beloved colleagues. We hope you'll surf by!

- Cynthia Leitich Smith's books for young adults include *Tantalize* (Candlewick, 2007) and *Rain Is Not My Indian Name* (HarperCollins, 2001), while Greg is the author of *Ninjas, Piranhas, and Galileo* (Little, Brown, 2003) and *Tofu and T. rex* (Little, Brown, 2005), both for preteens.

was flying back to Salt Lake to spend the night at home with the rest of her family. When someone asked if it was hard being both famous and a mother, she gave a disclaimer to the fame part, but then laughingly confessed that one of her relatives had figured out that she was known by more people than was the Pope in the 1300s.

The Internet, especially author websites and blogs, makes a huge difference in connecting writers and readers. For an illustration, see Cynthia Leitich Smith's statement. We first got acquainted with her website when we read in *School Library Journal* that if someone wanted to keep up with only one website in YA or children's literature, Cynthia's was the one. As soon as we found it and spent a few minutes investigating we could understand the reason for the recommendation and also why the site is listed among the American Library Association's "Great Web Sites for Kids" and why *Writer's Digest* chose it as one of the top-ten author sites on the Internet. When we asked Cynthia to describe her site, the first thing she said was that from the beginning, she has received considerable

The Crow-Girl: The Children of Crow Cove by Bodil Breds-dorff, translated from Danish by Faith Ingwersen. Farrar, 2004. Young teens will be the ones to appreciate this historical tale set in a remote coastal area of Denmark. A young girl lives with her grandmother, who does everything she can to prepare the girl to survive when she dies, and with the help of the crows the girl manages.

Emil and Karl by Yankev Glatshteyn, translated from Yiddish by Jeffrey Shandler. Roaring Brook/A Neal Porter Book, 2006. Middle school students studying the Holocaust will be the ones to appreciate this novel written about two boys growing up in prewar Vienna. Glatshteyn wrote it after returning to America from a 1934 visit to Poland where he saw how Nazi persecution was changing all of Europe.

Inkheart by Cornelia Funke, translated from German by Anthea Bell. Scholastic, 2003. Twelve-year-old Meggie has a loving father, whom she calls Mo. He is a book mender, but unknown to her he has the accidental, and sometimes dangerous, talent of making characters come right out of a book into real life. Middle school readers especially like this charming fantasy, which is continued in *Inkspell*.

Over a Thousand Hills I Walk with You by Hanna Jansen, translated from German by Elizabeth D. Crawford. Carolrhoda Books, 2006. For mature students, this painful book was written by the author as she tried over and over to help her adopted daughter, Jeanne d'Arc Umubyeyi, recover from the sadness and the anger she feels toward the Hutu neighbors in Rwanda who participated in the 1994 genocide killing of Jeanne's family and destroying her home and life as she knew it.

The Pull of the Ocean by Jean-Claude Mourlevat, translated from French by Y. Maudet. Delacorte, 2006. Middle school readers who like mysteries and stories set in the past are likely to be charmed by this mysterious story of three sets of twins and their dwarf-sized little brother. When they learn that their father intends to kill them, they set off to sea.

Secrets in the Fire by Henning Mankell, translated from Swedish by Anne Connie Stuksrud. Annick, distributed by Firefly, 2003. This fictional account is based on the true story of Sofia Alface, a friend of the author who survived the civil war in Mozambique (1975–1992), only to lose both of her legs when she stepped on a landmine.

The Water Mirror by Kai Meyer, translated from German by Elizabeth D. Crawford. S&S/Margaret K. McElderry Books, 2005. Part of the Reflections series, this fantasy is set in medieval Venice. Protagonists are two orphans apprenticed to a maker of mirrors. One of them is blind. The adventure starts when the Egyptian Army invades and the survival of Venice is in doubt.

---

help from her husband, Greg, who, besides keeping his day job as a lawyer, also writes books for kids. But even with Greg's help, we wondered how Cynthia could possibly squeeze out the two or three hours a day she devotes to the site, and she smilingly said, "Some people garden. I link!" Then she went on to say that the work is possible because their "commitment is to the body of literature as a whole, not just our own—though we couldn't be more passionate about it."

Another difference today is the speed with which popular new books are being translated and sold in other countries. Within less than two years, Stephenie Meyer's 2005 *Twilight*, the first of three books about star-crossed lovers, had already been translated into over thirty languages. Readers can go online to amazon.com and buy Spanish, Dutch, and German versions as easily as the English one. Stephenie lives in metropolitan Phoenix and here at ASU we agreed to help host a spring "Prom" on May 10, 2007. The main event at the prom was Stephenie reading a chapter from the third book, *Eclipse*, which was not going to be released for three more months; however, attendees could buy an edition of the second book (*New Moon*) that would include the forthcoming chapter. The $8.00 tickets, which Meyer offered on her website, sold out so fast that the organizers quickly set up both a matinee and an evening event. Girls, mostly accompanied by a parent (a small number came with boyfriends), flew in from all over the country, with one girl coming from London. Just prior to the big event on our campus, Stephenie and her husband had been on a book signing trip to Rome. They had also been invited to go to South America, but had turned down the invitation, at least for the time being, because such a trip would keep them away from their three young sons as well as from the rigorous writing schedule that Stephenie is committed to.

Other evidence of a flat world in relation to young adult books is how many more YA books are being translated into English from other languages. See Focus Box 3.3 for recent translations that were given starred reviews in *School Library Journal*. And besides the translated books, more books from other English-speaking countries are being successfully marketed in the United States, as with Marcus Zusak's *The Book Thief* and Sonya Hartnett's *Surrender*, both of which were originally published in Australia, but made their way to our 2006 Honor List.

In three different sections of the survey we conducted in local high schools, students expressed positive feelings toward entertainment coming from Japan. When we asked about comic books, for example, one thirteen-year-old boy wrote that he liked reading the Japanese ones because they go backward and "they are good artists." When we asked about favorite magazines, a student listed three (to us, unrecognizable) names and explained, "they are all Japanese music magazines." Another listed *Shonen Jump*, praising it for including various manga, while another listed *Cure* (a Japanese fashion magazine). And then of course, in the section asking about computer games, many of the students' favorites were Japanese imports.

Some of the credit for American teenagers developing more of a worldview must also go to the Harry Potter books, which are now a worldwide phenomenon. When we attended the 2007 International Society for Humor Studies meeting, we talked with a woman from Spain whose research project was comparing the humor in the German, Spanish, and Portuguese translations with the original English version. Because we have studied J. K. Rowling's clever invention of names, we asked her about how the names were translated. For the most part, she said the names had stayed the same, so that readers would miss some of the jokes, but many of them were still understandable because the names were based on Latin roots, which have carried over into many other languages, especially the Romance languages of Spanish and Portuguese.

We wrote a letter to Scholastic, the American publishers of Harry Potter, to ask about the level of changes being made to accommodate American readers. We knew that several changes had been made in the first book, with fewer in the second one, which Scholastic decided to publish sooner than they planned because people were going online and buying the British version rather than waiting for the American one. Editor Arthur A. Levine responded that very few changes were being made between the British and the American versions, not because of Scholastic's fear of losing sales, but because by now American readers are so well acquainted with the setting and the vocabulary that they feel comfortable with "Britishisms."

More evidence of Americans developing more of a worldview is the publication of *The Real Revolution: The Global Story of American Independence*, by Marc Aronson. Aronson is one of our most thoughtful YA writers and editors and here he takes a second look at the American Revolution as he develops the point that America has always been part of a wider world and that the real revolution occurred not in the 1776 war but in the minds and hearts of the people who came from, and were influenced by people from, many different countries between 1760 and 1775.

At a 2006 meeting of the Children's Literature Association, we heard Cornelia Funke's name included in a list of celebrities who had suddenly begun to publish children's books just because they had name recognition. Actually, Cornelia Funke did not belong in that list because she had written some forty books in German before *The Thief Lord* was translated into English and into nearly thirty other languages. She compared seeing her books in other languages (she reads Italian, German, and English) to seeing them in a new dress. For the last edition of this textbook she wrote:

> So, with the help of many translators and publishers my stories have started traveling to places I've never been. They find their way to people I've never met who choose to spend some of their time walking in my imagination. In a world where borders still cut the world into artificial pieces, where differences are thought to be more important than the things that people share, it is wonderful that writers and readers can travel together for a while in their imaginations. It still feels like a miracle.[7]

We were surprised to read on the back of Listening Library's boxed set of CDs for *Inkspell* that "Funke lives in California, with her husband and children." When we received this statement from Funke for the 2005 edition of the text, we communicated through international mail, and she was still excited about her first trip to the United States in 2002.

Joan Bauer, whose *Thwonk*, *Squashed*, and *Hope Was Here* have been translated into several languages, compares seeing the translated editions of her books to seeing a friend who has gone off for plastic surgery and come home with a new face. Even though it takes her a while to get used to the new look, she loves seeing them and knowing that people are reading them in places very different from where she was when she wrote them. She took the Korean version of *Squashed* to a friend who read Korean, but the only thing he could figure out was that on the cover it promised a "better story than Jack and the Beanstalk." One of Bauer's most memorable experiences was a week that she spent at the American School in Shanghai where the students had read her books as part of their English studies. She was surprised when she arrived to see that the students were not Chinese, but were the children of diplomats and business people from all parts of the world. The one thing they had in common was that they had all been plucked from their homes and brought by their parents to Shanghai.

While not telling them about the American slang term *to be shanghaied*, she changed her speaking plans and worked mostly with *Hope Was Here*, the story of a girl plucked from Brooklyn and taken to a small town in Wisconsin. Many of the students had read the book, but had not connected it to their own lives. Bauer began by leading the students to talk about their own experiences of moving and adjusting to a new home and then they began talking about what similar feelings they had all experienced. As the week went on, they began writing a group story. Fortunately, Bauer's husband, a computer programmer, had come with her, and while the students were composing he would type their words into his computer and then project them onto the ceiling. She has since led similar activities in Croatia and in Kazakhstan on visits sponsored by the United States Department of State, which sometimes sends American authors on cultural exchange visits.

We wrote to several publishers asking them if they now sponsor their writers on overseas visits or if they paid to have "foreign" writers come to the United States. They mostly said they were not the ones sponsoring such visits, but that they were always happy when visits were arranged and they would be supportive in furnishing publicity handouts, and so forth. On rare occasions, for example, if an author were invited to appear on the *Today* show or to accept an award and speak at a big convention, they might help with expenses, but usually the bookstores or the host school or conference handles the finances.

We chatted with Linda Sue Park (author of *A Single Shard*) when she came to Phoenix to participate in our state library convention. She told us about feeling fortunate to be invited to a large conference in Hong Kong connected with the Man Booker Awards. She was invited as the Asian American children's writer, while Amy Tan was the Asian American general writer. Another international tidbit that we happened to hear about is that the Fitchburg State College in Massachusetts, whose library houses the Robert E. Cormier collection, holds an annual memorial service in which attendees stand and read a favorite portion of one of his books. A highlight of the program is when foreign students read some of Cormier's writing in their native languages.

A flat earth does not mean that the world is free from dangers and fears, but there is something comforting in knowing that young people around the world are reading many of the same books and being exposed to many of the same ideas and values. Even dictators are known to warm up to children's stories. As one author confided when he was invited for a two-week visit to a totalitarian country, the people who invited him tactfully explained that in order to get his visa approved, he should identify himself not as an "author," but as a "children's storyteller."

Deciding on the Literary Canon

The factors already mentioned in this chapter are contributing to an ongoing debate over what books should be taught. An oversimplification is to say that on one side are those who believe in acculturation or assimilation. They think that if we all read approximately the same books, we will come away with similar values and attitudes. On the other side are those who believe in diversity and want individuals and groups to find their own values, attitudes, and ways of life reflected in the literature they read. This latter group views the traditional literary canon as racist and sexist, with its promotion in schools serving to keep minorities and women in their place.

Katha Pollitt, a contributing editor of *The Nation*, wrote that "In a country of real readers a debate like the current one over the canon would not be taking place." She described an imaginary country where children grow up watching their parents read and going with them to well-supported public libraries where they borrow books and read and read and read. At the heart of every school is an attractive and well-used library, and in classrooms children have lively discussions about books they have read together, but they also read lots of books on their own, so that years later they don't remember whether "they read *Jane Eyre* at home and Judy Blume in class, or the other way around."

Pollitt wrote that in her imaginary country of "real readers—voluntary, active, self-determined readers"—a discussion of which books should be studied in school would be nothing more than a parlor game. It might even add to the aura of writers not to be included on school-assigned reading lists because this would mean that their books were "in one way or another too heady, too daring, too exciting to be ground up into institutional fodder for teenagers." The alternative would be millions of readers freely choosing millions of books, each book becoming just a tiny part of a lifetime of reading. Pollitt concluded that at the root of the current debate over the canon is the assumption that the only books that will be read are those assigned in school: "Becoming a textbook is a book's only chance: all sides take that for granted." She wonders why those educated scholars and critics who are currently debating this issue and must be readers themselves have conspired to keep secret two facts that they surely must know:

> . . . if you read only twenty-five, or fifty, or a hundred books, you can't understand them, however well chosen they are. And . . . if you don't have an independent reading life—and very few students do—you won't like reading the books on the list and will forget them the minute you finish them.[8]

Pollitt's argument puts even more of a burden on those of us who have as our professional responsibility the development of lifelong readers. We are the ones who should be raising our voices to explain the limitations of expecting children to read just what is assigned in class. We are also the ones with the responsibility of helping students develop into the kinds of committed and enthusiastic readers that Pollitt described in her imaginary country.

In the meantime, we also have an obligation to become knowledgeable about the issues underlying the current debate over the literary canon and to assist schools and libraries in making informed choices with the resources they have. We, as authors of this textbook, have already committed ourselves to the idea of an expanded canon. Some of the harshest critics of adolescent literature are those in favor of promoting only the traditional canon; others tolerate adolescent literature only because they view it as a means to the desired end of leading students to appreciate "real" literature.

At the 1991 National Council of Teachers of English convention in Seattle, Washington, Rudolfo Anaya, author of *Bless Me, Ultima* and a professor of creative writing at the University of New Mexico, talked about the incorporation of minority literature into the mainstream. He did not mean just the inclusion on book lists of the names of authors who are members of minority groups but also the incorporation of new styles and ideas into the writing of nonminority authors.

One example is the incorporation into mainstream literature of the kinds of magical realism that for a long time has been common in Hispanic literature. Another way is through the desegregation of characters as seen in several of the books listed in Focus Box 4.5, Relating across Cultures (p. 129).

Anaya went on to explain that Mexican Americans have a different worldview. When he was in college, he loved literature and read the standard literary canon with enthusiasm and respect, but when he went to write his own stories, he couldn't use Hemingway or Milton as models. He could create plots like theirs, but then he was at a standstill because nowhere in the literary canon did he find people like the ones he knew. His Spanish-speaking family has lived in eastern New Mexico for more than one hundred years. The harsh but strangely beautiful landscape and the spirit of the Pecos River had permeated his life, as had stories of La Grande, the wise old woman who had safely pulled him from his mother's body even though the umbilical cord was wrapped around his neck.

Anaya worked on *Bless Me, Ultima* for seven years, during which he felt he was "writing in a vacuum. I had no Chicano models to read and follow, no fellow writers to turn to for help. Even Faulkner, with his penchant for the fantastic world of the South, could not help me in Mexican/Indian New Mexico. I would have to build from what I knew best." He went on to explain:

> I began to discover that the lyric talent I possessed, as the poet I once aspired to be, could be used in writing fiction. The oral tradition which so enriched my imagination as a child could lend its rhythm to my narrative. Plot techniques learned in Saturday afternoon movies and comic books could help as much as the grand design of the classics I had read. Everything was valuable, nothing was lost.[9]

Anaya's observations about not having models to follow and being forced to create a new narrative style to tell a story coming from his own experience relates to the frustration that teachers and librarians often express when they go to look for young adult novels about minority characters. They look for the same kinds of coming-of-age stories that are typical in mainstream young adult literature except they want the characters to have brown skin and "different" names. The absence of such books, especially such books written by Native American authors, is in itself part of the cultural difference. We've noticed that the more closely a book with a Native American protagonist resembles what we described in Chapter 1 as a typical young adult book, the greater the chance that the author is not a Native American and that the protagonist is of mixed parentage or is living apart from the native culture.

Being in the blood line of a particular group does not guarantee acceptance by the group. Most high school teachers think they are contributing to an awareness of cultural diversity and the enlargement of the literary canon by leading students to read Maxine Hong Kingston's *Woman Warrior*. But noted Chinese writer Frank Chin criticizes Kingston, along with Amy Tan for *The Joy Luck Club* and David Henry Hwang for his plays, *F. O. B.* and *M. Butterfly*. He accuses these writers of "boldly faking" Chinese fairy tales and childhood literature. Then he goes on to ask and answer the question of why the most popular "Chinese" works in the United States are consistent with each other but inconsistent with Chinese culture and beliefs: "That's easy: (1) All the authors are Christian; (2) the only form of literature written by Chinese Americans that major publishers will publish (other than the cookbook) is autobiography, an exclusively Christian form [based on confession]; and (3) they all write to the specifications of the Christian stereotype of Asia being as opposite morally from the West as it is geographically."[10]

Chin's comments are in an essay, "Come All Ye Asian American Writers," that is used as an introduction to an anthology entitled *The Big Aiiieeeee!*, apparently put together for use in college classes. The 619-page book is too intimidating for most high school students, but they could appreciate many of the individual stories, poems, and essays. The book's title comes from the sound in movies, television, radio, and comic books assigned to "the yellow man" who "when wounded, sad, or angry, or swearing, or wondering" either "whined, shouted, or screamed, 'Aiiieeeee!'"

Chin's introductory essay illustrates the complexities involved in the whole matter of ethnic differences. As Chin goes on to state his case, he brings in religion and gender differences as well as differences caused by race, history, social class, and politics. In answer to the kind of criticism he offers, Kingston has explained:

> Sinologists have criticized me for not knowing myths and for distorting them; pirates [those who illegally translate her books for publication in Taiwan and China] correct my myths, revising them to make them conform to some traditional Chinese version. They don't understand that myths have to change, be useful or be forgotten. Like the people who carry them across oceans, the myths become American. The myths I write are new, American. That's why they often appear as cartoons and Kung Fu movies. I take the power I need from whatever myth. Thus Fa Mu Lan has the words cut into her back; in traditional story, it is the man, Ngak Fei the Patriot, whose parents cut vows on his back. I mean to take his power for women.[11]

Knowledge of these opposing viewpoints should not frighten teachers back into the comforts of the established canon; instead, it should help teachers prepare for meeting the challenges involved in going beyond the "tried and true."

Teaching Ethnic Literature

Most educators feel a duty to bring ethnic-based literature to young people in hopes of increasing general understanding. Besides that lofty goal, here are some additional reasons for making special efforts to bring ethnic books to young people:

- Young readers can identify with characters who straddle two worlds because they have similar experiences in going between the worlds of adulthood and childhood.
- Motifs that commonly appear in ethnic-based stories—including loneliness, fear of rejection, generational differences, and troubles in fitting into the larger society—are meaningful to teenagers.
- Nearly all teenagers feel that their families are somehow different, and so they can identify with the theme of family "differentness" that often finds its way into stories about immigrant families.
- Living in harmony with nature is a common theme, especially in Native American literature, and this theme appeals to today's ecology-minded youth.
- As movies, television programs, mass media books, and magazines inundate teens with stories and photos of people who are "all alike," readers find it refreshing to read about people who have their own individuality.
- Myths and legends that are often brought into ethnic-based literature satisfy some deep-down psychological and aesthetic needs that are not met with contemporary realism or with the romanticism masked as realism that currently makes up the main body of fiction provided for young adults.

One of the most important concepts that needs to be taught is that there are large differences among people typically identified as a group. When Europeans first came to the American continent, there were more than thirty distinct nations speaking perhaps a thousand different languages. During the past five hundred years, these people have had such common experiences as losing their lands, being forced to move to reservations, and having to adapt their beliefs and lifestyles to a technological society. These experiences may have affected their attitudes in similar ways, but still it is a gross overgeneralization to write about Native Americans as if they were one people holding the same religious and cultural views. Although in a single class it would be impossible to study dozens of different Native American tribes, a compromise solution might be to study the history and folklore of those tribes who lived, or are living, in the same geographical area as the students. With this approach, it is important for students to realize that they are looking at only one small part of a bigger group, and that if they studied a different group they would learn equally interesting but different facts.

Similar points could be made about the thoughtlessness of talking about Africa as if it were one country and as if one set of folktales could represent a continent that contains nearly twelve million square miles and over forty independent countries. Asian Americans also resent being lumped together. The Chinese and Japanese, the two groups who have been in the United States the longest, come from countries with a long history of hostility toward each other. A refugee from Vietnam or Cambodia has very little in common with someone whose ancestors came to California in the 1850s. Likewise, Puerto Ricans in New York have a different background from Mexican Americans. Even in the Southwest, people whose families have lived there from the days before Anglo settlers arrived resent being grouped with people who just came over the border from Mexico.

We need to teach about the histories of groups whose literature is being read to help readers understand the bitterness that finds its way into some ethnic literature. Readers who get impatient with Hispanic authors for including words and phrases in Spanish will probably be a little more tolerant if they realize that today's generation of Mexican American authors went to school in the days before bilingual education. In their childhoods, many of them heard nothing but Spanish and were amazed to arrive at English-speaking schools where they would be punished for speaking the only language they had ever known.

While Rudolfo Anaya broke new literary ground with his *Bless Me, Ultima*, many other minority writers are breaking new ground by changing the format of stories and translating them from an oral tradition into a written form. Before printing presses, typewriters, word processors, movies, radio, and television, people had more of an incentive to remember and tell the stories that communicated the traditions and values of a society. Even today, oral traditions play an important role, as seen on television talk shows as well as with kids telling stories and workers and travelers whiling away long, boring hours. Because minority writers are translating oral stories into written and printed formats, some of the first publications to come from particular groups are more likely to be poetry and short stories than novels.

There are many beautifully designed collections presenting art, poetry, photographs, essays, observations, interviews, and short stories. Besides the obvious advantage that anthologies present a variety of pieces short enough for classroom and library use, the differences in the statements demonstrate that members of groups are first and foremost individuals. They have their own thoughts, feelings, and values, just as do the members of one's own family, one's own church, and one's own neighborhood. A helpful new book is *Integrating Multicultural Literature in Libraries and Classrooms in Secondary Schools* by Kaa Vonia Hinton and Gail K. Dickinson. The authors include specific examples of fiction, nonfiction, poetry, screenplays, and picture books with suggestions of how to use them alongside the more standard offerings found in most textbooks.

This is probably a lesson that works better through demonstration than through lecturing. Jim Burke, in *The English Teacher's Companion*, gives two examples of ways that teachers might introduce Sandra Cisneros's *The House on Mango Street*.

Scenario One

Okay guys, today we're going to be getting a new book called *The House on Mango Street* by a Latina author. I thought it was really important that we read an author from a different culture since so many students here are Latino.

Scenario Two

[*after reading a brief section from Cisneros's book*] So, we've been talking about this whole idea of growing up, about creating an identity for oneself, what it means, how and when it happens. Huck Finn allowed us to talk about some important aspects of that whole experience. And Nathan McCall's book told us what it was like for him to grow up as a young black man in the sixties. I thought it would be interesting to see what this other book has to say about the experience since unlike Huck she didn't take off but stayed on Mango Street. I love this book a lot. It took her five years to write this 120-page book. It's like a poem almost, the language and images are so intense.[12]

As Burke explains, the second scenario is clearly better in that the teacher grabbed students' interest by reading an excerpt and then linked the book to what the class had been doing. By emphasizing the book's literary quality, the teacher helped students see why they were reading the book while the teacher in the first scenario left students with the idea that they were reading *The House on Mango Street* to be politically correct.

We'll conclude this section with a plea for all those working with books and young adults to continue seeking out and promoting the use of minority literature. Educators have shied away from working with minority literature because:

- They didn't study it when they were in school and so they feel less prepared than when teaching mainstream literature.
- They fear censorship both because of prejudice against minorities and because of the fact that some minority writers use language considered inappropriate for schoolbooks.
- Minority literature is harder to find, especially minority literature that has been given a "seal of approval" by the education establishment (i.e., positive reviews and suggestions for teaching).
- Ethnic identification is such a sensitive topic that teachers fear that when they are discussing a piece of literature either they or their students may say something that will offend some students or hurt their feelings.

Being a professional means that you do not shy away from responsibilities just because they are challenging. Instead, you prepare, so that you can be successful—at least most of the time. The fact that we are working in an exciting and changing field where we have to keep learning new things is something to be grateful for rather than afraid of. Pablo Casals, the great cellist, was still practicing three hours a day when he was ninety-four years old. When someone asked him why he was still practicing, he answered, "I'm beginning to notice some improvement."

Notes

1. Deirdre Donahue, "'Fame Junkies' Is Hooked on Celebrity Behavior," *USA TODAY*, January 5, 2007, p. 1.
2. Alleen Pace Nilsen, *Joan Bauer* (Greenwood Press, 2007), p. 11.
3. Louis Sachar, "On the Moral of the Story," *Literature for Today's Young Adults* by Alleen Pace Nilsen and Ken Donelson (Longman, 2001), p. 203.
4. "Letters to EJ" by Bruce C. Appleby, Heather Fitzgerald Jorgensen, and Wendell Ricketts, *English Journal* 94 (January 2005): 8–9.
5. *Washington Post*, July 6, 2007, p. 2.
6. Kathleen Kennedy Manzo, "The Bible Makes a Comeback," *Education Week*, May 16, 2007, pp. 25–27.
7. Cornelia Funke, "On the Miracle of Translation,"

Literature for Today's Young Adults 7th edition, by Kenneth L. Donelson and Alleen Pace Nilsen (Allyn and Bacon, 2005), p. 176.

8. Katha Pollitt, "Why We Read: Canon to the Right of Me . . . ," *The Nation*, September 23, 1991, reprinted in *The Chronicle of Higher Education*, October 12, 1991.

9. Rudolfo Anaya, *Autobiography: As Written in 1985*, TQS Publications, 1991, pp. 16–17.

10. *The Big Aiiieeeee! An Anthology of Chinese American and Japanese American Literature*, edited by Jeffery Paul Chan, Frank Chin, Lawson Fusao Inada, and Shawn Wong (New American Library, 1991), p. 8.

11. Maxine Hong Kingston, "Personal Statement," in *Approaches to Teaching Kingston's* The Woman Warrior, edited by Shirley Geok-lin Lim (Modern Language Association, 1991), p. 24.

12. Jim Burke, *The English Teacher's Companion: A Complete Guide to Classroom, Curriculum and the Profession* (Boynton Cook, 1999), p. 252.

Contemporary Realistic Fiction: From Tragedies to Romances

chapter **4**

As shown in Chapter 2, the development of the young adult problem novel is fairly recent. Before 1967, we had Mary Stolz—who wrote like an angel—but most other realistic books had to be "borrowed" by teens from books published for adults. But in 1967, young adult literature came of age in several ways. Nat Hentoff wrote a persuasive piece "Tell It as It Is" in the May 7 *New York Times Book Review*. Three months later, the *NYT Review* carried a piece by S. E. Hinton (see the write-up on her on p. 8), "Teen-Agers Are for Real."

And almost before we knew it, we had realistic YA books as good as Hinton's *The Outsiders*, Paul Zindel's *The Pigman*, Robert Lipsyte's *The Contender*, John Donovan's *I'll Get There. It Better Be Worth the Trip*, Virginia Hamilton's *The House of Dies Drear*, John Neufeld's *Lisa, Bright and Dark*, and Theodore Taylor's *The Cay*.

However, there was a problem in all this richness. Donovan's *I'll Get There . . .* the first YA novel dealing with homosexuality, caused some rumbles with parents and assorted pressure groups. More rumbles came with the publication of Ann Head's *Mr. and Mrs. Bo Jo Jones*—a book that talked openly about an unplanned pregnancy and a young couple in love. In retrospect, Patty Campbell in her March–April 2003 *Horn Book Magazine* column, called it "the most controversial and important book" of 1967.

Head's book and Donovan's book weren't alone in causing problems. Zindel's *My Darling, My Hamburger* and *I Never Loved Your Mind* added to the fuel and suddenly almost any YA book had the potential of being censored.

Today's general reaction to teenagers' interest in video games and fantasy is similar to how the public reacted in the 1970s when teenagers flocked to the new realism. Here P J Haarsma, author of the Softwire *fantasy books, is shown working with students in Kristina Bybee's senior English class at Desert Ridge High School in Gilbert, Arizona. They are working with ASU Professor James Blasingame on a research project searching for carryovers between reading science fiction and inventing and playing video games based on the books they've read.*

In the October 1989 *VOYA*, Dorothy Broderick chided the ultra conservative critics who were asking, "Why, oh why [do today's] authors have to deal with such depressing subjects? Why can't we go back to the good old days?" Then she went on to say:

> As one who has spent six decades on this planet, let me tell you an important fact: there were no good old days. Every problem confronted in a young adult novel today not only existed during my childhood and adolescence, but was known to most of us. There were drunks in families, there were wife abusers, there were child molesters, divorce, certainly death and dying, mental illness, premarital pregnancy, and, yes, abortions if you were among the elite. In high school, one of my classmates went home one day to find his father had hung himself in the garage; a couple of weeks later he went home to find his mother had done the same thing. (204)

Facing the problem of censorship locally was never easy, but the American Library Association and the National Council of Teachers of English faced it nationally and eased some of the problems of teachers and librarians, a topic treated more fully in Chapter 12. Many of us began to read *The Newsletter on Intellectual Freedom*, partly out of curiosity to find who and what was now under attack, mostly out of concern for what we could or would do if one of our favorite books had somewhere drawn the scorn of a parent or a pressure group. As Broderick went on to say, as individuals we profit from uniting with others who share our values, but as professionals we must be willing "to provide materials that allow us and our patrons access to ideas we love and ideas we loathe." As a final point, she jokingly advised librarians to put signs on their doors, "This library has something offensive to everyone."

What Do We Mean by Realism?

When critic Northrop Frye used the term *realism* in his *Anatomy of Criticism*, he put it in quotation marks because when it is applied to literature the term does not—or should not—mean the same thing that it does in other contexts. He argued that expecting literature simply to portray real life is a mistaken notion. The artist who can paint grapes so realistically that a bird will fly up and peck at the canvas is not highly acclaimed. Nor would people want to listen to a symphony in which all the instruments imitated "real" sounds from nature—the cooing of doves, the rushing of a waterfall, a clap of thunder, and the wind whistling through trees.

In the 1990s when Norman Mailer was being interviewed on CNN by Larry King, he said that as soon as a character—whether real or imagined—is written about, fiction results because the character now lives as imagined in people's minds rather than as a real person who can be talked to and touched. G. Robert Carlsen made a similar point when he said that a story exists first in the mind of its creator and then in the minds of its readers. Because it was never anything "real," it cannot be tested against an external reality, as can the plans for a building, a chemical formula, a case study, and so on.

If we evaluate literature by its realism alone, Carlsen said, we would be forced to abandon most of the truly great literature of the world: certainly most of tragedy, much of comedy, and all of romance. We would have to discard the Greek plays, the great epics, Shakespeare, Molière. They succeed because they go beyond the externals of living and instead reach out and touch the imaginative life deep down inside where we live.

He was irritated with readers and critics who took a simplistic view of YA books, particularly novels like *The Chocolate War.*

> I despair when a critic views *The Chocolate War* as a realistic novel, saying "Life doesn't happen that way." This book should be approached as a tragic vision exemplifying Shakespeare's horrifying line [from *Lear*], "We are flies to the gods; they kill us for their sport." Or Swift's statement, "Man is the most pernicious race of little odious vermin that nature ever suffered to crawl upon the earth." You may not like such visions, but that does not make them *dishonest* or *failures* as literature. The arts are beyond external reality. They deal with that mysterious realm of consciousness for which we seek adequate expression.[1]

Even though respected authors and critics argue against realism as a literary concept, we are using the term mainly because we can't think of a better one. Also, because people commonly use *realism* to describe the books in this chapter we would be at a communication disadvantage if we invented a new term. We are writing about young adult fiction with real-world settings in historical periods not far removed from our own. The books feature young protagonists solving problems without the help of magic. Marc Aronson says that what makes realistic novels succeed is their level of intimacy. "Does a book have the potential to touch readers deeply so that, in the struggle with it, they begin to see and to shape themselves?"[2]

The Modern Problem Novel

The general public seems to have an almost subconscious belief that children will model their lives after what they read. Since all of us want our children to be happy, we feel more comfortable when they are reading "happy" books. The problem novel, however, is based on the philosophy that young people will have a better chance to be happy if they have realistic expectations and if they know both the bad and the good about the society in which they live. This changed attitude is what opened the door to writers of irony and even tragedy for young people. Irony is like a tennis serve that you can't return. You can admire its perfection, its appropriateness, and even the inevitability of the outcome, but you just can't cope with it. There is a refreshing honesty in stories that show readers they are not the only ones who get served that kind of ball and that the human spirit, although totally devastated in this particular set, may rise again to play another match.

When, in the late 1960s, publishers began feeling comfortable in encouraging writers to create serious coming-of-age stories to be read by teenagers themselves, they identified the books as new realism or as problem novels rather than as the more literary term of *bildungsroman*, which is formally defined as "novels dealing with the development of a young person usually from adolescence to maturity." The books are often autobiographical and are sometimes called "apprenticeship novels."

In addition to their candor and the selection of subject matter, these new problem novels differ from earlier books in four basic ways. The first difference lies in the choice of characters. The protagonists come from a variety of social and economic levels, which ties in with the second major difference—that of setting. Instead of living in idyllic, pleasant suburban homes, the characters come from settings that are harsh and difficult places to live. To get the point across about the characters and where and how they live, authors use colloquial language, which is the third difference. Many of today's authors write the way people really talk, including profanity and ungrammatical constructions. That the public has generally allowed these changes shows that people are drawing away from the idea that the main purpose of fiction for young readers is to set an example of proper middle-class behavior.

The fourth difference also relates to this change in attitude, and that is the change in mode. As it became acceptable to provide readers with more vicarious experiences than would be either desirable or possible in real life, the mode of YA novels changed. Most of the books for young readers—at least those endorsed by parents and educators—used to be written in the comic and romantic modes. Statistically, this may still be true, but several of the books currently getting critical attention are written in the ironic or tragic modes.

For example, John Green's *Looking for Alaska*, which won a Printz Award, is far from a happy story. It is told by sixteen-year-old Miles Halter, who leaves his family home in Florida to attend the Culver Creek Boarding School in suburban Alabama. His roommate, Chip, is a poor but brilliant scholarship student who delights in "getting even" with the rich kids at Culver Creek. Both Chip and Miles—and most of the other boys in school—fall madly in love with Alaska Young, a beautiful and full of life—and death—young woman who chooses to hang out with Chip and Miles. There is no happy ending for Alaska and the whole book is organized around the number of days before and after the tragedy that befalls her.

When the problem novel was first developing as *the* genre in young adult literature, it played a relatively unique role in openly acknowledging that many young people's lives are far removed from the happy-go-lucky images shown in television commercials and sitcoms. The best-known books from the 1960s and 1970s were new and interesting because they vividly demonstrated that young people worried about sex, drugs, money, peer pressure, and health problems. Such information does not come as news today because the mass media does a thorough job of communicating that many adults are less than perfect and that many young people are facing problems ranging from minor to severe. In fact, talk shows, reality shows, courtroom TV, soap operas, and even news programs and magazines make us privy to so many people's problems that we simply do not have the energy to empathize with all the sad stories that we hear. We shrug our shoulders and turn off our tear ducts, which leaves us feeling alienated and dehumanized. Also, most media treatments present a one-shot portrait chosen to tug at the emotions of viewers or readers. To increase the drama, they make a virtue of suffering and pain by portraying people as victims unable to move beyond their pain. In contrast, in the best of the problem novels authors take the space to develop various strands of their stories and to show differing viewpoints and alternate solutions. This differs from television sitcoms as well as from most series books, which preserve the status quo so that at the end the producer or the author can start all over again with a similar story.

In relation to the term *realism*, it is only fair to mention that some critics have justifiably pointed out that the large majority of high school readers are more likely to experience something akin to a wish-fulfilling romance than to the experiences described in many of the so-called realistic novels shown in this sampling of recent books and in those described in Focus Box 4.1, Challenges: Physical and Mental.

- Meg Rosoff's *How I Live Now* (winner of the 2005 Printz Award) is about a futuristic war that breaks out in England where Daisy has been sent in hopes that with the help of her aunt and her cousins and the fresh country air, she will recover from her eating disorder. She says her food problem started when she was afraid that her father's new wife was trying to poison her, but then she confesses it became very satisfying to see both parents worrying about her. When she arrives at the old family farm, her aunt, who is active in a peace movement, is just rushing off to Oslo to give a speech and Daisy is left with her cousins. A strange kind of war breaks out and the teenage children are left to fend for themselves, which they do but only with some terrible consequences. An interesting technique is the way that Rasoff uses vague language when talking about the enemy so that readers are left to fill in their own images with whoever or whatever they fear the most.
- One of our students who read E. R. Frank's *America* responded with "grim, grim, grim." A fifteen-year-old boy named America was born to a drug-addicted woman who abandoned him, but nevertheless reappears for

Focus Box 4.1

Challenges: Physical and Mental

Accidents of Nature by Harriet McBryde. Holt, 2006. A summer at Camp Courage, which is designed for teenagers with disabilities, proves to be life-changing for seventeen-year-old Jean. She has cerebral palsy and is assigned to share a cabin with the intelligent and thoughtful Sara, who is in a wheelchair and has a different "take" on the matter of disability.

Boy Toy by Barry Lyga. Houghton, 2007. Seventeen-year-old Joshua Mendel is almost ready to graduate from high school, but he is still struggling emotionally with the fallout from being sexually abused by Eve, the woman who was his seventh-grade history teacher. Older teens will be fascinated at how their relationship developed and its long-term effects.

A Corner of the Universe by Ann Martin. Scholastic, 2002. Hattie looks back on her thirteenth summer when Uncle Adam, someone she had never been told about, comes "home" to live with her grandparents because his "school" has closed. In this powerful look at mental illness, tragedy ensues when Hattie invites Uncle Adam to sneak out with her to a carnival.

Cut by Patricia McCormick. Front Street, 2000. This picture of life in a mental-health facility for teenagers is far from pretty with its constant smell of vomit, its lack of privacy, and the hostility and sadness of the patients. Callie, a girl who secretly cuts herself, is the narrator.

Dreamland by Sarah Dessen. Viking, 2000. Vivid characterization makes this story of Caitlin's drift into passivity all the more memorable and haunting.

Every Time a Rainbow Dies by Rita Williams-Garcia. HarperCollins, 2001. Thulani's mother died three years ago, and he is a relatively unwelcome "guest" in the apartment of his older brother and the brother's wife. Thulani spends hours with the pigeons he raises on the roof of their apartment house. When he witnesses a brutal rape, he rushes down to "rescue" the girl and takes an important first step toward reentering life.

Inside Out by Terry Trueman. HarperTempest, 2003. Zach, who is schizophrenic, waits every day for his mother to pick him up in a small restaurant where he gets caught in the midst of a holdup. Although he comes close to being a hero in this particular situation, there is no happy ending.

Invisible by Pete Hautman. Simon & Schuster, 2005. Seventeen-year-old Dougie has one good friend, and readers hope that will be enough to help him maintain his focus. When he hides his medication and resists help from his psychiatrist, readers begin to realize that Dougie has a secret too awful to reveal.

Saving Francesca by Melina Marchetta. Knopf/Borzoi, 2004. Francesca's mother, who used to be strong and successful, is so depressed that she cannot function and so Francesca has little help from home when she changes schools and experiences her first romance. Nevertheless, readers come away feeling positive for Francesca.

The Sibling Slam Book edited by Don Meyer. Woodbine, 2005. Although this is nonfiction, it fits with the books in this section. Eighty-one young people offer insights from

terrifying episodes. The boy's best memories are of living with Mrs. Harper and her half-brother. However, the half-brother introduces the preteen America to vodka and sex, and in guilt and rage, America sets the man's blanket on fire and escapes. Years later, a capable therapist is coaxing America's story from the reluctant fifteen-year-old, who is living in a residential treatment center and trying to gain control over his suicidal depression. Readers are left with hope for a boy who, so far, has been a survivor against incredible odds.

- In *Hush*, Jacqueline Woodson uses a similar situation to the one that Robert Cormier used in *The Cheese Stands Alone*, in which a family is uprooted and put into the Federal Witness Protection Program. In Wood-

having grown up in a family with a special needs child. The focused chapters reveal not only feelings of embarrassment, but also of protectiveness and of pride because of learning things that other kids don't know and of making a real contribution to one's family.

Slam by Nick Hornby. Putnam, 2007. A sixteen-year-old skateboarder gets slammed with something new—he's about to become a father. Hornby is being praised for treating such a serious subject with warmth as well as respectful humor.

A Small White Scar by K. A. Nuzum. HarperCollins/Joanna Cotler Books, 2006. Besides being responsible for his disabled twin brother, fifteen-year-old Will wants to be free to ride in a rodeo and to work like a man on his father's 1940s Colorado ranch. Nuzum has written a fictional account of many of the feelings treated in the real-life accounts in *The Sibling Slam Book*.

Story of a Girl by Sara Zarr. Little, Brown, 2007. Older teens will be touched by this story of a girl whose life is drastically changed when her father catches her at age thirteen having sex in a car, and she is immediately "branded" by her own family as well as by the school community as a slut.

Stuck in Neutral by Terry Trueman. HarperCollins, 2000. Fourteen-year-old Shawn McDaniel thinks his father is planning to kill him, a suspicion that readers gradually grow to share in this story of a boy who is born with cerebral palsy. The story is continued in *Cruise Control* (HarperCollins, 2004) told from the viewpoint of older brother Paul, who hates his father and is striving to learn to control his own violent behavior both on and off the basketball court.

Surrender by Sonya Hartnett. Candlewick, 2006. Fire and a haunting secret from the past play a part in this powerful story, which is on the Honor List. A major character is a dog named *Surrender*, and readers are left wondering whether the book is named after the dog or after the mental attitude of the twenty-year-old protagonist who lies dying.

Under the Wolf, under the Dog by Adam Rapp. Candlewick, 2004. A sixteen-year-old boy is living at a therapeutic facility for teens who have tried suicide and/or have troubles connected to substance abuse. The circumstances are dreadful, but a little more hopeful than the ones in Rapp's *33 Snowfish*, *Little Chicago*, and *The Buffalo Tree*.

Wasteland by Francesca Lia Block. Joanna Cotler/HarperCollins, 2003. People who think YA lit is easy to read and easy to understand need to immerse themselves in this powerful and sad story about Marina and her brother, Lex.

The Very Ordered Existence of Merilee Marvelous by Suzanne Crowley. HarperCollins/Greenwillow, 2007. Thirteen-year-old Merilee Monroe has her life in order, but then all kinds of troubles start intruding and readers get glimpses into the condition known as Asperger's Syndrome (not identified by name), alcoholism, senility, and plain old meanness.

Wild Roses by Deb Caletti. Simon & Schuster, 2005. Cassie Morgan is a normal seventeen-year-old with ambitions of becoming an astronomer, but then her mother marries a famous and arrogant violinist, whose attitudes and behavior cross way over the line of what the world is willing to accept from people with artistic temperaments.

son's story, the family is African American, and the protagonist, Evie Thomas (née Toswiah Green), is twelve years old when her father testifies against other African Americans in a racially motivated murder. Instead of creating the kind of dramatic situation that Cormier created, Woodson shows the tedium and the depression that sets in when a family is torn from its past and has yet to build a future. Evie's mother finds a kind of solace in the Seventh Day Adventist Church, but her father spends his days staring out the front window, while her older sister plots how she can escape from this nonlife. Rather than being left with a happy ending, readers are left pondering what is a less-than-perfect solution to a very real family problem.

Of contemporary authors, Adam Rapp probably writes the most "downer" books. *Little Chicago* is the grim story of eleven-year-old Blacky, who is sexually abused by his mother's boyfriend. Although he is brave enough to tell "all the right people," no one helps him. His best friend makes it even worse by telling kids at school, who cruelly taunt him. He gets a gun and, with no money for ammunition, performs a sexual act to get bullets. His one friend, who suffers almost as much as he does, has told him that if you follow a deer long enough it will lead you to paradise. The book ends with Blacky following a deer into a forest, but only the most optimistic of readers can believe that this is going to make Blacky's life better. Tyrrell Burns closed her *School Library Journal* review with, "The sense of hopelessness in this disturbing novel is almost physically painful."[3] For *VOYA*, Kathleen Beck wrote that Rapp's books are valuable because of their honest recognition that young people can suffer and face really difficult questions, but "Forget using them as bibliotherapy. . . . There are no solutions here."[4]

In the February issue of *VOYA* when the "Top-Shelf Fiction for Middle School Readers 2002" (a list of twenty-four "best books") was published, *Little Chicago* received twice as much space as the other books, but its annotation was in a gray box under the unusual heading, "Adult Reader Recommendation." The committee's idea was that adults should read the book to keep such a story from ever happening. Their closing line was, "This book is not to be handed to young readers without forethought—not because it is unrealistic but precisely because it shows how heartlessly unprotected they might find themselves to be."[5]

Rapp's *33 Snowfish* is about four kids on the run. One of them has killed his parents and stolen their car. One is a prostitute; one has recently escaped from a pedophile, while the youngest is just a baby, whom the others think they might sell. Reviewer Joel Shoemaker said that the book is bound to be controversial: "The fearsome elements escape the pages like nightmares loosed into daylight, . . . but for those readers who are ready to be challenged by a serious work of shockingly realistic fiction, it invites both an emotional and intellectual response, and begs to be discussed."[6]

In traditional literary criticism, tragedies have three distinct elements. First, there is a noble character who, no matter what happens, maintains the qualities that the society considers praiseworthy; second, there is an inevitable force that works against the character; and third, there is a struggle and an outcome. The reader of a tragedy is usually filled with pity and fear—pity for the hero and fear for oneself that the same thing might happen. The intensity of this involvement causes the reader to undergo an emotional release as the outcome of the story unfolds. This release, or catharsis, has the effect of draining away dangerous human emotions and filling the reader with a sense of exaltation or amazed pride in what the human spirit is called on to endure.

But rather than writing pure tragedies, most young adult authors soften their stories with hopeful endings. Even the books that include death, as with those listed in Focus Box 4.2, Dying Is Easy; Surviving Is Hard (p. 120), focus on recovery and the future. This goes along with the cherished belief that young readers deserve books with happy endings. Virginia Hamilton illustrated this belief when she was awarded the Newbery Medal for *M. C. Higgins the Great*, and a reporter asked her if she really thought that the retaining wall that M. C. was building on the mountain above the house would keep the mine tailings from sliding down and ruining the family's home. She responded with something to the effect, that "Probably not, but this is a book for kids. They have to have hope."

Her statement illustrates a long-cherished belief that young readers deserve books with happy endings. These are the kinds of books that serve as a counterbalance to the depressing realism of the "true" problem novel. There is nothing magical in the books, so they are "real" in that sense, but as Richard Peck has observed, teenagers' favorite books are "romances disguised as realism." He was not saying this as a negative, because he was describing his own books along with those of many other well-respected writers. It is understandable that teenagers want both the happy endings and the assurance that happy endings are possible. Actually, most readers prefer happy endings, but it is assumed that adults have had more experience in coping with difficult life experiences so that they might be "turned off" by endings that come across as falsely hopeful. See Table 4.1 for suggestions of how to evaluate problem novels.

TABLE 4.1 Suggestions for Evaluating the Problem Novel

A good problem novel usually has:	A poor problem novel may have:
A strong, interesting, and believable plot centering around a problem that a young person might really have.	A totally predictable plot with nothing new and interesting to entice the reader.
The power to transport the reader into another person's thoughts and feelings.	Characters who are cardboardlike exaggerations of people and are too good or too bad to be believed.
Rich characterization. The characters "come alive" as believable with a balance of good and negative qualities.	More characters than the reader can keep straight comfortably.
A setting that enhances the story and is described so that the reader can get the intended picture.	Many stereotypes.
A worthwhile theme. The reader is left with something to think about.	Lengthy chapters or descriptive paragraphs that add bulk but not substance to the book.
A smoothness of style that flows steadily and easily, carrying the reader along.	A preachy message. The author spells out the attitudes and conclusions with which he or she wants each reader to leave the book.
A universal appeal so that it speaks to more than a single group of readers.	Nothing that stays with the reader after the book has been put down.
A subtlety that stimulates the reader to think about the various aspects of the story.	A subject that is of interest only because it is topical or trendy.
A way of dealing with the problems so that the reader is left with insights into either society or individuals or both.	Inconsistent points of view. The author's sympathies change with no justification.
	Dialogue that sounds forced or inappropriate to the characters.
	"Facts" that do not jibe with those of the real world.
	Unlikely coincidences or changes in characters' personalities for the sake of the plot.
	Exaggerations that result in sensationalism.

Before I Die by Jenny Downham. Random/David Fickling, 2007. Sixteen-year-old Tessa has only a few months to live and she sorrowfully tries to cram in all the life experiences that she's not going to have. Except for the plot, this touching book has little in common with the 2007 *Bucket List* film starring Jack Nicholson and Morgan Freeman.

The Bell Jar by Sylvia Plath. HarperCollins, 1971. A young woman who has become famous for her writing commits suicide. Plath's partly autobiographical story continues to fascinate readers as shown by the enthusiastic reception of Stephanie Hemphill's 2007 *Your Own Sylvia: A Verse Portrait of Sylvia Plath*.

A Brief Chapter in My Impossible Life by Dana Reinhardt. Random, 2006. A sixteen-year-old girl has always known she was adopted, but hasn't thought much about it. Then her birth mother calls and wants to meet her. Everything changes when she learns that the woman is dying.

Cures for Heartbreak by Margo Rabb. Delacorte, 2007. A bonus for readers is the touching afterword that tells how closely this sad story follows the real events of the author's teenage years when she lost her mother to cancer and her father develops heart trouble. A vibrant New York City set-ting, flashes of dark humor, and beautiful characterization make this a wonderful read for older teens.

The Dark Light by Mette Newth, translated by Faith Ingwer-son. Farrar, Straus and Giroux, 1998. In Norway more than a century ago, a thirteen-year-old girl tries to work out the meaning of life, God, happiness, and revenge as she lies in a bed dying of leprosy.

A Death in the Family by James Agee. McDowell, Obolensky, 1957. Set in Knoxville, Tennessee, back at the turn of the last century, the Follet family with their two children lead a comfortable life until the father is struck down.

Double Helix: A Novel by Nancy Werlin. Dial, 2004. Eli Samuels is about to lose his mother to Huntington's Disease, but this is just the background for Werlin's mystery. Eli goes to work for Wyatt Transgenics Lab and gradually discovers why his father doesn't want him to work there. Werlin brings up some intriguing bioethical issues.

Ghost Girl: A Blue Ridge Mountain Story by Delia Ray. Clarion, 2003. It's the 1930s and pale April Sloane with her white-blonde hair and her light blue eyes feels like a ghost, especially since the death of her younger brother a year ago. Her mother has fallen into a deep depression and during the four years that are covered in the story, it's pretty much up to April to pull herself out of her problems.

Three popular stories about young protagonists that were published as somber adult novels are J. D. Salinger's *The Catcher in the Rye*, Hannah Green's *I Never Promised You a Rose Garden*, and Judith Guest's *Ordinary People*. In all three, worthy young heroes set out to find wisdom and understanding. They make physical sacrifices, including suicide attempts, and even though they receive help from wise and kindly psychiatrists (today's counterpart to the white witches, the wizards, and the helpful gods and goddesses of traditional romances), they must prove their worthiness through hard, painstaking work. This is what Deborah Blau's psychiatrist communicates in the sentence used for the book's title, *I Never Promised You a Rose Garden*. If Green had intended her book for teenagers, she would have been more likely to have ended the book with Deborah leaving the mental institution to "live happily ever after."

It is the details of a story and the author's attitude as much as the plot that determines whether a book is realistic or romanticized. For example, the plot of Joyce Carol Oates's *Freaky Green Eyes* is as somber as any tragedy, but Oates devised several techniques to soften the story of a girl whose father murders her mother and is sent to prison. First, the family is wealthy and the father is a celebrity so that Francesca (aka Franky) lives in a house and goes to the kinds of

Green Angel by Alice Hoffman. Scholastic, 2003. Mature readers will grieve with the fifteen-year-old girl who is now ashamed of her sullen behavior when she didn't get to go with her parents and sister to the city. They never came back.

The Key to the Golden Firebird: A Novel by Maureen Johnson. HarperCollins, 2004. After their father's death, three sisters—sensible May, frightened Palmer, and rebellious Brooks—are left pretty much on their own while their mother works to provide financial support. Their father's Pontiac Firebird helps each one heal in her own way.

The Lightkeeper's Daughter by Iain Lawrence. Delacorte, 2002. When the lightkeeper's daughter returns home to the island lighthouse with a three-year-old daughter in tow, she not only has to reestablish relations with her parents, but also has to come to terms with the death of her beloved brother.

Missing May by Cynthia Rylant. Orchard, 1992. Summer has been tossed from relative to relative. Then Uncle Ob and Aunt May take her into their loving home, and May dies. Uncle Ob is so devastated that Summer is afraid she will lose him too.

My Brother Stealing Second by Jim Naughton. HarperCollins, 1989. While star athlete and favorite son Billy is drunk, he kills himself along with a couple celebrating their wedding anniversary. Billy's family and the daughter of the couple are left to suffer.

Strays by Ron Koertge. Candlewick, 2007. Fifteen-year-old Ted O'Connor would rather communicate with animals than people. His situation is understandable in that he worked in his parents' pet store until they were killed in an accident and he was placed in an inappropriate foster home. But in a basically optimistic book, Ted gradually learns that he doesn't have to be a "stray."

A Summer to Die by Lois Lowery. Houghton Mifflin, 1977. While her older sister is dying of leukemia, Meg finds comfort and solace in the help of a seventy-year-old landlord, handyman, and photographer.

The Truth about Forever by Sarah Dessen. Viking, 2004. Always in control, Macy witnesses the death of her father, but does not allow herself to grieve. Then she goes to work for a catering service, where things are a lot more unpredictable. The job—and the people Macy works with—help her make her way back to life and living.

Walk Softly, Rachel by Kate Banks. Farrar, 2003. Three Rachels—One, a grandmother coming to live with a family; Two, the mother in the family who is a lawyer and a judge; and Three, the fourteen-year-old daughter. The change works as a catalyst to bring the Rachels together as they face the possibility of dismantling and remodeling a bedroom for Rachel One. The bedroom in question has been preserved as a kind of shrine to older brother Jake, who died seven years ago.

parties that other kids only dream about. Readers get to see her as a take-charge girl, both for herself and for wild animals that are being kept in cages simply for amusement. At the end she has a loving aunt to provide a new home for her and her sister. And most important of all, she now has Garret as a boyfriend. She met him when she went to visit her mother. They had made arrangements for an informal date, but her enraged father came and took her and her sister away before she could go out with him. She met Garret again only after her mother's death when she came with her aunt to take away her mother's belongings, and Garret wandered over and helped them load the U-Haul trailer. They exchanged email addresses, and at the end of the book she lets readers know that they keep in touch—"Sometimes daily." Also, Garret's family is going to change its usual plan of vacationing at Aspen and going to ski at Taos, where Frankie now lives, so "Garret and I will see each other then."

Devising happy, or at least hopeful, endings for tragic stories is a challenge for authors. Even a good book such as Laurie Halse Anderson's 1999 *Speak*, which was a finalist for the National Book Award and a Printz Honor Book, has a coincidence at the very end that stretches believability. Thirteen-year-old Melinda is raped at a summer party. When she calls the police, who come and break up the party, she becomes a social outcast. No one knows why she called the police, and out of shame she hides behind silence for almost a whole year. Finally, a wonderful art teacher helps her not only to "speak," but to speak about the incident. The boy who raped her is furious and vengeful. He stalks her and after school one day pulls her into a janitor's closet and slams the door. She is saved from a severe beating or another rape—if not from death—by her own efforts, including cries for help, and the arrival of the girls' lacrosse team. They are coming in from the field and when they hear Melinda, they pound with their sticks on the closet door, calling for additional help.

Another challenge for writers of problem novels is that they most often write the books in first person. Thoughtful readers must surely question how these malfunctioning and troubled kids can write so well. In A. M. Jenkins's *Out of Order*, Colt, who is a star baseball player, tells the story of his senior year in high school. The story is beautifully written, but Colt's main problem is that he has little interest and little aptitude for academics. Readers have to enter into a willing suspension of disbelief when they compare the pitiful essay he wrote for his English class with the rest of the beautifully written book.

What Are the Problems?

The best authors treat candidly and with respect problems that belong specifically to young adults in today's world. Many of the problems that go along with modern adolescence did not exist in the nineteenth century, so at least in this one area, there is ample justification for books directed specifically to youthful audiences as in several of the new books mentioned in Chapter 1, including Patricia McCormick's *Sold*, Alan Stratton's *Chanda's Secrets*, and Pete Hautman's *Godless*.

If authors have a teaching goal when they are creating problem novels, it is probably to help young readers develop an internal locus of control through which they assume that their own actions and characteristics will shape their lives. They ask the question, "What am I going to do with my life?" while people with an external locus of control depend on luck, chance, or what others do. Their major life question is "What will happen to me?"

Although we all know adults who blame others for whatever happens to them, most of us would agree that we want to help young people feel responsible for their own lives. Books cannot substitute for real-life experiences, and one or two books, no matter how well written, are not enough to change a teenager's view of life. Skilled authors, however, can show what is going on in characters' minds, whereas cameras can show only what is externally visible. The title of Laurie Halse Anderson's *Catalyst* hints at the idea that what happens from outside can trigger changes, but the changes actually come from within. *Catalyst* is the story of Kate Malone, who, through her minister father, becomes involved with Terri, a classmate who has been touched by such problems as incest, pregnancy, abuse, and mental illness. Kate is on the track team and the honor roll, and when the book opens her main concern is whether she will be admitted to MIT, the only college she has applied to. Anderson's thought-provoking character study

 *Now that it is so easy to download information and to scan book covers, both teachers and students enjoy making posters to help them share information about favorite books.*

shows how experiences can trigger changes, but it is Kate who is responsible for the growth that allows those changes.

Other examples include Janet McDonald's *Spellbound*, in which a teenage mother who lives in the projects decides to turn her life around by studying for a spelling bee and getting in line for a program that might lead to a college scholarship. Ruth White's *Tadpole* is set in Appalachia in the 1950s. It is the story of a thirteen-year-old orphan and the effect he has on his four cousins and their mother when he seeks them out as a refuge from an uncle who beats him and uses him as free labor. Sometimes, in spite of all the protagonist does, help is still needed, as in Kimberly Willis Holt's *Keeper of the Night*. When thirteen-year-old Isabel Moreno's mother commits suicide, Isabel struggles to care for her seven-year-old sister and her twelve-year-old brother. The story is set in Guam and there are some interesting cultural differences, one of which is Aunt Bernadette, who is a traditional healer. Isabel does not take as much help from her as she might because she is determined to prove that she is stronger than was her mother. Isabel's grief-stricken father avoids the family problems by spending long hours on his fishing boat, but after the brother collapses, Isabel and her family get some of the help they need.

Peer Groups

Peer groups become increasingly important to teenagers as they move beyond social and emotional dependence on their parents. By becoming part of a group, clique, or gang, teenagers take a step toward emotional independence. Even though they are not making truly independent decisions, as parts of different groups they try out various roles, ranging from conformist to nonconformist and from follower to leader. Young adult literature can extend the peer group by giving teenagers a chance to participate vicariously in more personal relationships than are possible for most youngsters in the relatively short time that they spend in high school. When they were children, parents were responsible for locating in the "right" neighborhood near "good schools," so that children had no reason to give particular thoughts to differences in social and economic classes or ethnic backgrounds. Then quite suddenly their environments are expanded, not only through larger, more diverse schools but also through jobs, extracurricular activities, public entertainment, shopping in malls, and church or community activities.

While high school students have always known that some of their fellow students were truly scary, the Columbine tragedy forced adults to pay attention to a problem that many of us had preferred to ignore. Tackling the problem in 1974 of school bullies and peer pressure was what made Robert Cormier's *The Chocolate War* so unusual for its time. When Cormier was asked at a meeting of English teachers about the changing nature of school violence now that kids were bringing guns to school, he sadly admitted that he was as troubled as everyone else. However, one of the teachers in the group pointed out that it is actually the beginnings of the alienation and the hostility that are interesting. The simplest of video games can show people getting shot, but it takes great literature to help people understand the intensity of the emotions that might trigger such actions.

Today, virtually everyone is aware that tough kids, mean kids, frightened kids, and plain old nutty kids are "out there," but we are still unsure about what to do. The increased awareness of the problem and the formation of school policies and procedures to deal with incidents may help, but Michael Cart (see his statement on p. 5) says, in the introduction to his book *Necessary Noise*, that what is needed is something that will help "kids who are living outside the mainstream in radically nontraditional families deal with their circumstances—circumstances that often result in their being marginalized, rendered invisible, regarded as unacceptably different, or even being persecuted by peers." And equally important is helping "mainstream kids begin to comprehend—intellectually and emotionally—the dramatic differences that now define the daily lives of so many other teens. Kids need to learn empathy. They need to learn how the other can become us."[7] One approach, he thinks, "is through reading fiction that captures—artfully, authentically, and unsparingly—the circumstances of kids" whose lives are different. See Focus Box 4.3, Buddies and Bullies, for books whose authors are trying to do this.

Although Louis Sachar's 2006 *Small Steps* is not the great book that *Holes* is, it nevertheless does a good job of illustrating different kids in different situations taking on the responsibility of making their own decisions. It is a follow-up or companion book to *Holes* with the focus being on Armpit and X-Ray, two of the boys from Camp Green Lake, who are back home living in Austin, Texas. Armpit has a job (putting in irrigation pipes for a lawn service company) and is going to school and being friends with a ten-year-old disabled girl who lives next door. X-Ray hangs around trying to involve Armpit in a get-rich-quick scheme photocopying and selling concert tickets. Through some rather unlikely events, Armpit becomes friends with singer Kaira DeLeon and through his experiences with her learns that not even the rich and talented are immune from bullies and frauds.

Big Mouth and Ugly Girl by Joyce Carol Oates. Harper-Collins, 2002. Popular Matt Donaghy says something in the school cafeteria that is interpreted as a threat to school safety. He is ostracized, except by Ugly Girl Ursula Riggs, who knows a thing or two about being on the outside.

Boys Lie by John Neufeld. DK, Ink, 1999. Gina is traumatized by being sexually assaulted in a New York swimming pool. Rumors follow her to California where her family moves to help her start over.

The Brimstone Journals by Ron Koertge. Candlewick, 2001. Fifteen students at Branston (aka Brimstone) High reveal themselves and their problems through poetic journal entries. Their problems cover the waterfront, but angry Boyd is the most frightening because he has already made a mental hit-list of students to "get even" with.

Buddha Boy by Kathe Koja. Farrar, Straus and Giroux, 2003. This book would be way too grim if not for the friendship that develops between Justin and the very different Jinsen, the Buddha Boy of the title, who is victimized by most kids at school.

Fat Kid Rules the World by K. L. Going. Putnam, 2003. Troy Billings weighs nearly three hundred pounds and is contemplating jumping off a subway platform. To his surprise, he is stopped by a punk-rock guitarist and occasional fellow student from W. T. Watson High School. And so begins a strange friendship.

Freak Show by James St. James. Dutton, 2007. Billy calls himself a "Gender Obscurist," even though other people at the Eisenhower Academy are more direct. Reviewers used such adjectives as "fast-paced," "snarky," and "playfully naughty" for this story about a queen who turns things upside down by running for Homecoming Queen.

Friction by E. R. Frank. Simon & Schuster, 2003. Stacy enters the eighth grade at Forest Alternative School and disproves the stereotype that it is always the newcomer who gets bullied. She also demonstrates that bullying can be done through words as well as actions.

Inexcusable by Chris Lynch. S&S/Atheneum/Ginee Seo Bks., 2005. While Keir, the protagonist, is indeed a bully, the more chilling part of Lynch's powerful book is the way that Keir rationalizes his behavior and views himself as a "lovable rogue."

Leap of Faith by Kimberly Brubaker Bradley. Dial, 2007. An extra bonus to this story about a sixth-grade girl who pulls a pocketknife on a boy who has been sexually harassing her, is that the author follows the girl into a Catholic school and an exploration of both the comfort and the questions that this new experience brings to a girl who has been raised in a nonreligious family.

Racing the Past by Sis Deans. Holt, 2001. To avoid being picked on by a school-bus bully, eleven-year-old Ricky starts walking, and then jogging, and finally running to school. He manages to make a success story out of what could have been a downward slide into the apathy and hopelessness of his alcoholic father.

Rat by Jan Cheripko. Boyds Mills Press, 2002. Fifteen-year-old Jeremy Chandler was called Rat (short for gym rat) because he spent so much time hanging around the gym. He was the basketball team's manager, and for a kid with one useless arm (a birth defect) was a pretty good player himself. His nickname takes on a whole new meaning because he happens to see the coach molesting one of the cheerleaders. The team turns against him when he testifies against their popular coach.

Scorpions by Walter Dean Myers. HarperCollins, 1988. Jamal's brother is in jail, and an old gang leader brings word to Jamal that he is to take over as leader of the Scorpions. He also brings Jamal a gun.

Touching Spirit Bear by Ben Mikaelsen. HarperCollins, 2001. Cole Matthews is a street-wise bully who permanently damages a classmate in a beating. He chooses to participate in Circle Justice, an alternative program for Native American offenders because he mistakenly thinks he can outsmart the system.

The Tulip Touch by Anne Fine. Little, Brown, 1997. As Natalie looks back on the intense relationship she shared over the years with a classmate named Tulip, she gains important insights about friendship, accountability, and manipulation.

Who the Man by Chris Lynch. HarperCollins, 2002. An alternate title might be *A Week in the Life of a Thirteen-Year-Old Bully*. Lynch does an excellent job of characterization, and by the end even Earl (the thirteen-year-old bully) has a bit more understanding of what drives him.

Family Relationships

For his *Necessary Noise* collection of short stories, Cart asked leading YA authors to contribute stories that would illustrate "the abiding importance of dialogue, of discussion, of talking about our circumstances, of leaving room, in short, for some necessary noise."[8] In his introduction, he comments on all the changes in "family" that have come about since he grew up in the 1950s' world of *Ozzie and Harriet*, *Father Knows Best*, and *Leave It to Beaver*. Well into the 1970s, 45 percent of American households were headed by a husband and a wife living together with their offspring. Today that is true for only 24 percent of U.S. households. Some of the reasons include changing attitudes toward same-sex parents, less restrictive rules on who can be foster parents, and new immigration patterns that have resulted in many partial families or people with different ideas of "family" coming to the United States.

A look at mythology, folklore, and classical and religious literature shows that stories featuring inadequate or absent parents appeal to young readers because they provide opportunities for the protagonists to assert their independence and prove that they can take care of themselves. Nevertheless, in real life, most kids want to be closer to their parents than they are. A news story in July 2003 reported that 75 percent of the nearly 1,500 teenagers contacted in a national survey really liked their parents and wanted to have more to do with them. Still, in many young adult novels, good relationships between teenagers and their parents are the exception. If they are there, the focus is more likely to be on one than on both parents as in Virginia Euwer Wolff's *Make Lemonade* and *True Believer*, in which LaVaughn's mother is a pillar of common sense. In Paul Fleischman's *Seek*, Rob puts tremendous importance on the family he has grown up in while still wanting to find the father he has never known. In Carolyn Coman's *Many Stones*, Berry's father is wise and generous as he plans a trip to help both himself and Berry come to terms with the death of older daughter/sister Laura. The emphasis on relating mainly to one parent is not so much a reflection of real life as of the literary limitations of not crowding stories with more characters than readers can relate to.

Of course, with the problem novel, just as with today's news stories, the focus is going to be on the more dramatic stories about family relationships as in Will Weaver's *Claws*. The story starts with a description of the "perfect" life of Jed Berg, the top player on the school's tennis team. He has a popular girlfriend and is an honors student and the son of adoring and successful parents. His father is an architect and his mother an attorney. Then Jed receives an email from a girl asking Jed to confront his father about the affair he is having with the girl's mother. This is the beginning of what a caustic classmate describes as the fun of watching a preppie "in a downward spiral." See Focus Box 4.4, Family Ties, for other examples that support the old saying that troubled families are all dysfunctional in their own ways.

One of the freshest new books about family relationships is Christopher Paul Curtis's *Bucking the Sarge.* Fifteen-year-old Luther T. Farrell is stuck working for his mother, "The Sarge." She is a scheming, huckster-type landlady in Flint, Michigan. She runs Happy Neighbor Group Homes where she cheats on the food and the clothes she is supposed to buy for the residents, several of whom are

Between Mom and Jo by Julie Anne Peters. Little, Brown, 2006. A boy has two mothers and when they decide to separate, the boy (Nicholas Nathaniel Thomas Tyler) goes through all the pain normally associated with a family breakup, but since he is biologically related to only one of his mothers, there are extra problems.

Blind Sighted by Peter Moore. Viking, 2002. The title comes from sixteen-year-old Kirk's involuntary job of reading to a blind woman. Kirk narrates this story of three very different friendships that help him get through the year that his alcoholic mother decides it is time for her to get her life together.

Comfort by Carolee Dean. Houghton, 2002. Comfort is the name of the town, not the emotion, in this coming-of-age story about a boy whose mother forces him to lie about his age so he can drive his father to AA meetings when he comes home from the penitentiary.

Honey, Baby, Sweetheart by Deb Caletti. Simon & Schuster, 2004. In a summer romance, Ruby gets involved with a bad boy on a motorcycle and then with her mother's book group, the Casserole Queens. It's a toss-up as to which of these atypical relationships will have the longest influence on Ruby's life.

In Spite of Killer Bees by Julie Johnston. Tundra, 2001. The lives of three sisters, ages twenty-two, seventeen, and fourteen, are suddenly thrown into what many people would think was a dream-come-true. A grandfather they've never met dies and leaves them a fortune, but with strings attached.

Looking for JJ by Anne Cassidy. Harcourt, 2007. Alice Tully is seventeen and has been given a new identity and a new chance in life. Her troubles started in her childhood when she alternated between living with a resentful grandmother and following her emotionally disconnected and transient mother. Even with all the new chances, her old life when she was Jennifer Jones, or JJ, keeps intruding.

Lord of the Deep by Graham Salisbury. Delacorte, 2001. Thirteen-year-old Mikey Donovan helps his stepdad charter his boat to Hawaiian tourists for deep-sea fishing. Mikey feels betrayed when his father lets a customer claim a record he did not really earn. Thoughtful readers will recognize the situation as more complex than Mikey realizes.

Miracle's Boys by Jacqueline Woodson. Putnam, 2000. Two orphaned brothers are holding on as they manage their individual grief; then a third brother is released from a three-year term at a detention center. The boys have to start over in building a tenuous new relationship.

Not Like You by Deborah Davis. Clarion, 2007. Fifteen-year-old Kayla has always resented her unpredictable mother, and when they move to New Mexico in hopes of getting a new start, Kayla is helped by the new environment to take a look at her own behavior and how tempted she is to follow in her mother's footsteps.

Pool Boy by Michael Simmons. Millbrook/Roaring Brook, 2003. Fifteen-year-old Brett has a major lifestyle change when his father is convicted of white-collar crime, and Brett and his mother and sister have to leave their posh neighborhood and move in with a great-aunt. Brett takes a job cleaning swimming pools in his old neighborhood, hence the nickname.

Saving Francesca by Melina Marchetta. Knopf/Borzoi, 2004. Francesca's mother, who used to be strong and successful, is so depressed that she cannot function and so Francesca has little help from home when she changes schools and experiences her first romance. Nevertheless, readers come away feeling optimistic for Francesca.

Sonny's House of Spies by George Ella Lyon. Simon & Schuster, 2004. It is the 1950s in Alabama and thirteen-year-old Sonny has not seen his father for six years. When he confronts a family friend for information, secrets come out with some harsh results.

Tending to Grace by Kimberly Newton Fusco. Knopf/Borzoi, 2004. A shy, lonely, and awkward girl is taken out of ninth grade and dropped off with a great-aunt in rural New England. They argue and fuss and the girl even gets ready to run away, but eventually Aunt Agatha and her niece Cornelia unwind and manage a mutually beneficial relationship.

Tyrell by Coe Booth. Scholastic/Push, 2006. Booth said that she wrote this book in a language that she thought would resonate with her younger brother and his friends. Before entering the writing program in The New School in New York, Booth was a social worker often pulled into emergency situations so she knows the kinds of situations that she writes about in this vibrant problem novel.

elderly men that Luther has to take care of, including driving them around in a pretty cool van. He doesn't get much pleasure from the van since it's always for "business," and his driver's license is a fake, so he's always nervous. When we sent an audiotape so our grandsons could listen in their car, the parents enjoyed the quirky humor as much as the boys did.

Living in a Multicultural World

Kids are probably more aware than are their parents of changing demographics. During the 1970s when the parents of today's teenagers were in school, 4.7 percent of Americans were foreign born. In 1990 the figure was 8.6 percent, while in 2040 it is predicted to be 14.2 percent.[9] Today's immigrants are primarily Asian or Hispanic, with increasing numbers coming from the Middle East. By the year 2020, the fastest-growing segment of the population will be the very old—those over age 80. Marriage is being postponed or not even considered, and over 25 percent of new births are occurring outside of marriage. The population is being divided into extremes, with the middle class shrinking and the numbers growing for those in "permanent" poverty and "permanent" affluence. This is especially true for African Americans; many well-educated professionals' lives are in sharp contrast with large numbers living under conditions as painful as anything known since the days of slavery.[10]

Many people find these changes threatening. One result has been an increase in incidents of racism on high school and college campuses. While those are the incidents that grab public attention, there have also been many incidents showing the development of friendship and understanding across cultural and ethnic lines. See Focus Box 4.5, Relating across Cultures. These are powerful books because they explore the edges where young people brush up against values and practices different from their own.

Among the most critically acclaimed books of the 1960s and early 1970s were Eldridge Cleaver's *Soul on Ice*, William H. Armstrong's *Sounder*, Maya Angelou's *I Know Why the Caged Bird Sings*, Sharon Bell Mathis's *A Teacup Full of Roses*, Alice Childress's *A Hero Ain't Nothin' but a Sandwich*, and Rosa Guy's *The Friends*. As powerful as these books were, they had a grimness to them, and the protagonists were mostly segregated from mainstream culture. It is refreshing today to have books in which a variety of characters from different backgrounds face problems by working together.

Cynthia Kadohata's *Weedflower* reveals a three-way relationship among Japanese families being sent to internment camps just before World War II, their "American" neighbors, and the Native Americans who manage the Poston Internment Camp where Sumiko's family is sent. This is the camp where Kadohata's father was sent and so she relates to it in a special way even though her story is fictional. Several internment camps were placed on Indian Reservations, but only at Poston were the Indians in charge.

Within a few days of being at the camp, Sumiko makes friends with a girl named Sachi, and together they go to look at the bean fields, which have been planted by people who arrived at the camp earlier. The green foliage is like a miracle in the dry desert. Suddenly Sachi hisses, "Shh! Hide!" Three Indian boys are

Bat 6 by Virginia Euwer Wolff. Scholastic, 1998. World War II has been over for nearly four years, but pockets of prejudice are very much alive in the towns of Barlow and Bear Creek Ridge in rural Oregon. People choose not to notice until the prejudice erupts during the annual Bat 6 girls' softball championship.

The Arrival by Shaun Tan. Scholastic, 2007. In this unusual graphic novel, which is wordless except for an invented alphabet, Tan uses sepia drawings to depict the emotions and the challenges faced by a man bringing his family to a new country. While there is a sense of fear, there is also a sense of warmth and caring for others.

Bone by Bone by Bone by Tony Johnston. Roaring Brook, 2007. Set in the 1950s in small-town Tennessee, this haunting novel tells about the friendship of two boys, white David, age nine, and black Malcolm, age eight. Readers will be left with a deeper understanding of how far we've come.

Born Blue by Han Nolan. Harcourt, 2001. Blue-eyed and blonde Janie is abandoned by her heroin-addicted mother. Her one friend is an African American boy who has a set of blues tapes that he and Janie listen to so often and so deeply that Janie decides she is African American.

Born Confused by Tanuja Desai Hidier. Scholastic, 2003. A summer of growing up has some interesting new angles when the protagonist is an Indian American.

Children of the River by Linda Crew. Delacorte, 1989. Crew's story is about seventeen-year-old Sundara's life in Oregon after fleeing the Khmer Rouge in Cambodia.

The Circuit: Stories from the Life of a Migrant Child by Francisco Jimenez. University of New Mexico Press, 1997. Even though this collection of autobiographical stories was published by a university press, which meant it received only limited publicity, within several years it was in its fifth printing.

Esperanza Rising by Pam Muñoz Ryan. Scholastic, 2000. Ryan's engaging novel about how her Mexican family became Americans is both joyous and lyrical. A *Publisher's Weekly* reviewer noted that only by the end of the story do readers recognize how carefully "Abuelita's pearls of wisdom" have been strung.

Jubilee Journey by Carolyn Meyer. Harcourt Brace, 1997. Going on a family trip from Connecticut to a small town in Texas proves to be educational for thirteen-year-old Emily Rose Chartier, who learns about both racism and her family.

Mister Pip by Lloyd Jones. Dial, 2007. It's in the early 1990s when there's a civil war on the island community of Bougainville. Thanks to one white teacher who stays because he's married to one of the natives, thirteen-year-old Matilda is in love with Charles Dickens's *Great Expectations,* but even this contributes to misunderstandings.

Seedfolks by Paul Fleischman. HarperCollins, 1997. Fleischman traces the sprouting of the Bigg Street community garden in inner city Cleveland through the voices of thirteen young and old neighbors—Mexican, Haitian, Black, Vietnamese, Korean, British, Guatemalan, Rumanian, Indian, and Polish.

Tasting the Sky: A Palestinian Childhood by Ibtisam Barakat. Farrar, 2007. Barakat was three years old in 1967 when her family fled their home as the six-day war broke out. She now lives in the United States and tells her story through childhood memories, which are being praised for their power and at the same time for their lack of sentimentality and exploitation.

Zack by William Bell. Simon & Schuster, 1999. It is Zack's senior year in high school and his family (a black mother and a white father) move from the city of Toronto to a small town where, for the first time, Zack stands out because of his color.

also exploring the bean field, and Sachi explains that "they're not supposed to be in our camp. If they catch us, we'll get scalped. . . . After they scalp us, they'll cut off our fingers and boil them."

Then, the girls hear a rattlesnake. Sachi screams and runs, but Sumiko trips on the vines and finds herself sitting "on her rear end a foot from the snake," which rises into the air and hisses. A calm voice says, "Walk back slowly. *Slowly.*

It doesn't want to hurt you," and someone from behind lifts her onto her feet and partly walks/drags her backward.

This is Sumiko's introduction to a boy called Frank. Over the months that Sumiko is in the camp she and Frank slowly develop a kind of respectful friendship, which on the day she leaves, he acknowledges by sharing with her his "Indian" name of "Huulus, which means 'lightning.'"

A multicultural book that older teens are reading is Khaled Hosseini's *The Kite Runner*, a book written by a young American immigrant from Afghanistan. It was published in 2003 as a book for general audiences. Even though it is fiction, readers can't help but believe that much of it is autobiographical as Hosseini writes about a young boy living in Kabul during the 1960s and 1970s and watching and adjusting to the changes that came to his country. The Nilsen family lived in Afghanistan between 1967 and 1969 and so, of course, we found the book especially meaningful because it was set at about the same time we were there. But Hosseini is such a good writer that as we think back on the book (we listened to a recorded version), we have in our minds vivid mental images from both California and Afghanistan.

It is expecting too much from any one book to think that its reading will change a bigoted bully into a sensitive and loving individual. However, for the majority of young readers such books can serve as conversation starters and as ways to focus needed attention on matters of hostility related to racial, ethnic, and class differences. It is good that some authors prefer to focus on the similarities among all people rather than on differences between particular groups. For example, African American author Lorenz Graham is quoted in Anne Commire's *Something about the Author* as saying

> My personal problem with publishers has been the difference between my image and theirs. Publishers have told me that my characters, African and Negro, are "too much like white people." And I say, "If you look closely, you will see that people are people."[11]

Jamake Highwater expresses a counterbalancing view:

> In the process of trying to unify the world we must be exceedingly careful not to destroy the diversity of the many cultures of man that give human life meaning, focus, and vitality. . . . Today we are beginning to look into the ideas of groups outside the dominant culture, and we are finding different kinds of "truth" that make the world we live in far bigger than we ever dreamed it could be—for the greatest distance between people is not geographical space but culture.[12]

Teachers, librarians, and reviewers should not present and discuss any single book as if it represents the African American point of view or the Asian American point of view. Adults need to help young readers realize that there are many points of view. This concept is further discussed in Chapter 10, along with the increased willingness of today's teenagers to read about protagonists in countries other than the United States.

The Physical Body

Among the books listed in Focus Box 4.1, Challenges: Physical and Mental, are several relating to sex, but we do not wish to imply that we consider the whole matter of sex to be a problem. We realize that sex also has something to do with the books in Focus Box 4.7, Love and Friendship (on p. 141). In trying to satisfy their curiosity, teenagers seek out and read vivid descriptions of sexual activities, as hinted at by the students in our survey who commented about liking particular magazine because of the "fine boys," or because of "learning about and talking about girls."

In the first edition of this textbook, we wrote that the three sexual issues treated in problem novels were rape, pregnancy, and homosexuality. We stand corrected by a reader who wrote to us and made the persuasive point that the problem is not homosexuality, but homophobia. In addition to these concerns, we now see problem novels treating disease, incest, and child abuse, and, in a big change, we also see teen protagonists being written about as parents. In the earlier books, pregnant girls had an abortion, as in Paul Zindel's *My Darling, My Hamburger*; the baby died as in Ann Head's *Mr. and Mrs. Bo Jo Jones*; or the baby was given up for adoption as in Richard Peck's *Don't Look and It Won't Hurt*. In today's books the babies actually appear as in the highly acclaimed *Make Lemonade* by Virginia Euwer Wolff, *Gypsy Davey* by Chris Lynch, and *Like Sisters on the Home Front* by Rita Williams Garcia. In *Hanging on to Max*, by Margaret Bechard, seventeen-year-old Sam is a single parent struggling to keep his infant son. *A School Library Journal* reviewer praised the book because "In a world where much of YA literature is fraught with noir plots peopled with dysfunctional characters caught in tragic situations, *Hanging on to Max* is a breath of fresh air."[13] It is a book "peopled with human beings all struggling to make their lives work." One of these people is Sam's father who agrees to support Sam and Max for one year if Sam will stay in high school and graduate.

The reason we refer to the problems that are the topics of the books in Focus Box 4.1 as both physical and mental is that the two usually go together. Several years ago when Paul Zindel was speaking in Arizona, he commented on the fact that next to *The Pigman*, his most popular book was *My Darling, My Hamburger*, which is about pregnancy and abortion. Soon after the book was published in 1969, a Supreme Court decision made most abortions legal, and Zindel thought that would be the end of all sales because his book would seem terribly old-fashioned. It did not turn out that way, however, because rather than settling the issue, the legalization of abortions increased interest in the moral and psychological aspects of the problem. Decision making was passed from the courts to every woman with an unwanted pregnancy. It is not only the woman herself who is involved, but also the father, the grandparents, and the friends.

In any area of life, it is hardly possible for someone to have a severe physical problem without also having an accompanying emotional problem. A vivid example is Priscilla Cummings's *A Face First*. It tells the story of twelve-year-old Kelley waking up from her affluent and "beautiful people" world to a Baltimore hospital's burn unit. She has been in a horrific automobile accident and fire, and experts are working to peel off the skin that melted, along with her earrings. Even worse than the pain and the physical therapy is the day when a clear mask is strapped onto her ruined face. In shock and depression, she ceases all human communication. But finally, she starts her long road to emotional recovery when she empathizes with a crying baby who is brought into the burn unit.

More Optimistic Novels

In one sense, all novels are problem stories because the problems provide the tension and the interest; without a problem there would be no plot. The difference in the books we will mention in this section is that the problems are not as grave as are the ones described earlier, and there is some force or some individual in the story who helps the young person through the experience. Authors frequently use nature or animals as the helper or the catalyst. Many children come to high school already familiar with such stories as Frances Hodgson Burnett's *The Secret Garden* and Kenneth Grahame's *The Wind in the Willows*. Animals play major roles in Allan Eckert's *Incident at Hawk's Hill*, Fred Gipson's *Old Yeller*, Sterling North's *Rascal*, Marjorie Rawlings's *The Yearling*, and Wilson Rawls's *Where the Red Fern Grows*. In many such stories, the animals are sacrificed as a symbol of the loss the young person undergoes in exchange for wisdom. Gordon Korman makes fun of this literary custom in his *No More Dead Dogs*, written for middle school readers, but fortunately some animals in stories live long, happy lives, providing companionship and even inspiration to the humans with whom they share the planet.

Jack London's *The Call of the Wild* is still enjoyed by many readers. More recent books in which animals have helped teens move forward in their understanding of life are Kathy Koja's *Straydog*, which is told through the voice of Rachel, a smart and angry loner who identifies with a fierce wild dog brought into the animal shelter where she volunteers. The theme of Cynthia Voigt's *A Solitary Blue* is established by Jeff Greene's looking at a beautiful blue heron in a Carolina marsh and then learning more about himself, his parents, and the way herons live. In Gary Paulsen's *Brian's Hunt*, Brian is hunting a bear, but if not for the help of his companion dog, Brian would have been the prey instead of the hunter. In Marilyn Halvorson's *Bull Rider*, sixteen-year-old Layne sneaks out to ride rodeo bulls even though his father was killed in a national championship. After Layne comes close to getting seriously injured, his grandfather agrees to help him develop the skills he needs.

A different kind of story is the one in which a young person is helped through a religious experience, as in Cynthia Rylant's *A Fine White Dust*. The book's title comes from the chalklike dust that gets on Pete's fingers when he handles the "little bitty pieces of broken ceramic" that used to be a cross he had painted in Vacation Bible School—back before he got so old that it was not cool to go any more. His best friend is a confirmed atheist, and he has "half-washed Christians for parents." Nevertheless, the summer that Preacher Man comes to town, "something religious" begins itching Pete, something that going to church could not cure.

Rylant's skill in developing Pete's character and revealing the depths of his emotions when he is saved and wooed and then betrayed by the Preacher Man won for her a well-deserved Newbery Honor Award. The twelve short chapters are almost an outline for a traditional quest story beginning with "Dust" and a sense of ennui, moving through "The Joy," "The Wait," and "Hell," and ending with "The Light" and "Amen." In the end, Pete decides that "The Preacher Man is behind me. But God is still right there, in front."

Books that unabashedly explore religious themes are relatively rare, which is one reason that Pete Hautman's *Godless*, discussed in Chapter 1 as an Honor List book, attracted such immediate attention. One reason for their rarity is that public schools and librarians fear spending taxpayer's money on religious material. Also, mainstream publishers fear cutting into potential sales by printing books with protagonists whose religious beliefs may offend or make readers uncomfortable. It has been easier for schools to include religious books with historical settings, such as Lloyd Douglas's *The Robe*, Scott O'Dell's *The Hawk That Dare Not Hunt by Day*, Elizabeth George Speare's *The Bronze Bow*, and Jessamyn West's *Friendly Persuasion*. Accepted also are books with contemporary settings that have proved themselves with adult readers—for example, Margaret Craven's *I Heard the Owl Call My Name*, Catherine Marshall's *A Man Called Peter*, and William Barrett's *Lilies of the Field*. In lamenting the shortage of young adult books treating religious themes, author Dean Hughes wrote

> We need to be careful that, in effect, we do not say to young people that they should be most concerned about pimples and clothes and dates and football games—or even sex. Part of being human is addressing oneself to questions about justice, creation, morality, and the existence of divinity.[14]

Patty Campbell made a similar point when she wrote that although nearly 60 percent of Americans attend some type of religious services, young adult fiction presents a world almost devoid of either personal or organized religious practices. "Where," she asks, "are the church youth groups, the Hebrew or confirmation classes, the Bible study meetings that are so much a part of middle-class teenage American life? Where, too, is the mainstream liberal Protestant or Catholic practice and sensibility?" Practically the only religious characters developed in young adult books are villains who are "presented as despicable in direct proportion to the degree of their religious involvement."[15]

Examples of the "despicable" characters she was thinking about include the fanatical and unbending parents who make life miserable for their kids in Suzanne Newton's *I Will Call It Georgie's Blues*; Norma Howe's *God, The Universe, and Hot Fudge Sundaes*; and Kathryn Lasky's *Memoirs of a Bookbat*. In Stephanie Tolan's *A Good Courage*, Tie-Dye's hippie mother ends up in a religious commune that forces Tie-Dye to take control of his own future, whereas in M. E. Kerr's *Is That You, Miss Blue?* the hypocritical attitudes of the faculty members at a religious school inspire the students to come to the aid of a teacher who is fired because she "believes." In Bette Greene's *The Drowning of Stephan Jones*, homophobic ministers are at the heart of the evil treatment of two gay men, while in Lois Ruby's *Miriam's Well*, religious leaders do not let Miriam receive medical help. Jane Yolen and Bruce Coville's *Armageddon Summer* is not only about religion gone awry but also about love and survival. Marina and Jed are two teenagers caught up among the 144 "True Believers" chosen by Reverend Beelson to wait with him in an armed camp for the end of the world, predicted to occur on July 27, 2000.

In many ways, the negative portrayal of religion in books for teenagers is similar to the negative portrayal of parents and other authority figures. Such presentations serve as a foil to make the good qualities of the young protagonists shine all the brighter. Authors rely on the general assumption that religious people are good to provide contrast, as when the evil in Robert Cormier's *The Chocolate War* is all the heavier because of the book's setting in a religious school.

Another reason that books for teenagers appear to have so many religious characters portrayed in a negative light is that the good characters go unnoticed. For example, in M. E. Kerr's *Little Little* one of Little Little's suitors is a dishonest evangelical preacher. When Kerr was criticized for this negative portrayal, she pointed out that Little Little's grandfather—the only person in the whole book who approached Little Little's dwarfism with common sense—was also a minister, but few readers noticed because he did his work in the manner expected from a competent clergyman in a mainstream church. Although there are some good books focusing on broad religious themes and questions about whether there is a God and an afterlife (e.g., Aidan Chambers's *NIK: Now I Know*, Iris Rosofsky's *Miriam*, and Phyllis Reynolds Naylor's *A String of Chances*), what is more common is for an author to bring in religion as a small part of a bigger story. In Jim Naughton's *My Brother Stealing Second*, Bobby reminisces about his family's church experiences before his brother was killed, and in Sue Ellen Bridgers's *Permanent Connections*, Rob finds comfort by visiting a little country church. Katherine Paterson, who has attended theological school and served as a missionary in China, includes both implicit and explicit religious references in her books, most directly in *Jacob Have I Loved* and *Bridge to Terabithia*. Her 1999 *Preacher's Boy* is set in rural Vermont between May 1899 and January 1900. The excitement of a new century is part of the story, but this excitement includes worries about Darwin's theory of evolution and what is predicted to be the end of the world.

Madeleine L'Engle was devout, and along with some other writers of fantasy and science fiction, includes religious overtones in her books; for example, the struggle between good and evil in *A Wrinkle in Time* and Vicky's hard-won acceptance of her grandfather's dying of leukemia in *A Ring of Endless Light*. Other books that include casual references to religious people and beliefs are Alice Childress's *Rainbow Jordan*, J. D. Salinger's *Franny and Zooey: Two Novellas*, Mary Stolz's *Land's End*, and Jill Paton Walsh's *Unleaving*. Chaim Potok's *The Chosen*, *My Name Is Asher Lev*, and *In the Beginning* show what it is to come of age in a Hasidic Jewish community. Cynthia Voigt's *David and Jonathan* asks questions about religious and cultural differences; Marc Talbert's *A Sunburned Prayer* is about eleven-year-old Eloy making a seventeen-mile pilgrimage on Good Friday to pray for his grandmother, who is dying of cancer.

Of course, religious publishing houses provide books focusing on religious themes, but these are seldom useful in schools because they are aimed directly at believers of a particular faith, and sometimes in their zeal to convert potential believers, the authors write polemics against other groups. Nevertheless, teachers and librarians are advised to visit religious bookstores to see the upscale marketing techniques currently in fashion. An especially troublesome group of books about religion are the books in which a misguided life is set right by an end-of-the-book conversion. Teachers hesitate to discuss the credibility of such stories because they fear that in the process of building up literary sophistication, they may tear down religious faith. Because so many people turn a blind eye, it is all the more important that educators seek out and support those authors and publishers who treat religious motifs with honesty as well as with respect for literary quality. We also need to help parents and other critics realize that strong religious feelings, including doubts, are part of the maturation process and that reading about the doubts that others have or about imperfections in organized religion does not necessarily destroy one's own faith.

Kathleen Beck, a young adult librarian in Colorado, wrote an article for *VOYA* in which she recommended "Young Adult Fiction for Questioning Christians."[16] Her article was responding to the comment of one of the members of her ecumenical congregation who had observed about the teen members, "They don't know all the answers, but they sure know all the questions." Among the books she recommended were Bruce Brooks's *Asylum for Nightface*, in which a boy develops his own religious faith based on the orderliness of the world and in spite of his "self-indulgent, yuppy parents"; Cynthia Voigt's *Tree by Leaf*, in which teenager Clothilde gets help in coming to terms with the wounds her father received fighting in World War I; Neal Shusterman's *What Daddy Did*, in which a boy begins to understand the complexities of forgiveness when he goes to live with his grandparents after his father had killed his mother; and Gary Schmidt's *The Sin Eater*, in which a boy is aided in understanding his father's suicide by the members of the Albion Grace Church of the Holy Open Bible, "whose theology is strict but who know the meaning of grace and compassion." In Han Nolan's *Send Me Down a Miracle*, M. E. Kerr's *What I Really Think of You*, and Gary Paulsen's *The Tent*, young people look questioningly at their parents' careers as evangelical preachers.

The Romantic Quest

The archetypal story of The Journey or The Quest as outlined by Joseph Campbell[17] is well illustrated in Cynthia Voigt's *Homecoming* series (see her write-up on p. 137), as well as in some of the books discussed in Chapter 10 and in Chapter 8 where we write about the experience of young American soldiers in Vietnam. These stories are especially appealing to young readers because many romantic symbols relate to youthfulness and hope, and many of the protagonists in traditional and classic tales are in their teens. They have reached the age at which they leave home or anticipate leaving to embark on a new way of life. Today, this is more likely to be called "moving out" than going on a romantic quest, but the results are much the same. Seeking and securing a "true love" usually, but not always, takes up a greater proportion of the time and energy of young adults than of middle-aged adults. And the exaggeration that is part of the romantic mode is quite honestly felt by teenagers. Robert Cormier once said that he began writing about young protagonists when he observed that in one afternoon at the beach his own children could go through what to an adult would be a whole month of emotional experiences.

A distinguishing feature of such romances is the happy ending, achieved only after the hero's worth is proven through a crisis or an ordeal. The suffering nearly always purchases some kind of wisdom, even though wisdom is not what the hero set out to find. Authors like to send young people on trips, not just for the symbolism of a quest, but because the trip provides the protagonists with a new environment, new challenges, and new acquaintances, all of which add interest. More than any other author, Sharon Creech has worked with journeys. For the last edition of this text, she wrote

> I love the way that each book—any book—is its own journey. You open the book, and off you go. You don't know who you're going to meet along the way, nor where you will go, and when you finish a book, you feel as if you've been on a journey. You are changed in some way—large or small—by having traveled with those characters, by having walked in their moccasins a while, by having seen what they've seen, heard what they've heard, felt what they've felt. These journeys echo all of our daily journeys: not knowing who we will meet today, tomorrow; who will affect our lives in small ways and profound ways; where we will go; what we will feel; what will happen to us.[18]

She went on to say that the journey motive extends to her writing process as well as to the way she builds her plots. In *Walk Two Moons*, which won the Newbery Medal, thirteen-year-old Sal takes a car trip with her grandparents from Ohio to Idaho. This is a gift of genuine love as they help Sal come to terms with the terrible question of what happened to her mother. *The Wanderer* is the name of a forty-five-foot sailboat in which a contemporary "family" crosses the Atlantic. The chapters alternate between Sophie and her cousin Cody. What lifts *The Wanderer* above a simple adventure tale is the subtle way that Creech develops the mystery of Sophie's past and the reason that her reluctant parents viewed this voyage as one of those things that Sophie "just had to do."

As you read the stories in Focus Box 4.6, Literal Journeys/Figurative Quests, notice the different ways that creative authors have figured out how to adapt ancient literary customs into modern life. For example, in traditional romances the protagonist usually receives the vision or insight in a high or isolated place like a mountain top, an island, or a tower. In Hamilton's *M. C. Higgins, the Great*, the boy, M. C., comes to his realization about his family and his role while he contemplates the surrounding countryside from a special bicycle seat affixed to the top of a tall steel pole standing in the yard of his mountain home. The unique pole was given to M. C. by his father as a reward for having swum across the Ohio River. Another characteristic is that the young person is shown to be "special," something that Robert Lipsyte communicated in *The Contender* by starting with Mr. Donatelli, the manager of a boxing gym, listening to the confident sound of young Alfred Brooks climbing the steps to his gym. Donatelli says he can tell who has what it takes to be a contender (readers are to interpret this as meaning a contender in life as well as in the boxing ring) by how they climb those stairs. Young heroes receive unexpected help as did Jerome in Bruce Brooks's *The Moves Make the Man*. Through a wager on his basketball skills, he won a railroad

Margaret A. Edwards Award
Winner (1995)

Cynthia Voigt, **A Writer Who Keeps on Learning**

Cynthia Voigt ties with Anne McCaffrey in being honored for the most books, a total of seven, including *Homecoming*; *Dicey's Song*; *A Solitary Blue*; *Building Blocks*; *The Runner*; *Jackaroo*; and *Izzy Willy-Nilly*. A surprising fact is that these seven are fewer than one-third of the books that Voigt has published. Besides having written more than a dozen independent novels, between 1973 and 1989 Voigt wrote six books about the Tillermans and their associates; one of which (*Dicey's Song*) won the 1983 Newbery Medal. Between 1985 and 1999, she wrote four fantasy stories in the Kingdom series, while between 1996 and 2006, she wrote the Bad Girl series about Mikey and Margolo, who are really more "inconvenient" than "bad." They are based on some of the students Voigt remembers from the years that she taught middle school.

Another surprising fact about Voigt's books was noted by Jaime Hylton in "Exploring the 'Academic Side' of Cynthia Voigt" in *The ALAN Review* (Fall 2005, pp. 50–55). Hylton wrote that "After nearly a quarter of a century, every book that Voigt has published is still in print." She went on to give credit for this happy event to the fact that Voigt does all that we expect from an excellent writer; plus she provides a richness that "transcends topical stories with teen-oriented, identity-focused themes." Hylton's thesis is that Voigt achieves this kind of transcendency by suffusing her books "with allegory, literary allusion, classical mythology, and traditional folk and fairy tales."

Hylton's observation sent us back to check out a Focus Box statement that Voigt wrote for the third edition of this textbook under the title of "Learning and Knowing." In it she explored "a central and an essential difference" between adults and young people. She said that the real difference between the two is that kids expect themselves to *be learning* while adults expect themselves *to know*. For herself, Voigt chooses to be in the kid category so that her "attitude towards experiences, people, the whole side show, is characterized by questions and curiosity," which will guarantee that she will keep changing and adding to herself—"perpet-ually growing up with no end in sight to the arduous and uneasy occupation."

At the beginning of *Izzy Willy-Nilly*, which is the story of a young girl who has been in an automobile accident and lost a leg, Voigt acknowledges learning a great deal from medical personnel who taught her about physical and mental aspects of amputation. And it is obvious that while writing *Come a Stranger* and *Building Blocks*, Voigt had to learn a lot about slavery and the Underground Railroad, and that while writing *David and Jonathan* she learned new things about the Holocaust. But as Hylton points out, the real power of Voigt's learning is in the uses she makes of her deep knowledge of the world as revealed through its great thinkers and writers. This is what keeps Voigt's books fresh and interesting year after year.

David and Jonathan is an allegorical story filled with biblical and Talmudic parables. In *Homecoming*, Voigt uses sailing as an extended metaphor, while in *The Runner*, she uses cross-country track. In *A Solitary Blue*, she builds the whole story around a glimpse of a blue heron that her protagonist, Jeff, gets. The heron, who is half-hidden in the marsh, seems to be all by herself, but as Jeff works his way toward an understanding of his two very different parents, he realizes that each of them has a place in his life. One of the things that helps him begin to accept both of his parents is his realization that the heron was not really solitary; herons build their nests in colonies "all of them together."

The literary allusions that Voigt uses to help put across her points range from Shakespeare's *Macbeth*, *The Tempest*, and *Hamlet* to Hemingway's *The Old Man and the Sea* and de Saint Exupéry's *The Little Prince*. In her later books, she includes pop culture references. Both Emily Dickinson and Judy Blume are alluded to in *Izzy, Willy-Nilly*, while one of Virginia Hamilton's books makes it into *Bad Girls*. Voigt's *Orfe* is a modern telling of the myth of Orpheus and Eurydice, while *Homecoming* has many similarities to the Greek myth of Odysseus. In an interesting reversal, Voigt puts females in the place of the traditional male heroes. ●

An Abundance of Katherines by John Green. Dutton, 2006. Colin Singleton is a budding genius but when he graduates from high school, he feels as though he's already wilting. So far he's had way too many girls—all named Katherine—give him the heave-ho, but as he and his buddy drive across the country, he finally meets a girl whose name is not Katherine.

Chasing Redbird by Sharon Creech. HarperCollins, 1997. Zinny does not travel far, only on an old Appalachian trail that she discovers and works to rebuild. Nevertheless, there's plenty to think about in this story of family relationships and young romance. Other Creech books based on journeys include *Bloomability* (HarperCollins, 1998), *Walk Two Moons* (HarperCollins, 1994), and *The Wanderer* (HarperCollins, 2000).

Defining Dulcie by Paul Acampora. Dial, 2006. When Dulcie's father dies, she and her mother move from Connecticut to California as a way of starting over. When it doesn't work for Dulcie, she takes the truck and in a somewhat mad-cap adventure drives back home. Although she learns that she cannot pick up the pieces of her old life, she nevertheless begins to heal.

Dunk by David Lubar. Clarion, 2002. Chad's trip is only to the Boardwalk in a Jersey beach town where he takes a summer job running a dunking tank. He learns some subtle lessons about the difference between using humor to insult and recruit potential customers and using a different kind of humor to help his best friend who is seriously ill.

Ghost Boy by Iain Lawrence. Random House, Delacorte, 2000. It is just after WWII and Harold Kline, a partially orphaned albino, becomes friends with three sideshow performers in a traveling circus. He thinks that joining the circus will solve his problems, and in ways it does, but mainly because of the lessons he learns about the difference between outside appearances and inside beauty.

Gingerbread by Rachel Cohn. Simon & Schuster, 2002. Gingerbread is the rag doll that Cyd's biological father, who was almost a stranger, gave her when she was five. Now as a teenaged "recovering hellion," she is sent from her San Francisco home to New York City to get acquainted with him and his family.

The Great Turkey Walk by Kathleen Karr. Farrar, Straus and Giroux, 1998. In this wish-fulfilling and lively quest story set in 1860, fifteen-year-old Simon Green becomes partners with his school teacher to buy 1,000 turkeys in Missouri, hoping to sell them to turkey-starved miners in Denver.

Homeless Bird by Gloria Whelan. HarperCollins, 2000. This winner of the National Book Award is set in India and is about thirteen-year-old Koly, who through an arranged marriage that turns out badly, is forced on a journey toward making a life for herself.

Hope Was Here by Joan Bauer. Putnam's, 2000. Sixteen-year-old Hope and her Aunt Addie leave New York City for promised jobs in Wisconsin—Addie as a cook and Hope as a waitress. They find their jobs—and much more. *Rules of the Road* (1998), along with its companion book, *Best Foot Forward* (2005) and *Backwater* (1999), all from Putnam, are also highly recommended Bauer books in which journeys play a role.

A Long Way from Chicago (1998) and *A Year Down Yonder* (2000) by Richard Peck. Dial/Penguin Putnam. These books, one of which won the Newbery Medal, are set during the Great Depression when Mary Alice is sent to live in rural Illinois with her larger-than-life grandmother.

Many Stones by Carolyn Coman. Front Street, 2000. Berry and her father travel to South Africa to attend a memorial service for Berry's older sister, who was killed while working at a church school in Cape Town. The title comes from the stones that Berry places on her chest each night, one at a time, to calm her troubled mind.

The Orpheus Obsession by Dakota Lane. HarperCollins/Katherine Tegen Books, 2005. Sixteen-year-old Anooshka Stargirl lives in a small town in New York State, but when she goes to New York City to visit her older sister, ZZ Moon, she gets introduced to a twenty-one-year-old singer called Orpheus. She pores over his website and develops an obsession for him.

True Confessions of a Heartless Girl by Martha Brooks. Farrar/Melanie Kroupa Books, 2003. A plot summary would make this book seem grimmer than it is. Brooks's main point is to demonstrate the power of community in the process of healing.

Whirligig by Paul Fleischman. Holt, 1998. This is a perfect story to show how a journey provides time for reflection and growth. A boy who in a fit of rage causes an automobile accident that kills a girl sets out on a journey to memorialize her in each corner of the United States.

lantern that he named Spin Light. It enabled him to go to a hidden, lonely court and play basketball after dark, which also enabled him to see more than his way around the basketball court.

The idea of a sacrifice is shown in Jean George's *Julie of the Wolves* when Julie learns that her father still lives and that she has arrived at his village. When she learns that he has married a "gussack" and now pilots planes for hunters, the disillusioned Julie grieves for the wolves and the other hunted animals and vows to return and live on the tundra. However, the temperature falls far below zero and the "ice thundered and boomed, roaring like drumbeats across the Arctic." Despite all that Julie does to save him, Tornait, Julie's golden plover, who has been her faithful companion, dies from the cold. Tornait is the last symbol of Julie's innocence, and as she mourns his death, she comes to accept the fact that the lives of both the wolves and her people are changing, and she points her boots toward her father and the life he now leads.

Success is demonstrated in Chris Crutcher's *The Crazy Horse Electric Game*, in which pitching star Willie Weaver is seriously injured in a water skiing accident. He runs away from home when it appears that he is also losing his girlfriend. At first he is only concerned with surviving, but then he gets involved with other people and attends an alternative school where, with help, he recovers many of his motor skills. He returns home strong enough to cope with all the changes that have occurred.

Some critics fear that when authors use such physical changes as Willie Weaver's almost miraculous recovery as a tangible or metaphorical way to communicate emotional or mental accomplishment, young readers interpret the physical achievement literally rather than figuratively. Teenagers are already overly concerned about their bodies and any defects they might have. Many physical challenges, including the common motif of obesity, cannot be totally overcome, so these critics prefer stories in which the protagonist comes to terms with the problem as does Izzy in Cynthia Voigt's *Izzy Willy-Nilly*, about a young girl who loses her leg, and the young Native American boy in Anne Eliot Crompton's historical *The Sorcerer*. The boy is named Lefthand because he was injured by a bear and cannot hunt. In his tribe, this is a serious problem, because hunting is what the men do. There is no miraculous cure for his disability, but he gains both his own and his tribe's respect when he develops enough skill as an artist to draw the pictures of animals needed for the tribe's hunting rituals.

The acceptance of the compromised dream is an element of the romantic quest particularly meaningful to teenagers who are just beginning to achieve some of their goals and to discover the illusory nature of the end of the rainbow, which is a symbolic way of saying such things as, "When I graduate," "When we get married," "When I'm eighteen," or "When I have my own apartment." Like the characters in the romances, they are not sorry they have ventured, for they have indeed found something worthwhile, but it is seldom the pot of gold they had imagined.

Stories of Friendship and Love

When people hear the term *romance*, their first thought is usually of a love story, which with young readers probably includes friendship as well as love. This is because in the old romances, which were stories coming from such romance languages as Latin, Italian, Spanish, and especially French, the climax of the story was often the uniting of a young couple. A common motif was for successful adventurers to be rewarded with the love of a beautiful maiden. While few of us have the ability or the means to go on a grand adventure or to compete and win against incredible odds, most of us can imagine finding a true love. Because of the universality of this wish to love and be loved, this element of adventure stories became the feature that many readers, especially females, came to identify with the term *romance*. The challenge or problem is invariably the successful pairing of a likable young couple. An old definition of the love-romance pattern is, "Boy meets girl, boy loses girl, boy wins girl." But with teenage love, the pattern is often reversed because most of the romances are told from the girls' point of view. She is the one who meets, loses, and finally wins a boy.

The tone of most love romances, see Focus Box 4.7, Love and Friendship, is lighter than that of the adventure romance. Its power lies in its wish fulfillment, although critics worry that we may be setting young girls up for disappointment when we consistently reward girls who have had a disappointment or who have worked their way through a difficult time with a boyfriend who appears out of nowhere. They also worry about the stories in which an ugly duckling girl is suddenly transformed by the love of a boy into a swan. In her new role as swan, she is not only popular but also happy.

For the writer of a love story, probably no talent is more important than the ability to create believable characters. If readers do not feel that they know the boy and girl or the man and woman as individuals, they cannot identify with them, and consequently will not care whether they make it. Another characteristic of the good love story is that it provides something beyond the simple pairing of two individuals. This something extra may be interesting historical facts, introduction to a social issue, glimpses into the complexity of human nature, or any of the understandings and concepts that might be found in quality books or movies.

Although most formula romances are aimed at a female audience, comparable to the way that most pornography is aimed at a male audience, some writers are trying to write romances that will also be read by boys. The most obvious difference between these boy-oriented romances and the larger body of love stories written from a girl's point of view is that their authors, who are mostly men, tend to put less emphasis on courtship and romance and more on sexuality. Rather than relying on discreet fade-outs, they allow their readers to know what happens, which sometimes means sexual intercourse. For the most part, the descriptions are neither pornographic nor lovingly romantic, but in such books as Chris Crutcher's *Running Loose*, Robert Lehrman's *Juggling*, Terry Davis's *Vision Quest*, and Aidan Chambers's *The Toll Bridge*, there is little doubt about the abundance of sexual feelings that the characters experience.

As an antidote to the lopsidedness of books that are either overly romantic or overly sexy, some adult critics suggest offering books in which boys and girls are as much friends as lovers. This is especially true in lighter books read by tweeners where the romantic relationship is only part of a bigger story. Also, neither partner exploits or manipulates the other, as often happens in exaggerated romances or in pornographic or sex-oriented stories. As a ploy to attract male

Freak the Mighty by Rodman Philbrick. Scholastic, 1993. Opposites attract in this heartwarming but sad story about a "giant" and a "midget" who become the best of friends.

Cold Sassy Tree by Olive Ann Burns. Ticknor & Fields, 1984. Teenagers like this book that was published for adults and made into a successful film. It is the story of Will Tweedy's growing up, as well as his grandfather's love story.

Heart on My Sleeve by Ellen Wittlinger. Simon and Schuster, 2004. The author of the Printz Honor Book *Hard Love* uses emails, postcards, IMs, and regular old letters to tell the story of Chloe and Julian's spring and summer relationship after they meet when Chloe is on a trip to scout out a college.

If Beale Street Could Talk by James Baldwin. Doubleday, 1974. In this mature story told in frank, black English, pregnant Tish loves Fonny, who has been jailed on a false charge.

If You Come Softly by Jacqueline Woodson. Putnam, 1998. This story of love between a white girl and a black boy was chosen as one of the top-ten books of 1998 by the Young Adult Library Services Association.

My Heartbeat by Garret Freymann-Weyr. Houghton, 2002. Fourteen-year-old Ellen has a crush on her brother's best friend, but things get complicated when she finds out that her brother and his friend are more than friends. Nevertheless, she and the friend go ahead with their own sexual relationship and readers are left to ponder the difficulties of trying to put people in boxes.

The Plain Janes by Cecil Castellucci, illus. by Jim Rugg. Minx, 2007. This amusing and quirky graphic novel is about the friendship of four girls who all feel like misfits until they form their secret club, the Plain Janes. This may be just the book to convince regular readers of realistic YA fiction that graphic novels can have their own kind of power.

Prom by Laurie Halse Anderson. Viking, 2005. Readers were happily surprised to learn that the author of such a serious book as *Speak* could also write a lighthearted

and humorous book about Ashley and what she does to save the prom—all because it means so much to Nat, her best friend. The trouble started when a dishonest teacher stole the prom money and most people were ready to give up.

Son of the Mob by Gordon Korman. Hyperion, 2002. Seventeen-year-old Vince Luca, whose father could easily be part of the Sopranos, usually manages to stay out of his father's business ventures, but then he falls in love with the daughter of an FBI agent.

The True Meaning of Cleavage by Mariah Fredericks. Atheneum/S & S, 2003. A reviewer for *VOYA* compared Fredericks's book to Judy Blume's *Forever*, but predicted that this one would escape the censor's sword because it is filled with chuckles minus graphic descriptions.

The Unlikely Romance of Kate Bjorkman by Louise Plummer. Delacorte Press, 1995. Kate Bjorkman is a high school senior who is six feet tall and much too smart and too funny to write a typical romance, but that's what makes this first-person story refreshing.

Vote for Larry by Janet Tashjian. Holt, 2004. In this sequel to *The Gospel According to Larry* (Holt, 2001), seventeen-year-old Josh Swenson comes back (he had committed *pseudocide* by faking the death of his online alter ego, Larry) to work with his friend, Beth, in hopes of mobilizing young voters and getting them to reject the commercialism that surrounds them.

When Zachary Beaver Came to Town by Kimberly Willis Holt. Henry Holt, 1999. It is the 1970s and the world is thinking about Vietnam, but thirteen-year-old Toby is much more interested in Zachary Beaver, a boy billed as the fattest boy in the world, who gets left by his manager in the parking lot of the neighborhood bowling alley.

Who Am I without Him? Short Stories about Girls and the Boys in Their Lives by Sharon G. Flake. Hyperion, 2004. Flake's stories aren't all wish-fulfilling; instead, she makes girls take a second look at what they are willing to give up to please the boys.

---

readers (publishers already feel confident that girls will read romances), authors often tell the story through the boy's eyes or perhaps through chapters that alternate back and forth between the boy and the girl, as Paul Zindel did in *The Pigman* and M. E. Kerr did in *I'll Love You When You're More Like Me*. Zindel

While many realistic books are problem novels, popular authors including Polly Horvath, Louis Sachar, Gary Paulsen, and M. E. Kerr use humor to bring smiles in between the solemn parts.

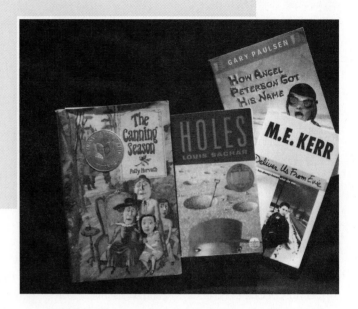

told us that he wrote his books for girls to read, but he always kept in mind the fact that girls recommend books to their boyfriends, and he did not want those girls to be disappointed when their boyfriends didn't like the book. He therefore tried to avoid including things that would be an automatic turn-off to boys. If more authors followed his example, we would probably have more "love stories" that could be appreciated by readers of both sexes.

Wish-Fulfilling Stories

The most wish-fulfilling stories for males are most likely to be the sports and adventure stories found in Chapter 6, while for females wish-fulfilling stories are usually about friendship or love. Especially for young teens, friendship books are more appealing than love stories because they are free from the complications of sex. It was the friendships that a decade ago kept many girls reading the Babysitters Club and the Sweet Valley High series. A few years ago in one of our classes, Ann Brashares's *The Sisterhood of the Traveling Pants* turned into "The Sisterhood of the Traveling Book." While no males borrowed it, the women passed it from friend to friend, even to roommates not taking the class. When we asked for it back, there was always one more student wanting to read it. The book is a coming-of-age story in four parts. Lena, Tibby, Bridget, and Carmen have been "best friends" ever since their mothers took the same aerobics class for pregnant women. By the time the mothers begin drifting apart, the girls are old enough to maintain their own close friendship, and the book opens with them being in high school and getting ready for the first summer they will be apart. Carmen had purchased a pair of jeans at a thrift shop, and as the girls gather to help Carmen pack (she's the first to leave, going to South Carolina to spend the summer with her divorced father), each one playfully tries on the pants. Even though the four friends have different body builds, they are happily surprised to find that the pants "fit" and, in fact, make each girl feel elegantly fashionable. Carmen had offered to give the pants to whoever wanted them, but now everybody wants them and so the girls come up with the idea of taking turns. Each one will have the pants for a few weeks.

Part of the charm of the book is Brashares's writing, which lends credibility and interest to the four stories, but more important are the wish-fulfilling aspects of the supportive friendship. All of the girls experience rough times: Lena in Greece with her grandparents; Bridget at soccer camp in Baja, California; and Tibby staying home with her first real job in a discount store. The supportive friendship of the girls, as symbolized through the traveling pants and shown through their letters, notes, and candid observations, helps them survive and, in some ways, thrive.

Ever since the biblical story of David and Jonathan, we have had stories about boys' friendships. It is a refreshing change to read about girls helping each other. And because readers came to know and like the girls, it was to be expected that Brashares would continue their story, which she did in 2003 with *The Second Summer of the Sisterhood*, in 2005 with *The Third Summer of the Sisterhood*, and in 2007 with the final book *Forever in Blue: The Fourth Summer of the Sisterhood*. The success of the 2005 film also helped to garner readers, but in relation to the third and fourth books we did hear some worries from junior high teachers who felt uncomfortable about twelve- and thirteen-year-old girls racing through the series, which ends with the girls being away at college and having mature sexual experiences.

Author Meg Cabot came up with the ultimate in wish-fulfilling stories when she created The Princess Diaries series about five-foot-nine, flat-chested Mia Thermopolis, who suddenly learns that she is a real princess and is heir to the throne of the small but wealthy European country of Genovia. The books are frivolous and fun "diaries," of Meg's experiences as she trains to be a princess. The books have been best sellers and led Cabot to also write *All-American Girl*, the story of how Samantha (aka Sam) Madison, the awkward middle daughter in an upper-

The best story that Ann Brashares told when she came to Tempe's Changing Hands Bookstore to promote Forever in Blue: The Fourth Summer of the Sisterhood *was about her mother's passing a display of* Traveling Pants *books in a New York bookstore and confiding to a nearby clerk, "Those are my daughter's books!" The clerk responded with, "Mine too. How old is your daughter? Mine is fourteen."*

Margaret A. Edwards Award
Winner (2008)
Orson Scott Card, **A Writer with Talent and Versatility**

When the American Library Association announced that it was honoring Orson Scott Card with the 2008 Award, specifically for *Ender's Game* and *Ender's Shadow,* the committee praised him for writing two books that "continually capture the imagination and interest of teens." Tor published *Ender's Game* in 1985 and *Ender's Shadow* in 1999, with the later book being not a sequel but a companion book because it tells the same story except from the perspective of Bean, a boy who becomes Ender's friend and helper.

Ender's Game is set in a somewhat vague future time when humans fear another attack from the insect-like buggers. Seventy years earlier, a military genius in Earth's army saved the world, and military leaders are now looking for one more child genius who can be trained to repeat the act. Peter and Valentine Wiggin have the military genius but the wrong temperament to be the proper choice. However, their little brother Andrew, who is called Ender because that's how his two-year-old sister pronounces his name, has both the temperament and the genius. Government officials take him to Battle School in hopes that he will be the one to prevent the attack that seems imminent.

The announcement that the American Library Association had chosen Card as the 2008 winner was made on January 14, which coincided with the first day of our young adult literature class in the spring semester. We always start a new semester with students introducing themselves by telling about a favorite book, one that has meant something in their lives. This year one of the first students spoke lovingly about how much she, along with the rest of her family, loved *Ender's Game* and *Ender's Shadow*. Her concluding comment was that her older brother had just come back from two years in Poland and the only souvenirs—the only thing Polish—that he brought back were *Ender's Game* and *Ender's Shadow* translated into Polish.

It was fun to tell the class that just that morning the American Library Association, which was meeting in Philadelphia, had announced that Card was being honored for the very books that the student's brother had brought home from Poland. The conversation reminded other students of Card favorites, including ones that they or their spouses have gone on to read as adults. The next day a graduate student stopped by and reminded us of how prescient she had been when in our Symbols and Archetypes class she had written her paper on the "Duality of the Warrior/Destroyer Archetype" in the two Ender books. But perhaps a more interesting point she made was that gifted children love the Ender books because Card so skillfully shows his characters grappling with a desire for belonging while at the same time being "different."

Card is a man of many talents and many ambitions. To get a hint of his wide-ranging interests check out his website at www.hatrack.com/osc/about-more.shtml. He has written nearly three dozen plays, and if not for his love of drama, we might never have had his science fiction. One reason is that by writing plays and hearing his words spoken on stage he developed an awareness of how careful he had to be to keep his words from being misinterpreted by the reader. The other reason is more mundane. After college, he took a job as a copy editor, but in his spare time he established a theater company that performed on an outdoor, public stage that had been built during the Depression in Provo, Utah. The company did fine during the summer when they did not have to pay rent, but when winter came their expenses increased and debts piled up. Card knew he could never pay the debts from his modest salary and so he gave himself another part-time job of writing and selling science fiction.

When the short story that eventually turned into *Ender's Game* was accepted, the editor wanted to use the title "Professional Soldier," but even though Card was desperate to sell the story he insisted on keeping the title of "Ender's Game." He had devised the boy's name and the story title so as to make readers think about the "endgame" in chess. Fortunately the name also works for people who play more football than chess because it is reminiscent of an "end run." and as one of the boys says when he first meets Ender at school, "Not a bad name here. Ender. Finisher. Hey," which is exactly what Ender turns out to be when he plays the all-important video game named *The End of the World*."

class family, happens to save the life of the president of the United States and then have his son fall in love with her.

Today most adults are so pleased to see young people reading anything at all that they won't complain at girls who are reading one-sided love stories or such romanticized books as the Princess Diaries or *All-American Girl*. But still it requires restraint not to point out that such stories aren't very realistic. If we do that, we run the risk of insulting the reader because young people are as sensitive as anyone else to hints that they are gullible and lacking in taste and sophistication. Of course they don't really expect to suddenly become real-life princesses or to "go down in history" by having "David + Sam" carved into a windowsill of the White House. It is nevertheless fun to see how many things they have in common with someone who just might do these things. And as shown by the line in a review for The Princess Diaries published on Amazon.com by a Toronto teenager, "This book was, I think, one of the cutest little reads I have ever read," young people are aware of the difference between *little reads* and *big reads*.

One of the points we made in Chapter 1, where we outlined the stages of developing literary appreciation, is that throughout life people keep reading at all the different levels. No one wants to read seriously taxing material all the time. It is our job to surround young readers with many books of different types and to give them time and encouragement to read a wide variety. Virtually all of the studies that have been made of people who read widely and with pleasure and understanding, shows that in their lives they have done a fair amount of "pleasure reading."

Concluding Comments

The books written about in this chapter make up the large body of what the general public views as young adult literature. Such books will undoubtedly continue to be published, but, as we demonstrated in Chapter 3, adolescent literature does not exist in a vacuum separate from the literature of the rest of the world. One reason that the creators of the Printz Award did not specify criteria other than "the best" book of each year, is that they did not want to limit the creativity of authors for young adults. As producers of realistic books try not to repeat themselves while at the same time plucking psychic strings that remain untouched by superficial media stories, they are pulled in the same directions as writers for adults. Many of them are rejecting boundaries between realism and fantasy. Annette Curtis Klause, in her 1990 *The Silver Kiss*, created a vampire ghost to help Zoë adjust to her mother's death. Robert Cormier in his 1988 *Fade* wrote about the struggles of young Paul Moreaux, who through his inherited ability to be invisible begins to understand the difference between good and evil. Francesca Lia Block focuses on such problems as loneliness, alienation, sexual confusion, and love, but she accepts wholeheartedly the deconstructionist idea of creating her own world and then working within it. Readers who are puzzled or troubled by her books are usually those accustomed to looking for a kind of "realism" that can be tested against their own observations or against statistics of probability. This does not work for the many writers who are now experimenting with stretching their readers' imaginations by writing in the style of everyday realism and then slipping in fantasy elements as does Stephenie Meyer with her popular books *Twilight*, *New Moon*, and *Eclipse*, which have all the characteristics of the modern, realistic problem novel, along with some very "real" vampires and werewolves. Authors are incorporating multiple genres in their pieces as they lead readers directly from the consideration of serious everyday problems into magical realism. A contributing factor to such changes is the new freedom that authors feel to mix art work and story as in Peter Sis's *The Wall: Growing Up Behind the Iron Curtain* and Brian Selznick's *The Invention of Hugo Cabret: A Novel*.

These various examples of imaginative stories will be further discussed in later chapters. We mention them here to illustrate that the lines between genres are fading, and while we, along with many readers, continue to appreciate well-done realistic books, we are at the same time pleased to realize that the field is not standing still. Many of today's writers are finding new ways to treat old stories.

Notes

1. G. Robert Carlsen, "Bait/Rebait: Literature Isn't Supposed to Be Realistic," *English Journal* 70 (January 1981): 8.
2. Marc Aronson, *Exploding the Myths: The Truth about Teenage Reading* (Scarecrow Press, 2001), p. 20.
3. Tyrrell Burns, *School Library Journal*, August 2002, p. 197.
4. Kathleen Beck, *VOYA* 25:3 (August 2002): 197.
5. *VOYA* 25:6 (February 2003): 437.
6. Joel Shoemaker, *School Library Journal,* April 2003, p. 166.
7. Michael Cart, *Necessary Noise: Stories about Our Families as They Really Are* (Joanna Cotler/HarperCollins, 2003), p. x.
8. Michael Cart, pp. x, xiii.
9. "Immigrant Impact Grows on U. S. Population," *Wall Street Journal*, March 16, 1992.
10. George Keller, director of Strategic Planning for the University of Pennsylvania, outlined these changes in a workshop at Arizona State University, February 24, 1992.
11. Anne Commire, *Something about the Author*, Vol. 1 (Gale Research, 1971), pp. 122–123.
12. Jamake Highwater, *Many Smokes, Many Moons* (Lippincott, 1978), pp. 13–14.
13. *School Library Journal*, May 2002, p. 146.
14. Dean Hughes, "Bait/Rebait: Books with Religious Themes," *English Journal* 70 (December, 1981): 14–17.
15. Patty Campbell, "The Sand in the Oyster," *The Horn Book Magazine* (September/October 1994): 619.
16. Kathleen Beck, "I Believe It, I Doubt It: Young Adult Fiction for Questioning Christians," *VOYA* 21:2 (June 1998): 103–104.
17. Joseph Campbell, *A Hero with a Thousand Faces* (Princeton University Press, 1968), pp. 145–156.
18. Sharon Creech, "On Journeys in Literature," in *Literature for Today's Young Adults* by Alleen Pace Nilsen and Kenneth L. Donelson (Longman, 2001), p. 149.

Poetry, Drama, Humor, and New Media

The genres in this chapter are primarily social, and for the most part are shared orally, being transferred to paper mainly for safekeeping and preservation. Poetry, drama, and humor all existed before the printing press, and if we want students to enjoy them for their emotional impact, as well as for their intellectual content, we need to do whatever we can to bring them alive through talk and oral presentations. In the section on New Media we are writing briefly about comics, graphic novels, manga, animation, DVDs, and video games. And with these latter items, many of the stories being told are basic—even primitive—in contrast to the high-tech equipment through which they are being shared.

A New Day for Poetry

One of the happiest surprises we had when we tabulated the results of our survey was that 155 out of 266 respondents had written a poem within the last two years. Sixty-four had acted in a play, and twenty-seven had attended a poetry slam, although one boy apologized that it "was just in school." It's mostly older teens and college students who attend "real" poetry slams (or jams) at bars, coffee houses, and theaters, but schools and libraries also host such events and students seem to have positive reactions to such experiences.

A *Time* magazine article (September 13, 1999), "Who Are the New Beat Poets? Hint: They're Blue," told how the Chicago police department began sponsoring poetry readings in local station houses in hopes of establishing better relations with teenagers. While teenagers as well as invited professional poets were the main participants, police officers also began stepping forward to share their thoughts. The article quoted Officer Linda Griffith:

> He allows me to walk the danger,
> He lets me extend help to a stranger,
> My flesh crawls and I miss him when he's not under my wing.
> I don't let people see or touch him, it's a private thing.
> So you should be grateful and understand what I've done.
> If and when I let you touch the butt of my gun.

A surprising best seller of the 1990s was Lori M. Carlson's *Cool Salsa: Bilingual Poems on Growing Up Latino in the United States*. In 2005, she followed up with *Red Hot Salsa: Bilingual Poems on Being Young and Latino in the United States*. The poems are in both Spanish and English by such well-known poets as Gary Soto, Martín Espada, and José Antonio Burciaga, plus she included a few written by teenagers in New York City's public schools.

In speaking about *Cool Salsa*, editor Marc Aronson gave part of the credit for its success to the fact that Carlson had found hip poems in three languages: English, Spanish, and Spanglish. He then explained:

> Poetry has been out of favor in America for a good long time. It was seen as either incredibly boring, or impossibly difficult to understand. Neither made it a good match for teenagers. But that has changed. The popularity of rap music has made adolescents very conscious of the power of words, rhythm, and rhyme. The revival of the Beat poets as emblems of rebellion, sexuality, and coolness has encouraged teenagers to drink espresso, grow beards, read Kerouac, and recite their own poetry.[1]

Sarah Flowers, a librarian in Santa Clara County, California, gives some of the credit for the new enthusiasm for poetry to two recent poet laureates: Robert Pinsky and Billy Collins.[2] When, in the late 90s, Pinsky was Poet Laureate he started the Favorite Poem Projects, in which Americans shared their favorite poems and told why they liked them or how they related to their lives. *The News Hour with Jim Lehrer* on National Public Television regularly showcased these three- to six-minute presentations. Twenty-seven of these presentations, many featuring young people, are available on a DVD, *An Invitation to Poetry* (Legacy Productions, Inc., 2004), edited by Pinsky and Maggie Dietz.

When Billy Collins was the Poet Laureate between 2001 and 2003, he initiated the Poetry 180 project, hoping to bring a poem a day to American classrooms (see www.loc.gov/poetry/180). Another good DVD to bring into class is *Billy Collins: On the Road with the Poet Laureate* (Checkerboard Film Foundation, 2003). It briefly mentions the Poetry 180 project, but most of it shows Collins giving readings and talking to college students. Flowers describes his poems as "nonthreatening but meaty." For example, "The Lanyard" is about a boy making a lanyard at summer camp and giving it to his mother as a gift. As he explains on screen, writing about his mother was "too big, too difficult," but Collins could write a poem about "a little thing like a lanyard," and in doing so, say something important about his relationship with his mother.

Other DVDs that Flowers recommended are *The Poetry Lounge: Self-Expression Through the Spoken Word* (distributed by Home Vision Cinema/Public Media, Inc.), *Russell Simmons Presents Def Poetry Season 3* (distributed by HBO, Inc.), *Furious Flower II*, a three-part program about African American poetry (distributed by California Newsreel), and a new DVD version of the 1982 film *Poetry in Motion* (distributed by Home Vision Cinema). These were all given a thumbs-up by the Young Adult Library Services Association media review committee, where Flowers served for four years.

One of the jobs of the Poet Laureate, who is appointed by the Librarian of Congress, is to promote poetry in the United States. Charles Simic, a Serbian American Pulitzer Prize–winning poet, was appointed the fifteenth Poet Laureate in the summer of 2007. In an August 5 interview on National Public Radio, he was asked for his plans. He laughingly said he hadn't decided but that people were already sending him ideas. The best so far was that anyone who wrote a really heartfelt love poem to a spouse, lover, or pet should get a tax break. And then, as an add-on, he suggested that any spouse, lover, or pet who listens to the love poem should also get a tax break.

New poetry books are as varied as are these DVDs. Books that represent the increased awareness of the world at large include, for example, *A Thousand Peaks: Poems from China* by Siyu Liu and Orel Protopopescu. Thirty-five poems are selected from two millennia of Chinese literature, each with its own illustrated page, along with prose explanations including information about selected Chinese characters and the challenges of translation. *The Poet Slave of Cuba: A Biography of Juan Francisco Manzano*, by Margarita Engle, was described by the *School Library Journal* reviewer as "an absolutely lovely book about the unlovely subject of slavery." It is another example of how the formality of poetry can give readers the distance they need to continue reading a truly sad story.

Engle's book is representative of the popular new genre of telling stories through free-verse poetry (see Focus Box 5.1, Stories Told through Free-Verse Poetry). So is Jen Bryant's 2000 *Pieces of Georgia*. Georgia's artist mother named her after artist Georgia O'Keefe, but when her mother died and her broken-hearted father emotionally abandons her, Georgia isn't sure she can continue her artistic endeavors. She is shocked to be assigned to weekly meetings with the school counselor, but she nevertheless accepts the notebook that the counselor gives her with the instructions, "Write down what you might tell, or what you might ask, your mother if she were here."

A Bad Boy Can Be Good for a Girl, by Tanya Lee Stone, might be read as a companion book to Laurie Halse Anderson's *Speak*. Three high school girls—a freshman, a senior, and a junior—are all courted by the same hot jock, only to be dropped when his lusts are satisfied. Josie, a happy and confident freshman, was first. In her disappointment, she checks out Judy Blume's *Forever*, and when she finds a few blank pages at the back of the book, she writes her story, which is later added to by Nicolette, the junior, and Aviva, the senior. In some new books, poetry plays a role in the plot as with Ron Koertge's *Shakespeare Bats Cleanup*. Koertge is a humorous writer who tells the story of a baseball player sidelined by a bad case of mononucleosis. Out of boredom as he waits to get well enough to play ball again, he starts messing around with poetry and looking for words "like some guy pawing through his sock drawer/for a pair that matched."

Fortune's Bones: The Manumission Requiem by Marilyn Nelson. Front Street, 2004. Nelson tells the true story of a slave who in the late 1700s was owned by a Connecticut doctor. When he died, the doctor dissected his body and boiled down the bones to use for anatomy studies. Nelson's rich telling of this unique story could be an effective reader's theater production.

Frida: Viva la Vida! by Carmen T. Bernier-Grand, Marshall Cavendish, 2007. Free-verse poems, each paired with one of Frida Kahlo's paintings, do a good job of introducing a new generation to this famous Mexican painter.

Heartbeat by Sharon Creech. HarperCollins, 2004. Middle school readers will enjoy the rhythm of the verses in this story of twelve-year-old Annie who loves to run, not to win a race, but to feel the earth and sky.

Hoop Kings by Charles R. Smith, Jr. Candlewick, 2004. Shaq O'Neal's shoe sole (actual size) is featured as a fold-out in this gorgeous book of sports poems. The pages feature twelve super-heroic basketball players with equally vibrant poems.

Locomotion by Jacqueline Woodson. Putnam's, 2003. Woodson uses a teen voice to create the free verse, the sonnets, and the haiku that tell Lonnie's story as he moves through group and teen homes.

Make Lemonade by Virginia Euwer Wolff (Holt, 1993), winner of the National Book Award, was one of the earliest books in which the author lent dignity to a problem novel by using a spacious free-verse format. In the sequel, *True*

Believer (2001), LaVaughn's horizons extend beyond her neighborhood, but she does not lose her determination.

Out of the Dust by Karen Hesse. Scholastic, 1996. In diary-like entries, Billie Jo tells how her dreams get lost in the swirling winds of the 1930s Oklahoma dustbowl. The book won the Newbery Medal.

Split Image by Mel Glenn. Morrow/HarperCollins, 2000. Poems from observers show how Laura Li, a dutiful Asian daughter, has a hard time figuring out how to manage her heritage and her new life. Glenn's other poetic stories include *Foreign Exchange: A Mystery in Poems* (1999), *The Taking of Room 114: A Hostage Drama in Poems* (1997), *Jump Ball: A Basketball Season in Poems* (1997), and *Who Killed Mr. Chippendale?* (1996).

The Voyage of the Arctic Tern by Hugh Montgomery. Candlewick, 2002. Unlike most of the new prose poets who are writing realistic problem stories, Montgomery spins a high-seas adventure story.

The Way a Door Closes by Hope Anita Smith, illustrated by Shane W. Evans. Holt, 2003. The first twelve poems are about the happiness that C. J. experiences in his family, but the thirteenth, "The Way a Door Closes," lets readers know that the father of the family is leaving. The rest of the book (twenty-two more poems) describe C. J.'s up-and-down emotions.

Who Will Tell My Brother? by Marlene Carvel. Hyperion, 2002. Carvel's sensitive story treats the issue of offensive Indian mascots used by sports teams.

In Sonya Sones's *One of Those Hideous Books Where the Mother Dies*, the mother has actually died before the book starts, and far from being the kind of predictable melodrama implied by the title, Sones has written an honest book whose basic sadness is relieved by the protagonist's lively writing, much of which is in the form of emails that she sends to her friends in Boston after she has flown out to California to live with a father she hardly knows.

A standard assignment in our YA literature class has been to ask students to start making their own poetry collections. We ask them to collect at least ten poems that they can imagine using in their own classes, either as part of academic units or simply as a way to enjoy a few minutes of class time. On the day they turn in the assignment, we arrange an in-class poetry slam, in which, both the performers and the audience have fun. Sara Holbrook and Michael Salinger's

Poetry slams, whether held in classes, libraries, parks, or even police stations, are bringing new life to the sharing of poetry.

Outspoken! How to Improve Writing and Speaking Skills through Poetry Performance and Marc Smith and Mark Eleveld's *The Spoken Word Revolution: Slam, Hip Hop and the Poetry of a New Generation* may be confidence builders for teachers or other group leaders wanting to get kids interested in performance poetry. But we simply follow the pattern we have seen colleague Lynn Nelson do with his Greater Phoenix Area Writing Project. Here is what is required:

1. An uninhibited volunteer to act as master of ceremonies.

2. Numbered participation tickets on which students write their name and the name of their poem. They hand their "tickets" to the MC just before they step "on stage." The numbering helps them know when their turn is coming, and the job of the MC is easier because of having the information needed for an introduction.

3. Minimal room decorations and simple refreshments lend a festive air and add to the coffee-house atmosphere.

4. Two sets of double judging cards—the kind used for Olympics scoring—add to the fun and suspense as everyone waits to see if the judges (two uninhibited students seated on opposite sides of the room) will agree on their scores.

5. For prizes, we give away pencils and big erasers since it comes near the end of the semester just before final exams.

In our first poetry slam, the students had so much fun that we waited until the next class period to share our disappointment about where they found the poems for their collections. Virtually all the students took their ten poems from Internet sources. This was fine for the poetry slam because most of the poems were written in first person and therefore had a kind of drama and urgency to them. However, as we explained when we brought back the cartload of poetry books for them to browse, they had missed out on many of the world's best poems as well as on the appealing designs and organizational structures of the best new books. Obviously, students found some enjoyable poetry on the Internet, but as we tried to convince them, they had handicapped themselves because Internet poems are likely to be either too old to be in copyright or too new and too undervalued to be protected with copyrights. We now specify that at least half of their poems come from a print source.

Among the books we felt the worst about our students missing are collections put together by Paul Janeczko and, more recently, Naomi Shihab Nye (see Nye's statement). These two wonderful poets and collectors joined forces in 1996 when they went searching for poems from around the world that would present male and female points of view on similar topics. The resulting book is *I Feel a Little Jumpy Around You: A Book of Her Poems and His Poems Collected in Pairs.* As an explanation of why he collects poems, Janeczko has explained that long before he created his first anthology in 1977 he was hooked on poetry, believing the words of James Dickey, "What you have to realize if you love poetry, is that poetry is just naturally the greatest goddamn thing that ever was in the whole universe. If you love it, there's no substitute for it." And if you love it, you have to pass it along.[3]

Readers' appreciation for poetry develops in much the same way as their appreciation for prose. They begin with an unconscious delight in sounds—the repetition and rhythm of nursery rhymes, songs, and television commercials. Then they go on to the fun of riddles, puns, playground chants, and autograph rhyme. Soon they get involved in such simple plots as those found in limericks and the humorous verses of Jack Prelutsky and Shel Silverstein. By the time children are in the middle grades, their favorite poems are those that tell stories, for example, Robert Browning's "The Pied Piper of Hamelin," Henry Wadsworth Longfellow's "Hiawatha's Childhood" and "The Midnight Ride of Paul Revere," Robert Service's "The Cremation of Sam McGee," James Whitcomb Riley's "Little Orphant Annie," and Edgar Allan Poe's "The Raven."

Novels written as prose poetry are a kind of extension of these early stories. Such books are popular for both young readers and adults. David Lehman, series editor of the Best American Poetry series published by Scribner, said in the March/April 2003 issue of *The American Poetry Review* that the genre goes back to the nineteenth-century French poets Charles Baudelaire and Arthur Rimbaud and that English influences are as diverse as the King James Bible, Shakespeare's plays, and John Donne's sermons. However, the new American variant "in all its glorious variety," is keeping its distance from these earlier traditions. It is "saturated" with American culture and vernacular, and while the poets lose much, they also "gain in relaxation, in the possibilities of humor and incongruity, in narrative compression, and in the feeling of escape or release from tradition or expectation."[4]

In writing about the popularity of the new genre, librarian Ed Sullivan stated that the poetry in these books "is not like what most students are forced to study in class—it does not require analysis and explication." They are so different from kids' present idea of poetry that Sullivan catalogs them in his library as fiction so that kids will be more apt to find them. He says the genre is popular because

> It is straightforward, but it retains the rhythm and succinctness of traditional poetry. By writing their stories in verse, authors offer readers a voyeuristic perspective not possible with prose. Poetry lends itself well to introspection and intense emotion. There is also a more practical attraction for students—novels in verse are a shorter and faster read. The substantial white space on the pages of these books certainly appeals to reluctant readers.[5]

Young Adult Authors Speak Out

Naomi Shihab Nye on the

Poetry Bridge

To cross the Mississippi River when I was a child, my family could drive over a noisy bridge with a strange surface that made tires rattle and squeal, or a silent humming bridge with elegant spires. Of course, we all cheered for the noisy bridge, but once I started reading and writing poetry at age six, I realized quiet bridges had a deeper appeal.

Simply by reading a poem written long ago, one could feel transported into the heart and mind of another time. Emily Dickinson or William Blake offered startling wisdom-sparks that made a whole day swerve, sit up, take on a shinier, more attentive tone.

Or by reading a poem by a poet from another country—Rabindranath Tagore of Bengal was a childhood favorite of mine, and Robert Louis Stevenson from Scotland—one felt connected. Distances dissolved as the bridge of shared experience and insight linked us. I also knew what it was like to swing high in a swing or stare into a stream. So these far-away people were my secret friends.

Of course, the reality of connectedness is only one of the tragedies that haunts devoted readers during a time of war. How many details and impulses do we really have in common with all the people who are dying? What shared understandings might have moved us past whatever desperation leads human beings to commit acts of violence against one another? What could we have done better?

I am interested in the bridges between images and ideas, layers of thinking, reality and metaphor—the unexpected seams that writing helps us sew. I am interested in how writing about one thing so often opens a door to another thing. The act of writing itself is an opening. Even if you don't like what you write first, you may move around within words on a paper and allow them to lead you somewhere else. I am interested in placement of parts of language, and the shining unspoken stream of meaning that often flows brightly right below the little bridges we carefully construct.

When I write about the Middle East, or anywhere else on earth, the poem or story is only trying to shine a little light on human realities which exist for all people in the world, not just some of us—that is the ground the poem grows out of. Not a "message"—not a "slogan"—as in politics—but creation of a simple scene. The people in the Middle East appreciate their homes, like good food, love children, want to water their plants and tend their trees and have friends in school and be respected in work, just as we do over here. It is impossible to explain the desperation that creates so much violence, but it is *possible* to describe regular human life and its hopes and fears.

I would hope readers feel at home in my poems, wherever the poem is taking place. "Oh, I know that feeling" or "That's sort of like me." Poetry is not jut a surface glance at something, it is a deeper gaze. It tries to look *into*, not just at something. It slows us down, which is good, since we usually move too fast anyway. It helps us see something worth seeing everywhere, whether inside or outside us.

A girl in Calgary, Canada, wrote to me that after reading my work she could never look at the world headlines in the same way again. She would always be thinking about "regular people" everywhere—not "enemies" or "foreigners" or "strangers." Her letter, in which she also mentioned she had asked her mom to cook only Middle Eastern food for her while she was reading *Habibi* the second time, was the best review I ever got.

My happiest moment as a writer is when someone else sees something of their *own* in one of my stories or poems.

That's the bridge—and it doesn't make a lot of noise.

- Naomi Shihab Nye's books include her *Habibi* (Simon and Schuster, 1997), *19 Varieties of Gazelle—Poems of the Middle East* (Greenwillow, 2002), *A Maze Me* (Greenwillow, 2005), and *I'll Ask You Three Times, Are You OK?* (Greenwillow, 2007).

The Teaching of Poetry

When we ask our college students about their in-school experiences with poetry, on the negative side they tell us about teachers who did not like poetry themselves and so flooded lessons with technical terms or turned poems into guessing games that made students feel stupid. On the positive side, they tell us about teachers who seemed to take genuine pleasure in poems and shared them with students as a gift. Their actions match the advice of Richard W. Beach and James D. Marshall:

1. Never teach a poem you don't like.
2. Teach poems that you're not certain you understand. Teach poems about which you may have some real doubt.
3. Teach poems that are new to you as well as your store of "old standards."
4. Become a daily reader of poems, a habitué of used bookstores, a scavenger of old *New Yorkers* and other magazines that contain poetry.
5. Give students the freedom to dislike great poetry.[6]

Books about teaching literature inevitably give suggestions on teaching this or that genre, but readers can almost palpably sense the urgency of suggestions for teaching poetry. Recommended books include Louise Rosenblatt's seminal *The Reader, the Text, the Poem: The Transactional Theory of the Literary Work*; Patrick Dias and Michael Hayhoe's *Developing Response to Poetry*; and Stephen Dunning's *Teaching Literature to Adolescents: Poetry*. See Chapter 11 for helpful ideas on writing poetry. With the help of these books and poems gleaned from teachers' reading, any teacher can soon have several hundred poems worth reading and using in class. Here we offer some other suggestions.

1. Avoid units on poetry. Poems deserve to be used frequently but not en masse. It is better to use poems in thematic units where they can be tied in with short stories or drama.
2. Drop a funny poem—or a monster poem—into class just for the fun of it.
3. Let students, at least occasionally, help choose the poems that a class will study.
4. Remember that poetry takes time and plan accordingly. This is not to see how many poems you can knock off in one class, but to allow students to hear poems again and again and to talk about them. We saw one teacher who obviously hated poetry set a record by killing thirty-six Emily Dickinson poems in less than one class period. It takes time to recognize kinship with a poet, to find someone who expresses a feeling or makes an observation that the reader has come close to but has not quite been able to put into words.
5. Surround your students with as many beautifully designed poetry books as you can borrow from libraries, scrounge from friends and neighbors, or buy. For suggestions, see Focus Box 5.2, More Poets and Poetry.

Even though the age range of those who can read and enjoy a particular poem is usually much wider than for prose, there is still a subtle dividing line between children's and young adult books. While teenagers may be amused by the humorous poetry of Shel Silverstein and Jack Prelutsky, they are likely to feel slightly insulted if offered serious children's poetry. Many young adults are ready to read and enjoy the same poetry that educated adults enjoy, especially if teachers smooth the way by first providing access to poets whose allusions they are likely to understand and then gradually leading them into poetry representing cultures and times different from their own. It may help to ease students into appreciating the work of some poets by first offering various kinds of biographical reading, as with Neil Baldwin's *To All Gentleness: William Carlos Williams, The Doctor-Poet*; Jean Gould's *American Women Poets: Pioneers of Modern Poetry*; or Paul Janeczko's *Poetspeak: In Their Work, About Their Work*. In a similar way, someone who has read Alice Walker's *The Color Purple* will probably be ready to appreciate the poems in her *Good Night, Willie Lee, I'll See You in the Morning: Poems*. Readers of Ray Bradbury's science fiction may want to read his fifty-plus poems in *When Elephants Last in the Dooryard Bloomed*. Students who have read Maya Angelou's autobiographical *I Know Why the Caged Bird Sings* will probably be interested in her poetry.

One of the delights and challenges of working with modern poetry is that students (and teachers) have no source to turn to for determining the meaning or worth of the poems. Comments on a T. S. Eliot poem are easy to come by, and a glance at criticism tells us whether this poem is major Eliot or minor Eliot. We hardly need to read the poem to comment on it, to determine its place in the canon, or to chase down all those wonderful symbols and allusions. With a modern poem, teachers and students must fall back on honest responses to the poem. Years ago, Luella Cook, one of the great people in English education, warned teachers about the dishonesty of canned responses to literature, and although she referred to students alone, her warning might be extended to teachers as well.

The problem of teaching literature realistically faced, then, becomes one of widening the range of responses to literature, of guiding reading experience so that reaction to books will be vivid, sharp, compelling, provocative. The great tragedy of the English classroom is not that students may have the "wrong" reactions—that is, veer from accepted judgment—but that they will have no original reaction at all, or only the most obvious ones, or that they will mimic the accepted evaluations of criticism.[7]

Making Drama a Class Act

We used to say that playwrights did not write plays for teenagers because teenagers were not the ones buying tickets to Broadway plays or flying to London on theater tours. That's still true, but as we discussed in Chapter 3, teenagers make up a healthy portion of television and movie audiences, so that talented writers are now writing serious plays designed for young people either to read or to perform.

Crush: Love Poems by Kwame Alexander. Word of Mouth, 2007. Naomi Shihab Nye wrote the title poem; other featured poets are Pablo Neruda, Nikki Giovanni, and Sherman Alexie. An intriguing variety of verbal formulas may inspire teens to submit their own poems to a related website.

Good Poems, compiled by Garrison Keillor. Viking, 2002. After a lighthearted introduction, Keillor presents three hundred poems that he has read on his PBS radio show, *A Prairie Home Companion*. They range from the well-known to the obscure, but they are all accessible.

Heart to Heart: New Poems Inspired by Twentieth-Century American Art, edited by Jan Greenberg. Abrams, 2001. In this Printz Honor Book, Greenberg commissioned poets to write in response to some of the greatest twentieth-century American paintings. She arranged the paintings and the poems according to the poet's approach.

I Am the Darker Brother: An Anthology of Modern Poems by African Americans, revised edition, edited by Arnold Adoff, illustrated by Benny Andrews. Simon & Schuster, 1997. Since its publication in 1968, this has been the premier anthology of black poetry. Twenty-one new poems are included with pieces coming from nine women, including Rita Dove and Maya Angelou.

I, Too, Sing America: Three Centuries of African American Poetry, edited by Catherine Clinton, illustrated by Stephen Lalcorn. Houghton Mifflin, 1998. This attractive, large-sized book is a good resource for classrooms and libraries.

Immersed in Verse: An Informative, Slightly Irreverent and Totally Tremendous Guide to Living the Poet's Life by Allan Wolf, Illustrated by Tuesday Mourning. Sterling/Lark, 2006. This is both a how-to and a book of encouragement for anyone who's even slightly tempted to write a poem. The illustrations add an upbeat tone.

Love Speaks Its Name: Gay and Lesbian Love Poems, edited by J. D. McClatchy. Knopf, 2001. The 144 poets include Sappho, Walt Whitman, Frank O'Hara, and Muriel Rukeyser.

Pierced by a Ray of Sun: Poems about the Times We Feel Alone, selected by Ruth Gordon. HarperCollins, 1995. These seventy-three poems all explore human loneliness. Also recommended are Gordon's earlier collections including *Time Is the Longest Distance* (1991), *Under All Silences* (1987), and *Peeling the Onion* (1993), all HarperCollins.

Be warned, however, that these are not the kinds of nondescript plays that were found in books for high school students a generation ago. In an *English Journal* article, "Toward a Young Adult Drama," Rick E. Amidon described them as "works which question fitting in, popularity, sex, drugs, making choices, taking chances." He labeled Jerome McDonough the "father of young adult drama" because of his dozen "powerful, practical-to-produce, and effective plays for the young adult stage."[8] His plays differ from those typically produced at high schools in that they are shorter (fifty to seventy minutes long); they deal with topics dear to the hearts of teenagers; most of the casts are flexible, so the plays can be adapted to how many actors are available; and they have contemporary settings. Hindi Brooks, who has been a writer for television's *Fame* and *Eight Is Enough*, has also written plays specifically for young adults. (Both McDonough's and Brooks's plays are available from I. E. Clark in Schulenberg, Texas.) Samuel French in Hollywood and Dramatists Play Service in New York also offer play scripts written for teenagers. For the first time, the ALAN Workshop was held in New York City in November, 2007, and included a panel of playwrights talking about their

Poetry Speaks: Hear Great Poets Read Their Work from Tennyson to Plath, edited by Elise Pashen and Rebekah Presson Mosby. Source Books, 2001. A bonus to this book are the three CDs presenting many of the forty-two poets doing interpretive readings.

Reflections on a Gift of Watermelon Pickle, edited by Stephen Dunning and others. Scott, Foresman, 1967, reissued, 1994. A landmark book, this collection proved that young readers could enjoy modern poetry without the help (or hindrance) of teachers. Its sequel, *Some Haystacks Don't Even Have Any Needles and Other Complete Modern Poems* (Lothrop, 1969) is almost as good.

Red Hot Salsa: Bilingual Poems on Being Young and Latino in the United States, edited by Lori M. Carlson. Holt, 2005. Continuing along the lines of her popular 1994 *Cool Salsa*, Carlson has gathered another wonderful collection of poems in both Spanish and English.

Revenge and Forgiveness: An Anthology of Poems, edited by Patrice Vecchione. Holt, 2004. Contemporary poets including Naomi Shihab Nye, Lucille Clifton, and editor Vecchione join "classic" poets ranging from the creator of a Native American myth song to William Shakespeare and Ezra Pound in illustrating different ways of dealing with grief and anger. The collection was inspired by the events of September 11, 2001.

Tour America: A Journey through Poems and Art by Diane Siebert, illustrated by Stephen T. Johnson. CIP Chronicle, 2006. Children, teens, and adults can all enjoy this book of poems and paintings that take readers to 26 of the author's favorite places in America—ranging from Alaska and a view of the aurora borealis to Chicago and a view of the El.

Truth and Lies: An Anthology of Poems, edited by Patrice Vecchione. Holt, 2001. Vecchione adds illuminating notes to help young readers enjoy the poems that she carefully chose from across centuries and across cultures.

Wáchale! Poetry and Prose About Growing Up Latino in America, edited by Ilan Stavans. Cricket Books/Carus Publishing, 2001. A reviewer described the vivid word pictures in this bilingual collection as speaking from the heart and lingering in the mind.

Walt Whitman: Words for America by Barbara Kerley, illustrated by Brian Selznick. Scholastic, 2004. Beautiful pictures and a generous format make this a good book for introducing one of America's most famous poets.

Why War Is Never a Good Idea by Alice Walker, illustrated by Stefano Vitale. HarperCollins, 2007. Folk art paintings make Walker's poem especially powerful. Skilled teachers can use the book to bring both an artistic and a thought-provoking experience to groups from ages eight or nine on up.

scripts. Aaron Levy (see his statement on p. 158) was responsible for bringing the event together.

Without encouragement from teachers, few teenagers read drama because it needs to be read aloud with different voices and it is hard to visualize the scenery and the stage directions. One of our graduate students, Alison Babusci, who came to study in Arizona State University's well-known program in Children's Theater, drew up these five suggestions for teachers who are planning to have students read and study such plays as those listed in Focus Box 5.3.

1. Make students feel like they are "on the inside" of the theatrical world by bringing in photocopies of sets and costume designs. Obtain a stage diagram and teach students stage directions; the more they know about the production of a play they are reading, the more interested they will be.

2. Become "friends" with the cast by having students copy the cast list (dramatis personae) from the beginning of the play and then write their own descriptions of the characters and their relationships.

Young Adult Authors Speak Out

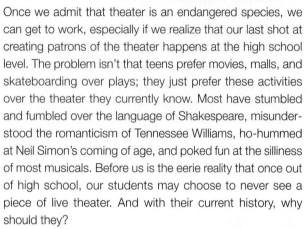

Aaron Levy, Dramatist

Speaks to English Teachers and Librarians

Once we admit that theater is an endangered species, we can get to work, especially if we realize that our last shot at creating patrons of the theater happens at the high school level. The problem isn't that teens prefer movies, malls, and skateboarding over plays; they just prefer these activities over the theater they currently know. Most have stumbled and fumbled over the language of Shakespeare, misunderstood the romanticism of Tennessee Williams, ho-hummed at Neil Simon's coming of age, and poked fun at the silliness of most musicals. Before us is the eerie reality that once out of high school, our students may choose to never see a piece of live theater. And with their current history, why should they?

I can identify with their attitude because I have a similar history. In high school, I didn't even know where the theater was, but then in college I started writing dialogue and so I ventured over to the theater. On many a night, I was surprised at the magic of a live story unfolding before me. I connected with the actors and the characters they portrayed in a way I've never done with a movie. In the one-woman play by Jane Wagner, *Search for Signs of Intelligent Life in the Universe,* one of the characters played by Lily Tomlin is the bag lady, Trudy, who admits that going crazy and dropping out of corporate America was the best thing she ever did. The play has Trudy taking visiting aliens on tours of *our* universe. They end their visit with a night in the theater where her charges wind up watching the audience instead of the play because Trudy hadn't thought to tell them otherwise. At the end of the evening one of them shows Trudy his goose bumps. Trudy reflects, "Yeah, to see a group of strangers sitting together in the dark, laughing and crying about the same things . . . that just knocked 'em out. . . . So

they're taking goose bumps home with 'em. Goose bumps! Quite a souvenir."

That's a great lesson that the aliens teach us about our own theater—the audience is the real art, and it's our job to make sure with every production (and every reading in our classrooms) we keep it that way. When I work with students either in class or on the stage, we talk every day about audience. Unlike other literary forms, without an audience, theater does not exist.

Too often, high school theater perpetuates archaic notions about theater with slow-moving dramas, repetitive musicals, and plays that don't speak to the teenage experience. We do not need to acquiesce to the MTV style of telling stories in quick snippets, but we have to be aware of certain trends in the teenage attention span. If we want them to actually turn their cell phones all the way off and sit there for an hour-and-a-half, we had best deliver goose bumps or lose them forever.

Before we can deliver the goose bump experience and make it so teenagers leave high school craving theater, we've got to figure out a way to get them into high school auditoriums in the first place. We also have to make it so that when we read plays in English classes, it feels like something stronger than a requirement. We need to read drama with such fervor that students are actually curious to see it produced.

Here are a few suggestions for ways that English teachers and drama teachers can work together.

- Invite the drama teacher to your very first English department meeting. Get acquainted and make plans for him or her to come to your class to promote the first play. Some teachers send students around to pitch the play or perform a scene, but I think that's risky because students often feel silly performing without the benefit of a stage. If their performance falls flat, the visit has had adverse effects, and even when it succeeds, it has taken away some of the surprise of the performance.

- Offer extra credit for students to attend the plays. If you don't believe in extra credit, make two assignments for homework, one a textbook type and the other attending the play. Inform students early and often of the play dates so they can get off work and/or make other arrangements. Most productions run three or four performances so students should be able to attend at least one if they plan ahead.

- Attend the performance yourself. This is big. I know (believe me I know) that an English teacher's job, if performed perfectly, would never end. We could grade until our heads drop into our morning cereal. But think of your attendance as a built-in lesson plan. If you attend, your students are twice as likely to attend, and you can use the performance as an actual piece of literature. Your theater teacher might be able to provide you with some background information, study guides, or quizzes.

- Suggest and support a theater teacher's opportunity to select some riskier plays that speak closer to the teen experience or tell a story in a nontraditional structure. If you and/or your theater teacher scout the catalogues, you can order several plays besides the usual ones that are produced over and over, sometimes by schools in the same district during the same academic year.

- As a way of returning the favor of your tireless support of the theater program, many theater teachers are willing to work with their students to perform a scene or two from one of the plays in *your* curriculum. After reading and dissecting a play like *Death of*

a *Salesman,* wouldn't it be a breath of fresh air to see and hear Willy Loman on his feet?

- Suggest and support library collaboration with theater productions. When I produce a play, I always visit our librarian and explain the play's plot and themes to see if she can help us set up a promotional display. When I did Jim Leonard's *The Diviners,* a humorous and touching story about a mentally challenged teenager who had a gift for divining, the librarian displayed books about the Depression (that's when the play is set) and about the art of divining.

- Help with press releases for promotion. While newspapers won't write articles on high school plays, they will if you spin it in an interesting way. When we produced my comedy-drama about teen suicide, *Pizza with Shrimp on Top,* we wrote the header for the press release something like, "Valley students reach out to community to fight against teen suicide." Both reporters and photographers showed up at our rehearsals.

- Invite and engage the community. Too often we produce plays whose quality suffers supposedly for the sake of "education." But I wonder if we're teaching our theater students the right things when we choose boring scripts, produce them at a low level of cost and effort, and then present them in half-filled arenas.

When I am teaching theater, I try to include my students in every aspect of production, especially marketing. The most important marketing lesson we learn is that if we are going to invite the whole school and the community, our product needs to make patrons want to see our next play.

- As a prize-winning playwright and director, Aaron Levy specializes in plays for the teen audience. He is on the faculty at Kennesaw State University and can be reached with comments and questions at Levycurio@aol.com. His *Pizza with Shrimp on Top* is published by Dramatic.

Children of a Lesser God by Mark Medoff. Dramatists, 1980. Especially since the success of the movie, students appreciate this Tony Award–winning play about a deaf young woman and her relationship with a hearing teacher.

Driving Miss Daisy by Alfred Uhry. Dramatists, 1988. The impressive film serves as a backdrop for reading this play that helps students learn what is involved in a lasting friendship.

The Effect of Gamma Rays on Man-in-the-Moon Marigolds by Paul Zindel. Dramatists, 1970. This moving story of the damaging forms that parent–child love can take brought Paul Zindel to the attention of the literary world.

Fences by August Wilson. Drama Book Shop and New American Library paperback, 1995. Wilson's play won the Pulitzer Prize for the way it shows an African American family losing its dreams in the 1950s.

Inherit the Wind by Jerome Lawrence and Robert E. Lee. Dramatists, 1955. Based on the Scopes trial, this play is especially interesting in relation to current controversies over creationism versus evolution. The lines are easy to read aloud, and there is a good balance between sharp wit and high drama.

Les Misérables by Tim Kelly. Dramatists, 1987. With eleventh and twelfth graders, the boys like action, the girls like romance, and they all like music. So here's a play that answers everyone's needs.

A Man for All Seasons by Robert Bolt, 1960. Baker (also French), 1960. It's good for its portrayal of one of the most famous periods of English history and for its exploration of a hero. Interesting comparisons can be drawn to works treating heroes of noble birth, as in *Antigone* and *Hamlet,* and heroes of ordinary birth, as in *Death of a Salesman* and *The Stranger.*

"Master Harold" . . . and the Boys by Athol Fugard. Penguin, 1982. This powerful one-act play asks students to examine the psychological effects of racism on whites.

The Miracle Worker by William Gibson. Baker (also French), 1951. Students love the poignancy of the story of Helen Keller and Annie Sullivan, but it is also a good illustration of flashbacks, foreshadowing, symbolism, and dramatic license when compared to such biographies as Nella Braddy's *Annie Sullivan Macy* and Helen Keller's *The Story of My Life.* Gibson's *Monday After the Miracle,* a continuation of the story, is also a good read.

Sorry, Wrong Number by Lucille Fletcher in *Fifteen American One-Act Plays,* edited by Paul Kozelka. Pocket Books, 1971. Because it is a radio play written to be heard and not seen, it is ideal for reading aloud.

A Storm in Summer by Rod Serling in *Great Television Plays,* Vol. 2, edited by Ned E. Hoopes and Patricia Neale Gordon. Dell, 1975. Students like the way Serling relates an encounter between a ten-year-old Harlem boy and a bitter, sarcastic, Jewish delicatessen owner in upstate New York.

The Teahouse of the August Moon by John Patrick. Dramatists, 1953. The way Patrick lightheartedly pokes fun at American customs and values is refreshing.

Visit to a Small Planet by Gore Vidal, in *Visit to a Small Planet and Other Television Plays.* Little, Brown, 1956. Because this play was written for television, the action is easy to visualize and the stage directions simple enough to discuss as an important aspect of the drama itself.

What I Did Last Summer by A. R. Gurney, Jr. Dramatists, 1983. As Anna tells fourteen-year-old Charlie in this play about the last summer of World War II, "All choices are important. They tell you who you are."

3. Involve students by leading them to form their own opinions and images.

4. Let students see the play. Before deciding on what play to read, contact theater groups in your area and find out what plays they will be producing over the next year, or choose a play available on video.

5. Instead of always having students read parts aloud, try letting them improvise selected scenes. Also think of ways to combine drama with

music, fine arts, dance, or other physical activities. People do not fall asleep when their bodies are active.

Her concluding advice was that teachers have to be excited by drama. Students will quickly identify and adopt the teacher's attitude: If the teacher is bored, students will be bored. Because so many students work after school and are involved in extra heavy academic loads, some high schools are trying alternative ways to get drama included; for example, offering theater programs during the summer or as extracurricular events.

Paul Zindel's career (see his Margaret A. Edwards Award write-up on p. 164) as a popular playwright, screen writer, and author of young adult books is a good illustration of how teen readers appreciate the immediacy and the directness of characters talking with each other as they do in films and plays. See Focus Box 5.4, Books Recommended for Reading Aloud or Adapting into Reader's Theater for books that include this kind of vivid language.

A favorite play for reading aloud is Reginald Rose's three-act television play *Twelve Angry Men*, the story of a jury making a decision on the future of a nineteen-year-old boy charged with murder. Some classes affectionately refer to the play as *Twelve Angry People* because girls as well as boys are assigned parts. Teachers have offered the following reasons for the play's success, which can serve as guides when predicting the potential of other scripts.

1. It calls for twelve continual parts, enough to satisfy all students who like to read aloud.
2. It teaches practical lessons of value to students' lives.
3. It may serve as a springboard for research and further discussion on how the judicial system works.
4. It creates a forum for students to prove the psychology of group dynamics and peer behavior.
5. It sparks student excitement from the beginning and sustains it throughout.
6. It can be read in two-and-a-half class sessions.
7. The "business" is minimal and can be easily carried out as students read from scripts.
8. Pertinent questions can be asked when the jury recesses after Acts I and II.
9. Students are attracted to the realism, and they can relate to a motherless slum youth of nineteen.
10. The excellent characterization allows students to discover a kaleidoscope of lifelike personalities.

Play scripts are sold through distributors, most of whom will happily send free catalogues to teachers who request them. A typical script price for a one-act play is $7.50 with a typical royalty charge of $75.00 for the initial production and less for each subsequent production. Teachers wanting scripts for in-class reading rather than for production should so note at the time of ordering so that no royalty is charged. If the play is to be produced, whether admission is charged or not, the producer should pay the fee when the scripts are ordered. A royalty

Black Cat Bone: The Life of Blues Legend Robert Johnson by J. Patrick Lewis, illustrated by Gary Kelley. Creative Editions, 2006. This story of Robert Johnson, a blues musician, could be used as a wonderful introduction to a music event.

Talkin' about Bessie: The Story of Aviator Elizabeth Coleman by Nikki Grimes, illustrated by E. B. Lewis. Scholastic, 2002. An unusual biography is presented through twenty-one poetic speeches given at the funeral parlor where people have come to mourn the early death of the first African American woman to become a licensed pilot. See also Grimes's *Stepping Out with Grandma Mac* (Scholastic/Orchard, 2001) in which poems capture and celebrate the experiences shared by a teenaged girl and her grandmother.

Carver: A Life in Poems by Marilyn Nelson. Nikki Giovanni praised this winner of the 2001 Boston Globe Horn Book Award by writing, "Oh, Marilyn Nelson, what a magnificent job you have done to bring the past so alive it looks like our future." The individual poems make for an easy way of dividing up this biography of George Washington Carver for a class presentation.

A Gift from Zeus: Sixteen Favorite Myths by Jeanne Steig, pictures by William Steig. Joanna Cotler Books/HarperCollins, 2001. William Steig's drawings, as in *Sylvester and the Magic Pebble*, and his Dr. DeSoto books have always been brute art. Now that he is in his nineties, his style is even more succinct and could serve as a model for kids to do their own giant-sized drawings to assist them in storytelling.

Here in Harlem: Poems in Many Voices by Walter Dean Myers. Holiday House, 2004. Myers did for Harlem what Edgar Lee Masters did in his 1915 *Spoon River Anthology.* The rich text and the variety of voices (up to fifty) make it appealing either for choral readings, individual presentations, or a mixture of both.

The Hitchhiker's Guide to the Galaxy by Douglas Adams. Ballantine, 1980. Arthur Dent and Ford Prefect are on a perilous and very funny journey through the galaxy. The stories were originally produced in England as radio shows and so work well as read-alouds.

Keesha's House by Helen Frost. Frances Foster Books/FSG, 2003. These first-person accounts from seven teenagers show that kids who are pushed out of their own homes and are dealing with such "heavy" issues as abandonment, racism, addiction, delinquency, and sexual consequences can still come together and help each other.

Joyful Noise: Poems for Two Voices by Paul Fleischman. HarperCollins, 1998. Fleischman designed his book as a way of "forcing" readers to approach poetry out loud because he had such fond memories of the storytelling and wordplay his family participated in when he was a boy.

Short Circuits: Thirteen Shocking Stories by Outstanding Writers for Young Adults, edited by Donald R. Gallo. HarperCollins, 1992. Several of these suspenseful and ghostly stories can be used for humorous read-alouds. Alvin Schwartz's *Scary Stories to Tell in the Dark*, *More Scary Stories to Tell in the Dark*, and *Scary Stories 3: More Tales to Chill Your Bones* (HarperCollins, 1981, 1984, and 1992) are also the kind that will make the hair on listeners' arms stand up straight.

The Song Shoots Out of My Mouth: A Celebration of Music by Jamie Adoff, illustrated by Martin French. Dutton, 2002. Jamie Adoff is the son of Virginia Hamilton and Arnold Adoff and as a musician has put together a poetic tribute to all kinds of music.

Tough Boy Sonatas by Curtis L. Crisler, illustrated by Floyd Cooper. Boyds Mills/Wordsong, 2007. Driving through the Industrial town of Gary, Indiana, will not be the same for readers who absorb these thirty-eight fierce and muscular poems about the boys who run in this harsh town and who, like LaRoy, sing "I am not a failing flashlight. I am an Inspired/Inspiration."

What My Mother Doesn't Know by Sonya Sones. Simon & Schuster, 2001. These free-verse poems can stand on their own, but when read all together they tell the story of fourteen-year-old Sophie's longings as well as her adventures.

Witness by Karen Hesse. Scholastic, 2001. It is 1924 and a small town in Vermont is caught up in intrigue and prejudice. Hesse uses carefully constructed free verse to present a little-known piece of U.S. history through the eyes and voices of eleven different townspeople.

contract is mailed along with the scripts. Check online for information from such distributors as Samuel French, Dramatists Play Service, Inc., Anchorage Press, and Contemporary Drama Service.

But even better than launching yourself on a solitary tour of such guides as these is to go and visit the theater teacher, who will probably have several catalogues that have arrived in the mail. Borrow them. Read the quick plot summaries and order some plays to read with your classes. Perhaps you can share costs with the theater department, while your students serve as first readers—as scouts—for appealing new scripts. Reading new plays from professionally prepared scripts is one of the simplest ways to follow Alison Babusci's suggestion that we make students feel "on the inside" of the theatrical world. Another way is to let students create their own plays from such books as those listed in Focus Box 5.4.

Humor Matters

Despite what must seem obvious truth to good teachers and librarians—that a sense of humor is essential for the survival of educators and students—some deadly serious people wonder if this (or any other time, presumably) is the time for levity. The answer is, of course, yes. Given their enforced world of school and an ever-demanding society, young people need laughter every bit as much as—maybe even more than—adults.

What do young people find funny? Lance M. Gentile and Merna M. McMillan's article, "Humor and the Reading Program," offers a starting point. Their stages of children's and young adults' interest in humor, somewhat supplemented, are as follows:

1. Ages ten to eleven. Literal humor, slapstick (e.g., The Three Stooges), laughing at accidents (banana-peel humor) and misbehavior, sometimes mildly lewd jokes (usually called "dirty jokes"), and grossness.

2. Ages twelve to thirteen. Practical jokes, teasing, goofs, sarcasm, more lewd jokes, joke-riddles, sick jokes, elephant jokes, grape jokes, tongue twisters, knock-knock jokes, moron jokes, TV blooper shows, and grossness piled on grossness.

3. Ages fourteen to fifteen. More and more lewd jokes (some approaching a mature recognition of the humor inherent in sex); humor aimed at schools, parents, and other adults in authority, as in television's *Malcolm in the Middle*; and grossness piled on even greater grossness. Young adults may still prefer their own humor to their parents' humor, but they are increasingly catching on to adult humor and may prefer it to their own.

4. Ages sixteen and up. More subtle humor; satire and parody now acceptable and maybe even preferable, witticisms (rather than last year's half-witticisms, which they now detest in their young brothers and sisters). Adult humor is increasingly part of their repertoire, partly because they are anxious to appear sophisticated, partly because they are growing up.[9]

Margaret A. Edwards Award
Winner (2002)

Paul Zindel **and His Legacy**

Paul Zindel's Margaret A. Edwards Honor Books include *The Pigman*, *The Pigman's Legacy*, *The Pigman and Me*; *My Darling, My Hamburger*; and *The Effect of Gamma Rays on Man-in-the-Moon Marigolds: A Drama in Two Acts*. Zindel also wrote many other books and several successful screen plays including the 1972 *Up the Sandbox*, the 1973 *Mame*, and the 1986 *Runaway Train*.

Zindel graduated from Wagner College on Staten Island where, even though he majored in chemistry, he took a concentrated ten-day course in playwriting from Edward Albee. At the time, Albee was well known for his one-act plays *The Zoo Story* and *The Death of Bessie Smith*, and would soon be even better known for *Who's Afraid of Virginia Woolf?* Zindel was entranced. He said he wanted to be Edward Albee. He wanted his career, and his popularity, and most of all, his money!

After graduation, Zindel taught chemistry for ten years at Tottenville High School on Staten Island, while moonlighting by writing plays. In one of his classes, a girl had answered an ad from the back of a comic book that promised for one dollar to send seeds that had been exposed to gamma rays at Oak Ridge Laboratories. She got the seeds and grew them for her science fair exhibit, which she named "The Effect of Gamma Rays on Man-in-the-Moon Marigolds and Celestial Cabbage." Zindel loved her title—once he dropped off the part about cabbage—and his first successful play grew out of his love for this title. It was the story about the relationship between a sensitive girl, her epileptic sister, and their bitter and controlling mother. It opened in 1965 at the Alley Theatre in Houston and went on to win the Pulitzer Prize, a New York Drama Critics Circle Award, and an Obie. When, in 1970, it opened off-Broadway, it played 819 performances. In 1966, a shortened screen version was produced on public television. Harper and Collins editor Charlotte Zolotow saw it and was so impressed at Zindel's skill in creating interesting and believable teenage dialogue that she contacted Zindel and convinced him to try his hand at writing a book for young adults. Her invitation resulted in *The Pigman*, which was published to widespread acclaim in 1968.

At the time of the invitation, Zindel was saving on his rent money by living in and "guarding" empty houses that were up for sale and when he saw a teenaged boy trespass onto the property he went out to scold him, but instead ended up listening to the boy's many adventures. Zindel thought of a girl in one of his classes who was named Lorraine and who was so sensitive that she would cry at any mention of death or sadness. He was struck with the idea of putting two such different people in a book and having them interact with an eccentric, old man whose character Zindel based on an Italian neighbor that he remembered. Zindel later wrote more about this same neighbor in *The Pigman and Me* and in *The Pigman's Legacy*.

Both Robert Cormier and M. E. Kerr acknowledged that before they decided to enter the field of young adult literature they read Zindel's *The Pigman* and weighed the fact that a Pulitzer Prize–winning playwright was putting forth his best efforts for teenagers. Joan Bauer has said that the first respect as an author that she received from her teenage daughter was when in 1994 she was asked to be on a panel about creating humor with Zindel. And at the time of his death in 2003, other writers of YA books spoke about his influence on their own careers. Will Hobbs described Zindel as a "chemistry teacher turned alchemist," and went on to say that Paul was "so good I couldn't stand it; I had to try writing young adult novels of my own." Alex Flinn said that Zindel was one of only three YA authors that he remembers reading when he was young. He feels as if he "met John and Lorraine just yesterday." Lauren L. Wohl, the marketing director for Roaring Brook Press, thanked Zindel in the June 2003 *VOYA* for allowing her to finally score with her teenaged son when she mentioned that she was working with Paul Zindel.

> "The Pigman *Paul Zindel?*"
> *I nodded.*
> "You're kidding."
> "Nope. Really!"
> "Cool!" ●

Dramatic Publishing (www .dramaticpublishing.com) has printed scripts for several new plays aimed at young adult audiences including The Wrestling Season, Everyday Heroes, *and* Deadly Weapons *by Laurie Brooks;* Zen Junior High *by Kirk Lynn; and* The Bully Show! *by Brian Guehring. Paul Fleischman has also adapted his book* Seek *into a play that the company is offering.*

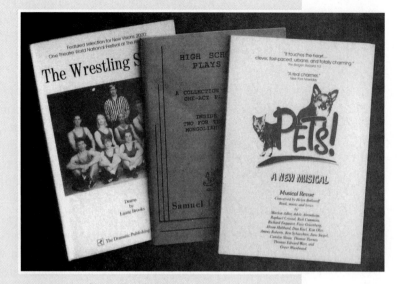

From Chills to Giggles

Something in the human mind encourages crossovers between fear and amusement, as shown by how often people who have suffered a fright burst out laughing as soon as the danger is over. Humor about death can be traced back at least as far as the early Greeks. English speakers refer to this blend of humor and horror as Gothic because they associate it with the grotesque gargoyles and other frightening figures in tapestries, paintings, sculptures, and stained glass windows, which were created to represent the devil and to frighten people into "proper" beliefs and behavior. Instead, people coped with their fears by turning such icons into objects of amusement.

People still do this at Halloween with spiderwebs, skeletons, black cats, bats, rats, ghosts, coffins, tombstones, monsters, and haunted houses. Halloween developed out of the sacred or "hallowed" evening preceding All Saints Day, which falls on November 1. The holiday is now second only to Christmas in the amount of money expended for costumes, parties, and candy to be given to trick-or-treaters.

The world has had great fun with Mary Shelley's story *Frankenstein: Or, the Modern Prometheus,* but when it was written many people viewed it as a cautionary tale against medical experimentation. Shelley's story followed close on the heels of the development of autopsies and of dissection for purposes of medical study. Such practices made people nervous and fearful. One way of calming such fears was by laughing at them. While Shelley's story was itself rich in Gothic details with a complex plot and fully developed characters, hundreds of parodies and imitations are comic in nature.

Gothic novels underwent a similar kind of transformation from scary to funny when the same year that Shelley published *Frankenstein* (1818), Jane Austen published *Northanger Abbey* as a gleeful parody of the earlier novels.

Later Gothic stories in the mid and late 1800s included some darkly humorous moments caused by visits from the dead as in Edgar Allan Poe's "The Fall of the House of Usher," Emily Brontë's *Wuthering Heights*, and Charles Dickens's *A Christmas Carol* with its Ghosts of Christmas Past, Christmas Present, and Christmas Future. In *Bleak House*, Dickens creates a character who spontaneously combusts; in *Little Dorrit*, the prison resembles a haunted castle; and in *Great Expectations*, Pip meets the criminal in a graveyard and has a hallucinatory vision of Miss Havisham's hanged body "with but one shoe to the feet."

Bram Stoker's 1897 *Dracula* is not the first story about a vampire, but it is the one that established such Western traditions as vampire's need for periodically sucking blood, the requirements of a prolonged relationship before a human can be turned into a vampire, vampires sleeping in coffins during the day and arising for action only after dark, the impossibility of killing vampires with ordinary human weapons, and the use of such conventional techniques for repelling vampires as garlic, a silver crucifix, and a wooden stake through the heart.

Bud Abbott and Lou Costello were among the earliest film comedians to take advantage of the possibilities of film for stretching viewers' emotions between the frightening and the ridiculous. Their 1948 *Abbott and Costello Meet Frankenstein* still appears on all-time best comedy lists. In the mid 1960s, *The Munsters* was a popular television show. Also, Charles Addams's ghoulish cartoons, which had been published in the *New Yorker*, were adapted into the pseudoscary *The Addams Family*. Laughs come mostly from the surprise of seeing ordinary family life conducted in a spooky old mansion by scary-looking individuals with such names as Uncle Fester, Morticia, Gomez, Wednesday, and Pugsley.

Other Gothic movies that made people both shiver and laugh include the 1973 *Rocky Horror Picture Show*, a spoof of a Gothic novel, which originally failed at the box office, but soon developed a cult following. The 1984 *Ghostbusters* starred Bill Murray and Dan Aykroyd, while the 1986 *Little Shop of Horrors* starred Steve Martin, Rick Moranis, and a plant that eats people. Also in 1986, *The Witches of Eastwick*, based on John Updike's novel, starred Jack Nicholson, Cher, Susan Sarandon, Michelle Pfeiffer, and Veronica Cartwright. This fascination with horror led right into the Batman movies of the 1990s, in which New York City was renamed Gotham City. Its underground tunnels and sewer systems were made to serve as modern substitutes for the secret passageways, hidden entries, and basement crypts of the castles and mansions in Gothic novels.

In 1975, folklore collector Alvin Schwartz was happily surprised when his 1981 *Scary Stories to Tell in the Dark* and its sequels, *More Scary Stories to Tell in the Dark* and *Scary Stories 3: More Tales to Chill Your Bones*, started winning state contests where children voted on their favorite books. Today, Schwartz's books are still on the American Library Association's list of frequently banned books, but kids still love them. They are kids' versions of some of the scary urban legends published in such adult books as Jan Harold Brunvand's *The Vanishing Hitchhiker: American Urban Legends and Their Meanings* and Joseph C. Goulden's *There Are Alligators in Our Sewers and Other American Credos*. A similar, but newer, book that includes such stories as "The Stolen Kidney," "The Scuba Diver in the Forest Fire," and "Aliens in Roswell, New Mexico," is Thomas Craughwell's *Alligators in the Sewer: And 222 Other Urban Legends*. In the mid 1980s writer Robert Lawrence Stine, who had written joke books for Scholastic as well as a *How to Be Funny* manual under the pen name of Jovial Bob Stine, created the Goosebumps series for eight-, nine-, and ten-year-olds and the Fear Street series for young teens. Although by now, interest in Gothic humor has peaked, Stine is still a publishing phenomenon. We recently heard that when Laura Bush was invited to a book promotion event with Mrs. Putin in Russia, she offered to bring an American author with her. She was told that the only author Russian children would know was R. L. Stine, and so Mrs. Bush and Mr. Stine went on a goodwill tour to Russia.

Ethnic-Based Humor

Discussions and news stories about political correctness have made everyone aware of the fact that ethnic-based humor can be used in negative ways. However, the other side of the coin is that such humor can also be used for positive purposes. Among members of their own groups, people use ethnic-based humor as a way of bonding and as a sign of solidarity and group pride. For example, humorous undertones often run through the Spanglish that young Hispanics use and through the exaggerated slang that is part of Black English.

An important point is that positive uses of ethnic humor usually come from within the group itself. This does not mean that all elements of criticism are avoided. Just as individuals sometimes use self-deprecating humor, they also use group-deprecating humor. The difference, when such humor comes from inside versus outside a group, is that the insider is probably chiding the group to change, while the outsider is making fun of, and cementing, old stereotypes.

When ethnic-based joking finds its way into books or films, thoughtful readers or viewers can learn a lot about each other. Henry Spalding has described the way that Jews use self-deprecating humor as "honey-coated barbs" at the people and things Jews love most. He says they "verbally attack their loved ones and their religion—all done with the grandest sense of affection—a kiss with salt on the lips, but a kiss nevertheless."[10] Sherman Alexie's 1998 movie *Smoke Signals*, based on a short story from his book *The Lone Ranger and Tonto Fistfight in Heaven*, has some of this same kind of humor in it. The story is set on the Coeur d'Alene Indian Reservation in northern Idaho, and while it is about such serious problems as alcoholism, alienation, and broken dreams, it does not shy away from wry humor. When we went to see the film in Scottsdale, Arizona, the audience was almost equally divided between whites and Native Americans. Both groups laughed at such parodies as a T-shirt advertising "Fry Bread Power" and at "the miracle of the fry bread" when Victor's mother magically feeds a crowd that is twice as big as she had expected. She simply raises her arms heavenward and solemnly rips each piece of bread in half. Both groups also laughed at the KREZ radio station announcer who sounds like Robin Williams when he shouts, "It's a great day to be indigenous!" Indian viewers seemed more amused by Victor's telling Thomas to shut off the television, "There's only one thing more pathetic than Indians on TV and that's Indians watching Indians on TV."

Indian viewers also laughed uninhibitedly at the two gum-chewing, soda-drinking sisters who sat sideways facing each other in the front seat of their old car as they listened to rock music and drove backward. While white viewers were troubled by such practical questions as, "Is the gear shift broken?" and "Can't they afford to get it fixed?" the Indian viewers appeared to accept the women as genuinely funny versions of contrary clowns. Several tribes rely for humor on contraries. These are clowns that do the opposite of what is expected. They dress in buffalo robes in the summer and go stand naked in winter snow. In Thomas Berger's 1964 *Little Big Man*, made into a film of the same name, a contrary clown arrives riding backward on a horse with his body painted in motley colors. He says "Goodbye" for "Hello," "I'm glad I did it!" for "I'm sorry," and cleans himself with sand before striding off by walking through the river.

The point is that humor is a powerful literary technique that can be used for a multitude of purposes as in the books listed in Focus Box 5.5, p. 170. Because humor is so intimately tied to the culture of particular groups, it will probably be one of the last things that outsiders catch onto. Nevertheless, it is well worth whatever attention we can give to it, whether working with middle-school readers (see Focus Box 5.6, p. 172) or with older students.

Teaching Literary Humor

Students are sometimes disappointed because an adult recommends a "funny" book. When they read it, they don't feel like laughing all the way through. The fact is that for people to laugh, they have to be surprised, and there is no way that an author can surprise a reader on every page. Instead, authors sprinkle humor throughout their books. The greater the contrast between the rest of the book and the humor, then the bigger the surprise and the more pleasure it will bring to the reader. Our job at school is not just to repeat the same kinds of humor that students get on the Comedy Channel or through lists of jokes on the Internet but to help students mature in their taste and appreciation. We need to educate students to catch onto a multitude of allusions and to have the patience required for reading and appreciating subtle kinds of humor.

At one of the International Society for Humor Studies meetings, Jacque Hughes, who teaches at Central Oklahoma University in Edmond, presented an example of how drawing relationships between raucous humor and more subtle humor can help students move to new levels of appreciation. She was having a hard time getting her eighteen-year-old freshmen to understand the dark humor in Flannery O'Connor's "A Good Man Is Hard to Find." Then she happened to see National Lampoon's *Vacation* starring Chevy Chase. It was wonderfully funny, and because most of her students had seen the movie, class members were able to compare the personalities and the incidents. When they realized that the similarities were too extensive—and too funny—to be coincidental, they gained a new appreciation for O'Connor's skill to do only with words what cost the movie producers millions of dollars to do with words and film.

It takes skill and practice, along with a broad, cultural background of knowledge, to understand a full range of humor. In *New York* magazine (July 17, 1995), readers sent in some thoughtful letters as a follow-up to an article on today's depressing state of stand-up comedy. One writer answered his own question of "Why were the Bennys, the Aces, the Allens (Steve and Fred, both), Berles, Benchleys, Parkers, Woollcotts intuitively brilliant and where are their kind now?" with the observation that these earlier comedians "were the products of a literate society, widely read or with extensive cultural experience, which gave them backgrounds upon which to draw. . . . They knew how to think and were well edited, either by erudite editors or by perceptive audiences." Another reader wrote that the place to look for delightful wit today is not in the comedy clubs but "in written form, in comic novels and essays." Most of our students aren't going to find this kind of humor unless we help prepare them.

Several creators of humor for general adult audiences can be appreciated by young readers if their teachers genuinely enjoy bringing their work into class and sharing a few paragraphs. Richard Lederer's *Anguished English* is fun, and so are stories written by Garrison Keillor and the newspaper columns written by Dave Barry and Erma Bombeck.

While few people appreciate having jokes explained to them, analyzing humor can be a good way to entice students into other kinds of literary analysis. Humor is an obvious emotion, and students are genuinely interested in figuring out what causes them to smile or laugh. While philosophers, psychologists, linguists, anthropologists, writers, actors, and comedians have all tried to answer this question, no one has come up with a proven system. All the reviewers we know, however, have come to agreement that Louis Sachar's *Holes* is a very funny book. It won both the Newbery Medal and the National Book Award and was listed on practically every "Best Book" list created for 1998. *Holes* consists of two stories. One is set in the present and features young Stanley Yelnats, while the other one is set in the past and is about Stanley's ancestors. When the contemporary story got too grim, Sachar would slip in a chapter from the past.

As explained very early in *Holes*, Stanley and his family seem to have more than their share of bad luck "all because of his no-good-dirty-rotten-pig-stealing-great-great-grandfather!" The very next line says that Stanley smiled when he thought of this because "It was a family joke," but as shown in a later statement by Louis Sachar, some readers are just like Stanley and his family in forgetting that this is a joke.

Stanley is mistakenly accused of theft, found guilty, and sentenced to Camp Green Lake Juvenile Correction Facility, where every day each of the boys must dig a five-foot-by-five-foot hole, supposedly to strengthen their character. Actually, the warden is forcing the boys to help her (yes, the warden is a woman) look for buried treasure. Stanley figures he'll lose weight or die digging, but his friend and fellow criminal Zero tries another way: He runs away. Stanley sets out after Zero, knowing little about the environment and forgetting to fill up his canteen. Stanley and Zero save themselves, partly through their own devices and partly through a series of coincidences that even Sachar admits is a bit much. However, he lets readers in on the joke by entitling his denouement "Filling in the Holes."

To illustrate the complexity and the interrelatedness of narrative humor, in Table 5.1 (p. 173) we list several of the features that humor scholars identify as being what people find funny. We illustrate them with examples from Sachar's *Holes*. The chart will, of course, be more meaningful to those who have read the book, so if nothing else, we hope it will encourage you to do just that.

Evidence of the power of Sachar's humor is the difficulty we had in pulling out succinct examples of humor because a well-developed book differs from

Books to Make Readers Smile

Angus, Thongs, and Full-Frontal Snogging and *On the Bright Side, I'm Now the Girlfriend of a Sex God: Further Confessions of Georgia Nicolson* by Louise Rennison. HarperCollins, 2000 and 2001. There's also a third book in the series, but it doesn't have quite the sparkle of these first two British imports.

Bucking the Sarge by Christopher Paul Curtis. Random/Wendy Lamb, 2004. "The Sarge" is Luther's mother who is a big-time landlady and a master at running scams on both her tenants and her business associates. Luther has to use his own creative abilities to establish his independence and break free from his mother's deviousness.

Gilda Joyce: Psychic Investigator by Jennifer Allison. Dutton, 2005. Gilda is a cross between *Harriet the Spy* and the 2007 *Nancy Drew* film, especially in relation to moving to California and living in a grand old Victorian mansion that appears to be haunted.

How Angel Peterson Got His Name: And Other Outrageous Tales about Extreme Sports by Gary Paulsen. Random/Wendy Lamb Books, 2003. Paulsen is at his storytelling best in these entertaining sketches. His *Harris and Me: A Summer Remembered* (1993) and *Lawn Boy* (2007) are equally funny—and exaggerated.

Lemony Snicket's Series of Unfortunate Events from *Book the First: The Bad Beginning, or, the Orphans!* (1999) to *Book the Thirteenth: The End* (2006) by Daniel Handler (under the pseudonym of Lemony Snicket). HarperCollins. Written and illustrated as old-fashioned melodramas, the series, with its wry humor and unexpected allusions, began as books for children, but by and large Handler managed to retain his audience as they grew older by writing longer and more sophisticated stories. Handler's smart allusions refer to such pop culture icons as Monty Python and Isadora Duncan and to such authors as Edgar Allan Poe, T. S. Eliot, J. D. Salinger, George Orwell, Virginia Euwer Woolf, and Sappho.

I'm Not Joey Pigza by Jack Gantos. Farrar, Straus and Giroux, 2007. In his Joey books, all from FS&G, Gantos walks a fine line between creating humor and empathy for a hyperactive boy with more than his share of family troubles. Titles include *Joey Pigza Swallowed the Key* (1998), *Joey Loses Control* (2000), and *What Would Joey Do?* (2002).

Martyn Pig by Kevin Brooks. Scholastic, 2002. The humor is pretty dark, but it's here in the story of a boy and the girl next door (an aspiring actress) who work to cover up the accidental death of Martyn's drunken and mean father.

stand-up comedy in being more than a series of one-liners. For example, Sachar carried some of his jokes throughout the entire book as when Stanley first gets to camp and the guard tells him, "You're not in the Girl Scouts any more." The guard regularly repeats this idea sometimes by just reminding the boys they aren't Girl Scouts, while at other times he asks, "You Girl Scouts having a good time?" Near the end of the book, when Stanley's lawyer and the attorney general drive into the camp and the warden wonders if it's "them," the guard tells her, "It ain't Girl Scouts selling cookies." This all leads up to the ironic denouement when readers are told that the camp is "bought by a national organization dedicated to the well-being of young girls. In a few years, Camp Green Lake will become a Girl Scout camp."

Another difficulty in making the chart was matching specific examples with the designated features because many of Sachar's jokes serve several purposes. At the same time Sachar is surprising readers or making them feel superior to a particular character, he is puzzling them with incongruous details, which he later

No More Dead Dogs by Gordon Korman. Hyperion, 2000. Twelve-year-old Wallace is tired of reading books in which the dog always dies. He gets in trouble at school when the drama club decides to put on a play about Old Shep and Wallace takes steps to keep the fictional dog alive.

Son of the Mob by Gordon Korman. Hyperion, 2002. Television's *Sopranos* has nothing on this story about seventeen-year-old Vince Luca, whose "family" business keeps interfering with his regular life.

Surviving the Applewhites by Stephanie S. Tolan. Harper-Collins, 2002. As a last resort, twelve-year-old Jake Semple, complete with spiked hair, numerous body piercings, and "attitude" is sent to an extremely loose and creative "academy" run by the Applewhite family.

The Misadventures of Maude March, or, Trouble Rides a Fast Horse by Audrey Couloumbis. Random, 2005. This historical piece resembles a dime novel, partly because the pioneer heroine has grown up reading such stories and therefore uses them as the basis for decision making. She and her sister steal two horses and head out for Independence, Missouri, where "nobody cares about your past."

The Secret Diary of Adrian Mole, Aged 13¾ and *The Growing Pains of Adrian Mole* by Sue Townsend. First published in England in 1982, reissued as HarperTempest, 2003. These very funny books are taken from Adrian's diaries as he recounts his life struggles, in which no one (especially the BBC) fully appreciates the value of his sensitive writings, in which the beloved Pandora does not long for Adrian's caresses as much as Adrian longs to caress Pandora.

The Vacation by Polly Horvath. Farrar, 2005. As she did with her 2003 National Book Award winner, *The Canning Season*, Horvath places a parentless young person under the care of some very strange, but not purposefully harmful, relatives. Readers probably find the situations funnier than do the characters, who are forced to rethink some of their basic beliefs about adults and how they act.

Uncle Boris in the Yukon and Other Shaggy Dog Stories by Daniel Pinkwater, illustrations by Jill Pinkwater. Simon & Schuster, 2001. In his usual style, Pinkwater starts with a smidgin of autobiography and then adds large helpings of exaggeration.

Zen and the Art of Faking It by Jordan Sonnenblick. Scholastic, 2007. Middle schoolers love the unpretentious style of Sonneblick's writing. Here he tells the realistic story of San Lee, an adopted Chinese kid whose con-artist father is in jail. As San Lee starts a new school he vows to stand out instead of slinking into the background.

resolves, thereby bringing more smiles. For example, on first seeing this description of the animals who share the amenities of Camp Green Lake Detention Center, readers probably do not realize they are being let in on a crucial plot element. Instead they just sit back and enjoy a standard three-part joke in which a comedian sets up a pattern and then surprises listeners by breaking the pattern.

> Here's a good rule to remember about rattlesnakes and scorpions: If you don't bother them, they won't bother you.
>
> Usually.
>
> Being bitten by a scorpion or even a rattlesnake is not the worst thing that can happen to you. You won't die.
>
> Usually. . . .
>
> But you don't want to be bitten by a yellow-spotted lizard. That's the worst thing that can happen to you. You will die a slow and painful death.
>
> Always.

The American Library Association website. Use any search engine to find the American Library Association, then type in *graphic novels* and you will find a wealth of information coming from three different units of the organization: The Intellectual Freedom Committee, the Young Adult Library Services Association (YALSA), and the American Association of School Libraries (AASL). The Intellectual Freedom committee has a site on "Dealing with Challenges to Graphic Novels," which is part of a larger project, "Graphic Novels: Suggestions for Librarians" (PDF), created by the National Coalition against Censorship, the Comic Book Legal Defense Fund, and ALA. YALSA prepares yearly lists of "Great Graphic Novels for Teens," including an annotated and a "Top Ten" list. The "Graphic novels—Professional Tips" (http://wikis.ala.org/professionaltips/index.php/Graphic_novels) is especially helpful, providing a bibliography of recently published articles and a guide to current sources of reviews. AASL, which works mostly with elementary school librarians, also has a helpful site, "Graphic Novels, Manga, and Anime: What's New and Cool for Your Library."

Art Spiegelman (http://lambiek.net/artists/s/spiegelman.htm) provides a good discussion of graphic novels and underground comix in general, as well as of his Pulitzer Prize–winning graphic novel *Maus.*

Attack of the Political Cartoonists: Insights and Assaults from Today's Editorial Pages, edited by J. P. Trostle. Dork Storm Press, 2004. Trostle gives a short history of political cartoons and then discusses the work of 150 members of the Association of American Editorial Cartoonists.

Best Editorial Cartoons of the Year, edited by Charles Brooks. Pelican, 1979–2007. Every year, Charles Brooks publishes a selection of the best political cartoons of the year in such categories as "The Administration," "Iraq/Terrorism," "Natural Disasters," "Media/Entertainment," "Foreign Affairs," and "Society."

Comedy: A Geographic and Historical Guide, 2 Volumes, edited by Maurice Charney. Praeger, 2005. The humor of ethnic groups, geographies, genres, nationalities, periods, and social groupings are discussed in great detail.

Comic Books for Young Adults (ublib.buffalo.edu/lml/comics/pages). This site explores the question, "Do comic books belong in libraries?" Geared toward comics for young adults, the site is maintained by Michael R. Lavin of the Lockwood Memorial Library at the State University at Buffalo.

Encyclopedia of 20th Century American Humor by Alleen Pace Nilsen and Don L. F. Nilsen. Oryx, 2000. Chosen as an ALA Best Reference book, this encyclopedia treats humor in children's and adolescent literature and also discusses humorous poetry, irony, parody, and satire.

Graphic Novels (www.graphicnovels.brodart.com) Brodart, a supplier of books to libraries, sponsors this commercial site, which includes core lists of "must have" graphic novels as well as a monthly evaluation of "the best, most appropriate new materials."

MAD *Magazine (www.dccomics.com/mad)* presents a tongue-in-cheek view of current politics, movies, television programs, books, and social movements.

No Flying, No Tights (www.noflyingnotights.com). Robin Brenner, a library technician and graphic novel enthusiast at Brookline Public Library in Brookline, Massachusetts, maintains this site, which reviews graphic novels especially for teens.

The Onion (www.theonion.com) looks so much like a regular news site that it is often mistaken as legitimate even though its main purpose is to satirize the news. A couple of years ago in Florida, a clearly identified excerpt from The *Onion* tripped up high school students when it was put on the state's high-stakes test.

The Psychology of Humor: An Integrative Approach by Rod A. Martin. Elsevier, 2007. Psychology is demonstrataed to interact with a number of other disciplines such as linguistics, sociology, medicine, and anthropology.

Topsy-Turvy Optical Illusions by Al Seckel. Sterling, 2006. Al Seckel is the world's leading authority on visual and other types of sensory illusions. His other books include *Ambiguous Optical Illusions* (Sterling, 2005), *Impossible Optical Illusions* (Sterling 2005), and *More Optical Illusions* (Carlton Books, 2002).

Wry Harvest: An Anthology of Midwest Humor edited by Chris Lamb. Indiana University Press, 2006. Lamb shows how the humor of people as different as Mike Royko, Erma Bombeck, Garrison Keillor, and James Thurber has been influenced by their Midwestern backgrounds.

TABLE 5.1 Some Features of Narrative Humor as Illustrated by Incidents in Louis Sachar's *Holes*

Ambiguity	*Stanley Yelnats* is the name of either Stanley, his father, or his grandfather.
	The whole story would have collapsed if *Zero*'s name hadn't been a shortened form of *Zeroni* instead of a reference to the contents of his brain.
	When Stanley finds the gold cap with *K.B.* on it, he thinks it might be the cap to the pen of a famous writer, but readers figure out that the *K.B.* stands for both *Kate Barlow* and the *Kissing Bandit*.
	Upon seeing the name *Mary Lou* on the back of the sunken boat, Stanley and Zero imagine a boy rowing across the lake with a beautiful girlfriend; readers know that *Mary Lou* was a fifty-year-old donkey who lived on onions.
Exaggeration	The digging of five-foot-by-five-foot holes every day by every boy was surely an exaggeration.
	The characters are eccentrics, especially those bigger-than-life ones from the 1890s including the Kissing Bandit, Kate Barlow, who "died laughing," the mean sheriff, the too-good-to-be-true "onion man," and the too-bad-to-be-true townspeople including Trout Walker and Linda.
	Equally exaggerated is Stanley's great-grandfather who carried his wealth in his suitcase and after losing it to Kate Barlow spent three weeks wandering in the desert. He was saved by the "Thumb of God," and married the nurse who took care of him at the hospital because he thought she was an angel—literally.
Hostility	There is enough hostility to go all around. When Stanley first gets to camp, the guard asks him if he's thirsty and when Stanley gratefully says, "Yes, thanks," the guard tells him to get used to it because "You're going to be thirsty for the next eighteen months."
	Stanley fantasizes about his new "friends" coming to his old school and intimidating his nemesis.
	The warden puts rattlesnake venom in her nail polish so when she slaps Mr. Sir and scratches his face, he writhes in pain and his face is swollen for days.
Incongruity	There could hardly be a more incongruous set of characters ranging from Clyde "Sweet Feet" Livingston to Warden Walker and from Madame Zeroni to poor lovesick Elya Yelnats.
	Stanley had thought about becoming an F.B.I. agent, but he realizes the group meeting with Mr. Pendanski is not "the appropriate place to mention that."
	Readers laugh right along with the other boys when Stanley innocently responds to Mr. Pendanski's lecture about there being only one person responsible for Stanley's predicament: "My no-good-dirty-rotten-pig-stealing-great-great-grandfather."
Incongruity Resolution	The whole story revolves around Sachar's resolving such incongruities as the boys being covered with the dreaded lizards but not being bitten, why the warden made the boys dig so many holes, why Zero never learned to read, how Zero and Stanley were tied together by "fate," how Stanley's great-grandfather was saved on the desert, and why the curse is now lifted.
Irony	Not only is there no lake at Camp Green Lake, there is no greenery except in the two trees whose shade is owned by the warden.
	The townspeople of Green Lake said that God would punish Kate Barlow for kissing a black man, but instead God punishes the town so that no rain falls and the Lake dries up so that not only its shape but also its surface is like a frying pan.
	In his search for Zero, when Stanley comes up on the old, wrecked boat, he realizes that someone probably drowned in the very spot where he might die of thirst.

(Continues)

Superiority	Throughout the story kids feel superior to the adults, and well they might, judging by the Warden, Mr. Sir, and Mr. Pendanski.
	The whole adult society is made to look ridiculous so that readers agree with Stanley's "Well, duh!" when he reads the sign at the entrance to the camp declaring it "a violation of the Texas Penal Code to bring guns, explosives, weapons, drugs, or alcohol onto the premises."
	Readers cheer when Zero and Stanley, who are the lowest on the totem pole of the camp, are the ones who get out and become something less—"but not a lot less"—than millionaires.
	Everyone feels superior to the pot-headed Myra, who does not have sense enough to choose to marry Stanley's great-great-grandfather.
Surprise or Shock	Readers are as surprised as is Stanley at the sneakers falling from the sky and hitting him on the head.
	When Zero tells Stanley that he knows he didn't steal Clyde Livingston's sneakers, Stanley shakes his head because when he tells the truth nobody believes him, and now when he lies, he still isn't believed.
	Stanley and Zero's adventure is one surprise after another starting with Stanley finding Zero and Zero finding the "Sploosh" and ending with their finding the trunk with Stanley Yelnats's name on it.
A Trick or a Twist	An intriguing new setting is provided for the old trick of convincing someone that by lifting a calf every day, his strength will increase at the same rate that the animal gains weight.
Word Play	The recreation hall is named the *W-R-E-C-K* room.
	The boys all have descriptive names: *Zigzag, Magnet, Squid, Armpit, Caveman, Barf Bag,* and *Xray*.
	The macho guard is named *Mr. Sir* (he's doubly a man), while the boys call *Mr. Pendanski* ("pen-dance-key") *Mom*.
	Sachar constantly plays with the word *holes* as when Stanley finds the lipstick tube initialed with *K.B.* and "digs that hole into his memory," and Sachar entitles the denouement, "Filling in the Holes."

Comic Books and Graphic Novels

The idea of telling continuing stories and showing the passing of time by drawing pictures in different boxes, as opposed to having just a single cartoon, was a turn-of-the-last-century innovation. In America, Richard F. Outcault is generally credited with the creation of newspaper comic strips. He had been a scientific and technical illustrator for Thomas Edison's laboratories but wanted to combine his drafting skills with his keen social observations and so began creating comic art. In April of 1895, Joseph Pulitzer's *New York World* agreed to carry Outcault's *Hogan's Alley*, which started as a single panel but gradually evolved into a "strip." One of the characters was a buck-toothed street urchin named Mickey Dugan. He wore an oversized shirt and had his head shaved, which was a common practice to prevent head lice. What "The Kid" said was either printed on the front of his shirt or in a cut line underneath.

The newspaper had just purchased a color press with the intention of printing great art pieces and explaining them to the public, but the technology was not advanced enough to get satisfactory color separations and so the newspaper looked for other ways to get a return on its investment. Yellow was the easiest color to reproduce and a pressman took it upon himself to color Mickey Dugan's shirt yellow. Mickey Dugan became so famous as "The Yellow Kid" that the name of the strip was changed, and the bidding back and forth between Joseph Pulitzer and William Randolph Hearst to print "The Yellow Kid" became so vitriolic and unethical that it contributed to the acceptance of the term *yellow journalism*, which was first used in 1898 to refer to the competition between Pulitzer's *New York World* and Hearst's *New York Journal* and the sensationalized stories that both papers were printing about Spanish atrocities in Cuba.

Bill Blackbeard, who edited a 1995 book celebrating the centennial of comic strips, *R. F. Outcault's The Yellow Kid: A Centennial Celebration of the Kid Who Started the Comics* by Richard Felton Outcault described The Kid as "the first great newspaper comic character" and the "lucrative predecessor" to such other characters as Maggie and Jiggs, Popeye, Blondie, the Gumps, Dick Tracy, Flash Gordon, Buck Rogers, and Charlie Brown and Snoopy. In the 1930s, such storytelling was banned in Italy by Mussolini, while in the 1950s comic books were investigated and castigated for their moral content in an investigation led by U.S. Senator Estes Kefauver of Tennessee. When radio arrived, comics were counted for dead; again their demise was predicted when movies started to talk, and then again when television programming was developed. Today's big threat to comic strips is the shrunken space in newspapers and the desire of editors to cram in a comic strip to please every taste. Some newspapers crowd as many as twenty or thirty strips onto a double-page spread, so that they all end up practically unreadable.

In November of 2006, Pulitzer Prize–winning cartoonist Jules Feiffer spent a week as visiting artist for the Honors College at Arizona State University. When we talked with him, he questioned the idea that we are now in what some people are calling "a golden age of comics." He said that of course he is glad to walk into bookstores and see well-stocked comic sections and to see that after many years this art form is being recognized by the United States Postal Service with a set of stamps honoring superheroes, "but it's a bad set." Even Superman is not represented by the original creators: Jerry Siegel and Joe Shuster. They were two "Clark Kents" from Ohio, who brought their own dreams to a fantastic idea.

He thinks the golden age of comics was the 1930s when the Sunday supplements devoted whole pages to Prince Valiant, Tarzan, and Gasoline Alley. In the 1920s, cars were still relatively rare and people were obsessed with them, which made Gasoline Alley as exciting for its time as space travel is today. When he mentioned Skeezix as the first baby to grow up in the comics, several people in one of his "older" audiences smiled because they remembered babies in their own families being called Skeezix.

One of the points Feiffer made was how important writing is to comics. Of course the drawings are what people see first, but the comic strip has its own form of language. He said that when he first read Samuel Becket's *Waiting for Godot*, he recognized it as comic strip dialogue. He couldn't believe the way it resonated with him, the way the phrases stuck in his head. Becket was the best cartoonist he ever read—even though he did not draw.

The increasing popularity of comics and graphic novels inspires students to try their own hand at drawing as with this illustration of the metaphorical meaning of turf *that students drew in one of our language classes.*

Feiffer said he learned a lot from Becket, including that what you're not telling the reader is as important as what you reveal. Suspense is when you don't know what's happening. In *Waiting for Godot*, nothing is happening, like in Seinfeld, which would never have been on the air if it had not been for Samuel Becket. In a similar way, *Star Wars* would never have been made if not for Alex Raymond's *Flash Gordon*.

Another aspect of comic strips that he finds fascinating is the crossover among genres. Milton Caniff, with his *Terry and the Pirates*, was a genius when he created the adventure strip by turning comic art into a storyboard. His Dragon Lady came straight from the movies and for generations circled back around in the popular culture. Soldiers in Vietnam were still using her as a reference point, and Anne McCaffrey (see her Margaret A. Edwards Award, p. 225) jokingly refers to herself as the Dragon Lady.

Comic books were a natural outgrowth of comic strips and almost from the very beginning newspapers began reprinting their strips, binding them together, and selling them through newsstands on a monthly, bimonthly, or quarterly basis. The term "comic magazine" was also used. It was the 1930s before original material was prepared and whole books were devoted to single characters.

The terms *comic strips* and *comic books* became so firmly entrenched that they continued to be used even when creators moved away from the kinds of humorous events and jokes that had been the norm in such "innocent" strips as *Mutt and Jeff*, *The Yellow Kid*, and *Krazy Kat*. What comic books have in common is their format and binding, not the subject matter or the attitudes that their creators take toward their stories. Every possible genre—adventure, romance, tragedy, informative nonfiction, horror, science fiction and fantasy—has been treated in so-called comic books.

Graphic novels are comic books that have gone off to college and come back with new sophistication and respect. Actually, many of them are not so different from comic books except that they have more durable bindings and cost more money. One of the reasons that the new term is coming into popularity is that it is more accurate because it focuses on what such books have in common, which is the drawings. The *Merriam Webster Collegiate Dictionary* (tenth edition, 2001) dates the term *graphic novel* at 1978 and defines it as "a fictional story for adults that is presented in comic-strip format and published as a book." Feiffer said while many graphic novels are junk, they are still the place where the most interesting forms of cartooning are being done today, especially with the alternative presses.

He thinks highly of Chris Ware (whose real name is Jimmy Corrigan) and The ACME Novelty Library series, which are being put together from Ware's comic strips supplemented by a few extras. Michael Chabon, who won the 2001 Pulitzer Prize for *The Amazing Adventures of Kavalier and Clay*, had an early love of comics, which he put into the plot of his adult book, set just before World War II when comic books were rising in popularity. Back in 1991, Jeff Smith, who was also a lover of comics, especially Walt Kelly's *Pogo*, started independently publishing his Bone books (Sample titles include *Out from Boneville* and *The Great Cow Race*) for a general adult audience. The characters are a surprising mixture of human and imaginary creatures engaged in activities reminiscent of Tolkien's *The Lord of the Rings* trilogy.

It's not just boys who are reading graphic novels. Marvel Comics has published *Spider-Girl*, Volumes 1 through 6, by Tom DeFalco and Pat Olliffe. The subtitles are *Legacy*, *Like Father Like Daughter*, *Avenging Allies*, *Turning Point*, *Endgame*, and *Too Many Spiders!* The Spider Girl comics are the longest-running Marvel comic books starring a female superhero. A bonus is that they offer a world where even villains can find redemption and heroes can retain their moral scruples. The most charming graphic novel we've seen is *To Dance: A Ballerina's Graphic Novel*, by Siena Cherson Siegel, illustrated by Mark Siegel. It is an autobiographical story being marketed to fourth through seventh graders, but we've seen older girls and adults enjoying it while also learning about the American dance scene in the 1970s and 1980s.

Graphic Novels: Stories to Change Your Life, by Paul Gravett, is a good introduction to graphic novels appropriate for either adult or high school readers interested in learning about the genre and about the thirty graphic novels Gravett considers "classics." Feiffer suggests we offer books to students that will give them some historical benchmarks from which to view today's comics. He went back to Windsor McKay as a model for some of his early drawings and he also looked at the work of Thomas Nast, not for his style of art but to get the feeling of rage that Nast expressed. One of his happiest moments was to hear that both Woody Allen and Gary Trudeau have said that they went to some of Feiffer's work for inspiration as they developed their own kinds of humor. For a different kind of graphic novel, see Stefanie Craig's description of manga on pp. 178–179.

Video Games as Interactive Literature

Starting with the third edition of this textbook, we began mentioning interactive fiction, something that would go way beyond those Choose Your Own Adventure novels that kids had fun with back in the 1970s. But we always

A Young Adult Reader Speaks Out

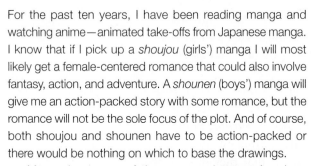

Stefanie Craig, **A Manga Lover**

Speaks to Teachers

For the past ten years, I have been reading manga and watching anime—animated take-offs from Japanese manga. I know that if I pick up a *shoujou* (girls') manga I will most likely get a female-centered romance that could also involve fantasy, action, and adventure. A *shounen* (boys') manga will give me an action-packed story with some romance, but the romance will not be the sole focus of the plot. And of course, both shoujou and shounen have to be action-packed or there would be nothing on which to base the drawings.

Manga has many of the same archetypes (warriors, heroes, sages, magicians, creators, innocent fools, etc.) that are in Western young adult literature, but one difference is that because manga is produced over many years in weekly, biweekly, or monthly magazines, the creator has time to develop a larger supporting cast than is usual in a book. It is a process-approach to storytelling. For example, *Fruits Basket*, a graphic novel just published in November of 2006, ran for seven years in the *Hana to Yume* magazine in Japan. At least twelve important characters help the protagonist with her quest. *Bleach*, which has run in *Weekly Shounen Jump* magazine since 2001, has five protagonists and nearly twenty important supporting characters.

Another difference is that while manga has a wide range of "good" and "bad" characters, there are more char-

acters in between, which makes it harder to label them. For example, the "innocent fool" in American stories is often held up as a negative example—someone whose behavior should be avoided. In manga, this is less true, probably because in Japan it is considered rude to point out someone's flaws.

Also, the main character of a series is not going to be purely good. The protagonist from *Slayers*, which is a popular franchise that has spanned novels, manga, and anime, is Lina Inverse, a character who is rude, brash, selfish, and loud. She beats up her partner if he stops listening to her (maybe this is why she's one of my favorite characters). Lina is a grey, as opposed to a black or white, character. Although she has lots of faults, she looks out for not only herself, but others around her, and ultimately the world, although it is always through her own skewed sense of justice.

One of the reasons that the in-between or grey characters are more interesting is that they are often the targets of influence by other characters who want to convince the neutral character to join their side. Once grey characters come under someone else's control, they are no longer considered grey because they are working for other people's priorities and are being controlled by some type of magical or technological means.

sort of begged off from writing about it because the idea wasn't fully developed yet. But now that full-blown interactive fiction has arrived by way of video games played either on computers or on game platforms such as the Nintendo Game Cube or a Sony PlayStation, many of us hesitate to embrace it. We're frightened away by such names as Warcraft, Gears of War, Counterstrike, and Grand Theft Auto.

With manga, there are extra complications because symbols and practices commonly understood to mean one thing in Japan may be understood to mean something different in America. For example, in the United States nudity usually connotes some kind of a sexual situation, while in Japan nudity may simply be a matter of efficiency because of longtime traditions of communal baths and family living arrangements. Also, Japanese has several different writing systems from which creators pick and choose to achieve different effects. *Kanji* is a system based on Chinese characters, while *hiragana* and *katakana* are different systems of Japanese characters. Some writers might also borrow from English or Romanized Japanese, and today most of the manga brought to the United States keeps the right-to-left sequencing that is the standard pattern in Japan. Early on, Japanese importers rearranged the panels to go from left to right, but then characters in the drawings appeared to be going the wrong way, and besides, we fans like a little reminder that we are reading something "different."

Japan's current market for manga began shortly after the end of World War II when a young doctor named Osamu Tezuka began to write and draw *Diary of Ma-chan.* He later became known as "the god of manga" because of the way present day manga styles can be traced back to his original artwork. During postwar Japan the popularity of manga grew, both because of its accessibility and also because it was inexpensive.

Manga are published typically every week or every month in large magazines, which sometimes include over a dozen different stories, most likely aimed at a specific audience by age and gender, although some manga such as the ones by Rumiko Takahashi, are read by both boys and girls. Takahashi's current series, *Inuyasha*, is published weekly in *Shounen Sunday* and is usually about eighteen pages long. Natsuki Takaya, creator of *Fruits Basket*, which ended its run in November of 2006, usually had thirty or more pages because her story ran only once a month.

Manga can be a single chapter of a short story or can run for decades. *Dragonball* by Akira Toriyama had a run from 1984 to 1995 and was collected into forty-two graphic novels in those eleven years. The longest-running manga in history, *This Is the Police Station in Front of Kameari Park in Katsushika* (not available in English), has been running continuously since 1976 with over 1400 chapters published. These types of publications are unusual, though, when you consider that other manga, such as Naoko Takeuchi's *Sailor Moon*, only ran for five years.

Unlike American comics, manga are almost exclusively black and white. Sometimes a creator will color the first few pages of a chapter for a week, but this is a rare occurrence. If a manga is considered successful and well liked by fans they are collected into *tankouban*, or graphic novels. It usually takes several months for this to occur because a graphic novel has many chapters of the weekly or monthly publication in it, and the magazine style publication does not stop once they are being republished. These graphic novels are what we Americans see when we go to buy our own translated manga.

Some of the most current manga hits are Rumiko Takahashi's *Inuyasha*, Kubo Tite's *Bleach*, Natsuki Takaya's *Fruits Basket*, Masashi Kishimoto's *Naruto*, and *Nana*, by Ai Yazawa. With new manga coming out each day there is something for every student, from science fiction and fantasy to romantic drama.

• Stefanie Craig may be the only college student in the United States who won a scholarship based on her knowledge of manga. Here at Arizona State University she won a Sun Angel Award because of her proposal to teach English teachers what they need to know about this new genre.

In the survey we took of 266 local high school students, we asked those who played video games to list a favorite and tell why they liked it. Eighty-four of the students responded, with hardly any of them listing the same game, which made us nostalgic for the old days when our grandchildren were all playing Pokémon and we had a chance of joining in their conversations. One of the boys filling out the survey had obviously had experience with negative adult judgments because he appended a note after he wrote that Stalker was fun: "No—you don't stalk people." Another boy said he liked Day of Defeat because he owns *noobs*, which he kindly explained are "beginners, like *newbys*." Another boy said he didn't like to play the games, but he loved "hunting for them online."

Besides the online card games, which seven students mentioned and which we understand are played by millions of women, there are basically four kinds of video games: first-person shooter games, fantasy role-playing games, real-time strategy games, and simulation games. The shooter games came first because they are the easiest to program, but as designers are getting more skilled and are figuring out how to let their characters talk, both the number and the variety of games have expanded so much that the video-game industry now makes as much or more money than does the film industry. We heard on an NPR broadcast that the 2006 Japanese economy was saved by the marketing of manga, anime, and computer games around the world, especially to the United States.

James Paul Gee makes the point, in *What Video Games Have to Teach Us about Learning and Literacy*, that many adults are looking at the games from the wrong perspective. We think the games must be a waste of time because they are not teaching content as textbooks do. However, Gee says, in fact, some of them do teach content while at the same time involving players in the kinds of active and critical learning that prepares them for the decision making and the modes of operation that are an increasingly big part of modern life. He organizes his book around over thirty "Learning Principles," a few of which he discusses in each chapter under such titles as Semiotic Domains, Learning and Identity, Situated Meaning and Learning, and The Social Mind.

A point he makes throughout the book is that video games often have a greater potential for learning than does much of what happens in school. His principles illustrate *active* learning. As an illustration of what he means by active learning, Gee says that when game players pick up the direction manual that accompany the games, they find the reading tough going. Younger players just start experimenting and playing the games in different ways, while older players who have grown up with different attitudes read the manuals over and over and fret if they cannot foresee exactly what they should do. Finally, out of frustration, they turn to the game and start playing. Then when they go back to the manual to check on some detail, they are happily surprised to discover that it is now much easier to read and understand.

We kept Gee's claims about active learning in mind as we read the reasons that students in our survey wrote for liking particular games. Two students said they were learning history from Age of Empires, while several mentioned cognitive processes in relation to particular games.

- Feeding Frenzy: "It takes multitasking."
- Warrior Worlds: "It's fast paced and allows for strategy."
- Ragdog Avalanche: "Because it's challenging."
- Gameball: "Because you have to pay attention."

- Command and Conquer: "Strategic, real-time overview, fun and challenging."
- Monopoly Tycoon: "Because it tests my brain."

When we adults walk by and see kids focusing so intently on their computers, we worry that they are growing up as loners or as antisocial beings, but students countered this idea with comments related to particular games:

- Starcraft: "I love this game because I can verve my friends online and it's strategic."
- Guild Wars: "I can communicate with people around the world and build teamwork, skills, and strategies."
- Infantry: "Because it's a shooting game and you have to use strategy. Your opponents are other people online."
- Runescape: "It's fun. You walk around and talk to other players, get your skills up and do quests."
- Gears of War: "I play with about fifteen of my friends."
- Action: "I love the challenge and puzzles that come."

The simulation games appear to come the closest to what English teachers would define as interactive fiction, and these were also the ones mentioned the most by girls as with these four who commented on some version of Sims.

- Sims: "It's fun and challenging," "Because you can control people. I get to build houses and the people who live in them, ha ha!" "Building and designing homes and defining what happens."
- Star Wars 2: "It's cool to change your characters and they're funny."
- World of Warcraft: "I like the fiction and the ability to create your own character."
- Axis and Allies: "I like it because you can be either of these two teams."

While twelve students mentioned having fun, only a couple mentioned humor. At the 2007 International Society of Humor Studies conference held at Salve Regina University in Newport, Rhode Island, we heard a panel presentation on the humor (or lack of humor) in video games. The presenters explained that because the figures are so small, it is hard to reproduce the facial expressions which bring much of the humor to comics and cartoons. And while some of the best designers are starting to bring in humor, for now the humor is coming mostly from the way players mock the characters and create their own parody stories.

Related to this, authors who grew up playing video games are bringing them into their writing as with Conor Kostick's 2007 *Epic*, a fantasy story about a society where violence is forbidden and people must solve their differences through the game world of Epic, while simultaneously trying to accumulate wealth and status in both the real world and the fantasy world. See Chapter 7 on science fiction and fantasy for other books where the authors have used computer gaming as part of the plot.

Concluding Comments

Of all the chapters in this book, this is the one that begs for some kind of out-loud sharing. We hope that in class you can have a poetry slam (or jam) and that selected students will perform an excerpt or an improvised scene from a play or do a humorous reader's theater presentation. It would also be a good experience for you to go to a local high school production of a play, and by making a few phone calls to the central administration of your local library to locate a teen poetry slam that you could observe. And in relation to the new media of graphic novels and video games, you might follow what we did with Stefanie Craig in asking her to help educate us on the genre of manga. Remember when, as English teachers, we used to assign students to write a follow-the-direction essay telling us how to make a peanut butter sandwich? Surely, it would be more interesting all the way around if you invited students to write a follow-the-direction essay telling you how to play their favorite video game or a comparison/contrast piece on two graphic novels.

Notes

1. Marc Aronson, "When Coming of Age Meets the Age That's Coming: One Editor's View of How Young Adult Publishing Developed in America," *VOYA* 21:5 (December 1998): 340–342.

2. Sarah Flowers, "Poetry Speaks," a "Teen Screen" feature, *VOYA* 29:1 (April 2006): 32–33. Flowers served for four years on YALSA's Selected DVDs and Video for Young Adults Committee, a group worth looking up on the American Library Association's home page.

3. Paul Janeczko, "On Collecting Poems," in *Literature for Today's Young Adults*, by Kenneth L. Donelson and Alleen Pace Nilsen (Longman, 1997), p. 345.

4. David Lehman, "The American Prose Poem," from *The American Poetry Review*, March/April 2003, quoted in "This Week's Chronicle" at http://chronicle.com/chronicle, April 18, 2003.

5. Ed Sullivan, "Up for Discussion: Fiction or Poetry: A Librarian Looks at the Profusion of Novels Written in Verse," *School Library Journal August*, 2003, pp. 44–45.

6. Richard W. Beach and James D. Marshall, *Teaching Literature in the Secondary School* (Harcourt Brace Jovanovich, 1991), p. 384.

7. Luella B. Cook, "Reading for Experience," *English Journal* 25 (April 1936): 280.

8. Rick E. Amidon, "Toward a Young Adult Drama," *English Journal* 76 (September 1987): 59.

9. Lance M. Gentile and Merna M. McMillan, "Humor and the Reading Program," *Journal of Reading* 21 (January 1978): 343–350.

10. Henry Spalding, quoted in *Encyclopedia of 20th Century American Humor*, by Alleen Pace Nilsen and Don L. F. Nilsen (Oryx Press, 2000), p. 173.

Adventure, Sports, Mysteries, and the Supernatural

Remembering English teachers who pleaded with us to "read only the best—the classics," many of us feel vaguely worried when we read books simply to enjoy characters and their adventures. Somewhat defensively, we make claims that are hard to substantiate. For example, we claim that reading about adventures makes us more interesting people, sports books teach us the game of life, mysteries are psychologically helpful to our inner well-being, and horror stories are a substitute for aggression. These claims may have some truth, but they are hard to prove. We would be on safer ground if we simply accepted "Rosenberg's First Law of Reading: Never apologize for your reading tastes"[1] and promoted the idea that reading for pleasure is a worthy activity and goal in and of itself. If we, or our students, gain something more than pleasure, we should be grateful that serendipity is still at work in today's complex world.

Adventure Stories

"Once upon a time" is a magical phrase. In one way or another, it opens every adventure tale and suggests actions and excitement. While we may care about the people in these adventures, we care equally—or more—about the actions to come. The greatest of these is implied violence, things we fear that will happen. The pace and tempo force the action to move faster and faster and to speed us into the tale.

Adventure books sell well, for good reason. Anthony Brandt, in *American Heritage*, noted that the country was mad for adventure.

> The whole country seems bent on getting out there and having adventures, and if you can't do it, you can read about it. Magazines like *Men's Journal* and *Outside* that specialize in the subject are thriving. The staid old National Geographic Society has launched its own magazine, *National Geographic Adventure*, to take advantage of what has reached the state of a craze.[2]

The author then added, "A taste for adventure is as old as the human race itself, a function of an evolutionary development that rewards risk takers over the timid and the meek." Readers of adventure tales feel much the same way about taking chances as did Susan Hiscock. For fifty years she and her husband sailed the globe, never letting loose of their wanderlust. She was a fan of Arthur Ransome's books and one of his mottos was painted over their cabin door: "Grab a chance and you won't be sorry for a might-have-been." That's a great motto for living—and for reading, too.

The best adventure story takes us outside ourselves (see Table 6.1). In an article on the dangers of being in Yosemite National Park, an ecologist and wilderness guide said, "There are incredible benefits to our life of modern luxury. But we pay for it by domesticating ourselves. When we set out in a park like Yosemite, we enter a world for which we are not very well trained. You don't practice sitting on top of 3,000-foot-high cliffs. You don't get that at the office."[3]

He's right, of course. We don't prepare for outdoor adventure by going to the office. That's why we crave all sorts of excitement by reading about people who do not go to the office. They live adventure and the thrills and chills we have denied ourselves by living in our comfortable and safe world.

The best adventure tales demand more than a plot and a series of actions. Good writers provide believable characters amid those thrills and chills, at least

TABLE 6.1 Suggestions for Evaluating Adventure Stories

A good adventure story has most of the positive qualities generally associated with good fiction. In addition it usually has:	A poor adventure story may have the negative qualities generally associated with poor fiction. It is particularly prone to have:
A likable protagonist with whom young readers identify	A protagonist who is too exaggerated or too stereotyped to be believable
An adventure that readers can imagine happening to themselves	Nothing really exciting about the adventure
Efficient characterization	Only stereotyped characters
An interesting setting that enhances the story without being in the way of the plot	A long drawn-out conclusion after the climax has been reached
Action that draws readers into the plot within the first page or so of the story	

a likable and imperfect (and probably young) protagonist and a wily and dangerous antagonist (or villain). Because we are primarily interested in action, we're likely to be irritated by long descriptive or meditative passages. Writers must reveal characterization through the plot—what could happen, what might happen, how all incidents tie together. We want surprises and turns of the screw. Heroes become trapped, and the only way to safety is through even greater jeopardy. Adventure tales usually focus either on person-against-person or on person-against-nature, with person-against-self becoming important only as the tale unfolds and the protagonist faces frustration and possible failure.

The most important literary device found in adventure stories is verisimilitude. With so much emphasis on danger, writers must provide realistic details galore to assure us, despite some inner misgivings, that the tale is possible and believable. We must believe that whatever the hero's frustrations, the cliffhanging scenes are possible.

Robb White's *Deathwatch* epitomizes the elements of adventure novels— person versus person, person versus nature, person versus self, conflicts, tension, thrills, chills, and a hero frustrated at every turn by an inventive, devious, and cruel villain. The first paragraph forces us into the action and introduces the two actors:

> "There he is!" Madec whispered. "Keep still!" There had been a movement up on the ridge of the mountain. For a moment something had appeared between the two rock outcrops.
> "I didn't see any horns," Ben said.
> "Keep quiet!" Madec whispered fiercely.

We know from those few words that *Deathwatch* has something to do with hunting, although we have no reason yet to suspect that hunting will become an ominous metaphor. We recognize that the name Madec sounds harsh and seems vaguely related to the word *mad*, again without recognizing how prescient we are. Within the next few pages, we learn how carefully White has placed the clues before us. Ben crouches with his little .22 Hornet and watches Madec with his "beautifully made .385 Magnum Mauser action on a Winchester 70 stock with enough power to knock down an elephant—or turn a sleeping Gila monster into a splatter" and remembers that Madec had been willing to shoot anything that moved.

> Madec huddled over his gun. There was an intensity in his eyes far beyond that of just hunting a sheep. It was the look of murder.

And murder is present. Before long, Madec takes a shot at a bighorn sheep, which turns out to be an old desert prospector—now quite dead—and he asks Ben to quash the incident and forget it ever happened. Ben refuses, and the book is off and running. So is Ben, running for his life, without gun, water, or food, amid hostile desert mountains and sand and a killing gun.

Madec personifies the maddened but crafty villain, able to read Ben's mind and forestall his attempts to get clothes, weapons, or water. We are almost certain Ben will win, but we wonder because Madec is an extraordinary opponent.

We see Ben change from a calm, rational young man to a frightened, desperate animal and then into a cold, dangerous person who must think as Madec thinks to win out over the villain. Madec begins with all the power on his side—guns, water, food, and wealth. Given reality, we know that Madec must win, but given our sense of rightness and justice, we know that he cannot be allowed to win. Ben has little interest in right or wrong after the first few pages. His interest is more elemental and believable—survival until he can escape.

Gary Paulsen leads all other YA writers in adventure tales. See p. 187 for the write-up on him as a Margaret A. Edwards Award winner. Coming in a close second is Will Hobbs, whose interests in hiking, white-water rafting, archaeology, and natural history are reflected in his books. *Bearstone*, about a Native American boy sent to live with an old rancher whose wife has died, combines adventure with a story of growth and friendship. His stories are more action-packed than Paulsen's and sometimes less introspective, though in *Downriver* the change that Jessie makes in her life is impressive. In *Far North* and *Jason's Gold*, readers learn what it is like to be really cold. *Jackie's Wild Seattle* is about mountain climbing, while both *Ghost Canoe* and *Down the Yukon* are canoeing adventures.

Hobbs's 2002 *Wild Man Island* may not wind up precisely as an adventure tale, but it begins with all that makes a book an adventure. Andy Galloway, fourteen, sneaks off from his kayaking tour group early one morning to find Hidden Falls on Baranof Island, Alaska, where his father had died. He should have been back in plenty of time to join the group, but he hadn't counted on hostile sea lions or a wind that mightily came at him and drove him off course as he headed back to his group. Sea lions wreck his kayak and he swims to the beach, almost dead from exposure.

From there on, Andy has a run-in with a grizzly bear; he hears wolves howling; he sees a dog where none should be; he finds an abandoned cannery, and more frightening—and intriguing—he runs into "a giant of a man overgrown with gray hair." *Wild Man Island* becomes a combination of adventure mixed with Andy's need to justify his father's archeological theories.

One of Hobbs's later books is *Crossing the Wire*. In *Crossing*, adventure is imposed on fifteen-year-old Victor Flores. Victor's father is dead, he is the sole breadwinner of his family, and that means he must illegally cross the border, the "wire" into the United States to find work. He has no green card, no command of English, no trade skills, and no money to pay the "coyotes" to guide him. His struggle to cross the border and to face drug smugglers, gang violence, and starvation makes for a compelling and disturbing novel.

Part of the charm of adventure stories is their variety of settings—both in time and space. Cornelia Funke's *The Thief Lord* is set on the watery "streets" of modern Venice. Two orphans, who are fleeing from cruel relatives, meet a group of other kids and a charismatic young man who calls himself the Thief Lord. She uses puckish humor to make the Thief Lord different from Charles Dickens's Artful Dodger in *Oliver Twist*.

In Kenneth Oppel's *Airborn*, fifteen-year-old Matt Cruse, a cabin boy on the luxury airship *Aurora*, watches a balloon sink slowly. Matt saves the old balloonist, but he dies that night. A year later, Kate, the granddaughter of the balloonist, travels on the *Aurora*, hoping to learn more about her grandfather's last voyage. *Skybreaker* carries on the story with Matt and Kate joining forces with

Margaret A. Edwards Award
Winner (1997)

Gary Paulsen, **Adventurer and More**

Among Paulsen's two hundred plus-or-minus books, the ones honored by the Margaret A. Edwards Award are *Hatchet, Woodsong, The Winter Room, The Crossing, Canyons,* and *Dancing Cart.* We would add to the list of his very best *Harris and Me, Brian's Winter, Soldier's Heart: A Novel of the Civil War, The River, The Beet Fields,* and *Guts.*

Gary Paulsen is most famous for the survival story that he tells in *Hatchet,* about thirteen-year-old Brian, who is flying to visit his father in the Canadian wilderness. The pilot has a fatal heart attack and the plane goes down. Brian's only survival tool is a hatchet that was a gift from his mother. While that wasn't much, it allowed him to survive.

Hatchet seems likely to become a classic adventure and survival story, probably for boys but it would work for most readers. Paulsen received a number of letters from readers who liked the book but questioned if Paulsen had taken the easy way out by having Brian rescued at the end of summer. They asked, what if Brian had not been rescued? Could he have survived a winter? Paulsen answered by writing another book, *Brian's Winter,* in which Brian is not rescued and has to face a bleak winter.

If that wasn't enough, Paulsen wrote other books about Brian, the most impressive being the nonfiction *Guts: The True Story behind Hatchet and the Brian Books.* Maybe a reader questioned Paulsen on the accuracy of *Hatchet* or the likelihood that Brian would survive, given the odds against him. In *Guts,* Paulsen writes about his own adventures that parallel Brians's problems. In successive chapters, Paulsen recalls his own near plane crashes, his tangles with a moose, his run-in with mosquitoes, and his ability to handle a gun—or a bow—when it was necessary. His education learning to eat in the wilderness is announced by the title of Chapter Five, "Eating Eyeballs and Guts or Starving."

Young people love Paulsen and his books. Some of that adulation comes from a simple fact, that Paulsen has lived a rugged life and has done most of the things that appear in his book. He has lived in the Canadian wilderness and in mountains and in canyons. He has sailed around Cape Horn. He has owned a motorcycle. He rides horses. He has played professional poker. He loves dogs and has raced them in the Alaskan Iditarod, and one dog, Cookie, saved his life. He has worked in a beet field, and he has worked for a carnival.

Paulsen is a master writer of adventure books, all essentially rite-of-passage. But he has written other kinds of books as well. *Harris and Me* is an autobiographical story of his early youth when he was dumped off on some relatives because his own folks were drunks. He learns to love his relations, particularly his cousin, Harris, who has a wild scheme for every occasion. Both boys learn the questionable fun of peeing on an electric fence or wrestling three hundred-pound pigs. *The Beet Fields* is as likely to be read and enjoyed by adults as young people, It's the story of Paulsen's sixteenth year, when he goes to work in the beet fields and learns that migrants can go up and down the rows much faster than he, and he will never get rich at weeding beets. It's the story of his working for a carnival and meeting Ruby. It's a gritty autobiography, and as Paulsen says this is "as real as I can write it, and as real as I can remember it happening."

Gary Paulsen writes for young adults, and they recognize honesty and goodness in his words. In *The Winter Room,* he tells the reader, "If books could have more, give more, be more, show more, they would still need readers, who bring to them sound and smell and light and all the rest that can't be in books. The book needs you."

The book always needs the reader, and Paulsen provides books that find the reader over and over. ●

a pirate's daughter and a swashbuckling ship's captain to salvage a ghost airship that disappeared forty years earlier.

Adventurous Girls

In Avi's Newbery Medal–winning *The True Confessions of Charlotte Doyle*, a young girl is forced to overcome circumstances before they overcome her. Charlotte is raised in an upper-class family with a strong father. Even though she is warned not to board the brig *Seahawk*, bound from Liverpool, England, to Providence, Rhode Island, her father has told her to take the ship, and so she goes on board, the only female on a ship commanded by evil and cruel Captain Jaggers. Trapped by the captain, she evades his plan to kill her and watches as the ship tips and plunges in a storm and the captain goes overboard. The crew makes her the ship's new captain—mostly because Charlotte is the daughter of an officer of the ship's company—but also because she has shown courage in facing down the captain and aiding the crew.

While most readers enjoyed Charlotte's adventures, at least one reviewer had qualms. Anne Scott MacLeod said, "It's a fine and vicarious adventure story. It is also preposterous."[4] Avi took exception to the exception and in the Summer 1999 *Signal*, wrote, "It is a legitimate task . . . of fiction to re-invent the past, if you will, so as to better define the future . . . Historical fiction—among other things—is about today's possibilities."[5] Perhaps both MacLeod's and Avi's statements illustrate the truth of critic Henry Seidel Canby's words, which are more than seventy years old, "Historical fiction, like history, is more likely to register an exact truth about the writer's present than the exact truth of the past."[6]

Another girl at sea is the heroine of L. A. Meyer's books about Bloody Jacky who starts her adventures as a ship's boy. The first book begins with Mary Faber's childhood in late eighteenth-century London, where her family has died from the plague. After cutting off her hair, and being a member of Rooster Charlie's gang, she spots a way out of London and her dreary world. She sees a ship, *The Dolphin*, and she tells a member of the crew that she can read (her father taught her). She becomes the ship's cabin boy, and off she sails, facing the wind and all the problems destined to come her way. She receives the inevitable rough treatment from the crew, she has no idea what life at sea is like, and she has no notion of the duties of a ship's boy, and—most of all—she puts off the inevitable discovery of her sex almost longer than readers can believe. She has adventures aplenty, all of them well handled by Meyer. Her later adventures are told in three books—*Curse of the Blue Tattoo: Being an Account of the Misadventures of Jacky Faber, Midshipman and Fine Lady*; *Under the Jolly Roger: Being an Account of the Further Nautical Adventures of Jacky Faber*; and *In the Belly of the Bloodhound, Being an Account of the Particularly Peculiar Adventure in the Life of Jacky Faber*.

In 2002, Nancy Farmer proved in *The House of the Scorpion* that she could write an exciting survival story, but since this was a science fiction dystopian novel, readers had other things to focus on besides the adventure. But in her 1997 *A Girl Named Disaster*, survival—physical as well as emotional—is the main focus. The realistic story takes place in the early 1980s in Mozambique and Zimbabwe, when there was considerable hostility among white people, the Shona, and the Matebele, and crossing borders was dangerous because of land mines. The protagonist is an eleven-year-old orphan, Nhamo, who lives with her deceased mother's relatives, but with the encouragement of her grandmother flees when the village decides that to ward off the evil spirits that have brought a plague to their area, Nhamo must marry a villainous older man with three older wives who everyone knows will resent Nhamo.

Nhamo follows her grandmother's instructions on how to escape in a fishing boat, but she misses the place where two rivers come together just before emptying into the huge Lake Cabora Bassa, which was formed when dams were built. When the rivers joined, Nhamo was supposed to paddle against the current, but instead she ends up lost in the lake. She lives for almost a year on a small island where she has to find her own food and deal with baboons and also a leopard. Finally, with the kind of strength that would have made her grandmother proud, Nhamo builds herself a new boat and sets out to find the river she had missed before.

Ship Ahoy! The Excitement of Pirate Stories

Johnny Depp has starred in three pirate films—*Pirates of the Caribbean: The Curse of the Black Pearl* (2003); *Pirates of the Caribbean: Dead Man's Chest* (2000); and *Pirates of the Caribbean: At World's End* (2007)—that have made multimillions of dollars along with millions of happy fans. Pirates are big business in film. They are equally entertaining to read about in books, as long as their cruelty and their bloodshed is confined to the printed page.

Howard Pyle's *Book of Pirates: Fiction, Fact, and Fancy Concerning the Buccaneers and Marooners of the Spanish Main*, first published in 1891, is one of the earliest books on pirates for young people, and in his preface he made the life of the pirate ambivalently distasteful and attractive:

> What a life of adventure is his, to be sure! A life of constant alertness, constant danger, constant escape! An ocean Ishmaelite, he wanders forever aimlessly, homelessly; now unheard of for months, now careening, his boat on some lonely uninhabited shore, now appearing suddenly to swoop down on some merchant vessel with rattle of musketry, shouting, yells, and a hell of unbridled passion, let loose to rend and tear.

YA writers have not ignored the attraction of pirates to young people. Tanith Lee's *Piratica: Being a Daring Tale of a Singular Girl's Adventure Upon the High Seas* is the tale of sixteen-year-old Artemesia Fitz-Willoughby's dream of taking on her dead mother's pirate lifestyle. A blow to the head brings back memories of sea storms and sword fights, all fantasy but all real to the eager girl. *Piratica II: Return to Parrot Island* is a delightful sequel. In Celia Rees's *Pirates*, Nancy Kington runs off from an arranged marriage to an evil man to join a pirate crew. When pirates begin raiding Savage Island in Lenore Hunt's *The Treasure of Savage Island*, fifteen-year-old Molly warns the settlers, saves her father, and finds a long-lost treasure. And in William Gilkerson's *Pirate's Passage*, when Captain Johnson of the good ship *Merry Adventure* washes up in Nova Scotia, a boy and his mother welcome him, but while the captain's extensive knowledge of pirates and pirates' ways excites the boy, it also makes him suspicious.

In Iain Lawrence's *The Wreckers*, a young man who longs for the sea but is denied it by his businessman father becomes involved in the dangerous business of looting wrecked ships. His adventures continue in *The Smugglers* and *The Buccaneers*. Lawrence's *The Convicts* begins with Tom, a fourteen-year-old boy charged with murder and sentenced to the Lachesis, a prison ship for boys. In the sequel, *The Cannibals*, the boys' lives are even more brutal as they plot to escape from a convict ship taking them to Australia.

Geraldine McCaughrean's *The Pirate's Son*, set in the 1800s and packed with derring-do, opens with the death of Nathan Gull's father. Nathan must leave school since he has no money, but luckily for him, Tamo White, son of a pirate, decides to leave school, too, and take Nathan with him. The first half of McCaughrean's *The Kite Rider* is even more action packed. The setting is thirteenth-century China, after the Mongols have conquered it, and hatred and distrust between Chinese and Mongols permeate the land. When twelve-year-old Haoyou's father takes his son to see his ship, the boy is thrilled until the first mate takes offense when the father insults the Khan's wife. The mate kicks Haoyou off the ship and, worse yet, attaches the father to a kite hoisted over the ship to determine whether the winds augur a profitable voyage for the ship and the crew. Horrifying as this is, Haoyou is unprepared when his father catches the wind and is lifted high aloft, only to be as suddenly plummeted to his death. It is now up to Haoyou to carry on the duties of the family and the honor of his father. He manages admirably, and a bonus for readers is that they get to meet Mipeng, a girl cousin, who is clever, funny, and wise in ways that save Haoyou from himself.

Pirates were so popular that even the American Library Association jumped on board by using a pirate theme for its 2007 Banned Books Week celebration. The children's poster, which read "Discover Buried Treasure," featured an open pirate's chest of gold surrounding four frequently censored books: Alvin Schwartz's *In a Dark, Dark Room*, Harry Allard's *The Stupids Step Out*, Dav Pilkey's *Captain Underpants and the Preposterous Plight of the Purple Potty People*, and Robie Harris's *It's Perfectly Normal*. The next page features another young adult poster reprinted by permission of the American Library Association.

Nonfiction Adventures

Nonfiction adventures in which people set out to challenge nature (see Focus Box 6.1, Real People Challenging Nature, p. 192) have an extra level of excitement because readers know that human lives are at stake. While young people seldom have what it takes to embark on such purposeful adventures, they can nevertheless read about them. They can also imagine what they would do if they happen to be forced into such an adventure, as were the young people whose story is told in *Alive* (see the discussion in Chapter 9, pp. 283–284).

Climbing mountains is one of the ways that people face off against nature because, as Reinhold Messner reminds us, "In all true adventure, the path between the summit and the grave is a narrow one indeed."[7] Nowhere is that clearer than in Jon Krakauer's *Into Thin Air: A Personal Account of the Mount*

ALA's young adult poster, under the banner, "Get Hooked on a Banned Book," featured Judy Blume's Forever, *Lois Lowry's* The Giver, *and Chris Crutcher's* Whale Talk, *all dressed as pirates. The adult poster used the banner "Set Sail on the Ship O' the Banned" and showed a large ship with sails made from Amy Tan's* The Joy Luck Club, *Maya Angelou's* I Know Why the Caged Bird Sings, *John Steinbeck's* Of Mice and Men, *and Sandra Cisneros's* The House on Mango Street.

Everest Disaster. In the spring of 1996, fourteen groups of climbers were making their way up Mount Everest. Krakauer reached the summit on May 10, as did five teammates, but five others died, and nineteen others were stranded for a time when a freak storm hit and left them to survive temperatures of 100 degrees below zero. Ultimately, Everest took twelve lives that spring. Krakauer describes the work that went into planning and setting up the camps, the difficulties of the climb, the heroism shown by many of the climbers—and some incidents that exhibited cowardice or selfishness—but he cannot explain fully why anyone should take such risks.

Krakauer had agreed to take part as a climber and writer for *Outside* magazine, but when he delivered his article—on time—he learned how bitter were many of the friends and relatives of those who died. *Into Thin Air* is an attempt to get the story straight and to explain what role Krakauer had in saving a few climbers and in being unable to save others. It is also one more effort to explain why it is that anyone would climb a mountain, specifically Everest.

> People who don't climb mountains—the great majority of humankind, that is to say—tend to assume that the sport is a reckless, Dionysian pursuit of ever-escalating thrills. But the notion that climbers are merely adrenaline junkies chasing a righteous fix is a fallacy, at least in the case of Everest. What I was doing up

Real People Challenging Nature

Annapurna: A Woman's Place by Arlene Blum. Sierra Club, Books 1980. Thirteen women climbers tackle one of the world's greatest challenges. Two reached the top. Two died.

Breaking Trail by Arlene Blum. Scribner, 2005. Blum organized and helped lead climbs on Mount McKinley, Annapurna, Everest, and more.

Clouds from Both Sides by Julie Tullis. Sierra Club Books, 1987. Tulis wrote the biography of a woman who, at age forty-seven, conquered K2 and died two days later.

Endurance: Shackleton's Incredible Journey by Alfred Lansing. McGraw-Hill, 1959. When his ship was crushed by ice in 1915, Sir Ernest Shackleton and his twenty-seven-member crew camped for five months on Antarctic ice floes and drifted at sea.

Ghosts of Everest: The Search for Mallory and Irvine by Jochen Hemmleb, Larry A. Johnson, and Eric Simonson. The Mountaineers, 1999. The authors set out to find the bodies of two climbers—George Mallory and Andrew Irvine—who died on Everest on June 4, 1924.

The Last Gentleman Adventurer by Edward Beauclerk Maurice. Houghton Mifflin, 2005. In this autobiography, a man joined the Hudson Bay Company in 1930 and was assigned to a remote trading post on Baffin Island. Despite his early tendency to fall into ice holes, he adjusted to his world, living with the Inuit and becoming involved with their culture.

The Long Exile: A Tale of Inuit Betrayal and Survival in the High Arctic by Melanie McGrath. Knopf, 2007. When Inuit hunters on the Ungava Peninsula in the east Arctic found game increasingly harder to find, the Canadian government decided to move 1,200 of them to Ellesmere Island where there were no permanent residents. This forced relocation to a place the Inuits had no understanding of and led to disaster.

Mountains of the Mind by Robert Macfarlane. Pantheon, 2003. Macfarlane writes about the history of the relationship between humanity and mountains from when mountains were seen as eyesores or obstacles to now, when they are regarded with awe.

No Shortcuts to the Top by Ed Viesturs. Broadway, 2006. Viesturs set out to climb the summits of the world's fourteen highest mountains without using bottled oxygen. He accomplished his quest in 2005.

Off the Map: Tales of Endurance and Exploration by Fergus Fleming. Atlantic Monthly Press, 2005. Fleming's book includes forty-five biographical essays covering the history of geographical discovery.

Savage Summit: The True Stories of the First Five Women Who Climbed K2, the World's Most Feared Mountain by Jennifer Jordan. Morrow, 2005. All five who climbed K2 died, three on the descent, two while climbing other mountains.

Scott of the Antarctic by David Crane. Knopf, 2006. Scott's background—middle-class upbringing amid genteel poverty, and the navy he joined which, in peacetime, recruited upper-class officers—made life difficult for him during the expedition to the Antarctic.

there had almost nothing to do with bungee jumping or skydiving or riding a motorcycle at 120 miles per hour. Above the comforts of Base Camp, the expedition in fact became an almost Calvinistic undertaking. The ratio of misery to pleasure was greater by an order of magnitude than any other mountain I'd been on. I quickly came to understand that climbing Everest was primarily about enduring pain. And in subjecting ourselves to week after week of toil, tedium, and suffering, it struck me that most of us were probably seeking, above all, something like a state of grace.[8]

Adventure stories are popular because boredom chafes at our souls and crowds out of our minds such practical concerns as safety and caution; however, the human body reminds us all too quickly of the risks. This may be why we prefer our adventures to come through books or, even better, through movies in which trick photography and special effects can make it easier for viewers to forget that losing is more common than winning.

Sports and the Game of Life

Because we lack the space to say everything that adults working with young people need to know about sports books, we recommend that interested readers find Chris Crowe's *More Than a Game: Sports Literature for Young Adults*. Several of the most popular and most talented YA writers tell sports stories. For example see the Margaret A. Edwards Award pages on Chris Crutcher and on Robert Lipsyte (pp. 195 and 197). As shown by the listing in Focus Box 6.2, An Armful of YA Sports Fiction, most sports books, whether fiction or nonfiction, include information about the training that is needed, the expected rewards, tangible or not, and the inevitable disappointments that make the rewards even sweeter. Early sports books in the 1800s and 1900s focused on the character-changing possibilities of sports along with an inning-by-inning or quarter-by-quarter account. The minute-by-minute account was almost never successful. But the excitement and the euphoria that sometimes comes to players has remained. Occasional nonfiction writers have focused almost exclusively on a player's character flaws, an iconoclastic approach that seems to have had its day.

The excitement of sports is what readers want, just as winning is the only acceptable verdict for fans. Way back on June 5, 1974, the *Los Angeles Times* headlined the sports section, "There's Nothing Like the Euphoria of Accomplishment." The *New York Times* for August 11, 1974, headlined its sports section with an article (first published in *Dial* in 1919): "Baseball: A Boys' Game, a Pro Sport and a National Religion." And scholar—and baseball fan—Jacques Barzun had the final say, "Whoever wants to know the heart and mind of America had better learn baseball, the rules and realities of the game."[9]

To deny or even to question the significant place of sports in many American lives is to misunderstand American life or values. In the 1950s and early 1960s such writers as H. D. Francis and John Carson wrote good novels filled with heroes reeking of sweat. Their heroes often examined the price of fame and the temptation to believe—always doomed—that fame would last. Writers as powerful as John Updike killed that dream much as F. Scott Fitzgerald had killed other dreams of society or business and glory and permanence. The sentimental fiction of the 1950s and 1960s was never real, but it had a charm that we have lost, and with it some readers of more innocent sports books.

Two particularly impressive books about baseball that mature high school students can appreciate are about love and friendship and fatherhood. They are Mark Harris's *Bang the Drum Slowly* and Donald Hall's *Fathers Playing Catch with Sons*. Harris's story of a second- or third-string catcher dying of leukemia is touching, just as it is good baseball. Hall, a major poet, offers a warm and almost sentimental account of his love for sports, particularly baseball. The first two sentences of his introduction tie together the two worlds he loves and needs: writing and baseball: "Half of my poet-friends think I am insane to waste my time

Ball Don't Lie by Matt De La Peña. Delacorte, 2005. A seventeen-year-old white boy, Sticky, lives mostly on the street and, because of his basketball skill, is pretty much accepted by black peers. However, his situation is far more precarious than is that of Maniac McGee in Spinelli's book for younger readers. Still, readers come away feeling optimistic.

Becoming Joe DiMaggio by Maria Testa. Candlewick, 2002. While the father is in prison during World War II, an Italian American family struggles to move on, with DiMaggio and radio always in the background.

The Boxer by Kathleen Karr. Farrar, Straus and Giroux, 2002. In New York City of the 1880s, John Aloysius Xavier Woods works in a sweatshop, but daily he goes by a saloon soliciting would-be bare-fisted boxers. Because boxing is illegal in New York, he's tossed in jail. When he comes out, he's now Johnny "The Chopper" Woods.

Crackback by John Coy. Scholastic, 2005. Coaches challenge and taunt players at Miles's school. His best friend tries steroids and Miles's father pushes Miles to play. When Miles is benched, he discovers how much he likes schoolwork and how little he likes football.

Dairy Queen by Catherine Gilbert Murdock. Houghton Mifflin, 2006. D. J. Schwenk takes on her father's dairy work when he is injured, but her heart is set on training Brian, the rival school's quarterback, and even going out for her own school's football team. Her story is continued in *The Off Season* (2007), where life becomes more challenging.

Fighting Ruben Wolfe by Markus Zusak. Scholastic, 2001. This story of two brothers joining an illegal fight circuit to earn money for their family received positive votes from all fifteen members of the Best Books for Young Adults committee of ALA.

Friends Till the End by Todd Strasser. Delacorte, 1981. A soccer star agrees reluctantly to visit Howie, who is dying of leukemia. A wonderful friendship develops.

Gym Candy by Carl Deuker. Houghton Mifflin, 2007. It's ironic that the name of the gym where running back Mick Johnson works out is named Popeye's because this is where he figures out that popping supplements isn't enough. But when he moves to injecting himself with steroids, he gets more than he bargained for. Readers who like *Gym Candy* will probably also enjoy Deuker's 2003 *High Heat* about a baseball pitcher.

Home of the Braves by David Klass. Farrar, Straus and Giroux, 2002. Jo Brickman, captain of the soccer and wrestling teams, faces a Brazilian transfer student who's a whiz at soccer and ready to sweep Jo's would-be girlfriend off her feet.

In Lane Three, Alex Archer by Tessa Duder. Houghton Mifflin, 1987. Swimmer Alex (short for Alexandra) trains for the 1960 Olympic Games in Rome.

Love, Football, and Other Contact Sports by Alden R. Carter. Holiday, 2006. A collection of short stories developed around Argyle West High School's football team. Realistic and ironic and sometimes funny.

The Passing Game by Richard Blessing. Little, Brown, 1982. In one of the best YA novels ever, Craig Warren has potential greatness but his play is erratic.

Slam by Nick Hornby. Putnam, 2007. Fifteen-year-old Sam is a skateboarding whiz who hits a bump when his girlfriend gets pregnant. Luckily, Sam has Tony Hawk, the world's greatest skater, to talk to him from the giant poster on Sam's wall.

Three Clams and an Oyster by Randy Powell. Farrar, Straus and Giroux, 2002. Flint is captain of a four-man flag-football team faced with a real problem, namely how to get rid of a teammate who is unreliable.

Ultimate Sports: Short Stories by Outstanding Writers for Young Adults, edited by Don Gallo. Delacorte, 1995. Stories by Robert Lipsyte, Chris Crutcher, Tessa Duder, and Norma Fox Mazer are included.

Under the Baseball Moon by John Ritter. Philomel, 2006. Andy Ramon's love life consists of Glory Martinez. He loves music, and Glory loves playing softball. The arrangement works for both of them; Andy plays his trumpet and that inspires Glory's hitting and pitching.

Wrestling Sturbridge by Rich Wallace. Knopf, 1996. Ben and Al are best friends. The only problem is that they are the two best 135-pound wrestlers in the state, and they attend the same high school.

Margaret A. Edwards Award
Winner (2000)
Chris Crutcher and His Sports-Plus Novels

Margaret A. Edwards Honor books include his *Staying Fat for Sarah Byrnes*, *Athletic Shorts: Six Short Stories*, *Chinese Handcuffs*, *The Crazy Horse Electric Game*, *Stotan*, and *Running Loose*. We want to add *Ironman*, *Whale Talk*, and *The Sledding Hill*.

When *Running Loose* was published in 1983, reviewers recognized that an accomplished first novelist had arrived on the YA scene, and it did not take long before teachers found Crutcher and began recommending him to their students. Critics began to call his books "honest" and "intense" and to argue over whether *Running Loose* or later books were his best. *Running Loose* is at least partly autobiographical. Few YA novels have parents so decent and so understanding as does Louis Banks. He also has a warm and believable girlfriend in Becky Sanders, but on the down side he has a vindictive football coach willing to do anything to win games, and that includes taking the opposition's star player out through dirty play. Louie protests the foul, but the coach ignores him, and the coach is supported by the principal. Louie is no longer on the team, and then he faces a far greater problem when Becky is killed in a car crash. Later, at the funeral, Louie is almost comatose until he hears the minister saying a litany of funeral clichés about God's moving in "strange and mysterious ways." Louie yells, "He doesn't move in strange and mysterious ways. He doesn't move at all! He sits up there on His fat butt and lets guys like you earn a living making excuses for all the rotten things that happen." No applause follows.

That scene is almost topped by a brief interlude when Louie learns that the principal plans to erect a plaque in Becky's memory and set it in concrete. Later, as Louie leaves school, he sees the plaque and reads all the stuff on it about Becky's work on cheerleading and student council and Honor Society and more. It's too much for Louie, partly because the principal had signed his name at the bottom of the plaque. He was the one school official that both Louie and Becky disliked and so at night Louie takes a sledge-hammer to the school. He hammers the plaque loose from the concrete, puts it in the back of his pickup, and dumps it in the river where Becky died.

One of our college students who picked up *Running Loose* expected to write a negative review because she had always hated sports books. She ended up admitting she was wrong because instead of being about sports, this was a book "about so many things—love, death, loyalty, anger, compassion, and courage. It's about being responsible. It was not about my boy friend. It was about me." She concluded with, "Crutcher asks the right questions that young people need somehow to find answers to. That's what I learned from reading *Running Loose*."

Stotan carries on with Crutcher's tests of endurance, loyalty, and challenge. In it, four young men begin the Stotan, a test of physical and emotional strength to develop their swimming team. Each swimmer is also faced with a significant personal problem. In *Staying Fat for Sarah Byrnes*, Sarah has been horribly burned and pretends to be catatonic to escape her evil father. In *Ironman*, Bo writes letters to radio talk-show host Larry King at the same time he is constantly angry with his father and his English teacher (an ex-football coach). In *Whale Talk*, a young male—black, white, and Japanese—refuses to be in organized sports but joins a swimming team and talks other outsiders into joining him.

In the third edition of this text (1989), Chris Crutcher wrote, "I think it is incredibly disrespectful and potentially damaging to foster the myths of our society—myths of the unconditional sanctity of the family, myths of the innate good of any particular institutional spirituality, myths of unexamined patriotism, and on and on. In other words, we owe the same thing to young adult readers as we do to adult readers: that is the honest depiction of our observations—the truth as we see it."

In *Deadline*, eighteen-year-old Ben Wolfe is diagnosed with an incurable kind of leukemia. Because he's of legal age, he doesn't have to let his parents know and so he sets out on his own to pack a lifetime of experience into his senior year at his small Idaho high school. When he contemplates playing on the football team and courting Dallas Suzuki—the girl of his dreams—he has to keep reminding himself that some insects live only one day. ●

writing about sports and to loiter in the company of professional athletes. The other half would murder to take my place." Later, he distinguishes between baseball and football to the detriment of the latter: "Baseball is fathers and sons. Football is brothers beating each other up in the backyard, violent and superficial."

Angry and Nostalgic Sports Books

Anger is part of sports—anger at oneself, anger at teammates, anger at coaches, anger at the opposing team. These three books are angry in quite a different way. They are angry with the system, with unfeeling parents who care only that their son or daughter is a star, never just a member of a team, with people who take the fun out of sports and replace it with a machine, with people who pretend that sports will build character, and with people who lead young people to embrace the violence that is at the heart of sport.

James Bennett's *The Squared Circle* focuses on Sonny Youngblood, a high school star basketball player now entering Southern Illinois University as the hope of the athletic department. Whether Sonny even likes the sport is a question that Sonny avoids asking, mostly out of fear for the consequences of the answer. His father long ago walked out on the family. Sonny did not like his high school coach; he is the only non–African American player on the squad; he hates the fraternity he is ready to join, and if all that were not bad enough, his cousin, who is an art professor at the university, wants Sonny to work out for himself what he wants to do with his life. Sonny is slow to act, but when he does act, he solves several problems all at once. A powerful book.

Chris Lynch's *Inexcusable* is also powerful. Keir Sarafian has bought into the world of football. He knows that violence is very much a part of his world. Keir knows that he is a good boy, and he adds what others would say—that Keir is "rock solid, the kind of guy you want behind you, a straight shooter, loyal, polite, funny, good manners, he was brought up the right way, that boy was." Keir has also crippled an opposing player and now has the nickname Killer. Keir likes being liked, though his sisters do not like him. His only fan is his father, oblivious to what Keir has become. When he and his friends tear down a statue, they know it's a prank. When they get drunk, as Keir regularly does, he and his friends pass it off as boyish fun.

He's also apparently deaf. When he starts to rape Gigi, she says no, but he refuses to admit that he hears anything that will stop him. Nobody says no to a football icon. So he rapes her, as readers will know by the end of the novel's first page.

Since 1967 when Robert Lipsyte wrote *The Contender*, he has had dual careers—one as a professional sports writer and commentator, and the other as an author of powerful young adult books, mostly about sports. His angriest book, *Raiders Night,* was published in 2007. It is the story of a football team and what one team member does to another team member and then what fear and shame can do to the entire team. For more about *Raiders Night* and Lipsyte's other sports books see the write-up on his Margaret A. Edwards Award.

Sports books with a touch of nostalgia come from the opposite end of the spectrum. One of the best in recent years is a slim work of nonfiction, David Halberstam's *The Teammates: A Portrait of a Friendship.* The only baseball player that young people are likely to recognize is Ted Williams, late of the Boston Red Sox

Margaret A. Edwards Award
Winner (2001)
Robert Lipsyte, **A Contender**
All the Way

Honored books include *The Contender*, *The Brave*, *The Chief*, and *One Fat Summer*. If the award were given today, we would vote that *Raiders Night* also be on the list. Lipsyte is a professional sports writer and television and radio commentator who, in 1967, was inspired to write *The Contender* when he was in a gymnasium and one of the grand old boxing coaches put a finger to his lips so they could both listen to the way a boy was running up the stairs. As they listened, the coach shared his judgment that this newcomer was going to be "a contender." He could tell from the energy that he put into running up the stairs.

The Contender made Lipsyte a name in YA literature because the story of a would-be fighter wandering into a gym in hopes of becoming a contender is a fresh allegory that fit the role filled by many young men in real life. For earlier editions of this text, Lipsyte wrote that he thinks boys don't read as much as we'd like them to partly because current books do not deal with the real problems and fears of boys. And then as educators we tend to treat boys as a group—which is where males are at their absolute worst. He suggests that boys "have to be led into reading secretly and one at a time." *The Contender*, *The Brave*, and *The Chief* are about individuals who suffer from being in a group. They find hope as soon as someone recognizes them as individuals.

Lipsyte's most recent book, *Raiders Night*, is about being an individual and speaking out when it is needed. The book may seem like yet another football story until a terrifying and crucial event. Matt Rydek is cocaptain of the Nearmont High School Raiders football team. He and the other players are treated royally by fans who love them unconditionally. Matt, however, has two problems. First is his pushy father, who does not know or understand his son, and second is his cocaptain, Ramp, who is mean and more sadistic than anyone suspects. In the locker room, Ramp singles out a new player named Chris for humiliation because he has made Ramp look bad. Ramp marches around during a team initiation waving a small white plastic bat, and when

Chris will not humble himself, Ramp pulls down Chris's shorts and sodomizes him with the white plastic bat. Vomit rises in Matt's throat, but even though he has always disliked and distrusted Ramp, he does nothing except feel guilty.

When the coaches and others learn of Ramp's actions on Raider Pride Night, Matt's first impulse is to keep his mouth shut and pretend that nothing happened. Matt's father tells Matt to keep "it in the locker room." At the book's end, when Matt stands up for Chris and himself, his father calls him an "ungrateful little sonuabitch," and says, "Everything I did was for you, busting my back so you could have everything you ever needed, best equipment, baseball and football camps, money in your account, you know how much safe steroids cost. I'm not going to let you throw it away." Matt says, "It's my call."

Of all the ugly episodes in *Raiders Night*, none is more nauseatingly unctuous than Pastor Jim's homily at the Welcome Home Rally. Long after the sodomy scene, Pastor Jim "asked God to give the Raiders the strength to get back up when they were knocked down, to forgive cheap shots, and to win clean." He added, "You know, if Jesus came back, he'd be a Raider, hitting hard and hitting clean."

When Lipsyte was asked if he was surprised that *Raiders Night* was a subject of censorship, he said that *censorship* is too strong of a word for what he has been experiencing. It has been more insidious as when he is invited to a school by a librarian or an English teacher and then is uninvited by a coach, an athletic director, or a principal. He does not think it is because of the language or the sex or the mention of steroids. Instead it is because the book takes a negative look at jock culture, which is something those guys are really invested in.

Is *Raiders Night* working? Yes it is. It must be to attract the attention of the greatest advocates of American sportsmanship, these holy three—coaches, athletic directors, and principals. ●

and now dying. Dom DiMaggio, also late of the Red Sox—Joe's brother but a far more complex and intriguing person—sets out to travel from Massachusetts to see his dying friend and former teammate, Ted Williams. This is the simple story of two road trips by old men who had been something in their youth—and in Halberstam's language—gain a nobility as ballplayers and decent men and, most important, as teammates and friends.

The story lines of two other books about athletes who were somebodies, but who as time flies become nobodies, are hardly new, but they come highly recommended by us: Jay Acton's *The Forgettables* and Martin Ralbovsky's *Destiny's Darlings*. Acton's book is about the Pottstown, Pennsylvania, Firebirds who, even in their glory, were rejects of professional football and yet athletes worth watching. The subtitle on Ralbovsky's book spells out the point—"A World Championship Little League Team Twenty Years Later." Growing old happens to all of us, world champions or not, but Ralbovsky's books powerfully remind us of the evanescence of victory.

Because sports is a subject where high school readers admire adult athletes and look forward to joining their ranks, both YA and adult books are included in Focus Box 6.3, Sports Nonfiction—Real-Life Dreams. What also is worth remembering, periodically, is that sports are enjoyable, a way of relaxing with friends, a way of becoming part of the majority, and a chance to exchange ideas about what the coaches, or players, should have done last Sunday, or Saturday.

We should also remind ourselves, again periodically, that sports are easily overvalued. In books published from the early days of the last century, boys—and men—were reminded that sports were ennobling because they built moral character. A boy who did not play games would, presumably, need to find some other source to develop his moral fiber. So the belief went, widely accepted by coaches, players, fans, and families. Is it true? Here's a modern response.

Although many coaches and administrators state that they stress ethical play, research finds that little or no concentrated moral education exists in sports.

Nor has research been favorable concerning the development of moral character through sports, even though this is universally expressed as a primary purpose of sport. For many years, the belief has existed that sport builds character and promotes moral growth. . . . Most sports and physical education texts, teachings, and programs for the past 150 years have supported this belief. A strong body of qualitative and quantitative research exists, however, supporting that the longer athletes participate in sport, the more their moral reasoning is adversely affected by the competitive experience.[10]

Actually, anyone who has ever been clobbered in a pickup basketball game already knows about sports and character building.

Mysteries

Why are mysteries so enduringly popular? Basically they are unrealistic and, as mystery writers cheerfully admit, usually have almost nothing to do with

Sports Nonfiction—Real-Life Dreams

Babe Didrikson Zaharias: The Making of a Champion by Russell Freedman. Clarion, 1999. Freedman's biographies are a pleasure to read because of the care he takes with the research and the writing as well as with the design of the book.

Between Boardslides and Burnout: My Notes from the Road by Tony Hawk. HarperCollins, 2002. Full-color photographs add to this realistic journal of a skateboarding champion.

A Biography of Red Smith: The Life and Times of a Great American Writer by Ira Berkow. New York Times Books, 1986. Present-day sports writers learned from this master whose columns are reprinted from the *New York Times*, the *New York Herald Tribune*, and assorted other places.

The Boys of October: How the 1975 Boston Red Sox Embodied Baseball's Ideals—and Restored our Spirits by Doug Hornig. Contemporary Books, 2003. Hornig prepared a hymn to the glories of his favorite team.

The Boys of Summer, rev. ed., by Roger Kahn. HarperCollins, 1998. One of baseball's finest writers tells this story of the great Brooklyn Dodgers. Where have they gone?

Crazy '08: How a Cast of Crooks, Rogues, Boneheads, and Magnates Created the Greatest Year in Baseball History by Cait Murphy. Smithsonian Books, 2007. Fans of the Chicago Cubs have a strange rallying cry: "Remember 1908!" the last time the Cubs won the World Series. A marvelous and wacky book about a marvelous and wacky time.

Game Time: A Baseball Companion by Roger Angell. Harcourt Brace, 2003. Angell again proves that he is one of baseball's greatest writers in this book about spring training, the World Series, and lots of other things.

The Greatest: Muhammad Ali by Walter Dean Myers. Scholastic, 2001. Myers brings his skill as a writer to this biography, along with his knowledge of what Muhammad Ali meant to African Americans.

Indian Summer: The Forgotten Story of Louis Sockalexis, the First Native American in Major League Baseball by Brian McDonald. Rodale, 2003. Sockalexis was recruited by the Cleveland Spiders in 1897 and drank himself out of baseball by 1910. A sad story.

Let Me Play: The Story of Title IX: The Law That Changed the Future of Girls in America by Karen Blumenthal.

S&S/Atheneum, 2005. A law that started as almost an accident has made a profound difference in the lives of America's young women. Blumenthal's take on the matter is shown both through facts and human interest stories.

The Meaning of Sports: Why Americans Watch Baseball, Football, and Basketball and What They See When They Do by Michael Mandelbaum. Public Affairs, 2004. The meaning of sports as a diversion, as a bonding with their fellows, or as a religious rite.

Race across Alaska: First Woman to Win the Iditarod Tells Her Story by Libby Riddels and Tim Jones. Stackpole Books, 1998. Readers who know Gary Paulsen's *Woodsong* (Bradbury, 1990) will enjoy this different perspective on the race.

The Story of Negro League Baseball by William Brashler. Ticknor & Fields, 1994. Brashler takes up the history of Negro baseball and its important players, e.g., Bob Gibson and Smokey Joe Williams. Neil J. Sullivan does something similar in his *The Minors: The Struggles and the Triumphs of Baseball's Poor Relations from 1876 to the Present* (St. Martin's, 1990). An introductory book for younger readers is *The Journal of Biddy Owens: The Negro Leagues, Birmingham, Alabama, 1948*, which is part of the My Name Is America series (Scholastic, 2001).

Triumph and Tragedy in Mudville by Stephen Jay Gould. Norton, 2003. The Harvard scientist takes off on his favorite avocation, baseball, and particular aspects of it that fascinate him, e.g., Joe DiMaggio's fifty-six-game hitting streak.

Wait Till Next Year: A Memoir by Doris Kearns Goodwin. Simon & Schuster, 1997. A historian remembers growing up in Rockville Center, New York, and her passion for the Brooklyn Dodgers. A truly lovely book.

Why Is the Foul Pole Fair? by Vince Staten. Simon and Schuster, 2003. The author takes up an incredible number of questions about the game and its history and answers them all. For example, why is the distance from the pitching rubber to the plate sixty feet and six inches?

Winning Ways: A Photohistory of American Women in Sports by Sue Macy. Holt, 1996. Both in this book and in her *A Whole New Ball Game* (Holt, 1993), Macy presents wonderful photos and intriguing details to show that women have a sports heritage.

real-life detection by police or private agents. They demand that we suspend most of our disbelief, and we gladly do so. Mysteries are mere games, but we love games. Some of us claim that we want to beat the detective to the murderer, but we rarely do, and when we succeed, we feel cheated.

The popularity of mystery movies and the number of hotels, ships, and individuals who sponsor parties in which a mock murder takes place, with the partygoers playing detectives, shows the entertainment value of mayhem, murder, and suspense. Because of the high entertainment value of mysteries and their sometimes easy reading level, many mysteries published for a general audience find their way into the hands of young adults. For examples, see Focus Box 6.4, A Century of Accessible Adult Mysteries.

Daniel's detection of the guilty Elders in "The Story of Susanna" in the Apocrypha may be the world's first detective story. Critics generally agree, however, that the modern mystery begins with Edgar Allan Poe's "The Murders in the Rue Morgue," although "The Purloined Letter" is more satisfying today. Poe's detective, C. Auguste Dupin, is unquestionably the first criminal investigator.

Writer and critic Hillary Waugh has said that the skeletons on which mysteries hang are "nothing more nor less than a series of ironclad rules." The rules are essential to present the puzzle properly and to ensure fair play. He lists them as follows:

Rule One: All clues discovered by the detective must be made available to the reader.

Rule Two: The murderer must be introduced early.

Rule Three: The crime must be significant.

Rule Four: There must be detection.

Rule Five: The number of suspects must be known, and the murderer must be among them.

Rule Six: The reader, as part of the game of fair play, has the right to expect that nothing will be included in the book that does not relate to or in some way bear on the puzzle.[11]

Types of Mysteries

The characteristics of the traditional murder mystery are well known and relatively fixed, although devotees are always interested in variations on the theme of murder. A mystery short story may settle for theft, but a novel, of course, demands murder. Accompanying crimes such as blackmail or embezzlement may add to the delights of murder, but they never replace murder. The ultimate crime normally takes place a few chapters into the book, after readers have been introduced to major and minor characters, including the victim and those who might long for his death. The detective appears, clues are scattered, the investigation proceeds, the detective solves the case, the guilty are punished, the innocent are restored to their rightful place, and the world becomes right again.

Shannon Ocork classifies mysteries into these six types:

1. *The amateur detective:*   At least in the older stories, the amateur detective was male (e.g., C. Auguste Dupin or Sherlock Holmes and, later, Rex

Focus Box 6.4

A Century of Accessible Adult Mysteries (Listed Chronologically)

The Circular Staircase by Mary Roberts Rinehart. Bobbs-Merrill, 1908. The first of the Had-I-but-Known genre of mystery, this story of a lonely house, a dead body, and blooming love reads far better today than readers have any right to expect.

The Greek Coffin Mystery by Ellery Queen. Stokes, 1932. Frederic Dannay and Manfred B. Lee, writing under the joint pseudonym of Ellery Queen, find Queen investigating a natural death with a missing will. When the coffin is exhumed, a second body is found and the mystery begins.

And Then There Were None by Agatha Christie. Dodd, Mead, 1939. Ten men and women come to an isolated island to spend a weekend. Each person has a dark secret and one by one they die in strange ways.

The Big Sleep by Raymond Chandler. Knopf, 1939. This study in power and corruption is the first Philip Marlowe mystery with Marlowe trying to determine the truth from two quite different women and a missing man.

Buried for Pleasure by Edmund Crispin (pen name of Bruce Montgomery). Harper and Row, 1949. Gervase Fen, Oxford professor, has been talked into standing for Parliament. After encountering a strange group of small-town eccentrics, he also encounters a murder in this very funny mystery.

Death in the Fifth Position by Edgar Box (pen name of Gore Vidal). Dutton, 1952. Press agent Peter Sargeant turns detective to solve the murder of a ballerina.

The Willow Pattern by Robert Van Gulik. Scribner, 1964. Judge Dee is administering a Chinese city in the midst of a plague and a rash of crime. Though here fictionalized, Dee was a real seventh-century judge in the T'ang dynasty.

An Unsuitable Job for a Woman by P. D. James. Scribner, 1972. In this remarkable book, Cordelia Gray learns that her partner has committed suicide, leaving her the business. Although she's a newcomer to the private investigator world, she is hired to find out about another suicide.

Dance Hall of the Dead by Tony Hillerman. Harper and Row, 1973. Reservation policeman Joe Leaphorn investigates the death of a young runner training for a religious ceremony.

Funeral Urn by June Drummond. Walker, 1976. By chance, Margaret Wooten finds herself in a lovely English village, and in the churchyard she finds a funeral urn filled with poisonous flowers.

Murder on the Yellow Brick Road by Stuart Kaminsky. St. Martin's, 1977. In 1940, a munchkin has been murdered on the set of *The Wizard of Oz*, and Judy Garland is frightened. Toby Peters comes to the rescue in the best of the series.

Strike Three, You're Dead by R. D. Rosen. Walker, 1984. Relief pitcher Rudy Furth is killed in the Providence Jewels's clubhouse, and outfielder Harvey Blissberg plays detective.

I Am the Only Running Footman by Martha Grimes. Little, Brown, 1986. The body of a young girl strangled with her own scarf is found near an old pub called I Am the Only Running Footman. Scotland Yard's Richard Jury is reminded of another murder, similar to this one, committed in Devon.

The Ritual Bath by Faye Kellerman. Morrow, 1986. A yeshiva in the Los Angeles hills is despoiled when a woman leaving the ritual bath is raped. Detective Peter Decker becomes involved.

The Master of the House by Robert Barnard. Scribner, 1994. A mother dies in childbirth, leaving four children and a crazy and ineffectual husband. When townspeople suspect something is wrong, two of the children find a body in the backyard.

Stout's Nero Wolfe). These detectives are altruistic and usually optimistic. They are bright and see what others do not. Sometimes called traditional, golden-age, or classic mysteries, these flourished from the 1920s through the 1940s.

2. *The cozy mystery:*   These stories are close to the amateur detective stories. They are usually set in a small English village, although New

England is increasingly popular. Agatha Christie, who began writing in the 1920s, is the most obvious writer of cozies. She scattered her best books throughout her life. Her 1939 *And Then There Were None* is her best book without a detective. Others include her 1950 *A Murder Is Announced*, a Miss Marple book, and her 1968 *By the Pricking of My Thumbs*, in which the usually tiresome Tommy and Tuppence Beresford stumble into a believable mystery.

3. *The puzzle:*   These stories are exercises in ingenuity as we are led into an intricate murder, with the detective daring us to figure out the end of the story. Ellery Queen's early mysteries had a "Challenge to the Reader" about three or four chapters from the end, when the writer announced that we had all the clues Queen had and should be able to solve the mystery. Luckily, we rarely succeeded.

4. *The private detective:*   These hard-boiled mysteries differ from other mysteries in significant ways. Private detectives lack altruistic motives. They enter cases for pay rather than for love of the chase or intellectual fondness for the puzzle. Working out of a cheerless office and around even less cheerful people, they are tired and cynical about the courts, the police, class distinctions, and life in general. Many are former police officers who left the force under a cloud. They have seen too much of the seamy world to feel hope for anything or anyone, and they know that detective work is hard and mostly routine and dull. With patience, any bright person could do what they do. Not only does violence come with the territory, it is the territory. Moreover, we are surprised, even disappointed, if the violence is not there.

5. *The police procedural:*   Police procedurals are often the most believable mysteries because the central characters are officers doing their mundane jobs and tracking down murderers with scientific methods and machines available only to the police. The books of Ed McBain are probably the most popular police procedurals today.

6. *The thriller:*   These are usually spy thrillers. They may have bits of mystery tucked into them, but as in Ian Fleming's James Bond series, the mystery involves not so much who did it as how our hero can escape his latest impossible situation with even more than his usual derring-do.[12]

Some Popular Mystery Writers

Sue Grafton has been among the hottest mystery writers since 1982 when *"A" Is for Alibi* appeared. Her alphabetical series (e.g., *"M" Is for Malice* and *"T" Is for Trespass*) shows Kinsey Millhone working as an insurance investigator in Santa Teresa (the name Ross Macdonald gave Santa Barbara in his mysteries). Readers met Kinsey in *"A" Is for Alibi.*

My name is Kinsey Millhone. I'm a private investigator, licensed by the state of California. I'm thirty-two years old, twice divorced, no kids. The day before yesterday I killed someone and the fact weighs heavily on my mind. I'm a nice person and I have a lot of friends. My apartment is small but I like living in a cramped space. I've lived in trailers most of my life, but lately they've been getting too elaborate for my taste, so now I live in one room, a "bachelorette." I don't have houseplants. I spend a lot of time on the road and I don't like leaving things behind. Aside from the hazards of my profession, my life has always been ordinary, uneventful, and good.

Killing someone feels odd to me and I haven't quite sorted it through. I've already given a statement to the police, which I initialed page by page and then signed. I filled out a similar report for the office files. The language in both documents is neutral, the terminology oblique, and neither says quite enough.

In these brief paragraphs, Grafton lets us know who Kinsey is with details that tell us about the real Kinsey—her taste in apartments, her dislike for stuff she'll have to leave behind, the effect of killing another human being, and her pawky wit when she says, "The day before yesterday I killed someone and the fact weighs heavily on my mind."

Grafton was following the advice of one of the best writing teachers in history, the Roman poet and critic Horace, who urged writers to begin in *medias res*, that is the middle of the story.

Nevada Barr created Park Ranger Anna Pigeon out of her own experiences as a park ranger. Since 2000, Anna Pigeon has been a ranger and amateur sleuth in various national parks. In 2000, Pigeon was assigned to the Natchez Trace Parkway in *Deep South*; in 2003, she was assigned to the Dry Tortugas in *Flashback*; and in 2005 she was assigned to Rocky Mountain National Park in *Hard Truth*. Barr's books combine love of the environment and lore of the place mixed with first class suspense.

Kathy Reichs is a forensic anthropologist who works professionally out of North Carolina and Montreal. Her detective is Temperance (Tempe) Brennan, also a forensic anthropologist, in books like *Fatal Voyage*, *Monday Mourning: A Novel*, *Cross Bones*, and *Break No Bones*. Reichs is a relative newcomer to the field, but her readers know that her mysteries are well plotted and accurate.

Tony Hillerman holds an honored place in the community of mystery writers. His books breathe of the desert and sand and lonely and quiet places and are inevitably about Hopi or Navajo Indians in the Four-Corners area of the Southwest. In the February 1992 *English Journal*, the editors published responses to "Who is your favorite writer of detective stories?" Hillerman won by a margin of ten to one. *The Blessing Way* in 1970 was his first book, where we meet Officer Joe Leaphorn. His later novels, including *The Wailing Wind* in 2002 and *Skeleton Man* in 2004, rarely disappoint.

No one writes police procedurals like Ed McBain, who has delighted fans since 1956, and his later books, like *The Frumious Bandersnatch* and *Fiddlers*, seem to be getting better and better. Part of his skill lies in his characters' names—Steve Carella, Cotton Hawes (from Cotton Mather) and Meyer Meyer, whose parents apparently took delight in duplicating the first and last names. Part of the charm lies in McBain's knowledge of his imaginary city, Isola, presumably New York City, and anyone and everyone who might want to live there. Two of his recent 87th Precinct novels illustrate the breadth of his city. In *The Last Dance* detectives Carella and Meyer investigate the killing of an old man, and in *Money*,

Money, Money a woman's body is dumped into the lions' cage in the city zoo and a trashcan is stuffed with the body of a book salesman.

Sherlock Holmes and His Descendants

Arthur Conan Doyle wrote two kinds of books, popular books of his times, like *The White Company*, which he considered literary and made him proud, and potboilers like the Sherlock Holmes adventures and mysteries, which gave him little pleasure though much money and whose popularity annoyed him. So he took the easy way out, he killed Holmes at the Reichenbach Falls in Switzerland, but the public outcry at Holmes's apparent death made Doyle rethink the matter.

Doyle had written five collections of Sherlock Holmes stories—*The Adventures of Sherlock Holmes* (1892), *The Memoirs of Sherlock Holmes* (1894), *The Return of Sherlock Holmes* (1905), and *The Case Book of Sherlock Holmes* (1927)—and one excellent novel about Holmes, *The Hound of the Baskervilles* (1902). That was all from Doyle.

But it was not the end of Sherlock Holmes. His admirers in England and America founded an organization called the Baker Street Irregulars devoted to Holmes's memory and to writing scholarly (mostly pseudoscholarly) articles mixed with the occasional imitation Holmes story published in the *Baker Street Journal*. Over the years, the articles and the stories (some of them now parodies and pastiches) multiplied. Many of the best were published under the editorship of Ellery Queen as *The Misadventures of Sherlock Holmes* (Little, Brown, 1944) and more recently under the editorship of Peter Ridgway Watt as *The Alternative Sherlock Holmes* (Ashgate, 2003).

One of the most successful Holmes imitators was the prolific and often superb August Derleth who created a detective sometimes rivaling Holmes in collections of short stories about Solar Pons; for example, *The Adventures of Solar Pons* (Pinnacle, reprinted 1974), *The Comeback of Solar Pons* (Pinnacle, 1975), and *The Reminiscences of Solar Pons* (Pinnacle, 1975). Adrian Doyle and John Dickson Carr provided another collection of Holmes imitations in *The Exploits of Sherlock Holmes* (Random House, 1952). It was not the last imitation to be published.

Three recent Sherlock Holmes books deserve mention. Cheng Xiaoqing's *Sherlock in Shanghai: Stories of Crime and Detection* is set in 1920s and 1930s Shanghai. It features a Chinese Holmes imitator, Huo. Steve Hockensmith's *Holmes on the Range* (St. Martin's, 2006) is set in the Old West of the 1880s with two brothers working as ranch hands. When a body is discovered, one brother prepares to solve the crime. In Mark Haddon's *The Curious Incident of the Dog in the Night-Time*, Christopher John Francis Boone—fifteen, autistic, and a Sherlock Holmes devotee—sets out to solve the murder of a poodle in a rich and warm and often funny novel.

The most successful writer who has taken on Holmes is Laurie R. King, who wrote *The Beekeeper's Apprentice* (1994). King's protagonist is Mary Russell, a brilliant fifteen-year-old who stumbles onto Sherlock Holmes, now a beekeeper in Sussex. The two soon become a team and ultimately solve the case of the kidnapping of the daughter of an American senator. In *A Monstrous Regiment of Women* (1995), Mary Russell has finished her studies at Oxford and is nearly twenty-one. She meets the charismatic leader of the New Temple of God. When several women in the leader's clique are murdered, Mary persuades Holmes to help. *The Game* (2006), eighth in the series, sets Mary and Sherlock in San Francisco. When someone takes a shot at Mary, Holmes hires detective Dashiell Hammet for protection. King's Mary Russell series is superb. It's great history mixed with humor, adventure, suspense, and the certainty that love will develop between Mary Russell and Sherlock Holmes.

Middle grades readers might get introduced to the whole genre through Tracy Mack and Michael Citrin's *Sherlock Holmes and the Baker Street Irregulars*. The "Irregulars" are a gang of street urchins who help the great detective. Casebook No. 1 (which implies more are coming) was published in 2006. The authors spoke at the 2006 ALAN workshop in Nashville and left even some of the grown-ups eager to start solving the "Three Gruesome Deaths" that are promised in Chapter 1.

Mysteries Written for Young Adults

While many teenagers have fond memories of such detectives as Encyclopedia Brown and Nancy Drew, and young teens happily read the Sammy Keyes books by Wendelin Van Draanen, most teenagers are looking for something a bit more complex. However, YA authors shy away from doing whole books focused on murder and mayhem, which means that most YA mysteries are concerned with more than the crime. They are also shorter than mysteries for adults, and instead of having professional detectives, the protagonists are likely to be bright and energetic young people, not yet cynical about the world. The violence is more likely to be underplayed, possibly at the edge of the story. The victim is often connected to the protagonist—a family member, a friend, an admired adult, a boyfriend or girlfriend—and the protagonist is virtually forced to enter the game and examine the puzzle.

Robert Cormier's *The Rag and Bone Shop* illustrates most of these characteristics. Seven-year-old Alicia is found murdered only a few hundred yards from her home, and the police have no physical evidence and no suspects. Twelve-year-old Jason, a neighbor and friend, was the last person to see her. To satisfy community pressure, the police arrest him and then bring in an out-of-town interrogator who has a reputation for getting confessions out of suspects. The interrogator, named Trent, works more quickly than did the psychiatrist/interrogator in Cormier's earlier mystery *I Am the Cheese*. In *The Rag and Bone Shop*, there is some evidence that Jason has antisocial attitudes, but mostly he is just shy. It is because he can't stand up to the neighborhood bullies that he spent so much time with the younger Alicia.

The interrogator is particularly motivated because he is hoping that solving this high-profile case will bring him a political appointment. His behavior is all the more repulsive when he keeps pursuing the "confession," even after readers suspect that he knows Jason is innocent. But, thankfully, readers—and Jason—get a reprieve in the very last sentence.

Francesca Lia Block's *Wasteland* is a moving but somber story of a sister, a brother, family secrets, love, and death. Block's beautifully enigmatic style of writing heightens the tension and adds to the mystery as Marina (the sister) gets closer and closer to the truth about her brother's death.

Two young adult mystery writers who stand out are Patricia Windsor and Joan Lowery Nixon. Windsor's *The Christmas Killer* is set in a Connecticut town terrorized by a killer. Rose Potter has a series of dreams in which a murdered girl appears and hints at where her body can be found. The police question whether Rose is believable, or even sane, wonder if she is involved in the murder, and finally realize that Rose is in danger. Sections dealing with Rose alternate with the ramblings of the deranged killer about his need for blood. At one point he says,

> Killing is not a bad thing. Death is easeful, death is kind. I am friends with death. It cools the boiling blood. Blood is as red as a Christmas ribbon. Blood ties a body like a Christmas package. Blood is the color of Christmas berries, baubles, all things of joy. Why shouldn't I find joy in blood?

He finds joy in all things red, and in the last two paragraphs of the book, imprisoned though he is, readers learn that the story may have yet another chapter.

> Let a little time pass. I will send her a letter, tied up in my own blood and sealing wax. She will know me from my work. And she will think of me again.
> And, before long, I will escape this place, and I will be seeing her again.

Here's a fine story, not long on mystery but full of suspense and wonders and fears. It's an eerie and scary book, just right for the night when a reader is home alone with the fierce wind and the blowing shutters and the creaking house.

Joan Lowery Nixon's thrillers are even more popular with young people. *Whispers from the Dead* is about a near-death drowning and a spirit who seems to shadow the protagonist thereafter. *The Dark and Deadly Pool* concerns a young girl who discovers a body floating in a pool, a typical ploy for Nixon, who is eager to grab her readers' attention. Cody Garnett's friend in *Spirit Seeker* is accused of murder, and Cody sets out to find the truth. In *The Kidnapping of Christina Lattimore*, Christina is kidnapped and safely returned, but then she is accused of setting up the whole thing to extract money from her wealthy grandmother.

In Carol Plum-Ucci's *The Body of Christopher Creed*, popular Torey Adams, age sixteen, is thrown into a whole new life and a new way of looking at people. He is drawn into a mystery when an unpopular classmate disappears after posting a cryptic email message to the school principal in which he mentions Torey and some of his friends. In Elaine Marie Alphin's *Counterfeit Son*, a boy's father (a serial killer himself) is killed by the police, and the boy tries to assume the identity of one of his father's victims. Of course, there are too many complications for such a plan to work.

See the page on Margaret A. Edwards Award–winner Lois Duncan. Her *Killing Mr. Griffin* is still the favorite of many young readers. Four other YA mysteries that teens are fond of include

1. Kevin Brooks's *The Road of the Dead* features fourteen-year-old Ruben who knows absolutely that his sister has been murdered. Ruben and his brother, Cole, travel to Dartmoor to bring her body home and to find her killer.

2. Joaquin Dorfman's *Playing It Cool* focuses on Sebastian who solves problems for his friends. When he agrees to track down a friend's birth father,

Margaret A. Edwards Award
Winner (1992)

Lois Duncan, **A True Storyteller**

The Margaret A. Edwards committee honored Duncan for her autobiographical *Chapters: My Growth as a Writer* and for her mystery/suspense books, *I Know What You Did Last Summer*; *Killing Mr. Griffin*; *Ransom*; *Summer of Fear*; and *The Twisted Window*.

Of all the Edwards Award winners, Duncan probably became a professional at the youngest age. She began submitting stories to magazines when she was ten. She sold her first short story when she was thirteen to *Calling All Girls*, and her first young adult novel, *Debutante Hill*, when she was twenty. At age twenty-seven, she found herself a single mother needing to support three young children. As she told Roger Sutton in a June 1992 *School Library Journal* interview, she grew up fast while learning to write not only the page-turners that kids love her for, but in between children's books and articles for women's magazines including *Ladies Home Journal*, *McCall's*, *Redbook*, and *Reader's Digest*. She did not want to be the kind of author who wrote the same story over and over again and so as soon as she finishes with one book, she refreshes her palate with a different kind of writing and then goes back to telling a new YA story.

Killing Mr. Griffin is one of her best-known books. She said it was inspired by her oldest daughter's first real boyfriend. While he was "the most charming young man you could ever meet," he was also a budding psychopath—"the kind of guy who would swerve in the road to run over a dog." She began wondering what a boy like this could do, how he could influence other teenagers, if he put his mind to it. Out of this wondering came a book that since 1978 has been read by hundreds of thousands of teenagers in spite of the fact that it regularly makes its way onto lists of censored books.

I Know What You Did Last Summer is also well known, partly because it was made into a major film. For an earlier edition of this textbook, Duncan confessed that one of the most exciting evenings of her life was going to the theater to see "her" story, but her excitement soon turned into such disappointment that she forgot to eat her popcorn. The film was so different from the book that at first she thought she was in the wrong theater, but then she recognized some of her teenage characters, just not the adults or the setting. She had no boat in her story, but most of the movie takes place on a fishing boat owned by an insane man who chases the teenagers with a large meat hook. A boy, new to the story, gets shoved into a vat of boiling water, and when her heroine opens the trunk of a car she finds a corpse with crabs coming out of its mouth. But this is nothing compared to when she has to hide in a bin of ice surrounded by the cut-off heads of her friends.

Duncan said that she has always taken pride in being professional about the business side of her career and she understands that changes sometimes have to be made between a print edition and a film edition. For the sixth edition of this textbook, she wrote, "But the soul of a story should not be destroyed in the process. For a book that has been a mainstay in middle school literature classes for over 23 years, to be transformed into a slasher film without the knowledge and consent of the author goes past what is acceptable" (p. 100).

Duncan has a special reason for not wanting to desensitize young people to violence. In 1989, her youngest daughter, eighteen-year-old Kaitlyn, was murdered in what the Albuquerque Police Department classified as a random drive-by shooting. Duncan recounted the awful experience in a 1992 book for adults *Who Killed My Daughter?*, which many of her teen fans have also read. In hopes of keeping the case open and finding out who did the shooting, the Arquette family (Duncan's married name) has a website that asks for comments or clues. As of the end of May, 2007, nearly a thousand people had responded, but as of this writing the case is still unsolved. ●

he also agrees to switch identities with his friend, and that is when the trouble begins.

3. Peter Abrahams's *Down the Rabbit Hole: An Echo Falls Mystery* has a protagonist, Ingrid Levin-Hill, who is also a devoted fan of Sherlock Holmes. In a delicious and suspenseful book, Ingrid sets out to find the murderer of a strange old woman associated with a theater group.

4. *The Perfect Shot*, by Elaine Marie Alphin, could also be considered a sports book because Brian is a basketball player, but far more important at the moment is that his girlfriend, Amanda, along with her sister and their mother, is shot to death in the family garage. Amanda's father is charged with the murder, but Brian has seen something that tells a different story, and so in the midst of trying to lead his team to victory he faces the dilemma of whether or not he should tell.

Stories of the Supernatural

Fears of death, the unknown, and the supernatural probably go back to prehistoric times, when shadows in a cave and light and dark mystified and frightened humans. We have demanded answers to the unknown but have rarely found them, and so we have settled on myths and legends about superior and unseen beings. Such explanations are satisfying (see Focus Box 6.5, The Supernatural in YA Fiction) because when we are fighting the inexplicable, they make winning more pleasing and losing more acceptable.

Amid all our modern knowledge and sophistication, we hold on to our fascination with the unknowable. We delight in chambers of horrors, tunnels of terror, and haunted houses. We claim to be rational beings, yet we read astrology charts. We mock the superstitions of others yet hold as pets one or two of our own, joking all the time while we toss salt over our shoulder, avoid walking under ladders, and knock on wood. We follow customs without wondering why they came about. Black is assumed to be the appropriate dress for funerals because it is dark and gloomy and demonstrates solemnity. We may not know that black was worn at a time lost in history because spirits, sometimes malignant or perhaps indignant, were thought to linger near a corpse for a year. Wearing black made it more difficult for these evil spirits to see the living. As long as spirits were around, danger lurked; hence, long mourning periods in black dress.

Greek and Roman literature abounds with supernatural elements, but so does Elizabethan literature. Whether Shakespeare believed in ghosts or witches is anyone's guess. Certainly, his audiences often did, and they apparently delighted in or were frightened by them in plays such as *Macbeth*, *Hamlet*, and *The Tempest*.

Few people will admit to believing in supernatural elements, yet they listen eagerly to urban legends and stories about mysterious happenings. Alvin Schwartz was happily surprised when his books *Scary Stories to Tell in the Dark*, *More Scary Stories to Tell in the Dark*, and *Scary Stories 3: More Tales to Chill Your Bones* began winning statewide contests as kids' favorite books. At the same time, the books also climbed to the top of the American Library Association's list of

The Supernatural in YA Fiction

All Hallows' Eve by Vivian Vande Velde. Harcourt, 2006. In this collection of thirteen stories, a master writer has created ghosts, goblins, and witches galore.

Beowulf by Gareth Hinds. Candlewick, 2007. This beautifully created graphic novel made its way to several "Best Book" lists, at least partly because it coincided with the release of Robert Zemeckis's 2007 *Beowulf* film. The book was praised for keeping the rhythm and the tone of the original story even though it is considerably abridged. The story is told in boxes near each painting instead of inside speech bubbles.

Beware! R. L. Stine Picks His Favorite Scary Stories, edited by R. L. Stine. HarperCollins, 2002. Stine's name is meant to grab young readers who loved his earlier books. He wrote original stories for Nightmare Hour and *The Haunting House* (HarperCollins, 1999, 2001).

The Entertainer and the Dybbuk by Sid Fleischman. Harper-Collins, Greenwillow, 2007. In this highly original book, readers get a new look at the anti-Semitism of the World War II era. Former American pilot Freddie Birch works as a ventriloquist and is surprised to find himself partnering with a dybbuk—a spirit or ghost—of a murdered Jewish boy who once helped Freddie escape from a POW camp.

Fade by Robert Cormier. Delacorte, 1988. Paul Moreaux, a young French Canadian, discovers that he has inherited a family gift/curse that comes to only one person in each generation: the ability to be invisible.

The Ghost Belonged to Me, *Ghosts I Have Been*, *The Dreadful Future of Blossom Culp*, and *Blossom Culp and the Sleep of Death* by Richard Peck. Delacorte, 1975, 1977, 1983, 1986. These delightfully funny books for middle school readers are about a boy who finds a charming, although somewhat outspoken, young woman from the past century living in the family barn.

The Great Blue Yonder by Alex Shearer. Clarion, 2002. Once tweeners get over the sadness of twelve-year-old Harry's being killed on his bicycle, they will love—and laugh—at the story of how he returns home as a ghost.

Horowitz Horror Stories: Stories You'll Wish You'd Never Read by Anthony Horowitz. Philomel, 2006. Horror is out of control in these nine tales of kids and the unknown.

In Camera and Other Stories by Robert Westall, Scholastic, 1992. Readers who enjoy these stories will want to read Westall's *The Haunting of Chas McGill and Other Stories* (Greenwillow, 1993) and *Rachel and the Angel and Other Stories* (Scholastic, 1988).

The Last Treasure by Janet S. Anderson. Dutton, 2003. Wealthy John Matthew Smith died in 1881, but that doesn't keep his spirit from returning for an annual visit to see how the family is doing and to nudge things along in hopes of helping his descendants appreciate each other.

The Lion Tamer's Daughter and Other Stories by Peter Dickinson. Delacorte, 1997. In the title story, Keith is drawn into the dark side of the circus when he meets a duplicate of a longtime friend.

The Lovely Bones by Alice Sebold. Little, Brown, 2002. Fourteen-year-old Susie Salmon is on her way to school when she is raped and murdered in a cornfield. She tells her story from heaven as she watches over her family.

The Presence: A Ghost Story by Eve Bunting. Clarion, 2003. A young girl, injured and her best friend dead in a car crash, goes to a beloved church for solace and finds an evil presence instead.

Restless: A Ghost's Story by Rich Wallace. Viking, 2003. A cross-country runner running in a graveyard feels someone following him. Later the ghost of a young man touches him. He begins to see other spirits, including his older brother, dead for ten years.

Skeleton Man by Joseph Bruchac. HarperCollins, 2001. Young teens may get nightmares from this story based on a Mohawk legend about a man so hungry that he eats himself down to the bone. Fortunately, Molly manages to outwit the stranger and save herself and her parents.

Skellig by David Almond. Delacorte, 1999. When Michael goes out to explore new property his family has bought, he discovers Skellig in an old shed. Skellig first appears to be a sick old man, but later he appears to be something more. *Kit's Wilderness* (Delacorte, 2000) also has some intriguing supernatural elements.

Vampires, edited by Jane Yolen. HarperCollins, 1991. This wonderful collection of short stories will make readers shudder and, sometimes, laugh. Yolen's series for Harcourt Brace, *Here There Be Ghosts*, . . . *Dragons*, . . . *Unicorns*, . . . *Angels*, and . . . *Witches*, is beautifully put together.

banned books. Stephen Gammell's creepy illustrations are probably as much to blame as are the stories themselves.

Let's hope that Derek Landy's 2007 *Skulduggery Pleasant* does not meet the same fate even though it too has a skeleton on the cover and is written for young teens. Twelve-year-old Stephanie Edgley inherits an estate from her uncle and is plunged into danger and violence with a touch of magic, thanks to a skeleton-detective who shows up at the funeral and sticks around for what happens after the reading of the will.

Supernatural novels have well-established ground rules. Settings are usually in an eerie or haunted house or in a place where a mysterious event occurred years ago. Some thrillers occur in more mundane places, perhaps a brownstone in New York City or a hotel shut down for the season, but readers know the mundane remains calm only for a short time before frightening events begin and strange people come out to play. Darkness is usually essential, but not always physical darkness. The protagonist is oblivious to evil for a time but ultimately recognizes the pervasive power of the darkness of the soul. Sometimes the wife or husband sells out to evil and entices the spouse to join in a black mass. Rituals or ceremonies are essential. Family curses or pacts with the devil have become commonplaces of the genre. Alfred Hitchcock, that master of suspense, reminds us over and over that the most terrifying things can happen in the most commonplace settings. In *North by Northwest*, on a lovely day in the middle of a South Dakota cornfield, Cary Grant is suddenly attacked by a crop-dusting airplane. In *The Birds*, a placid setting alongside the ocean suddenly turns to a scene of terror when sweet little birds begin to tear into human flesh.

In the 1989 edition of this textbook, Robert Westall observed that supernatural books break quite naturally into horror stories and ghost stories. The horror stories make the point that "the human organism is a frail thing of flesh subject to an infinity of abuse, and that it is painful and undignified for the human spirit to have to dwell in it." Such a depressing fact may be well worth saying but not over and over again. Even the books by such ingenious and powerful writers as Poe and Lovecraft, he noted, are not something you would want to read if you are "on the way to build the Taj Mahal, or paint the Sistine Chapel ceiling, or even have a happy love affair."

> On the other hand, the ghost story is about the undying spirit, not the dying flesh. . . . [Ghosts] add an exciting fifth dimension to the often-boring four dimensions of real life. They make it possible for us to escape into the land of the impossible where, delightfully, anything can happen. They are also a comfort: a reassurance of our own immortality. I would adore to spend my first few years of death as a ghost, drifting round the world painlessly in the company of other friendly ghosts, seeing all the things I never got round to seeing in life because there were other boring earthbound things to be done.

Westall went on to explain that we need ghost stories:

> In terms of love and the passing of time, we are all haunted houses, full of rooms we have shut off because of loss, or fear, or regret. To spend all our time wander-

ing through such rooms would lead to madness. But to wander sometimes can be agonizingly sweet and rich. And never to dare to wander through them can make life a dusty boring hell.[13]

Vampires, Werewolves, and Other Supernaturals

The most promising new star in the firmament of YA supernatural writing would seem to be the prolific Vivian Vande Velde. Her books cross several genres but always touch base at the supernatural. *Never Trust a Dead Man* presents a young loser. Selwyn has had a terrible week. His girlfriend—or at least the person he'd like to be his girlfriend—has turned him down and plans to marry Farold. Farold follows this news by beating up Selwyn. And as if all that weren't bad enough, Farold is found dead with a knife in his back, and the knife belongs to Selwyn. It is at the point when Selwyn sets out to prove his innocence that the mystery becomes supernatural. In Vande Velde's *Companions of the Night*, a teenage girl is an unwitting accomplice to a vampire, while her *Being Dead* is a compilation of seven creepy stories.

Another rising star is Neil Gaiman, who is already famous for his graphic novels. His 2002 *Coraline* was on nearly a dozen best-book lists and earned endorsements from the likes of Philip Pullman, Orson Scott Card, and Diana Wynne Jones. A girl discovers a door in the house where her family has moved. When she steps through, she is in another house, much like her own, but seemingly newer and better. There's also a new set of parents who want her to stay and be their child. As the *San Francisco Chronicle* wrote, it is a book that is both "creepy and funny" and "bittersweet and playful." It will linger long in the memory, even for readers who rush through it to see what happens.

Annette Curtis Klause's *The Silver Kiss* is a purer illustration of a supernatural story. Nearly every night Zoë comes home to a dark and empty house. Her mother is in the hospital dying of cancer, and as early as on page 2 readers get clues about supernatural elements. Zoë is almost as thin as her mother, "a sympathy death perhaps, she wondered half seriously. . . . Wouldn't it be ironic if she died, too, fading out suddenly when her look-alike went?" On page 3, Zoë remembers happier times with her mother, but even here there's a shadow: "You're a dark one," her mother said sometimes with amused wonder. "You're a mystery." Zoë likes to walk in the neighborhood park and sit in front of the old-fashioned gazebo, where one night "a shadow crept inside, independent of natural shades." Then she saw his face.

> He was young, more boy than man, slight and pale, made elfin by the moon. He noticed her and froze like a deer before the gun. They were trapped in each other's gaze. His eyes were dark, full of wilderness and stars. But his face was ashen. Almost as pale as his silver hair.

In her first meeting with Simon, a 200-year-old vampire from Bristol, England, Zoë recognizes how beautiful he is, he flees, and she cries. The story within a story, in which Simon explains how he became a vampire, is brilliant in its own right, but then so is the book's ending when Zoë and Simon must part.

Klause's *Blood and Chocolate* has also proved itself popular among young people and reviewers. A clan of werewolves, existing since time began, have lost their leader in a fire. They now intend to live in Virginia, led by Vivian, daughter of the late head of the clan. Going to school, she meets a boy who attracts her. She is sure she knows and can trust him, so Vivian shows him who and what she is, and he is frightened and repelled.

Stephenie Meyer, a new writer, published her first book, *Twilight*, in 2005. It immediately jumped to the top of the *New York Times* best-seller list and into the hearts of teenagers. The sequel, *New Moon*, was published in 2006 and *Eclipse* in 2007. The heroine is seventeen-year-old Bella, who lives in sunny Phoenix, Arizona, but when her mother's new boyfriend, a baseball player, has to go to Florida for winter training, Bella offers to go and live with her father, who is the sheriff in Forks, Washington. Forks is the place in the United States where there are the fewest days of sunshine, and so, of course, a gorgeous family of vampires has chosen to live there. The "father" in this family is something like four hundred years old, but he looks less than thirty. He works as a successful doctor in the local hospital where his unusual powers, including his finely honed sense of smell, help him diagnose illnesses. He hopes that by saving lives he can make up for his basic nature. Over the years, he and his "family" have learned in varying degrees to master their basic instincts and to drink only the blood of animals, which they regularly hunt. (There's no law against hunting animals year-round if you do not use weapons.) Edward, who has been pretending to be a high school student, falls in love with Bella, and all is well until a rival group of vampires without the refined tastes of the Cullen family discover the Cullens on a baseball outing—they have to play deep in the woods only during thunder storms that will cover the sounds of their powerful hits. The other gang "wants" Bella and so begins an exciting chase and a frantic fight for survival. In the second book, werewolves enter the plot as the legendary enemies of vampires, and we're left eager to read *Eclipse*, where the story moves from Forks to the city of Seattle, which is experiencing a health crisis, which gives Bella a lot more to sink her teeth into.

Other recent vampire stories include Cynthia Leitich Smith's *Tantalyze*. Seventeen-year-old Quincie lives with her uncle in Texas, and between the two of them they manage the Italian restaurant that was left to her when her parents died. Quincie decides to rename it Sanguinis and to decorate it with a vampire theme. But when the chef is mauled to death and replaced by a strange, fair-haired man with red eyes and some alarming recipes, readers know something is afoot. The *Publishers Weekly* reviewer described it as "campy," more like *Buffy the Vampire Slayer* than like Meyer's dignified romance.

Tantalyze is set in Texas, while the protagonist, Cal, in Scott Westerfeld's *Peeps*, leaves Texas—the home of shape-shifters—and moves to New York. Upon his arrival, he immediately loses his virginity and then learns that in the Big Apple a new kind of vampirism is an STD (Sexually Transmitted Disease). His kind prefers not to use the v-word, but instead call themselves Peeps, for "Parasite Positive." As the hero of the book, he of course comes over to the good side and becomes one of the Night Watchers, working to understand and defeat the condition. The sequel is *The Last Days*, which has the extra fun of involving rock music as a solution to the problem.

We've heard two theories about why teenagers are especially attracted to vampire and werewolf stories. One is that their bodies actually are undergoing tremendous changes and so they are attracted to stories where young characters change even more than they do. Another is the idea of forbidden love. Especially in Meyer's *Twilight*, girls can revel in all the satisfactions of being an ordinary girl who is suddenly courted and adored and yet does not have "to go all the way." The more-than-perfect Edward loves Bella so much that he exerts utmost control over his "natural" instincts so that he will not accidentally bite Bella and turn her into a vampire or lose control and kill her by sucking out all of her blood.

Stephen King—Leader of the Pack

The dilemma of most vampire and werewolf stories is whether we can accept someone disturbingly different even when we mostly admire and trust the person. Are we willing to go below the surface in judging people? That is the essence of much supernatural literature, from Frankenstein to Stephen King, who leads all the writers in the field of supernatural writing.

He is a former high school English teacher who frequently includes likable young people among his characters. The fact that he writes about them without condescension is not lost on the audience. "The Langoliers" (from *Four Past Midnight*) is the story of a late-night flight from Los Angeles to Boston. The plane goes through a time rip, and the only passengers who survive are the ten who happened to be sleeping. Fortunately, one of them is a pilot; otherwise there wouldn't have been much of a story to tell. There is also the blind Dinah, a young girl on her way to Boston for an operation on her eyes. She has such a super-developed sense of hearing that she is mistaken by the mad Craig Toomy, the ultimate yuppie gone awry, as the chief Langolier. The character most closely filling the role of a young adult hero on a romantic quest is Albert Kaussner, a gifted violinist on his way to enroll in a Boston music conservatory. In his own mind, he's not Albert or Al, but Ace Kaussner, "The Arizona Jew" and "The Fastest Hebrew West of the Mississippi." The journey turns out to be much more difficult than anything faced by Ace's mythical heroes of the Old West, and it even requires him to sacrifice his beloved violin. At the end of the trip, he is rewarded with his first love and the feeling of growth and confidence that comes with having passed a difficult test.

Stephen King's first book, *Carrie*, appeared in 1974 and sold well for a then-unknown writer. From that point on, King maintained his place as *the* writer of the genre. Carrie is a young outsider, the daughter of religious fanatics, and the brunt of cruel jokes. She possesses the power of telekinesis, and she uses it to destroy the school, the students, and the town in a fit of justified rage. *Firestarter* is far better, with its portrait of an eight-year-old girl with the power to start fires merely by looking at an object. A government agency, "The Shop," learns about the child and launches a search for her. King effectively demonstrates how the government agency has disintegrated into evil. *Firestarter* may not be King's best book, but it is his most penetrating study of character and the United States.

Among young adult writers specializing in supernatural themes, Lois Duncan has been consistently popular. In *Summer of Fear*, Rachel Bryant's family is notified that relatives have died in a car crash, leaving seventeen-year-old Julia behind. The girl, who looks surprisingly mature, arrives and changes the lives of everyone around her. Trickle, the family dog, suspects something is wrong, but Trickle does not live too long, and neither does anyone else who gets in Julia's way. Duncan's *Stranger with My Face* and *The Third Eye* were enjoyable but lacked the power of *Summer of Fear*. See Focus Box 6.5 for other examples of supernatural stories written for teens.

Support for allowing young adults to read supernatural books comes from Jeanine Basinger, the chair of film studies at Wesleyan University. While her words were aimed at horror films, they apply equally well to books:

> It never really goes away, this appetite for horror . . . We have all of these tragedies on our minds. In modern life it's just one damn thing after another, and we seek to explain it to one another. And if there's some experience that gives closure to it, gives an explanation or at least gives us reassurance that we're not the only ones having the scaries, it reassures us.[14]

Concluding Comments

This chapter has been about literature that is sometimes treated as "nonessential," mostly because it tugs at emotional more than intellectual parts of our brains. In today's high-tech world, however, it may be that this is the very kind of reading that serves to remind us of our humanity and our need to reach out and understand the emotions of others.

Notes

1. Betty Rosenberg, *Genreflecting: A Guide to the Reading Interests in Genre Fiction* (Libraries Unlimited, 1982), written in place of a dedication.
2. Anthony Brandt, "The Adventure Craze," *American Heritage* 51 (December 2000/January 2001): 43.
3. London, *Independent*, June 30, 1995, p. 18.
4. Anne Scott MacLeod, "Writing Backward," *Horn Book Magazine* 76 (January/February 1998): 29.
5. Avi, "Writing Backward but Looking Ahead," *Signal* 23 (Summer 1999): 21.
6. Henry Seidel Canby, "What Is Truth?" *Saturday Review of Literature* 41 (December 31, 1927): 481.
7. Reinhold Messner, *Everest: Expedition to the Ultimate* (Oxford University Press, 1979), p. 460.
8. *Into Thin Air* (Villard, 1997), pp. 135–136.
9. Jacques Barzun, *God's Country and Mine* (Little, Brown, 1954), p. 159.
10. Angela Lumpkin, Sharon Kay Stoll, and Jennifer M. Beller, *Sports Ethics: Applications for Fair Play* (McGraw-Hill, 2003), p. 262.
11. Hillary Waugh, "What Is a Mystery?" *The Basics of Writing and Selling Mysteries and Suspense* 10 (1991): 6–8.
12. Shannon Ocork, "What Type of Mystery Are You Writing?" *The Basics of Writing and Selling Mysteries and Suspense* 10 (1991): 10–12.
13. Robert Westall, "On Nightmares for Money," in *Literature for Today's Young Adults* (Scott, Foresman, 1989): 166–167.
14. Rick Lyman, "The Chills! The Thrills! The Profits," *New York Times*, August 31, 1999, p. B-1.

Fantasy, Science Fiction, Utopias, and Dystopias

chapter 7

Fantasy and science fiction are related to each other and to humankind's deepest desires, but it is not always easy to draw a clear-cut line between the two. Ursula K. Le Guin offered this distinction:

> The basic concept of fantasy, of course, is this; you get to make up the rules, but then you've got to follow them. Science fiction refines the canon: You get to make up the rules, but within limits. A science-fiction story must not flout the evidence of science, must not, as Chip Delaney puts it, deny what is known to be known.[1]

Or, as Walter Wangerin, Jr., said in a lecture to a college audience: "Fantasy deals with the *immeasurable* while science fiction deals with the *measurable*."[2]

No matter what the definitions or distinctions, the boundaries between science fiction and fantasy are fuzzy, so that more often than not the two genres are treated together. Advertisements for the Science Fiction Book Club often mix choices of science fiction and fantasy with horror, the supernatural, mythology, folklore, and some selections that seem impossible to pigeonhole. Anyone who is around young people knows that in this area books cross genre lines and age lines. Young adults read what adults read, and books that may have been published for young readers (e.g., Robin McKinley's *Beauty* or Lloyd Alexander's Prydain series) are now also read by adults.[3]

What Is Fantasy?

Fantasy comes from a Greek word meaning "a making visible." Perhaps more than any other form of literature, fantasy refuses to accept the world as it is, so readers can see what could have been (and still might be), rather than merely what was or must be.

The appeal of fantasy may be, simply, that it is so elemental. Some see its most comparable form of communication in music, which may be why so many composers have been influenced by it. Fantasy sings of our need for heroes, for the good, and for success in our eternal fight against evil or the unknown. Composers of works as dissimilar as Stravinsky's *Firebird*, Mahler's *Song of the Earth*, and Strauss's *Thus Sprach Zarathustra* have sung that song. On its lighter side, musicians sing of beauty, love, and dreams and dreamers, as in Mozart's *The Magic Flute* or Ravel's *Daphnis and Chloë* and Tchaikovsky's *Swan Lake*. Writers sing their lighter tales through stories about Beauty and the Beast, the happier and younger life of Arthur, and many of the old folktales and legends that are childhood favorites. (See Focus Box 2.1, New Tellings of Old Stories, p. 44.)

Ray Bradbury maintains that fantasy is elemental and essential:

> The ability to "fantasize" is the ability to survive. It's wonderful to speak about this subject because there have been so many wrong-headed people dealing with it. We're going through a terrible period of art, in literature and living, in psychiatry and psychology. The so-called realists are trying to drive us insane, and I refuse to be driven insane. . . . We survive by fantasizing. Take that away from us and the whole damned human race goes down the drain.[4]

Fantasy allows us—even forces us—to become greater than we are, greater than we could hope to be. It confronts us with the major ambiguities and dualities of life—good and evil, light and dark, innocence and guilt, reality and appearance, heroism and cowardice, hard work and indolence, determination and vacillation, and order and anarchy. Fantasy presents all these, and it provides the means through which readers can consider both the polarities and the shadings in between.

Conventions of Fantasy

Jo-Anne Goodwin's comment about the nature of fantasy is worth repeating for its accuracy and succinctness.

> Classic fantasy is centered around quests. The quest may have any number of different motives—spiritual, political, sexual, material—but its presence in the text is essential. The quest expresses the desire to accomplish a thing fraught with difficulty and danger, and seemingly doomed to failure. It also enables fantasy writers to deal with rites of passage; the central figure grows in stature as the quest evolves. Typically, the journey will be full of magical, symbolic, and allegorical happenings which allow the hero to externalize his or her internal struggles: thus Odysseus must pass through Charybdis and Scylla and the Knight of Temperance must extricate himself from Acracia and the Bower of Bliss.

Fantasy also deals with flux. The central characters operate in a world turned upside down, amid great wars and events of a cataclysmic nature. The possible outcomes are open and endlessly variable; the responsibility carried by the hero is enormous. In fantasy, the imagined world is always a global village. No action can take place in isolation. Every decision taken by the hero affects someone else, and sometimes the fate of nations. It is a deeply social genre.[5]

Heroes must prove worthy of their quest, although early in the story they may be fumbling or unsure about both themselves and their quests. John Rowe Townsend, both a fine writer of young adult novels and one of the most perceptive and honored critics of the field, maintained that the quest motif is a powerful analogy of life's pattern:

> Life is a long journey, in the course of which one will assuredly have one's adventures, one's sorrows and joys, one's setbacks and triumphs, and perhaps, with luck and effort, the fulfillment of some major purpose.[6]

We all begin our quest, that long journey, seeking the good and being tempted by the evil that we know we must ultimately fight. We face obstacles and barriers throughout, hoping that we will find satisfaction and meaning during and after the quest. Our quests may not be as earthshaking as those of fantasy heroes, but our emotional and intellectual wrestling can shake our own personal worlds. In the December 1971 *Horn Book Magazine*, Lloyd Alexander wrote this kind of comparison:

> The fantasy hero is not only a doer of deeds, but he also operates within a framework of morality. His compassion is as great as his courage—greater, in fact. We might consider that his humane qualities, more than any other, are really what the hero is all about. I wonder if this reminds us of the best parts of ourselves?[7]

Fears of Fantasy

Attacks on fantasy are common and predictable. Fantasy is said to be childishly simple reading. It is true there are simple fantasies, but anyone who has read Walter Wangerin, Jr.'s, *The Book of the Dun Cow* or Evangeline Walton's Mabinogion series knows that fantasy need not be childish or simple. Fantasies are often difficult and demand close reading, filled as they are with strange beings and even stranger lands with mystical and moral overtones and ambiguities.

Fantasy has been labeled escapist literature, and, of course, it is in several ways. Fantasy allows readers to escape the mundane and to revel in glorious adventures. For some readers (perhaps for all readers at certain times), escape is all that's demanded. For other readers, venturing on those seemingly endless quests and encountering all those incredible obstacles leads to more than mere reading to pass time. The escape from reality sends those readers back to their own limited and literal worlds to face many of the same problems they found in fantasy.

Fantasy has come under attack because of its use of magic. Therefore, presumably, fantasy justifies young peoples' interest in magic. From that, censors jump to their easy conclusion that evil can only come from magic, and since fantasy usually focuses on the struggle between evil and good—and evil is almost always more intriguing than good in fantasy or real life—fantasy clearly attracts young people away from good and surely to evil. Thus goes the circuitous attack.

In the most illogical objection (and more common than we could have predicted only a few years ago), fantasy has been attacked for being unreal, untrue, and imaginative (the term *imaginative* seems to have replaced *secular humanism* as one of today's leading bogeymen). To critics who believe that using imagination leads to unwillingness to face reality, fantasy doubtless seems dangerous. But fantasy is about reality, as Ursula K. Le Guin explained over thirty years ago.

> For fantasy is true, of course. It isn't factual, but it is true. Children know that. Adults know it too, and that is precisely why many of them are afraid of fantasy. They know that its truth challenges, even threatens, all that is false, phony, unnecessary, and trivial in the life they have let themselves be forced into living. They are afraid of dragons because they are afraid of freedom.
>
> So I believe we should trust our children. Normal children do not confuse reality with fantasy—they confuse them much less often than we adults do (as a certain great fantasist pointed out in a story called "The Emperor's New Clothes"). Children know perfectly well that unicorns aren't real, but they also know that books, about unicorns, if they are good books are true books.[8]

Or as Marjorie N. Allen wrote, "Fantasies often have more to do with reality than any so-called realistic fiction. Like poetry, fantasy touches on universal truths."[9]

The Popularity of Fantasy in Schools

"Move over, Holden Caulfield. There's a new breed of teen heroes in town," wrote Anita Silvey in a feature article in the October 2006 issue of *School Library Journal*. She went on to explain:

> In fact, there's been such a shift in young adults' reading tastes that all of us are scrambling to figure out what truly appeals to teens. Of one thing I'm certain: instead of craving realistic stories about people like themselves, today's teens are crazy about characters (and scenarios) that have little in common with their own everyday lives. As one young reader put it, his peers are hunting for novels that will "take them away to another world, not like this one."[10]

Although Silvey was writing about suspense and mystery as well as fantasy, it is fantasy that has forced us, as well as many school librarians, to increase the size of our bookshelves. Certainly, the success of J. K. Rowling's Harry Potter books has something to do with it, but as Tamora Pierce told us at the 2006 ALAN meeting in Nashville, it is not so much that writers suddenly climbed onto the Harry Potter bandwagon. Instead, what happened is that Rowling's success made publishers, especially the publishers of children's books, look at fantasy with new respect and give more serious readings to the kinds of manuscripts they

Crispin: At the Edge of the World by Avi. Hyperion, 2006. In this continuation of *Crispin: The Cross of Lead* (Hyperion, 2002), Crispin and Bear are again hunted by men who have decided that Bear is traitor to their Brotherhood, which is working to overthrow England's oppressive rulers. Troth, a disfigured girl, joins Crispin and Bear in crossing the English channel.

Flame (The Farsala trilogy No. #1) by Hilari Bell. Simon & Schuster, 2003. Set in ancient Persia, this is the story of a kingdom (Farsala) striving to stay free from the oncoming Roman army. It is told through the eyes of two teenagers and a young merchant, each of whom have a role to play in the survival of their country. *Rise of a Hero* followed in 2005.

The Game by Diana Wynne Jones. Firebird/Penguin, 2007. A dangerous game, forbidden by the parents but played by wild young people, allows youngsters to enter the "mythosphere" and ride in and out of folktales and myths.

Gnat Stokes and the Foggy Bottom Swamp Queen by Sally M. Keehn. Philomel, 2005. Humor and irreverence rule this lively story of twelve-year-old Gnat and her determination to rescue Goodlow Pryce, who seven years earlier was stolen by the magical Swamp Queen.

The Golem's Eye by Jonathan Stroud (The Bartimaeus Trilogy). Hyperion/Miramax, 2004. In this sequel to *The Amulet of Samarkand* (2003), Nathaniel and Kitty are faced with challenges, including those provided by the demon Bartimaeus, whose presence also provides opportunities for humor and sarcasm.

Goose Chase by Patrice Kindl. Houghton Mifflin, 2001. Alexandra's life is suddenly changed when she becomes wildly rich and gorgeous, all because she helped an old woman.

A Hat Full of Sky by Terry Pratchett. HarperCollins, 2004. A would-be witch is threatened by a parasite that hopes to take over her mind and her magic.

The Old Willis Place: A Ghost Story by Mary Downing Hahn. Clarion, 2004. The events in this spooky and beautifully written story are told through the eyes of two girls, Diana and Lissa, who call the Old Willis Place home. While they keep to themselves and consider making friends "against the rules," their reasons are different.

Sign of the Qin by L. G. Bass (Outlaws of Moonshadow Marsh Series). Hyperion, 2004. This opening to the Moonshadow Series tells the story of Young Prince Zong in the traditions of classical Chinese epics and modern kung fu films.

Soul Eater Book Three of *The Chronicles of Ancient Darkness* by Michelle Paver. HarperCollins, 2007. Torak, a gifted boy, who lives 6,000 years ago in Northern Europe can inhabit the souls of animals. One of his best friends, Wolf, is captured by the Soul Eaters and Torak must save him.

Troll Fell by Katherine Langrish. HarperCollins, 2004. Viking ships and some fantastic creatures add a Scandinavian touch to this adventure about young Peer Ulfsson, who discovers after his father dies that his greedy uncles are going to sell him to the Troll king, who wants to give him as a slave to his newly married son.

Un Lun Dun by China Miéville. Del Rey, 2007. The title is really an allusion to a London that is not quite normal. Twelve-year-olds Zanna and Deeba find themselves in this alternate reality where typewriters "seep," umbrellas are sentient, and milk cartons make endearing pets. It is recommended to readers who liked Norton Juster's *The Phantom Tollbooth* and Neil Gaiman's *Coraline*.

The Unseen by Zilpha Keatley Snyder. Delacorte, 2004. The heart of this story is Xandra Hobson's feeling that she is unloved by her family, but the fun of the story is the way she finds this to be untrue after she rescues a bird from some hunters and it leaves her a feather, which is really a key to another world.

---

had been receiving all along. See Focus Box 7.1, New Fantasy for Young Teens. Books for slightly older readers are listed in Focus Box 7.2, Reality May Not Be Fantasy, But Fantasy Is Reality.

In an *English Journal* article, Melissa Thomas offered two reasons why fantasy works in schools.

Elsewhere by Gabrielle Zevin. Farrar, 2005. Liz Hall awakens in a strange bed near a strange companion who has a small red wound at the base of her skull. Both girls are dead and heading for Elsewhere and some unusual experiences.

Epic by Conor Kostick. Viking, 2007. In New Earth, everyone plays a fantasy computer game called Epic. An unfair ruling by the Central Allocations Committee leads young adults to challenge the committee and to eliminate Epic.

Everlost by Neal Shusterman. S & S, 2006. Nick and Allie are killed in an automobile accident and get acquainted as they head down that mythical tunnel toward "the light." They learn they are Afterlights, who cannot be seen or heard by the living.

The Forgotten Beasts of Eld by Patricia McKillip. Atheneum, 1974. The great-granddaughter of a wizard controls enchanted beasts, but she fears men who come into her private world.

Foundling (from Monster Blood Tattoo Series, Book No. #1) by D. M. Cornish. Putnam, 2006. In this new and refreshing series, Rossamünd Bookchild ventures out of the orphanage and into the fascinating but dangerous world of Half-Continent.

A Glory of Unicorns edited by Bruce Coville. Scholastic, 1998. Coville collected twelve stories about his favorite creature, the unicorn, and how it works with and affects people.

The Hunter's Moon by O. R. Melling (Chronicles of Faerie Series). Abrams/Amulet, 2004. Successfully published in Ireland in 1992 and in Canada in 1993, Melling's story about a teen who must save her unwilling cousin from the Faerie lands is a blend of Irish mythology and geography.

The Lion Hunter (The Mark of Solomon Series Bk. #1) by Elizabeth Wein. Viking, 2007. Set in sixth century Africa, this story has all the intrigue and imagination of an Arthurian legend but in a very different part of the world. It continues the story of the boy Telemakos, whom readers met in *The Sunbird* (Viking, 2004).

Listening at the Gate written and illustrated by Betsy James (The Seeker Chronicles Series). S&S/Atheneum, 2006. In this sequel to *Long Night Dance* and *Dark Heart*, Kat falls in love with a seal/man, not at all like her father's repressive fellow merchants. The starred review in *School Library Journal* gives James credit for "redrawing the pattern of the classic hero's quest."

London Calling by Edward Bloor. Knopf, 2006. When an old radio takes Martin back in time to London during World War II, he makes some startling discoveries.

Magic of Madness by Justine Larbalestier. Penguin/Razorbill, 2005. A girl named Reason grows up in the Australian bush fearing and avoiding her grandmother, but when she is fifteen, her mother goes insane and Reason is sent to live with her frightening grandmother. She escapes through a magic door, only to find herself in New York City.

The Naming by Alison Croggon. Candlewick, 2005. When sixteen-year-old Maerad meets Cadvan, her life changes because he is a magically gifted Bard who begins teaching her about her own gifts and abilities and the responsibility he sees for her future.

The Navigator by Eoin McNamee. Houghton Mifflin, 2007. Owen, the Navigator, is chosen by the resisters to save the world from their enemies, the Harsh.

The Sea of Trolls by Nancy Farmer. Simon & Schuster/Atheneum, 2004. Farmer melds mythology, humor, and suspense in this fantasy that starts when Jack and his sister are kidnapped from their Saxon village by Vikings. A sequel, *Land of the Silver Apple* (2007) was also well received.

Summerland by Michael Chabon. Hyperion/Talk Miramax, 2002. In this original story, a Little League baseball player is recruited by an old-timer from the Negro leagues to play in a game that has the potential to save the world.

The Turning by Gillian Chan. Kids Can/KCP Fiction, 2005. After his mother's death, sixteen-year-old Ben Larsson goes reluctantly with his folklorist father on a sabbatical to England. He learns that he has inherited "old blood, hero's blood" from his Icelandic grandfather and now is needed to combat the evil designs of the Faerie folk.

Wicked Lovely by Melissa Marr. HarperCollins, 2007. Aislinn is a human who can see fairies. When the Summer King decides Aislinn is the Summer Queen he has long lusted for, the Winter Queen sets out to destroy her.

The Wish List by Eoin Colfer. Hyperion/Miramax, 2003. When Meg and her friend Belch try to rob their elderly neighbor, Lowrie McCall, a nearby gas tank explodes and sends Meg through that long tunnel to the afterlife. However, Saint Peter and Beelzebub can't decide who should get Meg and so they send her back to patch things up with Lowrie McCall.

1. Students like it.

2. It is a metaphor for the human condition—rife with mythic structures, heroic cycles, and social and religious commentary.[11]

We might not have needed another endorsement of fantasy, though all such endorsements are welcome. In recent years, as fantasy has moved to the center of YA interest, Tolkien has virtually been awarded sainthood, and given the steady or growing popularity of such writers as Ursula K. Le Guin (see p. 222) and Anne McCaffrey (see p. 225), both winners of the Margaret A. Edwards Award. Other popular fantasy writers include Cornelia Funke, Tamora Pierce, and Diana Wynne Jones. And if there's a more popular writer in the world than J. K. Rowling, we have no idea who it could be.

The summer of 2007 was a Harry Potter summer around the world. Since Rowling's first, *Harry Potter and the Sorcerer's Stone* in 1997, Rowling has written six other Potter books, all of them incredibly successful. By October 1999, the first three books had been translated into twenty-eight languages (the figure was sixty-four by the time Book Seven was sold), while on July 18, 2005, an estimated 6.9 million copies of *Harry Potter and the Half-Blood Prince* were sold in the United States within the first twenty-four hours the book was on the market.

Stephen King wrote a rousing review of *Harry Potter and the Order of the Phoenix* in the July 11, 2003, *Entertainment Weekly*, and ended by writing, "My own feeling is that they are much better than Philip Pullman's *His Dark Materials* trilogy, which is their only contemporary competitor."[12] Two years later in the July 19, 2005, *Entertainment Weekly*, Christopher Paolini went gaga for *Harry Potter and the Half-Blood Prince*. Even the French, who are notoriously suspicious of everything English, fell under the Potter spell as a *London Times* headline revealed on July 1, 2003. Worse yet, some adults—real adults—read Harry Potter with great enthusiasm, much to the disdain of English novelist A. S. Byatt, who wrote an op-ed in the July 7, 2003, *New York Times* lamenting the number of adults who enjoyed Harry as much as their kids. One young woman, who was twelve, was not amused by Byatt and wrote,

> I see nothing wrong with grown-ups liking J. K. Rowling's books. . . . My parents have both read the Harry Potter books and enjoyed them. I do not appreciate a stranger calling my parents childish for reading (in my opinion) wonderful books that our whole family and many others enjoy.[13]

Why is Harry so popular? Even a cursory reading of the series would suggest some answers. Harry is a remarkable character. He is almost impossible to dislike; he's an incredibly apt student of magic at the Hogwarts School of Witchcraft and Wizardy; he's athletic in the game of Quidditch (played in midair by students on broomsticks); he's clearly a fighter; and he has friends that are attractive to readers.

His parents were murdered by the evil Voldemort, and there are enough reminders of Luke Skywalker and Darth Vader and other aspects of *Star Wars* to fascinate readers for years. In a *School Library Journal* interview, Rowling was asked what young readers are most curious about. She answered, "They were very keen to know whom I'm going to kill." And shortly, a related question was

Margaret A. Edwards Award
Winner (2004)
Ursula K. Le Guin, **Master of Fantasy**

Le Guin was honored for *A Wizard of Earthsea*, *The Farthest Shore*, *The Tombs of Atuan*, *Tehanu*, *The Left Hand of Darkness*, and *The Beginning Place*. The books were praised for having helped adolescents address questions about their role and their importance in society and in the world. Honors previously given to these books include a Newbery Book Award, the Boston Globe–Horn Book Award, the National Book Award for Children's Books, and the Lewis Carroll Shelf Award. If we had been making the list we would have also added Le Guin's realistic *Very Far Away from Anywhere Else* and her two later books, *Tales from Earthsea* and *The Other Wind*.

In 2004, Le Guin began her Annals of the Western Shore with *Gifts,* followed in 2006 with *Voices* and in 2007 with *Powers,* which received starred reviews from both *Publisher's Weekly* and *School Library Journal.* In praising *Powers,* which features a dark-skinned and hook-nosed slave boy named Gav, the *PW* reviewer wrote that Le Guin's fans have ample reason to hope that her new saga is building toward a fantasy cycle as ambitious and as satisfying as are the beloved Chronicles of Earthsea.

The same year that YALSA honored Ursula K. Le Guin with the Margaret A. Edwards Award, the Children's Services Division selected her to give the May Hill Arbuthnot Honor Lecture based on the richness that she has added to books for young readers. We were fortunate that the Maricopa County Libraries were chosen to host the event and that they invited our English department to coordinate a daylong seminar on Le Guin and her writing. In getting ready for the symposium, we developed a whole new appreciation for the amount and the variety in Le Guin's books, which include short stories, novels, poetry, translations, criticism, and books of essays. When we first announced the symposium and sent out a call for papers, we were surprised at the variety of inquiries and responses that came in, and at how many people felt so close to her books that they offered us advice, as with one man who sent an email reminding us not to forget her children's books. When we shared his message with her, she responded:

> It is interesting that [your correspondent] feels people ignore my kids' books; a good many people pay attention only to them. But then there are many critical-type people who ignore YA and kidlit on prin-

posed, "The first two Harry Potter books are very lighthearted. Will the series remain that way?" Rowling answered,

> The books are getting darker, and that's inevitable. If you are writing about Good and Evil, there comes a point where you have to get serious. This is something I really have had to think about.[14]

Other Significant Writers of Fantasy Listed Alphabetically

Lloyd Alexander   Lloyd Alexander, who died on May 17, 2007, is best known for his *Chronicles of Prydain*. Alexander grew up in Pennsylvania, but in World War II was trained in Wales to work as a staff sergeant in intelligence and counterintelligence. His years in Wales provided him with knowledge of the Mabino-

ciple, . . . as others ignore SF, or fantasy, or realism, or historical. Mostly people want to recognize one of the kinds of writing I do and to dismiss the rest as unimportant, which is tiresome, but what's the use protesting?

One of the speakers at the symposium was science fiction writer Nancy Farmer, who on the following day would be an honored guest, along with Le Guin, at the Arizona Book Festival. It was a pleasure to see these two brilliant and like-minded women meet in person for the first time. Le Guin's praise for Farmer's 2002 *The House of the Scorpion* had already been printed on the back cover of Farmer's book and reveals what Le Guin values in both her own and other people's writing:

It is a pleasure to read science fiction that's full of warm, strong characters—people who are really fond of one another, children who are ignorant and vulnerable, powerful evildoers whom one can pity, good people who make awful mistakes. It's a pleasure to read science fiction that doesn't rely on violence as the solution to complex problems of right and wrong. It's a pleasure to read science fiction that gets the science right. It's a pleasure to read The House of the Scorpion.

The six books of the Earthsea series make up an amazing myth, full of love and danger and anger and evil and goodness and the need for balance, for individuals and society. For readers, Tenar and Ged are real people, not mere characters in books. Though aimed at young adults, the books make no apologies for posing difficult and unanswerable and universal questions and dilemmas.

When for the June 2004 *School Library Journal,* Francisca Goldsmith asked Le Guin what she wanted to teach in the Earthsea books, Le Guin explained that she sees herself as a storyteller, but that in a sense the story tells itself.

I am responsible for telling it right. The words that I work in are the words of the story. I'm not a philosopher. I'm not a moralist. If my story seems to begin preaching, I make it stop, if I notice it. I'm not a preacher either. My responsibility is to my art and to the people who perceive it, the readers. That's an aesthetic responsibility and if it's aesthetically right, then it will probably also be morally right. ●

gion, a collection of Welsh legends and myths, as well as some interesting settings, both of which he later used in his fantasies. The Prydain chronicles consist of five volumes about Taran, the young Assistant Pig-Keeper. The opening book of this rich fantasy, *The Book of Three*, introduces Taran and sends him on his quest to save his land of Prydain from evil. Taran also seeks his own identity, for none know his heritage. Taran's early impatience is understandable but vexing to his master, Dalben, who counsels patience "for the time being."

"For the time being," Taran burst out. "I think it will always be for the time being, and it will be vegetables and horseshoes all my life."

"Tut," said Dalben, "there are worse things. Do you set yourself to be a glorious hero? Do you believe it is all flashing swords and galloping about on horses? As for being glorious. . . ."

"What of Prince Gwydion?" cried Taran. "Yes, I wish I might be like him."

So many people at Kings Cross Station in London were asking for Track 9¾ (the track to Hogwarts School) that officials provided a photo op for tourists by hanging up a sign and cutting a luggage cart in two.

"I fear," Dalben said, "that is entirely out of the question."

"But why?" Taran sprang to his feet. "I know if I had the chance. . . ."

"Why?" Dalben interrupted. "In some cases," he said, "we learn more by looking for the answer to a question and not finding it than we do from learning the answer itself."

Taran, youthful impetuousness and righteous indignation aglow, is bored by Dalben's thoughts and wants action, and that he finds soon enough in the books that follow: *The Black Cauldron*, *The Castle of Llyr*, *Taran Wanderer*, and *The High King*, which was awarded the Newbery Medal in 1969.

Peter Dickinson   Readers are presented with adventures and ideas and an initiation rite in *The Ropemaker*. For twenty generations, the Valley has been safe from barbarians to the north and the evil Empire to the south through powerful magic, but now that the magic grows thin, people from the Valley set out to find help. In this fantastic, scary, and satisfying novel, they learn of the Ropemaker, a powerful magician who has been protecting their Valley. They set out to find him, but in the end, it is a young girl, Tilja, who becomes responsible for protecting her people. In *A Bone from a Dry Sea*, Dickinson uses two narrators, one contemporary, one historic. Vinny joins his archeologist father in Africa searching for signs of earlier life. Li, a prehistoric figure, shows evidence of earlier forms of reasoning and imagination that may help her and her people survive. In *Water: Tales of Elemental Spirits*, Dickinson and his wife, Robin McKinley, further

Margaret A. Edwards Award
Winner (1999)
Anne McCaffrey, **The Dragon Lady**

Honored novels include *Dragonflight*, *The White Dragon*, *The Ship Who Sang*, *Dragonquest*, *Dragonsong*, *Dragonsinger*, and *Dragondrums*. Like other science fiction and fantasy writers, Anne McCaffrey created a fictional world that took over many of the books that followed. Her world of PERN (Parallel Earth Resources Negligible) was created for a short story and that, supposedly, was that, but it has since been used for fifteen novels, three more short stories, three reference works, and one CD. The novels are required reading for anyone into fantasy.

Every two hundred years PERN is threatened by shimmering spores—organisms that devour all organic matter. The only protection is the dragons, who are able to destroy the threads as they fall. Beginning with *Dragonflight* in 1968, followed by *Dragonsong*, the books have considerable science fiction mixed with fantasy. This is not unusual for writers working either genre, but McCaffrey has long maintained that she writes science fiction, not fantasy.

When she was interviewed for the June 1999 *School Library Journal*, Michael Cart asked her again in which genre she wrote. She answered,

> We keep having to settle that question. I write science fiction. It may seem like fantasy because I use dragons, but mine were biogenetically engineered; ergo, the story is science fiction.

In *Dragonflight*, Lessa sees her parents killed and pursues the killer. Having succeeded, she searches for something fulfilling and becomes the female leader of Benden Weyur, the home of the dragons. *Dragonquest* illustrates the conflict that follows when the dragonriders, brought forward two hundred years into their future by Lessa, try to force the new society to return to the old and nobler ways.

Dragonsong is a favorite of many McCaffrey fans because of its especially intriguing heroine, which McCaffrey modeled after two of her youthful friends. Her name is Menolly and she wants nothing more than to become a musician on PERN, but only men are allowed to become harpers. As punishment for her ambitions, her father beats Menolly, but she is rescued by a dragonrider. When the Master Harper of PERN lis-

tens to her music, he invites Menolly to become the first female harper. It's not surprising that Menolly, with her talents and her obstacles and her bravery, is a model for female readers. She deserves to be.

Dragonsinger carries Menolly's story into her studies at Harper Hall and the obstacles caused by her teachers and jealous students. Menolly emerges even more admirable and engaging.

McCaffrey's dragons are almost as attractive to readers as are her characters. One of her friends told McCaffrey that dragons may have universal appeal but they have had bad press for years. So McCaffrey created dragons that are attractive to readers and gentle and devoted to their riders. McCaffrey agrees that given her fascination with dragons, it's no great stretch to call her the dragon lady. (The original Dragon Lady was a bewitching but dangerous woman in *Terry and the Pirates*, a comic strip of the 1940s.)

McCaffrey says that *The Ship That Sang* is her favorite because her father had fought in three wars and then died at age sixty-three. McCaffrey has said that in the grieving for the death of a character in *The Ship That Sang*, she was grieving for her father's death and for the lost chance to prove to him that she would amount to something. In this novel, shell persons—crippled females—and their brawns—males chosen to aid them in their jobs—give up their lives to run ships with their minds. Heroism and devoting one's life to the good of others is a theme that runs through her books, and no place is that better illustrated than in *The Ship That Sang*.

Her more than sixty books translated into twenty-one languages have brought her fame, security, and a legion of loyal fans. She was the first science fiction writer to receive the Margaret A. Edwards Award and to win both the Hugo and the Nebula awards. For the second edition (1985) of this textbook, she told us that she writes love stories that are "xenophilic, rather than xenophobic since I do feel that we shall, one day or another, encounter other sentient beings. I can devoutly hope that our species will greet them with tolerance and an overwhelming desire to understand alien minds and mores." Yes, no question about it, Anne McCaffrey is committed to science fiction. ●

explore some of their favorite themes through six short stories about mermaids and the Kraken and sea serpents. Dickinson's *Eva*, which may be his most popular book, is a blend of fantasy and science fiction.

Alan Garner   One of the most widely respected writers in the genre, Alan Garner is known largely for *The Owl Service* (1968), which appeared in the early days of modern adolescent literature in the United States and created something of a sensation among the teachers and librarians who read it. Based on the Mabinogion legends, the three young characters in the story find a set of dishes. As the three get to know each other better, they also find that the pattern reflects a story of love and jealousy and hatred, one of the Mabinogion's tales of a triangular love that ends disastrously.

Diana Wynne Jones   Diana Wynne Jones's versatility delights her readers. She always tells a good story, and each story somehow reminds readers of the last Jones book except that it is somehow different. In *Howl's Moving Castle*, Sophie is changed into an old crone by the Wicked Witch and finds shelter in a strange moving castle owned by a wizard named Howl, who has also been cursed by Wicked Witch. *Howl's Moving Castle* is a fantastic story, which was later filmed in animation by Hayao Miyazaki. *A Charmed Life*, about young witch Gwendolyn Chant and her brother, Cat, is set in an enchanted England where the government is in charge of magic.

Robin McKinley   *Beauty: A Retelling of the Story of Beauty and the Beast* and the more recent *Rose Daughter* are so amusing and so spirited that in this one narrow niche of fantasy, Robin McKinley leads all the rest. McKinley's Beauty is strong and unafraid and loving. When her father steals a rose from the Beast's garden and forfeits his life, Beauty, who is thinking of ways to save him, says about the beast:

> "He cannot be so bad if he loves roses."
>   "But he is a beast," said her father helplessly.
>   I saw that he was weakening, and wishing only to comfort him, I said, "Cannot a Beast be tamed?"

The answer to that question, in both *Beauty* and *Rose Daughter*, is yes, with time and kindness and love.

Early in her writing career, McKinley created the mythical kingdom of Damar. Her first heroic fantasy set in Damar was *The Blue Sword*, the story of Harry, a female orphan, kidnapped by the Hillfolk and slowly convinced that she should take up the legendary blue sword to free the Hillfolk. McKinley writes that on her first day of warrior training Harry's "heart rose up, despite her fears, to greet the adventure she rode into." Cathi Dunn MacRae noted in her book *Presenting Young Adult Fantasy Fiction* that this could be an epigraph for all of McKinley's heroic protagonists. McKinley won the 1985 Newbery Medal for *The Hero and the Crown*, a prequel to *The Blue Sword*.

Christopher Paolini   In 2003 Christopher Paolini surprised the world with *Eragon*, a quest fantasy, and the first book in the *Inheritance* trilogy. Paolini was

In our ASU classes, we've been holding Harry Potter Day right after Halloween, when we can get bargain prices on decorations, food, and costumes. Last year, the student committee in charge decorated the room and performed magic tricks. They used a sorting hat to divide us into houses, and then had us compete in a trivia contest and in creating new charms and spells and manufacturing our own wands.

a home-schooled boy living in Montana who, when he was fifteen, began writing the story of a middle-ages farm boy who finds a strange blue stone. He takes it home, where it hatches into a dragon. The boy keeps the dragon secret, but then terrible things start happening. In 2002, when Paolini was seventeen, his parents helped him self-publish and sell 10,000 copies of the 500-page book. At this stage, the book came to the attention of Knopf, a major publishing house, which edited and promoted the book worldwide. The 2006 movie was also well received, as has been *Eldest*, the second book in the trilogy. However, the video game that was introduced alongside the film has not been as successful.

Tamora Pierce   When she was in high school and college, Tamora Pierce fell under the influence of J. R. R. Tolkien and began to write. In every one of our young adult literature classes, we have at least a couple of students who are Tamora Pierce fans. The books they have mentioned most recently are the ones about Beka Cooper, including *Bloodhound: The Legend of Beka Cooper* and *Terrier*, along with *Trickster's Choice* and *Trickster's Queen*. We especially like *Shatterglass*, the concluding volume of her second quartet of the Circle Opens series, because of the way it combines mystery and magic when Keth's glass balls reveal the past, including some brutal murders. For an October 1993 article in *School Library Journal* titled "Fantasy: Why Kids Read It, Why Kids Need It," Pierce wrote:

> Fantasy, more than any other genre, is a literature of empowerment. In the real
> world, kids have little say. This is a given; it is the nature of childhood. In fantasy,

however short, fat, unbeautiful, weak, dreamy, or unlearned individuals may be, they find a realm in which those things are negated by strength. The catch—there is always a catch—is that empowerment brings trials. Good novels in this genre never revolve around heroes who, once they receive the "Spatula of Power," call the rains to fill dry wells, end all war, and clear up all acne. Heroes and heroines contend as much with their granted wishes as readers do in normal life.

Philip Pullman   After writing several excellent historical novels for young adults, Philip Pullman turned his attention to fantasy and a three-part series he called His Dark Materials. They are dark indeed. *The Golden Compass* introduces readers to Lyra Belacqua, her Oxford University education, and her daemon (something akin to a soul but in an animal form that reflects both its own and its owner's personalities). *The Subtle Knife* introduces readers to Will Parry, whose father has been lost in the Arctic. Will sets out to find his father, and in the journey, he slides into another universe and meets Lyra. The trilogy ends with *The Amber Spyglass*, not entirely successfully.

Pullman's books are filled with adventures and a constant stream of wonders and magic. In the first book, readers learn about the golden compass, or Aletheometer, which can foretell the future. In the second, the subtle knife, called Aesahaetr, is entrusted to Will. It can cut through anything, real or magical. The significance of the knife and the seriousness of Pullman's books are revealed when a witch remarks that the name of the knife "sounds as if it meant *god-destroyer*." Almost a year in advance, the publishers began an ambitious campaign hoping that the release of the *Golden Compass* film in December of 2007, which had been in the making since 2002, would boost sales of the trilogy.

J. R. R. Tolkien   For many readers J. R. R. Tolkien is the writer against whom all other fantasy writers are measured. *The Hobbit, or There and Back Again*, began in 1933 as a series of stories that Tolkien told his children at night about

Some teachers and librarians were surprised to open up their mail and find a Golden Compass *T-shirt, along with other materials, for promoting the ten-year anniversary of Pullman's book and the upcoming film.*

a strange being, Bilbo the Hobbit. *The Lord of the Rings*, his three-part series, is even better known, especially with the release of three movies made from the *Ring* series revealing his love of adventure and his fascination with language. But Tolkien is not done with us yet. The Associated Press reported on May 6, 2007, that more than 900,000 copies had been printed of *The Children of Hurin*, a prequel to *The Lord of the Rings*. Tolkien had started *The Children of Hurin* in 1918 and eventually abandoned it. His son, Christopher, edited it for publication.

Specific Kinds of Fantasy

Animal Fantasies   Animal stories aimed at instructing humans are as old as Aesop and as recent as yesterday's book review. Many teenagers have fond memories of such books as E. B. White's *Charlotte's Web*, Jane Langton's *The Fledgling*, Robert C. O'Brien's *Mrs. Frisby and the Rats of NIMH*, Kenneth Grahame's *The Wind in the Willows*, and Richard Adams's *Watership Down*. They may be ready to read Walter Wangerin, Jr.'s, *The Book of the Dun Cow*, a delightfully funny theological thriller retelling the story of Chauntecleer the Rooster. Supposedly the leader for good against evil (the half-snake, half-cock—Cockatrice—and the black serpent—Wyrm), Chauntecleer is beset by doubts. He is aided by the humble dog Mondo Cani, some hilariously pouting turkeys, and assorted other barnyard animals.

Several other fantasies have focused on animals. Clare Bell sets her *Ratha's Creature* books twenty-five million years ago. Ratha leads a group of intelligent wild cats who have developed their society and who have learned to herd and keep other animals. Erin Hunter's *Warriors: Into the Wild* portrays four clans of wild cats living in a loose harmony with each other as they share a forest, but when one clan becomes too powerful, the equilibrium is threatened. *Warriors: Fire and Ice* continues the saga. *Fire Bringer* by David Clement-Davies is about intelligent deer who have developed a complex society predicated on their own myths. He later wrote *The Sight*, about an intelligent wolf society. The birth of two pups, Fell, who is black, and Larka, who is white, leads to the acceptance of an ancient myth about foreseeing the future. A 2007 sequel, *Fell*, tells the story of one of the grown-up pups, his betrayal of the family, and then his redemption.

Eoin Colfer's books about Artemis Fowl go against the old idea that fantasy has to be highly serious. They are playful mysteries, as well as fantasies. And surely a large part of the pleasure in Philip Pullman's *Golden Compass* trilogy comes from the animal daemon that each human has, while much of the fun in the Harry Potter books comes from the animals, including Fang, Hedwig, Scabbers, Greyback, Pigwidgeon, and Crookshanks. The animages, Prongs, Padfoot, Moony, and Wormtail, play important parts in the plot, while a good joke is when Hagrid's hippogriff, Buckbeak, is on the Ministry's "Wanted" list and Hagrid thinks he can hide or at least disguise this huge flying creature by changing his name from Buckbeak to Witherwings.

Fantasy and the Mabinogion   The *Mabinogion* is a collection of medieval Welsh tales, first published in English in 1838 to 1849 by Lady Charlotte Guest. The eleven stories deal with Celtic legends, myths, and personalities. There are also four independent tales and four Arthurian romances. These stories are important for the influence that they have had on later writers, including Lloyd Alexander, whose *Prydain Chronicles* go back to the old stories.

Evangeline Walton also used the *Mabinogion* as a basis for her four-part series, *The Prince of Annwin: The First Branch of the Mabinogion*, *The Children of Llyr: The Second Branch of the Mabinogion*, *The Song of Rhiannon: The Third Branch of the Mabinogion*, and *The Virgin and the Swine: The Fourth Branch of the Mabinogion*. This last volume was reprinted in 1970 as *The Island of the Mighty: The Fourth Branch of the Mabinogion*. It is among the best of the retellings of the old Welsh legends.

Walton's quartet is both mythology and ecology, a pattern being followed by several contemporary writers who are worried about sustaining the earth. She makes the earth a divinity that must not be despoiled by humanity. In an afterword to the first book, she wrote "When we were superstitious enough to hold the earth sacred and worship her, we did nothing to endanger our future upon her, as we do now."

King Arthur and Other Myths in Fantasy   Arthurian legends have long been staples of fantasy. T. H. White's *The Once and Future King* (a source, for which it can hardly be blamed, for that dismal musical *Camelot*) is basic to any reading of fantasy. In four parts, *The Sword in the Stone*, *The Witch in the Wood*, *The Ill-Made Knight*, and *The Candle in the Wind*, White retells the story of Arthur—his boyhood, his prolonged education at the hands of Merlin, his seduction by Queen Morgause, his love for Guinevere and her affair with Lancelot, and Mordred's revenge and Arthur's fall.

Marion Zimmer Bradley's *The Mists of Avalon* focuses on the conflict between the old religion of the Celtics, represented by Morgan Le Fay (here called Morgaine) and the new religion of Christianity, represented by Guinevere (here called Gwenhyfar). Young readers curious about the Arthurian world have a choice of several good books. Leading the list, as usual, is Katherine Paterson, whose *Parzival: The Quest of the Grail Knight* complements our knowledge of Arthur's knights and Richard Wagner's *Parsifal* opera. Nancy Springer's *I Am Mordred* related the sad, even accursed life of Arthur's bastard son.

Two recent Arthurian fantasies should appeal to young readers, Alice Borchardt's *The Dragon Queen: The Tales of Guinevere* shows a powerful and magical Guinevere battling against Merlin to prove she's worthy of being Arthur's queen. In Diana Wynne Jones's *The Merlin Conspiracy*, Roddy and Grundo wonder if a conspiracy is behind the death of Merlin, but who will believe them, since they are only children?

Fantasy on Other Worlds: Here There Be Dragons   Several other writers have written marvelous tales of dragons and fantastic worlds. Jane Yolen's *Dragon's Blood*, *Heart's Blood*, and *A Sending of Dragons* comprise a series with two extraordinarily likable young people fighting for their lives and for their dragons. Patricia C. Wrede's *Dealing with Dragons* and *Talking to Dragons* are funny adventure stories. Her best work can be found in *Book of Enchantments*.

What Is Science Fiction?

As a follow-up to the audio recording of Orson Scott Card's *Ender's Game*, which was released as part of a twentieth-year celebration of the book's publication, Card laughingly told about the difference between science fiction and fantasy. He said it was a matter of rivets versus trees. If the cover of a book shows trees, it is a fantasy, but if it shows rivets holding pieces of metal together, then it is science fiction.

With his mention of rivets, Card was alluding to space travel and the related idea that other planets have intelligent or frightening life forms that may differ drastically from Earth's humans. Contemporary problems are projected hundreds or thousands of years into the future, and those new views of overpopulation, pollution, religious bickering, political machinations, and sexual disharmony often give readers a quite different perspective on our world and our problems.

The prime requirement for "good" science fiction (the kind listed in Focus Box 7.3) has been the idea that the technology in science fiction must fit into natural laws, that is, readers must be able to believe in at least the possibility of the events that occur in a story. In a 1983 *Nightcap* talk show on Arts Cable Television, Isaac Asimov agreed that "The best kind of sci-fi involves science," but then he went on to say that even though he knows that "Time travel is theoretically impossible," he wouldn't want to give it up as a plot gimmick. What he was saying is that "rules" count, but that plot and excitement count even more. The internal consistency and plausibility of a postulated imaginary society creates its own reality.

Science fiction was never as popular on radio as it deserved to be, although *Dimension-X* and *X Minus One* had many fans. Television was a different story. From Rod Serling's *The Twilight Zone* on through the ever-new casts of *Star Trek*, viewers seemed to find TV science fiction irresistible. A more recent entry in the field, *The X-Files*, was different enough that it found an audience. N. E. Genge's *The Unofficial X-Files Companion* is a record of the plots and characters along with the serial killers, cults, werewolves, robots, and other strangenesses that have roamed through *X-Files* episodes.

Because of the increasing abilities of filmmakers to create special effects, science fiction is a natural source for films (see Film Box 7.1 for some all-time favorites). In March 2007, even the United States Postal Service joined in a *Star Wars* celebration. To soften the blow that postage was being increased, the postal service remodeled selected mailboxes around the country to look like R2-D2, and at the Star Wars Celebration IV fan conference held in the Los Angeles Convention Center, they released a page of fifteen Star Wars stamps and let the fans be the first to vote on which stamp would be made permanent. On the back of the sheet was information about each of the pictured characters and the overall explanation:

> For 30 years, the *Star Wars* Saga has thrilled moviegoers with its epic story of good versus evil. Set across a fantastic galaxy of exotic planets and bizarre creatures, the saga tells the mythic tale of the disintegration of the Old Republic, the creation of

The Alien Years by Robert Silverberg. Prism, 1998. Aliens landing on the Earth and controlling it may spell the end of humanity.

The Best Alternate History Stories of the 20th Century edited by Harry Turtledove and Martin H. Greenberg. Del Rey, 2001. History is turned on its head in this anthology; e.g., what if the South had won the Civil War, what if the Nazis had won World War II.

Black Hole written and illustrated by Charles Burns. Pantheon, 2005. In this powerful graphic novel, suburban teens are faced with "The bug," a sexually transmitted disease that causes mutations.

Crossfire by Nancy Kress. Tor, 2003. On an interstellar planet, human colonists must decide which of two alien societies they will support.

Coyote by Allen M. Steele. Ace, 2003. Three stories tell about the right-wing government that has overtaken the constitutional government of the United States and a lonely planet called Coyote.

Darkover Landfall by Marion Zimmer Bradley. DAW Books, 1972. In this introduction to a well received series, colonists from Earth travel to the planet Darkover with its one sun and four multicolored moons. Over 2,000 years, they lose touch with their home planet and evolve new cultures and new myths.

Doppelganger by David Stahler, Jr. HarperCollins, 2007. After killing and possessing the body of a popular athlete, the shape-shifting killer becomes involved with the dead boy's life.

Dust by Arthur Slade. Random/Wendy Lamb, 2003. The very real setting of a dry and dusty summer during the Great Depression gradually becomes evil and scary when "traders" from the stars begin taking children.

Firestorm by David Klass. Farrar/Frances Foster Books, 2006. This fast-moving science fiction thriller (the first of three in a planned series) will appeal to readers who have always suspected that they were somehow "different" from their parents.

Fire-Us: The Kiln by Jennifer Armstrong and Nancy Butcher. Eos, 2003. The *Fire-Us* title of this trilogy, which also contains *The Kindling* and *The Keepers of the Flame*, is a pun on the virus that has killed almost everyone on earth. A small group of kids in Florida managed to survive the virus and now must survive the other "survivors."

Larklight: A Rousing Tale of Dauntless Pluck in the Farthest Reaches of Space by Philip Reeve, illustrated by David Wyatt. Bloomsbury, 2006. Here's a rousing pirate story even more fantastic than those in the movies. It is set in 1851 when the British Empire included extraterrestrial territories and rambling old houses floating through space.

The People of Sparks by Jeanne Duprau. Random, 2004. In a sequel to *The City of Ember*, Lina and Doon face the challenge of helping the four hundred people they have brought from their underground city avoid the escalation of conflicts arising between the low-tech farmers in Sparks and the high-tech people from Ember.

Singing the Dogstar Blues by Alison Goodman. Viking, 2003. Eighteen-year-old Joss Aaronson is the sarcastic and funny heroine of this Australian novel that combines time travel and alien relationships with the elements of a mystery thriller.

The Sky So Big and Black by John Barnes. TOR, 2002. A young Marswoman wants to become an ecospector who will find ways of releasing gasses and water to make Mars more habitable.

Tomorrowland, edited by Michael Cart. Scholastic, 1999. Prominent YA authors contributed these ten stories about the future.

True Talents by David Lubar. Tor, 2007. The sequel to *Hidden Talents* finds Eddie can move things with his mind, but when he's kidnapped, his friends at Edgeview Alternative school save him with their own psychic powers.

Wintersmith by Terry Pratchett. Harper, 2007. Tiffany Aching, a witch in training, is attracted to the dreaded one who threatens her family.

Wizards of the Game by David Lubar. Philomel, 2003. Junior high boys ignore their fantasy games for a time so they can help real aliens return to their planet.

Who Goes Home? by Sylvia Waugh. Delacorte, 2004. In this British sequel to *Space Race* (2000) and *Earthborn* (2002), thirteen-year-old Jacob Bradwell discovers that his father is from the planet Ormingat and that he is expected to return to Ormingat with his father.

Z for Zachariah by Robert C. O'Brien. Atheneum, 1975. Ann Burden lives in an isolated and geologically protected valley. She believes that she is the sole survivor of a nuclear blast, but then she discovers another survivor and learns that she is in more danger from him than from all the other problems she faces.

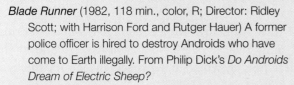

Fantasy, Science Fiction, and Dystopias

Blade Runner (1982, 118 min., color, R; Director: Ridley Scott; with Harrison Ford and Rutger Hauer) A former police officer is hired to destroy Androids who have come to Earth illegally. From Philip Dick's *Do Androids Dream of Electric Sheep?*

Children of Men (2006, 100 min., color, R; Director: Alfonso Cuaron; with Clive Owen and Julianne Moore) By 2027 women can no longer become pregnant. Then a young girl is found pregnant, and Theo devotes his life to saving her. From P. D. James's novel.

Cloverfield (2008, 84 min., color, PG-13; Director Matt Reeves; with Lizzy Caplan, Jessica Lucas, and T. J. Miller) Five young people are attending a going-away party for a friend when a monster the size of a sky-scraper attacks New York City. They are the tellers and the photographers of this truly scary story.

Pan's Labyrinth (2007, 112 min., color, R; Director: Guilleremo del Toro; with Ivana Naquero, Sergi Lopez, Maribel Verdu, and Doug Jones) Ofelia meets a tall faun who tells her she must complete three tasks to return to the underworld.

Frankenstein (1931, 71 min., black and white; Director: James Whale; with Boris Karloff) Mary Shelley's story of a man-created being and what he did.

Groundhog Day (1993, 102 min., color, PG; Director: Harold Ramis; with Bill Murray) A bored TV weather-man finds he is trapped, repeatedly replaying the same day.

Howl's Moving Castle (1994, 119 min., color, PG; Direc-tor: Hayao Miyazaki; with the voices of Jean Simmons

and Christian Bale). A young girl falls under a witch's spell and discovers a moving castle. From Diana Wynne Jones's novel.

Ladyhawke (1985, 124 min., color, PG; Director: Richard Donner; with Michelle Pfeiffer and Rutger Hauer). A medieval story about two lovers caught up in an evil spell.

Pleasantville (1998, 123 min., color/black and white, PG-13; Director: Gary Ross; with Reese Witherspoon, Tobey Maguire, and Jeff Daniels) A brother and sister are transported within their TV to a 1950s happy sit-com, *Pleasantville.*

The Purple Rose of Cairo (1985, 87 min., black and white/color; Director: Woody Allen; with Mia Farrow and Jeff Daniels). A Depression-era waitress finds relief from her misery in films until her favorite actor walks out of his film.

Stranger Than Fiction (2006, 105 min., color, PG-13; Director: Marc Foster; with Will Ferrell, Dustin Hoffman, and Emma Thompson) An IRS auditor hears an audi-ble voice repeating his own thoughts.

The Time Machine (1960, 103 min., color; Director: George Pal; with Rod Taylor and Yvette Mimieux) A sci-entist creates a time machine that can go forward to see what humanity has done to itself.

Young Frankenstein (1974, 105 min., black and white, PG; Director: Mel Brooks; with Gene Wilder, Peter Boyle, Cloris Leachman) A loving parody of Frankenstein with touches of *Bride of Frankenstein* tossed in.

the Empire, the rise of the evil Darth Vader, and the ultimate victory of the Rebel Alliance. From the wisdom and power of Yoda to the brave deeds of Jedi Knights and improbable heroes, *Star Wars* has inspired generations of fans with its unbri-dled sense of adventure, advancing the art of filmmaking while leaving an indeli-ble mark on our cultural imagination.

Carl Sagan, the late Cornell University astronomer/author has said that sci-ence fiction is what brought him to science. Kurt Vonnegut, Jr., also applauded science fiction through having his character Eliot Rosewater, in *God Bless You, Mr. Rosewater*, stumble into a convention of science fiction writers and drunk-enly announce that he loves them because they are the only ones who:

. . . know that life is a space voyage, and not a short one either, but one that'll last billions of years. You're the only ones with guts enough to really care about the future, who really notice what machines do to us, what wars do to us, what cities do to us, what big, simple ideas do to us, what tremendous misunderstanding, mistakes, accidents and catastrophes do to us.

Then he goes on to praise them for being "zany enough to agonize over time and distances without limit" and "over mysteries that will never die, over the fact that we are right now determining whether the space voyage for the next billion years or so is going to be Heaven or Hell."

Why does science fiction appeal to young adults and to adults? First and probably most important, it is exciting. Science fiction may have begun with the "rah-rah-we're-off-to-Venus-with-Buck-Rogers" sensational fiction, and although it has gone far beyond that, the thrill of adventure is still there. Science fiction writers do not write down to their audience, and this is recognized and admired. Science fiction allows anyone to read imaginative fiction without feeling the material is kid stuff. Science fiction presents real heroes to readers who find their own world often devoid of anyone worth admiring, of heroes doing something brave, going to the ultimate frontiers, even pushing these frontiers farther back, all important at a time when many young people wonder if any new frontiers exist.

Science fiction has a heritage of fine writers and important books. Some critics maintain that the genre began with Mary Wollstonecraft Shelley's *Frankenstein: Or, The Modern Prometheus* in 1818. Others argue for Swift's *Gulliver's Travels* in 1726 or the much earlier Lucian's *The True History* in the second century AD. No matter, for nearly everyone agrees that the first major and widely read writer was Jules Verne, whose *Journey to the Center of the Earth* in 1864 and *Twenty Thousand Leagues Under the Sea* in 1870 pleased readers on several continents.

The first American science fiction came with Edgar Allan Poe's short story "The Unparalleled Adventures of One Hans Pfaall," which appeared in the June 1835 issue of the *Southern Literary Messenger* and was included in *Tales of the Grotesque and Arabesque* in 1840. Hans Pfaall's balloon trip to the moon in a nineteen-day voyage may be a hoax, but the early trappings of science fiction are there. Dime novels occasionally used science fiction, particularly in the Frank Reade series, as did some books from the Stratemeyer Literary Syndicate, particularly in the Tom Swift and Great Marvel series.

These books were readable and fun, and they were read over and over by many people who had no idea how good most of the stories were. Most critics, however, were snobs about science fiction. Some fans didn't consider the genre respectable, but the fact that science fiction, or whatever it was called in the early days, was not part of mainstream writing may have made it more attractive to readers who were not seeking literary respectability so much as they were looking for books that were entertaining.

For better or worse, academic respectability came to science fiction in December 1959, when the prestigious and often stuffy Modern Language Association began its science fiction journal, *Extrapolation*. Two other journals, *Foundation* (in England) and *Science-Fiction Studies* (in Canada), began publishing in the early

1970s. Colleges and secondary schools offered courses in the genre, and major publishers and significant magazines recognized and published science fiction.

Types of Science Fiction

The most obvious type, and probably the first to be read by many later fans of science fiction, is the simpleminded but effective story of wild adventure, usually with a touch of sociological or environmental concerns. H. G. Wells's *The War of the Worlds* spawned many imitations as we read, for example, about this group of aliens invading Earth and that group of aliens attacking another threatened outpost of civilization. Such books combine the best of two worlds—science fiction and horror.

Time travel has been a theme in science fiction since H. G. Wells's *The Time Machine*, while in many other books authors work with the wonder and danger of space travel. For example in Larry Niven and Jerry Pourelle's *The Mote in God's Eye*, humans have colonized the galaxy and an alien society sends emissaries to work with the humans. When the aliens accidentally die, the humans must send representatives dashing through space to ward off disaster and war.

Another kind of story is about the mad scientist or the threat of science gone sour or insane. Philip K. Dick's *Do Androids Dream of Electric Sheep?* (reissued as *Blade Runner* in 1982 when the film adaptation came out) presents a gloomy view of the future. A cop/bounty hunter searches for human-created androids who have escaped from another planet to come back to a horribly drizzling and bleak Earth.

Harry Turtledove's *Worldwar: In the Balance* is a kind of "what if" science fiction. The author changes history as when Turtledove sets his story in 1942 when the Allies are at war with the Axis powers. An alien force of lizard-like things invades Earth with a technology that far surpasses human knowledge.

Cyberpunk is one of the wildest, rampaging kinds of science fiction today. Gene LaFaille defines cyberpunk as

> A subgenre of science fiction that incorporates our concern about the future impact of advanced technologies, especially cybernetics, bionics, genetic engineering, and the designer drug culture, upon the individual, who is competing with the increasing power and control of the multinational corporations that are extending their stranglehold on the world's supply of information.[15]

Cyberpunk is about technology and the power of communication, particularly power used to manipulate people. William Gibson's 1984 *Neuromancer* was the novel that brought cyberpunk to readers' attention.

Humor is not often the strongest feature of science fiction, but Douglas Adams's *The Hitchhiker's Guide to the Galaxy* is a genuinely funny spoof of the genre. The book began as a BBC radio script, progressed to a television script, and ultimately became a novel. When Arthur Dent's house is due for demolition to make way for a highway, he finds Ford Prefect, a strange friend, anxiously seeking a drink at a nearby pub. Ford seems totally indifferent to Arthur's plight because, as he explains, the world will soon be destroyed to make way for a new galactic freeway. Soon the pair are safe aboard a Vogon Construction Fleet Battleship, and that is the most easily explained of the many improbabilities that follow.

Many people think of science fiction as a male genre, but Jane Donawerth countered this idea in an *English Journal* article, where she noted that between 1818, when Mary Wollstonecraft Shelley published *Frankenstein: Or, The Modern Prometheus*, and the 1930s, women were among the most important writers dealing with technological utopias and similar topics that foreshadowed science fiction:

> But the times when such visions were welcomed did not last; at least in *Amazing Stories* and in *Wonder Stories*, the women virtually disappeared by the mid-1930s. I think that editorial policy, or simply civic pressure on the women, kept their stories from earning money that could go, instead, to a man supporting a family during the Depression.[16]

By the time women returned to science fiction in the 1940s, they used masculine-sounding pen names, for example, Andre Norton and Leigh Brackett. Today, however, science fiction readers have a number of women writers, as shown by the fact that winners of the Margaret A. Edwards Award include: Madeleine L'Engle, Ursula K. Le Guin, Lois Lowry, and Anne McCaffrey.

Significant Science Fiction Writers Other Than the Margaret A. Edwards Award Winners

Isaac Asimov   Isaac Asimov's response to a question of what he would do if he knew he were going to die the next day, is said to have been "Type faster!" And before his death in 1992, he indeed typed fast. He wrote more than five hundred books in so many fields that he comes close to being a truly Renaissance figure. But whatever his contributions to the study of the Bible or Shakespeare, no one can question his contributions to science fiction. The several volumes in his Foundation series established the basis for a multidimensional society that an incredible number of readers have temporarily inhabited and accepted. Asimov's *The Ugly Little Boy* is a combination horror and science fiction story in which scientists trap a young Neanderthal boy and bring him back to our time. A nurse is hired to take care of him until he will be sent back to his own time. The boy is a terrified mess, and the nurse is horrified by him, but her native compassion and his normal need for a friend bring the two together. Asimov's first book of short stories was entitled *I, Robot*, and when in 2004 Twentieth Century-Fox released the film, *I, Robot*, starring Will Smith, they credited Isaac Asimov's stories.

Ray Bradbury   While arguably less interested in the mechanics of science fiction than any other major writer, Ray Bradbury may have been the most sensitive of them all about humanity's ability to befoul Earth and the rest of the universe. He seemed to have almost no interest in how his characters moved from Earth to Mars, but *The Martian Chronicles* is a wonderful set of semirelated short stories about the problems of being human in a universe that does not treasure our humanity. In a prefatory note to Bantam's 1954 edition, Clifton Fadiman described Bradbury as "a moralist who has caught hold of a simple, obvious, but overwhelmingly important moral idea—that we are in the grip of a psychosis, a technology-mania, the final consequences of which can only be universal murder and quite conceivably the destruction of our planet."

Bradbury argues that the appeal of science fiction is understandable because science fiction is important literature, not merely popular stuff. Opening his essay "Science Fiction: Why Bother?" he compared himself to a fourth-rate George Bernard Shaw who makes an outrageous statement and then tries to prove it. The outrageous statement that he went on to make is that "Science fiction is the most important fiction being written today. . . . It is not part of the Main Stream. It *is* the Main Stream."[17]

Arthur C. Clarke   Regarded as one of the fathers of science fiction, Arthur C. Clarke's *Childhood's End* is one of the classics in the field, and his short story *2001: A Space Odyssey*, which was developed into a full-length film, is perhaps the most widely cited of any work in science fiction. In the introduction to his *Profiles of the Future*, Clarke wrote:

> A critical—the adjective is important—reading of science-fiction is essential training for anyone wishing to look more than ten years ahead. The facts of the future can hardly be imagined *ab initio* by those who are unfamiliar with the fantasies of the past.
>
> This claim may produce indignation, especially among those second-rate scientists who sometimes make fun of science-fiction (I have never known a first-rate one to do so—and I know several who write it). But the simple fact is that anyone with sufficient imagination to assess the future realistically would inevitably be attracted to this form of literature. I do not for a moment suggest that more than one percent of science-fiction readers would be reliable prophets; but I do suggest that almost a hundred percent of reliable prophets will be science-fiction readers—or writers.[18]

We thought of Clarke's statement when, just after the September 11, 2001, terrorist attack, we heard a commentator say that readers of science fiction did not take nearly as long as did other Americans to realize that an airplane flying into one of the Twin Towers was not an accident.

Robert Heinlein   In 1953 Robert Heinlein defined science fiction as speculative fiction based on the real world, with all its "established facts and natural laws." He went on to say that while the result can be extremely fantastic in content, "it is not fantasy: it is legitimate—and often very tightly reasoned—speculation about the possibilities of the real world."[19] Heinlein began his career writing young adult books, and then moved on to adult material and never looked back. Books for the young such as *Farmer in the Sky* and *Pokayne of Mars* may be largely forgotten, but for many young people, these books provided a vision of the future new to them. Later books, particularly *The Moon Is a Harsh Mistress* and *Stranger in a Strange Land*, are both better written and far more powerful visions of a deeply troubled universe. And while Heinlein may have been unable to picture a believable, strong woman, as critics claim, he wrote exceptionally fine science fiction.

William Sleator   William Sleator's books are in the genre spawned by H. G. Wells's *The War of the Worlds* in which a group of aliens invade Earth. The genre combines science fiction and horror. Sleator's *Interstellar Pig* may sound like an odd or funny book, but it is not. Sixteen-year-old Barney is intrigued to discover that three different neighbors moved next door. Soon, Barney and the three are playing a board game called Interstellar Pig, and Barney learns fast enough that he stands between the neighbors and the destruction of Earth. *Parasite Pig* is an intelligent sequel. Sleator's *House of Stairs* illustrates how mad psychologists can become to prove their point. Five young people are brought to an experimental house made up almost entirely of stairs madly going everywhere, and the young people learn that adults can be truly cruel. There are similar emotions in Sleator's *The Last Universe*, in which a mysterious maze in the garden behind Susan's house terrifies her.

Scott Westerfeld   The Westerfeld set of books that our YA students are the most enchanted with started with *Uglies* in 2005, followed the same year by *Pretties*, then in 2006 by *Specials*, and in 2007 by *Extras*. They are set in a futuristic society where all sixteen-year-olds can have an operation to make them beautiful, but not everyone wants to lose what makes them unique. The job of the *Specials* is to keep the *Uglies* down and the *Pretties* stupid. *Extras* gets its title from the large adoring crowds that in the old days were hired for films. The economy is fame-based, which reminds readers of the way amazon.com assigns numerical sales rankings to authors' books and to the way people keep track of the number of viewers checking into their websites.

Westerfeld's *Peeps*, on the 2005 Honor List, is set in New York City, where *peeps* is slang for people who are "parasite-positive," a euphemism for various kinds of scientifically based vampirism. Luckily some of the peeps can maintain an almost normal life and can use their specialized abilities to help save New York City from mutant creatures much worse than the old alligators in the sewers. Rock music plays a part in a follow-up book, *The Last Days*.

Utopias and Dystopias

Utopias and dystopias are neither science fiction nor fantasy, but they share characteristics with both. Readers must suspend disbelief and buy into the author's vision, at least for the duration of the story. As with science fiction, utopian and dystopian books are usually set in the future, with technology having played a role in establishing the conditions out of which the story grows. Unlike science fiction, and more like fantasy, however, once the situation is established, authors focus less on technology and more on sociological and psychological or emotional aspects of the story.

The centuries-old fascination with utopias is suggested by the Greek origin of the word, which includes two meanings, "no place" and "good place." Most of us, in idle moments, dream of a perfect land, a perfect society, a place that

Lois Lowry, **Who Gave Us**
The Giver

Most of Lois Lowry's books are written for children, although young teens love both *Number the Stars* (a Holocaust story that won the 1990 Newbery Medal) and her first book, the 1977 *A Summer to Die*, in which she shares the emotions, although not the actual events, connected to the death of her sister, Helen. The Margaret A. Edwards Award committee honored Lowry for *The Giver*, which won the 1994 Newbery Medal, and is accessible to readers as young as twelve or thirteen, while at the same time being rich enough to stimulate serious thinking on the part of adults and college students.

The Giver is set in a futuristic society which has as its goal to make everything "the same." Babies are born to designated birth mothers and raised in a nursery until at age two they are either "released" (a euphemism for *killed*) or assigned to a "family," which will consist of two parents and a son and a daughter. The society is so controlled that the citizens are conditioned not to see colors and not to question authority or such things as "releases" and the making of lifelong work assignments when children turn twelve. At school, the children learn the values of their culture, but not its history or anything about neighboring societies. The group's memories are entrusted to a single individual, a man designated as The Giver.

The book's protagonist is a twelve-year-old named Jonas, who is startled when at the society's annual end-of-the-year ceremonies he is designated to be the next Giver. He is to start training immediately to become the Receiver of the community's memories. Lowry told Anita Silvey, who interviewed her for the June 2007 *School Library Journal*, that this unusual idea was inspired by visits she made in the early 1990s to her mother and father when they were in their late eighties and living in a nursing home in Staunton, Virginia. Lowry would fly down from Boston and on the trip home always had things to ponder.

Her mother was blind and very frail, but her mind was intact and she shared many experiences with her daughter, even talking about the painful ones including the death of Lois's older sister, Helen. In contrast, Lowry's father was physically healthy but his memory was gone and so as they would look at the scrapbook that Lowry and her brother had put together for him, she would have to tell him over and over again about such things as Helen's death. He would feel sad for a few minutes, but then in contrast to the deep sadness with which Lowry's mother would relive some of her experiences, he would soon forget and ask again about the girl in the scrapbook.

This unpredictability of memory and what goes on in the human mind is what Lowry set out to explore when she wrote *The Giver.* She says she had no intention of writing a dystopian novel; it just turned out that way. This may be why the first few pages of the book seem so bright and why readers feel the negative aspects all the more strongly when they become privy to the memories that Jonas receives from The Giver. Lowry further explores the mystery of memory in her 2006 *Gossamer*, in which a girl called Littlest is being trained as a dream giver to bring better dreams to a troubled boy. In 2000, she published *Gathering Blue* as a companion volume to *The Giver.* The protagonist is a crippled girl who is skilled at embroidery and is taken from her village to the palace where her job of restoring the ceremonial robes that tell the story of her people is made more difficult by the ruling powers and their philosophy of "management."

When we brought *The Giver* to class after it won the 1994 Newbery Medal, our YA students predicted that it had a great future as a book for common reading. They were correct in this prediction, but they were wrong in their companion prediction, which was that teachers would have no censorship problems because the book has "no sex, no violence, and no objectionable language." Within a couple of years, *The Giver* had become a frequently censored book. We suspect that the dystopian vision of a society that bears some resemblance to our own frightens and depresses some adults, but because this is a difficult concept to recognize, much less communicate, they look for specific incidents to protest such as the use of "released" as a *euphemism* for "death" and the mention of the pills that children take as they reach puberty and begin to feel "the stirrings." ●

After by Francine Prose. HarperCollins, 2003. After a nearby school shooting, Central High School receives a threat and administrators vow to protect the students. And protect them they do with random locker searches and urine tests, and a whole list of restricted items including wearing anything colored red because it's a gang color. When J. D. Salinger's *The Catcher in the Rye* is found in a locker, it is confiscated and removed from the literature curriculum because "Studies have proved that it has a terribly deleterious—*destructive*—effect on students too young to realize that Holden Caulfield is a highly negative role model."

The Dirt Eaters by Dennis Foon (The Longlight Legacy Trilogy Series Book No. #1). Annick, distributed by Firefly, 2003. In this dystopian story, fifteen-year-old Roan is forced to leave his peace-loving village after it is destroyed and his younger sister is taken to the city. At first he thinks he has been rescued by the leader of a band of warriors, but the more he learns the more certain he is that he must leave. Follow-up books include *Freewalker*, and *The Keeper's Shadow*.

Dreamquake: Book Two of the Dreamhunter Duet by Elizabeth Knox. Farrar, 2007. *Booklist* editors, as well as the YALSA committee, chose Knox's *Dreamquake* as one of the best books of the year. Dreamhunter was published in 2006, and both books are praised for their unique blend of fantasy and history. Edwardian heroines Rose and Laura uncover a government plot involving the Place where horrible dreams are created and used for such nefarious purposes as controlling prisoners.

Eva by Peter Dickinson. Delacorte, 1989. A famous scientist is devoting his life to working with chimpanzees, which in this futuristic world are the biggest of the remaining animals. The scientist, his wife, and Eva (their thirteen-year-old daughter) are in a horrible wreck and when Eva wakes up she slowly discovers that her brain has been transferred to the body of the chimpanzee. The rest of the book is about the next thirty years of Eva's life; the psychological and social aspects of the story are even more interesting than the technological.

Feed by M. T. Anderson. Candlewick, 2004. Modern life, particularly the corporate world, is satirized as a group of young people are connected to each other through the "feed," an implant in their brains that provides whatever they want to know. When they arrive on the moon they receive "feeds" on where to stay and who to know and what to eat and what's hot in styles and more.

Firestorm by David Klass. Farrar, 2006. Jack learns he is not an all-American boy but rather a visitor from the future sent to save Earth.

The House of the Scorpion by Nancy Farmer. Atheneum, 2002. This prize-winning book is a grim, futuristic novel set mostly on an opium farm along the Mexican border of the United States. The owner, Matteo Alacrán, also known as El Patron, is nearly 110 years old. He has lived so long because of taking replacement parts from young people raised as "clones." Readers meet Matt, a future clone, when he is six years old and follow him through his escape and "rescue" as part of a work camp that is a modern equivalent of the kinds of orphanages that Charles Dickens wrote about.

Life as We Knew It by Susan Beth Pfeffer. Harcourt, 2006. A family survives when a meteor hits our Moon and causes floods and assorted other catastrophes.

The New Policeman by Kate Thompson. HarperCollins/Greenwillow, 2007. In this lively Irish story, a fifteen-year-old musician sets out to find where all the time has gone in hopes of filling his mother's birthday request of having more time. And while Liddy makes it to the Land of Eternal Youth, he is surprised that it isn't the utopia he expected, but it is filled with fantasy, folklore, and music.

Rash by Pete Hautman. Simon, 2006. Bo examines a future society that's given up freedom in favor of safety. Sent to a prison, he survives by his own athletic ability and an artificial intelligence program.

The Secret under My Skin by Janet McNaughton. HarperCollins, 2005. The year is 2368 when a technocaust has destroyed most of the technology. Scientists are blamed for the disaster and sent to concentration camps, but as the world begins to heal a new class of specialists develops. Blay, who tells the story, starts out as a young orphan scrounging through garbage, but then she becomes an assistant and an observer in her own right.

would solve all our personal problems and, if we are altruistic enough, all of the world's problems as well. In our nightmares, we also dream of the opposite, the dystopias, which are diseased or bad land. But few of us do more than dream, which may explain why readers appreciate authors who transfer their dreams to the printed page.

We used to say that dystopian stories are not likely to be popular with teenagers because young people are basically optimistic and have not lived long enough to become disgruntled about the aspects of modern society most likely to be satirized in dystopian novels. However, Lois Lowry's *The Giver* proved us wrong. It is a prototypical dystopian novel, but also one of the all-time most popular books for both school and independent reading. See the page on Lois Lowry as winner of the Margaret A. Edwards Award. Also see Focus Box 7.4 for descriptions of other dystopian novels that young people appreciate.

In his *Republic* in the fifth century BC, Plato presented his vision of the ideal world, offering suggestions for educating the ruling class. With wise philosopher-kings, so Plato maintained, the people would prosper, intellectual joys would flourish (along with censorship, for Plato would ban poets and dramatists from his perfect society), and the land would be permanently safe. Later utopias were geared less to a ruling class and more to a society that would preserve its peace and create harmony and happiness for the people. Sir Thomas More's *Utopia* (1516) argued for mental equality of the sexes, simple laws understandable to all, and common ownership of everything. Whether More intended his book as a practical solution to society's problems is doubtful, but he probably did mean it as a criticism of contemporary English life.

Yearning for the simpler life in which we dream of being part of something greater than ourselves is natural. For some young people, however, the search has led to religious groups less like communes and more like cults. Robert Coover explored the power and madness of a cult in *The Origin of the Brunists*. In that novel, a mining explosion kills ninety-seven people, but one survivor believes that God has saved him to proclaim the approaching end of the world.

Dystopias are more dramatic and exaggerated than their counterparts and for that reason are more successful in attracting young adults. Dystopias warn us of society's drift toward a particularly horrifying or sick world lying just over the horizon. They are sometimes misinterpreted as prophecies alone, but books such as Aldous Huxley's *Brave New World* and George Orwell's *Nineteen Eighty-Four* and *Animal Farm* are part prophecy, part warning. Readers who have engaged with the characters are never again able to regard a discussion of individual freedom in an abstract way.

Concluding Comments

The books we've talked about in this chapter start with life as we know it and attempt to stretch readers' imaginations. All of us need to dream, not to waste our lives but to enrich them. To dream is to recognize humanity's possibilities. In a world hardly characterized by undue optimism, the genres treated here offer us challenges and hope, not the sappy sentimentalism of "everything always works out for the best" (for it often does not) but realistic hope based on our noblest dreams of surviving. If we go down, we do it knowing that we have cared and dreamed and found something for which we are willing to struggle.

Another comforting thought about the books in this chapter is how truly international they are. This is sometimes inconvenient as when we have trouble getting publication dates because they are different from country to country, or we are confused when we send for audiotapes because, for example, our favorite Garth Nix books are known in Australia as The Old Kingdom or Ancelstierr series while in the United States they are called the Abhorsen trilogy. The Nix books we are talking about are *Sabriel, Lirael: Daughter of the Clayr*, and *Abhorsen*, but soon we won't be able to talk about them as a trilogy because Nix has signed a contract to do both a prequel and a sequel, scheduled for publication in 2010 and 2011. We learned this from his author blog, which gave us a new appreciation for the ability to communicate with authors about real-world, practical matters at the same time that we are sharing their most intimate dreams and imaginings through their books. Surely, this is as fantastic as are many of the miracles that until now have been discussed only as science fiction or fantasy.

Notes

1. Ursula K. Le Guin, "On Teaching Science Fiction" in *Teaching Science Fiction: Education for Tomorrow,* ed. Jack Williamson (Oswick Press, 1980), p. 22.
2. Walter Wangerin, Jr., in a lecture, "By Faith, Fantasy," quoted in *Other Worlds: The Fantasy Genre*, by John H. Timmerman (Bowling Green University Popular Press, 1983), p. 21.
3. This point, with many more examples, is made by Leslie E. Owen in "Children's Science Fiction and Fantasy Grow Up," *Publishers Weekly* 232 (October 30, 1987): 32–37.
4. Mary Harrington Hall, "A Conversation with Ray Bradbury and Chuck Jones," *Psychology Today* 1 (April 1969): 28–29.
5. Jo-Anne Goodwin, "In Defence of Fantasy," *Independent Magazine*, London, July 25, 1993, p. 32.
6. John Rowe Townsend, "Heights of Fantasy" in *Children's Review* 5, ed. Gerard J. Senick (Gale Research, 1983), p. 7.
7. Lloyd Alexander, "High Fantasy and Heroic Romance," *Horn Book Magazine* 47 (December 1971): 483.
8. Ursula K. Le Guin, "Why Are Americans So Afraid of Dragons?" *PNLA* (Pacific Northwest Library Association) *Quarterly* 38 (Winter 1974): 18.
9. Marjorie N. Allen, *What Are Little Girls Made Of? A Guide to Female Role Models in Children's Books* (Facts on File, 1999), p. 41.
10. Anita Silvey, "The Unreal Deal," *School Library Journal* 52:10 (October, 2006): 44–47.
11. Melissa Thomas, "Teaching Fantasy: Overcoming the Stigma of Fluff," *English Journal* 92 (May 2003): 60.
12. Stephen King, "Potter Gold," *Entertainment Weekly*, July 11, 2003, pp. 80–81.
13. *New York Times*, July 12, 2003, p. A-22.
14. Roxanne Feldman, "The Truth about Harry," *School Library Journal* 45 (September 1999): 139.
15. Gene LaFaille, "Science Fiction: Top Guns of the 1980s," *Wilson Library Bulletin* 65 (December 1990): 34.
16. Jane Donawerth, "Teaching Science Fiction by Women," *English Journal* 79 (March 1990): 39–40.
17. Ray Bradbury, "Science Fiction: Why Bother?" *Teachers' Guide: Science Fiction* (Bantam, n.d.), p. 1.
18. Arthur Clarke, *Profiles of the Future* (Holt, 1984) p. 9.
19. Robert Heinlein, "Ray Guns and Rocket Ships," *Library Journal* 78 (July 1953): 1188.

History and History Makers: Of People and Places

chapter 8

The United States has always viewed history in its own way.
More than a century ago, Ralph Waldo Emerson described the
great American tradition as "trampling on tradition," and Abraham Lincoln
said that Americans had a "perfect rage for the new." But by the beginning of
the twentieth century, Americans were feeling more confident and began to
look back. U.S. history became a standard part of the school curriculum, thousands of towns erected statues of Abraham Lincoln and Ulysses S. Grant, and
historical pageants flourished, including in the South, where Confederates
began to look back with pride on their role in the Civil War.

We are including both fiction and nonfiction in this chapter because the
two genres complement each other. And especially in relation to war, it is
almost impossible to separate memoirs and autobiographical writings from fiction. We are also including materials written for both adults and young adults
because the reporting of history for a general audience is often done in a manner accessible to young readers. We will first write a general introduction to
historical fiction, then head to the American West, and then look at books
about war, the Holocaust, and Vietnam.

Historical Fiction

Reading historical novels satisfies our curiosity about other times, places,
and people, and even more important, it provides adventure, suspense, and mystery. As with any literary form, there are standards for judging historical novels

TABLE 8.1 Suggestions for Evaluating Historical Fiction

A good historical novel usually has	A poor historical novel may have
A setting that is integral to the story	A story that could have happened any time or any place. The historical setting is for visual appeal and to compensate for a weak story
An authentic rendition of the time, place, and people being featured	Anachronisms in which the author illogically mixes up people, events, speaking styles, social values, or technological developments from different time periods
An author who is so thoroughly steeped in the history of the period that he or she can be comfortably creative without making mistakes	Awkward narrations and exposition as the author tries to teach history through characters' conversations
Believable characters with whom young readers can identify	Oversimplification of the historical issues and a stereotyping of the "bad" and the "good" guys
Evidence that even across great time spans people share similar emotions	Characters who fail to come alive as individuals having something in common with the readers. They are just stereotyped representatives of a particular period
References to well-known events or people or other clues through which the reader can place the happenings in their correct historic framework	
Readers who come away with the feeling that they know a time or place better. It is as if they have lived in it for at least a few hours	

(see Table 8.1). They should be historically accurate and steeped in time and place. We should recognize totems and taboos, food, clothing, vocations, leisure activities, customs, smells, religions, literature, and all that goes into making one time and one place unique. Enthusiasts forgive no anachronism, no matter how slight. Historical novels should give a sense of history's continuity, a feeling for the flow of history from one time into another. Historical novels should tell a lively story with a sense of impending danger, mystery, suspense, or romance. Because of the excitement and romance involved, some stories in this chapter could have been included in Chapter 6 on Adventure.

Historical novels allow us—at their best they force us—to make connections and to realize that despair is as old and as new as hope, that loyalty and treachery, love and hatred, compassion and cruelty were and are inherent in humanity, whether it be in ancient Greece, Elizabethan England, or post–World War I Germany. As with most writers, historical novelists may want to teach particular lessons. Christopher Collier, for example, makes no pretense about why he and his brother write about the American Revolution in their historical novels:

The books I write with my brother are written with a didactic purpose to teach about ideals and values that have been important in shaping the course of American history. This is in no way intended to denigrate the importance of the dramatic and literary elements of historical novels. Nothing will be taught, and certainly nothing learned, if no one reads the books.[1]

Collier later added that "there is no better way to teach history than to embrace potential readers and fling them into a living past."[2]

Novelist Patricia Lee Gauch has a theory about why the historical novel may appeal to readers. She is talking about adults, but her idea might be worth springing on bright young people at the right time.

> Surely the appeal of historical story has something to do with the ironies of history. Because we know the ending, the twists of fate, the upside downness of history, and the unpredictability, it is particularly poignant. Not only is there craziness . . . but add to the games of history the obvious capriciousness that a long look at historical events reveals.[3]

Commenting on the historical novel and why some young people don't seem to care for the genre, Cathi MacRae wrote in the *Wilson Library Bulletin*, September 1991, p. 102:

> Harvard psychologist Diana Paolitto reported her research on children's developing concepts of time. The results astonished her no less than her audience. Her teenage subjects revealed an inability to conceive of a past unless someone they knew personally had lived then. In other words, the furthest back most young adults can extend credibility is the lifetime of the oldest people they know, probably grandparents. This late in the century, that means that teenagers hardly believe that any time prior to the twentieth century existed. Is there research to indicate at what age people begin to believe in history? Could it be when individuals have lived long enough to have a history of their own?[4]

Perhaps one explanation for student indifference to historical novels may be the first sentence of the Prologue to L. P. Hartley's *The Go-Between*. "The past is a foreign country: they do things differently there."

In our adolescent literature classes, we have students read something like twenty books in a semester spread across various genres. Historical fiction is often one of the last blanks to get filled in, but when students complain that they cannot find a good piece of historical fiction to read, we ask them which books they've read, and invariably they tell us about two or three that we consider to be historical fiction but that they had not recognized as such. One reason for their surprise is their stereotyped view that historical fictions must be grand and imposing, like a movie spectacle exaggerated, like a "bodice-ripper" romance. Actually, historical fiction includes mysteries, comedies, adventures, realistic problem stories, and whatever other genres can be listed. The only thing they have in common is that they are set in the past. We once defined historical fiction as any story that happened before or during World War II, but as we have grown older and readers of YA fiction seem to have grown younger, we find ourselves using the Vietnam era as the dividing line between "historical" and "contemporary."

Historical novels can take readers any place they want to go—or fear to go—and in any period of time they would like. In the last few years, a virtual industry of books about Shakespeare and his time have appeared. Gary Blackwood's

Bread and Roses, Too by Katherine Paterson. Clarion, 2006. As she did in her 1992 *Lyddie*, Paterson writes about the awful labor conditions that existed in the New England mills at the turn of the last century when prejudices and ethnic rivalries added a new layer of danger to already tense labor protests.

Copper Sun by Sharon Draper. S & S/Atheneum, 2006. The worst aspects of slavery and the best sides of friendship are illustrated through this story of a fifteen-year-old girl taken to a Carolina plantation from her African home.

Counting on Grace by Elizabeth Winthrop. Random, 2006. Winthrop's story was inspired by a Lewis Hines 1910 photo of a French Canadian girl, who was one of the "mill rats," working long hours in terrible conditions.

Hattie Big Sky by Kirby Larson. Delacorte, 2006. Hattie is an orphan who at age sixteen inherits a land claim in Montana. When she sets out from Iowa, she has no idea of the hardships ahead or of the kinds of prejudice, as well as the kinds of support and help, that she will receive from strangers as she works to save her claim.

The Horse Thief: A Novel by Robert Newton Peck. HarperCollins, 2002. It is 1938 in Chickalooke, Florida, and seventeen-year-old Tullis Yoder has a job taking care of the horses in a rodeo. When the owner falls on hard times and decides to sell the horses to a slaughterhouse, Tullis and various "helpers" steal the horses and lead them to life.

How It Happened in Peach Hill by Marthe Jocelyn. Random, 2007. During the Roaring Twenties, fifteen-year-old Annie travels through upstate New York with her mother who advertises herself as a spiritual adviser and fortune-teller. In a short-lived scheme, Annie pretends to be severely retarded so she can tell her mother what she overhears.

Lizzie Bright and the Buckminster Boy by Gary D. Schmidt. Clarion, 2004. Schmidt was on summer vacation in Maine when he heard the haunting story of how at the turn of the century an African American community was "cleared off" from a Maine island so that a nearby community could develop its tourist industry.

Lyddie by Katherine Paterson. Dutton, 1992. Lyddie goes to work in a Massachusetts textile mill when her family goes broke and finds a cause in a labor movement.

No Promises in the Wind by Irene Hunt. Follett, 1970. During the Great Depression, fifteen-year-old Josh leaves home with his brother and a friend to find shelter and food.

Sacrifice by Kathleen Benner Duble. Simon and Schuster, 2005. In 1692 Massachusetts, Abigail and her sister are accused and imprisoned for being witches. Their mother comes up with a terrible plan to free them.

Uncommon Faith by Trudy Krisher. Holiday House, 2003. Cataclysmic events nearly always have repercussions long after the event itself, and Krisher's book does a wonderful job of illustrating this in relation to a Millbrook, Massachusetts, livery fire that in the summer of 1837 killed six people and injured many others.

An Unlikely Friendship: A Novel of Mary Todd Lincoln and Elizabeth Keckley by Ann Rinaldi. Harcourt, 2007. After Abraham Lincoln is assassinated, Mary Todd Lincoln asks to have her best friend, former slave, and dressmaker Elizabeth Keckley, brought to her. This is the story of both women.

The Unresolved by T. K. Welsh. Dutton, 2006. On June 15, 1904, more than a thousand people from the German section of New York City die in a terrible fire that during an afternoon pleasure cruise sweeps the *General Slocum* steamship. Welsh gives the story a supernatural slant through the part played by the ghost of fifteen-year-old Mallory Meer, whose Jewish boyfriend (a survivor) is accused of starting the fire.

The Shakespeare Stealer and its sequels, *The Shakespeare Scribe* and *Shakespeare's Spy*, introduced readers to fourteen-year-old Widge, who knows a form of shorthand, becomes a member of Shakespeare's company, falls in love with Shakespeare's daughter, and attempts to finish a play begun by Shakespeare. Lisa Fiedler's *Dating Hamlet: Ophelia's Story* revealed a new view of Ophelia, a woman who loves and stands by Hamlet and is willing to act mad to move Hamlet's plan forward. Fiedler's *Romeo's Ex: Rosaline* moved Romeo and Juliet to the

The Book of Mordred by Vivian Vande Velde. Houghton Mifflin, 2005. After the fall of Camelot, a young widow seeks help from young Sir Mordred. Velde portrays a lost time when King Arthur and Mordred disagree on what is right for Camelot.

The Book of the Lion by Michael Cadnum. Viking, 2000. Seventeen-year-old Edmund goes to the Holy Land as knight crusader's squire and takes part in the bloody Battle of Arsuf.

Broken Song by Kathryn Lasky. Viking, 2005. Reuven, a Jewish boy in Russia at the turn of the last century, made his first appearance in Lasky's 1981 *The Night Journey*, but now he's back for this well-researched account of anti-Semitism in Russia and what it took for him to save his sister and himself.

The Canterbury Papers by Judith Koll Healey. Morrow, 2004. Queen Eleanor of Aquitaine asks Princess Alais of France to bring back a packet of letters hidden in Canterbury Cathedral. Alais learns that she is not the only one interested in the letters.

Dante's Daughter by Kimberley Burton Heuston. Front Street, 2003. This fictional memoir is a good illustration of how an author can make a story more interesting to young readers by having it told through the eyes of a young person, in this case, Dante's only daughter, Antonia Alighieri, who eventually entered a convent.

The Edge on the Sword by Rebecca Tingle. Putnam, 2001. Set in late ninth-century England, this is the imagined story of the teen years of Ethelflaed of Mercia, an extraordinarily accomplished woman noted in the Anglo-Saxon Chronicle.

Frontier Wolf by Rosemary Sutcliff. Dutton, 1980. A young Roman commander of a group of scouts in northern England must begin a retreat from the forces of native tribes.

Incantation by Alice Hoffman. Little, Brown, 2006. Hoffman uses the background of the Spanish Inquisition to tell a powerful story of friendship, faith, jealousy, resilience, and love. The protagonist is sixteen-year-old Estrella, whose family pretends to be Catholic but secretly keeps their Jewish faith.

A Single Shard by Linda Sue Park. Clarion, 2001. This winner of the Newbery Medal is set in twelfth-century Korea and is a good illustration of the archetypal journey. A young orphan apprentices himself to a master craftsman of celadon pottery and the journey occurs when he must take a sample of his master's work to the royal palace.

The Squire, His Knight, and His Lady by Gerald Morris. Houghton Mifflin, 1999. Along with *The Squire's Tale* (Houghton Mifflin, 1998), this lively and humorous book straddles historical fiction and fantasy.

Thursday's Child by Sonya Hartnett. Candlewick, 2002. This novel makes clear that life in the Australian Depression was no better than that during the American Depression.

sidelines and focuses on the fair Rosaline and her many suitors. Carolyn Meyer's *Loving Will Shakespeare* gives insights into Anne Hathaway's fear of being unloved and her recognition that Will Shakespeare at eighteen is handsome and intelligent. Philip Gooden sets *Alms for Oblivion: A Shakespearean Murder Mystery* in Shakespeare's company where a young member finds another member murdered and other bodies soon appear.

Donna Jo Napoli's *Daughter of Venice* is set in late sixteenth-century Venice with all its sinister intrigues. A trip to King Arthur's time can easily be had through Sarah L. Thomson's *The Dragon's Son*, with its newly created legends about Arthur. An equally easy trip can be made to the Crusades in *The Book of the Lion*, by the prolific and reliable Michael Cadnum, with his portrait of the adventures and horrors experienced in the Holy Land by a seventeen-year-old knight crusader's squire. Howard Fast's *April Morning* is more than forty years old, but it is still worth reading by anybody who cares about young people and their place in the Revolutionary War. Kathryn Lasky's *Beyond the Burning Time* is a fine novel focusing on the terrors of the Salem witch trials. The most frightening of the new historical fiction, because it is set only half a century ago in our country and at one of our most shameful times, is Chris Crowe's *Mississippi Trial 1955*, about the killing of Emmett Till, a black teenager from the North who had the foolish, or bad, manners to joke with a white Southern girl.

Two Recent and Important Historical Novels

M. T. Anderson's *The Astonishing Life of Octavian Nothing, Traitor to the Nation* is the first of two (possibly more) novels set in 1760s and 1770s New England. Octavian, the narrator; his mother, the lovely Cassiopeia; and Mr. Gitney, a member of the Novanglian College of Lucidity, live in a luxurious house. Members of the College divine secrets of the universe by writing poetry, drawing, and performing sundry experiments. One such experiment consisted of taking a dog in, showing it affection, and then drowning it to see how long it took to die. Their experiments are heartless and pointless, and their absurdity may remind readers of *Gulliver's Travels* and the Grand Academy of Lagoda with all its madness.

Octavian is taught Greek, Latin, mathematics, botany, and music—he plays the violin superbly. His food is weighed before he eats, and his excrement is also weighed (caught on a golden platter). Gitney assures Octavian his education equals that of the princes of Europe. The boy has no idea who or what he is, but Gitney's black valet assures Octavian that he is as African as the valet. Asked why he is treated as he is, Mr. Gitney replies, "We wish to divine whether you are a separate and distinct species." Unsure what that means, Octavian asks, "You wish to prove that I am the equal of any other?" Gitney corrects the boy, "We wish to prove nothing. We simply aim at discovering the truth."

Later, when the College desperately needs money, the money comes from a consortium anxious to prove that Africans are inferior to white people, and at that point, Octavian's education changes and the novel opens up. It's a sweeping novel that takes in the Revolutionary War, several forms of patriotism, rumors that slaves are preparing to revolt, and far more. Anderson is a born storyteller. His plot, full of convolutions, horrors, and surprisingly enough humor, will keep readers alert.

So will Markus Zusak's *The Book Thief*, in some ways an even more complicated novel than *Octavian Nothing*. On the first page, Zusak introduces his narrator, Death, who immediately says,

> HERE IS A SMALL FACT
> You are going to die.
> I am in all truthfulness attempting to be cheerful about this whole topic, though most people find themselves hindered in believing me, no matter my protestations. Please trust me. I most definitely can be cheerful. I can be amiable. Agreeable. Affable. And that's only the A's.

The book thief is Liesel, a little German girl who finds a book, *The Gravedigger's Handbook*, which she treasures as her own and from which she learns to read. She steals other books periodically. She is adopted by Rosa Huberman, who is profane but who loves Liesel, and Hans Huberman, who adores Liesel.

In 1930s Germany, Nazis are in power and they cause misery for Jews in Zusak's book. Bombs rain down as war comes, and Death becomes an even more omnipresent narrator as the war goes on.

The book seems sprawling at times as more characters are introduced, but the cast of major characters remains small—Liesel; the Hubermans; Rudy Steiner, who desires only to kiss Liesel; and Death, always Death. Zusak's novel is long and complex and rich. Some readers will be confused, but most will not forget Liesel.

Some Consistently Good Writers of YA Historical Fiction

Laurie Halse Anderson *Fever 1793*, which tells how fourteen-year-old Mattie's life changes, is a wonderful example of good writing. Church bells ring out, announcing the yellow fever that strikes down hundreds of people in Philadelphia, including one of Mattie's friends. Mattie's family struggles to keep their coffee-house open, but when Mattie's mother becomes ill, Mattie tried to escape. Laurie Halse Anderson's novel, as teachers and librarians have recognized, pairs naturally with Jim Murphy's *An American Plague: The True and Terrifying Story of the Yellow Fever Epidemic of 1793.*

Tracy Chevalier Although a writer of books for adults, Tracey Chevalier has been found by many teenagers who read her novels and consider her one of their own. Two of her historical novels are especially fine and deserve to be recommended. *Girl with a Pearl Earring* is about sixteen-year-old Griet, who must help to support her family. She is hired by the Johannes Vermeer family and immediately disliked by the wife and daughter. Vermeer is constantly in debt, mostly because he paints so slowly and produces few canvases. Griet grows closer to the painter as she mixes and prepares paints, and Vermeer uses Griet as a model for his most famous painting. *Girl with a Pearl Earring* was filmed in 2003 and is almost as good as the book.

In *The Lady and the Unicorn*, the impecunious Nicholas des Innocents convinces a nobleman to commission six tapestries of unicorns—with Nicholas's designs—to be placed in the nobleman's mansion. Nicholas goes to Brussels to visit a master weaver. In all these travels, the successfully virile Nicholas meets and seduces women, all of whom become part of his designs in the tapestries. The novel is full of the sights and sounds and beauty and ugliness of the last years of the fifteenth century. As Wendy Smith concluded her review of Chevalier's book in the December 21, 2003, *New York Times Book Review*, acknowledging that Nicholas has changed: "He's still no saint, but through him, Chevalier reminds us that art has the power to illuminate the understanding of those who make it as well as those who view it."

Bruce Clements In *The Treasure of Plunderell Manor*, Bruce Clements has written a very funny book that is at once an historical novel and a spoof of historical and Gothic novels. It begins with Laurel heading for Plunderell Manor to become the maid of Alice, heir to the manor. Laurel meets Lord and Lady Stayne who ask Laurel to spy on Alice. Later, sanctimonious Lady Stayne asks Alice if she is well. Then she turns to Laurel, who is Catholic, and says,

> And you? We must concern ourselves with your soul, too. Catholics go to hell, from the Pope on down. Just because you are simple and ignorant and weak, God will not forgive you for being a child of Rome. You may do as you wish, of course, but my advice is that you join the Anglican Church immediately.

Here the adventures begin. The Staynes drop Laurel and Alice at a deserted monastery, assuming the girls will soon die of cold or starvation. Alice is incapable of doing anything remotely helpful, but Laurel saves the day. In fact, she's forced to save several days during the rest of the book.

Christopher and James Lincoln Collier These two brothers specialize in historical fiction. Their best-known book, *My Brother Sam Is Dead,* comes from the time of the Civil War and was a Newbery Award book. *The Bloody Country* and *The Winter Hero* continue the story. Another trilogy, *War Comes to Willy Freeman, Jump Ship to Freedom,* and *Who Is Carrie?* focuses on African Americans and their role in early American history. Throughout the 1990s, the two produced the *Drama of American History* series for Benchmark Books.

Karen Cushman Karen Cushman has chosen to write about girls embarking on journeys to discover themselves. Her first two books are set in medieval Europe. *Catherine Called Birdy* (Newbery Award book) is the diary of a fourteen-year-old daughter of a knight whose feisty and witty observations bring the thirteenth century to life in ways that few historians could. In *The Midwife's Apprentice,* Cushman looks at the same period, but at a different part of the social scale. She writes about an orphan who manages to get herself apprenticed to a midwife. Her 2003 *Rodzina* has a similar plot, except that it is set in the American West in 1881. Rodzina is a large, ungainly Polish American girl who is sent west on an orphan train. As the train moves along, she sees the younger and more attractive children adopted. The two invitations she receives are disastrous and she runs away and returns to the train, finally making herself so useful that she becomes an assistant to the woman she calls "Miss Doctor." California's gold rush is the setting for *The Ballad of Lucy Whipple.* Lucy, whose original name was California Morning Whipple, finds herself dragged "like a barrel of lard" from Massachusetts to Lucky Diggings, California. The gold she finds is in pie-baking.

The Loud Silence of Francine Green is a recent work by Cushman. Set in 1949 in Los Angeles during an early anti-communist hysteria mixed with worries about the atomic bomb, thirteen-year-old Francine is an average girl until she meets Sophie, a thorough-going nonconformist. Francine learns about freedom and life, and she begins to question everything from her parents' indifference to Sister Basil's punishment of Sophie for the "sin of intellectual curiosity."

Jennifer Donnelly Donnelly has a single historical novel but one of the best. *A Northern Light* is based in part on the sensational murder of Grace Brown, whose body was found in Big Moose Lake in the Adirondack Mountains. While not the

One of the ways that Karen Cushman establishes her historical books is to choose names that fit into the period. The names in her *Catherine Called Birdy* were different from those in *The Ballad of Lucy Whipple*, shown on the right, but they were created through similar linguistic processes.

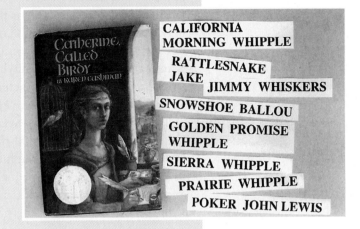

CALIFORNIA MORNING WHIPPLE

RATTLESNAKE JAKE

JIMMY WHISKERS

SNOWSHOE BALLOU

GOLDEN PROMISE WHIPPLE

SIERRA WHIPPLE

PRAIRIE WHIPPLE

POKER JOHN LEWIS

center of Donnelly's novel, the murder is always there, lurking in the background. It's better known to most adults as the basis for Theodore Dreiser's *An American Tragedy*.

Donnelly's novel is about sixteen-year-old Mattie, who lives a life of near poverty in 1906. Her mother is dead, and her father has hardened and is almost unreachable. Mattie, her sister Beth, and Weaver, a young African American boy who is Mattie's closest friend, love to play with language. Each day, one of them selects a word, like *inquisition*, and the three duel back and forth, supplying synonyms until they are bored.

When Mattie's friend has twins and Mattie helps, Mattie learns an important distinction between reality and literature. Of all the books she had read, "not one of them tells the truth about babies. Dickens doesn't. Oliver's mother just dies in childbirth and that's that. Brontë doesn't. Catherine Earnshaw just had her daughter and that was that. There's no blood, no sweat, no pain, no fear, no stink. Writers are damned liars. Every single one of them."

Mattie takes a job as a waiter at a resort on Big Moose Lake. She meets Grace Brown, a resort guest, who leaves a packet of letters with Mattie. Before she goes boating with her boyfriend, Grace asks Mattie to burn these letters if she doesn't return. Grace doesn't return.

When her teacher, Miss Wilcox, who loves Jane Austen, asks Mattie what she thinks of books, Mattie answers,

> Well, it seems to me that there are books that tell stories, and then there are books that tell truths. . . . The first kind, they show you life like you want it to be. With villains getting what they deserve and the hero seeing what a fool he's been and marrying the heiress and happy endings and all that. Like *Sense and Sensibility* and *Persuasion*. But the second kind, they show you life like it is. Like in *Huckleberry Finn* where Huck's Pa is a no-good drunk and Jim suffers so. The first kind makes you cheerful and contented but the second kind shakes you up.

Leon Garfield   Wit, humor, and liveliness permeate Leon Garfield's books. His world is the eighteenth century, with an occasional detour into early nineteenth-century England. Garfield set a standard for historical writing that few can match. Garfield's eighteenth century is the world of Fielding and Smollett—lusty, squalid, ugly, bustling, and swollen, full of life and adventure and the possibility that being born an orphan may lead you ultimately to fame and fortune. His stories play with reality versus illusion, daylight versus dreams, flesh versus fantasy. His ability to sketch out minor characters in a line or two is impressive. Of a man in *The Sound of Coaches,* he wrote, "He was one of those gentlemen who [e]ffect great gallantry to all the fair sex except their wives." Of the protagonist we are told, "although jealousy was ordinarily foreign to Sam's nature, they did, on occasion, talk the same language." The funniest of Garfield's books are *The Strange Affair of Adelaide Harris* and its sequel, *The Night of the Comet.* In *Adelaide,* Bostock and Harris, two nasty pupils in Dr. Bunnion's Academy, become so entranced with stories of Spartan babies abandoned on mountaintops, there to be suckled by wolves, that they borrow Harris's baby sister to determine for themselves the truth of the old tales. Therein begins a wild comedy of errors and an even wilder series of coincidences and near duels and wild threats that hardly let up until the last lines.

Carolyn Meyer   When Carolyn Meyer wrote nonfiction books, she frequently found herself coming up against blank walls where she could find no more information. Because she wanted the stories to continue, she began asking, "What if?" and so began her career as a writer of fiction. Her most highly acclaimed books are probably *White Lilacs,* about the dismantling of a black community in early Texas; *Mary, Bloody Mary,* about the youth of the woman who became one of England's most unpopular rulers; and *Where the Broken Heart Still Beats: The Story of Cynthia Ann Parker,* about a woman who was captured by Comanche Indians at age nine and unsuccessfully "rescued" by white settlers years later. Two recent Meyer books are *Patience, Princess Catherine,* in which the young princess goes to England to become queen, only to have her young husband die, which leaves her waiting seven years to learn what the new king has planned for her. In *Marie, Dancing,* Meyer writes a fictional portrait of the ballet dancer who was the model for Degas's statue, "The Little Dancer."

Scott O'Dell   *The King's Fifth* is probably Scott O'Dell's most convincing work, with its picture of sixteenth-century Spaniards and the moral strains put on anyone involved in the search for gold and fame. It is convincing, often disturbing, and, like most of O'Dell's historical novels, generally worth pursuing. Students coming to high school with a good reading background probably already know O'Dell from his *Island of the Blue Dolphins* and *Sing Down the Moon,* both of which present original and positive portrayals of young Native American women suffering at the hands of white settlers in the middle to late 1800s. He was a pioneer in featuring strong young women in these two books, and within the last couple of decades several good writers have followed his lead.

Ann Rinaldi   Among Ann Rinaldi's best books are *A Break with Charity: A Story about the Salem Witch Trials* and *Cast Two Shadows,* a Civil War story. She tackled a particularly ambitious subject in *Wolf by the Ears,* a fictional story of Sally Hemmings's family. Sally was a mulatto slave in Thomas Jefferson's household, and some historians believe that Jefferson fathered several of her children. Rinaldi's book implies that this is true, but the question is never clearly answered, even though the protagonist, supposedly Jefferson's daughter, asks it often enough. The book's title comes from Jefferson's statement about slavery: "as it is, we have the wolf by the ears and we can neither hold him, nor safely let him go. Justice is in one scale, and self-preservation the other." Most of Rinaldi's numerous books deal with some aspect of the Revolutionary or the Civil War.

Mildred D. Taylor   Her own family history provided Mildred D. Taylor with material for her prize-winning series. *The Land* won the 2002 Coretta Scott King Award. It was written as a prequel to the earlier books *Song of the Trees*; *Roll of Thunder, Hear My Cry*; *Let the Circle Be Unbroken*; and *The Road to Memphis*. Together, the series chronicles the generations of the Logan family, African American landowners near Vicksburg, Mississippi. *The Land* opens in post–Civil War Georgia when Paul-Edward Logan is about to leave his childhood behind. He is the son of a white plantation owner and a former slave of African American and Native American descent, and he is confused by his station in society. He has always been treated much like his white brothers, but now that he is approaching manhood, his father begins to treat him differently. The father thinks he might save the boy's life by teaching him that his welfare will always be subject to the whims and desires of white men. As reviewer James Blasingame said in *The English Journal*, "The author is fair to her characters, creating good and bad people of all races and genders, while keeping the reality of place and time. Rereading the previously written novels will be even more enjoyable after reading *The Land*."[5]

Rosemary Sutcliff   From her excellent early novel in 1954, *The Eagle of the Ninth*, through her 1990 *The Shining Company*, Rosemary Sutcliff has been acclaimed as the finest writer of British historical fiction for young people. We must find ways for librarians and teachers to get her books to the right young readers, those who care about history and a rattling good story, and who are not put off by a period of time they know little about. *The Shining Company* may be harder to sell than her earlier books about the Normans and the Saxons (e.g., *The Shield Ring* and *Dawn Wind*) because it is set in a more obscure time, seventh-century Britain. Sutcliff knew about the cries of men and the screams of stricken horses and the smell of blood and filth, and she cared about people who make history, whether knaves or villains or, in this case, naïve men who trusted their king and themselves beyond common sense.

Frances Temple   *The Ramsay Scallop* is a wonderful book about medieval Europe. In it, Frances Temple describes the apprehension that thirteen-year-old Eleanor of Ramsay feels as she awaits marriage to twenty-two-year-old Lord Thomas of Thornham. Thomas is no happier about his upcoming marriage because he has become cynical about life and religion after fighting in the Crusades. Father Gregory sends them off on a pilgrimage to the cathedral in Santiago, Spain, and asks that they remain chaste during the trip. Temple's portraits of the people and the time and the friendships they form and the deceit and pain

Focus Box 8.3

New Books about the History of the Civil Rights Movement

Cause: Reconstruction America 1863–1877 by Tonya Bolden. Alfred Knopf, 2005. Archival photos, excellent graphics, and political cartoons help Bolden achieve a sense of storytelling as she writes about the Civil Rights Act of 1866, the plight of Native Americans and freed slaves, and the women's suffrage movement during a time of national expansion. Chapter titles are intriguing quotes as with "Why Is This, Ma?" a question that a black child asks about the family's treatment at a train station.

Day of Tears: A Novel in Dialogue by Julius Lester. Hyperion, 2005. The book begins with the largest slave auction in United States history, which was held in 1859 on Pierce Butler's plantation in Georgia. The book is recommended for reading aloud or for reader's theater because so much of the story is told through monologues and reminiscences.

Elijah of Buxton by Christopher Paul Curtis. Scholastic, 2007. Web links that will bring added meaning to Curtis's story of an eleven-year-old boy, who was born free in the Buxton Settlement in Canada, and then became the youngest "conductor" on the underground railroad include www.blackhistoricalmuseum.com/history.htm; www. undergroundrailroadconductor.com; www.nps.gov/ archive/frdo/freddoug.html; www.buxtonmuseum.com and www.asu.edu/clas/english/englished/yalit/elijah/index. html/. This last one was prepared as a webquest by our students at Arizona State University.

Fire from the Rock by Sharon Draper. Dutton, 2007. Draper tells the fictional story of a young girl chosen in 1957 to be one of the first black students to enroll in Central High School in Little Rock, Arkansas. Chapters alternate between the girl's journal and third-person accounts of the events.

5,000 Miles to Freedom: Ellen and William Craft's Flight from Slavery by Judith Fradin. National Geographic, 2006. In this true story from 1848, a fair-skinned black woman disguises herself as Mr. William Johnson, accompanied by a black slave, who was really her husband. They first escaped to the North and then went on to England where they gave speeches and worked for abolition. After the Civil War, they returned to Georgia to run a farm and open a school.

Freedom Riders: John Lewis and Jim Zwerg on the Front Lines of the Civil Rights Movement by Ann Bausum. National Geographic, 2006. Bausum tells the story of the 1960s Civil Rights movement through the eyes of two young men—one white and one black—who joined in the freedom rides of the 1960s. Bausum's book was honored as the most distinguished piece of youth literature written in 2006 by a Wisconsin resident.

Getting Away with Murder: The True Story of the Emmett Till Case by Chris Crowe. Phyllis Fogelman, 2003. Crowe regretted that he never heard about Emmett Till's death

---

they meet are brilliant. Temple has written several more contemporary books about young refugees as in *Grab Hands and Run* and *A Taste of Salt*.

Current Historical Interests

Just as there are fashions and fads in clothing, toys, dances, and music, the world of book publishing also has its trends. An issue or a concern gets in the news with people talking about it on television and online and articles appearing in magazines and newspapers. Pretty soon someone writes a book that is well received and then someone else writes another well-received book, which inspires further investigation and writing. Over the past decade, this happened with two subjects as shown by Focus Box 8.3, New Books about the History of the Civil Rights Movement, and Focus Box 8.4, New Books about Native Americans. As much as any other YA author Walter Dean Myers is responsible for bringing

until forty years after it happened. He wrote his well-researched book in hopes that other kids would not grow up as uninformed as he was. A year later, he also told the story in fiction form in *Mississippi Trial, 1955.*

My Mother the Cheerleader by Robert Sharenow. Harper-Collins, 2007. The year is 1960 and the city is New Orleans. Thirteen-year-old Louise is yanked out of school because an African American child, Ruby Bridges, has enrolled in her school. Louise's mother runs a boarding house, but thanks to Louise taking over many of her chores, every morning she joins the other "cheerleaders" as they heckle Ruby Bridges and shout racial epithets. Louise gradually comes to sees the situation from new angles.

New Boy by Julian Houston. Houghton, 2005. It is the 1950s and fifteen-year-old Rob Garrett comes from the South to be the first African American to attend a prestigious Connecticut boarding school. He learns that prejudice wears different faces, especially when he visits a cousin in Harlem and meets Malcolm X and his followers.

The Power of One: Daisy Bates and the Little Rock Nine by Judith Fradin and Dennis Brindell Fradin. Clarion, 2004. Daisy Bates and her husband, L. C. Bates, published the *Arkansas State Press*, which in the 1950s presented news from the local black community not only for Little Rock, but for the world. She was the mentor and constant supporter of the nine African American students who in 1957 integrated Central High School in Little Rock.

A Summer of Kings by Han Nolan. Harcourt, 2006. Nolan uses her skill in characterization to present two believable teens living in New York City and traveling different routes leading up to the 1963 march in Washington, D.C., and Martin Luther King, Jr.'s, "I Have a Dream" speech.

We Are One: The Story of Bayard Rustin by Larry Dane Brimmer. Boyds Mills/Calkins Creek, 2007. Many people believe that Bayard Rustin, a lifelong advisor to Martin Luther King, Jr., was the intellect behind the Civil Rights movement.

We Shall Overcome: A Living History of the Civil Rights Struggle Told in Words, Pictures and the Voices of the Participants by Herb Boyd. Sourcebooks MediaFusion, 2004. Boyd uses a clear, journalistic style to tell his living history which begins with the murder of Emmett Till in 1955 and ends with the assassination of Dr. Martin Luther King, Jr., in 1968. Each chapter is dedicated to a specific person or event.

A Wreath for Emmett Till by Marilyn Nelson, illustrated by Philippe Lardy. Houghton, 2005. Nelson used an arcane poetic form to prepare a crown of sonnets to honor Emmett Till. The last line of each of the fifteen poems becomes the first line of the next. Both the artwork and the formality provide readers with the distance they need to absorb the tragedy of the situation and to contemplate its implications.

African American characters into many highly acclaimed books—both fiction and nonfiction. See his write-up on p. 257.

Westerns

The appeal of the American West is as old as the first explorer who saw it and marveled. Dime novelists of the 1870s and 1880s glorified the wildness and vitality of miners, cowboys, mountain men, soldiers, and outlaws. From the beginning, "westerns" were written for mass appeal, so they are easily accessible to teen readers.

If anything else were needed to make the West the heartland of adventure, movies provided rootin'-tootin'-shootin' cowboys and rustlers, good guys and

The Absolutely True Diary of a Part-Time Indian by Sherman Alexie, art by Ellen Forney. Little, Brown, 2007. Although teens had already been reading Alexie's short stories which were the basis of the 1998 *Smoke Signals* film, this is the first of Alexie's books published as YA. In 2005, the Grove Press published a new and fuller edition of *The Lone Ranger and Tonto Fistfight in Heaven*, which had earlier been published by the Atlantic Monthly Press and also by HarperPerennial.

The Buffalo and the Indians: A Shared Destiny by Dorothy Hinshaw Patent, illustrated by William Muñoz. Clarion, 2006. Patent starts each chapter by retelling a Native myth. She is such a good writer, that she is able to communicate both the spiritual and the very practical ways in which the Plains Indians were connected to the bison that roamed the plains before Europeans came to America.

Crooked River by Shelley Pearsall. Knopf, 2005. This well-written piece of historical fiction for young teens is set in 1812 Ohio and tells the story of a slowly developing friendship between thirteen-year-old Rebecca Carver and Amik, an Indian man accused of murder and chained in the loft of the Carvers' cabin.

The Great Circle: A History of the First Nations by Neil Philip. Clarion, 2006. Readers will come away with a new appreciation for the difference between the doctrine of possession that seemed so natural to Europeans when they came to the "New World" and the view held by First Nation cultures that the earth is a great wheel with all people and animals joined together in a connected web.

Jim Thorpe: Original All-American by Joseph Bruchac. Dial, 2006. Bruchac tells Thorpe's story in first person, but sticks close to documented sources for the life of this most famous football player at the Carlisle Indian Industrial School. Kids will enjoy the fact that Pop Warner was the Carlisle coach.

The Relocation of the North American Indians by John M. Dunn. World History Series, 2005. An *SLJ* reviewer predicted that readers would find this carefully researched and well-balanced presentation, "anything but a textbook experience." There's good documentation, boxed quotes, and good-sized illustrations, maps, and photos.

Remember Little Bighorn: Indians, Soldiers, and Scouts Tell Their Stories by Paul Robert Walker. National Geographic, 2006. Walker tells a two-year story that runs from the summer of 1874 until June of 1876 and gives some new perspectives to an old story.

Saving the Buffalo by Albert Marrin. Scholastic, 2006. Although his title presents current attitudes toward the "Lord of the Great Plains," much of the book is about the earlier destruction of these animals. Marrin writes with vigor and does not shrink from the violence that was involved in "harvesting" buffalo and the desire to weaken Native Americans who depended on the buffalo for many things.

Wabi: A Hero's Tale by Joseph Bruchac. Dial, 2006. Tweeners are especially apt to enjoy this journey of self discovery. It is told through the character of Wabi, a horned owl with some unusual characteristics. When his great-grandmother tells him that some of his ancestors were human, he decides to become human so that he can court Dojihla, a girl from the Abenaki village. Of course there are complications.

Where the Great Hawk Flies by Liza Ketchum. Clarion, 2005. Two boys in 1782 are enemies and later friends—one white and one half-Indian.

The Winter People by Joseph Bruchac. Dial, 2002. Based on a true incident in the fall of 1759, Bruchac's coming-of-age story is about fourteen-year-old Saxso, an Abenaki boy, who is trying to rescue his mother and sisters who have been taken by the English. Bruchac's more contemporary *Bearwalker* (HarperCollins, 2007) is a teen mystery/adventure, which received starred reviews.

Wounded Knee by Neil Waldman. Atheneum, 2001. Waldman gives different viewpoints about the events that led up to the infamous slaughter of Native Americans.

Walter Dean Myers, Bringing the Arts to a Second Generation

Hoops, *Motown and Didi: A Love Story*, *Fallen Angels*, and *Scorpions* were the books the Margaret A. Edwards committee honored, but Myers also has many other well-received YA books. His name dominates the list of Coretta Scott King Awards. His first YA book, *Fast Sam, Cool Clyde, and Stuff*, was a King Honor book in 1976, while King winners include *The Young Landlords*, in 1980; *Motown and Didi*, in 1985; *Fallen Angels*, in 1989; *Now Is Your Time! The African American Struggle for Freedom*, in 1992; and *Slam!*, in 1994. Other King Honor books include *Somewhere in the Darkness*, in 1993; *Malcolm X: By Any Means Necessary*, in 1994; and *Monster*, in 2000. His most recent book is *What They Found: Love on 145th Street* (Random, 2007).

Myers has frequently told audiences of booklovers how, when he was in something like third or fourth grade, he discovered from reading and from looking at the pictures in books that he was "different." He seldom found a black face in a book, and if it was there, it was a picture of someone he could not identify with. He set out to change this by becoming a writer about African Americans, first the people he knew in everyday life, and then later he was brave enough to go back and look into historical events.

His best known book is *Monster*, which was a nominee for the American Book Award and winner of the 2000 Printz Award. It is about a sixteen-year-old boy charged with being an accomplice in the murder of a Harlem drugstore owner. What makes the book so unusual is that the boy (Steve Harmon) is a budding screenwriter and so finds it easier to talk about his alleged crime as if it were being played out in a movie rather than in real life. Steve goes over and over his actions as he puts them into the script he is writing. The underlying question that he tries to push away from his mind is whether he is the monster that the prosecuting attorney describes.

Myers got the idea for the book and the way the boy uses third person whenever he is thinking or talking about the crime through interviewing inmates in New York and New Jersey prisons. In a February 4, 2000, interview for www.teenreads.com, Myers said he was struck by how frequently the young men denied being responsible for their actions. They used all kinds of verbal tricks to maintain their belief that they were really good people just caught up in bad circumstances.

In another interview published in the May 2007 *Journal of Adolescent and Adult Literacy*, interviewers Keith Miller and Allison Parker noted that in several of Myers's books, the main characters have artistic inclinations. Steve Harmon in *Monster* is learning to make films, Spoon and Gabi in *The Beast* share a love for poetry, Crystal in the book named after her sings in a church choir and writes poetry, and Mark Purvis in *Harlem Summer* loves to play the saxophone and aspires to a career as a jazz musician. The interviewers asked Myers if he was trying to appeal to readers who gravitate toward the arts or if he was simply trying to give support to the arts at a time of reduced funding.

Myers answered, "My characters are often involved with the arts because of my own preoccupation with writing, music, and the graphic arts." Both Myers's wife and his son, Christopher, are fine artists, and he often collaborates with Christopher—as when Christopher did the illustrations for Myers's 2003 *Time to Love: Stories from the Old Testament*, his 2006 *Jazz*, and his 2005 *Autobiography of My Dead Brother*, the contemporary story of fifteen-year-old Jesse who lives in today's Harlem. He loves cartooning and sketching, while one of his friends is into music. But Rise, who is two years older and Jesse's best friend, moves away from the group and into a life of violence. Christopher Myers's realistic drawings of such characters as Jesse's worried parents, a local policeman, and kids in the neighborhood, along with a comic strip, inspired one reviewer to describe the book as "photorealism." ●

bad guys—always easy to spot by who wore white hats versus who wore black. Edwin S. Porter's *The Great Train Robbery*, produced in 1903, even though filmed in New Jersey, helped develop the myth of the West, while later films like James Cruze's *The Covered Wagon* in 1923, and John Ford's *Stagecoach* in 1939 elaborated on it.

Films may not have been needed, at least not at first, because Owen Wister's *The Virginian,* written in 1902, had already established the central characters of too many westerns. There is the quiet and noble hero, the schoolmarm heroine, the hero's weak friend, the villain, and rustlers, along with such basic plot devices as cattle drives, the inevitable showdown between hero and villain, violence aplenty, and revenge and more revenge. Andy Adams's *Log of a Cowboy: A Narrative of the Old Trail Days* (1903) brought a semblance of honesty to the field, and that was heightened by the fine novels of Eugene Manlove Rhodes, particularly *Paso Por Aqui* (1927). For the most part, realism was rare in westerns—note the romanticized but highly popular novels of Zane Grey. *The Heritage of the Desert* (1910) and *Riders of the Purple Sage* (1912) are far and away his most popular books.

But an amazing number of fine writers lived and breathed the real West and wrote accurate and nonromanticized novels—for example, Oliver LaFarge with *Laughing Boy* (1929), A. B. Guthrie with *The Way West* (1949), and Charles L. McNichols with *Crazy Weather* (1944). The prototype of the western came with Jack Schaefer's *Shane* (1949), much overrated but consistently praised by critics and teachers. Frank Waters, one of the best writers of his time, wrote a loving and lyrical novel of a young man caught between two cultures in *The Man Who Killed the Deer* (1942).

Conventions of the western were so well established by this time that writers knew what was expected. The setting is obviously the West, preferably some time between 1880 and 1895, the high point of cowboy life. Suspense and excitement pervades the novel, as it rarely did for real cowboys back then—rustlers, lynchings, bank robberies, jailbreaks, crooked lawyers, ladies of the evening, the cavalry riding to the rescue, and on and on. Violence was more likely portrayed than implied. The hero (a marshal, ex-gunman, drifter, wagonmaster) will be moral, though that may have come after a reformation, which he will rarely be willing to talk about save to the heroine and only then in a particularly trying or tender moment. Morality will ultimately triumph as the hero plays a successful Hamlet and puts the world aright.

Fortunately, some western writers have been able to ignore or work around these conventions. Louis L'Amour continues to sell well, though he has been dead for a number of years. He is a far better writer than most librarians or English teachers realize, hardly a surprise since he has gone almost unread by educators. L'Amour knows the West as a historian, so the West he writes about is accurate. *Down the Long Hills* is one of his best. In it, a seven-year-old goes searching for his horse, which has wandered away. He returns to find his entire wagon train massacred. He and his sister head west, facing starvation, blizzards, and wild animals. It's a remarkable survival tale.

Three writers have focused on gunfighters and violence in small towns. E. L. Doctorow's *Welcome to Hard Times* shows how dismal a dying western town can be when an outlaw sets out to destroy it over and over. Charles O. Locke's *The*

Hell Bent Kid is about a man who kills a man in self-defense and then must flee for his life. The best known of the three is Glendon Swarthout's *The Shootist,* about a gunfighter dying of cancer who in his last shootout rids the town of some rough gunfighters. It may be more famous for being the last film made by John Wayne, but its renown is well deserved either as book or film.

Two great books are about a West that is dead. Robert Flynn's *North to Yesterday* is the story of a group of misfits who gather to ride old cattle drive trails long after they have dried up. Edward Abbey's *The Brave Cowboy* is a portrait of a cowboy who has outlived the wide open plains. He hates barbed wire fences and anything that encloses anything or anyone. He breaks into jail to free a friend, but when the friend indicates he is willing to serve his term, the cowboy breaks himself out and a long manhunt begins.

Westerns are so often serious that it is pleasant to read two books that are genuinely funny—deliberately so. David Wagoner's *The Road to Many a Wonder* is simply one of the funniest books in English. Ike Bender, age twenty, leaves home to find gold and is soon followed by his soon-to-be bride. Their struggles to get to Colorado and find the pot at the end of their rainbow are believable, generally, and utterly delightful. Bruce Clements's *I Tell a Lie Every So Often* is about a fourteen-year-old boy who begins his tale with this long and complex paragraph, which is a reasonably accurate description of the book that follows:

> I tell a lie every so often, and almost always nothing happens, but last spring I told a lie that carried me five hundred miles and made a lot of things happen. Somebody got shot because of it, and I had a visit with a beautiful naked girl who stood up in front of me early in the morning and talked in a foreign tongue, and I saw a ball game with a hundred men on one side and a hundred men and one girl on the other side, and a boat sank, somewhat, under me, and my brother Clayton started acting strangely and sleeping with a loaded rifle, and there were some more things, too.

Kathryn Lasky's *Beyond the Divide* is a YA novel of the western movement. Another good western written from the perspective of a young person is Marian Calabro's *The Perilous Journey of the Donner Party.* Calabro tells her meticulously researched story of a group of unfortunate western settlers stranded in an early California snowstorm. Her heroine is twelve-year-old Virginia Reed, the young survivor who throughout the months of the ordeal hid her rag doll inside her clothes. For other examples, see Focus Box 8.5, Westerns Too Tough to Die.

Books about War

It is increasingly difficult to distinguish between fiction and nonfiction, especially in memoirs and reminiscences and fiction about war. Struggling to survive in war is not an adventure we would choose, but so many people have been forced into horrible circumstances that books about war—histories, diaries, letters, interviews, fiction—are among the most powerful books young people can read. War is one of the topics treated in the movies, starting with D. W. Griffith's 1915 *The Birth of a Nation* and continuing on to Steven Spielberg's 1998 *Saving*

American Massacre by Sally Denton. Knopf, 2003. Based on the Mountain Meadows Massacre of September 1857, this novel tells the story of a group of pioneers who were misled and then killed by Utah settlers who wanted to discourage travel through their state. The book has the power to raise voices in support of—and opposed to—her interpretation.

Borderlands by Peter Carter. Farrar Straus & Giroux, 1990. Ben Curtis joins a cattle drive in 1871, meets an African American he learns to respect, and loses his brother in a gunfight.

Clem's Chances by Sonia Levitin. Orchard, 2001. With his father chasing gold in California, his mother dead, and Clem being cheated by another family, Clem Fontayne decides his best option is to go west.

I Should Be Extremely Happy in Your Company: A Novel of Lewis and Clark by Brian Hall. Viking, 2003. Brian tells the story of the famous expedition from the viewpoints of Lewis, Clark, Sacagawea, and her interpreter husband. Jealousy erupts when Clark learns that President Jefferson had clearly chosen Lewis as the expedition's leader.

The Last Picture Show by Larry McMurtry. Dial, 1966. The end of the West comes to dusty and drying up Thalia, Texas, where even the movie house shuts down.

Little Big Man by Thomas Berger. Dial, 1964. An old-timer tells of his life in the Old West, his capture by the Cheyennes, his work as a scout for General Custer, and other realities and myths.

North to Yesterday by Robert Flynn. Knopf, 1967. A band of misfits are determined to drive cattle on the old trails—shut down ten years. It's a Western adventure with touches of Don Quixote.

The Professor's House by Willa Cather. Knopf, 1925. The most intriguing part of the novel is about Tom Outland and the discovery of what we now call Mesa Verde National Park.

Stop the Train by Geraldine McCaughrean. HarperCollins, 2001. In this rollicking adventure about the Oklahoma Land Rush in 1893, city slickers try to steal land from settlers.

Wagons West by Frank McLynn. Grove, 2002. McLynn describes the first overland wagon train to California in 1841 (and later ones as well) along with all the irritations and terrors of the journey across America.

Walking Up a Rainbow by Theodore Taylor. Harcourt, Brace, 1994. In the 1850s, fourteen-year-old Susan Darden Carlisle is left an orphan in Iowa. To save her family home, she sets out to drive several thousand sheep from Iowa to California.

West of Everything: The Inner Life of Westerns by Jane Tompkins. Oxford University Press, 1992. Tompkins writes about western literature, films, and everything in between or around or near. It is a wonderful book of scholarship—readable and enlightening.

Wounded Knee by Neil Waldman. Atheneum, 2001. Waldman gives different viewpoints about the events that led up to the infamous slaughter of Native Americans.

Private Ryan. Newspaper and magazine banner headlines of this or that war and TV assault us with horrible scenes of carnage and tearful scenes of survivors.

Young adults may be conscious of the nearness of war, although they likely know little of the realities of war and even less about the details of past wars. Reading literature about war, fiction or not, acquaints young people with the ambiguous nature of war, on one hand illustrating humanity's evil and horror, on the other hand revealing humanity's decency and heroism.

Civil War literature, once pretty well summarized by Stephen Crane's *The Red Badge of Courage*, has several books worth young people's time. Three of the best are Milton Meltzer's *Voices from the Civil War: A Documentary History of the Great American Conflict*, Annette Tapert's *The Brothers' War: Civil War Letters to Their Loved Ones from the Blue and the Gray*, and Gary Paulsen's

Soldier's Heart: Being the Story of the Enlistment and Due Service of the Boy Charley Goddard in the First Minnesota Volunteers.

Meltzer's book combines his own voice with voices of those alive during the war—in journals, public records, ballads, and letters. It brilliantly covers virtually everything about the war, for example, slavery, politics, songs, battles, death, and civilians. Tapert's collection of letters is even more personal and touching. David Ash served with the 37th Illinois Volunteer Infantry. On March 11, 1862, three days after the Union victory at the Battle of Pea Ridge in Arkansas, Ash wrote about the aftermath of the battle.

> It is the hardest sight a person could behold to see the dead lying round after they bring them in. They lay them in a pile until they get time to bury them. There was twenty-one killed out of one regiment and one hundred and nineteen wounded. Albert Hilliard was laying alongside of me when he was shot, says he, "Oh, Dave, I am shot." It was the hardest thing I have done to call the roll the first time after the battle, so many of our boys killed or wounded.

Paulsen's work is an understated account of fifteen-year-old Charley, who enlists and is acclaimed by women and young boys for his bravery and rides in trains and wonders if he will ever get into battle. At his first battle at Manassas he learns what carnage can be with bullets whispering of death and a cannon ball neatly removing the head of a soldier next to him. Charley lived through the war, but he came out physically and mentally wounded and died in his mid-twenties.

World War I inspired some honest and realistic novels. Rudolph Frank's *No Hero for the Kaiser* was so powerful that Hitler banned it in Nazi Germany in the 1930s. Fourteen-year-old Jan and his dog are the only survivors when German troops take his Russian village. The troops befriend him and save him from being sent to a prison camp. He helps them, and they talk of the Kaiser's making him a German citizen. At a great ceremony, the soldiers learn what he thinks of war, and they are deeply troubled.

The most frequently cited book about World War I is again told from the German point of view. Erich Maria Remarque's *All Quiet on the Western Front* is a bitter account of a young German student Paul and his friends and fellow students who are persuaded to join the army by their teacher Kantorek, who fills them with nationalistic propaganda and patriotic fervor. They march off, find what war is really like, and die, one by one.

Pat Barker's award-winning British trilogy—*Regeneration, The Eye in the Door,* and *The Ghost Road*—convey the spirit of the times that led men to enlist for King and country and the inevitable horror and insanity that followed. Lt. Billy Prior is the center of the books, a bright young man from the wrong side of the railroad tracks, a man ordinarily unlikely to be allowed to move up in society. The books are about both the war and the apparently eternal social order before the war and the changing society after it.

During World War II, Ernie Pyle was the American soldier's favorite war correspondent, partly because he preferred talking to soldiers in the ranks rather than to officers, and partly because he reported honestly what he saw, not what was good for the morale of soldiers or civilians. For example, in *Ernie's War:*

The Best of Ernie Pyle's World War II Dispatches (edited by David Nichols) he writes about the death of Captain Henry T. Waskow, one of the most "beloved" men Pyle found in the war. He told of Waskow's men coming in, gently, to see and honor the body. Pyle ended his account this way:

> Then a soldier came and stood beside the officer, and bent over, and he spoke to the dead captain, not in a whisper but awfully tenderly, and he said: "I sure am sorry, sir." Then the first man squatted down, and he reached down and took the dead hand, and he sat there for a full five minutes, holding the dead hand in his own and looking intently into the dead face, and he never uttered a sound all the time he sat there.
>
> And finally he put the hand down, and then reached up and gently straightened the points of the captain's shirt collar, and then he sort of rearranged the tattered edges of his uniform around the wound. And then he got up and walked away down the road in the moonlight, all alone.
>
> After that the rest of us went back into the cowshed, leaving the five dead men lying in a line, end to end, in the shadow of the low stone wall. We lay down on the straw in the cowshed, and pretty soon we were all asleep.

Few books about World War II, or any other war, succeed so well in creating a revulsion to the blood and messiness as does Farley Mowat's *And No Birds Sang*. After Mowat's company encountered and killed six truckloads of German soldiers, Mowat said,

> It was not the dead that distressed me most—it was the German wounded. There were a great many of these, and most seemed to have been hard hit.
>
> One ghastly vignette from that shambles haunts me still: the driver of a truck hanging over his steering wheel and hiccuping great gouts of cherry-pink foam through a smashed windscreen, to the accompaniment of a sound like a slush pump sucking air as his perforated lungs labored to expel his own heart's blood . . . in which he was slowly drowning.

Mowat's book is not the only honest account, but it reeks of death and lost dreams, and anyone wanting to know what war is like should not miss it.

Several novels about World War II are especially worth reading. William Wharton's *A Midnight Clear* is about six high-IQ American soldiers in an intelligence and reconnaissance platoon sent to determine whether there are German troops near a French chateau. The six play bridge and chess and word games and begin to believe they have nothing to do with the war. Then the Germans show up, and instead of warfare, everyone engages in a snowball fight. They sing Christmas carols and set up a Christmas tree and wonderful peace reigns. Then war starts again and the killing resumes, and what had been warm is now bloody.

English novelist Robert Westall writes about young people who refuse to stay outside the war in *The Machine Gunners* and the sequel, *Fathom Five*. The first novel begins in an English coastal town during 1940 and 1941. Rumors of a German invasion are rife, and Chas McGill wants to help win the war. Chas and his friends locate a downed German plane, find the machine gun in working order, and hide it. When a school is hit by a German plane somewhat later, Chas steals sandbags to create a fortress, a safe place to display the machine gun. The rear gunner of the downed plane stumbles into their fortress and becomes the boys' prisoner. All this childish innocence dies when adults discover the fortress, the German is shot, and the young people are rounded up by their parents. *Fathom Five* is a rousing spy story set later in the war and the story of Chas's lost love and lost innocence. Westall had an amazing ability to portray the ambivalence of young people and the alienation they feel, mixed with love and duty.

Harry Mazer's *The Last Mission* is set near the end of World War II. Jack Raab uses his older brother's identification to lie his way into the Air Force to destroy Hitler and to save democracy, all by himself. That dream lasts only a short time before Jack learns that the Air Force involves more training and boredom than fighting. When Jack does go to war, his first twenty-four bombing raids go well, but on the last mission, his plane is hit, all his buddies die, and he is captured. When he returns home, the principal at his old high school asks him to talk.

> "I'm glad we won," he said. "We couldn't let Hitler keep going. We had to stop him. But most of all, I'm glad it's over." Had he said enough? There was a silence. . . a waiting silence. There was something more he had to say.
>
> "I don't like war. I thought I'd like it before. But war is stupid. War is one stupid thing after another. I saw my best friend killed. His name was Chuckie O'Brien. My whole crew was killed." Now he was talking, it was coming out, all the things he'd thought about for so long. "A lot of people were killed. Millions of people. Ordinary people. Not only by Hitler. Not only on our side. War isn't like the movies. It's not fun and songs. It's not about heroes. It's about awful, sad things, like my friend Chuckie that I'm never going to see again." His voice faltered.
>
> "I hope war never happens again," he said after a moment. "That's all I've got to say."
>
> He sat down. He hardly heard the applause. The floor of the radio room was still slippery with Chuckie's blood . . . Dave was still fumbling with his chute . . . the plane was still falling through the sky.

Many years after writing *The Last Mission*, Mazer wrote a trilogy about World War II. In *A Boy at War: A Novel of Pearl Harbor*, Adam Pelko signs up for high school classes while his father is on duty on the Battleship Arizona in Pearl Harbor, Hawaii. Adam is tired of being a military brat, but at least he finds a good friend in Davi Mori. Davi explains to Adam that he, Davi, was born in Hawaii and is *nisei* while his parents were born in Japan and are *issei*. Out fishing one day, Adam sees the bombing of Pearl Harbor and the sinking of the *Arizona*.

In *A Boy No More*, Adam and his mother live in Bakersfield. Davi writes from Hawaii that his father is being held by authorities and, later, that his father has been taken to the United States. Adam finds that the Mori family is at Manzanar, an internment camp in the California desert, and he visits them. Davi tells Adam that he always thinks about his father, "the way they treated him like a traitor. For nothing. They put him in prison for nothing. He never says anything, but it hurts him."

In the third book, *Heroes Don't Run*, Adam goes back to his grandfather in upper New York State and then joins the marines. In the meantime, Davi joins the army. When Adam's unit fights in Okinawa, Adam's life becomes violent, explosive, and at times bloody.

> It never stopped raining. We were in mud all the time. We fought in the wet, slept in it, ate our soggy, cold rations in it. We lived with the shells and the mortars and the screams of the wounded.

Later, as he slogs uphill and witnesses the Japanese dead, he observes, "There were too many bodies. So many shattered bodies. So many bodies without arms or legs." Mazer's trilogy is helpful in teaching young adults about Pearl Harbor, Japanese internment camps, and World War II in the Pacific, but it does not have the power of *The Last Mission*, which is a story that Mazer actually lived when he snuck into the World War II army as a teenager.

Aidan Chambers's *Postcards from No Man's Land* (winner of the 2002 Printz Award) has reminded young people of the ugliness of World War II, and particularly the long-term effects war can have on us. Chambers tells his story in alternating chapters set in 1944 and 1995. In the latter year, seventeen-year-old Jacob Todd travels to Holland to visit his grandfather's grave on the fifty-first anniversary of the Battle of Arnheim and to see Geertrui Wesseling, the last person to see his grandfather alive. Jacob has no presumption that this trip will be at all interesting, but a Dutch saying he hears early on in Amsterdam—"Nothing in Amsterdam is what it appears to be"—should have alerted him to all he would find out about his grandfather, the war, and Jacob himself.

James Forman's finest work, too little known, is *Ceremony of Innocence*. Hans and Sophie Scholl, brother and sister in Nazi Germany, print and distribute literature attacking Hitler. Arrested by the Gestapo, they are urged by friends to escape. A lawyer, who Hans suspects is a Nazi, encourages them to plead insanity. They refuse, endure the mock trial, are found guilty, and are taken away to be executed. Hans is the last to die by the guillotine.

> Hans heard the sound of rollers, and at last there burst from his throat a cry, uttered in a great voice, a voice that combined anger, reproof, and an overwhelming conviction for which he was willing to die.
> "Long live freedom!"
> Then the greased blade fell. His teeth met through his tongue, and it was over.

Readers curious about the White Rose, a German movement to end the war, can find information in Richard Hanser's *A Noble Treason: The Revolt of the Munich Students Against Hitler;* Hermann Vinke's *The Short Life of Sophie Scholl;* Annette E. Dumbach and Jud Newborn's *Shattering the German Night: The Story of the White Rose;* and Inge Jens's *At the Heart of the White Rose: Letters and Diaries of Hans and Sophie Scholl.* Sebastian Haffner's memoirs of his life in Germany during World War II, *Defying Hitler,* reveals a young man at first enthusiastic about German nationalism and later growing disillusioned about what Hitler represented. At one point, he lies about being a Jew and is horribly shocked by his lie. That leads to his leaving Germany in 1938.

A short book by John Wilson may have the most effect on young readers. *And in the Morning* is a simple and direct story about young John Hay, who thinks war must be a glorious romp, but when his father is killed in World War I and his mother has a mental breakdown, John goes into the service and soon learns in the trenches of France how dismally wrong he was. The remainder of the book is about the death of almost everyone around him that he cares for, and worse yet, after another bombardment and the death of yet another friend, John walks off and is captured by his own side and taken for a deserter. His court martial is brief, John is found guilty and sentenced to die before a firing squad. In a letter to his wife, John writes:

> *Sunday, July 9, Bouzincourt*
> Dear Anne: The decision of the court martial has been confirmed by General Haig. He said that soldiers who avoid their comrades' dangers cannot be tolerated. What nonsense—all my comrades are dead—I avoid their dangers simply by living. But not for long. I am to be shot tomorrow.

On August 20, 2006, the Associated Press reported that the British Government was preparing to pardon 306 men who were executed for desertion or cowardice after summary trials during World War I. Defense Secretary Des Browne announced, "The circumstances [of World War I] were terrible, and I believe it is better to acknowledge that injustices were clearly done in some cases, even if we cannot say which, and to acknowledge that all these men were victims of war." A retired teacher who founded a pressure group, Shot at Dawn, said the government had relented after three lawsuits were filed by families. Records show that the wartime trials were speedy, some lasted no more than twenty minutes, and in one case, a soldier was tried and executed on the same day. Michael Morpurgo's *Private Peaceful*, a 2004 Honor List book, is another excellent book telling a story from this period.

John Devaney and Peter Arnett have both written straightforward books about war. Devaney's *America Storms the Beaches: 1944* is an account of the period between September and December of 1944, which was a turning point. In his *Live from the Battlefield: From Vietnam to Baghdad, 35 Years in the World's War Zones*, a respected reporter gives his up-close view of war and soldiers and politics.

Of all the many books on war, none has a more horrible indictment of the absurdity and cruelty of war than Roger Rosenblatt's *Children of War*. Rosenblatt circled the globe seeking out children in Belfast, Israel, Cambodia, Hong Kong, and Lebanon whom he asked about themselves and what war had done to them. A nine-year-old girl in Cambodia had made a drawing, and after a year of help by an American psychologist, she was able to explain how the instrument in the drawing worked. Rosenblatt writes:

> The children harvesting rice include Peov. She is the largest of the three. Whenever a child refused to work, he was punished with the circular device. The soldiers would place it over the child's head. Three people would hold it steady by means of ropes. . . . A fourth would grab hold of the ring at the end of the other

Ain't Gonna Study War No More by Milton Meltzer. Harper and Row, 1985. Meltzer traces pacifism in the United States starting with the Quakers.

Climb to Conquer: The Untold Story of World War II's 10th Mountain Division Ski Troops by Peter Shelton. Scribner, 2003. Young men, expert skiers, became part of the army in World War II and fought in Italy. At one time, the division had ten or fifteen of the top skiers in the world.

The Deserter's Tale: The Story of an Ordinary Soldier Who Walked Away from the War by Joshua Key and Lawrence Hill. Atlantic Monthly, 2007. Key enlisted in the army on the assurance that he would be sent to a "nondeployable" base and would never see combat. Instead, he was sent to Iraq to hunt terrorists. So he walked away.

Hiroshima: A Novella by Laurence Yep. Scholastic, 1995. Though the story is centered around Hiroshima residents, Yep also tells the story of the bomb itself.

Johnny Got His Gun by Dalton Trumbo. Lippincott, 1939. Filled with patriotic fervor, Joe enlists, but after the battle, he has no arms or legs, and he is blind, deaf, and mute.

Lord of the Nutcracker by Iain Lawrence. Delacorte, 2001. It is 1914 and a ten-year-old London boy is sent, for safety, to live with his aunt in the country. He lives the war, first its patriotism and then its horror, through tin soldiers that his toymaker father sends to him.

Kipling's Choice by Geert Spillbeen. Houghton Mifflin, 2005. John Kipling is determined to get into World War I. His father, Rudyard Kipling, helps him join the Irish Guards. He is wounded and dies slowly on the battlefield.

The Loud Silence of Francine Green by Karen Cushman. Clarion, 2006. It is August of 1949 and Francine is an eighth grader at All Saints School for Girls in Los Angeles. It is the Cold War and she gets in trouble for challenging her teachers' descriptions of "the Godless" communists.

Manzanar by John Armor and Peter Wright. Time Books, 1989. The two authors use Ansel Adams photographs and a commentary by John Hersey to create a record of this Japanese internment camp.

Or Give Me Death: A Novel of Patrick Henry's Family by Ann Rinaldi. Harcourt, 2003. Patty and Anne, the daughters of Patrick Henry and his mentally ill wife, tell their moving story in this book that found a place on *VOYA*'s Top Shelf Fiction for Middle School Readers.

Red Scarf Girl: A Memoir of the Cultural Revolution by Ji Li Jiang. HarperCollins, 1997. A young girl tells how she was asked to betray her Chinese family.

Slap Your Sides by M. E. Kerr. HarperCollins, 2002. Jubal Shoemaker is a Quaker who, in the midst of the patriotism of World War II, has mixed feelings about his brother's being a conscientious objector. See also Kerr's *Linger* (HarperCollins, 1993) about patriotism during the Persian Gulf War.

Soldier Boys by Dean Hughes. Atheneum, 2001. Parallel stories tell about two young soldiers, American Spencer Morgan and German Dieter Hedrick, who enter their country's service full of idealism, only to learn how hellish war is.

Under the Blood-Red Sun by Graham Salisbury. Delacorte, 1994. The bombing of Pearl Harbor on December 7, 1941, changes the life of a young Japanese American as he searches for his father and grandfather.

Unknown Soldiers: The Story of the Missing of the First World War by Neil Hanson. Knopf, 2006. Hanson writes about three soldiers—an American, a Frenchman, and a German—using letters to families to draw a picture of the horrors of war, the gas and explosives in one of the worst sectors of the Western Front.

When My Name Was Keoko: A Novel of Korea in World War II by Linda Sue Park. Clarion, 2002. A brother and a sister use the loss of their Korean names as the focus of their memories of the 1940s when Japan occupied Korea.

Zlata's Diary: A Child's Life in Sarajevo by Zlata Filipovic. Penguin, 1994. A fifth-grade girl kept a diary of the horrors, the friendships, and the love and the blood that she saw during the Serbian-Croatian war.

rope. . . . When the rope with the ring was pulled . . . the child would be decapitated. A portable guillotine.

But it wasn't the soldiers who worked the device. It was the children.

Literature of the Holocaust

Not many years ago, anyone wishing to read about the Holocaust would read Anne Frank's *The Diary of a Young Girl*. Today an outpouring of films and books about the Holocaust means that no one can pretend not to know about the happenings and the evils that went with it.

One part of that outpouring is the 1995 definitive edition of *Anne Frank's Diary*, in which Anne becomes far more human and far less saintly. A number of passages touch on Anne's interest in sex and love, and Anne's entry for March 24, 1944, is sexual and analytical. The definitive edition should please readers who want to read about a human being with all her faults. It should almost equally please censors, who will have new reasons to find fault with a nearly perfect book. Miep Gies's *Anne Frank Remembered,* the autobiography of the woman who helped hide the Frank family, adds more detail and should be read alongside Anne's *Diary.*

Most young adults seek out books about young people caught in the Holocaust because they are better able to identify with people their own age or slightly older. A book that is similar to Anne Frank's Diary is Etty Hillesum's *An Interrupted Life: The Diaries of Etty Hillesum, 1941–1943*. Being twenty-seven years old, Hillesum probably knew precisely what her fate was to be. Her diary begins, "Here goes, then," and she writes of her love affairs, her graduate study at the University of Amsterdam, and her friends and ideas. She seems to have had little interest in politics until Jews were required to wear the yellow star. That jolted her, but she never sought to escape. In her last days, she volunteered to go with a group of condemned Jews to Westerbork Camp. She must have known that Westerbork was the usual first step to Auschwitz. Her journal complements Anne's *Diary;* Etty's irony and sophistication neatly counterpoint Anne's simplicity and innocence. *An Interrupted Life* is completed in *Letters from Westerbork.*

Students continue to read and love Johanna Reiss's *The Upstairs Room* and its sequel *The Journey Back*. The first book is a true story of the author and her sister, two young Jewish girls in Holland, kept safely in hiding by a gentile family for over two years during the Nazi occupation. The girls detest having to stay inside all the time, but when they learn from an underground newspaper what is happening to Jews across Europe, they realize how precarious is their life. The second book is about their trip back to their hiding place after the war. Karen Ray's *To Cross a Line* is about Egon Katz, a seventeen-year-old Jewish baker's apprentice who was certain that if he followed all the rules, he'd be safe. Then the Gestapo shows up with a warrant for him. Kati David's *A Child's War: World War II Through the Eyes of Children* is an account of World War II through the eyes of eight girls and seven boys, who saw fear and death and every horror that war brings about.

Thomas Keneally's *Schindler's List* should be read alongside any work about the Holocaust. But then so should the accounts of inmates of the concentration camps in Sylvia Rothchild's *Voices from the Holocaust*. Hazel Rochman and Darlene Z. McCampbell's *Bearing Witness: Stories of the Holocaust* is a marvelous collection of material that will shock readers just as other selections will give them pictures of real heroes. Hanna Volavkova's *I Never Saw Another Butterfly: Children's Drawings and Poems from Terezin Concentration Camp, 1941–1944* and Chana Byers Abells's *The Children We Remember* are unquestionably the most painful reading because they detail the massacre of the innocent.

Milton Meltzer does his usual fine job of collection and reporting in *Never to Forget: The Jews of the Holocaust*. Ten years later, he wrote a book about a much smaller number of people, *Rescue: The Story of How Gentiles Saved Jews in the Holocaust*. As he explained in the introduction:

> Now I have come to realize the great importance of recording not just the evidence of evil, but also the evidence of human nobility. Love, not hatred, is what the world needs. Rescue, not destruction. The stories in the book offer reason to hope. And hope is what we need, the way plants need sunlight.

Two other books deserve to be read alongside Meltzer—Eva Fogelman's *Conscience and Courage: Rescuers of Jews During the Holocaust* and Maxine B. Rosenberg's *Hiding to Survive: Stories of Jewish Children Rescued from the Holocaust*. Ina R. Friedman's *The Other Victims: First Person Stories of Non-Jews Persecuted by the Nazis* is a worthy addition to Holocaust literature.

Anyone considering a unit or a project on the Holocaust ought to be aware of two movies, a short film that is generally well known and a feature-length film considerably less known. *Night and Fog* (31 minutes, color and black and white, 1955, not rated, Director: Alain Resnais) is a documentary on Nazi concentration camps with color scenes of present-day ruins of Auschwitz played against German black-and-white footage when the camps were active, prisoners arrived, and smoke and death reigned and footage shot by Allied soldiers as they freed the camps and all their prisoners. The voice-over commentary by Jean Cayrol, himself once an inmate, is wonderfully quiet, allowing the film to shock the viewer. One can only guess why so much explicit film was shot by the Germans, but presumably they assumed they would win the war, and the film was a historic record of their work on the home front during World War II.

Night and Fog is a tough film to watch, even nearly sixty years after it was made and seventy years after the events it captures on film. Decapitated heads, mounds of prisoners' hair, huge piles of dead nude bodies being pushed into a long earthen grave—but the horror is intrinsic to the film and necessary for our reactions to the horrors of these concentration camps and the horrors that people do to each other. We'd hate to think that students could view the film dispassionately—though we've seen that happen.

We know from firsthand experience that some students get sick or begin to cry—we've seen that as well. Teachers who consider using the film should see it before showing it and then, judging the film and the sophistication of the students, determine their course of action.

The longer film is quieter, but it is also a record of the cold-blooded decision of a small group of Nazis about what to do with Jews in Europe, the so-called "final solution." *Conspiracy* (95 minutes, color, 2001, not rated; Director: Frank Pierson) shows how on January 20, 1942, fifteen highly ranked Nazis met at Wannsee on the outskirts of Berlin to determine the future of Jews. The meeting was organized by S.S. Major Adolf Eichmann and directed by Chief of Security Reinhard Heydrich. It was a civilized meeting with food and wine and lots of talk, but the meeting had only one item on its agenda, the extermination of six million European Jews. The text for the film was taken from minutes at the meeting found after the end of the war.

Kenneth Branagh, who played Heydrich, described his role as the most difficult and abhorrent of any he had played. It's a distinguished cast with Stanley Tucci, Colin Firth, and David Threlfall. The same topic is covered in a German film, *The Wannsee Conference* (87 minutes, color, 1984; Director: Heinz Schirk).

Some recent YA novels have focused on the obvious fact that bigotry endures. In Lois Ruby's *Skin Deep*, Dan comes from a fatherless home. When multiethnic quotas keep him off the swimming team and from getting a job at the University of Colorado, he turns to the local skinheads for support, adopting their dress code but never quite accepting their racism. Han Nolan's *If I Should Die Before I Wake* portrays a young girl, a neo-Nazi initiate, who is in a coma from a motor-

These three memoirs, all published to positive acclaim in 2007, illustrate how books about war are not limited to the participation of adults in officially declared global conflicts. They include Ibtisam Barakat's Tasting the Sky: A Palestinian Childhood, *Peter Sis's* The Wall: Growing Up Behind the Iron Curtain, *and Ishmael Beah's* A Long Way Gone: Memoirs of a Boy Soldier.

cycle accident. In her dreams in the hospital, she becomes a young Jewish girl whose family lives in a ghetto and then Auschwitz. *The Wave* by Morton Rhue (pen name of Todd Strasser) has proved incredibly popular with many young people. In a high school history class, students wonder why the non-Nazi Germans let the Holocaust happen. The teacher responds by introducing students to a new movement, The Wave, which captures the imaginations and the hearts of students apparently longing for indoctrination and belief in certainties.

The best of these books is Fran Arrick's *Chernowitz!* Bob Cherno, fifteen, looked back on his fights with Emmett Sundback, a bigot who ridiculed Bob's Jewishness. When Bob's school shows a film about the concentration camps, some students who have ridiculed Bob leave in tears because they understand the horrors of the Nazis' treatment of Jews and other minorities. To Arrick's credit, Sundback does not change and remains the creep that he was. See Focus Box 8.7, Experiencing the Holocaust to Keep It from Happening Again for further examples.

Some flippant person once argued that if we wanted to cut down sexual exuberance in the young, we ought to hire English teachers to teach about sex, preferably in lectures with copious black-and-white diagrams. In theory, that would kill any interest in sex for years.

In a more serious vein, that may also apply to teaching about the Holocaust. Most teachers would agree that it is good to teach about the Holocaust, though what to teach and how to teach it has always been the question, not simply whether we ought to teach this book or that. There is a weightier matter to consider. Few schools do much with the history of Christian anti-Semitism although that was an issue in Hitler's plan to exterminate Jews, and it was significant in the lack of support Jews had from their neighbors when the Nazis appeared. Of course, it just might "rile up" the community, as a teacher is quoted saying in Simone Schweber's excellent article, "'Holocaust Fatigue' in Teaching Today" in the January/February 2006 *Social Education*, an article worth reading by anyone who teaches the Holocaust or cares about the subject. Samuel Totten's "What Will Students Remember? Closing a Lesson on the Holocaust" in the November/December 2002 *Social Education* is less provocative but certainly helpful.

Internment of Japanese Americans in World War II

The most shameful American action during World War II began in January 1942 when President Roosevelt ordered the forced evacuation of anyone of Japanese ancestry on the West Coast into detention camps scattered in desolate places. More than 120,000 people were moved from their homes into the meager and arid camps. Lt. General John L. DeWitt spoke for many ignorant people when he maintained that there was no difference between people in Japan and Japanese Americans. "A Jap's a Jap," DeWitt said, "It makes no difference whether he is an American citizen or not." Always a crowd-pleaser, Dewitt especially pleased people who were eager to buy out Japanese farmers or merchants on their way to internment camps for a few cents on the dollar.

Jeanne Wakatsuki Houston and her husband James D. Houston's *Farewell to Manzanar* describes the first author's life in a camp ringed by barbed wire and

Experiencing the Holocaust to Keep It from Happening Again

After the Holocaust by Howard Greenfield. Greenwillow, 2001. Eight survivors of the Holocaust share their experiences on what happened to them after the defeat of Hitler.

After the War by Carol Matas. Simon and Schuster, 1996. A survivor of Buchenwald returns to her small town in Poland. When she can find no news of her relatives, she joins an underground group who smuggle her into Palestine.

Auschwitz: The Story of a Nazi Death Camp by Clive A. Lawton. Candlewick, 2002. Lawton has written a good introductory book with two-page chapters, which are arranged chronologically so that the book moves from mundane facts about building an organization to horrendous information about medical experiments and the disposing of bodies.

The Beautiful Days of My Youth: My Six Months in Auschwitz and Plaszow by Ana Novac. Holt, 1997. As Nazis kill and cremate concentration camp victims, Novac keeps a diary of the horrors.

The Boy in the Striped Pajamas: A Fable by John Boyne. Random/David Fickling Books, 2006. Nine-year-old Bruno, the only child in an affluent German family, is shocked when his family moves to a place in Poland where, from his new bedroom window, he can see a high wire fence and hundreds of people wearing striped pajamas.

Dancing on the Bridge of Avignon by Ida Vos. Houghton Mifflin, 1995. In Nazi-occupied Holland, Rosa finds solace in her violin while being Jewish becomes more and more dangerous. Read also *Anna Is Still Here* (Houghton Mifflin, 1993) and *Hide and Seek* (Houghton Mifflin, 1991).

Hidden Child by Isaac Millman. Farrar/Frances FosterBooks, 2005. For middle school students, this seventy-three-page biography tells the story of a Jewish boy whose Parisian mother bribed officials to take him out of the deportation line and to a hospital. Six years later when he is fifteen, he is adopted by an American Jewish family.

Hiding to Survive: Stories of Jewish Children Rescued from the Holocaust by Maxine B. Rosenberg. Clarion, 1994. Fourteen Americans, now in their fifties and sixties, remember what they can of being hidden.

In Kindling Flame: The Story of Hannah Senesh, 1921–1944 by Linda Atkinson. Lothrop, Lee and Shepard, 1985. Senesh, a Hungarian Jew, was a resistance fighter. See also *Hannah Senesh: Her Life and Diary* (Schocken, 1972).

The Key Is Lost by Ida Vos, translated by Terese Eddelstein. HarperCollins, 2000. The author writes from her own childhood memories when she and her sister were separated from their parents and forced into hiding during the Nazi occupation of Holland.

One, by One, by One: Facing the Holocaust by Judith Miller. Simon and Schuster, 1990. A journalist examines how West Germany, Austria, France, the Netherlands, Russia, and the United States each handled its responsibility for the Holocaust.

Return to Auschwitz by Kitty Hart. Atheneum, 1982. Thirty years after surviving the Holocaust, Hart returns to the camp to help make an English documentary.

The Righteous: The Unsung Heroes of the Holocaust by Martin Gilbert. Holt, 2003. The author collected stories of people who helped save Jews from Hitler's killing machine.

Sala's Gift: My Mother's Holocaust Story by Ann Kirschner. Free Press, 2006. At sixty-seven, Sala Garncarz Kirschner gave her daughter a present, a collection of papers about her life from 1940 when she thought she would be working six weeks in a Nazi labor camp to 1946 when she arrived in New York as a war bride.

Someone Named Eve by Joan M. Wolf. Clarion, 2007. Wolf tells a fictionalized story of a young Jewish girl from the Czechoslovakian village of Lidice who was one of the ten children chosen from the doomed village to be taken to a Lebensborn center for "Germanization."

Suite Française by Irène Némirovsky. Knopf, 2004. Nemirovsky, a Russian born Jew who migrated to France at an early age, was an accomplished novelist when she was arrested and taken to Auschwitz where she died at the age of 39. Her daughters saved her notebooks but did not read them until sixty years later when they were surprised to discover in their mother's tiny handwriting the polished story now published as *Suite Française*.

Surviving Hitler: A Boy in the Nazi Death Camps by Andrea Warren. HarperColllins, 2001. The many photographs will help middle school students relate to this account of a boy's experiences in one of the death camps.

Yellow Star by Jennifer Roy. Marshall Cavendish, 2006. Middle schoolers will appreciate the detailed observations in this moving retelling of the experiences of Jennifer Roy's Aunt Syvia in the Lodz Ghetto during the Nazi occupation of Poland.

guard towers and with open latrines. The three-year ordeal destroyed the family's unity and left them with a burdening sense of personal inadequacy that took years to remove.

John Armor and Peter Wright discovered many photographs taken by Ansel Adams for his ironically titled 1944 book *Born Free and Equal*. They added a text to go with the photographs and titled their book *Manzanar*. With a commentary by John Hersey, *Manzanar* is a record of a people who had a right to be bitter but who were instead generally making conditions at the camp work for them.

In February 1983, a Congressional committee concluded deliberations and agreed that the internment of Japanese Americans was a "grave injustice." The commission noted that the relocation was motivated by "racial prejudice, war hysteria, and failure of political leadership," not by any military considerations.[6]

Five years later, the House passed and sent on to President Reagan legislation giving apologies and $20,000 tax-free payments to Japanese American survivors of World War II internment camps. Typical of bureaucratic bumbling, it was 1990 before the first checks were issued. American justice may be slow—in this case forty-five years—but it may arrive.

Two novels about the internment are outstanding:

Cynthia Kadohata's *Weedflower* opens just before the bombing of Pearl Harbor. Sumiko's family grow flowers in California, and after the bombing they are sent to the bleak, dusty, and very hot internment camp in Poston, Arizona. Sumiko and Frank, a Mohave boy, become friends. Boredom set in for many internees, as it did for Sumiko, but she was strong enough to make her way through depression and out into the sunlight.

Each chapter in Julie Otsuka's *When the Emperor Was Divine* is narrated by a member of the family who was sent to an internment camp called Topaz in the Utah desert in 1942. They spent three years and five months at Topaz. And when they left and returned to what their home was, neighbors and former friends cut them almost as deep as Topaz did.

One other novel about internment camps is often forgotten, a shame because it was written at a time when befriending or being fair to the Japanese was not in fashion. Florence Crannell Means had written many books about minorities, but *The Moved-Outers* (1945) may be her best work. It's about how Sue Ohara's life changed after December 7, 1941, and Pearl Harbor. Her father was taken into custody by the F.B.I. and Sue, her brother Kim, and her mother were taken to a Relocation Camp (doesn't sound unpleasant, does it?) and then to a camp in Arizona. Conditions could not be worse, but the family survives. Means's novel has its problems. It is dated—few YA books survive more than fifty years—and at times it seems condescending, but it was one of the few contemporary books, YA or adult, that took a moral stand against the treatment of Japanese Americans.

Books about Vietnam

Two YA novels about Vietnam stand out. Valerie Hobbs's *Sonny's War* is about a garage mechanic who ignores his younger sister's advice to flee to

Canada and ignore the draft; he is subsequently sent to Vietnam. What makes this novel different is the author's attention to the antiwar movement as it is preached by a local history teacher. The other outstanding YA novel is Walter Dean Myers's *Fallen Angels*. Harlem is hard on Richie Perry, so he flees Harlem and joins the army. To his surprise, Richie finds himself dreaming of Harlem and wanting to get back to a world he thought he wanted to forget.

Larry R. Johannessen, a Vietnam veteran who came home to teach high school in suburban Chicago and now prepares teachers at Northern Illinois University, has been teaching nonfiction from the Vietnam War since the early 1980s. He is the author of *Illumination Rounds: Teaching the Literature of the Vietnam War* and in an article for the *English Journal*, "When History Talks Back: Teaching Nonfiction Literature of the Vietnam War,"[7] he explained that this material appeals to mature high school students because:

1. The Vietnam War was a "teenage" war. The average age of soldiers was nineteen, as compared to twenty-six for World War II. Because "many of these young people were not mentally prepared for the carnage and terror that marked the Vietnam experience . . . they describe the idealism, loneliness, homesickness, fear, terror, isolation, abandonment, and betrayal in ways that speak directly to students."

2. The oral histories are especially powerful because the speakers establish "a confidential, intimate relationship with readers in a voice that seems to be speaking directly to them."

3. Many students have relatives, teachers, or family friends who were in Vietnam, and so they have a personal interest in understanding what these people experienced.

4. The experience that in a year-and-a-half turned young, idealistic men and women into disillusioned "old kids," was in many ways the archetypal journey that we described in Chapter 4 as the romantic quest. Johannessen identified the stages as
   - The mystique of preinduction or the John Wayne syndrome.
   - The initiation into the military culture during training.
   - The dislocation of arrival in Vietnam—culture shock.
   - The confrontation with mortality in the first firefight.
   - The confrontation with moral dilemmas, moving from innocence to experience and consideration, or from innocence to numbness and madness.
   - The phenomenon of coming home and learning to live with the legacies of the war, with the guilt and the loss of faith and innocence.
   - Putting it together by finding a central meaning.

See Focus Box 8.8, Nonfiction Books about Vietnam, for some of the books that Johannessen recommends, along with our own recommendations. There are enough different books that when a class works on this subject, students can choose which book(s) they want to read, and chances are they can check them out from libraries. There are also good films that can provide common experiences for the whole class. Besides such famous films as those directed by Oliver Stone

American Daughter Gone to War: On the Front Lines with an Army Nurse in Vietnam by Winnie Smith. Pocket Books, 1994. As an idealistic twenty-one-year-old, Smith requested assignment as a combat nurse. She went on duty in an intensive care unit in Saigon caring for soldiers flown directly in from the battlefield.

Bloods: An Oral History of the Vietnam War by Black Veterans by Wallace Terry. Ballantine, 1984. As a reporter in Vietnam, Terry began interviewing African American soldiers. He continued the practice when he returned home and has arranged the interviews in a book that speaks to such issues as race relations and media manipulation.

Born on the Fourth of July by Ron Kovic. Pocket Books, 1976. Because of the powerful 1989 movie made by Oliver Stone (starring Tom Cruise) students will already be aware of how Kovic came home from Vietnam in a wheelchair, how he was embittered by the way the Veteran's Administration treated him, and how he became involved in the antiwar movement.

Dispatches by Michael Herr. Vintage, 1991. Larry Johannessen says that of all the books he has taught, this is the one that does the best job of capturing the *feel* of Vietnam.

Everything We Had: An Oral History of the Vietnam War by Thirty-Three American Solders Who Fought It by Al Santoli. Ballantine, 1981. Santoli's interviews with men and women take readers through the war from 1962 until the fall of Saigon in 1971.

Homecoming: When the Soldiers Returned from Vietnam by Bob Greene. Ballantine, 1990. Greene is a syndicated columnist who solicited letters from soldiers asking them to tell about their coming-home experiences. The letters document the double war that the veterans had to fight—the one in Asia and the one at home.

If I Die in a Combat Zone by Tim O'Brien. Dell, 1987. O'Brien's book will help students see how Vietnam literature fits into the bigger body of war literature because it starts with O'Brien's going to war identifying with the hero of Ernest Hemingway's *A Farewell to Arms*.

In the Combat Zone: An Oral History of American Women in Vietnam by Kathryn Marshall. Little, Brown, 1987. Marshall interviewed twenty women veterans and lets their diverse experiences and the way they tell them speak to an often overlooked part of the war.

Nam: The Vietnam War in the Words of the Men and Women Who Fought There by Mark Baker. Morrow, 1981. Berkley paperback. The interviewees come from a wide spectrum, and the interviews are so well done that many people feel this is the "classic" answer to the question of "What was Vietnam really like?"

Offerings at the Wall: Artifacts from the Vietnam Veterans Memorial Collection by Thomas B. Allen. Times Publishing, 1995. Allen took colored pictures of items left at the Wall and wrote the accompanying texts.

Patriots: The Vietnam War Remembered from All Sides by Christian G. Appy. Viking, 2003. A collection of 135 interviews from generals down (or up) to rag-tag soldiers allows readers to come to their own conclusions on what the war was or was not.

A Rumor of War by Philip Caputo. Ballantine, 1977. Caputo went to Vietnam as a young Marine infantry officer in 1965. His book documents his descent from innocence and idealism to disillusionment and despair, all within sixteen months.

Shrapnel in the Heart: Letters and Remembrances from the Vietnam Veterans Memorial by Laura Palmer. Random House, 1987. Palmer was a journalist who covered the war. Afterwards, she gathered 100 letters left at the Vietnam Memorial, traced down the writers, and then interviewed them for her book.

365 Days by Ronald J. Glasser, M. D. Bantam, 1971. Glasser was an Army doctor whose indictment of the war is built on elements of memoir, oral history, and fiction.

10,000 Days of Thunder: A History of the Vietnam War by Philip Caputo. Atheneum, 2005. Photos and maps add to Caputo's account of the war along with a superb bibliography.

Voices from Vietnam by Barry Denenberg. Scholastic, 1995. Anecdotes and horror stories all from Vietnam during the longest war in our history.

What Should We Tell Our Children about Vietnam? by Bill McCloud. University of Oklahoma Press, 1989. McCloud is a junior high social studies teacher who wrote letters to military leaders, ordinary and extraordinary veterans, politicians, protesters, and journalists, asking them to help him decide what to tell his students about Vietnam. The 128 published letters form one of the most readable records of the war.

When I Was a Young Man by Bob Kerry. Harcourt, 2002. An innocent young man sees the Vietnam War as good and patriotic, until on February 25, 1969, he leads his Navy Seal team on a raid into a Vietnamese village and kills thirteen women and children. In the process, he becomes someone he can no longer recognize.

Margaret A. Edwards Award
Winner (1990)
Richard Peck and the Magic of the Journey

Honored books included *Are You in the House Alone?*, *Father Figure*, *The Ghost Belonged to Me*, *Ghosts I Have Been*, *Secrets of the Shopping Mall*, and *Remembering the Good Times.* Since winning the Margaret A. Edwards Award, Peck has written several other wonderful books, including *A Long Way from Chicago* (Dial, 1999) and its follow-up, *A Year Down Yonder* (Dial, 2000), which won the Newbery Medal. These last two books are set during the Depression. Joey and Mary Alice Doudel are young teens who live in Chicago, but for the past few years have traveled by train to spend time during summer vacations with their Grandmother Doudel who lives in a rural area of downstate Illinois. At the height of the Depression in 1937, Joey and Mary Alice's parents are having terrible financial problems, and so, in *A Year Down Yonder*, Joey goes to work in a government-sponsored Civilian Conservation Corps (CCC) camp while Mary Alice is sent by herself (except for her pet cat) to spend a year or more with Grandma Doudel. Even though her coat is ragged and she has come as a kind of charity case, the local kids view her as the rich girl from Chicago, so life isn't easy, but thanks to Grandma Doudel, neither is it boring.

Several years ago when Peck came to Tempe, he spoke to one of our classes at ASU and explained that authors like to write journey stories, not just because the archetypal journey is inherently pleasing, but because such plots provide room for interesting developments as protagonists are removed from their old associates and patterns of life and are challenged by meeting new people and new situations. The two books about Joey and Mary Alice are perfect examples of this. He followed these two books with *Fair Weather* (Dial, 2001), which is a reversal on the idea of city kids going to farm country. In this one a farm family receives a surprising invitation from a rich relative to come to Chicago and attend the 1893 Chicago Columbian Exposition.

In our ASU visit with Peck, he also shared an interesting insight based on a bell curve. He showed how his readers come from the high middle of the curve where lots of kids fit in, but the plots of his stories come from the flat ends of the curve. The most exciting stories are about young people who are "different," people who are doing unusual and out-of-the-ordinary things. When he can, he writes about these "different" characters from the perspective of someone from the middle. For example, in *Don't Look and It Won't Hurt* (Holt, 1999), the story is about a pregnant teenager who is sent away to live in a home for unwed mothers, but it is told through the voice of her sister. In his 2007 *The Wings of Heroes* (Dial, 2007), which is set in the 1940s during WWII, the story is about a soldier going to war, but it is told through the eyes of Davy Bowman, the soldier's younger brother, who is left at home to collect tin cans for shell casings and milkweed for stuffing life jackets.

Peck told Linda Castellitto in a 2003 interview for Book Sense.com that he couldn't imagine writing for young people without having spent several years teaching them. Spending time with junior high readers convinced him that they wouldn't be interested in reading the kind of living autobiography that many first novelists offer the public. He had to go looking for something else, and in a large part that something else has been humor. He told Castellitto that his real goal has been to write a book that would make a teacher "break down and weep with laughter." Of course he wants young readers to laugh too, but he thinks this is a greater challenge because kids aren't used to laughing, except at each other, which is something he has tried to change, especially in his ghost stories and in the ones about Grandma Doudel.

For an example of how Peck combines what he knows about writing with what he knows about teaching, see p. 368 for his list of ten questions—accompanied by Ulterior Motives—to ask students about a book they have read. You might also want to find his 2004 *Past Perfect, Present Tense: New and Collected Stories.* It includes eleven previously published stories and two new ones, along with information and inspiration to help aspiring authors. ●

(*Platoon* in 1986 and *Born on the Fourth of July* in 1989), HBO produced a film version of *Dear America: Letters Home from Vietnam* by Bernard Edelman that works well in class. So does the 1999 *Regret to Inform,* a seventy-two-minute film directed by Barbara Sonneborn. In 1968 her husband was killed in Vietnam. In 1992 she went to Vietnam to document what other war widows—American and Vietnamese—suffered.

Concluding Comments

In historical books, fiction and nonfiction are often so intertwined that it is hard to tell the difference. And rather than naming a discrete genre, *historical fiction* is an umbrella concept covering genres as different as romance, adventure, mystery, humor, and biography. What the writing has in common is that it is set in the past, but this could be as long ago as Jean M. Auel's prehistorical *Clan of the Cave Bear* or as recent as the Vietnam War, as with Walter Dean Myers's *Fallen Angels.* A common topic for historical fiction is that of war; however, in relation to recent wars, readers seem to prefer memoirs and nonfiction accounts, much like the material seen on the History Channel. Another recent trend is for authors to look past the movers and shakers involved in big dramatic events and to focus instead on ordinary people and show how their lives have been affected by natural disasters and by developments and changes in society.

Notes

1. Christopher Collier, "Criteria for Historical Novels," *School Library Journal* 27 (August 1982): 32.
2. Christopher Collier, "Fact, Fiction, and History: The Role of the Historian, Writer, Teacher, and Reader," *ALAN Review* 14 (Winter 1987): 5.
3. Patricia Lee Gauch, "Why Writers Write of War: Looking into the Eye of Historical Fiction," *ALAN Review* 21 (Fall 1993): 13.
4. Cathy MacRae, "The Young Adult Perplex," *Wilson Library Bulletin* 66 (September 1991): 102.
5. James Blasingame, "2001 Honor List: A Vote for Diversity," *English Journal* 92.2 (November, 2001): 128–134.
6. A helpful article to understand the internment of Japanese Americans during World War II is Judith Miller's "Wartime Internment of Japanese Was Grave Injustice, Panel Says," *New York Times,* February 25, 1983, p. 1. For more details, see Roger Daniels, "Incarcerating Japanese Americans," *Magazine of History* 16 (Spring 2002): 19–23, and "Incarceration of Japanese Americans: A Sixty-Year Perspective," *The History Teacher* 35 (May 2002): 297–310. Two helpful books on the subject are Roger Daniels's *Prisoners without Trial: Japanese Americans in World War II* (Hill and Wang, 1993) and Sarah C. Taylor's *Jewel of the Desert: Japanese Intern-*

ment at Topaz (University of California Press, 1993). Two articles by Eugene V. Rostow at the time of the internment are worth reading for background: "The Japanese American Cases—A Disaster," *Yale Law Journal* 54 (July 1945): 480–533, and "Our Worst Wartime Mistake," *Harper's* 191 (August 1945): 193–201.
7. Larry Johannessen's *Illumination Rounds: Teaching the Literature of the Vietnam War* (NCTE, 1992) is an uncommonly helpful source of information on teaching or using material in secondary schools. So are Johannessen's articles, "When History Talks Back: Teaching Nonfiction Literature of the Vietnam War," *English Journal* 91:4 (March, 2002) 39–48; and "Young Adult Literature and the Vietnam War," *English Journal* 82 (September 1993): 43–49. Other good articles are by Perry Oldham, "Some Further Thoughts on Teaching Vietnam Literature," *English Journal* 82 (September 1993): 65–67; Christie N. Bradley, "Teaching Our Longest War: Constructive Views from Vietnam," *English Journal* 78 (April 1989): 35–38; and Frank A. Wilcox, "Pedagogical Implications of Teaching Literature of the Vietnam War," *Social Education* 52 (January 1988): 39–40.

Nonfiction
Information, Literary Nonfiction, Biographies, and Self-Help Books

chapter 9

If you are studying this textbook in the order that it is written, then you have already come in contact with several kinds of nonfiction. In the first chapter, Focus Box 1.1 lists memoirs by authors whose books, or memoirs, have found their way to our Honor List. And in Chapter 3, many of the books listed as coming from "Teen Voices" are first-person accounts of young people's experiences and feelings. And in a technical sense, the poetry and drama discussed in Chapter 5, along with much of the humor, is nonfiction, as are many of the historical books and the memoirs discussed in Chapter 8. In this chapter, we will look at four major categories of nonfiction: information books, literary nonfiction, biographies, and self-help books.

While fiction usually gets the lion's share of attention when it comes to reviewing and recommending books for teenagers, in libraries and schools, nonfiction gets the lion's share of the budget. Many adults go for years without reading a novel or even a short story, but virtually everyone reads nonfiction whether in newspapers, magazines, on the Internet, or on a cereal box. The March 2002 issue of *English Journal* had as its theme "The Truth about Nonfiction." Paul Hirth wrote the introductory piece in which he defended what Louise Rosenblatt labels *efferent* reading as compared to *aesthetic* reading. English teachers usually feel more inspired or more challenged when they focus on aesthetics, but he thinks it can be just as satisfying to help students revel in the "joy of facts" and the "poetry of prose." Teachers scoff, he says, because they think students "are already versed in reading for the literal." But he knows that students need help in reading for irony, in recognizing the subtleties of an argument, and applying facts and details to the development and interpretation of thought.

Hirth likes to pair nonfiction pieces with fiction. For example, Julius Lester's essay "Huckleberry Finn" from *Falling Pieces of the Broken Sky* is a good way to help students understand the controversial nature of Twain's book. Rollo May's *The Cry for Myth* has a wonderful section on *The Great Gatsby*. Other writers whose nonfiction he likes to bring to his students include Annie Dillard, Stephen J. Gould, Anne Morrow Lindbergh, Neil Postman, Richard Selzer, Susan Sontag, George Will, and Gary Wills, along with that of major columnists in magazines and newspapers. "Too often," Hirth says, teachers "begin with the assumption that students can't or won't read anything with a text more demanding than a billboard, yet they seem to devour the Internet with ease." He concluded that "just as the study of fiction, drama, and poetry help students explore their thoughts and feelings, nonfiction can offer a reality check—a second opinion, if you will," with which students, and their teachers, can measure their individual responses.[1]

Information Books

When the American Library Association made history by awarding its coveted 1988 Newbery Medal to Russell Freedman's *Lincoln: A Photobiography*, Milton Meltzer, who has long championed the cause of nonfiction, applauded by saying,

> It was a terrific thing to do, but it took fifty years to do it. The few books they gave prizes to before, that were called nonfiction, really were not. Instead, they were books written in the outmoded vein of biography that was highly fictionalized, had invented dialogue, and sometimes concocted scenes. That's all changed today, but it took a long time.[2]

In their *Nonfiction for Young Adults: From Delight to Wisdom*, Betty Carter and Richard F. Abrahamson cited twenty-two research studies. Among the reported findings:

- An interest in reading nonfiction emerges at about the fourth grade and grows during adolescence.
- Interest in reading nonfiction crosses ability levels; one study showed that nonfiction made up 34 percent of the leisure reading of academically able teenagers and 54 percent of the control group's leisure reading.
- Nonfiction makes up a much larger proportion of boys' reading than of girls' reading.
- One study categorized the seven most popular types of nonfiction as cartoon and comic books, weird-but-true stories, rock stars, ghosts, magic, stories about famous people, and explorations of the unknown.
- Remedial readers prefer informative nonfiction and read "primarily to learn new things."
- Students choose nonfiction for a variety of reasons often unrelated to school curricular matters.

As shown by this booth at an International Reading Association convention, reading teachers and publishers are beginning to pay more attention to what it takes to read and understand nonfiction.

- When students gave reasons for reading particular books, it became clear that the purpose of the reading is guided more by the student than by the type of book. One boy read books on subjects he already knew about because it made him feel smart; others preferred how-to books so that they could interact with the author while learning to draw, care for a pet, program a computer, make a paper airplane, and so on; and still others preferred *The Guinness Book of World Records*. Even here purposes differed. Some read the book to discover amazing facts, but others read it to imagine themselves undergoing strange experiences.

Students are sometimes seeking the kinds of information that can supplement what they are learning in school as in Ann Bausum's *With Courage and Cloth: Winning the Fight for a Woman's Right to Vote*, or if they want something closer to their own lives, they will pick up Jacqui Bailey's *Sex, Puberty and All That Stuff: A Guide to Growing Up*. Other times they might just want to feel mystified and so will pick up Judy Allen's *Unexplained: An Encyclopedia of Curious Phenomena, Strange Superstitions, and Ancient Mysteries* or some of the other books listed in Focus Box 9.1, Intriguing Facts.

And just as students have various reasons for seeking out different kinds of nonfiction, authors also have various reasons for choosing the topics they write about. See James Cross Giblin's comments on p. 281.

Narrative or Storytelling in Nonfiction

When Thomas Keneally's 1982 *Schindler's List* won a Pulitzer Prize in fiction, there was considerable controversy over whether the book was eligible because it was supposedly a journalistic account of a true event. E. L. Doctorow spoke to the same issue when he said in his acceptance speech for the National

Intriguing Facts

Alone in the World: Orphans and Orphanages in America by Catherine Reef. Clarion, 2005. Reef's informative and well-done book takes up where the accounts of orphan trains leave off. Relatively few children were sent on orphan trains; the others lived in poorhouses or almshouses right next to criminals and people judged to be insane.

An Inconvenient Truth: The Crisis of Global Warming by Al Gore, adapted by Jane O'Connor. Viking/Rodale, 2007. O'Connor's book is much shorter than the adult version, but it preserves the message, as well as many of its striking visuals.

Behind the Mask of Spider-Man: The Secrets of the Movie by Mark Cotta Vaz. Ballantine, 2002. Photos and production drawings add interest to this intriguing look at both the human and the technological challenges faced by the producers and the actors of the blockbuster movie.

Black and White Airmen: Their True History by John Fleischman. Houghton Mifflin, 2007. John Leahr was black and Herb Heilbrun was white in a time when racism was rampant. They grew up together and went into the WW II Air Force, successfully flying fifty missions as partners. Theirs is only one of the many fascinating stories about black and white airmen fighting together after Pearl Harbor.

Body Marks: Tattooing, Piercing, and Scarifying by Kathlyn Gay and Christine Whittington. 21st Century Books, 2002. One of the most interesting parts of this 112-page book is its explanation of how body markings both separate and unite cultures and generations.

Chew on This: Everything You Don't Want to Know about Fast Food by Eric Schlosser and Charles Wilson. Houghton Mifflin, 2006. Schlosser and Wilson give colorful stories, photographs, anecdotes and other eye-opening information to explain such slogans as "supersize me," "have it your way," and "everything you don't want to know about fast food."

Hurricane Force: Tracking America's Killer Storms by Joseph B. Treaster. New York Times, 2007. Treaster starts with the Galveston storm in 1900 and goes through Katrina and Rita in 2005.

Quotations for Kids, edited and compiled by J. A. Senn, illustrated by Steve Pica. Millbrook, 1999. Humorous full-color cartoons add interest to over 2,000 quotations in this 256-page book.

Skyscraper by Lynn Curlee. Atheneum, 2007. Dramatic acrylic illustrations and lucid prose tell the history of skyscrapers.

Steven Caney's Ultimate Building Book by Steven Caney, illustrated by Lauren House. Running Press, 2006. *Building* is examined in its broadest sense, encompassing everything from skyscrapers and bridges to bird feeders and peanut-shell "bricks."

Tracking Trash: Flotsam, Jetsam, and the Science of Ocean Motion by Loree Griffin Burns. Houghton Mifflin, 2007. Burns shows how currents, weather, climate, and the environment are interrelated. Read this book if you want to find out about ghost nets, nurdles, and the differences between flotsam, jetsam, plankton, ice floes, and other debris.

Who Was First? Discovering the Americas by Russell Freedman. Clarion, 2007. Freedman is the consummate researcher and his stories about Christopher Columbus, Chinese treasure-ships, and the wanderings of Leif Eriksson and the Vikings, along with clues about the origins of the first Native Americans, may inspire young readers to share his enthusiasm for researching historical mysteries.

Book Critics Circle Award for *Ragtime,* "There is no more fiction or nonfiction, only narrative."

Three hundred English teachers who responded to a survey asking for ten adolescent novels and ten adult novels worthy of recommendation to teenagers gave further evidence that in people's minds fiction and nonfiction are blending together. Among twenty nonfiction titles recommended as novels were Piers Paul Read's *Alive,* James Herriot's *All Creatures Great and Small,* Robin Graham's *Dove,* Peter Maas's *Serpico,* Doris Lund's *Eric,* Alvin Toffler's *Future Shock,* Maya Angelou's *I Know Why the Caged Bird Sings,* Dee Brown's *Bury My Heart*

Young Adult Authors Speak Out

James Cross Giblin **on an Author's Motivations**

In question-and-answer sessions, authors are almost always asked where they get their ideas. I think a more interesting question is, "Why did you want to write this book?" For ideas often come easily, and many are discarded along the way. But strong motivations are what keep authors going during the weeks, months, and years it takes to research and write a young adult nonfiction book.

For example, if you asked me where I got the idea to write *The Life and Death of Adolf Hitler*, which won the 2003 Robert F. Sibert Informational Book Award, I'm not sure I could tell you. Frankly, I don't remember. But if you asked me *why* I wanted to write a YA biography of Hitler, I could give you lots of reasons.

I was in elementary school during World War II, and the image of Hitler was all around me—in movie newsreels, on recruiting posters, and on the covers of weekly news-magazines. In almost all of them, he was portrayed as a raving monster, foaming at the mouth, and barking out commands.

Even as a boy, I found these portrayals hard to accept. Too often they made Hitler seem funny rather than frightening. I knew that wasn't a true picture because I'd read a lot of articles about his brutal actions during the war. (I hadn't heard about the Holocaust yet; its horrors weren't revealed until the war's end, in 1945.)

Years later, when I told friends I was planning a biography of Hitler, they almost invariably asked, "Why would you want to write about such a monster?" I had an answer ready: "I don't believe any human being is born a monster. So how and why did Hitler become one? That's what intrigues me—and that's what I want to try to find out."

There you have it: the chief motivation that got me started on in-depth research for *The Life and Death of Adolf Hitler* and that sustained me during the three years I spent writing and rewriting the manuscript, and gathering the more than eighty historical photographs that illustrate the book.

Did I succeed in my goal? Did I finally unearth the roots of Hitler's evil behavior—those dark elements in his nature that made him launch World War II and keep on spreading destruction long after it was clear Germany had been defeated? What fed his irrational hatred of the Jews and led him to seek their extermination?

Probably not—but I'm not sure anyone could. None of the authors of adult books about Hitler that I read felt they had arrived at a final, definitive portrait of the Nazi leader. The man often seemed mediocre, yet he was capable of the most enormous crimes. The usual rules of cause-and-effect didn't seem to apply.

Still, I did feel I had laid out Hitler's character and actions in a way that would hold the interest of young readers and provoke some stimulating discussions. That goal has been a key motivating factor behind all my young adult nonfiction books, and never more so than in the case of the Hitler biography.

It dismays me when I read of studies that say young people today find history boring and unrelated to their lives. Nothing could be further from the truth. As I point out in the book, another Hitler—another ruthless, power-mad leader with a destructive vision—might easily arise today or in the future if the social and political conditions are right and if the public has failed to learn the lessons of the past.

I've loved history since I was a boy in Ohio, trying to understand what was happening in World War II. Through my books, I hope to inspire the same sort of love in my readers. Nothing makes me happier than to get a letter from one of those readers, asking me thoughtful questions about Hitler or one of the other historical figures I've portrayed. Such letters provide stronger confirmation than even the most glowing reviews that I've achieved my goal.

- James Cross Giblin's other young adult nonfiction titles include *Good Brother, Bad Brother: The Story of Edwin Booth and John Wilkes Booth* (Clarion, 2005), *The Mystery of the Mammoth Bones, and How It Was Solved* (HarperCollins, 1999), *Charles A. Lindbergh, a Human Hero* (Clarion, 1997), and *When Plague Strikes: The Black Death, Smallpox, AIDS* (HarperCollins, 1995).

Matching fiction and nonfiction on the same subject adds to the value of each. Here is Michael L. Cooper's Fighting for Honor: Japanese Americans and World War II *and Cynthia Kadohata's* Weedflower, *about a Japanese American girl from California whose family is sent to the Poston internment camp in Arizona.*

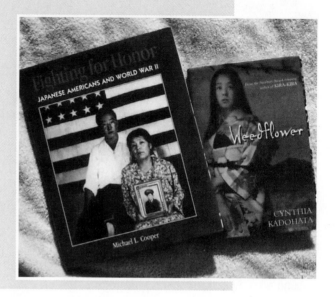

at Wounded Knee, Claude Brown's *Manchild in the Promised Land,* Eldridge Cleaver's *Soul on Ice,* and John H. Griffin's *Black Like Me.*

The blending of fiction and nonfiction has occurred from both directions. On one side are the nonfiction writers who use the techniques of fiction, including suspense, careful plotting and characterization, and literary devices, such as symbolism and metaphor. At the beginning of *Izzy, Willy-Nilly,* Cynthia Voigt acknowledged help from medical personnel who taught her about physical and mental aspects of amputation. And in *A Single Shard,* it is obvious that Linda Sue Park has done extensive research on celadon pottery.

Good novels are fiction in the sense that fictional names are used and they combine bits and pieces of many individual stories. Nevertheless, in another sense, these stories are more real and actually present a more honest portrayal than some pieces labeled nonfiction that are true accounts of bizarre or strange happenings.

Literature—fiction and nonfiction—is more than a simple recounting or replaying of the life that surrounds the writer. It is a distillation and a crystallization. Only when an author skillfully chooses descriptive details and develops believable dialogue does an account of an actual event become real to the reader. Alex Haley's *Roots* became real to millions of television viewers as well as to millions of readers, yet the book contains many fictional elements in both subject matter and presentation. Part of Haley's success comes from his ability to select powerful incidents and details. Good writers of nonfiction do not simply record everything they know or can uncover. With Haley's book, readers' imaginations were captured by the fact that on September 29, 1967, he "stood on the dock in Annapolis where his great-great-great-great-great-grandfather was taken ashore on September 29, 1767," and sold as a slave to a Virginia plantation owner. From this point, Haley set out to trace backward the six generations that connected him to a sixteen-year-old "prince" newly arrived from Africa. What the public might not stop to consider as they read about this dramatic incident is that it is setting the stage for only a small portion of Haley's "roots." In the generation in which Haley started his story with the young couple, Omoro and Binta Kinte, and the birth of their first son, Kunta, there were 256 parents giving birth to 128 children, each one of whom is also a great-great-great-great-great-grandfather or grandmother to Alex Haley. The point is that even though Haley was writing nonfiction, he had an almost unlimited range of possibilities from which to choose, and he made his choices with the instinct of a storyteller rather than a clerk, who might have put together a more complete but less interesting family history.

New Journalism

Roots is part of the genre sometimes labelled *new journalism*. Truman Capote called it the "most avant-garde form of writing existent today" and coined the term *nonfiction novel* for *In Cold Blood*, an account of an especially brutal murder and the subsequent trial. Other terms that are used include *creative nonfiction*, *literary journalism*, *journalistic fiction*, and *advocacy journalism*. Although its roots were growing right along with journalism in general, it did not begin to flower until the 1950s and 1960s. Part of the reason for its development is the increased educational level of the American public. Newspaper readers and television viewers, including young adults, are not satisfied with simplistic explanations. They want enough background information that they can feel confident in coming to their own conclusions.

Affluence, combined with modern technology, helps make the new journalism possible. Compare similar incidents that happened 126 years apart. In 1846, a group of travelers who came to be known as the Donner party were trapped in the high Sierras by an early snow. They had to stay there all winter without food except for the flesh of their dead companions. After they were rescued, word of their ordeal gradually trickled back east, so that for years afterward sensationalized accounts were made up by writers who had no chance to come to the scene or interview the survivors.

In 1972, a planeload of Uruguayan travelers crashed in the Andes mountains. As in the Donner party, some people knew each other before the trip, but others were strangers. During the terrible weeks of waiting to be rescued, they all got to know each other and to develop intense relationships revolving around leadership roles and roles of rebellion or giving up. They endured unspeakable hardships. Many died; those who lived did so because they ate the flesh of those who died. In this situation, however, the people were rescued by helicopters after two of the men made their way out of the mountains. Word of their 2 1/2-month ordeal was flashed around the world, and by the time the sixteen survivors, mostly members of a rugby team, had been flown back to Uruguay, reporters from many nations were there. A press conference was held, and the journalists were told about the cannibalism.

This was the second surprise in the story. The first had been their survival. The drama of the situation naturally fired imaginations all around the world. Lippincott suggested to author Piers Paul Read that this was the kind of story that would make a good book. He went to Uruguay, where he stayed for several months interviewing survivors, rescuers, family, and friends of both the deceased and the survivors, and the government officials who had been in charge of the search. More than a year later, Lippincott published *Alive: The Story of the Andes Survivors*, which was on the *New York Times* best-seller list for seven months, was made into a movie, and will probably continue to be read by young adults for the next several years, both in and out of school.

The fact that the survivors were in their early twenties undoubtedly helps teenagers to identify with the story, but so do the literary techniques that Read used. He focused on certain individuals, presenting miniature character sketches of some and fully developed portraits of others. The setting was crucial to the story, and he described it vividly. He was also careful to write so that the natural suspense of the situation came through. His tone was consistent throughout the book. He admired the survivors but did not shy away from showing the negative aspects of human nature when it is sorely tried. In a preface he said that the only liberty he allowed himself was the creation of dialogue between the characters, although, whenever possible, he relied on diaries and remembered comments and quarrels as well as his acquaintance with the speaking styles of the survivors.

"New journalism" combines factual information with emotional appeal. Such books might be classified as biography, history, drama, essay, or personal experience, but regardless of classification, they serve as a bridge between childhood and adult reading because of the straightforward, noncondescending style that is characteristic of good journalism.

Nonfiction best sellers often outsell fiction best sellers, and television producers have learned the appeal of "reality" shows and they know they can add millions of viewers if they advertise a program as "a documentary" rather than "a drama."

Even the success of the tabloids depends on their nonfiction format. The majority of readers do not really believe all those stories about Elvis Presley still being alive or about women giving birth to aliens or apricot pits curing cancer; yet, for the fun of it they are willing to give themselves over to a momentary suspension of disbelief, something we used to talk about mainly in relation to fantasy and science fiction.

Evaluation of Nonfiction

Evaluating nonfiction for young readers is more complicated than evaluating fiction because

1. People select informational books primarily on the basis of the subject matter, and because there is such a variety in subjects, people's choices vary tremendously, resulting in a lack of consensus on what is "the best."

2. Informative books on such topics as computers and car repair become dated more quickly than fiction books. Students preparing to take the SAT tests, wanting advice on handling money, or planning for a career need the most recent information. The constant turnover of informative books leaves us with few touchstone examples.

3. The transitory nature of informative nonfiction books discourages teachers and critics from giving them serious consideration as instructional materials. Although well-written personal experience narratives have

longer life spans, people who have made up their minds that they are not interested in nonfiction find it easy to ignore all nonfiction.

4. Reviewers and prize givers may not feel competent to judge the technical or other specialized information presented in many informative books. Also, many reviewers, especially those working with educational journals, come from an English-teaching tradition, and they tend to focus on books that would be used in conjunction with literature rather than biology, home economics, social studies, industrial arts, history, or business classes.

5. In evaluating nonfiction, there is no generally agreed-upon theory of criticism or criteria for judgment.

We suggest that the evaluation situation can be improved by readers looking at the intended audience and the content of the book. (What is it about? What information does it present?) Then look at the appropriateness and success with which each of the following is established. Examining a nonfiction book carefully enough to be able to describe the setting or scope and the theme, tone, and style will give you insights into how well it is written and packaged. Also, for information books, look at the more specific suggestions in Table 9.1.

Setting/Scope   Informative books may be historical, restricted to regional interests, or have a limited scope. In evaluating these, one needs to ask whether the author set realistic goals, considering the reading level of the intended audience and the amount of space and backup graphics available.

Theme   Informational books also have themes or purposes that are closely tied to the author's point of view. Authors may write in hopes of persuading someone to a particular belief or to inspire thoughtfulness, respect, or even curiosity. Some authors shout out their themes; others are more subtle. You need to consider consistency as you evaluate the theme. Did the author build on a consistent theme throughout the book?

Tone   The manner in which an author achieves a desired goal—whether it is to persuade, inform, inspire, or amuse—sets the tone of a book. Is it hard-sell, strident, one-sided, humorous, loving, sympathetic, adulatory, scholarly, pedantic, energetic, or leisurely? Authors of informative books for children used to take a leisurely approach as they tried to entice children into becoming interested in their subject. Today's young readers, however, are just as busy as their parents and most likely go to informative books for quick information rather than leisure time entertainment. A boy or girl who wants to repair a bicycle does not want to read the history of the Wright brothers and their bicycle shop before getting to the part on slipped gears.

Style   The best informative books also have style. As author Jane Langton said when she was asked to serve as a judge, the good books "exude some kind of passion or love or caring . . . and they have the potential for leaving a mark on the readers, changing them in some way."[3] George A. Woods, former children's editor of the *New York Times Book Review,* said that he selected the informational books to be featured in his reviews mostly on his own "gut-level" reactions to what was "new or far better than what we have

TABLE 9.1 Suggestions for Evaluating Informative Nonfiction

A good piece of informative writing usually has:	A poor piece of informative writing may have:
A subject of interest to young readers, written about with zest. Information that is up-to-date and accurate.	Obsolete or inaccurate information or illustrations. Even one such occurrence causes the reader to lose faith in the rest of the book.
New information or information organized in such a way as to present a different point of view than in previously available books.	Evidence of cutting-and-pasting in which the author merely reorganized previously prepared material without developing anything new in content or viewpoint.
A reading level, vocabulary, and tone of writing that are at a consistent level appropriate to the intended audience.	Inconsistencies in style or content, for example, college-level vocabulary but a childish or cute style of writing.
An organization in which basic information is presented first so that chapters and sections build on each other.	An awkward mix of fiction and nonfiction techniques through which the author unsuccessfully tries to slip information in as an unnoticed part of the story.
An index and other aids to help readers look up facts if they want to return to the book for specific information or to glean ideas and facts without reading the entire book.	A reflection of out-of-date or socially unfair attitudes, for example, a history book that presents only the history of white upper-class men with a title and introduction that give the impression that it is a comprehensive history of the time period being covered.
Adequate documentation of the sources of information, including some original sources.	A biased presentation in which only one side of a controversial issue is presented with little or no acknowledgment that many people hold different viewpoints.
Information to help interested students locate further readings on the subject.	In how-to books, frustrating directions that oversimplify or set up unrealistic expectations so that the reader is disappointed in the result.
In how-to books, clear and accurate directions including complete lists of the equipment and supplies needed in a project.	
Illustrations that add interest as well as clarity to the text.	
A competent author with expertise in the subject matter.	

had before." He looked for a majesty of language and uniqueness and for books that would add to children's understanding by making them eyewitnesses to history.[4] A problem in examining an author's style is that each book must be judged according to the purpose the author had in mind. From book to book, purposes are so different that it is like the old problem of comparing apples and oranges. Some books are successful simply because they are different—more like a mango than an apple or an orange.

Contemporary Influences on the Publishing of Informational Books

Before the 1950s, what was published for young readers was in the main fiction (novels or short stories), poetry, or textbook material to be used in school. Few publishers thought that young readers would be interested in factual books unless they were forced to study them as part of their schoolwork. Then the Russians launched Sputnik, and Americans were sincerely frightened that Russia was scientifically and technologically ahead. In 1961, Congress passed the National

Defense Education Act, which gave millions of dollars to school libraries for the purchase of science and math books (later expanded to include all books). Publishers competed to create informative books that would qualify for purchase under the Act and would attract young readers.

The rise in the popularity of nonfiction has paralleled the information explosion and the rise in the power and influence of the mass media. Today there is simply more information to be shared between reader and writer. Television, radio, movies, newspapers, magazines, and now the Internet all communicate the same kinds of information as do books, but people expect more from books because the other media are limited in the amount of space and time that they can devote to information on any one topic. Moreover, whatever is produced by the mass media must be of interest to a *mass* audience, whereas individual readers select books. Of course, publishers want masses of individual readers to select their books. Nevertheless, there is more room for experimentation and the development of minority viewpoints in books than in the kinds of media that are supported by advertisers and that, therefore, must aim to attract the largest possible audience.

Many writers take the same subjects that are treated on television and write about them in more detail or from unexpected viewpoints. They try to answer the questions that cursory news reports do not have time or space to probe. (For example, see Focus Box 9.2, Careers.) Readers also have more faith in books than in news stories that are necessarily put together overnight or in Internet stories for which it is often impossible to check the sources.

Need for Scientific Literacy

At a meeting of the Conference on College Composition and Communication in St. Louis, science writer Jon Franklin spoke on a panel entitled "Nonfiction: The Genre of a Technological Age." Formerly a science writer for the *Evening Sun* in Baltimore and now a teacher of journalism at the University of Maryland in College Park, Franklin's topic was "Literary Structure: A Growing Force in Science Journalism." He pointed out how in the past decade, more than half the winners of the Pulitzer Prize in nonfiction had been science books and how the increasingly important role of scientific writing in newspapers and magazines is changing basic concepts of journalism. The upside-down pyramid, in which the key points are stated first with the details being filled in later so an editor can cut the story whenever the available space is filled, does not work for science writing because it results in oversimplification. Science stories have to be written inductively, building from the small to the large points because most scientific developments and concepts are too complex for readers to understand unless they get the supporting details first.

Franklin worries about the development of a new kind of elitism based on scientific literacy. He says that if people feel uncomfortable with scientific writing, they are likely to resent and reject scientific concepts. He gives as an example the censorship battles that have developed over beliefs in creationism versus evolution. He proposes a two-pronged approach to keep the gap from widening between the scientifically literate and those who reject all science. On the one hand, science writers have to work harder to find organizational patterns and

Air Force One: The Aircraft That Shaped the Modern Presidency by Von Hardesty. NorthWord, 2003. The curator of the Smithsonian National Air and Space Museum prepared this attractive book about what it takes to keep the president's airplane in the air. Eleanor Roosevelt was the first to use an airplane, which was named *Guess Where II.*

Bones Rock! Everything You Need to Know to Be a Paleontologist by Peter Larson and Kristin Donnan. Invisible Cities, 2004. New technologies, scientific methods and equipment, have changed the business of hunting fossils. Color photos and personal stories show the best sides of this profession.

Built to Last: Building America's Amazing Bridges, Dams, Tunnels, and Skyscrapers by George Sullivan. Scholastic, 2005. Starting with the building of the Erie Canal and ending with the New York City Tunnel, which will not be finished until 2020, Sullivan pays tribute to the builders while sharing anecdotes showing that they are human.

Count on Us: American Women in the Military by Amy Nathan. National Geographic, 2004. The time period ranges from the American Revolutionary War to the invasion of Iraq. The author neither glorifies the roles that women have played nor glosses over such challenges as sexual harassment.

ER Vets: Life in an Animal Emergency Room by Donna M. Jackson. Houghton, 2005. Animal lovers who have romantic fantasies of saving beautiful pets for grateful people, will come away from Jackson's book with a more balanced view of what's possible and what isn't. Jackson took her material from an emergency animal hospital in Colorado.

Healing Our World: Inside Doctors Without Borders by David Morley. Fitzhenry and Whiteside, 2007. The Canadian director of Doctors without Borders between 1998 and 2005 wrote this insider account of the organization. The first part is made up of general information while the second part is excerpted journal entries written during work in various disaster areas.

Hurricane Force: Tracking America's Killer Storms by Joseph B. Treaster. New York Times, 2007. Using books, source notes, and personal experiences as a reporter for the *New York Times* in South Florida,

Treaster shows readers what it takes to track storms and get paid for it.

In Their Shoes: Extraordinary Women Describe Their Amazing Careers by Deborah Reber. S/Pulse, 2007. This is a fun and accessible book for teenage girls who are exploring career possibilities. It includes interviews, sidebars, and lists on how to prepare and what an average day is like.

Let Me Play: The Story of Title IX: The Law that Changed the Future of Girls in America by Karen Blumenthal. S&S/Atheneum, 2005. A law that started as almost an accident really has made a profound difference in the lives of America's young women. Blumenthal's take on the matter is shown both through facts and human interest stories.

Looking for Seabirds: Journal from an Alaskan Voyage by Sophie Webb, illustrated by the author. Houghton, 2004. Readers go with this artist/biologist on a monthlong springtime voyage through the Aleutian Islands. Her 2000 book *My Season with Penguins* is equally well done.

The North Pole Was Here: Puzzles and Perils at the Top of the World by Andrew C. Revkin. New York Times, 2006. Revkin is a *New York Times* reporter who accompanied modern day scientists to the top of the world. His book tells not only the contemporary story, but also those of previous explorers as it introduces readers to what climatologists and oceanographers do.

Out-of-This-World Astronomy: 50 Amazing Activities and Projects by Joe Rhatigan and Rain Newcomb. Sterling/Lark, 2003. Middle school students are the ones most likely to be enthusiastic about the ideas and the projects and to appreciate the readable text and the spectacular color photos.

Prairie Grasslands and *Rocky Mountains* by Wayne Lynch. NorthWord, 2006. These books show the interconnectedness of the climate, soil, plants, and animals and the intricate adaptations of living things to their surroundings. Wetlands, badlands, grasslands, mountains, and other ecosystems are all discussed

The Tarantula Scientist by Sy Montgomery, photos by Nic Bishop. Houghton, 2004. The focus is more on tarantulas than on scientists, but still the book introduces readers to what arachnologists do. Excellent photos add interest.

literary techniques that make their material understandable and interesting. On the other hand, schools must bring the reading of technological and scientific information into the curriculum with the goal of preparing students to balance their lifetime reading.

Books to Support and Extend the School Curriculum

Informational books purchased by school libraries are usually referred to as "books to support the curriculum," but a more accurate description would probably be "books to extend the curriculum." These books seldom help students who are doing poorly in class. Instead, they provide challenges for successful students to go further than their classmates. They also serve as models for research, and they go beyond the obvious facts to present information that is too complicated, too detailed, too obscure, or too controversial to be included in textbooks. A legitimate complaint often voiced about history books is that they focus on war and violence and leave out life as it was lived by most people. Another complaint is that they leave out the experiences of women and minorities. For example, school history textbooks do not mention contraception, but nothing has changed women's lives more than the birth control pill. Well-written and well-illustrated trade books serve as a counterbalance to these omissions.

Teenagers are especially interested in books that present the extremes of life's experiences, which is why various editions and adaptations of *The Guinness Book of World Records* remain popular. Whatever is the biggest, the best, or the most unusual is of interest.

A good example is the *Junior Chronicle of the 20th Century*. In 336 oversized pages, each including several full-color photographs, the editors give the major events of each year. They were clever in finding at least one youth-oriented photo for each double-page spread.

Succinctness and easy accessibility are also selling points when encouraging teenagers to dip into collections of essays as opposed to books that need to be read in their entirety. Students who have enjoyed Robert Cormier's fiction might look on his *I Have Words to Spend: Reflections of a Small-Town Editor* as a chance to share thoughts with the kind of uncle or grandfather they wish they had been lucky enough to have. Teenagers can also enjoy Russell Baker's, Erma Bombeck's, and Andy Rooney's collections of newspaper columns.

Space in this text allows us to present only a sample of the many books available as companion reading, or even replacement reading, for typical textbooks (Focus Boxes 9.3, 9.4, and 9.5 provide some suggestions). When selecting such books, librarians and teachers should remember that teenagers most often pick them up to find specific information. Because young readers lack the kind of background knowledge that most adults have, it is especially important that informative books be well organized and indexed in such a way that readers can look up facts without reading the whole book. Unclear references or confusing directions are especially troublesome in how-to books, which range from books as practical and personal as Ron Volpe's *The Lady Mechanic's Total Car Care for*

American Popular Culture, 4 Volumes, edited by M. Thomas Inge and Dennis Hall. Greenwood Press, 2002. All aspects of American popular culture are investigated including almanacs, amusement parks, fairs, architecture, automobiles, books, business, politics, social customs, ethnic differences, music, museums, newspapers, magazines, movies, games, and toys—just to name a few.

Artist to Artist: 23 Major Illustrators Talk to Children about Their Art, by Eric Carle. Philomel, 2007. Let's hope that the word *children* in the title will not turn teen readers away from this collection of some of the best known picture book art explained and commented on by the artists themselves. The work was mostly taken from the Eric Carle Museum.

Cave Paintings to Picasso: The Inside Scoop on 50 Art Masterpieces by Henry Sayre. Chronicle, 2004. The paintings range from cave drawings dated 22,000 BC to Rene Magritte's *The Son of Man*, painted in 1964. Each one is explained and set in its own time period as well as charted on an overall timeline.

Don't Hold Me Back: My Life and Art written and illustrated by Winfred Rembert. Cricket/Marcato, 2003. The title comes from a Nikki Giovanni poem written for Rembert, who grew up in the segregated rural South of the 1950s and did not begin painting until the 1990s. He paints on leather, which increases the depth and tone of his work.

Extraordinary Ordinary People: Five American Masters of Traditional Arts by Alan Govenar. Candlewick, 2006. The photos in Govenar's beautifully designed book help readers feel they really know these unusual artists, who include a Mardi Gras performer, a wax-flower maker, a weaver, a boat builder, and a singer with the Bejing Opera.

Harlem Stomp! A Cultural History of the Harlem Renaissance by Laban Carrick Hill. Little, Brown/Megan Tingley Books, 2004. It is refreshing to find a history book that focuses not on conflicts and wars but on creativity in literature, drama, and the arts. Photos and reproductions add to the satisfying result.

Jazz A B Z: An A to Z Collection of Jazz Portraits by Wynton Marsalis, illustrated by Paul Rogers. Candlewick, 2005. This three-in-one (poetry, music, and modern art) book should please lots of readers. It is a joy to look at, plus it can be read aloud with all the rhythm and vigor of slam poetry.

Salvador Dalí and the Surrealists: Their Lives and Ideas; 21 Activities by Michael Elsohn Ross. Chicago Review, 2003. Other artists whose work is featured and explained in this handsome book include Miró, Éluard, and Picasso. Explanations and activities will help young readers understand Cubism, Abstract Expressionism, and Pop Art, along with their historical backgrounds.

Wake Up Our Souls: A Celebration of Black American Artists by Tonya Bolden. Abrams, 2004. The Smithsonian Art Museum helped compile this interesting and beautifully laid out book. Bolden does a good job of presenting historical backgrounds and explaining the role that artists played in the Civil Rights movement.

Websites that students might enjoy are the American Dialect Society, http://americandialect.org, which discusses how and why new words are coming into the language. The group annually chooses a word of the year in different categories. The Discovery Channel, http://dsc.discovery.com/, is also interesting.

---

the Clueless to such an ambitious social action book as Arlene Hirschfelder's *Kick Butts! A Kid's Action Guide to a Tobacco-Free America.*

How-to books are seldom best sellers, simply because they are so specialized that they appeal to fairly limited audiences. The challenge for the teacher or librarian is to let students know about their availability. Once students find their way into the library to check out a book that helps them accomplish a particular goal, they are likely to return for other books. If they are disappointed by ambiguous or hard-to-understand directions or come-on statements that make projects look easier than they are, they may lose interest in both the project and the library.

With sports books, obviously the first thing a reader looks for is the particular sport; consequently, authors choose titles that practically shout to potential readers. The sports books that stand out from the crowd, as with those discussed in Chapter 6, usually have a believable and likable personality behind them. Many such books are inspirational as much as instructive, but one thing to watch for in a how-to sports book is whether costs are mentioned. It is almost cruel for an author to write a glowing account of a child star in tennis, gymnastics, skating, swimming, or dancing and leave young readers with the impression that all it takes is hard work. Those readers whose parents do not have time or money for transportation, lessons, entry fees, equipment, and clothes should be let in on the secret that there's more to how you play the game than meets the eye. A similar warning needs to be given about books telling kids how to establish their own businesses or how to get into show business. Such wish-fulfilling books about unusual successes are likely to set the stage for disappointment among the thousands of more typical kids who find themselves working in fast-food restaurants or as grocery store courtesy clerks for minimum wages. There's a need for more books about these less glamorous jobs as well as for the kind of commonsense guidance found in Neale S. Godfrey's *Godfrey's Ultimate Kid's Money Book*.

For academically inclined high school students, it is important to bring books about college to their attention early on because the actual application process takes eighteen months, and its success or failure may depend on what classes a student took as a freshman. High school libraries should have recent editions of such books as *The Fiske Guide to Colleges* and the Princeton Review's guide to *Visiting College Campuses* as well as various practice books designed to help students do well on admissions examinations.

Books helping students plan their future careers are equally important. As with sports-related books, the ones that are the most fun to read are biographical or personal experience accounts, such as those written by James Herriot on his veterinary practice or by Farley Mowat on being a naturalist. For more complete information on a wider range of jobs, see the *Careers without College* series from Peterson's Guides, the *Career Horizons* books from VGM, and the *Careers and Opportunities* series from Rosen.

Memoirs and Personal Experiences

The best memoir that we have read in the last few years is Jack Gantos's *Hole in My Life* which was a runner-up for the 2002 Printz Award. As shown by the smoothness and the power of the writing, Gantos has written this story probably dozens of times, if not on paper, at least in his head. It is an account of the fifteen months he spent in a federal prison between high school and college. He had helped to sail a boatload of hashish from the Virgin Islands to New York City, where he used a shopping cart to make the deliveries that his employers, Ken and Hamilton, had set up. As Jack explains one morning after the ritual head-count at the prison,

I was in. Counted in. After breakfast I was counted. Before dinner I was counted. After dinner. Before lights out. Then while I slept. And even then I turned that phrase over and over in my mind: "Count me in." Those were three words I'd take back if I could. They were my words to Ken and Hamilton. "Count me in." Now I was counted in my cell every day, and I was counted on to be there morning, noon, and night.

The first time Jack wrote this story, he squeezed it in between the lines of a prison library copy of Dostoyevsky's *The Brothers Karamozov* (journals were not allowed). When he was released, the prison guard who searched his suitcase took out the book for return to the library. Although he never saw it again, it is likely that his memories are more vivid because he wrote them down. When he received an early release from prison because of good behavior and because he had gotten himself accepted at a junior college, he began writing "brutal stories about prison, about New York street life, about the men I knew who had hard lives and hard hearts." Then one day he grew "tired of all the blood and guts and hard lives and hard hearts and began to write more stories" about his childhood. Middle school readers know him best for *Joey Pigza Swallowed the Key* and *Joey Pigza Loses Control* (a 2001 Newbery Honor Book).

In recommending this book to readers, adults need to realize that it is written for mature high school students, not the kids who read the Joey Pigza books. When Gantos came and spoke to our students at Arizona State, he said that the book was as much a cautionary tale for adults as for kids. He wants adults to get the message that we should not give up on kids who are in trouble. With the right help, and a lot of luck, they may survive and go on to become the kind of adult who can make the world a better place.

Most personal experience stories are about adventures, successes, and experiences the writers feel so strongly that they wish to share them with readers. Some are career stories, for example, former surgeon-general C. Everett Koop's *Koop: The Memoirs of America's Family Doctor*. Partly because of their fondness for animals, many readers appreciate Jane Goodall's *My Life with the Chimpanzees*. Animal lovers might also like Anne E. Neimark's *Wild Heart: The Story of Joy Adamson* and Diane Ackerman's *The Moon by Whale Light: And Other Adventures Among Bats, Penguins, Crocodilians, and Whales*, and Candace Savage's *Wolves*.

Although Farley Mowat's books are not as upbeat, they make fascinating reading. In *A Whale for the Killing*, he thought he had found the perfect place to live until he discovered his neighbors were savages who took pleasure in killing a trapped whale. His angry prose also typifies *Never Cry Wolf* and *Sea of Slaughter*. He's less angry in his earlier *The Dog Who Wouldn't Be* and *Owls in the Family*. *Born Naked* is Mowat's childhood memories of 1920s and 1930s Canada. Given Mowat's irritation with people in most of his books, *Born Naked* is a relatively quiet and gentle book.

Some authors tell their own quite ordinary stories of growing up in ways that make young readers feel privileged to get acquainted with a new friend. Annie Dillard's *An American Childhood* tells about growing up in the 1950s and 1960s. Tobias Wolff's *This Boy's Life* is set at about the same time, in Seattle, where he grew up longing to be a "boy of dignity."

Sometimes memories are incredibly funny to readers, although just how amusing the events were to the writer early in his life is open to question. The first paragraph in Mark Salzman's *Lost in Place: Growing Up Absurd in Suburbia* is witty and certainly likely to grab the attention of most readers:

When I was thirteen years old I saw my first kung fu movie, and before it ended I decided that the life of a wandering Zen monk was the life for me. I announced my willingness to leave East Ridge Junior High School immediately and give up all material things, but my parents did not share my enthusiasm. They made it clear that I was not to become a wandering Zen monk until I had finished high school. In the meantime I could practice kung fu and meditate down in the basement. So I immersed myself in the study of Chinese boxing and philosophy with the kind of dedication that is possible only when you don't yet have to make a living, when you are too young to drive and when you don't have a girlfriend.

The success of personal experience books, as well as autobiographies, depends largely on the quality of the writing because there isn't a plot for readers to get excited about, and honest accounts lack the kinds of literary exaggeration that make for intriguing villains and heroes. One aspect of personal experience books that makes them attractive to young readers is that they are by people looking back on experiences they had when they were young. For example, Robin Graham, author of *Dove*, was only sixteen when he set sail on his own boat to go around the world. Steven Callahan, author of *Adrift: Seventy-Six Days Lost at Sea*, was twenty-nine when he set sail. Bruce Feiler in *Under the Big Top* is an adult, but he remembers back to his childhood when he learned to juggle with a handful of oranges and when he first developed his love affair with the circus.

In the personal experience books about adult protagonists that teenagers enjoy, the adults are likely to be unencumbered by family responsibilities. For example, mature young readers enjoy such travel books as Peter Matthiessen's *African Silences*, Charles Kuralt's *A Life on the Road*, and Bruce Chatwin's *What Am I Doing Here?*

Whether to consider a book a personal experience or an autobiography is often up to the reader. For example, Maya Angelou's *I Know Why the Caged Bird Sings* and its three sequels are usually considered to be autobiographies because they move chronologically through Angelou's life, but it might be argued that they are personal experience stories because each book is about only a part of her life.

Biographies

The Greeks enjoyed stories about the gods of Mount Olympus and hero tales about the moral descendants of the gods. Hero tales, however, had an added feature that helped listeners identify with the protagonists. Unlike the gods, who live forever, heroes had one human parent, which meant that they were mortal. The most that the gods could risk in any undertaking was their pride, but heroes could lose their lives.

When we're reading modern fiction, we know that the author can always bring the protagonist out alive; however, in true hero tales—biographies—protagonists risk their lives, just as readers would in the same situation. This adds credibility and intensity because the reader thinks, "If this happened to someone else, then it might happen to me."

John Dryden introduced the word *biography* to English readers in his 1683 edition of Plutarch's *Parallel Lives*. While the term may have been new, the form was well known to readers who had long read the lives of famous generals and politicians and religious leaders. People today remain fascinated by biographies. Where else can we see the uniqueness and authenticity of one person's life and, at the same time, emotions and problems that all human beings face.

Today's biographies for young adults are likely to provide a balance of both strengths and weaknesses. They demonstrate how the subject and the reader share similar emotions. Both have fears and insecurities, and both succumb to temptations and vanities. After reading a good biography, the reader feels a kinship with the subject, not so much in spite of as because of the character's human frailties.

To say that a biography is written "objectively" does not mean that it is written without feeling. For biographies to ring true, the author must become immersed in the subject's life so that he or she can write with passion and commitment. This implies a point of view, not one imposed by an author who set out to prove a preconceived idea but a unifying force that guided the person's life and was discovered by the author through his or her research.

Few of us admit to selecting the biographies we are going to purchase and promote on the basis of how we feel about the subject, but that's like the old cliché, "Never judge a book by its cover," which is honored more in word than in deed. Someone could write a Ph.D. dissertation on how American values have changed over the last thirty years as reflected by whose biographies were put on the shelves of libraries.

In the early 1960s, readers at almost any library would find a predominance of biographies about white men who were inventors, statesmen, soldiers, and business leaders. During the 1970s, the imbalance became so obvious, particularly in school libraries, that educators and publishers took steps to correct the situation by preparing biographies about previously unsung heroes, including members of minority groups, women, individuals with disabilities, and people whose contributions were not in military, political, or business spheres. Of course, there is still room for good books presenting new information on both traditional and nontraditional heroes.

Young readers who have particular favorite authors should enjoy biographies about those favorites. Many teens remember Roald Dahl's *Charlie and the Chocolate Factory* with fondness, but whether they will enjoy Jeremy Treglown's *Roald Dahl: A Biography*, learning that he was not a nice person, may be questionable. Almost certainly, fans of Dr. Seuss will love Judith Morgan and Neil Morgan's *Dr. Seuss and Mr. Geisel: A Biography*. Fans of *The Little Prince*,—and they are legion—who read Stacy Schiff's *Saint-Exupéry: A Biography* will get a picture of a man of action, a lover of flying, and a man who wrote some exceptional books. With Daniel Dyer's *Jack London: A Biography*, there's bound to be a circular effect with its readers searching out London's fiction and readers of his fiction getting extra pleasure from the biography. Whether Jay Parini's *John Steinbeck: A Biography* convinces readers that Steinbeck is a major writer is unclear, but young adults who love *Of Mice and Men* and *The Grapes of Wrath* will surely enjoy Parini's book. Catherine Reef has also written a biography, *John Steinbeck,* which is a large-size book with plenty of photos and brief excerpts from Steinbeck's writing. Sharon O'Brien's *Willa Cather,* published in part of Chelsea House's *Lives of Notable Gay Men and Lesbians* series, is a solid study of Cather's life and work, not just her sex life.

There is always a place for biographies about women and men who have changed the world. Patricia C. McKissack and Fredrick McKissack's *Sojourner Truth: Ain't I a Woman?* is a compelling life story of a woman who began as a slave and ultimately emerged as a powerful African American voice in the United States. Ellen Chesler's *Woman of Valor: Margaret Sanger and the Birth Control Movement in America* recounts the life of a nurse who became a militant socialist and ultimately saved many other women's lives. Carolyn G. Heilbrun's *The Education of a Woman: The Life of Gloria Steinem* portrays the woman who may have had more power in the women's movement than any other. See Focus Box 9.4, Recent Biographies, for other examples.

Collective Biographies

Collective biographies (i.e., one book presenting the stories of several individuals) have become increasingly popular because authors can write about individuals whose lives may not have been chronicled fully enough to provide information for an entire book. Collective biographies are also an efficient way to get information about previously ignored individuals into a library. Authors usually bring together the stories of people who have something in common. This development of a unifying theme may be the best way to show trends and connections among various subjects. For example, Russell Freedman's *Indian Chiefs,* the biographies of six western Indian chiefs during the 1800s, is a stronger condemnation of white treatment of Native Americans than it would have been had he told only one of the stories. In a similar way readers get a broader picture than if they were reading about only one first lady when they read *The Smithsonian Book of the First Ladies: Their Lives, Times, and Issues,* edited by Edith P. Mayo, curator of the Division of Political History in the American part of the Smithsonian Institution. Ruth Ashby and Deborah Gore Ohrn's *Herstory: Women Who Changed the World* is a marvelous collection of brief comments (1–3 pages) about women from Queen Hatshepsut in the fifteenth century BC to Rigoberta Menchú of contemporary Guatemala. Two collective biographies of writers by Rebecca Carroll should attract young people. *I Know What the Red Clay Looks Like: The Voice and Vision of Black Women Writers* has excerpts from fifteen black authors, including Rita Dove, Gloria Naylor, Lorene Cary, and Nikki Giovanni. *Swing Low: Black Men Writing* has works by sixteen authors, including Henry Louis Gates, Jr., Ishmael Reed, and August Wilson.

Gold Rush Women by Claire Rudolf Murphy and Jane G. Haigh takes a look at the women who flocked to Alaska in the 1890s, when gold was discovered. One-tenth of the adventurers looking for riches were women. The authors

The Adventures of Marco Polo by Russell Freedman, illustrated by Bagram Ibatoulline. Scholastic, 2006. Ibatoulline's paintings at the beginning of each chapter, along with the ornate calligraphy, lend a sense of dignity and authenticity to Freedman's telling.

Ben Franklin's Almanac: Being a True Account of the Good Gentleman's Life by Candace Fleming. Simon & Schuster/Atheneum, 2003. The author intended to write a straightforward account of Franklin's life, but the longer she worked the more she learned about him and his wide-ranging interests and activities. She ended up telling his story in a format much like the original *Poor Richard's Almanack.*

Dickens: His Work and His World by Michael Rosen, illustrated by Robert Ingpen. Candlewick, 2005. Teachers wanting to bring more life to their reading of a Charles Dickens piece would be wise to bring in Rosen's book. It is well written and well illustrated, plus Rosen discusses some of the literary devices that Dickens used.

Escape! The Story of the Great Houdini by Sid Fleischman. HarperCollins/Greenwillow, 2006. An extra plus to this book is that Fleischman was himself a magician and so he is able to tell just enough of Houdini's secrets to make readers feel they have the inside track. Fleischman's own biography, *The Abracadabra Kid: A Writer's Life* (Greenwillow, 1996), makes a good companion read.

Fight On! Mary Church Terrell's Battle for Integration by Dennis Brindell Fradin and Judith Bloom Fradin. Clarion, 2003. Mollie Terrell, born to former slaves in 1863, went to Oberlin College and was the first black woman appointed to the Washington, D.C., Board of Education. When she was ninety years old, she won a Supreme Court case that ended segregation in the District of Columbia's restaurants and theaters.

Jane Addams: Champion of Democracy by Judith Bloom Fradin and Dennis Brindell Fradin. Clarion, 2006. The Fradins are being praised for the way they "humanize" Addams while also putting her advocacy for the poor into physical and historical contexts. The book could serve as a research model for high school students.

John Lennon: All I Want Is the Truth by Elizabeth Partridge. Viking, 2005. For this handsomely put-together biography, Partridge relies on Lennon's own writings and interviews.

While not censoring out the sordid details of Lennon's life with and without the Beatles, Partridge keeps her focus on the music.

Old Hickory: Andrew Jackson and the American People by Albert Marrin. Dutton, 2004. In his usual style, Marrin does more than introduce readers to an individual. He uses the person as a hook on which to hang the whole historical period of the American Industrial Revolution and the railroads.

Onward: A Photobiography of African-American Polar Explorer Matthew Henson by Dolores Johnson. National Geographic, 2005. Henson was hired to go on Robert E. Peary's trip to the North Pole as Peary's manservant, but he became much more than that as the group faced terrifying conditions. He was posthumously awarded the National Geographic Society's Hubbard Medal.

Our Eleanor: A Scrapbook Look at Eleanor Roosevelt's Remarkable Life by Candace Fleming. S&S/Atheneum, 2005. Fleming's biography is similar in style to Russell Freedman's photobiography and is designed to inspire feelings of intimacy that are usually reserved for family scrapbooks.

Rachel Carson by Ellen Levine. Viking, 2007. Part of the Up Close Series, Levine does a good job of introducing Carson as a person readers would like to know as well as telling about her work, which many people credit with starting the environmental movement.

The Voice That Challenged a Nation: Marian Anderson and the Struggle for Equal Rights by Russell Freedman. Clarion, 2004. In his usual style, Russell Freedman creates a beautifully designed and well-told biography of the talented singer who became a star in the political as well as the entertainment world.

The Wright Sister: Katharine Wright and Her Famous Brothers by Richard Maurer. Millbrook/Roaring Brook, 2003. Maurer tells the story of the woman sometimes called "the third member of the team," but she also had accomplishments apart from her brothers' flying.

A useful website for background information is Almanac Biography, www.infoplease.com/people.html, which includes information on 30,000 people organized into ethnic, career, and social and cultural groups.

give short biographies of twenty-three women, including two native women who helped discover the gold and then taught survival skills to newcomers, two sisters who opened a bank, an African American woman who gave birth on the trail, and a woman who panned gold by lantern light and became one of the first millionaires. Ina Chang's *A Separate Battle: Women and the Civil War* looks beyond Scarlett O'Hara to show what real women did during the Civil War.

In *The Greatest Generation*, newscaster Tom Brokaw tells the stories of some fifty Americans who came of age during the Depression and World War II. Their stories are grouped into such categories as Ordinary People; Women in Uniform and Out; Heroes; Shame; and Love, Marriage, and Commitment. While the book was printed for an adult audience, it is accessible to older teens who might be interested in learning about their grandparents' generation. Studs Terkel's *Coming of Age: The Story of Our Century by Those Who've Lived It* includes the voices of more than seventy people, the youngest of whom is seventy and the oldest ninety-nine. Similar to all of Terkel's collective biographies, this one ranges from charming chitchat to resounding ideas. A more specific group is looked at in *Hell Fighters: African American Soldiers in World War I* by Michael L. Cooper. In 1916, when the Fifteenth New York Voluntary Infantry of the National Guard went to serve in France, it was segregated from other soldiers, deprived of basic uniforms and equipment, and controlled by white officers. General John J. Pershing intervened on the soldier's behalf, and in May 1918, they were renamed the 369th Regiment and, because of their bravery in combat, came home to a hero's welcome in Harlem.

We rarely think about young people changing the course of the world, but Ellen Levine's *Freedom's Children: Young Civil Rights Activists Tell Their Own Stories* should make young people proud of other young people. Joseph Berger's *The Young Scientists: America's Future and the Winning of the Westinghouse* tells of Berger's study of the winners of the annual national Westinghouse Science Talent Search. Berger becomes excited, and so will readers, as they learn how dedicated these young scientists are and how they have developed their own research.

Debunking versus Fawning Biographies

We need to keep our wits about us as we read biographies because the authors may have agendas not immediately clear to readers. We used to worry about fawning biographies filled with hero worship, but today's authors are more likely to write debunking books. They may want subtly to poison the reader or to vent their spleens about any number of things, from the subject of the biography to an institution or anything at all.

In the debunking biography, a popular hero or an institution or anything treasured by many people is taken down from a pedestal. Although such books are certainly "antihero," they differ from true examples of the literary meaning of the term in that the subject of a debunking biography is not written about with sympathy. Among the most famous are Kitty Kelley's *Nancy Reagan: The Unauthorized Biography* and Christina Crawford's *Mommie Dearest,* which debunked actress Joan Crawford for the way she played her real-life role of mother.

Borrowing a phrase from Freud, Joyce Carol Oates has called this disturbing new subgenre "pathography." Michiko Kakutani says that the motifs are "dysfunction and disaster, illnesses and pratfalls, failed marriages and failed careers, alcoholism and breakdowns and outrageous conduct." She went on to describe how sensationalized some of these books are "wallowing in squalor and foolishness," playing with the "shrill theme" of "failed promise," if not outright "tragedy."[5]

Autobiographies

Autobiographies have an immediate and obvious appeal to readers. "Who," we ask ourselves, "would know more about this person than the person? Who could better tell us this person's story?" The truth may be that almost any other good writer could have been more honest and could have written a better story. Even a tiny bit of thought might suggest to us that most people are poor witnesses of their own lives. Most of us want to look good to others. Most of us might even leave out a significant piece of our lives that still embarrasses us or humiliates us or leaves us feeling unsure of ourselves and our motives. Most of us know friends who are incapable of telling us precisely, much less accurately, what happened at certain turns in their lives.

This is not to say that autobiographies are automatically untrustworthy, only that they may not tell the whole story or that certain parts may be left out, possibly for good reason, possibly not. Writers of autobiographies are not necessarily out to con us, but they may be. Worse yet, they may even con themselves. In today's media-oriented world, autobiographies may simply be business ventures designed to promote a celebrity's fame. In the introduction to comedian Tim Allen's *Don't Stand Too Close to a Naked Man*, he jokingly explained that he was practically forced to write his book because:

> Hyperion [his publisher] is owned by Disney, which also owns my television show. Disney owns Disneyland and Disney World. Disney also owns Euro-Disney, Tokyo-Disney, and a Disney store in every city, town, and hamlet in the world. *They also have my cat.*

He ended his introductory chapter with, "And if all goes well and you buy lots and lots of copies, maybe Disney will give me back my cat."

It's probably a good idea for adults to discuss with students the whole concept of celebrity biographies and autobiographies and the role of ghost writers or "book doctors." An article in the *New York Times Book Review* (January 5, 1997) mentioned that Charles Barkley and O. J. Simpson, both "claimed to have been misquoted in their ghostwritten autobiographies—thus inviting jeers, catcalls and obloquy." John Callahan, the disabled cartoonist who shocks the sensibilities of the politically correct, was more than candid in acknowledging the help he received on his *Don't Worry, He Won't Get Far on Foot.* In his thank-yous, he wrote,

> Finally, David Kelly, working from hundreds of hours of my tapes, drafted each chapter and then rewrote it again and again and again and *again* until no trace of his own voice remained. "We're not going to have one of those goddam *as-told-to* books," he would snarl. And we don't.

While celebrity autobiographies and biographies are the ones that get in the news and are likely to be requested from libraries, some of them present problems for educators. By the time a biography or autobiography of some new celebrity has gone through a rigorous selection procedure, the subject may no longer be of interest.

Many of the books also present questionable or outright immoral concepts. For example, Wilt Chamberlain's *A View from Above* has a chapter, "On Sex and Love: What Rules the World," which makes clear that he believes he is lucky because he has had sexual relations with nearly 20,000 women. That may impress Chamberlain, but it is likely to bother most adults. Adults have also been bothered by the popularity of Vincent Bugliosi's *Helter Skelter: The True Story of the Manson Murders,* which is still read by young people as Charles Manson periodically pops up in the news.

With questionable books, it's usually better that teenagers have a chance to read the whole book rather than just get the smatterings of sexual or violent titillation that appear in the media. One thing we can feel confident in suggesting is that when it comes to selecting books about which you are unsure, check out your initial reaction with others. Talk to colleagues, parents, and students, especially students, because unless someone starts young people along such a line of thinking, they may never understand that reading about someone's life does not necessarily mean emulating everything about that person. As librarian Mary Mueller observed:

> Our past and present are full of personages who lived outside traditional rules. They often used poor judgment or acted in a less-than-exemplary fashion. . . . How can we expect our students to really see the personality of Harry Truman without letting them see the tenacity, salty language, and temper that so characterized him?[6]

Nonfiction to Help Teenagers Learn Who They Are and Where They Fit

When young adult specialist Patty Campbell spoke at an American Library Association annual meeting, she pointed out that teenagers are so wrapped up in what the psychologists have labeled the "adolescent identity crisis" that

Cyberbullying and Cyberthreats: Responding to the Challenge of Online Social Aggression, Threats, and Distress by Nancy E. Willard. Research Press, 2007. An especially interesting part of this is the kinds of rationalizations that kids use to justify various types of cyberbullying. The book is written for adults, but could certainly be shared with sophisticated students who are probably going to be the ones to solve the problem.

Eating Disorders Information for Teens edited by Sandra Augustyn Lawton. Teen Health, Omnigraphics, 2005. Chapters alternate between narrative overviews covering causes, symptoms, preventions, and treatments of different problems. Quick tips, FAQ, and "Remember!" boxes give direct advice.

For Teens Only: Quotes, Notes, and Advice You Can Use by Carol Weston. HarperTrophy, 2003. Each page starts with an intriguing quote from people as different as Homer Simpson and Edna St. Vincent Millay. Weston expounds on the quotes and concludes with a boldfaced moral, almost like those at the ends of fables. She did an earlier book, *Private and Personal: Questions and Answers for Girls Only* (HarperTrophy, 2000), based on letters and answers in her Help column in *Girls' Life*.

The Girls' Guide to Friends by Julie Taylor. Three Rivers Press, 2002. The subtitle is "Straight talk on making close pals, creating lasting ties, and being an all-around great friend." For older readers, Taylor wrote *The Girls' Guide to Guys: Straight Talk for Teens on Flirting, Dating, Breaking Up, Making Up and Finding True Love* (Three Rivers Press, 2000).

Inside Out: Portrait of an Eating Disorder written and illustrated by Nadia Shivack. S&S/Atheneum, 2007. Shivack named her eating disorder Ed, and over the years she kept track of Ed on whatever scraps of paper she could find. These are worked into the book, along with hindsight comments, websites, and lists of resources.

Is It a Choice? Answers to 300 of the Most Frequently Asked Questions about Gays and Lesbians, 3rd edition, by Eric Marcus. HarperCollins, 2005. Questions range from what to call same-sex parents to how people know if they are gay. Dating, telling parents, socializing, and political activism are all treated.

It's Okay to Say No: Choosing Sexual Abstinence by Eleanor Ayer. Rosen, 1997. Both physical and emotional health are touted as benefits of abstinence. While the message fits in with many religious teachings, the author does not focus on religion but instead on self-respect and preparing for a healthy marriage.

The Latina's Bible: The Nueva Latina's Guide to Love, Spirituality, Family, and La Vida by Sandra Guzman. Three

---

they have neither the time for nor the interest in sitting down and reading about the world in general. What they are looking for are books that help them decide on who they are and where they fit into the scheme of things. Informative books they judge to be helpful include sex education books, some physical and mental health books, selected how-to books, and biographies or true accounts of experiences teenagers can imagine themselves or their acquaintances having. Nearly all the other information books published for teenagers are read under duress—only because teachers assign reports and research papers.

Teenagers especially appreciate books that give advice on managing one's life and being successful right now. Marie Hardenbrook, librarian at McClintock High School in Tempe, Arizona, says that over the last few years her "Inspirational" display and booklist has been consistently popular. She includes such sports-related books as Richard E. Peck's *Something for Joey*, William Blinn's *Brian's Song*, Steve Cameron's *Brett Favre: Huck Finn Grows Up*, and Shannon Miller's *Winning Every Day: Gold Medal Advice for a Happy, Healthy Life.*

Rivers Press, 2002. One of the interesting facts presented in Guzman's book is that, according to 2000–2001 statistics, 30 percent of U.S. Latinas are under the age of fifteen and the median age for Latinos as a whole is 25.9 years. While there is a wealth of information here, at least one of our Latina students was offended by what she viewed as overgeneralizations about sexual beliefs and practices.

101 Questions about Sex and Sexuality: With Answers for the Curious, Cautious, and Confused by Faith Hickman Brynie. 21st Century Books, 2003. While emphasizing that abstinence is the only sure way to avoid STDs and pregnancies, Brynie also provides contraceptive information. The questions were collected from middle school and high school students.

The Sibling Slam Book edited by Don Meyer. Woodbine, 2005. Eighty-one young people offer insights from having grown up in a family with a special needs child. The focused chapters reveal not only feelings of embarrassment, but also of protectiveness and of pride because of learning things that other kids don't know and of making a real contribution to one's family.

Stay Strong: Simple Life Lessons for Teens by Terrie Williams with an introduction by Queen Latifah. Scholastic, 2001. Chapters include "Life Isn't Fair and Nothing You Do Matters," "How I Talk Is My Business," and "It's the 'In-Crowd' That Matters."

Staying Safe on Dates by Donna Chaiet. Rosen, 1996.

Chaiet's goal is to help girls, starting with those in middle school, develop safety skills. She shows girls the wisdom of setting and maintaining verbal, emotional, and physical boundaries.

Teen Fathers Today by Ted Gottfried. 21st Century Books, 2001. At last here is a book that acknowledges the contradictory feelings, the long-term implications, and the complexities of dealing with the baby's grandparents (both paternal and maternal). Contrary to the common notion that boys who father teen babies are interested only in casual sex, studies show that many have a continuing relationship with both the mother and the baby.

Teen Pregnancy, edited by Myra H. Immell. Gale/Greenhaven, 2001. Pregnant teens, health-care workers, educators, and professional writers for scientific journals are among the contributors to this book, which works well for both skimming and reading.

The "What's Happening to My Body?" Book for Boys and *The "What's Happening to My Body?" Book for Girls* by Lynda Madaras with Area Madaras. Newmarket, 2000. The prefaces encourage parents by giving them tips on how to talk to preteens and teens about their developing bodies and their changing emotions. These books are accessible to middle schoolers, while still acceptable to high schoolers. An especially good section in the book for girls talks about dealing with the kind of unwanted attention that is often given to girls who develop early.

The runaway best loaners, however, are Jack Canfield's books including two volumes of *Chicken Soup for the Teenage Soul: 101 Stories of Life, Love, and Learning*; *Chicken Soup for the Pet Lover's Soul: Stories about Pets as Teachers, Healers, Heroes, and Friends*; and *Chicken Soup for the Woman's Soul: 101 Stories to Open the Hearts and Rekindle the Spirits of Women*. See Focus Box 9.5, Information about Bodies and Minds, for books that answer the more specific kinds of questions that kids ask about both themselves and each other; for example,

Can I get AIDS from French kissing?

Do I have diabetes?

Why do I feel like crying all the time?

How serious is herpes?

What's the difference between just trying a drug and becoming addicted?

If I'm pregnant, what are my options?

What's an STD?

Is being fat really unhealthy?

What causes pimples?

What happens if someone has Hodgkin's disease?

My mother has breast cancer. Is she going to die?

Is anorexia nervosa just in a person's head?

Why does my grandfather say such strange things? Will I be like that when I'm old?

What will happen if I have venereal disease and don't go to the doctor?

The best books offering answers to such questions have good indexing, clear writing, suggestions for further reading, and, where appropriate, information about Web pages, telephone numbers, and support groups. The *Need to Know Library,* put out by Rosen publishers, is a dependable series of self-help books. Each book is sixty-four pages and includes a glossary, index, photos, and suggestions for further reading. With self-help books, girls make up the majority of readers; hence authors and publishers work hard to create such books as Erika V. Shearin Karres's *Mean Chicks, Cliques, and Dirty Tricks: A Real Girl's Guide to Getting Through the Day with Smarts and Style* and *Girlsource: A Book by and for Young Women About Relationships, Rights, Futures, Bodies, Minds, and Souls.* And even a more neutral sounding title such as Florence Cadier and Melissa Daly's *My Parents Are Getting Divorced: How to Keep It Together When Your Parents Are Splitting Up* will probably attract more girl than boy readers.

The exploration of sexual matters in books for young readers is an especially sensitive area for the following reasons:

1. Young adults are physically mature, but they probably have had little intellectual and emotional preparation for making sex-related decisions.

2. Parents are anxious to protect their children from making sex-related decisions that might prove harmful.

3. Old restraints and patterns of behavior and attitudes are being questioned, so that there is no clear-cut model to follow.

4. Sex is such an important part of American culture and the mass media that young people are forced to think about and take stands on such controversial issues as homosexuality, premarital sex, violence in relation to sex, and the role of sex in love and family relationships.

5. Talking about sexual attitudes and beliefs with their teenage children may make parents uncomfortable, especially if the father and the mother have different views. This means that many young people must get their information outside of the home.

While some books focus specifically on a problem such as AIDS or pregnancy, it is more common for books to cover emotional as well as physical aspects of sexual activity. No single book can satisfy all readers, and this is true of those

While nearly all self-help and advice books contain information about physical health and safe sex, what most kids are really interested in are the emotional aspects.

dealing with sex education. An entire collection must be evaluated and books provided for a wide range of interests, attitudes, beliefs, and lifestyles. Those who criticize libraries for including books that present teenage sexual activity as the norm have a justified complaint if the library does not also have sex education books that present, or even promote, abstinence as a normal route for young people.

Materials dealing with sex are judged quite differently from those on less controversial topics. For example, in most subject areas, books are given plus marks if they succeed in getting the reader emotionally involved, but with books about sex, some adults feel that it is better for young readers to be presented with straightforward, "plumbing manuals"—the less emotional involvement the better. Other adults argue that it is the emotional part that young people need to learn. Coming to agreement is not at all easy because adults have such varying attitudes and experiences.

Well-planned and well-written books can present information about different viewpoints, and teachers and librarians are performing a worthwhile service if they bring such books to the attention of young people. Over the last few years, we have noticed that women's magazines are increasingly using sex-related articles as a selling point. In magazines for young women, many of the articles are written as though their purpose is sex education, when in fact they border on what *Playboy* editors once described as "pious pornography." Women who have inhibitions or feel guilty about sex can think and talk about sexuality as long as they are doing it to learn something, especially if they are made to feel that they are being unselfish in learning to "please their man." We were talking about this in one of our summer school classes, which had an unusually large number of parents in it, and casually remarked that maybe there was no longer a need for sex-education books because kids could get all the information they wanted from the Internet. There was an immediate uproar with the parents in the class saying there was a greater need than ever for well-thought-out and well-designed books, if for nothing more than warning kids against entering into sex-related conversations on Web chat rooms, and so on. The consensus from the parents was that they wanted their children to have nothing at all to do with sexual information posted on the Internet.

When helping young adults make reading decisions in this area, we need to consider the reader's purpose. If the reader wants basic information, nonfiction is far superior because it can present a wider range of information in a clear, unambiguous way. But if the reader desires to understand the emotional and physical aspects of a particular relationship, an honest piece of fiction usually does a better job.

The important thing for adults to remember is that they should provide both kinds of material in conjunction with a listening ear and a willingness to discuss questions. Schools and libraries need to seek community help in exchanging ideas and developing policies. Family values must be respected, but honest, accurate information must also be available for those who seek it. Charting a course along this delicate line is more than any one individual should be expected to do, which is why people need to communicate with each other. Professionals working with books are also obligated to find and study the latest, most authentic information and to bring that information to those who are helping to shape policies and practices. The general public may get away with objecting to or endorsing ideas and books that they have never explored or read. Not so for the professional charged with leading a group to consensus or compromise. The more you know about the materials, and the more you understand about individual and group differences, the better able you are to participate in book selection, discussion, and, sometimes, defense.

Outstanding Authors of Nonfiction for Young Adults

In mid July 2007, Mark Aronson sent an email to *School Library Journal* in which he told about spending a happy afternoon at his local library. He and John W. Glenn had met with middle school students and a few adults to talk about their forthcoming book *The World Made New.* He said the "neat part" was how enthusiastic both the students and the adults were about finding new ways of thinking about history and the world that we live in.

Aronson is both an editor and an author of nonfiction books, so of course he has an interest in how nonfiction is promoted to young people. He worries about the fact that schools choose "safe and familiar" textbooks and that book stores seem to consider nonfiction for kids to be "owned" by the schools so they do little to promote it. Even parents and grandparents shy away from buying nonfiction books as gifts. He wrote:

> I suspect that the very size of the problem is the beginning of the solution. That is, the general ignorance of and aversion to nonfiction is so widespread that it is ripe

to be toppled. What I felt from the crowd today—and I've seen in other similar gatherings is . . . a craving that is all the stronger because people didn't even realize they had it—they simply did not know that nonfiction could come to them in exciting and new ways.[7]

Aronson is working to create a revolution of rising expectations in which people will "know that nonfiction can offer more, so they demand more." They will recognize "what is wrong with the mix of textbooks that have no narrative power and reading lists dominated by fiction."

A crucial element in Aronson's "revolution" is simply getting more people to read books that are written with passion and a deeply felt interest in the subject. Aronson chooses to write about topics that are complex and to present sides of the stories that haven't been told before as in his *The Real Revolution: The Global Story of American Independence* and his *Race: A History Beyond Black and White*. His biographies focus on a range of people as different as Bobby Kennedy, John Winthrop, and Oliver Cromwell. His *Sir Walter Ralegh and the Quest for El Dorado* won the 2000 Boston Globe/Horn Book Award and was praised for exploring a contradictory and complex Elizabethan figure who had a kind of passion that enabled him to be both a poet and a soldier. His *Art Attack: A Short Cultural History of the Avant-Garde* did an excellent job of tying together art, music, and literature with available Internet resources.

Here are brief write-ups in alphabetical order of some of the other authors who, in addition to Aronson, can consistently be counted on to provide this kind of passion in their writing.

Russell Freedman

Nearly thirty years elapsed between the time that Russell Freedman wrote his first book, *Teenagers Who Made History in 1961*, and when he won the Newbery Medal in 1988 for *Lincoln: A Photobiography*. Since then he has been honored with the Laura Ingalls Wilder Award, given every five years to honor a lifetime contribution. Among his most recent books are *Who Was First? Discovering the Americas*; *The Voice That Challenged a Nation: Marian Anderson and the Struggle for Equal Rights*; and *Children of the Great Depression*. His *Confucius: The Golden Rule*; *Martha Graham: A Dancer's Life*; and *Babe Didrikson Zaharias: The Making of a Champion* contain between 175 and 200 pages and, as such, are longer than his earlier books.

Freedman began his career by focusing mostly on books about animals for primary and middle grades readers. A turning point came when he attended an exhibition of historical photographs and found himself "communicating" with the young faces that stared out at him from the old photos. He searched out these and other pictures for a book, *Immigrant Kids*. Since then he has made a specialty of finding evocative photographs to use not as decoration but as an integral part of his books. He won the Orbis Pictus Award and the Boston Globe Honor Book award for his 1990 *Franklin Delano Roosevelt*. His 1991 *The Wright Brothers* was a Newbery Honor Book and so was his 1993 *Eleanor Roosevelt: A Life of Discovery*. In his 1994 *Kids at Work: Lewis Hine and the Crusade against Child Labor*, he wrote directly about the power of photography to document social conditions under which U. S. children labored. In 2003, his *In Defense of Freedom: The Story of the Bill of Rights* was praised for its timeliness.

James Cross Giblin

See Giblin's statement on p. 281 for an illustration of what we mean when we say that the best nonfiction authors are ones who choose topics that have been in their minds and in their hearts for a long time. Giblin is fascinated with telling two sides of a story, which he did admirably in his 2005 *Good Brother, Bad Brother: The Story of Edwin Booth and John Wilkes Booth*. The two brothers were in ways similar. They were both well known as talented actors, each with a commanding stage presence, but they were also different. The older brother Edwin was more introspective while John was passionate and impulsive. Edwin voted for Abraham Lincoln, while John strongly supported the Confederacy. Giblin does an excellent job of creating vivid images of the brothers and the events that led up to the assassination of President Lincoln and the effects on the nation in general and on the Booth family in particular.

In his *Secrets of the Sphinx*, Giblin shows readers a world before written history as he explores clues and various theories about the pyramids, the Rosetta Stone, and Atlantis. English teachers will be especially interested in the Rosetta Stone, a large slab covered with writing in three different languages which enabled linguists to decipher one of the world's first writing systems. His *The Truth about Unicorns* serves as an excellent model for research as it traces the history of beliefs, superstitions, stories, and art about this mythical creature. His *Charles A. Lindbergh, A Human Hero* was chosen for several best-book lists based on Giblin's meticulous research and the skillful way that he balanced information about "an all-too-human hero."

James Haskins

Although James Haskins died in 2005, many of the one hundred books that he wrote will continue to fill a need. He wrote for both children and young adults. His main contribution was to recognize the need for biographies and other books about minorities, and he set out to fill the gap. Since the mid-1970s, he consistently prepared books on African American heroes and African American history as well as on such topics as rights for people with disabilities, the U.S. labor movement, and women leaders in other countries including Corazon Aquino and Indira Gandhi. In 2005 he wrote *African Heroes* and coauthored with Ortha Richard Sullivan *African American Millionaires*. Earlier books included *Spike Lee: By Any Means Necessary*; *Bound for America: The Forced Migration of Africans to the New World* (illustrated by Floyd Cooper); *Get on Board: The Story of the Underground Railroad*; *I Have a Dream: The Life and Words of Martin Luther King, Jr.*; *Thurgood Marshall: A Life for Justice*; and *I Am Somebody! A Biography of Jesse Jackson*.

Albert Marrin

Albert Marrin earned a Ph.D. in history from Columbia University in 1968 and shortly thereafter began publishing history-related books. We've already mentioned his 2006 *Saving the Buffalo* in connection with the current interest in books about Native Americans and their history. One of the points he makes in this book is that Native Americans had more than a hundred uses for the buffalo and never killed more than they needed. In the same year, he wrote a fascinating book, *Oh, Rats! The Story of Rats and People*, while the year before he published *Old Hickory: Andrew Jackson and the American People*. In 1985, Marrin's *1812: The War Nobody Won* was given a Boston Globe/Horn Book Honor award for nonfiction.

Marrin has written well-received biographies on historical figures ranging from Abraham Lincoln to Adolf Hitler and from Sir Francis Drake to General Robert E. Lee. His *Dr. Jenner and the Speckled Monster: The Search for the Smallpox Vaccine* is a timely book because of fears about vials of frozen virus preserved in laboratories around the world. His *Secrets from the Rocks: Dinosaur Hunting with Roy Chapman Andrews* is the story of a pioneering paleontologist who led five expeditions into China between 1922 and 1930. Less-thoughtful writers would have been satisfied to focus on the excitement and danger of traveling into the Gobi Desert of Mongolia, but Marrin goes further and shows how the expeditions would have been different under today's sensibilities. For example, women were excluded from the expeditions, and Andrews had no compunctions about shooting rare animals or loading up treasures and bringing them out of the host countries he visited. A *School Library Journal* reviewer praised Marrin's *The Spanish American War* for delineating "how American jingoists, expansionists, 'big navy' advocates, yellow journalists, and filibusterers maneuvered the nations into taking part in what politicians called 'A splendid little war!'"

Milton Meltzer

Meltzer was born in 1915 and of all the nonfiction writers for young adults, he has the longest record of being a spokesperson and a champion of the genre. As of 2004, he was still publishing on interesting topics as shown by his *Hear that Train Whistle Blow! How the Railroad Changed the World*. Because of his thoroughness and the interesting way he presents his findings, many of his books will continue to be read for decades. He focuses on social issues and for the third edition of this textbook wrote that except for inventing facts, he uses almost all the same techniques as do writers of fiction. Literary devices help him draw readers into the situation and the story that he is telling, and they help to enrich and deepen readers' feelings for people whose lives may be far different. He believes that it is not so much a question of fiction versus fact, but of truth versus falseness. His conclusion was that both fiction and nonfiction can lie about reality; but they can also tell the truth.

His 1998 *Food: How We Hunt and Gather It, How We Grow and Eat It, How We Buy and Sell It, How We Preserve and Waste It, and How Some Have Too Much and Others Have Too Little of It* grabbed attention for the length of its title as well as for its subject matter. Meltzer pioneered an in-their-own-words technique using historical journals, diaries, letters, and news accounts to bring out the personalities of such subjects as Abraham Lincoln, Frederick Douglass, and Andrew Carnegie. Other books include *In the Days of the Pharaohs: A Look at*

Ancient Egypt; *Piracy and Plunder: A Murderous Business*; *Ferdinand Magellan: First to Sail around the World*; and two beautifully illustrated companion books, *Ten Queens: Portraits of Power* and *Ten Kings and the Worlds They Ruled*.

Jim Murphy

Murphy is living proof that authors of nonfiction use many of the same literary techniques as authors of fiction, because in 2006 he published a well-received piece of historical fiction entitled *Desperate Journey*. It is the story of twelve-year-old Maggie, her younger brother, and her pregnant mother having to get the family's mule-drawn barge to Buffalo on the nineteenth-century Erie Canal. Murphy had already earned his reputation as a historian in such books as *Gone A-Whaling: The Lure of the Sea and the Hunt for the Great Whale*. His *Blizzard!* (the story of the great storm of 1888) was described by reviewers as not only humorous, jaw-dropping, and thought-provoking, but also *chilling*. Just as in *The Great Fire*, he blended history and adventure through focusing on the stories of individuals. His well-done *An American Plague: The True and Terrifying Story of the Yellow Fever Epidemic of 1793* takes on more interest now that people are worried about the possibilities of biological terrorism. A good companion book would be Laurie Halse Anderson's novel *Fever 1793*, which is set during the same epidemic. Murphy's *Inside the Alamo* was praised for the way it models the sorting out of historical information between folklore and true history, while *Pick and Shovel Poet: The Journeys of Pascal D'Angelo* was praised especially for the photographs, which were taken by D'Angelo after he migrated to America from Italy in 1910.

Laurence Pringle

Pringle is a respected and prolific writer of science-related books for young readers. For an earlier edition of this text, he discussed the challenge of being "fair" when writing about decision making that involves both social and scientific knowledge and attitudes. Because idealistic young readers may be especially vulnerable to one-sided arguments, he says that writers have a responsibility to present all sides of an issue and to show the gray as well as the black and white. He quickly adds, however, that being fair is not the same as being objective: "anyone who is well informed on an issue is not neutral," but that does not mean that he or she cannot work "to help kids understand the issues so they can make their own decisions."[8] Among Pringle's recent well-received books is one for young teens, *American Slave, American Hero: York of the Lewis and Clark Expedition,* about the African American who was owned by William Clark and went on the Lewis and Clark expedition. He uses quotes from the expedition's journals to show the contributions made by York.

Other Pringle books include *Drinking, A Risky Business* and *Jackal Woman: Exploring the World of Jackals*, in which he introduces middle school readers to the life of a behavioral ecologist, Patricia Moehlman. She was trained by Jane Goodall and is doing for jackals what Goodall did for chimpanzees. Other titles include *Chemical and Biological Warfare: The Cruelest Weapons*; *Oil Spills: Damage, Recovery and Prevention*; *Living Treasure: Saving Earth's Threatened Biodiversity*; *Global Warming*.

Joseph Bruchac, who traces part of his ancestral heritage to the Abenaki tribe in the Adirondacks, is a prolific writer of books about Native Americans, several of which are appropriate to young teens. Marlinda White-Kaulaity, a Navajo teacher in Arizona, was especially happy to put up this poster advertising Bruchac's biography of Jim Thorpe, the great Indian athlete. She remembers being at a meeting of Indian educators where an elder was being honored as Educator of the Year. The woman had been a student at the Carlisle school in 1911 and in her acceptance speech said almost as an aside, "We had a good football team." The audience broke into laughter and cheers because they all knew about Jim Thorpe and his coach, Pop Warner, and how in 1911 the Carlisle team had beaten Harvard 18 to 15.

Catherine Reef

Reef is the modern counterpart of the frontier housewife who always saved a little dough from a batch of bread to serve as starter yeast for the next batch. On her website, Reef tells how her interest in African American history led her to write *This Our Dark Country: The American Settlers of Liberia*, and then to go on and write *William Grant Still: African-American Composer* and *African Americans in the Military*. In 2000, she wrote *Paul Laurence Dunbar: Portrait of a Poet* and then six years later she wrote *e. e. cummings: A Poet's Life*. Other successful books include *Alone in the World: Orphans and Orphanages in America*; *Childhood in America: An Eyewitness History*; *Sigmund Freud: Pioneer of the Mind*; and *George Gershwin: American Composer*.

Concluding Comments

We will simply repeat the plea that we made at the beginning of this chapter where we said that in the real world nonfiction gets a greater share of people's money and attention than does fiction. Because there is so much of it, adults working with young readers have an even greater responsibility to help to winnow the wheat from the chaff and to bring to students' attention the books that they are likely to want and need. We also have the obligation that Mary E. Mueller pointed out in an Up for Discussion piece, "History and History Makers" that she wrote for *School Library Journal*. With shrinking budgets, all of us know that we need to buy new computer books, but we hesitate to spend money on new historical and informative books and on new biographies. But with changing attitudes and outlooks—which, we add, is even more true for self-help books—these sections of a library need just as much loving care and attention, including weeding, replacing, and promoting, as do any other sections of a library.

Notes

1. Paul Hirth, "What's the Truth about Nonfiction?" *English Journal* 91:4 (March 2002): 20–22.
2. "A Conversation with Milton Meltzer," in *Nonfiction for Young Adults: From Delight to Wisdom* by Betty Carter and Richard F. Abrahamson (Oryx Press, 1990), pp. 53–54.
3. Milton Meltzer, "Where Do All the Prizes Go? The Case for Nonfiction," *Horn Book Magazine* 52 (February 1975): 23.
4. George A. Woods, personal correspondence to Alleen Pace Nilsen, Summer 1978.
5. Michiko Kakutani, "Biography as a Blood Sport," *New York Times*, May 20, 1994, pp. B1, B6.
6. Mary E. Mueller, "Up for Discussion: History and History Makers: Give YAs the Whole Picture," *School Library Journal* 37 (November 1991): 55–56.
7. Mark Aronson, "Nonfiction Matters, Web Gems," *School Library Journal* 54 (August 2007): 13.
8. Laurence Pringle, "Laurence Pringle on Trying to Be Fair," *Literature for Today's Young Adults*, 4th edition, by Alleen Pace Nilsen and Kenneth L. Donelson. (HarperCollins, 1993), p. 314.

Evaluating, Promoting, and Using Young Adult Books

Chances are that you are studying young adult literature because you expect to work, or are already working, in a situation that calls for you to bring teenagers in touch with books. This chapter begins with a report on a survey we took and then continues with sections on various skills and responsibilities common to the work of librarians, English teachers, reading teachers, social studies teachers, parents, and counselors or youth workers. (See Chapter 11 for more specific information for English teachers.) These areas were chosen to give focus and organization to the information, but there is considerable overlap. Everyone working with young readers and books needs to get in the habit of both writing and reading reviews of books so as to increase their efficiency and skill in being able to suggest the right book for the right student or to at least point someone in the right direction.

When two people are talking about a book they both enjoyed, there is no way to divide the conversation into such discrete categories as literary analysis, personal feelings, sociological implications, and evaluation of potential popularity. Librarians find themselves discussing books as if they were classroom teachers. Teachers can adopt some of the promotional techniques that librarians use, and librarians can use some book discussion tactics that teachers use. In short, the organization of this chapter may make it appear that librarians work with young readers and books quite differently from teachers or counselors. In reality, nearly all adults who work with young readers and books have much the same goals and share many of the same approaches.

As a prelude to revising this chapter, we conducted a survey in four different high schools: one rural, two suburban, and one inner-city; one suburban junior high school; and with individual teenagers recruited by our young adult literature students. Fortunately for us, the respondents were almost equally divided between males and females. At the top of our questionnaire we listed twelve descriptors and asked students to circle the ones that applied to them. The number preceding each of the italicized descriptors tells how many students out of the 266 circled the item. They are arranged in descending order of popularity with our thoughts appended underneath each statement.

Number of Positive Responses	Questionnaire Statement and Comments

166   *I like having some choice about what books I will read in class.*

The popularity of this descriptor was consistently high across all ages and both genders. It was explained in some of the open-ended comments at the very end of the survey when we asked students to give advice to librarians or teachers who are interested in helping teenagers with their reading.

121   *I like reading books by authors I already know.*

At the youngest level, males and females answered almost the same, but as students grew older, the percentage of girls circling this descriptor consistently increased. This gave us a new understanding of the popularity of series books and for the way that publishers are increasingly asking "hot" new authors to sign contracts for several books.

113   *My mother likes to read.*

We were a little surprised that males and females circled this descriptor in equal numbers. We had thought that perhaps girls would have paid more attention to whether their mothers were reading while boys would have paid more attention to whether their fathers were reading.

112   *I have listened to one or more recorded books.*

We were happily surprised that this descriptor was circled by so many students. In hindsight, we wish we had asked for a distinction between "in school" and "on your own." At about the same time we were conducting the survey, we happened to observe a student teacher introducing Harper Lee's *To Kill a Mockingbird*. She did a wonderful job and read aloud the first chapter. The students begged her to keep reading, but she said, "No, now it's your turn. You are going to read the rest of it on your own, but we'll stop and talk about the chapters." They kept begging for her to read it aloud. She demurred by saying her voice would give out. Then someone raised a hand and said, "Let's play it on tape." When she said the school didn't own the tape (Sissy Spacek is the reader) and it would cost something like $40, the students in all seriousness offered to bring in two dollars each. Our student teacher—wise beyond her years—laughingly declined the offer but promised to read aloud at least a couple more chapters over the course of the next two weeks.

103   *I like to read.*

All the way across girls were more likely than boys to circle this descriptor, especially at the oldest level where sixteen girls and only one boy agreed.

98   *In grade school I liked story time.*

Again, girls circled this more often than did boys, but the difference was not as extreme.

97   *As a little kid I went to the library.*

All the way across this was circled by more girls than boys. The highest percentage of agreement, and the most percentage of boys, came from the youngest students. Perhaps they are closer to being "little kids" and could remember better or maybe more recently parents have gotten the message about taking their children, both boys and girls, to libraries.

93   *I read mostly fiction for fun.*

Here the males and females response rate was very similar.

84   *I usually like the book better than the movie.*

Overall, forty-six girls and thirty-eight boys circled this, but we were encouraged that ten boys from the oldest group (the one where only one person circled "I like to read") said they liked the book better than the movie.

77   *My father likes to read.*

That only 77 students circled this question for fathers (as compared to 113 for the question about mothers), goes against the stereotypical portrayal of evenings at home presented in old cartoons where the tired father sits reading the newspaper and the mother putters around the house or sits in a chair knitting or mending socks. In similar cartoons from today, both parents are sitting on a couch watching television.

54   *After seeing a movie, I have read the book.*

Although this was circled by relatively few students, it is at least enough to show that some students do not automatically think that a movie takes the place of a book.

43   *I read mostly nonfiction for information.*

While this was circled by the lowest number of students, it is the only one circled by more boys (twenty-four) than girls (nineteen). And in retrospect, we probably should not have assigned a purpose to their reading by including the phrase, "for information." One girl crossed it out and wrote "for fun."

Favorite Authors and Favorite Books

One of the open-ended questions we asked was "If you have favorite authors, list two or three names." Some students left the space blank, while others wrote such comments as "Whoever it is that writes the Redwall series," and "Author of *Eragon*." In all, 276 names (144 different ones) were listed. While this looks as though it averages out to one author per student, it really does not because many students left the space blank while others wrote two or three names. The variety of names made for difficult tabulations, but at the same time, they brought home the point that teenagers are reading from a much wider range of books than most of us are acquainted with. Here listed in descending order of popularity are those authors listed more than five times, along with a brief identifier.

Number of Students	Title and Author
34	J. K. Rowling (Harry Potter books)
10	Stephenie Meyer (vampire-centered romances: *Twilight*, *New Moon*, and *Eclipse*)
9	Stephen King (novels and films with supernatural elements)
9	Lemony Snicket (pseudonym of Daniel Handler, author of the *Series of Unfortunate Events*)
8	Roald Dahl (*Charlie and the Chocolate Factory* and many other children's books)
7	Dan Brown (*The Da Vinci Code*)
7	J. R. R. Tolkien (*The Lord of the Rings*)
6	Dean Koontz (quirky mysteries)
6	Gary Paulsen (adventure stories)
6	Darren Shan (scary Cirque du Freak books)
6	C. S. Lewis (*The Chronicles of Narnia* and other books)

Authors listed by five students included F. Scott Fitzgerald, Edgar Allan Poe, and R. L. Stein. Four students said their favorite authors were Avi, Tom Clancy, Michael Crichton, Brian Jacques, and Christopher Paolini, while three students wrote in the names of Orson Scott Card, Tom Clancy, Matt Christopher, Dave Pelzer, Anne Rice, and Nicholas Sparks. Two students listed Jane Austen, Judy Blume, Agatha Christie, Andrew Clements, Eoin Colfer, Caroline Cooney, Sharon Creech, Charles Dickens, Lois Duncan, John Grisham, Jack London, Lois Lowry, Yann Martel, Anne McCaffrey, Lurlene McDaniel, Garth Nix, Jodi Picoult, John Steinbeck, and Richard Wright.

We were surprised at Roald Dahl's coming in fifth, but we probably should not have been because we recently read a news story about a survey of adults in

England that showed Dahl to be the British public's all-time favorite author. The reporter was appalled that Dahl had beaten out even William Shakespeare. Other children's authors listed as favorites included Dr. Seuss, and Dav Pilkey, the author of the Captain Underpants books.

We are not taking the space right here to identify all of the authors listed by only a single student (although most of them are mentioned somewhere in the pages of this book). However, that does not mean they are unimportant. Any author should be thrilled to know that he or she is a teenager's favorite writer, and what is important is that young readers are involved enough to have favorite authors. When James Paul Gee was on our campus in the spring of 2007, and people were asking questions that revealed their disapproval of some of the kinds of interactive fiction now available through computer games, he said that he isn't worried about what games students choose to play or how much time they spend. The students he is worried about are the ones who have "no interest, no passion, and no desire" to be involved in literacy activities of any kind.

Another thing that surprised us from the list was how few female authors were included. We've always thought it kind of silly—or at least old-fashioned and counter-productive—that publishers encourage women to hide the fact that they are female by using initials instead of their given names as with S. E. Hinton (Susan) and J. K. Rowling (Joanne), but these self-generated lists show a definite leaning toward male names. This was less the case with female readers and with younger readers. In the twelve-to-fifteen age range, girls listed 16 female names out of their total of 45 names, while the boys listed 5 female names out of their total of 45 names. In those ages sixteen to nineteen, girls listed 19 female names out of their total of 57, while on their list of 52 names, boys included only three females: Agatha Christie, Caroline Cooney, and J. K. Rowling.

We asked two questions about favorite books: one about favorite books read as part of a class assignment and one about favorite books read outside of class. We were surprised at the variety, especially for those read as assignments because we are accustomed to seeing articles and hearing complaints that students are still assigned the same "classics" that we read in high school. Also, if our students' grade levels had all been the same (ours went from eighth grade through seniors) there would undoubtedly have been more consistency. If we had worded the question to ask what was your *least* favorite book read as a class assignment, we would probably have gotten more consistency in the answers. Here are class assignment favorites identified by three or more students:

Number of Respondents	Title and Author
5	*Night* by Elie Wiesel
5	*Romeo and Juliet* by William Shakespeare
4	*The Great Gatsby* by F. Scott Fitzgerald
4	*Lord of the Flies* by William Golding

4	*Othello* by William Shakespeare
4	*The Outsiders* by S. E. Hinton
4	*To Kill a Mockingbird* by Harper Lee
3	*Down River* by Will Hobbs
3	The Harry Potter books by J. K. Rowling
3	*Killing Mr. Griffin* by Lois Duncan
3	*The Pearl* by John Steinbeck
3	*Tangerine* by Edward Bloor

The list of favorites read outside of English class was still more varied. The only crossovers were *The Outsiders* and the Harry Potter books, and with Harry Potter, students did not specify which of the books they were referring to. We had the same trouble with students who wrote "David Pelzer's Story" because he has three autobiographical books: *A Child Called It, The Lost Boy,* and *A Man Named Dave.* At the time of the survey, the Gossip Girl series was up to Number 11, and there are so many versions of the Nancy Drew books that we did not try to assign an author.

Number of Respondents	Title and Author
6	Harry Potter books by J. K. Rowling
4	*A Child Called It* by Dave Pelzer
4	*The Outsiders* by S. E. Hinton
3	*Holes* by Louis Sachar
3	*Twilight* by Stephenie Meyer
2	*B.F.G.* (Big Friendly Giant) by Roald Dahl
2	The Bible
2	*The Chronicles of Narnia* by C. S. Lewis
2	*My Story* by Dave Pelzer
2	*Eldest* by Christopher Paolini
2	*Ender's Game* by Orson Scott Card
2	*Eragon* by Christopher Paolini
2	Gossip Girl series by Cecily von Ziegesar
2	Nancy Drew books
2	*Please Stop Laughing at Me* by Jodee Blanco
2	*Survivor* by Chuck Palahniuk

Taking a similar survey with a group of your own students would probably be a good idea because if you find out what they are reading and go out of your way to read one of "their" favorite books or authors (e.g., we had to go find out who Darren Shan is) then they will be more amenable to reading one of your books.

However, we should warn that student preferences can be affected by any number of things. The timing of our survey probably helped put J. K. Rowling so far above everyone else because we took the survey in May 2007, when excitement was mounting for the release of the third film and also the final book in the series. Publicity had also begun for the summer release of the new Nancy Drew movie, and Stephenie Meyer's ranking was probably influenced by location because she is a young mother who lives in Phoenix and it is exciting for students to see their own neighborhoods put inside such exciting books as *Twilight* and *New Moon* (*Eclipse* had not yet been released). Also, she has gone out of her way to make school visits and to be available for bookstore signings and other local events.

Choosing Books to Read

Another reason for doing such a survey and involving students in the counting and posting of results is that kids like to talk to each other about their favorite books. When we asked, "Who is most likely to give you ideas for leisure reading?" 105 students circled friends, 103 circled family members, 81 circled a teacher, and 25 circled a librarian. On a similar question, in which we asked students where or how they obtained their books, older students were more likely to circle browsing in stores, while younger students circled browsing in libraries. The total numbers were:

129	Browsing in stores
81	Browsing in libraries
69	Using the Internet
29	Other

In the space by the *Other* category, students listed taking suggestions from boyfriends or girlfriends or just picking up whatever happens to be around. We were amused at one boy who wrote that if he hears of a good book, he just tells his grandmother and she gets it for him. Perhaps the biggest lesson to be learned from the wide range of the students' chosen "favorites" is how important it is for us to provide a variety of books and to give readers choices.

When we asked students how they decide whether to read a book that they have picked up, their answers ranged all the way from "reading fifty pages" to "reading the first chapter," or "a little bit of the first page." While we always tell students not to judge a book by its cover, we fully expect them to do exactly that, so we were impressed that more students (thirty-four as compared to the thirty-one who mentioned the cover) said they read the back of the book. Eight students mentioned the title as a factor, while four mentioned reviews, with one of those specifying a "Google synopsis."

When we read news stories like the ones cited in our Media Watch in Chapter 3, we get the impression that all teenagers are writing and responding to chat groups or posting their work online. But on our survey only 75 out of a total of 266 had posted some of their own writing online. To get this information, we listed fourteen literacy activities and asked the students to circle the ones they had participated in during the last two years. Here is the complete list showing how many students circled each activity:

Number of Respondents (out of 266)	Literacy Activity
230	Used Google to find information
202	Sent a text message to a friend
202	Used a cell phone to take a photo
200	Sent email to someone
193	Visited YouTube, MySpace, etc.
172	Wrote a book report
159	Wrote a friendly letter or card
155	Wrote a poem
148	Found information on Wikipedia
132	Filled out a job application
75	Put something you wrote online
71	Read about a book online, e.g., in Amazon.com
64	Acted a part in a play
27	Attended a poetry slam

Answers to Miscellaneous Questions

Three times as many students (139 to 45) said that when picking a book, the genre is more important than the author. When we asked what reading material was regularly available in their homes, the Internet topped the list with 132 responses; next came magazines, with 110 students; then books, with 100 students; and lastly, the daily newspaper, with 67 students. Younger students were less likely than older students to read the newspaper. Funnies and comics are read almost equally by males and females (total of 47), while the sports page is read by three times as many males (48) as compared to females (15). Twenty-four males and 14 females reported reading the front page and news stories, while six males and five females listed entertainment or movie reviews. This was similar to ads and classifieds, which were read by four females and five males. Two girls, but no boys, reported reading obituaries and horoscopes while only one girl (an eighteen-year-old) said she reads the editorials.

We concluded the survey by asking what advice students wanted to offer teachers and librarians. "Get books that are fun and interesting," was an idea that appeared again and again in the student responses. However, the teacher who helped us by administering the survey at the junior high school cautioned us against promoting the idea that reading should always be fun. Her husband is a math teacher, and his students expect to work hard even when they aren't having fun. In contrast, some of her students who have been taught to view reading as "fun," feel perfectly justified in choosing not to read if they think it would be more "fun" to listen to music or to go skateboarding. Her point was that we need to help students recognize the value in reading for information as well as for pleasure. Here are some of the student comments that centered on the idea of "fun."

- "When you ask us to look for specific things, it ruins the fun of reading." (girl, eighteen)
- "Find a book that is fun, adventurous, and mysterious. Also joke around a little to make it fun." (boy, sixteen)
- "Give us fun and easy-to-read books that really grab our attention. Also give us books on tape/CD and have us follow along." (boy, eighteen)
- "Make reading more fun by doing what our teacher did. She had us read a biography and make a CD, diary entries, or a board game of the person's life." (girl, sixteen)
- "Don't force us to read 'classics.' Also stop having students interpret every other sentence and constantly look for 'hidden meanings.' It is a waste of time and can turn some kids off from reading." (boy, eighteen)

As noted earlier, the most consistent finding from the survey was that students liked having some choice about what books they would read in class. Comments supporting this idea include:

- "Let us read what we want. I remember last year hating being told what to read. I want my own choice." (girl, fourteen)
- "When you ask students to give suggestions on books, try to keep track of them and try to get them ASAP." (girl, fifteen)
- "Ask us what we want to read about instead of providing something we don't want to read." (boy, fifteen)
- "At least once a year let students choose what book they want to read." (boy, fourteen)

One student hinted at wanting a feeling of accomplishment when he wrote nostalgically about the good feelings he got in elementary school when he would finish reading a book and then take a computerized test on it. Other students as well were interested in more than fun, as shown by these statements:

- "Encourage kids to read; it's the best thing to do." (boy, fifteen)
- "Librarians and English teachers can help us understand why reading a particular book is good for us." (girl, sixteen)
- "Take into consideration the appearance of said teenager, and really know some obscure genres and titles. Chances are, you'll be an accurate judge of young people's tastes." (girl, fifteen)
- "Help us find an author or certain genre of book so that we can get interested in it." (girl, fourteen)
- "Help us understand what's happening in a book by giving us reviews after each chapter." (boy, sixteen)
- "You should make students read outside of class." (boy, sixteen)
- "Constantly read books that teenagers like so that you have a broader idea of what is popular and can recommend new things to us." (boy, seventeen)

Borrowing a Philosophy from Teachers of Physical Education

Students' strong preference for choosing their own reading materials reminded us of what we've been hearing from our Arizona State University colleagues in the Department of Exercise and Wellness (what used to be called Physical Education). Modern PE teachers are now being trained under the PLAY (Promoting Lifelong Activity for Youth) philosophy. They no longer plan the kinds of activities that inspired Paula Danziger to write her funny YA novel about overweight Marcy, who, in *The Cat Ate My Gymsuit*, makes all kinds of excuses to keep from going to PE. While the PLAY acronym might not seem as appropriate for those of us working in literacy as it is for PE teachers, we are suggesting an analog because some of their good ideas, especially the focus on inspiring a lifelong commitment, are applicable to our goals as literacy teachers.

In the new PE classes, children no longer play elimination games in which the least skilled are the first to sit down. Our literacy equivalent—the spelling bee—is a perfect illustration of what's wrong with games where there is one winner and twenty-nine losers. Another literacy comparison is round-robin reading, dreaded by students who aren't good at oral reading in the same way that kids in PE dread getting laughed at for their inability to do push-ups or climb a rope. And our equivalent to the now-extinct game of Dodge Ball is the way we sometimes fire questions at harried students.

The most appropriate and far-reaching comparison is that, rather than waiting apprehensively to see if they will be assigned to run wind sprints or be the last one picked for a team, children are allowed to select their own activities from such sports as skating, jumping rope, juggling weighted scarves, keeping beach balls in the air, and playing with Frisbees, jacks, and hula hoops. Older students play badminton or tennis, jog or run, and work out on climbing walls and on the kinds of equipment now found in adult fitness clubs. The idea is that if students enjoy and understand the value of what they are doing, they are more likely to continue it when no teacher is applying pressure.

Physical education teachers are absolutely certain that when today's kids grow up they are going to need to exercise their bodies and control their diets, so they teach wellness and food management. We literacy teachers do not have such a specific view of our students' future needs, but we know that it is getting harder, rather than easier, to manage literacy needs. Modern media encourages divided attention as people multitask by taking their phone messages while handling their email and by listening to television newscasts while reading on-screen crawlers about different events. Also, today's world is filled with purposeful obfuscation in that many political, commercial, and philosophical messages are written more for persuasion than for clarification. And because of the complexity of such things as today's computer manuals, prescription drug warnings, and income tax forms, the reading material we need for managing our daily lives is more complicated than what our grandparents needed.

The major lesson we can learn from the PE teachers is the importance of student choice. The idea is unsettling because presiding over a gym or a room filled with students all engaged in the same activity gives teachers a satisfying sense of control. But whether students are doing the same calisthenics, chanting the same phonics lessons, or reading the same book, the activity is probably not something they will look forward to doing in their adult lives because humans, like cats, do not want to be herded.

When students are allowed to be the teacher's partner in choosing reading materials, they gain a sense of ownership and pleasure, plus they get practice in one of the most important literacy skills they will need in their adult lives. Because each day we are presented with so much to read, all of us are forced to perform triage: Category One—*Ignore*; Category Two—*Skim*; and Category Three—*Read*. Children seem less troubled by this than are most of us, but the problem is that many pieces find their way into students' Read category only because of pressure from us. Once students graduate, there will be no pressure from teachers and so it is important that we think ahead.

Instead of always assigning students to answer textbook or teacher-prepared questions, we need to give them practice in talking about their reading with small groups of fellow students so as to lay a foundation for future literary talk with friends about the movie they just saw, a TV series, or a book they have read. We also need to model and encourage students to show respect for different literary genres and tastes. What starts as a movie becomes a book and what starts as a cartoon becomes a video game and then a book, or vice versa. We need to extend the old saying about not judging a book by its cover to something like "Don't judge a story by the medium of its telling."

Of course, we want to offer books to readers that portray their own cultures and their own lifestyles, but we also need to provide readers with access to books beyond our own expectations. One of our best lessons in the diversity of reading tastes came from an Arizona woman who, as a volunteer, drove the

Reading-Is-Fundamental bookmobile through northern Arizona. One morning when she was parked high on a desert mesa on the Hopi Indian Reservation, she saw an elderly man leaning against a cedar tree. She assumed he had come with a grandchild, but a couple of hours later when he was still standing there she invited him to come in and pick a book for himself. He stayed quite a while and at last chose Robert Louis Stevenson's *Treasure Island*. He must have sensed her surprise because he offered an explanation: "I started it at boarding school, but I didn't get to finish it."

Probably not one of us would have "matched" this book to this particular reader, but the incident shows that there are many kinds of diversity and that if we want to succeed in turning people into lifelong readers, we need to provide many choices and then to respect those choices that students make.

Ways of Teaching While Offering Students Choices

Teri Lesense in her 2006 book for teachers in middle grade schools, *Naked Reading: Uncovering What Tweens Need to Become Lifelong Readers*, is well aware of how widely disparate are the literacy practices of young people and how much they want to have something to say about what they read. A good idea that she has for helping teachers cope with the new reading strategies is what she calls Template Activities, teaching techniques that can be used with a variety of books. Middle school teachers would do well to find her book and see which of her Template Activities might work for them. Here we will describe three Template Activities that have worked for us with older students.

Free Reading

In Ken Donelson's thirteen years of teaching high school English, free reading is the activity that won more students over to the satisfaction (and maybe even the joy) of reading than anything else he tried. He remembers it as the hardest work he did, but also the most satisfying. In today's world of high-stakes tests and accountability, some schools are tempted to label the activity—whether it's a whole semester's course or a couple of days each week—"guided" or "individualized reading." However, such titles go against the basic philosophy of the course, which in the mid 1930s grew out of Lou LaBrant's English teaching at Ohio State University's Lab School. The great benefit of "free reading" is that students have freedom of choice in what they read. Teachers can, of course, suggest or recommend books they feel are "better" or "more challenging" or "more mature," but if it's really a free-reading class teachers can do no more than suggest and then leave it to the student to make the final decision.

One of the chief reasons for providing students time to read in class is to prevent the dropoff in reading that usually occurs when students begin high school and their social and work schedules leave little time for reading. A classroom library is provided, containing multiple copies of popular young adult and adult titles from which students make their own selections. It is wise for teachers to send a note of explanation to parents that includes the statement that the choice of books is up to the student and his or her parents. It helps at the beginning for either the teacher or the librarian to give booktalks; once the class is started, students can recommend "good books" to each other.

When students finish a book, they hold a conference with the teacher, who preferably has also read the book. The purpose is not to test the student as much as it is to encourage thinking about the book and the author's intentions and to give teachers an opportunity to suggest other books that the student might enjoy. Teachers need to show that they respect the reading of popular young adult books by being familiar with many of them and by being genuinely interested in what students have to say about them. The class is doomed to failure if teachers view it as a kind of focused study hall in which their job is to do little more than keep control and keep kids reading. It's also doomed to failure if students view it as a "cake" class, and for this reason successful teachers are fairly stringent as they devise various systems for giving credit. Students keep records of the number of books (or number of pages) read, they assist the teacher in judging the difficulty of the material, they mark their improvement over the semester (perhaps shown by a test score or by the number of pages the student reads in a class period), and they receive grades on their preparation for the individual conferences.

Various studies summarized by Dick Abrahamson and Eleanor Tyson in "What Every English Teacher Should Know about Free Reading"[1] have shown:

1. Free reading is enjoyed by both students and teachers.

2. Over a semester, students pick a variety of books, ranging from easy to difficult and from recent to classic.

3. Reading skills improve, with some of this improvement undoubtedly related to attitude change.

4. Students taught through free reading are more likely to read as adults and to foster reading activities with their children.

5. Individual conferences help literature come alive for students.

6. The conferences also help to break down barriers between students and teachers.

7. Good teachers employ the concept of reading ladders (e.g., helping a girl move from a Sweet Dreams romance to a Norma Fox Mazer or an M. E. Kerr book and on to *Gone with the Wind* and *Jane Eyre*).

With so many benefits, why isn't the course taught more often? Part of the reason is an image problem. More people than we care to think about are sure that if students are having a good time they can't also be learning. Another problem is that the teacher's role is practically invisible. Being able to listen to students while working ever so subtly to suggest books that will raise levels of reading and improve skills without discouraging young readers takes a knowledge of hundreds of books plus tact and considerable talent in communication. Yet this teaching occurs in private sessions between two people. One of our favorite graduate students is a high school reading teacher who teaches an individualized reading class along with some of the more traditional remedial reading classes. She laughs in frustration about her principal's visits to her individualized reading class. After popping his head into her room on several different occasions and seeing the kids reading and her talking with a student at her desk, he sent her a note requesting that she let him know "when you are going to be teaching," so that he could come and observe.

She's still trying to educate him about the type of class she's teaching. It is not for the dysfunctional or disabled reader. It is for the average or above-average student who simply needs a chance to read and discuss books. In effect, it is one last try on the part of the school to instill in young people the habit of reading for pleasure. An alternative discussed in Chapter 11 is the organization of literature circles.

Archetypes in Literature and Pop Culture

Another template activity is to work with archetypes as they are reflected in literature and in pop culture. A benefit of supervising student teachers is that we get to see successful classroom activities, and the one that excited us this year was on archetypes taught by Cynthia Kiefer and her student teacher, Jessica Zellner, at Saguaro High School in Scottsdale. On our third visit, we walked in and found every bulletin board and practically every chalkboard and every inch of the wall covered with one-page "posters." Cynthia said it was the only assignment she had ever given where every student in every class followed through and brought in their work to be explained to the other students and pinned or taped up for everyone to see. Each poster had a downloaded picture of a celebrity or a character from a film, a television show, or an advertising campaign, plus the identification of an archetype and a couple of paragraphs written by the student explaining why this character fit into the particular archetype. The most surprising part was that we saw very few duplicates of the specific characters, but many repeats of particular archetypes being illustrated.

Studying archetypes is a perfect way to bring some consistency and commonality to discussions and considerations of the variety of literacy experiences illustrated through the Media Watch in Chapter 3 and in the comments from students taking our survey. Working with archetypes helps people understand the circular way in which literature and popular culture work together to create the collective unconscious, that is, those images related to the deepest, most permanent aspects of people's lives including death, fear, love, ambition, the biological family, and the unknown.

Carl Jung, Joseph Campbell, and Northrop Frye have all written on how these images find their way into people's minds and underlie the way we communicate with each other. People not privy to such cultural images could not understand the thirty-second commercials we watch on television, the cartoons that tell a whole story in one picture, and the cover lines that attract us to magazine stories, and so forth. The small "bubbles" from which comic strip characters speak allow for only a few words, while the small screens on cell phones used for Instant Messaging encourage the creation of even more succinct messages. This push toward efficient communication promotes a reliance on archetypal images in which just three or four words or the mention of a name is enough to trigger full-blown images in the minds of readers or listeners.

Beth Ricks, one of our Ph.D. graduates who now teaches at the University of Louisiana–Monroe, wrote to tell us about her frustrations in trying to get the high school students she was teaching to approach literature through a critical lens or perspective. They would lose interest long before she could teach them the backgrounds for Marxism or feminist theory, or even Reader-Response,

> But when I used archetype theory as a way to introduce mythology and Homer's *Odyssey*, they were actively involved. And I realized it's because they already have the foundation with archetypes because the archetypes are part of the subconscious and myth is part of who we are. They easily picked up the concept of looking at texts through an archetypal lens. So far, we have applied archetypes to film, music, the newspaper, magazines, and of course, the *Odyssey*. We watched *Shrek* in class, and they saw it through new eyes. . . . With my senior class, we watched an Adam Sandler movie and they wrote essays in which they traced the Innocent's Journey. They loved this exercise and from it realized that many of the books they had previously read included an Innocent embarking on a journey.[2]

In closing, she said the best part was that her students had fun and that for the first time they understood they could criticize literary texts without being negative. And long after the class studied archetypes, students were still identifying and arguing about the archetypal roles of particular characters. In a spillover to real life, one of her students reported on how she tried to calm her parents by explaining the nature of the archetypal Seeker when they were upset about their popular new minister's resigning and going to "find himself" in a different town. They weren't impressed until she explained the concept of a Shadow Seeker as someone who has the archetypal characteristics to such an extent that they go beyond reason—for example, the interfering mother-in-law as a Caregiver or the control freak or micromanager as a Leader or Ruler.

The following are brief descriptions of archetypes that we have found easy for students to understand and to "discover" in both the popular culture and in the literature we are reading. We took most of these from Carol S. Pearson's *Awakening the Heroes Within: Twelve Archetypes to Help Us Find Ourselves and Transform Our World* (HarperOne, 1991), but over the years we've changed the descriptions and added a couple of new ones, including the Junex versus the Senex.

The Innocent Embarking on a Journey This most archetypal of all stories begins with a young person setting out either willingly or through some kind of coercion on a journey or a quest and meeting frightening and terrible challenges. After proving his or her worth, the young person receives help from divine or unexpected sources. Even though a sacrifice is usually demanded, readers rejoice in the success of the young protagonist as when David slays Goliath, when Cinderella is united with the noble prince and given the fitting role of queen, and when Dorothy and Toto find their way back to Kansas. In every culture, legends, myths, and folk and fairy tales follow the pattern of the adventure/accomplishment romance. They are called romances because they contain exaggeration. The bad parts are like nightmares, while the good parts are like pleasant daydreams. Such romances came to be associated with love because the traditional reward for a successful hero on such a quest was the winning of a beautiful maiden.

The biblical story of Joseph is a prototypical example of a worthy young hero being forced to go on a journey. Early in life, Joseph was chosen and marked as a special person as shown by the prophetic dreams he related to his brothers and by his father's special love demonstrated through the multicolored coat. When Joseph was sold to the Egyptian traders, he embarked on his quest for wisdom and knowledge. Just when all seemed lost, Joseph was blessed with the ability to interpret dreams. This got him out of prison and into the Pharaoh's court. The climax came years later during the famine that brought Joseph's brothers to Egypt and the royal palace. Without recognizing Joseph, they begged for food. His forgiveness and his generosity were final proof of his worthiness.

A distinguishing feature of such romances is the happy ending achieved only after the hero's worth is proven through a crisis or an ordeal. Usually as part of the ordeal the hero must make a sacrifice, be wounded, or leave some part of his or her body, even if it is only sweat or tears. The real loss is that of innocence, but it is usually symbolized by a physical loss, as in Norse mythology when Odin gave one of his eyes to pay for knowledge. J. R. R. Tolkien used a similar theme in *The Lord of the Rings* when Frodo, who has already suffered many wounds, finds that he cannot throw back the ring and so must let Gollum take his finger along with the ring.

Among the world's great stories of journeys are Homer's *Iliad* and *The Odyssey*, John Bunyan's *The Pilgrim's Progress*, Jonathan Swift's *Gulliver's Travels*, and the biblical story of Adam and Eve being banished from the Garden of Eden. Modern children's journey stories include William Steig's *Sylvester and the Magic Pebble*, Ezra Jack Keats's *The Snowy Day*, and Maurice Sendak's *Where the Wild Things Are*. See Focus Box 4.6, Literal Journeys/Figurative Quests (p. 138), for examples of YA stories that follow this archetypal pattern.

The Archetypal Seeker   The Archetypal Seeker has much in common with the real lives of young adults because they know that sooner or later they must leave their parents' homes and make a life for themselves. Joseph, in the Bible story, was forced to go on his journey; in contrast, Moses, who led the Jews in their Exodus from Egypt, comes closer to being a Seeker because he chose to go forth and find a better life. The Pharaoh, who wanted the Jews to stay and work for him, represents the part of the human psyche that resists change and wants to preserve the status quo.

An important part of being a Seeker is knowing when to stop. Shadow Seekers—those for whom the grass is always greener on the other side—abound in modern culture as with marriage partners and the owners of cars and houses, who continuously "trade up." The boy in Willa Cather's short story "Paul's Case" is a Shadow Seeker who wants to live in the fantasy world of the theater and in the glamorous world that he imagines for the wealthy. Paul commits suicide rather than face the dreary life he foresees for himself after his father repays the money he stole to finance his trip to New York. The parents in Gary Paulsen's *The Island* are Shadow Seekers who have such wanderlust that they constantly move from one town to another in search of an idealized sense of community.

The Junex versus the Senex   This archetype simply represents another way of talking about the conflict that exists between young and old. From an adult viewpoint, this is the idea of the *Dennis the Menace* cartoons and *The Little Rascals* movie gang. From a child's viewpoint, this is perhaps what is behind referring to someone as a Scrooge, with implications of stinginess, to someone as an old Witch or a Grinch, with implications of mean-spiritedness, or to someone as a dirty old man, with implications of sexual exploitation. This archetype is often referred to as the generation gap, but in fact it does not have to cross a whole generation. With teenagers, only a few years can make a difference in one's attitudes and loyalties, as when high school seniors "lord" it over freshmen, or when older siblings make life miserable for younger brothers and sisters. Because of where they are on their life journeys, teenagers find this archetype important.

In an interesting switch, a reversal is sometimes shown in which young protagonists skip a generation and identify with people of their grandparents' ages. This may relate to the fact that teenagers and elderly people are both living on the edges. They are not really in control of their lives, and so as "outsiders" may join with each other to present a united front against the mainstream adults in the middle. Examples include Jimmy and his grandmother in Walter Dean Myers's *Somewhere in the Darkness*, Miracle McCloy and her grandfather in Han Nolan's *Dancing on the Edge*, and Tree and his grandfather in Joan Bauer's *Stand Tall*.

The Orphan The Orphan has always been a well-loved character, probably because deep in our subconscious all readers fear being the lost child. Harry Potter is the latest orphan to tug at our heartstrings, but before Harry, we had the orphans in Charles Dickens's *Little Dorrit* and *Oliver Twist*, the children in C. S. Lewis's *The Lion, the Witch, and the Wardrobe*, and the endearing young redhead in Lucy Maud Montgomery's *Anne of Green Gables*. The comic strip character Little Orphan Annie is so famous that she inspired a Broadway musical. To play the literary role of orphan, young protagonists can have lost both of their parents, as in Robert Cormier's *I Am the Cheese*, or only one parent, as in Mark Twain's *Huckleberry Finn*. A child might be a temporary orphan as was the boy in the *Home Alone* film, or the protagonist might still have one or both parents, but the parents are unable to play their role, as with the mother in Cynthia Voigt's Homecoming series. A higher percentage of orphans appear in children's literature than in real life because many authors do what Betsy Byars has confessed to. When planning a book, she says the first thing she does is figure out some way to get rid of the parents so that the children can be free to make decisions and get credit for their own actions.

The Caregiver From the world's bank of great stories, we have such caregivers as The Good Samaritan, Robin Hood, Snow White, Jiminy Cricket, Mary Poppins, Wendy from Peter Pan, and Charlotte from E. B. White's *Charlotte's Web*. From real life we occasionally hear someone referred to as a Florence Nightingale or a Mother Teresa. Even preschoolers know about Horton, the wonderfully patient elephant from Dr. Seuss's *Horton Hatches the Egg*, and about the mother duck who majestically leads her ducklings through Boston traffic in Robert McCloskey's *Make Way for Ducklings*. One of the most touching contemporary stories about a caregiver is Katherine Paterson's *The Great Gilly Hopkins*. Galadriel, shortened to Gilly, is in foster care because, as one of our students described the situation, her "flower-child parents went to seed in the garden of motherhood." While searching for her birthmother, Gilly fails to appreciate her larger-than-life foster mother until it is too late.

The Wicked Stepmother is a universally understood archetype of the Shadow Caregiver. Bruno Bettelheim, along with other critics, has suggested that she isn't a stepmother at all. Instead, she's the dark side of everyone's mother—the scapegoat for the resentments that build up as part of the Junex–Senex conflict. The character is portrayed as a wicked stepmother instead of a wicked stepfather because on a daily basis the mother enforces discipline and teaches children a sense of responsibility as well as the skills of daily living.

The Sage   Sages offer spiritual and intellectual care as opposed to the physical care that is thought of as being part of the Caregiver role. The Giver in Lois Lowry's book of that name is an archetypal Sage. By holding the community's memories, he shields the members from responsibilities. In his wisdom, he questions this role and leads Jonas, who has been chosen to be his successor, to also question it. In more traditional literature, Merlin is a Sage, and it could make an interesting study to compare how authors ranging from C. S. Lewis to T. H. White and from Mary Stewart to Walt Disney's scriptwriters have portrayed this legendary Sage. Jeff's father at the beginning of Cynthia Voigt's *A Solitary Blue* is portrayed as a Shadow Sage. In response to his wife's leaving the family, Jeff's father places himself in "an ivory tower," but finally, as the book progresses, he is able to come down and relate to his son. Our students have argued about whether Darth Vader from *Star Wars* is a Shadow Sage because he is obsessed with perfection and being right, but at the same time is cynical and wants to obtain wisdom not so he can help others, but so he can feel superior and criticize them.

A true Sage is wise enough to realize that people cannot search for just one truth, but instead must understand a multiplicity of truths. This is the point made in Hisako Matsubara's *Cranes at Dusk*, set in post–World War II Japan. When a Shinto priest allows his daughter to attend Christian services, the Christian missionaries are disappointed to learn that the daughter and her father are not being "converted." Instead, the father is just putting into practice his belief that "No religion is enough to answer all the questions."

The Friend   Friends in literature range from Robin Hood and his Merry Men to Harry Potter, Ron, and Hermione. Friendship is the theme of some of the most popular children's books—for example, Arnold Lobel's *Frog and Toad Are Friends*, Lois Lowry's Anastasia books, Barbara Parks's Junie B. Jones books, and Beverly Cleary's Ramona books. Middle school girls have loved the friendships shown in books by Judy Blume, Ellen Conford, and Paula Danziger. Friendship was also at the root of the success of The Babysitters' Club and the Sweet Valley High series. (See Focus Box 4.7, p. 141, for books that explore friendships among contemporary teens.) Since the story of David and Jonathan in the Old Testament, there have been strong stories about friendships between boys, as in John Knowles's *A Separate Peace*. The runaway success of Ann Brashares's 2001 *Sisterhood of the Traveling Pants* shows that friendships among girls can also be satisfying.

The Lover   Lovers are such popular protagonists that for general readers they have coopted the whole genre of romance. From a literary standpoint, the first romances were stories told in the Roman (or Latin) manner; that is, those told by speakers of Latin, Italian, Spanish, and French. These stories were often about bold adventurers slaying dragons, rescuing princesses from ogres, and defeating the wicked enemies of a righteous king. Love came into the stories because a successful knight was often rewarded by being given the hand of a beloved maiden. The world's lovers are as different as Adam and Eve, Beauty and the Beast, Jane Eyre and Rochester, Catherine and Heathcliff, and even Tarzan and Jane. Shadow Lovers, those whose love is out of control or damaging, might include Samson and Delilah, J. Gatsby and Daisy, Humber Humbert and Lolita, and perhaps even the gangsters Bonnie and Clyde.

Being rewarded with the love of a respected character is a common theme in YA books. Stories of star-crossed lovers, the most famous of which is Shakespeare's *Romeo and Juliet*, are intrinsically interesting because of the possibility for greater suspense and tension. Such protagonists come close to being Shadow Lovers if their actions bring about tragic results. The possibility for tragedy and conflict is frequently at the heart of YA books about love between characters of the same sex, but in fairly recent years YA authors have begun to portray lesbian and gay characters filling the role of Lovers rather than Shadow Lovers. When Nancy Garden was interviewed for *School Library Journal* after she won the Margaret A. Edwards Award (see p. 414), she showed how differently the two protagonists have been portrayed on the cover designs of three paperback editions of *Annie on My Mind*. Only on the most recent cover do the two girls look comfortable and equally interested in each other.

The Warrior, the Hero, the Villain or Destroyer   These archetypes are strong characters; people who will stand up and fight. Those who become heroes or Superheroes choose to fight on the side of good, as with Superman, Spiderman, Wonder Woman, and Batman and Robin. If warriors make the wrong choice and go in the other direction, they become Villains or Destroyers. Female villains are called such names as Jezebels or Witches, while male villains might be referred to as Hitlers or Devils. A fairly new eponym for a Destroyer Warrior is a Rambo, taken from the name of the lead character in David Morrell's *First Blood*, made famous in the Rambo movies starring Sylvester Stallone. Another reason the name caught on is that society was becoming aware of a new kind of Destroyer— young, hostile males who were not thieves or criminals in the old sense of the word, but instead were toughs and bullies. Thirty years after Morrell created his Rambo character, society is even more puzzled by these kinds of Destroyers and the ripple effects of their actions in schools and communities. (See Focus Box 4.3, Bullies and Buddies, p. 125.)

The Ruler   These characters are more likely to be called leaders in the United States because of the country's history as a haven for common people and its rejection of the idea of royalty and inherited power. The good ruler is like Aslan in C. S. Lewis's *The Lion, the Witch, and the Wardrobe* or like Simba in Walt Disney's *The Lion King*. Alison Lurie in her 1991 *Don't Tell the Grownups* observed that the great appeal of the Winnie the Pooh books to young children is that the child Christopher Robin gets to play the role of the beneficent dictator in charge of the whole "Hundred Akre Woods."

Great rulers make mistakes, but when this happens, they are mature enough to recognize their folly and to learn from it. A recognition of this fact has brought changes in the biographies written for young people. It used to be that authors put in only the positive aspects of leaders' lives, but today they include both the good and the bad, in the hopes that young people will be even more inspired to see that "imperfect" people, which all of us are, can still make great contributions.

The Fool and the Trickster These archetypes appear in American jokes about "The Little Moron," in some of the Muslim stories about Mullah Nasruddin (sometimes he's wise and other times he's foolish), in Jewish tales about the Fools of Chelm, and in European and American folktales about Foolish Jack. Readers and listeners enjoy the humor that comes from the surprise, incongruity, spontaneity, and violations of social norms that are part and parcel of stories about fools or clowns. While clowns play the role of the fool, they are really Tricksters, since they are only pretending to be ignorant. Children have an extra reason for enjoying stories about fools—because of their powerlessness and lack of experience, they are often left feeling foolish and so are glad when they find characters even more foolish than they are. Literary fools include such characters as Sheridan's Mrs. Malaprop, who always mixes up her words, and Thurber's Walter Mitty, whose mind keeps wandering away from real life and into fantasy daydreams.

Tricksters are only pretending to be fools so that they can get away with something, as when Tom Sawyer tricks the neighborhood boys into whitewashing the fence. Ulysses was a Trickster when he managed to escape with most of his men from the cave of the Cyclops. The Joker in the Batman movies is a trickster. In YA books, portrayals of fools and tricksters are fairly subtle and usually have the serious purpose of teaching young people not to be fools or to be tricked, a point discussed in more detail in relation to realistic problem novels in Chapter 4.

The Magician Magicians appear in stories of fantasy where authors create a make-believe world with no explanation of how the magic works. Internal consistency is all that is required. Ursula Le Guin's books about Earthsea are especially good at illustrating the role of the Magician. Ogion is the Magician/Sage, but readers are most interested in the young people who are training to become Magicians as when the boy Sparrowhawk becomes the archmage Ged, the girl Goha becomes the wise woman Tenar, and in the last book, an abused Orphan becomes Tehanu, destined to become the next archmage. Honest Magicians use their powers for good, while Shadow Magicians use their powers for evil or destructive purposes. Some stories about Magicians and Creators are cautionary tales that warn against humans trying to take the power of the gods for themselves, as illustrated by the host of troubles released when Dr. Frankenstein created his monster.

The Creator Creators do not lift a finger to their noses or bring out an array of helpers to make happy endings possible; instead they transform reality by

Margaret A. Edwards Award
Winner (1993)

M. E. Kerr, **A Genius with Names**

Edwards Honor Books include *Dinky Hocker Shoots Smack!*; *Gentlehands*; *ME, ME, ME, ME, ME: Not a Novel*; and *Night Kites*. Other highly acclaimed books include *Little Little*; *If I Love You, Am I Trapped Forever?*; and *Deliver Us from Evie*.

One of Kerr's first jobs when, in 1972, she wrote *Dinky Hocker Shoots Smack!* was to choose a penname to use with her YA books since she was already known as a writer of mysteries and of love stories about lesbians. Her real name is Marijane Meaker, and so for her penname she chose M. E. Kerr, a play on her surname. The next thing she had to do was to argue with her publishers who wanted a softer title than *Dinky Hocker Shoots Smack!*

The story is about a do-gooder mother who is oblivious to the needs of her own overweight daughter, who is ironically called Dinky. The title comes from what Dinky paints on the walls and the sidewalk for people to see when her mother exits a meeting where she is being honored for her work with drug addicts. In a lighter, naming incident, Dinky names the stray cat she finds cowering under a car Nader, in honor of Ralph Nader, who, as a critic of the American automobile industry, also spent considerable time under cars.

In *I'll Love You When You're More Like Me*, Wally has a crush on a girl who has created for herself the fancy sounding stage name of Sabra St. Amour—she used to be plain old Maggie Duggy. When Wally meets her at the beach and she asks him for a cigarette, he tells her she has to be a little crazy to let the cigarette companies manipulate her with such names as Merit and Vantage. She responds that she came to the beach for a swim and some sun, not for a lecture, but Wally goes right on asking her if True, More, and Now mean that she will get more out of life by living for the moment because she won't live long if she is being True to her filthy habit. While this isn't enough to convince Sabra to quit smoking, she becomes interested in Wally as a "thinker."

Kerr's *Gentlehands* is the story of a post-WWII hunt for one of the cruelest of the Nazi SS guards at Auschwitz. He taunted Jewish prisoners from Rome by playing Puccini's opera *Tosca* and singing "O dolci mani," which translates to "gentle hands." The plot centers around whether Buddy's mysterious German grandfather is this man. He has named his keeshond dog Mignon, a name that he says comes from an opera, but a more gruesome interpretation could be that it comes from filet mignon, as a reminder of how Gentlehands used to turn selected prisoners over to his dogs.

Deliver Us from Evie is the story of a lesbian relationship between Evie Burrman and Patsy Duff, two high school seniors who live in the fairly prosperous farming community of Duffton. A boy from a neighboring farm, Cord Whittle, would like to court Evie and when she turns him down he gets even with her in church during the recitation of "The Lord's Prayer." He stands near her and says in an extra loud voice, "Deliver us from Evie," and then laughs and nudges Evie as if he has made a good joke.

Kerr named the protagonist of her YA mysteries John Fell so she could have such titles as *Fell*, *Fell Back*, and *Fell Down*, and then make such additional puns as "fell apart," "fell to pieces," and "fell in love." *Little Little* is about a girl who is a dwarf and her relationship with Sidney Applebaum, a dwarf with a humpback who grew up in the Twin Oaks Orphans home run by Miss Lake. The boys, all deformed in some way, called their home Mistakes Cottage, and chose for themselves such names as Wheels, Cloud, Pill, and Worm. Miss Lake objects, but she does not understand that the boys have taken "naming rights" for themselves so as to take away the pain that might come from outsiders calling them names. In keeping with their attitude, they refer to "regular" people as Sara Lee, an acronym for "Similar And Regular And Like Everyone Else." ●

changing the way characters perceive matters, often with long-term effects on the real world. The Wizard in Frank Baum's *The Wonderful Wizard of Oz* was this kind of a magician when he convinced Dorothy's companions that he was giving them what they obviously already had: courage for the lion, brains for the scarecrow, and a heart for the tin woodman. In old folktales, the role of the magical Creator was filled by dwarves, elves, fairy godmothers, fortune-tellers, shamans, witches, healers, and priests and priestesses. In modern life, psychiatrists, therapists, religious leaders, politicians, teachers, friends, and parents are more likely to play these roles. Shadow Creators are the con artists and others who exploit people's emotional needs for selfish purposes. Both kinds of Creators are commonly included in YA books where authors explore some fairly subtle differences between Creators who play a positive role and those who play a negative role by killing others' dreams—usually through being overly controlling or overly negative. The power of Robert Lipsyte's *Raiders*, already discussed in Chapter 6, is the way it demonstrates the damage that can come to young athletes when parents and coaches are Shadow Creators.

Names and Naming in Young Adult Literature

Looking at names and naming in YA books is a third template activity for working with different books under an overall umbrella topic. The Nilsens (Don in his linguistics classes and Alleen in her literature classes) have had such success in looking at names of not only characters but also places and items that they wrote *Names and Naming in Young Adult Literature*, which was published in the summer of 2007 as part of the Scarecrow Studies in Young Adult Literature series, edited by Patty Campbell.

The book starts with the idea that names are discrete discourses—little epiphanies or stories in miniature. When authors create names for their characters, they have more freedom than they do in any other aspect of their writing. When people create new words, they mostly have to use sound combinations that have already been agreed upon, but when creating names for characters, places, or imagined items, authors can make up entirely new sound combinations and devise their own spellings. Chapters include "Names for Fun" (M. E. Kerr, Gary Paulsen, Louis Sachar, and Polly Horvath), "Names to Establish Tone and Mode" (Robert Cormier and Francesca Lia Block), "Names to Establish Time Periods" (Karen Cushman), "Names to Establish Realistic Settings" (Gary Soto, Adam Rapp, Meg Rosoff, and Nancy Farmer), "Names to Establish Imagined Settings" (Yann Martel, Orson Scott Card, and Ursula K. Le Guin), "Names to Reveal Ethnic Values" (Amy Tan, Sandra Cisneros, Maya Angelou, Cynthia Kadohata, Sherman Alexie, and others), "Names to Build a Dual Audience" (Daniel Handler and the Lemony Snicket books), and "Names as Memory Hooks" (J. K. Rowling and the Harry Potter books). People who are interested in pursuing this approach should find the book (many libraries have standing orders for the series), and also look at Focus Box 10.1, Names and Naming in Multicultural Books, and see the write-up on M. E. Kerr as a Margaret A. Edwards Award winner on p. 331.

Names and Naming in Multicultural Books

The Absolutely True Diary of a Part-Time Indian by Sherman Alexie. Little, Brown, 2007. Alexie's first book written specifically for teenagers won the 2007 National Book Award in the category of young people's literature. One of the ways he illustrates the mixing of cultures is to combine Indian naming practices with mainstream names when he writes about the mysterious Turtle Lake which he and his friend Rowdy dare each other to dive into. He explains that Indians love mysteries and that some people say that Turtle Lake, which no one has ever been able to find the bottom of, got its name because of being home to a giant snapping turtle that ate Indians. Then he shows the universality of such exaggerations by going on to call it "A Jurassic turtle," "A Steven Spielberg turtle," and "A King Kong versus the Giant Reservation Turtle turtle."

I Know Why the Caged Bird Sings by Maya Angelou. Random House, 1970. One of the stories does a wonderful job of explaining why Margaret and everyone she knew "had a hellish horror of being called out of his name." She was twelve years old and traumatized by having been raped when she was sent to work at Mrs. Cullinan's house. All went pretty well until Mrs. Cullinan's friends convinced her it would be easier to call Margaret, Mary.

Jip: His Story by Katherine Paterson. Lodestar, 1996. When the story starts, the year is 1855 and Jip West is probably eleven or twelve years old. No one knows for sure because he was abandoned on West Hill Road when he was a toddler. Townspeople named him Jip thinking that he must have fallen from a Gypsy wagon, but actually he was purposely left behind by his slave mother who was being taken back to the South and did not want her boy to be a slave.

The Joy Luck Club by Amy Tan. Random House, 1989. Waverly was named for the California street where her immigrant family lived. She is an adult before she learns that her mother named her oldest brother, Winston, because she "liked the meaning of those two words wins ton," and her second brother, Vincent, because it "sounds like win cent, the sound of making money."

The Lone Ranger and Tonto Fist Fight in Heaven by Sherman Alexie. Grove Press, 2005. Alexie's book is set on the Coeur d'Alene Indian Reservation in northern Idaho and much of the humor comes from the way he mixes Indian and white naming practices as when he writes, "I was always falling down; my Indian name was Junior Falls Down. Sometimes it was Bloody Nose or Steal-His-Lunch. Once, it was Cries-Like-a-White-Boy, even though none of us had seen a white boy cry."

The Meaning of Consuelo: A Novel by Judith Ortiz Cofer. Farrar, Straus and Giroux, 2003. Consuelo, whose Spanish name means "consolation" or "joy" is the older sister in a middle class Puerto Rican family. She is the "good one," while her younger sister, Mili, whose name is short for "miracle" or "wonder," drifts into increasingly bizarre behavior and then suicide. Consuelo must decide whether to stay and "console" her family or to move to New York and make her own life. *Call Me María: A Novel in Letters, Poems, and Prose* by Judith Ortiz Cofer (Orchard, 2004) is written for younger teens.

My Name Is Not Angelica by Scott O'Dell. Houghton Mifflin, 1990. O'Dell dedicated this historical novel "To Rosa Parks, who would not sit in the back of the bus." Raisha and her two young friends, Dondo and Kanje, are put on a slave ship and taken from Africa to St. Thomas. The boys' names are changed to Abraham and Apollo, and Raisha's to Angelica. When revolts and violence occur on the island, the boys commit suicide rather than return to slavery, but pregnant Raisha is determined to live and save her baby, but not ever to think of herself as Angelica.

Naming Maya by Uma Krishnaswami. Farrar, Straus and Giroux, 2004. Maya grew up in New Jersey, but now she finds herself back in India with her mother, who is intent on selling the family home after her parents' death. Maya's parents are divorced and Maya falsely thinks their problems started with a disagreement over her name.

Weedflower by Cynthia Kadahota. Atheneum, 2006. Sumiko is a young Japanese/American girl living in California during the years leading up to World War II. Sumiko's family is sent to the Poston Internment Camp, located on a Mohave Indian reservation near Parker, Arizona. The camp was run by Native Americans and Sumiko develops a shy friendship with an Indian boy named Frank. Names and their symbolic meanings are at the heart of several incidents in this well written piece of historical fiction.

When My Name Was Keoko: A Novel of Korea in World War II by Linda Sue Park. Clarion, 2002. Between 1940 and 1945, South Korea was occupied by Japan and the people were forced to adopt Japanese names and study the Japanese language. Chapters alternate between Keoko and her brother, who is trying to get used to his new name of Sun-hee.

Evaluating and Promoting Young Adult Literature

At the same time that we want to give young people choices, we want to do all that we can to make available the kinds of choices that will encourage them to read and help them make good use of the time they invest in it. It is ironic that, in a time when there are more books to choose from, most schools and libraries have less money to spend. Also, book prices have increased more than budgets, so that if a purchasing mistake is made, especially with a series or a set of books, a proportionately larger bite is taken out of school, library, and personal budgets.

Writing about Books

Teachers and librarians working with books for young people have more opportunity to be among the decision makers than do those working with books for adults because fewer than two dozen people in the United States are full-time reviewers of juvenile books. Most reviews of children's books (which is where in the publishing world YA lit is categorized) are written by teachers and librarians who evaluate books both as part of their assigned workloads and as a professionally related hobby. Here is a summary of the kinds of writing you will do over your career listed in ascending order of difficulty and challenge:

- Keeping a record of your own reading, probably by typing paragraph-length descriptions complete with publishing information (author, publisher, original year of publication), the genre of the book, and whatever information you anticipate wanting in the future. If the book might be controversial, jot down any prizes it has won or where you could find a review.

- Making annotations, little descriptions like the ones that are in the focus boxes throughout this textbook. Teachers and librarians often use these, reorganized to fit different purposes; for example giving a sheet of them to a teacher planning a unit on the Holocaust or making a flier to go with a display of love stories for Valentine's Day. Try not to start all your annotations with "This book . . ."

- Writing reviews for locally or nationally published newsletters, magazines, or journals. Thanks to amazon.com, both you and your students can send in reviews and get them posted for others to read. Also, thanks to several online services, you can also read different reviews of the same book and develop your own ideas of what makes a helpful review. One of the main things that people reading reviews want is for some sensible person to tell them whether or not this particular book is worth an investment of money, trouble, and time. Teachers and librarians also want to be alerted to potential censorship problems and if there is a tie-in with an upcoming movie or some other event.

- Writing pedagogical (teaching-related) articles for fellow educators about such matters as how you've been successful at using a particular book with

See Appendix B for magazines and journals devoted to the evaluation and promotion of literature for young readers.

a class or in finding three or four books that worked well together. These kinds of articles appear in such journals as those shown in the photo above including *Voices from the Middle*, *English Journal*, *Journal of Adult and Adolescent Literacy*, VOYA (Voice of Youth Advocates), *School Library Journal*, and *Horn Book Magazine*.

- Writing scholarly articles, i.e., engaging in literary criticism, in which you look more closely at the literature than at how it might be used in an educational setting. You can see articles of this type listed in Appendix C, "Some Outstanding Books and Articles about Young Adult Literature." Because young adult literature is a relatively new development, there is ample opportunity for original research and observation, whether from the viewpoint of a literary scholar, a teacher, a librarian, or a counselor or youth worker. The field as a whole will grow strong as a result of serious and competent criticism and analysis.

The field of juvenile reviewing is sometimes criticized for being too laudatory because the reviews are written by book lovers who are anxious to "sell" literature. One reason is that the publishers of well-established authors are the ones who can afford to send out review copies. Also, those editors who have room for only a limited number of reviews devote their space to the books they think are the best, so of course the reviews are usually positive.

The fact that juvenile books are reviewed mostly by librarians and teachers working on a part-time basis slows down the reviewing process, especially if they take time to incorporate the opinions of young readers. With adult books, reviews often come out before or simultaneously with the publication of the book, but with juvenile titles it is not uncommon to see reviews appearing a full year or more after the book was released. Once young adult books are launched, however, they are likely to stay afloat much longer than adult best sellers because teachers work the best ones into classroom units, librarians promote them, and paperback book clubs keep selling them for years. Children continue to grow older and to advance in their reading skill and taste, so that every year a whole new set of students is ready to read *A Separate Peace*, *The Catcher in the Rye*, and *The Outsiders*.

People generally evaluate books based on literary quality, reader interest, potential popularity, or what the book is teaching (i.e., its social and political philosophy). Evaluators should make clear their primary emphasis lest readers misunderstand them. For example, a critic may review a book positively because of its literary quality, but a reader will interpret the positive review as a prediction of popularity. The book is purchased and put on the shelf, where it is ignored by teenagers. Consequently, the purchaser feels cheated and loses confidence in the reviewing source. In an attempt to resolve that kind of conflict, when Mary K. Chelton and Dorothy M. Broderick founded *VOYA* (*Voice of Youth Advocates*), they devised the evaluation code shown in Table 10.1. Each review is preceded by a Q number, indicating quality, and a P number, indicating popularity. They suggest that a fringe benefit to using such a clearly outlined code is that it helps librarians analyze their buying patterns. Those who lean heavily toward either quality or popularity see their biases and are able to strike a more appropriate balance.

A quite different set of criteria from either popularity or literary quality is that of social or political values. Most reviewers—whether or not they realize it—are influenced by their personal feelings toward how a book treats social issues. Of course, none of us—neither authors nor reviewers—are free from personal biases. Note how all of the authors who have contributed pages to our "Young Adult Authors Speak Out" feature are making statements reflecting their own viewpoints. That's fine. The fun and excitement of working in a creative field is that we aren't expected to act like robots, but at the same time book reviewers need to be clear in their minds, and communicate to their readers what criteria they are using. Censors, for example, who might be offended about a philosophy or a life style in a particular book, will often avoid talking about their real discomfort and instead will focus on such matters as language and style.

TABLE 10.1 VOYA Evaluation Code

Quality	Popularity
5Q: Hard to imagine it being better written	5P: Every young adult was dying to read it yesterday
4Q: Better than most, marred only by occasional lapses	4P: Broad general young adult interest
3Q: Readable without serious defects	3P: Will appeal without pushing
2Q: A little better editing or work by the author would have made it 3Q	2P: For the young adult reader with a special interest in the subject
1Q: Hard to understand how it got published	1P: No young adult will read unless forced to for assignments

Young Adult Literature in the Library

When discussing public libraries, we used to assume that every library has a young adult librarian and a special section serving teenagers. Although this may be the ideal arrangement, there are certainly many libraries where this has never been the practice and many others where shrinking budgets are making young adult librarians an endangered species. A fairly common approach is for libraries to enlarge their children's sections to "Youth Sections" serving readers up to age fifteen or sixteen, while sending everyone else to the adult division. Some of the problems with such an arrangement were cited in a *Voice of Youth Advocates* article. Teenagers enter a children's section reluctantly, and their size, voices, and active natures intimidate the children who are there. Other issues raised include the following:

- The purpose of young adult services is to provide a transition from the children's collection to the resources of the total library, and when a librarian accompanies a teenager looking for something into the larger adult collection there's no one left to serve the children.

- It is difficult for the same person who runs programs for preschoolers, prepares story hours for older children, and reviews hundreds of children's books to switch gears to the fads and multiple interests of teenagers.

- Young adult librarians deal not only with "safe" young adult books, but also with adult materials of interest to young adults. These are often controversial and are likely to prove more problematic to a children's librarian whose training has engendered different perceptions and attitudes.

- Without "sponsorship" by knowledgeable young adult librarians, there may not be enough circulation for serious, high-quality books, which results in a greater reliance on popular taste (e.g., formula romances and series books).[3]

Certainly these worries are valid, and we all need to do what we can to persuade decision makers that young adult librarians serve an important role. If the choice is between having a library open only four days a week and having separate librarians for children and teenagers, most library boards vote to keep the library open. This dictates more flexibility and more challenge for the librarian who serves both age groups. Parents who have both teenagers and young children vouch for the differences between the two, yet they manage somehow. Many librarians have to do the same. We hope this textbook helps.

Matching Books with Readers

Commercial programs and CD-ROMs allow students to search for books using key words. Many YA authors have their own websites and blogs, and clever booksellers do on an international level the same kind of promotional work that teachers and librarians have for years been doing locally. Electronic aids are wonderful, but nothing can substitute for a large and varied reading background and the ability to draw relationships between what students tell or ask and what the librarian remembers about particular books. Experience sharpens this skill, and those librarians who make a consistent effort to read a few new books every month rapidly increase their repertoire of books.

With all their other responsibilities, few librarians have as much opportunity as they would like to guide individual reading on a one-to-one basis. The next best thing is to give presentations or booktalks to groups. A booktalk is a short introduction to a book, which usually includes one or two paragraphs read from the book. Booktalks are comparable to movie previews or teasers in presenting the characters and a hint of the plot, but they never reveal the ending. Joni Bodart has described booktalking as a kind of storytelling that resembles an unfinished murder mystery in being "enticing. It is a come-on. It is entertaining. And it is fun, for both the listener and the booktalker."[4]

The simplest kind of booktalk may last only sixty seconds. In giving it, the booktalker must let listeners know what to expect. For example, it would be unfair to present only the funniest moments in a serious book—a reader might check it out expecting a comedy. If a book is a love story, some clue should be given, but care needs to be taken because emotional scenes read out loud and out of context can sound silly. The cover of a book often reveals its tone, which is one of the reasons for holding up a book while it is being discussed or for showing PowerPoint slides or color overheads if a presentation is being given to a large audience.

Booktalks need to be prepared ahead of time. Selecting the "heart" of a story takes both concentration and skill. People who try to ad-lib have the advantage of sounding spontaneous, but they also run the risk of using up all their time telling about one or two books or of getting bogged down in telling the whole story, which would defeat the purpose. Most young readers do not want to hear a ten- or fifteen-minute talk on one book unless it is dramatic and used as a change of pace along with shorter booktalks. Even with short booktalks, people's minds begin to wander after they've listened for ten or fifteen minutes. The ideal approach is for the teacher or librarian to give booktalks frequently but in short chunks. This may not be practical, however, if the person giving the booktalk is a visitor such as a public librarian coming to a school to encourage students to sign up for library cards and begin to use the public library. A school librarian can arrive in class with a cart full of books ready to be checked out. A half-hour or so can be devoted to the booktalks, with the rest of the time saved for questions and answers, browsing, signup, and checkout. In cases like this, it's good to have a printed bibliography or bookmark to leave with students for later use in the library.

This kind of group presentation has the advantage of introducing students to the librarian. Students who already feel acquainted are more likely to initiate a one-to-one relationship, a valuable part of reading guidance. Group presentations also give students more freedom in choosing books that appeal to them. When a student asks a librarian to recommend a good book, the librarian has time to tell the student about only two or three titles, and the student probably feels obligated to take one of these books regardless of whether it sounds appealing. But when the librarian presents ten to fifteen different titles, students can choose from a much larger offering. This also enables students to learn about and to select books that might cause them embarrassment if they were recommended on a personal basis. For example, if a girl is suspected of having lesbian leanings, it may not help the situation for the librarian to hand her Nancy Garden's *Annie on My Mind*. But if this were included among several books introduced to the class and the student chose it herself, it might fill a real need. And when librarians talk about a book showing they have read it, the door is opened for students to initiate conversations either about a specific book or books in general.

Another advantage to group presentations is that they are efficient. If a social studies class is beginning a unit on World War II in which everyone in the class is required to read a novel having something to do with the war and also write a small research paper, it makes sense for the librarian to give the basic information in one group presentation. Being efficient in the beginning enables the librarian to spend time with individual students who have specific questions rather than making an almost identical presentation to thirty individuals. Table 10.2 gives some suggestions adapted from an article by Mary K. Chelton, "Booktalking: You Can Do It" (*School Library Journal*, April 1976).

Displays

In our survey, eighty-one students said that browsing in a library was one of the ways they gathered reading ideas. This hints at the importance of making displays that will at the least let browsers see the covers of books and know that someone thought these books were good enough to deserve special attention. Displays can be fairly simple, perhaps nothing more than a sign that says, "Like to watch Dr. Phil?—You'll Love These" (personal experiences and social issues books, although not identified in just that way), or "Kleenex Books" (books about sadness, death, and loss). Preparing displays can bring the same kind of personal satisfaction that comes from decorating a room or setting out a bouquet of flowers. People with negative feelings toward making displays and bulletin boards have probably had experiences in which the results did not adequately compensate for the amount of time and effort expended. Following are some general principles that will help to increase the returns on a display while cutting down on the work:

1. Go window shopping in the best stores—the ones that appeal to the young adults that you are wooing. When you see a display that you like, adapt its features to your own purposes.

2. Promote more than one book and have multiple copies available. Enthusiasm wanes if people have to put their names on a list and wait. As a backup, have color photocopies of the book jackets, so that as the books are checked out, your display won't look skimpy.

3. Tie displays into current happenings. Connect the books to popular movies, the school play, a neighborhood controversy, or various holiday celebrations.

4. Use displays to get people into the library. Offer free bibliographies and announce their availability through local media.

TABLE 10.2 Dos and Don'ts for Booktalking

Do	Don't
1. Prepare well. Either memorize your talks or practice them so much that you can easily maintain eye contact.	1. Don't introduce books that you haven't read or books that you wouldn't personally recommend to a good friend as interesting.
2. Organize your books so that you can show them as you talk. To keep from getting confused, you might clip a note card with your talk on it to the back of each book.	2. Don't "gush" over a book. If it's a good book and you have done an adequate job of selecting what to tell, it will sell itself.
3. When presenting excerpts, make sure they are representative of the tone and style of the book.	3. Don't tell the whole story. When listeners beg for the ending, hand them the book. Your purpose is to get them to read.
4. Even though you might sometimes like to focus on one or two themes, be sure, over the months you meet with any group, that you present a wide variety of books. Include informative books that young readers would probably like to know about but might be too embarrassed to ask for.	4. Don't categorize books as to who should read them, for example, "This is a book you girls will like"; or show by the books you have brought to a particular school that you expect only Asian Americans to read about Asian Americans and only Native Americans to read about Native Americans, and so forth.
5. Experiment with different formats, for example, a short movie, some poetry, or one longer presentation along with your regular booktalks.	5. Don't give literary criticisms. You have already evaluated the books for your own purposes, and if you do not think they are good, do not present them.
6. Keep a record of which books you have introduced to which groups. This can be part of your evaluation when you compare before and after circulation figures on the titles you have talked about. Also, good record keeping helps you not repeat yourself with a group.	
7. Be assertive in letting teachers know what you will and will not do. Perhaps distribute a printed policy statement explaining such things as how much lead time you need, the fact that the teacher is to remain with the group, and how willing you are to make the necessary preparation to do booktalks on requested themes or topics.	

5. Put displays in high-traffic areas where everyone, not just those who already use the young adult collection, will see them.

6. Get some height and variety into the display by using interchangeable parts such as leaning boards with hooks to hold books, or boxes covered with drapes. To focus attention on the books, plain backgrounds are better than figured ones.

7. Take advantage of modern technology. Buy stick-on letters, use your computer and your desktop publishing skills to prepare attractive bibliographies and signs, and for big events splurge on a banner at a copy store.

It is efficient to make a few interesting signs that can be stored flat (or hung) and then brought out for use with various sets of books.

The changing location of portable displays is in itself an attention getter. A portable display can be as small as a foot-square board set in the middle of a table or as large as a pup tent surrounded by books about camping, hiking, backpacking, ecology, and nature foods. If space is a problem, small bulletin boards can be hung from the ceiling or stood against pillars or walls. Involve students by displaying their art work or snapshots of their pets under such headings as "The Comforts and Delights of Owning a Dog," or ". . . of Being Owned by a Cat." And don't overlook the possibility of putting up posters such as those offered by the American Library Association or tying commercial posters in with books; remember the part that the poster message "Don't disturb the universe" played in Cormier's *The Chocolate War.*

Programs

Stores have special sales and events to get people into the marketplace, where they will be tempted to buy something. In the same way, ambitious librarians sponsor video-game nights and put on special programs both to do something special for regular library users and to bring nonusers into the library. Advice from people whose libraries have been especially active in arranging programs includes

Mary Wong, librarian at Explorer Middle School in suburban Phoenix, uses snapshots that she has taken of visiting authors as a conversation starter with students. She encourages students to find a picture of someone who looks interesting. When they come to her, she tells them something about the visit and helps the students find the author's books.

1. Take a survey, or better, talk with your teenage clientele to see what their interests and desires are.

2. Avoid duplicating the kinds of activities that students do in school and in conjunction with other community agencies.

3. Work with existing youth agencies to cosponsor events, or plan them in conjunction with school programs so as to have the beginning of an audience and the nucleus of a support group.

4. Do a good job of publicizing the event. The publicity may influence people unable to come so they will feel more inclined to visit the library at some other time.

5. Have a casual setting planned for a relatively small group, with extra chairs available in case more people come than you expect. Bustling around at the last minute to set up extra chairs gives an aura of success that is more desirable than having row on row of empty chairs.

6. Involve young people in the preparation and teach them to write thank-you notes.

Program possibilities include outdoor music concerts featuring local teenage bands, a film festival showing videos or films created by teens, poetry readings in a coffeehouse setting, or workshops in computer programming, photography, creative writing, bicycle repair, and so forth. Guest speakers are often invited to discuss subjects that schools tend to shy away from, such as self-defense and rape prevention, drug and birth control information, and introductions to various hot-lines and other agencies that help young adults. Regardless of the topic or format of a program, librarians should view programs as opportunities to encourage library visitors to become regular book users. It helps to route traffic past the young adult section, to pass out miniature bibliographies on bookmarks, and to arrange scheduling so that attendees have time to spend a few minutes in the library before or afterwards.

Some libraries have had success with book discussion groups in which teenagers serve as readers and critics. These usually work best if their evaluations can be shared, for example, put on the library's website, posted on a bulletin board, printed in a teen opinion magazine, or put on a handout that accompanies a display of recommended books.

When an author is invited to speak, the host librarian needs to begin publicity several weeks in advance to be sure that people are reading the author's books. English and reading teachers should be notified so that they can devote some class time to the author's work. A few teenagers might be invited to share in the presentation by asking questions or introducing the speaker. When Ann Brashares, author of *The Sisterhood of the Traveling Pants*, came to Arizona to speak at Changing Hands Book Store, four girls (Britney, Paula, Audrey, and Ashley), who were sharing a pair of $4.00 jeans purchased at Goodwill, were interviewed for a prepublicity news story in the local newspaper. At the presentation and book signing, they each gave a one-minute introduction of their favorite author. (See the photo in Chapter 4, p. 143.)

Many authors' websites tell how they can be contacted for school or library visits. Google the Children's Book Council and look under "Author and Illustrator Sites" for information on how to contact particular authors, including Pat Mora who speaks out about "Linguistic Wealth" on p. 346. See Focus Box 10.2 for several other helpful websites.

Magazines

In the survey we took for the seventh edition, ten different magazines were listed as favorites by three or more boys, while eight different magazines were listed as favorites by three or more girls. In our survey for this edition, there was much less consensus, but *Sports Illustrated* remained at the top for males, while *Seventeen* (along with *Cosmo*, and *Cosmo Girl*) remained at the top for females.

We gave the students the option of telling why they liked a particular magazine. In their comments, about half of them gave an explanation of their magazine, showing that they realized we probably would not know it. And many students did not list a particular name of a magazine, but instead a type such as sports, fashion, or gossip. A sampling of their comments hints at the wide range of interests among teenagers, and of all the questions we asked, magazine choices reflected the most difference between males and females. One reason is that magazines are read by one person at a time and so are basically free from the kinds of outside pressures that influence the reading of books in school or the viewing of television or movies, which is usually done by males and females in groups or as couples. Also, magazines are controlled by advertising money and so the publishers purposely aim them at one gender or the other so that they can sell ads for

Arizona State English Education Website

www.asu.edu/clas/english/englished/yalit/webquest.htm: Professor James Blasingame directs his YA literature students in creating WebQuests for outstanding new YA books. The best ones are posted for downloading.

Assembly on Literature for Adolescents

www.alan-ya.org: The National Council of Teachers of English's Assembly on Literature for Adolescents website offers activities, links to related websites, as well as online access to *The ALAN Review*. ALAN's webmaster is David Gill.

Authors 4 Teens

www.authors4teens.com: This subscription site by noted YA short story editor Don Gallo contains interviews and up-to-date author information.

Carol Hurst's Children's Literature Site

www.carolhurst.com: Professional educator Carol Hurst offers reviews, annotations, and lesson plans in this comprehensive site, featuring books geared toward the younger adolescent.

Children's Book Council

www.cbcbooks.org: An association of publishers presents classroom ideas, previews of new books, discussions about current issues and trends, links to authors' websites, bibliographies, and news about the publishing business and available promotional materials.

Children's Literature Web Guide

www.ucalgary.ca/~dkbrown: David Brown of the University of Calgary provides information on author resources, reader's theater, illustrators, and publishers.

Cynthia Leitich Smith

See Smith's YA Authors Speak Out statement on p. 98. Her site, www.cynthialeitichsmith.com, contains articles, interviews, reading recommendations, publishing news, and annotated links from the noted author.

Database of Award-Winning Children's Literature

www.dawcl.com: This useful site has many search options and includes YA lit. Frequently updated, it is maintained by Lisa R. Bartle, reference librarian at California State University, San Bernardino.

Lesson Plans and Resources for Adolescent and Young Adult Literature

www.cloudnet.com/~edrbsass/edadolescentlit.htm: This site features a collection of YA lit lesson plans and resources by Ed Sass, professor at the College of St. Benedict/St. John's University.

Notes from the Windowsill

www.armory.com/~web/notes.html: This e-magazine that reviews children's and YA lit is edited by Wendy Betts, librarian.

Vandergrift's YA Literature Page

www.scils.rutgers.edu/~kvander/YoungAdult: Kay Vandergrift's comprehensive site includes an overview of YA lit, a "top 100" list, bibliographies, and more.

The WebQuest Page

webquest.sdsu.edu/webquest.html: Maintained by Bernie Dodge, this is the definitive site for WebQuests (an online, process-oriented lesson). The WebQuest Page includes lessons for many YA books.

YALSA Booklists

www.ala.org/yalsa/booklists: This site contains book lists from the Young Adult Library Services Association of the ALA. It includes Quick Picks for reluctant readers as well as lists of award-winning books.

cosmetics and fashions in the girls' magazines and for sports equipment and car accessories, and so on, in the boys' magazines.

Comments from Boys

Alternative Press or AP—"It's appealing because it's about music and updates on tours and bands."

Car and Driver—"Because I like cars."

Cooking—"I like to cook."

Classic Trucks—"I'm rebuilding one."

Dirt Bike Magazine—"I like dirt bikes and going out riding so I love to read about it."

Four Wheeling—"Any dirt bike and jeep magazines."

Game Informer—"It's a video game magazine. I like it because it tells you what games are most favored and less favored." "Gives me great ideas on what's coming."

Low Rider—"Because of the articles and cars." "I like the art."

Snowboarder—"It brings the winter to me." "'Cause I love snowboarding."

Sports Illustrated—"Because it's about sports and I like sports." "Because of the pictures."

Comments from Girls

"Any magazine involving teenage actors and actresses. I like gossip."

Cosmo—"Because it's a girl thing." "It's interesting and funny."

Cosmo Girl—"I like to look at the makeup ads and read articles." "For the horoscope."

Modern Bride—"Because of all the beautiful dresses." "I love planning weddings."

New Era—"Gives inspiring ideas." "It relates to me and my basis of life." "It uplifts my mind and helps keep me on the right track."

People—"It is interesting." "It's true." "Fun and interesting."

Rolling Stone—"Because it has information on my favorite bands." "I love music."

Seventeen—"Because it gives you tips and tells you what is new and in style." "You can relate to it." "To see the outfits." "It has articles on relationships."

Teen Magazine—"Because of the fine boys." "Because it is more about us."

Vogue, Harper's Bazaar—"Any fashion magazine."

Many students who will not pick up books are eager to read the latest magazines in their areas of interest. Magazines help poor readers feel success with the printed word because much of the information is communicated through easy-to-read layouts and photographs. Also, the material—of prime interest to teens—is presented in short, digestible chunks.

There's no limit to the information that good students can find in magazines. A much higher percentage of adult Americans read magazines than books, and

Young Adult Authors Speak Out

Pat Mora on Linguistic Wealth

Let me share some stories, *cuentos*. My preference would be to share them with you in person, but our conversation will have to be on the page, not an unusual meeting place for a writer.

One of my many blessings is that I am bilingual. A native of El Paso, Texas, a city on the U.S./Mexico border, I've always spoken both English and Spanish. I wish I were trilingual, that I could find the time to learn one of the other Romance languages, French or Italian. I'm going to Finland soon, and as usual when I travel, I've purchased a simple phrase book and am signing my emails to my three grown children Äiti—Finnish for *mother*. I'll stumble along as I have in German and Japanese asking directions and ordering meals, delighted when I connect though haltingly. I majored in English because I love literature and wanted to teach it. I've also discovered that I love languages, the wonder of their sounds, complexities, wisdom.

I was stunned years ago when a fellow presenter on a West Virginia campus, the publisher of a small press, looked at me and said, "I understand that Spanish is a much simpler language than English. You know, English has many words for the color red, for example, but I hear that Spanish has just one word."

What? Could this woman really believe that the beautiful Spanish language lacks the richness of English? Could this educator be falling for the myth of a hierarchy of languages, the belief that certain languages are actually superior to others?

Now let's travel to Oklahoma. It was afternoon, and I was to meet with a small group of students in a high school library. Half of the students were Latinos, but when I asked them to translate a line in Spanish from my poem "Elena"—silence. We were in a building dedicated to education in which students with linguistic knowledge felt ashamed to share what they knew.

Some of the Latino students looked down, not I think because they didn't speak Spanish, but because they didn't want to be connected with a language perceived as second-class. No children are born ashamed of their home language, skin color, or religion. Sadly, societies throughout the world teach the young that knowledge including languages isn't valued if not used by those in power.

---

yet in school we give people little help in picking out the magazines they will get the most from. It is almost as if kids find magazines despite teachers, not because of them. We would do well to change our attitudes and look on magazines as taking up where books leave off in presenting up-to-date information on a wide variety of topics chosen to be especially interesting to young adults.

Young Adult Books in the Reading Classroom

Including a section on reading in this text is in some sense superfluous because this whole book is devoted to teaching and promoting reading, but the interests and responsibilities of teachers of reading differ in some ways from those

Let me also share a hopeful story, an example of the power of a teacher, your power, to create classrooms and ultimately schools that are psychologically safe for all our diverse students. I was going to say that we'd have to leave the issue of physical safety to others, but since I believe in the importance of words, I'll propose that what we do relates to physical safety too.

I visited a creative writing class at a private college in Ohio. Their professor, though monolingual, wanted her students to study America's diverse voices, and I'm sure she had honored her students' backgrounds and encouraged them to be open and curious about the many languages spoken in this country. The class had studied my adult poetry collection, *Agua Santa: Holy Water* and a student said, "I wish I spoke Spanish so that I could use those beautiful words in my poems."

You and I know that language issues are often political rather than educational. In a nativist social climate, in different eras and in different portions of the country, German, Italian, Vietnamese, Chinese, Spanish have been frowned on. What a sad irony that though one in five children in our country speaks a language other than English at home, and though any of us who have struggled with another language understand the concrete meaning of the words "foreign tongue" as a country, we don't value bilingualism as an intellectual skill and a literary asset. Well, actually, we do—depending on the language and the status of the speaker.

I feel fortunate to write for adults, teens, and children, and I always use Spanish in my work since it's part of who I am. Presently, I'm happily writing a collection of love poems for teens. What an array of linguistic options I have, not only the words and sayings, but poetic forms and other literary traditions. To deny myself that option would be like playing the piano without using the black keys. I would limit what I could create.

Would I have used Spanish in my work when I was in high school? No. Would I have encouraged my students to bring themselves fully to the page: their families, loves, fears, cultures, languages? No. Years ago, I hadn't learned what I know now.

A reason I didn't think about being a writer until I was a parent was because I'd never seen a writer who was like me, bilingual. I've been working on a manuscript, tentatively titled, "Dear Teacher: Seven Practices for Creative Educators." In it I say that to my utter surprise, when I began to write, I discovered that being from the desert, of Mexican descent, and from a close bilingual family were all *fuentes de inspiración*, fountains of inspiration. That sweet liquid has sustained me in the uphill struggle of sharing the U.S. Latina voice.

- Pat Mora's books include *Adobe Odes*, The University of Arizona Press, 2006; *My Own True Name: New and Selected Poems for Young Adults*, Piñata Books/Arte Público Press, 2000; *House of Houses*, Beacon Press, 1997; *Nepantla: Essays from the Land in the Middle*, University of New Mexico Press, 1993. www.patmora.com.

---

of English teachers or of librarians. One difference is that except for remedial programs, teaching reading as an academic discipline in the high schools is a fairly recent development. The assumption used to be that normal students had received enough formal instruction in reading by the time they completed elementary school. They were then turned over to English teachers who taught mostly literature, grammar, and composition. Certainly English teachers worked with reading skills, but they were not the primary focus. Today more and more states are passing laws setting minimal reading standards for high school graduation, and this has meant that reading has become almost a regular part of the high school curriculum. In some schools, all ninth graders now take a reading class; in other schools, such a class is reserved for those who test one or two years below grade level. Depending on how long it takes them to pass the test, students may take basic reading classes for several semesters.

In the teaching profession, the reluctant reader is nearly always stereotyped as a boy from the wrong side of town, someone S. E. Hinton would describe as an outsider, a greaser. Actually, reluctant readers come in both male and female varieties and from all social and IQ levels. Many of them have fairly good reading skills; they simply don't like to read. Others are poor readers partly because they get so little practice. What these students have in common is that they have been disappointed in their past reading. The rewards of reading—what they received either emotionally or intellectually—have not come up to their expectations, which were based on how hard they worked to read the material. They have therefore come away feeling cheated. The reading profession has recognized this problem and has attempted to solve it by lowering the price the student has to pay (i.e., by devising reading materials that demand less effort from the student). These are the controlled vocabulary books commonly known as "high-low books," meaning high interest, low vocabulary. They are only moderately successful because the authors are rarely creative artists; they are educators who have many priorities that come before telling a good story. An alternative approach is making the rewards greater rather than reducing the effort. This is where the best young adult literature comes into the picture. It has a good chance of succeeding with reluctant readers because:

1. It is written specifically to be interesting to teenagers. It is geared to their age level and their interests.

2. It is usually shorter and more simply written than adult material, yet it has no stigma attached to it. It isn't written down to anyone, nor does it look like a reading textbook.

3. There is so much of it that individual readers have a good chance of finding books that appeal to them.

4. As would be expected, because the best young adult books are the creations of talented, contemporary authors, the stories are more dramatic, better written, and easier to get involved in than the controlled vocabulary books.

5. The language used in good adolescent literature is more like the language that students are accustomed to hearing. In this day of mass-media communication, a student who does not read widely may still have a fairly high degree of literary and language sophistication gained from watching television and movies.

Taking all this into account, some types of adolescent literature will still be enjoyed more than others by reluctant readers. In general, reluctant readers want their stories told faster and in less space. If it's information they are looking for, they want it to be right there. If they are reading a book for thrills and chills, they want it to be really scary. If they're reading for humor, they want it to be really funny. And if they're not sure about committing themselves for a large chunk of time, they want books in which they can get a feeling of accomplishment from reading short sections, paragraphs, or even sentences, as with various kinds of trivia books.

The Young Adult Library Services Association (YALSA) puts together an annual list of "Quick Picks," based on the selection criteria of short sentences, short paragraphs, simplicity of plot, uncomplicated dialogue, a sense of timeliness, maturity of format, and appeal of content. Fiction must include "believability of character and plot as well as realistic dialogue." This list, along with another YALSA list, "Popular Paperbacks for Young Adults," can prove helpful for reading teachers. The lists are available on the American Library Association's (ALA) website, www.ala.org/yalsa. The ALA also publishes a yearly book, ALA's Guide to Great Reading, which includes all of their "Best Book" lists ready for photocopying. Reading teachers should also pay extra attention to the section on Free Reading on pp. 322–324 and take a look at Stephen Krashen's article, "Free Reading: Is It the Only Way to Make Kids More Literate?" in the September 2006 School Library Journal.

Young Adult Books in the Social Studies Classroom

Turning facts into believable stories that touch readers' emotions is the biggest contribution of fiction to the social studies class. It is important for readers to realize, however, that many different books need to be read because each book presents a limited perspective. Stereotypes exist in people's minds for two reasons. One is that the same attitudes are repeated over and over, so that they become a predominant image. Another is that an individual may have had only one exposure to a particular race, group, or country. For example, readers of Chaim Potok's The Chosen don't learn everything about Hasidic Jews, but they know a lot more than they did before they read the book, and their interest may have been piqued, so that they will continue to watch for information and to read other books.

Nearly everyone agrees that by reading widely and sharing their findings, social studies class members can lead each other to go beyond stereotypes. For this to happen on more than an ad hoc or serendipitous basis, however, the teacher needs to identify clear-cut goals and then seek help from professional sources and other teachers and librarians in drawing up a selective list of books to be offered to students.

Social studies teachers have always recognized the importance of biographies and of the kind of historical books featured in Chapter 8, but they may not be as aware of the many books, both fiction and nonfiction, that are available to help them teach students about contemporary social issues. See Chapter 9 for nonfiction books treating topics of interest to teenagers, such as ecology; issues related to pornography, rape, abuse, abortion, and prostitution; and medicine and health care, including questions about transplants, surrogate parenting, euthanasia, animal rights, cloning, stem cell research and experiments on humans. Books on government ask questions about individual rights as opposed to the welfare of the group. Such questions range from whether the state has a right to require motorcycle helmets and seatbelts to whether it should legislate drugs and sexual preference.

Social studies teachers also miss a powerful resource if they fail to bring in the kind of fiction discussed in Focus Box 10.3, Teenagers outside the

Chanda's Secrets by Allan Stratton. Annick, distributed by Firefly, 2004. Sixteen-year-old Chanda lives in sub-Saharan Africa, and is faced with arranging for the burial of her baby brother and eventually for her mother, both of whom succumb to AIDS.

City of the Beasts by Isabel Allende, translated from Spanish by Margeret Sayers Peden. HarperCollins, 2003. Allende's first novel for young readers is part magical realism and part contemporary politics. A fifteen-year-old boy accompanies his journalist grandmother on an expedition into an Amazon jungle in search of a legendary beast that is perhaps human.

Colibri by Ann Cameron. Farrar/Frances Foster Books, 2003. A twelve-year-old Guatemalan girl, whose original name meant "Hummingbird Star," learns that at age four she was kidnapped by "Uncle" Baltasar, a man who calls her Rosa and uses her as his assistant while he pretends to be blind.

Facing the Lion: Growing up Maasai on the African Savanna by Joseph Lemasolai Lekuton and Herman J. Viola. National Geographic, 2003. The author tells his own story of growing up in a nomadic subgroup within the Maasai people in Kenya. By law, each family designates a child to attend school, and he was the one chosen from his family. He went from the mission school to an elite high school and then to college in the United States.

Haveli by Suzanne Fisher Staples. Knopf, 1993. In this sequel to the well-received *Shabanu: Daughter of the Wind* (Knopf, 1989), Staples continues the story of the strong-willed young woman who because of custom and family needs becomes the fourth wife of a powerful land owner in the Cholistan desert of Pakistan.

Island Boyz: Short Stories by Graham Salisbury. Random House, 2002. The preface to these ten stories is a free-verse poem in which Salisbury establishes what it takes to qualify as "island boyz/not boys/boyz," and adds information about his own years of growing up in Hawaii, "I would not have traded places with anyone/not even God."

Our Stories, Our Songs by Deborah Ellis. Fitzhenry & Whiteside, 2005. In the summer of 2003, the author traveled to Malawi and Zambia to gather stories from children and teens whose lives have been touched by AIDS. Factual information, along with quotes, are woven through the book, but what will stick with readers are the stories told in the words of the interviewees, many of whom are orphans.

Red Glass by Laura Resau. Delacorte, 2007. A shy sixteen-year-old Arizona girl develops new strengths when she and her Bosnian great-aunt Dika get involved in helping a Guatemalan immigrant and his six-year-old son go back across the U.S. border that they had crossed illegally.

Running with the Reservoir Pups and *Bring Me the Head of Oliver Plunkett* by Colin Bateman. Delacorte, 2005. Bateman is a popular Irish writer for adults, but decided to do an *Eddie and the Gang with No Name* trilogy for tweeners. These are the first two books and are a welcome contrast to many of the more serious problem novels set in foreign countries.

The Sweet, Terrible, Glorious Year I Truly, Completely Lost It by Lisa Shanahan. Delacorte, 2007. Gemma Stone is Australian, but that does not explain why her older sister turns into bridezilla and why in her fourteenth year, Gemma learns that "Love is doves *and* dog poo."

Tasting the Sky: A Palestinian Childhood by Ibtisam Barakat. Farrar, 2007. A Palestinian woman who now lives and works in the United States tells the story of her life between 1967 and 1970 when, as a young child, she was caught during the Six-Day War.

Tonight by Sea by Frances Temple, Orchard, 1995. Temple writes about Paulie and her family trying to escape from their troubled Haitian community. She has also written *Taste of Salt: A Story of Modern Haiti* and *Grab Hands and Run*, which is about a family fleeing El Salvador.

What the Moon Saw by Laura Resau. Delacorte, 2006. Fourteen-year-old Clara Luna is invited to spend the summer with her father's parents, people she has never met, in a remote Mexican village. Readers get to share her experience as she learns about a life style foreign to the one she has in the United States.

Continental United States. Movies, television, and photographs allow people to see other places, but literature has the added dimension of allowing the reader to share the thoughts of another person. As today's jet age and the Internet shrink the distances between countries and cultures, it is more important than ever that people realize that members of the human race, regardless of where or how they live, have more similarities than differences.

Parents and Young Adult Literature

"Tell me a story."

"Read just one more!"

"Can we go to the library today?"

Such requests are among the pleasant memories that parents have of their young children. These memories become even more cherished when parents look at these same children, now teenagers rushing off to part-time jobs or after-school sports or spending so much time with friends that they no longer seem to have time to do required school assignments, much less read a book. When parents ask us what they can do to encourage their teenage children to read, we find it easier to tell them what not to do because we've observed at least three clear-cut roads to failure.

1. Don't nag. There's simply no way to force young adults to read, much less to enjoy it.
2. If you choose to read the books your teenagers are reading, don't do it as a censor or with the intent of checking up on your child or your child's school.
3. Don't suggest books to your teenager with the only purpose being to teach moral lessons.

Lest we appear unduly pessimistic, we hasten to add that we have also seen some genuinely rewarding reading partnerships between teenagers and their parents. These successful partnerships have resembled the kind of reading-based friendships that adults have with each other. Mutual respect is involved, and the partners take turns making suggestions of what will be good to read. Conversations about characters, plots, authors, and subject matter come up naturally, with no one asking teacher-type questions and no one feeling pressured to talk about what he or she has just read.

Teenagers enjoy being in a helping role (i.e., being experts whose opinions are valued). Some of the best partnerships we've seen have been between our students whose teenage children have volunteered to read and share their opinions on the books they've seen their mothers reading (sorry, we can't remember hearing of fathers in this role, although we have known fathers who do read and serve as examples). A key to enticing young people to read is simply to have lots of books and magazines available. But they need to be available for genuine browsing and reading by everyone in the family, not purchased and planted in a manner that will appear phony to the teenager. A teenager who has never seen his or her parents read for pleasure will surely be suspicious when parents suddenly become avid readers on the day after parent-teacher conferences.

Perhaps a more important benefit than modeling behavior is that when parents read some of the best new books (the Honor List is a good starting place), they gain an understanding of what is involved in being a teenager today. Parents who have read some of the realistic problem novels have things to discuss with their children regardless of whether their children have read the same books. Even when children are not interested in heart-to-heart discussions, parents are more understanding if they've read about the kinds of turmoil that teenagers face in struggling to become emotionally independent. In our own classes, and we understand the same is true for others teaching young adult literature, we are getting an increasing number of adult students who are there simply because they enjoy reading and talking about the young adult fiction that was not being written when they were teenagers. Those who are parents of teenagers consider it serendipitous if their teenagers also get interested and begin reading the same books.

A more structured approach is for parents to work with youth groups and church groups or to volunteer as a friend of either the public library or the school library. These kinds of activities provide parents with extra opportunities to involve young people in sharing reading experiences. In such situations, it is often a benefit to have other young people involved and for parents to trade off, so that they aren't always the leader for the particular group in which their child is a member.

Clarifying Human Relations and Values

Workers with church and civic youth groups, teachers of classes in human relations, and professional counselors working with young adults have all found that reading and discussing short stories or books can be useful. When we talk about using books to help students understand their own and other people's feelings and behavior, we sometimes use the term *bibliotherapy*. It is a word that goes in and out of fashion, at least in reference to the informal kind of work that most teachers and librarians do with young adults. Its technical meaning is the use of books by professionally trained psychologists and psychiatrists in working with people who are mentally ill. Because of this association with illness, many "book" people reject the term. They reason that if a young adult is mentally ill and in need of some kind of therapy, the therapy should come from someone trained in that field rather than from someone trained in the book business or in teaching and guiding normal and healthy young adults.

Most people agree, however, that normal and healthy young adults can benefit psychologically from reading and talking about the problems of fictional characters. All teenagers have problems of one type or another, and simply finding out that other people have them too provides some comfort. We are reassured to know that our fears and doubts have been experienced by others. David A. Williams, a communications professor at the University of Arizona, said in a newspaper interview that he would die happy if he could "prove that a positive correlation exists between the rise in anxiety in the country and the decline of pleasure reading." Research done during the 1950s and 1960s showed that anxiety is directly related to a poor concept of oneself. "It seems to me," he said, "that the human being's major concern in life is to determine what it means to be a human being." The paradox is that before people can see themselves, they have to get outside of themselves and look at the whole spectrum of human experience to see where they fit in. "When we are feeling anxious it is usually because we have a narrow perspective that sees only what it wants to see." Someone who is anxiety-ridden, paranoiac, or resentful selects experiences from life to validate those feelings. For people like this, reading can put things back into perspective. "When we read about others who have suffered similar anxieties, we don't feel so cut off and, although the world doesn't change, we change the way we look at it."[5]

As books put things back into perspective, they open up avenues of communication that successful discussion leaders tap into. It is important, however, for adults to be careful in guiding students to read and talk about personal problems. No one should be forced to participate in such a discussion, and a special effort should not be made to relate stories to the exact problem that a group member is having. In fact, it would probably be best to avoid matching up particular problems with particular students. When someone is in the midst of a crisis, chances are that he or she does not want to read and talk about someone else in a similar predicament. As a general rule, one would probably get the most from such a discussion before or after—rather than during—a time of actual crisis.

Such discussions are usually held in clubs, church groups, classes on preparation for marriage and human relations, and counseling and support group meetings at crisis centers and various institutions to which young people are sent. Because membership in these groups changes from meeting to meeting and there are no pressures for participants to do outside reading as "homework," a leader will probably be disappointed or frustrated if the discussion is planned around the expectation that everyone will have read the book. A more realistic plan is for the leader to use a short story or to give a summary of the book and a ten- to twenty-minute prepared reading of the part that best delineates the problem or the topic for discussion. Using fairly well-known books, including ones that have been made into movies, increases the chances of participation. Using popular books also makes it easier for students whose appetites have been whetted to find the book and read it on their own.

In an adult group of professionals, the same purpose would be accomplished by reading a case study that would then be discussed. But case studies are written for trained adults who know how to fill in the missing details and how to interpret the symptoms. Teenagers are not psychologists, and they are not social workers or philosophers. Literature may be as close as they will ever come to discussing the kinds of problems dealt with in these fields. What follows the oral presentation can be extremely varied, depending on the nature of the group, the leader's personality, and what the purpose or the goal of the discussion is. The literature provides the group—both teenagers and adults—with a common experience that can serve as the focus for discussion. Pressures and tensions are relieved because everyone is talking in the third person about the characters in the book, although in reality many of the comments will be about first-person problems.

TABLE 10.3 The Powers and Limitations of Young Adult Literature

What literature can do:

1. It can provide a common experience or a way in which a teenager and an adult can focus their attention on the same subject.

2. It can serve as a discussion topic and a way to relieve embarrassment by enabling people to talk in the third person about problems with which they are concerned.

3. It can give young readers confidence that, should they meet particular problems, they will be able to solve them.

4. It can increase a young person's understanding of the world and the many ways that individuals find their places in it.

5. It can comfort and reassure young adult readers by showing them that they are not the only ones who have fears and doubts.

6. It can give adults as well as teenagers insights into adolescent psychology and values.

What literature cannot do:

1. It cannot cure someone's emotional illness.

2. It cannot guarantee that readers will behave in socially approved ways.

3. It cannot directly solve readers' problems.

Reading and discussing books can in no way cure mental illness, but reading widely about all kinds of problems and all kinds of solutions helps keep young people involved in thinking about moral issues. Table 10.3 shows what young adult literature can and cannot do. When it is used as a tool to teach about human relations and values, the positives outweigh the negatives.

Concluding Comments

This chapter has shown that using and promoting books with young readers is a shared opportunity and responsibility. It belongs not only to librarians and English and reading teachers but also to everyone who works closely with young people and wants to understand them better. It can serve as a medium through which to open communication with young adults about their concerns.

Notes

1. Dick Abrahamson and Eleanor Tyson, "What Every English Teacher Should Know About Free Reading," *The ALAN Review* 14 (Fall 1986): 54–58, 69.
2. Beth Ricks. Personal email to Alleen Nilsen, April 30, 2002.
3. Dorothy M. Broderick, "Whose Job Is It Anyway?" *VOYA* 6 (February 1984): 320–326.
4. Joni Bodart, *Booktalk! Booktalking and School Visiting for Young Adult Audiences* (H. W. Wilson, 1980), pp. 2–3.
5. "Feeling Uptight, Anxious? Try Reading, UA Prof Says," *Tempe Daily News*, December 15, 1977.

Young Adult Literature in the English Class

In response to requests from previous users of this textbook, we devote this chapter to a discussion of young adult literature and how it can be a welcome addition to standard English classes in high schools. Although we recognize that there is no single best way to teach and that classes, students, and goals vary from school to school, from teacher to teacher, and from parent to parent, the methods of teaching literature to young people discussed here have proven their worth for large numbers of teachers and their students.

Principles of Teaching English

We believe in five principles about English teachers and the teaching of literature. These come from our own experiences and from the writings and thoughts of others in both books and journals.

1. *English teachers must never forget that literature should be both entertaining and challenging.* Teachers must alert students to literature they will find challenging and satisfying. Is this easy to do? No, not always, but it might convince students that teachers care about reading and kids. If the literature does not provide entertainment and challenge, English teachers have failed.

2. *English teachers must know a wide range of literature.* Teachers should know classics of English and American literature, of course; they should

also know American popular literature and young adult literature and something about Asian and European literature (e.g., Asian folktales, Norwegian drama, French short stories, or Russian novels). They should know women writers and ethnic writers, especially, but not exclusively from the United States, and what they do not know about literature, they should learn. That demands that English teachers read all sorts of literature—the great, the new, the popular, the demanding, and the puzzling. Why do they read? Because they are readers themselves and because they are always looking for books that might work with students.

3. *English teachers ought to know enough about dramatic techniques and oral interpretation to be comfortable reading aloud to students.* We need teachers eager and able to read material to students that just might interest, intrigue, amuse, or excite them, material that might make young people aware of new or old books or writers or techniques or ideas. Outside of speech or drama, no classes require so much oral performance from teachers as English classes. Poetry must be read aloud. So must drama. Reading fiction aloud is half the fun of teaching short stories. If students are to learn how to read poetry or drama, it will come from English teachers comfortable with their own oral reading. Obviously, the availability of poetry or fiction on tapes or CDs means other voices can be heard, but that does not mean the teacher's voice should be silent. Ian McKellen's reading of Shakespeare exceeds the grasp of us mortals, but McKellen is not there to explain why he read a passage from *Richard III* or *Macbeth* or *Othello* as he did.

4. *English teachers must remember the distance in education and sophistication between them and their students.* No matter what the rapport, it is almost equally easy for teachers to overestimate as to underestimate their students. Choosing material for an entire class is never easy. Some materials—say, a *New Yorker* short story or a T. S. Eliot poem or a Harold Pinter play—assume a sophistication that high school students often do not have, although sometimes their glibness in class temporarily fools a neophyte. Selecting literature for 15, 35, or 45 students is almost inevitably an exercise in frustration and failure. That comes with the territory, but it is no excuse for not trying to meet all students' needs with that one fabulous, never-to-be-forgotten classroom novel, poem, short story, or play.

5. Finally, *English teachers should teach and use only literature they enjoy.* Teachers should not fake enthusiasm or interest. If a teacher doesn't like Robert Frost's poetry or Stephen Crane's *The Red Badge of Courage*, the teacher has no business using Frost or Crane. It is permissible for both teachers and young people not to like a work or an author, assuming, of course, the teacher has read and responsibly considered the author or work in question (we can be a bit more charitable toward students on this point). If teachers do not like highly regarded modern works such as Raymond Carver's short stories or Athol Fugard's *"Master Harold" . . . and the Boys* or Sharon Olds's poetry, they shouldn't teach them. There are too many stories, plays, and poems out there about which teachers are pre-

sumably enthusiastic. Obviously, this point follows our second point, that teachers are incurable, wide readers. For help in making the best use of your reading time, look at the professional books listed in Focus Box 11.1.

None of this implies that teachers cannot change their minds about literature or writers, just as teachers know that occasionally it is great fun and profitable to work with literature about which they feel ambivalent. Nor does this imply that students should be discouraged from reading and talking about works for which the teacher has no great enthusiasm.

Our five principles for teaching literature extend to works in the curriculum guide as well as the literary canon of great books. We are not being unduly critical of the manner in which literature curriculum guides are developed by noting that they are created by human beings with strengths and weaknesses, and they can be changed. Assuming teachers have a wide knowledge of literature, they can find a variety of works of equal quality to teach. What is gained from a bored teacher presenting Poe's poetry to an equally bored class? It is better to assume that in the four years of high school these students will have one English teacher who likes Poe. And if it doesn't happen? There are worse disasters. What if no teacher wants to teach Shakespeare? We cannot imagine an English department so devoid of taste or ability, but if one exists, it is surely preferable that students leave school ignorant of Shakespeare than bored by him.

Literature that a teacher thinks worth teaching, however defined, ought to encourage honest teaching and honest responses from kids. As Louise Rosenblatt has pointed out, "No one else can read a literary work for us. The benefits of literature can emerge only from creative activity" on the part of each reader. Readers respond to the little black marks on the page, or to the sound of the words in their ears and "make something of them." The verbal symbols enable readers to combine their "past experiences with what the words point to in life and literature."[1]

Allowing young people time to respond to literature slows down the teacher and the lesson because thinking takes time and brainpower. Time is required to build trust, especially for students accustomed to memorizing and spitting back whatever the teacher has said. Some students simply do not believe that a teacher wants their opinions, sometimes for good reason. Students have to be convinced that responding honestly to literature is worth the trouble and hard work.

Using Young Adult Literature in English Classes

One of the reasons we endorse young adult literature for English classes is that students can believe a teacher who asks for their honest response to a book that features a contemporary young person facing a problem that students are likely to face. Young adult literature is often recommended as a bridge to appreciating literary techniques, but its role in developing the trust needed for a response-centered approach to literature may be even more important.

Adolescent literature has a place in the literature program because it appeals to young people. Why?

Authorizing Readers: Resistance and Respect in the Teaching of Literature by Peter J. Rabinowitz and Michael W. Smith. National Council of Teachers of English and Teachers College, Columbia University, 1998. This thoughtful book probes what goes on in the minds of both authors and readers as they meet unconventional ideas.

Books That Don't Bore 'Em: Young Adult Books That Speak to This Generation by James Blasingame. Scholastic, 2007. Blasingame, who edits the young adult literature column for IRA's *Journal of Adult and Adolescent Literature* and also coedits the *ALAN Review* shares his knowledge of contemporary books and authors.

The Heart Has Its Reasons: Young Adult Literature with Gay/Lesbian/Queer Content, 1969–2004 by Michael Cart and Christine A. Jenkins. Scarecrow Press, 2006. This is a fascinating look at how books for young people reflect cultural beliefs.

Literacy for the New Millennium edited by Barbara J. Guzzetti. Praeger Perspectives, 2007. The third volume in this set of four focuses on adolescents and include chapters written by leading scholars. Topics include blogging, literacy tutors, gender issues, digital literacy, and the "best books" for teenagers.

Naked Reading: Uncovering What Tweens Need to Become Lifelong Readers by Teri S. Lesesne. Stenhouse, 2006. Lesesne's 118-page book is filled with sensible advice and good ideas on how to keep kids reading as they move into their teen years.

Not Your Mother's Vampire: Vampires in Young Adult Fiction by Deborah Overstreet. Scarecrow Press, 2006. It's too bad that Stephenie Meyer's *Twilight* and Ellen Schreiber's *Vampire Kisses* series did not make it into Overstreet's book, but still for those of us wondering why vampires are so "hot," there's lots to bite into.

Once Upon a Time in a Different World: Issues and Ideas in African American Children's Literature by Neal A. Lester. Routledge, 2007. Both children's and YA books are discussed. Specific examples include interesting discussions of such issues as the treatment of hair and the absence of the n-word in books published for young readers.

Radical Change: Books for Youth in a Digital Age by Eliza T. Dresang. H. W. Wilson, 1999. Dresang made so many new and interesting observations about changes coming to the field of YA literature, that in the last edition we used her book as the organizing focus for a chapter on pop culture.

Rationales for Teaching Young Adult Literature edited by Louann Reid with Jamie Hayes Neufeld. Heinemann, 1999. In the introduction, Reid quotes the old advice that it takes a village to raise a child, and then adds that it takes only one complaint to raze a curriculum. Essays are presented in defense of nearly two dozen frequently challenged YA books.

Teaching and Learning about Multicultural Literature: Students Reading Outside Their Culture in a Middle School Classroom by Janice Hartwick Dressel. International Reading Association, 2003. Dressel worked with a teacher of 123 eighth graders, mostly from the dominant culture. They were reading a variety of multicultural literature and Dressel studied their responses, which focused as much on differences in power as on differences in color.

Teen Reads Series edited by James Blasingame, Jr. Greenwood Press. Books already published in 2007 include *Sharon Creech* by Pamela Sissi Carroll, *Walter Dean Myers* by Myrna Dee Marler, *Joan Bauer* by Alleen Pace Nilsen, *Tamora Pierce* by Bonnie Kunzel and Susan Fichtelberg, and *Gary Paulsen* by James Blasingame, Jr.

Thematic Guide to Young Adult Literature by Alice Trupe. Greenwood, 2006. Descriptions of both contemporary and historical titles are included under thirty-two categories or issues.

Using Picture Storybooks to Teach Literary Devices: Recommended Books for Children and Young Adults by Susan Hall. Oryx Press/Greenwood, 2002. Most high school students enjoy the change of pace that comes with looking at picture books from their childhood. The literary devices being taught include Black Humor, Hyperbole, Internal Rhyme, Parallel Story, and Serendipity.

Using Critical Perspectives to Teach Young Adult Literature by Anna O. Soter, Mark Faust, and Theresa Rogers. Christopher-Gordon, 2008. Several leading scholars have contributed essays that can serve as a motivation to further research and experimentation.

What Was It Like? Teaching History and Culture Through Young Adult Literature by Linda J. Rice. Teachers College Press, 2006. Part of TCCU's Language and Literature Series, Rice's book is filled with good ideas for activities and books connected to specific periods of history. English and social studies teachers can get some good ideas.

- YA novels are short, or at least shorter than most modern novels or classics studied in schools.
- YA books are easier to read (or so they seem at first reading) than most adult or classic novels.
- They are about young people the age of the readers and concerned with real issues and problems facing adolescents, which is often not true of adult books or classics.
- As shown in the photos on p. 360, many YA authors are happy to make in-person visits with teachers and students.
- The photos or paintings on young adult paperbacks are calculated to grab readers and there is also a blurb showing, for example, that the book is about a kid who has this wonderful brother who's dying of AIDS, or it is about a girl whose grandmother is senile, or it is about a boy and a girl enmeshed in a love affair against their parents' wishes.
- The last reason for their popularity with many young people is that the books are often perceived to be unacceptable to traditional teachers, and so they are as appealing as forbidden fruit.

Robert C. Small, Jr., offered an uncomfortable reason that some teachers resist bringing contemporary and YA literature into their classrooms. He said that teachers who want to establish themselves as the literary expert and translator of books to lowly students will be uncomfortable with YA literature because when young people read adolescent books, they are the experts, and they may need to serve as translators to adults who wish to understand the adolescent books.[2]

For many English teachers who use young adult literature in their classes, one exciting development is that students are more than merely willing to talk about the novels; they are excited and anxious to talk. That's also true for teachers who have used YA books and adult books together. Patricia Lee Gauch writes:

> Some of the best discussions in my classroom experience have been based on adolescent fiction. We have ranged from the use of animal imagery to the development of plot to the question of the alienated hero in American fiction. And I have found one of the best ways to use the "good stuff" of adolescent fiction is to yoke it with adult fare. *Roll of Thunder, Hear My Cry* with *I Know Why the Caged Bird Sings*; *Gentlehands* with *Night*; *The Chocolate War* with *The Oxbow Incident*. This isn't "babying kids into reading decent prose." It's yoking "good stuff" with "good stuff" to take advantage of the length and teen-centered subject of the younger books.[3]

For an imaginative teacher, young adult books have many uses. An individual title can be studied by the whole class, although that is comparatively rare. They can be paired with adult books, classics or not, as recommended by some of the books in Appendix C, and they work beautifully in free reading and thematic units. Their possibilities extend as far as the teachers' imaginations because they provide what other good novels do plus an almost guaranteed adolescent interest.

Attending presentations and relating to authors at conferences, book signings, or school visits is a wonderfully efficient way to get to know authors and to relate to their books. This sampling shows Stephenie Meyer after her presentation at an NCTE meeting; authors Coe Booth and David Levithan visiting with Professor Jim Blasingame at an ALAN function; Cynthia Kadohata signing an autograph at a Children's Literature Association meeting; and Yann Martel after giving a presentation as part of the One-Book Arizona celebration.

Richard Jackson, when he was editor-in-chief at Bradbury Press, explained that YA literature should illuminate rather than educate, raise questions rather than trot out answers. And it should entertain. Though society changes from one generation to another, its rites of passage remain quite fixed. Literature for young adults will endure because the impulse to record and reconsider those rites strikes us all. We can't resist it—and though they may not admit the fact, adolescents do hear us.[4]

Using Short Stories

Short story author Tim Wynne-Jones, who has been described as "the master of the glimpse," wrote for the sixth edition of this textbook,

> A good short isn't a lot of things. It isn't long, it isn't preachy, and it certainly isn't a novel wannabe. It isn't a sketch, it's a miniature. Not the whole season, just the big game. Not the whole sunset, just one straggler on the beach. It does not presume to grandeur. It is happy to invoke a gasp of surprise, a belly laugh, a single tear.[5]

While warning teachers not to overanalyze short stories, we suggest reading them aloud in class to introduce a topic for discussion or writing, to illustrate a point, fill out a thematic unit, provide material for reader's theater and dramatization, and give students enough experience in literary discussion that they can learn the meanings of literary terms from actual experience rather than from memorizing definitions.

For all of these reasons, short stories work well in classrooms where students can read fifteen short stories in the time it takes to read one or two novels. Through reading the larger number of short stories, they can meet a greater variety of viewpoints and representatives of different ethnic groups and cultures. Because the best of modern American authors have written short stories, students can experience high-quality writing in pieces that are short enough for comfortable reading.

If students are to enjoy and profit from reading short stories some preparation is necessary. Kids are not born with genes labeled "How to Read Short Stories Perceptively." Teachers must help students develop the skills to enter imaginative works. Tempting as simple solutions have been to curriculum designers, students should not be required to master a vocabulary list of "Thirty Magic Literary Terms That Will Change Your Life and Make You the Reader You Have Always Longed to Be." D. W. Harding argues that while there is a place for learning about verisimilitude, point of view, unreliable narrator, synecdoche, foreshadowing, and so on, memorizing the meanings of such terms often becomes a substitute for literature. We are in the business, he says, of teaching literature, not literary criticism. And he worries that "many students arrive at and leave universities with an unprofitable distrust of their personal responses to literature."[6]

Finding out about the codes that make one piece of literature succeed while another fails forces teachers to consider how they went about getting into a short story, for example, and how they get into a story that's new to them. There is no single way of getting at any literary work, and several approaches may need to be tried. Students may come to class already knowing how to listen, to take assiduous notes on what the teacher says is important, and to play all this back at test time, but none of that has much to do with reading. In many ways, a careful reading of a work by student A produces a different work from an equally careful reading by student B or student C because readers base their feelings on past experiences and present morality to yield a different story with each reader, and sometimes a greatly different story. These steps may help a class break the code in reading a short story.

1. Read the first sentence carefully (and the first paragraph). What do they tell you about the setting, characters, or tension?
2. Predict from the first paragraph what's likely to follow.
3. Speed-read the story to get some sense of what it's about and who the characters are (probably the only part that can be done outside of class).
4. Isolate the problems in reading the story (e.g., dialect, structure, conflicting characters).
5. Reread the story, doing parts or all of it aloud.

Going through this with students should help them learn how literary codes can be broken through careful reading. What can we safely say to our classes about virtually all short stories? We can tell students that all fiction is based on conflict, and we might begin by exploring with them different kinds of conflict. We can say, with some confidence, that the title of the story usually is significant.

We can tell students that first-person narrators are similar to readers in many ways—fallible mortals likely to make mistakes in judging people or letting their emotions get in the way. Students are sometimes puzzled when we raise this point, but it's essential because readers tend to take the narrator's word for almost anything.

We can also tell students how important those first words are in most short stories. It is the author's opportunity to grab the audience, and some readers (at least outside school) may decide to drop the story and the author based on those words. Most students rush through the first lines. In class we can force them to slow down by reading aloud the first lines over and over.

The questions English teachers pose for students should be carefully thought out and played with. Beginning teachers need to develop and practice the questions before class, while more experienced teachers can rely on mental notes of what makes the discussion worthwhile rather than mere chitchat to take up fifty-five minutes of class.

Many teachers ask students to keep journals and to respond to a question or a comment written on the board for the first five or ten minutes of class. This activity serves several purposes, including quieting students, turning their attention to the story, and focusing on an issue in the story (probably a key aspect). It helps students consider what they will say later in class when the question or comment is posed again. Journals also provide an opportunity for students to outline preliminary ideas for papers that may be developed later.

The first few moments of class discussion are often taken up with simple recall questions, reassuring to students and setting up details in the story that may have significance later on. One schema developed and recommended by Edward J. Gordon and Dwight L. Burton[7] suggests how teachers can move from concrete to abstract, as in the following example based on questions our students devised for teaching Nadine Gordimer's "A Company of Laughing Faces." Gordimer's short story is set at a beach resort in South Africa. A young girl has been brought there by her demanding mother to spend Christmas holidays with "nice" people. The girl is almost raped, finds the nice people dull and not all that nice, and finds a friend in a little boy who later drowns.

1. Questions requiring students to remember facts:
   - Describe the setting of the story.
   - Describe the protagonist and the other major characters.
   - What new things had Kathy's mother bought for her?
   - List the major events in the story.

2. Questions requiring students to prove or disprove a generalization made by someone else:
   - Although the story is set in a South African resort, I think it could have happened at any resort frequented by the upper middle class. Do you agree or disagree? What differences were there between this holiday and that of American college students going to Florida beaches during spring break? Are these differences crucial to the story?
   - Some readers have interpreted this story as saying that Kathy was a conformist. Do you agree? In what ways was she a conformist? In what ways was she different?
   - One interpretation is that the nameless young man in the story represents the anonymous crowds of young people at the resort. Do you agree or disagree? On what evidence?
   - When Kathy put on her new clothes, the author said that the "disguise worked perfectly." Was Kathy in "disguise" any more than the others? Support your answer with evidence from the story as well as from your own experiences.

3. Questions requiring students to derive their own generalizations:
   - What kind of relationship did Mrs. Hack and Kathy have?
   - What is Kathy's perception of being young? Who has shaped that perception? Do the events in the story change her perception?
   - Why doesn't the author give the "young man" a name?
   - Why does the author contrast the constant activity of the other young people with Kathy's stillness?

4. Questions requiring students to generalize about the relation of the total work to human experience:
   - What did Kathy mean when she said that the sight in the lagoon was the "one truth and the one beauty" in her holiday?

- Compare Kathy's relationship with the nameless young man to that of the Bute boy. What is the author saying by showing these two different relationships?
- Relate the different parts of the story to Kathy's development in life.
- What is the significance of the statement "The only need she [Kathy] had these days, it seemed, was to be where the gang was; then the question of what to do and how to feel solved itself"?
- Is Kathy satisfied with the answer the gang provides for her? Why or why not?

5. Questions requiring students to carry generalizations derived from the work into their own lives:
   - Have you been in a situation similar to the one experienced by Kathy? How did it make you feel?
   - What kinds of security do you get from a group? How hard is it to break away?
   - Have you seen parents like Kathy's mother? What are some ways that young people defend themselves from well-meaning parents who don't understand the situation?

While teachers should enter their classrooms having thought enough about a story to devise such questions and to have anticipated possible answers, they should not fire off the questions as if they are giving a spelling test, but instead should use them to provoke thinking and comments from the class. Observers of good literary discussions have found that students circle back around to all these levels and that while students seldom pose questions, they frequently make observations that stimulate other students to comment and add their own opinions.

Probably the most important part of a discussion—and unfortunately the most often ignored—is the summing up. In too many classes, the bell rings in the midst of a discussion and students rush away without gathering their thoughts. Such "fly-away" endings cause students to lose respect for class discussions. If they think the teacher is just filling in time until the bell rings, they won't put forth their best efforts. The successful teacher keeps an eye on the clock and saves at least a couple of minutes to draw things together before students are distracted from the topic at hand. Good teachers continually work to develop skill in summarizing throughout a discussion. They draw attention to those points that the class basically agrees on, they praise insightful comments that help the rest of the class see something they might have missed, they search out reasons for disagreement, and they lead students to see connections between the present discussion and previous ones about similar themes or topics.

Within the last two decades, publishers have produced several attractive collections of short stories written by young adult authors (see Focus Box 11.2, Old and New Recommended Collections of Short Stories). Because of all the reasons we've already given for liking young adult literature, we often recommend short stories by YA authors, but we also like to mix in stories about young people written for general adult audiences. Our favorite general anthology is Robert S. Gold's *Point of Departure*, which just came out in a new printing. Such stories as John Bell Clayton's "The White Circle," Bernard Malamud's "A Summer's Reading," William Saroyan's "Seventeen," Carson McCullers's "Sucker," John Updike's

Am I Blue? Coming Out from the Silence, edited by Marion Dane Bauer. HarperCollins, 1994. Several popular writers contributed stories centered on coming to terms with homosexuality.

The American Short Story, Volumes 1 and 2, edited by Calvin Skaggs. Dell, 1977 and 1980. Among the well-loved stories in these two collections are Faulkner's "Barn Burning," Thurber's "The Greatest Man in the World," Twain's "The Man Who Corrupted Hadleyburg," and Richard Wright's "Almos' a Man."

American Short Story Masterpieces, edited by Raymond Carver and Tom Jenks. Dell, 1987. Included are Flannery O'Connor's "A Good Man Is Hard to Find," Bernard Malamud's "The Magic Barrel," and Joyce Carol Oates's "Where Are You Going, Where Have You Been?"

Athletic Shorts: Six Short Stories by Chris Crutcher. Greenwillow, 1991. The athletes in these stories may attract readers to Crutcher's sports novels because several of the protagonists are the same.

Baseball in April and Other Stories by Gary Soto. Harcourt Brace Jovanovich, 1990. These eleven fairly simple stories are about everyday events in lives of Mexican American kids living in the Fresno, California, neighborhood where Soto grew up.

Best Shorts: Favorite Short Stories for Sharing edited by Avi. Houghton Mifflin, 2006. Avi chose such great read-alouds as Isaac Bashevis Singer's "Zlateh the Goat," Frank Stockton's "The Lady or the Tiger?" Robert D. San Souci's "The Caller," Lloyd Alexander's "The Town Cats," and Megan Whalen Turner's "The Baby in the Night Deposit Box."

Girl Goddess No. 9 by Francesca Lia Block. HarperCollins, 1996. From reading this collection of nine short stories, readers come away feeling acquainted with some young Los Angeles residents who are a lot more interesting than "the girl next door."

Gothic, edited by Deborah Noyes. Candlewick, 2004. Ten original dark tales are written by M. T. Anderson, Vivian Vande Velde, Garth Nix, Celia Rees, and six other masters.

Half-Human, compiled and edited by Bruce Coville. Scholastic, 2001. Each of these ten stories is appropriately illustrated with a surrealistic photograph. Coville's own story ends the collection. Earlier Coville collections include *Odder Than Ever,* 1999, and *Oddly Enough,* 1994, both from Harcourt Brace Jovanovich.

In Short: How to Teach the Young Adult Short Story by Suzanne I. Barchers. Heinemann, 2005. These fifteen short stories are by writers like Avi, Neal Shusterman, Gloria Skurzynski, and Vivian Vande Velde. Teaching helps on theme, literary forms, and discussion topics are appended.

Leaving Home: 15 Distinguished Authors Explore Personal Journeys,, selected by Hazel Rochman and Darlene Z. McCampbell. HarperCollins, 1997. Allan Sherman, Tim O'Brien, David St. John, Norma Fox Mazer, Gary Soto, and Toni Morrison are among the authors represented.

One Hot Second edited by Cathy Young. Knopf, 2002. Stories by Norma Fox Mazer, Ellen Wittlinger, Nancy Garden, Jacqueline Woodson, and others explore the nature of desire.

Point of Departure: 19 Stories of Youth and Discovery edited by Robert S. Gold. Dell, 1967 (New printing, Laurel Leaf, 2005). These stories, all featuring young protagonists, come from the pens (actually the typewriters) of a Who's Who of great American authors.

21 Proms, edited by David Levithan and Daniel Ehrenhaft. Scholastic, 2007. Here is the perfect centerpiece for a spring book display, but you'll need lots of copies. Several talented writers contributed unique takes on this traditional American rite of passage.

Short Stories in the Classroom, edited by Carole L. Hamilton and Peter Kratzke. National Council of Teachers of English, 1999. Essays offer advice on teaching the works of such writers as Toni Cade Bambara, Armistead Maupin, Tim O'Brien, and Sherman Alexie.

Sixteen: Short Stories by Outstanding Writers for Young Adults, edited by Donald R. Gallo. Delacorte, 1984. Gallo was the first person to reach a mass audience through inviting YA authors to contribute short stories. Since this first book, he has gone on to publish *Visions, Connections, Short Circuits, Join In: Multiethnic Short Stories, Within Reach, Ultimate Sports, No Easy Answers,* and *Time Capsule.* More recent collections include *On the Fringe* and *What Are You Afraid Of? Stories about Phobias.*

Working Days: Short Stories about Teenagers at Work, edited by Anne Mazer. Persea, 1997. Mazer's collection helps to counterbalance the way authors, except for Joan Bauer, have mostly ignored the importance of jobs in the lives of teenagers.

"A&P" and "Tomorrow and Tomorrow and So Forth" can go a long way toward helping young readers increase their literary sophistication while still being about teen interests. With sophisticated classes, teachers might lead students to detect the subtle differences in tone between a story written *for* young adults and stories written *about* young adults.

Right now there are so many books of YA short stories that we are hoping someone will come along and do for them what Stephen Dunning and his coeditors did for poetry back in the 1960s when they tried out hundreds of poems with teenagers and chose the ones that resonated the best to go in their *Reflections on a Gift of Watermelon Pickle*, which raised the bar on the production of poetry anthologies for teenagers. What has happened with many of the current collections of YA short stories is that the writing has been on assignment rather than coming from someone's heart and soul. For example, someone in the publishing world gets an idea for putting together a collection of short stories, or maybe they have one or two good stories and need a few more to make a book. They invite authors they know to write stories around a particular theme and voila! a collection is born. Some of them are excellent, but with others it looks as though the editor didn't have the nerve to reject or revise a story that didn't quite come together. Another difference between the new anthologies and something like *Point of Departure* is that the stories in *Point of Departure* were gleaned from the best magazines over something like forty years, while many of the new anthologies are put together in a matter of months.

The genres for short stories include realistic fiction, science fiction, fantasy, humor, animal stories, folklore, and myth. Students who are hung up on a particular kind of book can usually be enticed to try at least a short story in another genre. And within the same genre, students can be encouraged to select more challenging books. Stories by the best YA authors can also serve as introductions to authors, whose longer novels they might also enjoy.

Using Novels

Assigning one novel to be read by an entire class became a popular practice with teachers, partly because it seems reassuring to know what's on the agenda for the next few days or, in some classes, the next few weeks. After struggling with grammar and composition, in which class members' abilities are obviously at great distances from each other, it should be a treat for teachers and the students all to join in reading the same book, some in class and some at home. For students with reading difficulties, teachers might suggest that they try checking out an audiotape of the novel from a library. A surprisingly large number of books have been recorded. Students can read along with the tape or CD or just listen to it. Some are condensations, while others are full readings, but either way the listening experience will be better than resorting to *Cliff's Notes*.

Although many teachers assume that having specific novels read by the entire class has always been a standard part of the English curriculum, the practice is not universally accepted. One of the problems in using novels is the expense of acquiring a set of novels of your choice (e.g., Bernard Malamud's *The Assistant*,

Robin McKinley's *The Hero and the Crown*, or Mary Shelley's *Frankenstein: Or, the Modern Prometheus*) rather than inheriting whatever is left in the English department closet. Another problem is the length of time it takes for students to read the novel (rarely less than a week and more likely two or more). Adults have been known to stop reading when boredom sets in, but no such benediction comes to kids when they're reading a book for a class. More than sixty years ago, Howard Francis Seely wondered about our attraction to novels.

> Just why is it deemed imperative that a whole class read the same novels at the same time, anyway? I haven't heard a sound answer yet. . . . The burden of most of these answers can be recapitulated briefly. A frequent one is that reading one book permits class discussion (which discussion, however, more often than not turns out to be the answering of factual questions chiefly of a trifling nature). . . . A third answer indicates reading this one particular book in this particular class will enlighten the pupils to the structure of the novel as a literary form (which it won't, and which would be of doubtful immediate or ultimate value even if it did). . . . Perhaps the most frequent (and likely the most futile) argument of all is this: If Johnny hasn't read *The Talisman* in the ninth grade with his group, what will happen to him when he comes to *The Spy* in the tenth? That question is generally hurled at me with an air of utter, crushing finality. I can only faintly ask, "Well, just what would?" With that I'm given up as hopeless.[8]

A few years later, a teacher from England worried about teaching the novel on other grounds.

> Once the novelty has worn off a book, the child's interest in it can very easily flag. . . . Even the best novel rarely occupies us more than a few evenings. It is curious that teachers . . . should so often expect the restless mind of the child to possess a greater staying power in this respect than they possess themselves.[9]

English teachers who wish to use novels for common reading should choose books they believe will appeal to young people. Never choose something because it is reputedly a classic and, therefore, will somehow be magically good for students. Do not choose a book solely because it has won an award. Some teachers and librarians assume that an award-winning book is quality literature. Generally, there's merit in that, but winners are chosen by human beings, not gods, and human beings make mistakes, some of them wondrous to behold. Anyone who has been part of a committee charged with choosing a book award knows that books are removed from final consideration for reasons having nothing to do with literary merit or adolescent appeal. Controversial books, such as those with more than marginal profanity or mild sex, frighten committees, and compromise is inevitable.[10] This is as true of awards for adults as for young people; Pulitzer and Nobel winners have frequently been controversial and debated for years.

Some teachers do not have to worry about selection because choices are established by school or district curricula. Among the most widely used titles are Orson Scott Card's *Ender's Game*, Robert Cormier's *The Chocolate War*, Charles Dickens's *Great Expectations*, Harper Lee's *To Kill a Mockingbird*, and Mark Twain's *Adventures of Huckleberry Finn*. Not a bad selection, and all are popular with teachers and most students.

But what are teachers to do if none of these seems right for the class they now face? What if other novels, like one of the following, would have been their first choice: Chinua Achebe's *Things Fall Apart*, William Faulkner's *As I Lay Dying*, Lois Lowry's *The Giver*, Herman Melville's *Billy Budd*, Walter Dean Myers's *Fallen Angels*, Mildred Taylor's *Roll of Thunder, Hear My Cry*, or Kurt Vonnegut, Jr.'s, *Slaughterhouse-Five*? All seven of these novels have been widely used in American schools for one grade or another.

What can a teacher do in that situation? That depends on the school or the district. How rigid is the curriculum guide? Some may be more flexible than teachers expect. How rigid are the department chair or the curriculum coordinator? Isn't it worth finding out?

Author and former teacher Richard Peck (see his Margaret A. Edwards Award write-up in Chapter 8) devised the following ten questions which were published in the *ALAN Review*.[11] His goal was to help teachers move students past their I-liked-it or I-didn't-like-it reactions. Each question is followed by his UM (Ulterior Motive):

1. *What would this story be like if the main character were of the opposite sex?*

UM: To approach the thinking of the author, who must decide what kind of protagonist or narrator will best embody or express the viewpoint. Could the protagonist of *The Member of the Wedding* be a boy instead of a girl? Could Jerry Renault in *The Chocolate War* be a female victim of a female gang? Certainly, though each book would seem different in many superficial ways. Such a question might even temporarily defuse the sexual polarization rampant in junior high.

2. *Why is this story set where it is (not what is the setting)?*

UM: To point out the setting as an author's device to draw the reader into the action by means of recognizable trappings. The isolated setting of *The Lord of the Flies* is a clear, if negative, example. But why is a soap opera almost always placed in an upper-middle-class, suburban setting? Why do so few YA novels occur in historic or exotic settings?

3. *If you were to film this story, what characters would you eliminate if you couldn't use them all?*

UM: To contrast the human richness of a novel with the necessary simplification of a TV show. Confronted with the need to eliminate some of the characters who add texture, some readers may rise up in defense of their favorites.

4. *Would you film this story in black and white or in color?*

UM: To consider tone. The initial reaction in this florid age is to opt for color in everything. But some young readers may remember that the most chilling *Dracula* films are in black and white, perhaps in part because dark shadows are always darkest and black blood is more menacing than red.

5. *How is the main character different from you?*

UM: To relent for once in our attempts to get the young readers to identify on their own limited terms. Protagonists regularly embody traits for the reader to aspire to. In YA books, they typically have powers, insights, and surmountable drawbacks that readers will often respond to without processing the facts.

6. *Why or why not would this story make a good TV series?*

UM: To contrast the shaping of a book's sequential chapters in the larger shape of the plot to the episodes of a TV series that repeat narrowly but do not rise from their formula to a central conclusion.

7. *What's one thing in this story that's happened to you?*

UM: To elicit an anecdotal response that draws the reader into the book. YA novels typically deal with the shock of recognition in their depicting of highly realistic school, social, and personal situations. Science fiction and fantasy use very human situations to balance their more fabulous elements and to make room for the earthbound reader.

8. *Reread the first paragraph of Chapter 1. What's in it that makes you read on?*

UM: To begin a book where the author must, in assessing the need for immediate involvement in an age not known for its patient attention span. An even more wistful motive is to suggest that young people include in their own writing immediately attractive devices for gaining the attention of the reader, if only the poor teacher.

9. *If you had to design a new cover for this book, what would it look like?*

UM: To consider the often deceptive packaging of the book in this visual era, particularly the paperback cover, and to encourage a more skeptical eye among those who were being bombarded by packaging and commercial claims long before they could read.

10. *What does the title tell you about the book? Does it tell the truth?*

UM: To remind readers that the title may well be the most important words the author writes and to encourage their defenses against titles that titillate and oversell.

Literature Circles

While Free Reading is still our favorite approach for English classes (see pp. 322–324), we have also seen classroom success through the setting up of Literature Circles in which five or six students read and talk about the same book. Obvious advantages are that students feel more responsible for the conversation and many more students get to speak than when one teacher leads thirty students in a discussion. Another advantage is that each group can be reading a book, at least partially of its own choosing. Some teachers collect sets of books that are thematically related or that are written by the same author. For example, Jacqueline Woodson (see the Margaret A. Edwards Award description about her on p. 371) has written enough books that each of five or six groups in a class could be reading a different Woodson book. In a college class, students could do all of the reading outside of class and spend only an hour in a discussion with perhaps an extra half-period for group sharing. In high schools, the experience is usually spaced out over two weeks so that the students have time for reading both in and outside of class. Three or four days are spent in discussions, with the final discussion day being devoted to brief presentations by each group to the whole class.

In the six weeks usually devoted to a common reading of a single book, students can read and discuss two or three books. The law of averages, plus the fact that the readers help select the books they read, means that participants have a good chance of appreciating their reading experience. Also, when the program succeeds, students often choose to read on their own one or two of the books that their classmates have enjoyed.

The biggest resistance to this approach comes from teachers who feel that if a book is so simple that kids can read and discuss it on their own, there is no use in wasting class time on it. We hear less of this attitude than we used to because more and more teachers worry that if they do not lead students to enjoy reading books in school, these students will go through life getting both their enjoyment and their enlightenment from whatever their acquaintances happen to say, or from whatever snippets they happen to find on the Internet or hear through other mass media.

The fact that the teacher cannot be involved in all the groups at once puts greater responsibility on the students. This can be good in that students know that the success of the discussion depends on them, but it can also be a problem in that students are tempted to talk about other things. To encourage involvement, a common practice is to make a list of jobs that students either volunteer for or receive by assignment on a rotating basis. When setting up literature circles, you can choose from the following list of jobs or devise additional jobs of your own. While you will probably always want someone to fill the first three categories, be flexible with the others and make sure that over the course of a semester students are assigned to different responsibilities.

1. *The Discussion Leader* helps the members decide how far the participants should read before their next meeting, keeps the group on task, and makes sure all students have a chance to participate. These leaders are encouraged to start with the seeds provided by other students and are cautioned against asking simple fact questions or questions that can be answered with a yes or no.

2. *The Recorder* takes notes and is responsible for summarizing the group's observations either for the group itself or in a report to the whole class.

3. *Initiators* (probably two or three) make seed cards, on which they write questions or ideas for the group to begin discussion. They give these seeds to the discussion leader and stand ready to explain what they meant or what kinds of ideas they hope to elicit.

4. *Character Guides* come ready to describe the personality and the physical characteristics of the main characters and to lead the group in figuring out how and why these characters change.

5. *A Word Detective* watches for unusual words or ordinary words used in different senses. This person jots down the words and the page numbers

Margaret A. Edwards Award
Winner (2006)

Jacqueline Woodson, Writing
Against the Fear

Woodson's honored books include *I Hadn't Meant to Tell You This*; *Lena*; *From the Notebooks of Melanin Sun*; *If You Come Softly*; and *Miracle's Boys*. Among her other writings are several well-received children's books.

Woodson has described her goal as "writing against the fear," by which she means putting on paper the kinds of things that she knows young people worry about but seldom hear honestly discussed. When she was in high school, her favorite authors were James Baldwin, Toni Morrison, and Alice Walker. She wrote her first book at age seven (a book of poetry about butterflies) and carried it around in the back pocket of her jeans to show to whomever she could nab. In college she majored in English and minored in British literature, but all the time, she told Deborah Taylor, who interviewed her for the June 2006 issue of *School Library Journal*, she felt like it was a background for something bigger — something that she is just now beginning to understand.

I wrote because I loved writing and the power of writing. I wrote because there were people in my head saying stuff and I wanted to listen and understand. Call it madness. Call it a gift. Call it whatever society needs to call it to understand it. I watched the world and the world was big and amazing and attainable when I wrote.

One of the reasons that kids pick up Woodson's books is that they are thin. She jokes that she is so talkative that when she sits down to write she has used up all her words. In a more serious vein, she explains that she feels such urgency about the subjects she's treating that she has to strip away the descriptions and just get to the point. Her writing is spare, almost like free-verse poetry. Her succinctness — plus the fact that she treats subjects that other authors have shied away from — keeps kids reading. She includes both black and white characters as she writes about racism and homophobia, first love of an interracial couple, sexual abuse by a parent, and kids being on their own. Bad things happen in her books, but there are also some very good people who step in to help. In *I Hadn't Meant to Tell You This*, black Marie and white Lena become friends. They both live in homes without a mother. Marie's father is a black college professor and although he resists, Marie makes her affluent home a weekly refuge to the impoverished Lena and her little sister, Dion, who take their Saturday baths at Marie's. What Lena doesn't mean to tell Marie is that her father is sexually abusing her. In the sequel, *Lena*, which Woodson wrote after getting numerous letters from readers who wanted to know what happens, thirteen-year-old Lena takes her eight-year-old sister, Dion, and runs away. They cut their hair and pretend to be boys, unless they happen to be picked up by a woman. Lena's idea is that if they make it to the small town in Kentucky where she thinks their deceased mother grew up, surely some of her people will take them in. They don't go to authorities because they fear they will be separated. As they hitchhike, they make up lie after lie asking people to drop them off at the hospital in the next big town where they say their mother just had a new baby and has sent for them and they lost their bus money. Only after they are given a ride, two good meals and an overnight stay by a kindly woman who has cared for foster children and is concerned enough to question their unlikely story, does Lena's fear melt enough for her to come to her senses and realize that her dream of finding "family" is pretty unlikely. After all, she and Dion had never heard from any Kentucky relatives, nor did anyone send a card or acknowledge her mother's death. This realization makes Lena ready to accept help from the woman, who gets in touch with Marie's father. As with most of Woodson's book, while all the problems are not solved, they are at least recognized and readers go away with a little more knowledge about what the world needs to do. ●

and comes ready to lead the other students in seeing why these words are special.

6. *A Plot Guide* starts each day's discussion by summarizing events that have happened in the course of the day's reading. He or she invites other group members to speculate on the importance of the events and helps group members become comfortable with such words as exposition, rising action, climax, and denouement.

7. *Future Authors* select three or four passages that they wish they had written. They come ready to read the passages and to explain what they like about them. Are there interesting allusions or metaphors? Are they particularly surprising in how much information they present in so few words? Do they have underlying humor or foreshadowing?

8. *A Drama Director* suggests how the group might present their book to their classmates through a reader's theater presentation, a television talk show, or a short skit.

9. *A Graphic Designer* figures out and brings the needed supplies for the group to make some kind of a chart or poster that will help explain the idea of their book.

For several semesters here at Arizona State University we have conducted a service-learning class in which college students who are taking, or have taken, the class in young adult literature travel to a local high school to conduct literature circles in classes required of high school students whose reading scores were a couple of years below where they should have been. Everyone involved was pleased to have the experience, but we need to confess that even with literature circles being led by enthusiastic college students under the direction of one of our doctoral students, they did not succeed 100 percent of the time as shown by the following notes from a recent semester. The students went to the high school on Tuesday and Thursday afternoons. They came to the first class with multiple copies of several books including Glendon Swarthout's *Bless the Beasts and Children*; Rudolfo Anaya's *Bless Me, Ultima*; David Almond's *Kit's Wilderness*; Joan Bauer's *Rules of the Road*; Louis Sachar's *Holes*; S. E. Hinton's *The Outsiders*; Gary Soto's *Buried Onions*; and Paul Zindel's *My Darling, My Hamburger* and *The Pigman*. The college students gave booktalks, and the high school students then bid on which books they wanted to read. The ability to choose which books they read was important to the students, and the circles were off to a rocky start when students were assigned books other than their first choice.

Once the literature circles were organized, the procedures were explained and students were assigned the roles they would take for the first discussion. They were asked to write down their feelings and ideas in a reading journal and to put sticky notes on the pages where they had a question or came to a word they did not know.

When, at the end of the semester, the students wrote evaluation comments, nearly all of them expressed positive attitudes about working with the college interns such as "They were fun to talk to" and "They should come three or four times a week." Clearly positive comments included the following.

- You can learn things that you wouldn't learn if you read a book alone.
- Working together like this showed the differences in our reactions.
- If I missed something, then most likely we would talk about it in our group.

In answer to a question on how they felt themselves "improving as readers," students wrote:

- I actually read the books now.
- Since I have been reading more, I'm much faster than before.
- I find myself underlining words I don't know.

When asked to comment on their favorite book, three students listed *Bless Me, Ultima* because "It's a good book with mystery," "It's different from the books I'm used to reading," and "It had some intense stuff that kept me reading." Five students listed *Holes* as their favorite: "It was interesting," "It kept my attention," "The intern made it fun," and "It was easy." *The Outsiders* kept one reader "on my toes the whole time," while *My Darling, My Hamburger* was a favorite because "It's about people and I like books like that," "I like love stories," and "It's about teens."

As might be expected, the evaluative comments from the college interns were more fully developed:

- I know one of the goals is to get the students to talk, but I found it easier to discuss the books when they didn't "realize" they were talking about the book because we shadowed it with something else. I would love to see more possibilities for activities.
- I would improve the choice of books. I overhead one student say, "There aren't any good books to choose." I felt the same way—sorry!
- In my first group we read *Bless the Beasts and Children*. Group members seemed to have done their reading, but they were relatively quiet and didn't speak up unless I prodded them or let the discussion get off topic.
- The one thing that surprised me in my experience was the way all the students interacted with each other. Although once in a while I heard someone say something negative about another student, most of the time I felt the students were working as a team and helping each other out. I personally benefited from this because at first I felt shy and nervous in front of the students. However, I soon felt a connection with them, which allowed me to be more open. I never expected to lose my shyness so quickly.

Literature circles are one more technique to use with students, but as with everything else suggested in this book, they do not come with a guarantee and there is no exact recipe to follow. You will want to devise your own approach after considering our suggestions as well as those to be found in such books as *Literature Circles: Voice and Choice in the Student-Centered Classroom* by Harvey Daniels and *Literature Circles and Response*, edited by Bonnie Campbell

Hill, Nancy J. Johnson, and Katherine L. Schlick. In response to the interns' request for more activities, we drew up the following list:

1. Do a costumed presentation of your book. Dress either as the author or one of the characters.

2. Write a letter from one character to another character.

3. Outline a sequel.

4. Write a new conclusion or a new beginning.

5. If a journey was involved, draw a map with explanatory notes of significant places.

6. Make a diorama and explain what it shows.

7. Write a book review for a class publication.

8. Make and laminate a new book jacket with an original blurb.

9. Use email to tell a reading pen pal about the book.

10. Participate with three or four classmates in a television talk show about the book.

11. For fun, exaggerate either characteristics or events and write a tabloid-style news story related to your book.

12. Draft a letter to a television or movie producer suggesting that your book be considered for a mass-media production. (Note: S. E. Hinton's *The Outsiders* was made into a movie as the result of a letter written to Francis Ford Coppola by students at the Lone Star School in Fresno, California.)

13. Draw a comic strip about an incident in your book or make a graphic novel by working with a section of the book.

Many teachers like to have students write letters to authors or communicate with them via email, but before you make such an assignment read what Vivian Vande Velde has to say on p. 375.

Using Young Adult Literature in Creative Writing

In an Up for Discussion article in *School Library Journal*, contemporary author and creative writing teacher Jack Gantos told how, on the first day of class when he asks his college students about a book they've recently enjoyed, they try to impress him by citing *War and Peace, Crime and Punishment, Wuthering Heights*, and *The Sound and the Fury*. Gantos appreciates and teaches these books in his literature classes, but because not one of his creative writing students "was with Tolstoy when Napoleon retreated from Moscow, or spent part of their youth in a Siberian prison with Dostoyevsky, or wandered the imaginary moors with Emily Brontë while stuck in a parsonage, or sorted mail with Faulkner in Mississippi," he marches his students to the library where he takes them through the stacks and hands them young adult books to read "not for comprehension or analysis, but for inspiration." He wants them to "revel in the

Young Adult Authors Speak Out

Vivian Vande Velde on "Dear Cranky Author . . ."

I was shocked the first time I heard an author complain about fan letters. If a reader was touched enough by my stories to take the time to write to me (I thought in my just-published naiveté), I would be honored to write back.

"Dear Vivian Vande Valda, I like wrestling and X-Men but I don't care much for books, but as part of my writing project . . ."

School assignment letters fall into three categories:

1. The "I-don't-have-time-to-read-your-book/Please-send-me-a-list-of-important-events" category (Not much anybody can do here; the whole purpose of this letter is for the teacher not to know about it.)
2. The "author/dog groomer—same difference" category. Tell why you are an important person. What are your accomplishments? Have you won any major awards in your field? Do you enjoy your work? (Picture yourself answering these questions. Now picture answering them without getting sarcastic.)
3. The "friendly-advice" category, including: These are three things I liked about your story . . . These are three things I didn't like . . . This is something I inferred . . .

I know evaluating a story hones analytical ability. Noting what parts kept you interested versus when your mind wandered, questioning what makes you want to spend time with certain characters—these kinds of observations are valid and, in fact, could be the first step toward becoming a writer. But why send that report to the author? An author is no more likely to enjoy hearing three things you didn't like about her story than a teacher would relish hearing three things you don't like about her teaching techniques.

If learning to write—and send—a letter is part of the assignment, shouldn't the teacher read that letter? Some of my mail is almost illegible from erasures and spelling errors, with students asking for copies of my books (no, I don't get them free), or for me to visit their out-of-state school. Then they tell me their project mark depends on getting an answer from me. (. . . No offense, but what took you so long to get back to me? I sent my email yesterday . . .)

My suggestions? A teacher could, without stifling students' creativity, point out there's no need to ask an author for information that can be easily found elsewhere, such as what else she's written. Instead, this could be a chance to ask where she got the idea for the story or—if the students didn't like something, such as the ending—why she chose to do things the way she did.

On the other hand, if the student is unhappy with unpleasant characters and tense situations, this might be an opening for classroom discussion about conflict in a story and how boring it would be to read about an attractive, popular, healthy, happy child to whom only good things happen.

I cherish the heartfelt letters from students who say my books made them laugh, made them think, got them through a difficult time: the letters born from enthusiasm. Those are letters worth reading—long after the end of the marking period.

NOTE: All excerpts are from real letters.

> • Vivian Vande Velde has written more than twenty books for young readers. One of her most recent is *All Hallows' Eve: 13 Stories* (Harcourt, 2006). She won the Edgar Award for *Never Trust a Dead Man*. To learn more about her, visit www.vivianvandevelde.com.

One reason that books written by Sherman Alexie, Maya Angelou, and Amy Tan have become popular with teen readers is that young people identify with authors writing about the complications of living in two cultures. Also much of the writing is autobiographical with these adults including their own coming-of-age stories.

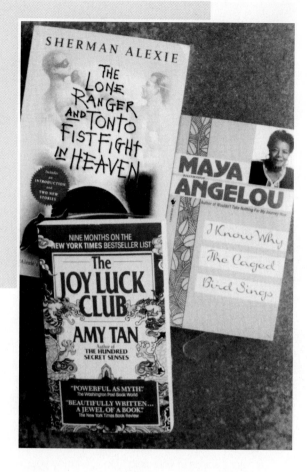

juicy details of life" that will help them value their own experiences "with family and friends, in their own communities, observing or participating in the human dramas of the moment."[12]

Language is a social phenomenon, and just as we learned to speak through imitation and trial and error, we learn to write in much the same way. Young adult literature can provide creative teens with inspiration and models to follow. See how the point about breaking stereotypes that Kimberly Willis Holt makes in her Young Adult Authors Speak Out statement is perfectly accessible to young writers. Furthermore,

- The problems in the books are likely to be ones that readers or their friends have experienced or thought about.
- A variety of ethnic backgrounds and settings enlarges the chance of students finding stories with which they can identify.
- Characters' conversations can serve as models for the writing of dialogue because the speech patterns come close to the everyday, spoken language of teenagers and to the I-wish-I-had-said-that kind of rejoinder.
- Even in historical fiction or in fantasy or science fiction, the protagonists are young, which means that their intellectual and emotional development is similar to that of teenage readers.

Young Adult Authors Speak Out

Kimberly Willis Holt on the Unexpected

While visiting schools, I'm frequently asked, "Why did you make Zachary Beaver neat?" The students are referring to the obese character in my novel *When Zachary Beaver Came to Town.*

I often begin my answer with a question—"Why wouldn't he be neat?" This query is usually met with a shrug from the somewhat embarrassed student. I know the answer, though. Many readers assume Zachary Beaver would be sloppy because of his large size. However, I wanted to give Zachary dignity. One way I tried to do this was to avoid the stereotyped characteristics that some people associate with an obese person. That's why Zachary is a neat-freak. He also has a dream. He wants to help grow the sideshow business that he shares with Paulie. Also, although Zachary views the world from his trailer window, he is able to expand those horizons by reading. He knows more about other places than most people do even though they do not have his limitations. By giving my characters unexpected traits, I hope I'm eliminating clichés while creating interesting people.

In *Part of Me*, I write about four generations of a family. Though each character is different they share a love of books and each tries to reach goals by planning. Rose wants to be a writer. Merle Henry wants to trap a mink. Annabeth merely wants to be popular. It seems those two traits are possessed by each family member until Kyle enters the story. Kyle is nothing like his predecessors. He is content spending the summer in bed, listening to Pink Floyd albums. And he hates to read.

Giving unexpected traits to my characters can be challenging so I sometimes use a system. I start by studying their physical features. What would readers assume about them just by their appearance? Then sometimes I give them the opposite personality traits. In *When Zachary Beaver Came to Town*, Scarlett is the beautiful girl who breaks Toby's heart. But before the story ends, I try to show the reader that she, too, has a heart, when she returns a gift and says, "Toby Wilson, you're the nicest boy in Antler."

In the same story, Miss Myrtie Mae, the town librarian and historian, betrays the narrow-minded nosy old woman stereotype that her elderly body might suggest. Instead she is tolerant with a passion for life. And much to Toby's surprise, she even had a past romance.

Sometimes I let an action give the reader the unexpected. When readers of *Keeper of the Night* experience calm Isabel snap and slap a friend over a comment, I hope they gasp. I hope they didn't see it coming.

Like most lessons I've learned about writing, this, too, comes from rereading books I love. Without exception, they are always stories with interesting characters that surprise me. They are not who they seem originally. The authors of those stories give the unexpected. They never forget the thrill of a surprise.

- Kimberly Willis Holt's books include *Part of Me: Stories of a Louisiana Family* (2006), for young teens; *Keeper of the Night* (2003); and National Book Award Winner *When Zachary Beaver Came to Town* (1999), all published by Holt.

- Most YA authors write in a succinct and straightforward style so that readers can "get" the story and still have some intellectual energy to expend in looking at the author's techniques.

- The intriguing details that professional writers include in their stories are the same kinds of details that clever and witty teenagers observe and relate to each other, which means they have a head start when it comes to incorporating such details into stories.

While teenagers seldom write scholarly papers, many of them enjoy writing scripts, poems, and short stories, or putting their observations online in blogs or even creating their own zines. See Focus Box 11.3, Encouragement for Student Writers and 11.4, Publication Opportunities for Young Writers.

Some teachers of creative writing have found that it works well to use a collection of YA short stories for the text because, for one thing, it's a lot easier to pick out figurative language from contemporary short stories than from Elizabethan drama or early American literature. A collection that has worked well for us is Don Gallo's *Sixteen: Short Stories by Outstanding Writers for Young Adults*. Gallo grouped the stories under the categories of friendships, turmoils, loves, decisions, and families, but for creative writing purposes, we regrouped them into types starting with what we judged to be the easiest for students to imitate, then moved on up to the hardest. We started with wish-fulfilling stories so that students could have fun thinking, talking, and then writing about their daydreams and fantasies. We next looked at stories filled with incongruity and surprise, followed by those showing contrasting points of view. The most sophisticated category of the stories, which we left until last, were the realistic explorations of human emotions.

How much work young writers do depends on their motivation as well as on the setting. Students in a semester- or yearlong class probably have more time to put into their writing than those in a six-week unit or in an after-school writing club sponsored by a library or other community organization. Those in extracurricular writing groups, however, may be more motivated and may be together over several years rather than just for a few months.

While an obvious goal may be the writing of a short story, less ambitious tasks can provide practice as well as feelings of success along the way. For example, students can work in small groups to improvise dialogue for a scene that might have occurred in one of the stories, or they can rework a story into a one-act play or a reader's theater production.

Students love to write scenes for movies or television, and now that there are so many teen-centered television shows, they might practice turning a short story into a TV script. Keeping a response journal helps students focus on a story. Prompts to help readers think of themselves as authors include:

1. The part of this story that comes the closest to something I might write is . . .
2. If I had written this story I would have . . .
3. If I were to write a sequel . . .
4. This author is especially skilled at (choose one) developing characters, writing conversations, describing settings, or creating interesting plots as shown by . . .

In anticipation of creating their own story titles, help students examine the titles in a collection. Which are the most intriguing? The most memorable? For

A Maze Me: Poems for Girls by Naomi Shihab Nye, illustrated by Terre Mahere. HarperCollins/Greenwillow, 2005. Nye not only shares her wonderfully fresh poetry, but also advises future poets. One of her sensible suggestions is "If you write three lines down in a notebook every day . . . you will find out what you notice." She started doing this when she was twelve and hasn't stopped yet. (See her Young Adult Authors Speak Out statement on p. 153).

Blood on the Forehead: What I Know about Writing by M. E. Kerr. HarperCollins, 1998. The title comes from the framed quotation that Kerr keeps above her desk, "Writing is easy: All you do is sit staring at a blank sheet of paper until the drops of blood form on your forehead."

Getting the Knack: 20 Poetry Writing Exercises by Stephen Dunning and William Stafford. National Council of Teachers of English, 1992. The book does exactly what it sets out to do, which is to give young writers specific details about different ways to write poems.

Immersed in Verse: An Informative, Slightly Irreverent and Totally Tremendous Guide to Living the Poet's Life by Allan Wolf, illustrated by Tuesday Mourning. Sterling/Lark, 2006. This is both a how-to and a book of encouragement for anyone who's even slightly tempted to write a poem. The illustrations add an upbeat tone.

A Kick in the Head: An Everyday Guide to Poetic Forms by Paul B. Janeczko, illustrated by Chris Raschka. Candlewick, 2005. In this follow-up to their 2001 *A Poke in the I*, these two creative men make the study of poetic forms so much fun that we predict kids will want to see if they can follow the "rules" while still being as original as are the sample poems in the book.

The Making of a Writer by Joan Lowery Nixon. Delacorte, 2002. This popular author of mysteries for young readers aimed her memoir at fans in junior high and middle school. All the way through she shares advice and tidbits, ending up with her "top ten" tips.

One Experience to Another: Stories about Turning Points, edited by M. Jerry Weiss and Helen S. Weiss. Forge, 1997. Top YA writers (e.g., Joan Bauer, Gordon Korman, Suzanne Fisher Staples, and Walter Dean Myers) contributed stories accompanied by introductory remarks tracing the routes their minds took in changing a real-life event into a fictional story.

Our Stories: A Fiction Workshop for Young Authors by Marion Dane Bauer. Clarion, 1996. In each of twelve chapters,

Bauer includes sample stories and essays from young people who are identified at the back of the book.

Poems from Homeroom: A Writer's Place to Start by Kathi Appelt. Henry Holt, 2002. Appelt is a successful writer for children and middle school students and uses her same fresh style in this encouraging book.

Poetry Matters: Writing a Poem from the Inside Out by Ralph Fletcher. HarperCollins, 2002. Fletcher describes poems as "emotional X-rays," and then sets out to equip readers with what they need to create the X-rays of their feelings and observations. Interviews with poets are inspiring as well as instructive.

Seeing the Blue Between: Advice and Inspiration for Young Poets, compiled by Paul B. Janeczko. Candlewick, 2002. Janeczko collected advice and models from thirty-two successful poets and put it all together with the same care that he has used in such previous books as *How to Write Poetry* (Scholastic, 1999), *The Place My Words Are Looking For* (Bradbury, 1990), and *Poetspeak: In Their Work, About Their Work* (Bradbury, 1983).

Technically, It's Not My Fault: Concrete Poems written and illustrated by John Grandits. Clarion, 2004. The title comes from a science experiment gone awry. Middle school students will be the ones most likely to be amused, but high school students might want to see how their own skills stack up with those of Grandits's.

A Teen's Guide to Getting Published: Publishing for Profit, Recognition, and Academic Success, 2nd edition by Jessica Dunn and Danielle Dunn. Prufrock Press, 2006. Although we aren't as enthused as some people are about encouraging teens to become published authors, we at least need to provide ambitious teens with the kind of information that is in this book.

Whatcha Mean What's a Zine? The Art of Making Zines and Mini-Comics by Mark Todd and Esther Pearl Watson. Graphia Books/Houghton Mifflin, 2006. Creative and/or artistic kids can get both inspiration and instruction from this book that is designed to look like a homemade zine. It is the book the authors wish they had run across when they started drawing and telling their own stories long before they knew there was a name for what they were making.

Writing Magic: Creating Stories That Fly by Gail Carson Levine. HarperCollins, 2006. Levine's chapter titles give the tone of her must-read for potential authors: "Liftoff," "Heart and Guts," "Plowing Through," "Digging Deeper," and "Writing Forever."

Amazon.com

www.amazon.com: Amazon is one of the original places on the Web where teens can submit book reviews. The List-mania! Lists allows users to create personalized book lists and suggestions on any topic.

Bookbrowse.com

www.bookbrowse.com: Teens can write and submit reviews about their favorite books at this site edited and owned by Davina Morgan-Witts.

BookDivas

www.bookdivas.com: A collaboration between Seventeen magazine and Electric Artists, BookDivas encourages girls to read, review, and discuss books or whatever strikes their fancy.

Book Raps

www.oz-teachernet.edu.au/projects/br: At this site, teens can discuss books that are nominated by teachers and librarians. "Book Raps" are scheduled on a monthly calendar and anyone can participate. Book Raps is part of the Oz-Teacher Net of Australia and is maintained by Margaret Lloyd, Jennifer Masters, and Shaun Nykvist.

Favorite Teenage Angst Books

www.grouchy.com/angst/: At this appealing site, teens can discuss books related to classic coming-of-age issues, such as relationships, drugs and alcohol, self-esteem, and family problems. The website author, Cathy Young, recently edited an anthology of stories called *One Hot Second: Stories of Desire.*

Guys Read

www.penguinputnam.com/static/packages/us/yreaders/guys read: Guys Read is an initiative to improve literacy in boys, created by Jon Scieszka. This site features booklists and tips to help improve literacy among boys.

Merlyn's Pen

www.merlynspen.org: Established long before the days of Internet printing, Merlyn's Pen publishes a yearly collection as well as more frequent issues featuring teenage writing.

Read! Literacy and Education for Life

www.weread.org/teens/Index.asp: Teens can read and submit stories and book reviews at this site. WE READ is an acronym for "World Enterprise for Reading, Education, and Academic Development" and is in the process of obtaining its nonprofit status.

Reading Rants!

www.readingrants.org: Maintained by Jennifer Hubert, middle school librarian at the Little Red School House and Elisabeth Irwin High School in Greenwich Village, Manhattan, Reading Rants! focuses on books geared toward girls.

TeenInk Magazine

TeenInk.com/Books/: A monthly print magazine and website written by teens for teens. The website accepts original poetry, fiction, and book reviews from teens.

TeensPoint.org

www.teenspoint.org/reviews/index.asp: At this library site teens have opportunities to read and write reviews of books, music, movies, and websites. It is maintained by the Central Rappahannock Regional Library in Fredericksburg, Virginia.

WordSmiths

http://teenlink.nypl.org/wordsmiths-current.cfm: Sponsored by the New York Public Library, WordSmiths is a site where teens can publish their own creative writing.

---

example, in Gallo's *Sixteen* collection, what are the extra meanings in Brancato's "Fourth of July" and Lipsyte's "Future Tense"? Which titles help establish setting by hinting at time and place? Which establish a light tone? How about a dark or serious tone? What is the effect of an author asking a question?

Does Cormier's "In the Heat" remind readers of the oxymoronic "In the heat of the night," while Major's "Three People and Two Seats" reminds them of the cliché "two's company, three's a crowd"? The point in relation to students' own writing is to illustrate how much thought authors put into creating titles that honestly convey the sense of their stories while arousing a readers' interest.

Thematic Units

Part of the reason that thematic units have become popular in English classes is that they provide a way to bind together a number of apparently dissimilar elements, including literature, language, media, and popular culture. First, however, we need to distinguish the thematic unit from two other kinds of units. The project unit has a clear end product, with all the steps that lead up to that end. For example, the production of a class play ends when the play is put on, a class-published slang dictionary ends when the booklet is put together and handed out, and reading and talking about a novel ends with the last discussion and the test. A subject-centered unit consists of a body of information the teacher feels is important for the class. For example, units on the history of the language, the rise of drama in Shakespeare's time, or "Our Friend, the Introductory Adverbial Clause" (the last is not made up; we saw it in action, if that's the right phrase). These units have no clear-cut ending, barring a test, but they do have generally clear limits of what is to be included.

The thematic unit is different in that it binds together many elements of English while centering on a theme or motif that runs through a body of literature. For example, a question most of us have asked ourselves is, "Why do some people want to manipulate others?" This question is also asked in Aldous Huxley's *Brave New World*, George Orwell's *1984*, Shakespeare's *Othello* and *King Lear*, F. Scott Fitzgerald's *The Great Gatsby*, Henrik Ibsen's *An Enemy of the People*, Robert Cormier's *Fade*, Sonya Hartnett's *Surrender*, M. E. Kerr's *If I Love You, Am I Trapped Forever?* and Sophocles's *Antigone*. Is this a theme deserving the four or five weeks' time that the usual thematic unit takes? Here are four criteria against which to stack such a question:

1. The theme needs to appeal to kids. If it is too easy, too hard, or too boring, the teacher will lose the students' interest and attention.

2. The theme needs to be worth doing—in other words, intellectually and emotionally respectable for these particular kids at this particular time of their development and at this particular time of the year.

3. There must be lots of easily located literature on the theme.

4. The theme needs to appeal to the teacher; if the teacher is not excited about it, the kids won't be either.

Assuming that the theme meets these four requirements, the teacher must search for literature on the theme that will challenge the students and that they will enjoy, composition topics (written and spoken) worth using and related to the theme, films (short and feature-length) related to the theme and worth viewing, and spelling and vocabulary lists related to the theme. That means the teacher must determine the following:

1. A list of sensible objectives (or learning outcomes or standards if you prefer) for this specific unit (not English classwork in general) that both kids and their parents can understand.

2. A work of some length (usually a short novel or a play) to open the unit and make clear to students what the unit is aiming at. Such a work is not essential, but it's customary and usually helpful.

3. A body of short works (poetry and short stories and essays) to be used throughout the unit because they are related to the theme.

4. A series of composition assignments (usually two or three written assignments and two or three oral assignments) on the theme.

5. A list of vocabulary words related to the unit topic, perhaps twenty to thirty or so, to be talked about and tested five at a time.

6. A list of spelling words related to the unit topic, perhaps twenty to thirty or so, to be talked about and tested about five at a time.

7. A way of beginning the unit that grabs students' attention and interest while focusing on the theme. Obviously, teachers can (and do) begin thematic units with "Hey, kids, how would you like to talk about _____?" or "Hey, kids, we're going to turn to something entirely different now, a unit on _____," but surely there's a slightly more fascinating way. A short film or the teacher reading aloud a short story (or a recent news clipping) might work.

8. A way of wrapping up the unit that ties all the strands together. Tests, the all-American way to wrap anything up, are always possible. Some classes find panel discussions useful, some might profit from a student evaluation of the unit and the literature read, and others might benefit from some creative art project or a dramatization.

9. The problems that the unit—and students—may encounter and how the teacher works through them. Perhaps it's time to incorporate peer editing into the class, and if this unit is as good a time as any other to introduce kids to peer evaluation and editing, the teacher needs to plan on preparing class members to work in small groups. Perhaps the short book chosen to get the unit started (e.g., Monica Hughes's *Hunter in the Dark*) has some vocabulary problems, or Nathaniel Hawthorne's short story "Young Goodman Brown" presents problems getting the kids to understand colonial life and religion. These and similar issues need to be worked through and solutions found.

Thematic units can range from complex and sophisticated topics for college-bound kids to simple topics that are appropriate for junior high. For example, a thematic unit on "Our Ability to Endure," which centers on the theme of survival and power, is a topic of immediate interest to eighth and ninth graders. It could open with words from William Faulkner's much-anthologized Nobel Prize speech and move to one of these as common reading and the remainder as supplementary reading: Avi's *The True Confessions of Charlotte Doyle*, Alice Childress's *Rainbow Jordan*, Robert Cormier's *After the First Death*, James Forman's *Ceremony of Innocence*, Anne Frank's *The Diary of a Young Girl*, Harry Mazer's *The Last Mission*, or Robb White's *Deathwatch*.

A more intellectually and emotionally complex thematic unit on "Redemption" might begin with reading and discussing Katherine Mansfield's "The Garden Party" or Nadine Gordimer's "A Company of Laughing Faces." This might be followed by the class reading Bernard Malamud's *The Assistant*, and sometime during the unit each student might be asked to read at least one supplementary work. Here there's room for a range in difficulty with advanced students doing Dante's *The Divine Comedy* or Dostoevsky's *Crime and Punishment*. Less challenging books include Hal Borland's *When the Legends Die*, F. Scott Fitzgerald's *The Great Gatsby*, Ursula K. Le Guin's *A Wizard of Earthsea*, Fran Arrick's *Tunnel Vision*, Judy Blume's *Tiger Eyes*, Margaret Mahy's *Memory*, and Paul Zindel's *The Pigman*.

Teachers wanting ideas for themes of interest to young people might skim through titles of some of the recent short story collections, many of which are thematically organized; for example Belinda Hollyer's *You're the Best: 14 Stories about Friendship*, M. Jerry Weiss and Helen Weiss's *Dreams and Visions*, Walter Dean Myers's *What They Found: Love on 145th Street*, and Michael Cart's *Tomorrowland: Stories about the Future*. Cart has made several thoughtful collections (see YA Authors Speak Out in Chapter 1). He worked with Marc Aronson and Marianne Carus to put together *911: The Book of Help*, in which authors wrote stories somehow relating to the 2001 terrorist attack. The editors grouped the stories under headings that could themselves become the themes for exploratory units:

- Healing: No one has been untouched . . . ;
- Searching for History: Putting 9/11 in the context of a personal past;
- Asking Why? Why? Why? Our persistent struggle to understand;
- Reacting and Recovering: It is a dangerous world but it's wonderful too.

Other well-received collections edited by Cart include *Necessary Noise: Stories about Our Families as They Really Are*, *Love and Sex: Ten Stories of Truth*, and *Rush Hour: Sin*.

Of course you want to have more than a collection of short stories from which to plan a unit, but it is comforting to have something to start with and to show students the possibilities for different interpretations. One of the benefits of thematic units should be that they are flexible enough to inspire different thinking by different students.

Film and Television

Studying the great plays of the world such as the Greek tragedies and Shakespeare's dramas has always been a part of teaching English, so it was to be expected that in the 1940s and 1950s, leaders in the field would suggest expanding drama studies to include the study of films, which were a much bigger part of students' lives than drama. During the 1960s and on into the 1970s, the idea of teaching about the making and viewing of films grew in popularity. Such terms as *film noir, cutting, film code, fade-out, camera tracking, outtakes, voice-over, gaffer, best boy,* and *trailer* were added to the literary terminology of high school English classes. In the 1980s, the VCR brought a wonderful new kind of freedom to film studies because teachers could now have at their fingertips most of the great movies of the world which they could use to supplement their study of novels or plays or to lend excitement to thematic units.

Today DVDs bring the same kind of freedom, plus the benefit of enabling teachers to pick out specific scenes to show or to come back to. In addition, some DVDs include background material showing interviews with producers, authors, or critics, and behind-the-camera scenes revealing how particular effects were achieved. Some—but not all—of this background material is worth showing and talking about because it resembles what knowledgeable teachers of film studies provide. Popular television serials are also on DVDs, and provide even more choice when bringing in something visual.

Showing a two-hour film in class has the advantage of telling the whole story, but it takes more time than is usually available and also has the disadvantage of lacking focus if a teacher wants to come back to talk about how a movie scene compares with the same scene in the book or why the producer chose to leave out a certain part, or to film another part from a particular angle. Also, today's students have so much access to movies of their own choosing that they aren't as likely to be thrilled at the prospect of sitting at a hard desk with no popcorn to see a movie that they aren't sure they are interested in.

A DVD allows teachers to show particular scenes for specific purposes. For example, a well-chosen five-minute scene can serve as an introduction or a book-talk to get students interested in reading the book that provided the inspiration for the film. Popular teen books are made into films surprisingly fast, and this goes a long way toward inspiring teens to read such books as Louis Sachar's *Holes* or Ann Brashares's *The Sisterhood of the Traveling Pants*. Kids interpret a film as a seal of approval or a guarantee of interest. When Brashares came to talk about her Traveling Pants books at the Changing Hands Bookstore in Tempe, Arizona, it was fun to see groups of girls walking up to the suburban bookstore. Ninety-nine percent of them were wearing jeans. We couldn't help but suspect that the girls who wore skirts hadn't read the book.

Clearly delineated scenes can also be used as the impetus for creative writing. Students can be asked to write what happens next, or you can show an incident with the sound off and ask students to create the dialogue. There's no end to the possibilities. An important lesson for students is that while many movies are based on novels, the movie version cannot be the same thing as the book. In putting across this point, we had one of our best teaching experiences when we brought in a DVD of the movie *Holes* and used it in conjunction with Table 5.1, on pp. 173–174, which illustrates some of Louis Sachar's techniques of creating humor. Our purpose in the lesson was to have students figure out which of the examples of humor could be transferred to the film and which ones were best left only in the book.

To get ready, we had to watch the DVD at home and make a list of the scenes as shown on the preview to the DVD and then jot down notes on which scenes we wanted to show because they included humor and which scenes we could simply tell about so that those who had not read the book could keep the plot straight. It was also revealing to find instances in the film of visual humor that were not in the book, such as the inclusion of Stanley's grandfather living with the Yelnats family and the decor of their crowded apartment, with all the old sneakers his dad was experimenting on.

Of course preparing this lesson was a lot more trouble than doing what many parents and administrators think teachers do when they take a film into class. These critics remember the days when they were in school and "movie day" was considered a treat for both teachers and students because all the teacher did was slip in the film and turn off the lights, and everyone felt free to watch or go to sleep. In modern schools, such movie days are rare partly because teachers feel pressured to be on task and many teachers have not dared to work with film enough to see that it can be a wonderful way to provide a classroom with a common literary experience.

The September 2007 *English Journal* printed an especially good article by John Golden, "Literature into Film (and Back Again): Another Look at an Old Dog." He wrote about laying the foundation for profitable class discussions by focusing attention on three different approaches: cinematic elements, theatrical elements, and literary elements. He gave suggestions for short scenes that can be used to illustrate each of these elements. See Appendix C for further information on Golden's article, as well as on other helpful books and articles.

Concluding Comments

We once had a student come to our office and announce that he wanted to learn everything that a good high school English teacher needed to know. He wondered where he should begin, and we suggested he start with literature. He agreed and wondered yet again where he should begin. We mentioned that good English teachers know the classics, lots of novels and plays and poetry, and lots of young adult literature. After we cleared up the confusion about the term classics—we weren't talking about Steinbeck yet—we turned to Sophocles, Euripides, and Aristophanes, none of whom he knew. Because he begged us to turn to the eighteenth century, where he claimed he knew the novel, we moved onward and upward only to hear his complaint when we brought up such writers as John Gay, William Blake, and Richard Brinsley Sheridan. A day later, we pointed out that good English teachers also know English and American literature, of course, but also know third-world literature and German, Japanese, Norwegian, and Russian literature, and young adult literature as well.

Somewhere as we rounded Russian literature, our earnest student gave up. After this catalogue of what he needed to know, he asked one last question before he disappeared: "How can anyone learn all that?" The answer, which he obviously did not want to hear, was that thousands of good people do it all the time, not in a few hasty weeks but in a lifetime. They are called English teachers.

Notes

1. Louise M. Rosenblatt, *Literature As Exploration*, 4th edition (Modern Language Association, 1983), pp. 278–279.
2. Robert C. Small, "Teaching the Junior Novel," *English Journal* 61 (February 1972): 222.
3. Patricia Lee Gauch, "Good Stuff in Adolescent Literature," *Top of the News* 40 (Winter 1984): 129.
4. Richard W. Jackson, *CBC Features* 39 (October 1984–July 1985): 5. A publication of the Children's Book Council.
5. Tim Wynne-Jones, "On Short Stories," *Literature for Today's Young Adults*, 6th edition, by Alleen Pace Nilsen and Kenneth L. Donelson (Longman, 2001), p. 364.
6. D. W. Harding, "Response to Literature; The Report of the Study Group," in James R. Squire, ed., *Response to Literature: Papers Relating to the Anglo-American Seminar on the Teaching of English at Dartmouth College, New Hampshire, 1966* (NCTE, 1968), p. 26.
7. Edward J. Gordon, "Levels of Teaching and Testing," *English Journal* 44 (September 1955): 330–334; Dwight L. Burton, "Well, Where Are We in Teaching Literature?" *English Journal* 63 (February 1974): 28–33.
8. Howard Francis Seely, "Our Novel Stock-in-Trade," *English Journal* 18 (November 1929): 724–725.
9. G. F. Lamb, "The Reading Habit," *Tomorrow* (England) 2 (July 1934): 10.
10. Three informative articles that comment on books that did not win awards (or were not nominated), although the books are popular today and deserve careful attention: Joni Bodart's "The Also-Rans: Or, 'What Happened to the Ones That Didn't Get Eight Votes?'" *Top of the News* 38 (Fall 1981): 70–73; Pam Spencer's "Winners in Their Own Right," *School Library Journal* 36 (July 1990): 23–27; and "Part II," *School Library Journal* 38 (March 1992): 163–167.
11. Richard Peck, "Ten Questions to Ask About a Novel," *ALAN Newsletter* 5 (Spring 1978): 1, 7.
12. Jack Gantos, "Up for Discussion: Warts and All," *School Library Journal* 42:3 (March, 1996): 128.

Censorship
Of Worrying and Wondering

chapter **12**

In public schools and libraries, nothing is more constant than censorship. Parents complain about the immorality of characters in books assigned, or books not assigned, or books that someday might be assigned. Violence in literature is unacceptable as is profanity and obscenity, both rarely defined. Books as different as Robert Cormier's *The Chocolate War* and *After the First Death*; Judy Blume's *Forever* and *Are You There God? It's Me, Margaret*; John Steinbeck's *The Grapes of Wrath* and *Of Mice and Men*; Mark Twain's *Tom Sawyer* and *The Adventures of Huckleberry Finn*; and Katherine Paterson's *Jacob Have I Loved* and *Bridge to Terabithia* easily and frequently come under attack. The Harry Potter series consistently is challenged supposedly for its attention to wizardry and magic, but what may be even more frightening is its popularity with young people and adults.

A Censorial Spirit

Teachers and librarians know that attacks on books are here to stay and are often deadly serious, increasingly so in the last decade or two. Colin Campbell's words from 1981 still ring true.

A censorial spirit is at work in the United States, and for the past year or so it has focused more and more on books. Efforts to remove certain titles from school and public libraries, from paperback racks and bookstores, from the eyes of adults as well as children, have increased measurably.[1]

Norma Fox Mazer recognized that censorship was as likely to happen today as it was in 1981. In a 2003 interview, she was asked, "Does censorship of YA literature continue to be a problem or is the situation improving?" Mazer responded, "Improving? I doubt it. Without being pessimistic, I think there will always be that core of people who long to press us all into their own small confined world, and there will always be those of us who resist." Her husband, writer Harry Mazer, added, "Censors are always out there. I don't know that they will ever go away or ever should. It's good to know that there are people who take books so seriously they want to burn them. Resisting censorship is part of the territory for all book lovers, be they publishers, writers, parents, teachers, or librarians. We need to stand our ground. There are more of us than there are of them."[2]

It is difficult for teachers and librarians not to overreact when another censorship incident hits the newspaper. On September 3, 1999, a story in the *Arizona Republic* revealed that at Carson Junior High School in Mesa, a suburb of Phoenix, a few parents had decided that a musical production of *Tom Sawyer* should close before it opened. One parent said, "The script was culturally insensitive." Why? Because *Tom* was clearly a product of another time and place, and it simply did not fit our politically correct time. Parents listed these objections. Injun Joe was a slam at Native Americans. Three female characters were described, respectively, as "extremely feminine," "an outrageous flirt," and "a large, warm, homey woman." Equally offensive, the constable was referred to as "a typical redneck." Also, several references to religion were impolite.

Four school board members supported the ban, although none had received a complaint from parents. Worse yet, the district's associate superintendent announced her view of drama: "A play in which the content and characterization becomes the focus steals the spotlight from the students. A play is entertainment. It's not in an instructional setting."[3] That's not quite what Aristotle wrote in the *Poetics*. It's not the view that Henrik Ibsen, Eugene O'Neill, and Tennessee Williams and their plays espouse. Maybe Arthur Miller and Tom Stoppard should reconsider what drama is all about and ensure that entertainment is all that drama should be.

While the reasoning of censors and the gibberish they produce frightens us, sometimes it is impossible to fathom the arguments underlying the censorship, as in these six episodes:

In April 2007 in Wilton High School, Connecticut, students prepared a play, a series of monologues by soldiers entitled "Voices in Conflict" only to learn that their principal had canceled the play because of "Concerns about political balance, sourcing, and the possibility of hurting Wilton residents who had lost "loved ones." The students were given a "Courage in Theater" award by the Music Theater International, and famous theater people including Edward Albee, Christopher Durang, and John Guare joined the National Coalition Against Censorship in urging school officials to let the play go on. In the meantime, the Public Theater, a New York City institution, scheduled the play to be shown off-Broadway in June.[4]

In July 2004 in Wake Count, North Carolina, a school district banned the *Cassell Dictionary of Slang* because of parental complaints. Jonathon Green, who compiled the 87,000 entries in the dictionary, said he was "very flattered" and added,

"It's not exactly book-burning, but in the great tradition of book censorship, there never seems to be the slightest logic to it."[5]

In March 2003 in Albuquerque, New Mexico, a high school teacher was fired and classes in poetry and the poetry club in Rio Rico High School were "permanently terminated." After a girl presented one of her poems at a Barnes and Noble bookstore and later over the school's closed-circuit TV channel, the principal and a school military liaison accused the girl of being un-American for criticizing the war in Iraq. The girl's mother, a teacher, was ordered by the principal to destroy her daughter's poem.[6]

In 1997 in Marysville, California, when the superintendent removed J. D. Salinger's *The Catcher in the Rye* from the required reading list of the district, he announced, "This is not an issue of book banning. Rather it is an opportunity for parents with varied viewpoints to come together, listen to each other, and define common values."[7]

In July 1966, the East Stroudsburg, Pennsylvania, School Board approved 8 to 0 to drop Robert Cormier's *The Chocolate War* and several other books from a new English curriculum. The assistant superintendent for curriculum announced that the book was eliminated because of scheduling conflicts, not because of the furor it had caused the previous school year.[8]

In May 1993, the Oskaloosa, Kansas, School Board voted 4 to 2 to enact a new policy requiring teachers to examine their required materials for profanities. They are expected to list each profanity and the number of times it's used in the book.[9]

Obviously, not everyone who questions or objects to a book is a censor. Most parents are concerned about the welfare of their children, but being forced to go to school to make a complaint may make them resentful or nervous or angry. If taking time from work were not enough reason to feel irritated, many parents have a built-in love-hate ambivalence toward schools. They may not have fond memories of English teachers when they were young. They may worry about being talked down to by a much younger teacher or librarian. They may wonder if anyone will take them or their complaints seriously. When parents arrive at the school or the library, it is hardly surprising that they may feel hostile. That's easily misread by equally nervous teachers, who may see aggressive censors where there are only concerned parents.

Keeping this possibility of mistaken identity in mind, educators need to be considerate and reasonable and to listen more than they talk, at least for the first few minutes. Everyone may learn, sometimes to the listener's surprise, that no one wants to ban anything, but parents do wonder why the teacher is using the book or why the librarian recommended it to their children. They may want their children to read something else but agree that they have no wish to control the reading of anyone else. The problem is easier to handle (not always easy, but certainly *easier*).

In such cases, teachers and librarians should remember that the announced objection may not always be the real objection. Censors might attack Huxley's

Brave New World or Orwell's *1984* for their sexual references when the real objection is to the frightening political attitudes the authors displayed (or were thought to display). It is human nature to fear things we do not understand; hence the discomfort that many parents feel over the recent popularity of scary, supernatural books.

The underlying reasons for objections to particular books often are more significant than teachers or librarians may suspect. Sometimes the complaining parents do not even realize why a particular author or book makes them feel uncomfortable. This is why it's so important for parents to talk and for educators to listen. Parents who are worried about the moral climate facing their children are painfully aware that they have little power to change the material on television, and they cannot successfully fight the movies offered by local theaters or do away with local "adult" bookstores. Who, then, can they fight? What can they change? An easy answer is to go to school and protect at least that little corner of their children's lives.

The American Library Association has been on record against censorship since the 1920s, but its strongest statement first appeared in 1939 as the Library Bill of Rights. The document has periodically been tightened and strengthened, and the latest version can be found in the *Intellectual Freedom Manual,* 7th ed. The entire *Intellectual Freedom Manual* is filled with provocative ideas and helpful suggestions and should be required reading for librarians and English teachers alike.

A Sampling of Early Attitudes toward Censorship

5th Century BC: In Book II of *The Republic,* Plato argued that banishing poets and dramatists was essential for the moral good of the young because writers often told lies about the gods or made the gods appear responsible for the evils and misfortunes of mortals. Plato's argument that fiction could be emotionally disturbing to the young is echoed by many censors today.

211 BC: In China, the Emperor Chi Huang Ti burned Confucius's *Analects.*

1555: The Catholic Index of Forbidden Works was first published.

1737: Prime Minister Walpole forced passage of a Licensing Act in 1737, which required that every English play be examined and approved before production.

1797: The *Monthly Mirror* published an attack on reading novels in its November issue—"Novel Reading: A Cause of Female Depravity," which opened, "I now begin to hope that I shall see good old days come round again—that moderately stiff stays, covered elbows, and concealed bosoms, will soon be the prevailing fashions, and what is of far greater importance, that chastity— pure and spotless CHASTITY! Once more be the darling attribute of women. . . . I find those who first made *novel-reading* an indispensable branch in forming the minds of young women, have a great deal to answer for. Without this poison instilled, as it were, into the blood, females in ordinary life, would never have been so much the slave of vice."[10]

1872: In the United States, reformer Anthony Comstock founded the Society for the Suppression of Vice in New York. The next year he went to Washington, D.C., to urge passage of a federal statute against obscenity, abortion, and contraceptive devices. He got himself appointed as a Special Agent of the Postmaster General and by 1914 had caused the arraignment of 3,697 people with 2,740 convictions. He raised $237,134.30 in fines, which helped somewhat to pay for the prison sentences totaling over 565 years. Even in his last year of life (1915) he remained active with 176 arrests and 140 convictions.[11]

1877: William Kite, librarian at the Friends Free Library in Germantown, Pennsylvania, worried about the influence of novels. He wrote, "I could tell of one young woman of my acquaintance, of fine education, who gratified a vitiated taste for novel-reading till her reason was overthrown, and she has, in consequence, been for several years an inmate of an insane asylum. . . . Instances could be furnished by the records of such institutions in too sad frequency, but we need not seek them. Have we the moral right to expose the young to such cancer?"[12]

1896: While Mark Twain was coming under widespread attack for his less-than-genteel characters, Stephen Crane's *The Red Badge of Courage* was heavily criticized for its profanity. On a panel at the annual meeting of the American Library Association, A. L. Peck said about Crane's book, "I never could see why it should be given into the hands of a boy." G. M. Jones questioned the praise that the book was receiving in the "literary papers" and surmised that the reviews were being "written by young men who know nothing about war, just as Mr. Crane himself knows nothing about war. Gen. McClurg, of Chicago, and Col. Nourse, of Massachusetts, both say that the story is not true to the life of the soldier. An article in the *Independent,* or perhaps the *Outlook,* says that no such profanity as given in the book was common in the army among the soldiers. Mr. Crane has since published two other books on New York life which are simply vulgar books. I consider the *Red Badge of Courage* a vulgar book, and nothing but vulgar."[13]

1897: "Let teachers strictly forbid the bringing of any literature, which is merely for entertainment, into the schoolroom. . . . Many a wild escapade has been hatched from a blood-and-thunder story-book under a boy's desk-lid. Many a feverish thought and impulse has come to the romantic school girl from the page of a light novel which she conceals beneath her text-book."[14]

1897: "If the public library is not first and foremost an educational institution, it has no right to exist. If it exists for mere entertainment, and for a low order of entertainment at that, it is simply a socialistic institution."[15]

1903: At the first Library Institute of the State of New Jersey, Father McMahoon, director of the Catholic library, spoke of "the idea of children browsing among books as an educational fad, susceptible of nothing but evil."[16]

1920: In the *English Journal,* which had been founded in 1912, a teacher discussed her junior high students' reaction to *Treasure Island*. While one girl thought it should be read because "it is considered a classic," a boy wrote "I like a cleaner story. In this story there is too much bloodshed, drinking, and swearing." A girl wrote, "This story full of murder, fighting, and wiping blood off of knives is not suitable for boys and girls to read and if these kinds of books were not written there would not be so many boys go wrong. I don't think there should be any more books written like it, because it don't learn you anything and nowadays we should read books that do us some good."[17]

1932: At a library meeting in Michigan, Mary Silverthorn recommended ten criteria for fiction if it were to be allowed in a library. Among them, "1. It was written in good English. . . . 3. It depicted experiences of life worthwhile for others to enter in vicariously. . . . 5. It was stimulating to right thinking and action. . . . 6. It satisfied natural desires and curiosities in a normal, wholesome way. . . . 10. The line between right and wrong was clear-cut and distinct, or there was called forth a judgment on the part of the reader when the issues were blurred."[18]

Readers curious about the history of censorship and the changing roles of the public or school librarian on censorship will find two books especially helpful and readable. Evelyn Geller's *Forbidden Books in American Public Libraries, 1876–1939: A Study in Cultural Change* (Greenwood, 1984) carries the story of the attitude of the ALA toward intellectual freedom, from the early fear of fiction through the questions about what the public library exists for and who should be its clients on to the development of the Library Bill of Rights in 1939. Louise S. Robbins's *Censorship and the American Public Library: The American Library Association's Response to Threats to Intellectual Freedom, 1939–1969* (Greenwood, 1996) provides all-too-many examples of the skirmishes and battles that the ALA has engaged in since 1939.

No such book describes what the English teacher has gone through on censorship from the nineteenth century on, but Lee Burress and Edward B. Jenkinson's *The Students' Right to Know* (NCTE, 1982) and Joan DelFattore's *What Johnny Shouldn't Read: Textbook Censorship in America* (Yale University Press, 1992) are useful places to begin. The National Council of Teachers of English was remiss in its professional obligations on intellectual freedom until 1962 when the first edition of *The Students' Right to Read* was published (later editions appeared in 1972 and 1982). With articles from the *English Journal* in the bibliography that concludes this chapter—beginning with Wayne Booth's March 1964 article—readers should be able to picture English teachers' contemporary attitude toward censorship.

A fast sketch of our country's history since the Great Depression would suggest times or events or people when censorship was likely to be an issue, sometimes a major problem, in our schools. In seventy-some years, we've witnessed *The Grapes of Wrath*, the cold war, *Slaughterhouse-Five*, the fall of the Berlin Wall, *The Catcher in the Rye*, segregation and integration, *Go Ask Alice*, Senator Joseph McCarthy, *To Kill a Mockingbird*, Vietnam, *Born on the Fourth of July*, Iraq, and Harry Potter. Some were, at the least, controversial. Often, merely being controversial was enough to spawn censorship.

See the "Starter Bibliography" at the end of this chapter for sources to help mitigate the negative effects of censorship.

More Recent Attitudes on Censorship

Before World War II, paperback books seemed to offer little of intellectual or pedagogical value to teachers. Even after the war many teachers blithely assumed that paperbacks had not changed, and given the often-lurid covers, teachers seemed to have a point, although it was more superficial than real. Administrators and parents continued to object even after the Bible, Plato's *Dialogues,* and *Four Tragedies of Shakespeare* proved to teachers and librarians that paperbacks had merit. Students discovered even earlier that paperbacks were handy to stick in a purse or back pocket, and paperback titles were appealing, not stodgy, as were most textbooks. So paperbacks came to schools, censors notwithstanding, and these cheap and ubiquitous books created problems galore for teachers.

Surveys of the state of censorship since 1963 reveal that censorship is either getting worse or fewer teachers and librarians are willing to lie quietly while the censor walks over them. Lee Burress's pioneer study "How Censorship Affects the School," in October 1963, was only the first of these surveys. Nyla H. Ahrens's doctoral study in 1965 was the first national survey. State surveys of Arizona censorship conditions appeared in the February 1969 and February 1975 *Arizona English Bulletin.* National studies appeared ever more often: L. B. Woods's "The Most Censored Materials in the U.S.," in the November 1, 1978, *Library Journal* and Burress's "A Brief Report of the 1977 NCTE Survey," in James Davis's *Dealing with Censorship.* The 1982 survey of high school librarians by Burress found that 34 percent of the librarians reported a challenge to at least one book compared to 30 percent in his 1977 survey. A survey of Canadian censorship by David Jenkinson published in the February 1986 *Canadian Library Journal* provided no optimism about censors. Two surveys by Donelson—one in the March 1985 *School Library Journal* of censorship for the previous thirteen years and comparing conclusions from six previous surveys and another in the October–November 1990 *High School Journal* summarizing the censorship incidents in the *Newsletter on Intellectual Freedom* from 1952 through 1989—provide little comfort to teachers or librarians.

The only way to keep up to date on what's happening with censorship is to stay alert to what's happening in the world. That means listening to TV and radio newscasts, reading newspapers and magazines, and keeping in touch with two professional organizations, the National Council of Teachers of English (NCTE) and the American Library Association (ALA). That's a lot of work to impose on English teachers and librarians already living hectic lives of quiet desperation, but it's necessary work. Some schools have been fortunate enough to have librarians who stay aware of their professional responsibilities as ALA members. English departments often have professionally active NCTE members in their midst, who know that being professional means keeping up to the moment on professional dangers, none of them more important than the threat of censorship.

No source provides more fast information about censorship than the *Newsletter on Intellectual Freedom*, where readers can find news about recent attacks on literature or films and news about court decisions that may affect us all. Occasionally, we may run across an item that is disturbing. For example, the November 2002 *Newsletter* summarized a survey of Americans' attitudes toward the First Amendment as reported in the *American Journalism Review*. Among findings that have some scary implications for censorship, almost half of those surveyed said they thought the First Amendment went too far in the rights it guaranteed, 42 percent said they thought the press in America had too much freedom, and about half of those surveyed thought the government should be able to monitor religious groups in the interests of national security.[19]

Some Assumptions about Censorship and Censors

Given the censorship attacks of the last twenty-plus years, we can safely make the following assumptions about censorship:

1. Any work is potentially censorable by someone, someplace, sometime, for some reason. Nothing is permanently safe from censorship, not even books most teachers and librarians would regard as far removed from censorial eyes—not *Hamlet, Julius Caesar, Silas Marner, Treasure Island,* or anything else.

2. The newer the work, the more likely it is to come under attack.

3. Censorship is capricious and arbitrary. Two teachers bearing much the same reputation and credentials and years of experience and using the

same work will not necessarily be equally free from attack (or equally likely to be attacked). Some schools in conservative areas go free from censorship problems even though teachers may use controversial books.

4. Censorship spreads a ripple of fear. The closer the censorship, the greater the likelihood of its effect on other teachers. If the newspaper coverage of the incident has been extensive, the greater the likelihood that schools many miles away will feel the effect. Administrators may gently (or loudly) let their teachers know it is time to be traditional or safe in whatever the teachers choose for the coming year.

5. Censorship does not come only from people outside the school. Administrators, other teachers or librarians, or the school board may initiate an incident. That often surprises some English teachers or librarians.

6. Censorship is, for too many educators, like cancer or a highway accident. It happens only to other people. Most incidents happen to people who know "it couldn't happen to me." It did and it will.

7. Schools without clear, established, school board–approved policies and procedures for handling censorship are accidents waiting to happen. Every school should develop a policy and a procedure that helps both educators and objectors when an incident arises. The aim of both policy and procedures should be to ensure that everyone has a fair hearing, not to stall or frustrate anyone.

8. If one book is removed from a classroom or library, no book is safe any longer. If a censor succeeds in getting one book out, every other person in the community who objects to another book should, in courtesy, be granted the same privilege. When everyone has walked out of the library carrying all those objectionable books, nothing of any consequence will be left no matter how many books remain. Some books are certain to offend some people and be ardently defended by others. Indeed, every library has books offensive to someone, maybe everyone. After all, ideas do offend many people.

9. Educators and parents should, ideally, coexist to help each other for the good of the young, but the clash of parents with some educators appears to be sadly inevitable. Some people would prefer to see young adults *educated,* which means allowing them to think and wonder about ideas and to consider the consequences of those ideas. Others would prefer to see young people *indoctrinated* into certain community or family values or beliefs or traditions and to eschew anything controversial. With so little in common between these two philosophies of schooling, disagreement is not only natural but certain.

Censors seem unwilling to accept the fact that the more they attack a book, the greater the publicity and likelihood that more young adults will read the offensive book. In their drive to eliminate a book, censors create a wider circle of readers. In some cases with older or more obscure works, they revive something that has been virtually dead for years.

Censors do not believe that in trying desperately to keep young people pure and innocent they often expose those young people to the very thing the censors abhor. Several years ago, in the Phoenix area, a group violently objected to a scholarly dictionary that contained some "offensive" words. Worried that others might not believe all those degrading, evil, pernicious words could be so easily found in one work, censors compiled a sort of digest of "The Best Dirty Words in _____," duplicated the list, and disseminated it to anyone curious, including the very students censors claimed to be protecting. More than one censor has read parts of a book that would "warp any young person's mind" aloud at a school board meeting to prove the point while young students raptly listened.

Censors often have a simplistic belief that there is an easily established and absolute relationship between books and deeds. A bad book, however defined, produces bad actions. What one reads, one immediately imitates. To read profane language automatically leads young people to swear. Presumably, nonreading youngsters who swear must eagerly await more literate fellows to instruct them in the art of the profane. To read about seduction is to wish to seduce or to be seduced (although it is possible the wish may precede the book). To read about crime is to wish to commit that crime or at least something vaguely antisocial. Anthony Comstock loved to visit boys in jail because when he asked what led them into the world of crime, they told him exactly what he wanted to hear (as they knew full well), that dime novels and drinking and shooting pool were *the* sources of all their present misery.

Censors seem to have limited faith in the ability of young adults to read and think. Censors wonder if young people can handle controversial books such as Huxley's *Brave New World* or Salinger's *The Catcher in the Rye* because the young are so innocent and pure and untainted by contact with reality. That may have been what caused one censor who objected to Ann Head's *Mr. and Mrs. Bo Jo Jones* and Paul Zindel's *The Pigman* to announce to an audience, "Teenagers are too young to learn about pregnancy."

Censors alternately love and hate English teachers and librarians. Censors would appear to hate what educators use, but censors would also appear to approve of great literature, particularly the classics. Being essentially nonreaders, they know little about literature but that it must be uplifting and noble and fine. They may claim to have read the uplifting when they were young, "back when schools knew what they were doing," but they often cannot remember titles; when they do their comments suggest the book was read in an emasculated child's edition. Censors assume that classics have no objectionable words or actions or ideas. So much for *Crime and Punishment, Oedipus Rex, Hamlet, Madame Bovary, Anna Karenina,* and most other classics. For censors, the real virtue of great literature is that it is old, dusty, and hard to read, in other words, good for young people.

Finally, censors use language carelessly or sloppily. Sometimes they cannot possibly mean what they say. The administrator who said, "We don't wish to have any controversial books in the bookstore or the library," either did not understand what the word *controversial* meant or was speaking gibberish (the native tongue of embarrassed administrators talking to reporters).

Three adjectives are likely to pop up in the censor's description of objectionable works—*filthy, obscene,* and *vulgar*—along with favored intensifiers such as *unbelievably, unquestionably,* and *hopelessly,* although a few censors favor oxymoronic expressions like *pure garbage* or *pure evil.* Not one of the adjectives is likely to be defined operationally by censors who assume that *filth* is *unquestionably filth*, and everyone shares their definition. Talking with censors is, thus, often difficult, which may disturb others, although it is often a matter of sublime indifference to the censors. If talking is difficult, communicating with them is sometimes nigh unto impossible.

Attacks on Materials

Who Are the Censors?

There are three reasonably distinct kinds of censors and pressure groups: (1) those from the right, the conservatives; (2) those from the left, the liberals; and (3) an amorphous band of educators, publishers, editors, and distributors who we might assume would be opposed to censorship. The first two groups operate from different guiding principles, or so one would assume. But it is sometimes easy for educators to be confused—whether the attack stems from the right or the left, the coercive methods, the censorial rhetoric, and the messianic fervor seem so similar. The third group is unorganized and functions on a personal, ad hoc, case-by-case approach, although people in the group are more likely than not to feel sympathetic to the conservative case for censorship.

An incredible number of tiny censorship or pressure groups on the right continue to *worry* educators (worry in the sense of alarm *and* harass). Many are better known for their acronyms, which often sound folksy or clever—for example, Save Our Schools (SOS); People of America Responding to Educational Needs of Today's Society (PARENTS); Citizens United for Responsible Education (CURE); Let's Improve Today's Education (LITE); American Christians in Education (ACE); and everyone's favorite, Let Our Values Emerge (LOVE).

With few exceptions, these groups seem united in wishing to protect young people from insidious forces that threaten the schools, to remove any vestiges of sex education and secular humanism from classes or libraries, to put God back into public schools, and to restore traditional values to education. Few announce openly that they favor censorship of books or teaching materials, although individual members of the groups may so proclaim. Indeed, what is particularly heartening about the groups is that many of them maintain that they are anti-censorship, although occasionally a public slip occurs. The president of the Utah chapter of Citizens for Decency was quoted as saying:

> I am opposed to censorship. We are not a censorship organization. But there are limits to the First Amendment. People have the right to see what they want on television, but that has nothing to do with the right to exhibit pornography on television. We're not stopping anyone from buying books and magazines or going to the movies they want. They just can't do it in Utah. Let them go to Nevada. Nobody there cares.[20]

Whether anyone from Nevada with a similar anti-censorial attitude responded with a suggestion that people from Nevada seeking cheap thrills should go to Utah is unknown. Something similar to the preceding comment came from the Rev. Ricky Pfeil. Wheeler, Texas, apparently has its moral problems with objectionable movies like *Porky's, Flashdance,* and *E.T.* (Pfeil's argument against the last-mentioned film was, "The film's an attempt to show something supernatural and it's not God. There's only one other power that's supernatural and that's Satan.") The good minister also is against censorship, as he said:

> You know, I am not for censorship. People have a right to see what they want or read what they want, but I'd just as soon they go to Los Angeles to get a copy of *Playboy* magazine. I'm responsible for here. Evil left unchecked will go rampant. God tells me what to do.[21]

Given the doublespeak of the Utah president and the Rev. Pfeil, readers will admire the honest and the original constitutional interpretation of the Rev. Vincent Strigas, co-leader of the Mesa (Arizona) Decency Coalition. Slashing merrily away at magazines that threatened the "moral fiber" of residents, the Rev. Strigas answered complaints about his approach:

> Some people are saying that we are in violation of First Amendment rights. I do not think that the First Amendment protects people [who sell] pornographic materials. The Constitution protects only the freedom to do what's right.[22]

Surely there is no ambiguity in that message.

Whatever else conservative groups may agree or disagree on, they seem united in opposing secular humanism, the New Age Movement, and the teaching of evolution. Secular humanism is both too large and too fuzzy to handle adequately in a few paragraphs (or even a short chapter). Briefly, if inexactly, conservatives appear to define secular humanism as any teaching material that denies the existence of (or ridicules the worth of) absolute values of right and wrong. Secular humanism is said to be negative, anti-God, anti-American, anti-phonics, and anti-afterlife and pro-permissive, pro-sexual freedom, pro-situation ethics, pro-socialism, and pro-one worldism. Conservatives hopelessly intolerant about secular humanism often have problems explaining what the term means to outsiders, or even insiders, usually defining the presumably philosophical term operationally and offering little more than additional examples of the horror that secular humanism implies.

The third kind of censorship or pressure group comes from within the schools: teachers, librarians, or school officials who either censor materials themselves or support others who do. Sometimes these educators do so fearing reprisals if they do not. Sometimes they do so because they fear being noticed, preferring anonymity at all costs. Sometimes they are fearful of dealing with reality in literature. Sometimes they regard themselves as highly moral and opposed to whatever they label immoral in literature and sometimes they prize (or so claim) literary merit. Fear permeates many of these people. A survey of late 1960s Arizona censorship conditions among teachers uncovered three marvelous specimens:

I would not recommend any book any parent might object to.

The Board of Education knows what our parents want their children to read. If teachers don't feel they can teach what the parents approve, they should move on.

The English teacher is hired by the school board, which represents the public. The public, therefore, has the right to ask any English teacher to avoid using any material repugnant to any parent or student.[23]

Lest readers assume that Arizona is unique, note these two Connecticut English Department Chairs quoted in Diane Shugert's "Censorship in Connecticut" in the Spring 1978 *Connecticut English Journal*:

At this level, I don't feel it's [censorship] a problem. We don't deal with controversial material, at least not in English class.

We have no problems at all in my department. The teachers order books directly and don't clear them with me or with a committee. But *I* receive the shipments. Copies of books that I think to be inappropriate simply disappear from the book room.[24]

So much for the good old days.

Publishers, too, have been guilty of rewriting texts or asking authors to delete certain words to make books or texts more palatable to highly moral librarians or communities. "Expurgation Practices of School Book Clubs" in the December 1983 *Voice of Youth Advocates* and Gayle Keresey's "School Book Club Expurgation Practices" in the Winter 1984 *Top of the News* uncovered censorship practices in Scholastic Book Club selections, as titles were changed and deletions of offensive words or ideas occurred between the hardback edition and its publication in a paperback club edition.

What Do the Censors Censor?

The answer to the question of what censors censor is easy—almost anything. Books, films,[25] magazines, anything that might be enjoyed by someone is likely to feel some censor's scorn and moral wrath.

Some works, however, are more likely to be attacked.

A nearly ten-year survey of books listed as under attack in the *Newsletter on Intellectual Freedom* between May 1986 and September 1995 revealed that several books were repeatedly questioned. The most obvious was John Steinbeck's *Of Mice and Men,* but a few others were also frequently listed. Mark Twain's *Adventures of Huckleberry Finn,* J. D. Salinger's *The Catcher in the Rye,* Maya Angelou's *I Know Why the Caged Bird Sings,* Judy Blume's *Forever,* and Robert Cormier's *The Chocolate War* were all listed at least ten times. Nancy Garden's *Annie on My Mind,* Alice Walker's *The Color Purple,* Kurt Vonnegut's *Slaughterhouse-Five,* Robert Newton Peck's *A Day No Pigs Would Die,* John Gardner's *Grendel,* and the anonymous *Go Ask Alice* followed soon thereafter.

Racism raises its ugly head on censorship lists, with titles such as Claude Brown's *Manchild in the Promised Land* and Gordon Parks's *The Learning Tree* and Harper Lee's *To Kill a Mockingbird* appearing with nauseating regularity. There are the usual suspects on every list of censored books—Joseph Heller's *Catch-22*, Aldous Huxley's *Brave New World*, George Orwell's *Animal Farm* and *1984*, and William Golding's *The Lord of the Flies*.

There are a few inevitable censorial favorites such as *The American Heritage Dictionary* or the much-hated story by Shirley Jackson, "The Lottery." Or modern plays such as Tennessee Williams's *The Glass Menagerie* or *Summer and Smoke* or Arthur Miller's *All My Sons* or *Death of a Salesman*.

Readers curious as to why a commonly censored title is not listed here should feel free to add whatever they wish. Anyone who wishes to expand the list could glance casually through any issue of the *Newsletter on Intellectual Freedom*.

Although most of the titles on these lists were published for adults, today's censors seem quite happy to attack books published for adolescents. Titles such as these now frequently appear on lists of censored books, rarely near the top but still disturbingly present:

Judy Blume: *Deenie, Forever*

Robert Cormier: *After the First Death, The Chocolate War, Fade, I Am the Cheese*

Chris Crutcher: *Athletic Shorts, Running Loose*

Lois Duncan: *Killing Mr. Griffin*

Paula Fox: *The Slave Dancer*

Nat Hentoff: *The Day They Came to Arrest the Book*

S. E. Hinton: *The Outsiders; That Was Then, This Is Now*

Robert Lipsyte: *The Contender*

Lois Lowry: *The Giver*

Harry Mazer: *The Last Mission*

Walter Dean Myers: *Fallen Angels*

Katherine Paterson: *Bridge to Terabithia*

Robert Newton Peck: *A Day No Pigs Would Die*

Mildred D. Taylor: *Roll of Thunder, Hear My Cry*

Paul Zindel: *My Darling, My Hamburger; The Pigman*

And, of course, any of the Harry Potter series.

English teachers and librarians are unlikely to be surprised that lists of censored works are largely made up of novels, but they may be unaware why that is so. A fast glance through early issues of educational journals will uncover a great truth—reading novels was regarded as an unhealthy pastime for anyone, particularly for young boys or girls. True, there were classics that some readers classified as fiction, but they were justifiable since they were, after all, classics, not unhealthy novels. Books of advice for the young were highly esteemed during the last half of the nineteenth century, and without exception, their authors damned fiction (a synonym of the time for novels). For example, Sylvanus Stall in *What a Young Man Ought to Know* (Vir, 1897) wrote, "No young man or young woman can afford to read fiction before they are twenty-five years of age. . . .

If fiction is begun before a correct taste is formed and foundation principles laid, the best books will never be read at all. The habit of reading rapidly for the simple sake of the story will destroy the power, and even the wish, to read thoughtfully and seriously" (pp. 268–269). "The Fiction Problem" or "The Fiction Question" on the suitability of novels—particularly popular and contemporary novels—for the public library as it was often called in the *Library Journal*, remained an issue from the 1850s until the late 1920s. One of the best articles on the place of the novel in early libraries and society is Steven Starker's "Fear of Fiction: The Novel," *Book Research Quarterly* 6 (Summer 1990): 44–59.

Why Do the Censors Censor What They Do?

Why censors censor what they do is far more important and far more complex than what they censor. Unfortunately, for readers who want simple answers and an easy-to-remember list of reasons, the next paragraphs may be disappointing.

In "Censorship in the 1970s: Some Ways to Handle It When It Comes (and It Will)" in early 1974, Donelson listed eight different kinds of materials that get censored, those that censors:

1. Deem offensive because of sex (usually calling it "filth" or "risqué" or "indecent").

2. See as an attack on the American dream or the country ("un-American" or "pro-commie").

3. Label peacenik or pacifistic (remember, the Vietnam War had not yet become unpopular with the masses).

4. Consider irreligious or against religion or, specifically, un-Christian.

5. Believe promote racial harmony or stress civil rights or the civil rights movement ("biased on social issues" or "do young people have to see all that ugliness?").

6. Regard as offensive in language ("profane" or "unfit for human ears").

7. Identify as drug books, pro or con ("kids wouldn't hear about or use drugs if it weren't for these books").

8. Regard as presenting inappropriate adolescent behavior and, therefore, likely to cause other young people to act inappropriately.[26]

In an article entitled "Dirty Dictionaries, Obscene Nursery Rhymes and Burned Books," published in James E. Davis's 1979 *Dealing with Censorship*, Ed Jenkinson added fourteen more likely targets, including young adult novels, works of "questionable" writers, literature about or by homosexuals, role playing, texts using improper grammar, sexist stereotypes, and sex education. In a *Publishers Weekly* article the same year,[27] Jenkinson listed forty targets, with new ones being sociology, anthropology, the humanities generally (if secular humanism is bad, so then must be humanism or anything that sounds like humanism, and that easily extends to humanities), ecology, world government, world history that mentions the United Nations, basal readers lacking phonics, basal readers with many pictures or drawings, situation ethics, violence, and books that do not promote the Protestant ethic or do not promote patriotism.

A year later, Jenkinson had expanded his list to sixty-seven, with additions including "Soviet propaganda," citizenship classes, African American dialects, uncaptioned pictures in history texts, concrete poetry, magazines that have ads for alcohol or contraceptives, songs and cartoons in textbooks, and "depressing thoughts."[28] The last of the objections is truly depressing, apparently for censors and educators alike.

For an earlier edition of this textbook, M. E. Kerr wrote about what happens when she goes to speak at schools. In the early 1990s, prior to the publication of her critically acclaimed *Deliver Us from Evie*, she came out publicly as a gay woman. At about the same time, publishers, as part of a marketing technique to take advantage of the large numbers of children in middle schools, began labeling YA literature "age ten-up" or "Junior High-up." This means that Kerr was often invited to speak to children in sixth, seventh, and eighth grades. In these situations, it was common for teachers to let her know they did not want her to talk about her gay novels. One principal met her in the parking lot and said, "We like your books a lot, Ms. Kerr, but these children are too young for *Night Kites, Delivers Us from Evie,* or *Hello, I Lied.*" Her response to this kind of censorship is:

> Of course kids know about gays; any kid who watches TV does. There are gay characters in sitcoms now, on soaps, on talk shows and featured in movies and made-for-TV dramas. Gay performers are on MTV, and there are gay rock stars, singers, and composers. The failure to mention us to children, and to discuss books about us, puts us in a special category. Kids know we're there, but they sense that somehow we're reprehensible. Educators are not protecting the child with this blackout, they are protecting the prejudice.[29]

Some Court Decisions Worth Knowing

Legal battles and court decisions often seem abstract and dull and irrelevant to practical matters for too many educators, but several court decisions have been significant and have affected thousands of educators who hardly knew the battles had taken place, much less their disposition. A brief run-through of two kinds of decisions, those involving attempts to define obscenity and its supposed influence on readers and viewers and those directly involving schools and school libraries, may be helpful to readers.

Court Decisions about Obscenity and Attempting to Define Obscenity

Because censors frequently bandy the word *obscene* in attacking books, teachers and librarians should know something about the history of courts vainly attempting to define the term.

Although it was hardly the first decision involving obscenity, the first decision announcing a definition of and a test for obscenity came about in an English case in 1868. *The Queen v. Hicklin* (L.R. 3Q.B. 360) concerned an ironmonger who was also an ardent antipapist. He sold copies of *The Confes-*

sional Unmasked: Showing the Depravity of the Romish Priesthood, the Iniquity of the Confessional and the Questions Put to Females in Confession, and although the Court agreed that his heart was pure, his publication was not. Judge Cockburn announced a test of obscenity that was to persist in British law for nearly a century and in American law until the 1930s:

> I think the test of obscenity is this, whether the tendency of the matter charged as obscenity is to deprave and corrupt those whose minds are open to such immoral influences, and into whose hands a publication of this sort may fall.

Clearly, but not exclusively, Cockburn was attempting to protect young people.

In 1913 in *United States v. Kennerly* (209 F. 119), Judge Learned Hand ruled against the defendant because his publication clearly fell under the limits of the Hicklin test, but he added:

> I hope it is not improper for me to say that the rule as laid down, however consonant it may be with mid-Victorian morals, does not seem to me to answer to the understanding and morality of the present time, as conveyed by the words, "obscene, lewd, or lascivious." I question whether in the end men will regard that as obscene which is honestly relevant to the adequate expression of innocent ideas, and whether they will not believe that truth and beauty are too precious to society at large to be mutilated in the interest of those most likely to pervert them to base uses.

Then in 1933 and 1934, two decisions (5 F. Supp. 182 and 72 F. 2d 705) overturned much of the Hicklin test. James Joyce's *Ulysses* had been regarded as obscene by most legal authorities since its publication, largely for Molly Bloom's soliloquy. The novel was confiscated by customs officials and tried before Judge John M. Woolsey of the Federal District Court for Southern New York. Woolsey found the book "sincere and honest" and "not dirt for dirt's sake" and ruled that in matters determining what is obscene, the work *must* be judged as a whole, not on the basis of its parts. An appeal to the Federal Circuit Court of Appeals in 1934 led to Judge Learned Hand's upholding Woolsey's decision.

In 1957 in *Butler v. Michigan* (352 U.S. 380), Butler challenged a Michigan statute that tested obscenity in terms of its effect on young people, arguing that this restricted adult reading to that fit only for children. Justice Felix Frankfurter agreed, and wrote:

> The State insists that, by thus quarantining the general reading public against books not too rugged for grown men and women in order to shield juvenile innocence, it is exercising its power to promote the general welfare. Surely, this is to burn the house to roast the pig. . . . The incidence of this enactment [the Michigan statute] is to reduce the adult population of Michigan to reading only what is fit for children.

Frankfurter agreed with Butler and declared the Michigan statute unconstitutional.

Later in 1957, in *Roth v. United States* (354 U.S. 476), the U.S. Supreme Court announced that obscenity was not protected by the Constitution, for "implicit in the history of the First Amendment is the rejection of obscenity as utterly without redeeming social importance." (That phrase, "without redeeming social importance" was to cause problems for several years thereafter.) Reading for the majority, Justice Brennan added a new definition of obscenity:

> Obscene material is material which deals with sex in a manner appealing to prurient interest.

And a new test:

> Whether to the average person, applying contemporary community standards, the dominant theme of the material taken as a whole appeals to prurient interest.

Roth rejected the Hicklin test (already in patches) as "unconstitutionally restrictive of the freedoms of speech and press."

Jacobellis v. Ohio (84 S. Ct. 1676) in 1964 further refined the *Roth* test when Justice Brennan announced that the "contemporary community" standard referred to national standards, not local standards although Chief Justice Warren angrily dissented, arguing that community standards meant local and nothing more.

In 1966, in *Memoirs v. Attorney General of Massachusetts* (86 S. Ct. 975), Justice Brennan further elaborated on the *Roth* test:

> Under this definition, as elaborated in subsequent cases, three elements must coalesce: it must be established that (a) the dominant theme of the material taken as a whole appeals to prurient interest in sex; (b) the material is patently offensive because it affronts contemporary community standards relating to the description or representation of sexual matters; and (c) the material is utterly without redeeming social value.

The *Ginsberg v. New York* (390 U.S. 692) decision in 1968 did not develop or alter the definition of obscenity, but it did introduce the concepts of variable obscenity and caused some concern for librarians and English teachers. Ginsberg, who operated a stationery store and luncheonette, had sold "girlie" magazines to a sixteen-year-old boy in violation of a New York statute that declared illegal the sale of anything "which depicts nudity" and "was harmful" to anyone under seventeen years of age. Ginsberg maintained that New York State was without power to draw the line at the age of seventeen. The Court dismissed his argument, sustained the New York statute, and wrote:

> The well-being of its children is of course a subject within the State's constitutional power to regulate.

The Court further noted, in lines that proved worrisome to anyone dealing in literature, classic, or modern or what-have-you:

> To be sure, there is no lack of "studies" which purport to demonstrate that obscenity is or is not "a basic factor in impairing the ethical and moral development of . . . youth and a clear and present danger to the people of the state." But the grow-

ing consensus of commentators is that "while these studies all agree that a causal link has not been demonstrated, they are equally agreed that a causal link has not been disproved either."

Those words were lovingly quoted by censors across the United States, although few of them bothered to read the citations in the decision that suggested the dangers of assuming too much either way about the matter.

Five U.S. Supreme Court decisions in 1973 brought forth a new test of obscenity. The most important, *Miller v. California* (413 U.S. 15) and *Paris Adult Theatre II v. Slaton* (413 U.S. 49), contained the refined test, one presumably designed to remove all ambiguities from past tests. That the test proved as ambiguous and as difficult to enforce and understand as previous tests should come as no surprise to readers. After attacking the 1957 *Roth* test, the majority decision read by Chief Justice Burger in *Miller* provided this three-pronged test of obscenity:

> The basic guidelines for the trier of fact must be: (a) whether "the average person, applying contemporary community standards" would find that the work, taken as a whole, appeals to the prurient interest; (b) whether the work depicts or describes in a patently offensive way, sexual conduct specifically defined by the applicable state law; and (c) whether the work taken as a whole lacks serious literary, artistic, political or scientific value.

To guide state legislatures with "a few plain examples of what a state statute could define for regulation under the second part (b) of the standard announced in this opinion," the Court provided these:

> a. Patently offensive representations or descriptions of ultimate sexual acts, normal or perverted, actual or simulated.
> b. Patently offensive representations or descriptions of masturbation, excretory functions, and lewd exhibition of the genitals.

After this so-called Miller catalogue, Burger announced that "contemporary community standards" meant state standards, not national standards.

Paris Adult Theatre II underscored *Miller* and added more worrisome words about the dangers of obscenity and what it can lead to. Chief Justice Burger, again, for the majority:

> But, it is argued, there is no scientific data which conclusively demonstrated that exposure to obscene material adversely affects men and women or their society. It is urged on behalf of the petitioner that, absent such a demonstration, any kind of state regulation is "impermissible." We reject this argument. It is not for us to resolve empirical uncertainties underlying state legislation, save in the exceptional case where that legislation plainly impinges upon rights protected by the Constitution itself. . . . Although there is no conclusive proof of any connection between antisocial behavior and obscene material, the legislature of Georgia could quite reasonably determine that such a connection does or might exist.

In other words, no proof exists that obscenity does (or does not) lead to anti-social actions (or nonactions), yet state legislatures can assume or guess that such a relationship may exist and pass legislation to that effect.

Justice Brennan dissented, noting that the dangers to "protected speech are very grave" and added that the decision would not halt further cases before the Court:

> The problem is that one cannot say with certainty that material is obscene until at least five members of this Court, applying inevitably obscure standards, have pronounced it so.

To few observers' surprise, Brennan's prophecy proved correct. On January 13, 1972, police in Albany, Georgia, seized the film *Carnal Knowledge* (starring Jack Nicholson) and charged the manager with violating a state statute against distributing obscene material. He was convicted in the Superior Court, and the decision was affirmed by a divided vote in the Georgia State Supreme Court. In 1974, the U.S. Supreme Court announced its decision in *Jenkins v. the State of Georgia* (94 S. Ct. 2750), Justice Rehnquist reading the unanimous decision to reverse the Georgia Supreme Court opinion. Although *Carnal Knowledge* had been declared obscene by state standards and although it had a scene showing simulated masturbation, Rehnquist stated that "juries do not have unbridled discretion" in determining obscenity and that *Carnal Knowledge* had nothing that fell "within either of the two examples given in *Miller.*"

The history of litigation and court decisions about obscenity and its definition are hardly models of clarity or consistency. Anyone interested in more details of this frustrating but fascinating story should read that marvelous book by Felice Flanery Lewis, *Literature, Obscenity and Law.*

Court Decisions about Teaching and School Libraries

If the implications of court decisions about obscenity are a bit vague, decisions about teaching and school libraries are not notably better. Courts are notoriously leery of decisions involving schools and libraries, lest they be regarded as a national school board, but a few decisions, not unsurprisingly ambiguous, are worth noting about school libraries.

The U.S. Supreme Court had ruled in *Tinker v. the Des Moines (Iowa) School District* (393 U.S. 503) in 1969:

> First Amendment rights, applied in light of the special characteristics of the school environment, are available to teachers and students. It can hardly be argued that either students or teachers shed their constitutional rights to freedom of speech or expression at the schoolhouse gate.

But courts, federal or state, seemed unwilling to extend those rights to the school library in *Presidents Council, District 25 v. Community School Board No. 25* (457 F. 2d 289) in 1972. A New York City school board voted 5–3 in 1971 to remove all copies of Piri Thomas's *Down These Mean Streets* from junior high libraries because of its offensive nature and language. The U.S. Court of Appeals,

Second Circuit, held for the school board. The book, so the Court decided, had dubious literary or educational merit, and because the state had delegated the selection of school materials to local school boards and there was no evidence of basic constitutional impingement by the board, the Court saw no merit in the opposing view.

Presidents Council was cited for several years thereafter as the definitive decision, but because it was not a Supreme Court decision, it served as precedent only for judges so inclined.

A different decision prevailed in *Minarcini v. Strongsville (Ohio) City School District* (541 F. 2d 577) in 1977. The school board refused to allow a teacher to use Heller's *Catch-22* or Vonnegut's *God Bless You, Mr. Rosewater*, ordered Vonnegut's *Cat's Cradle* and Heller's novel removed from the library, and proclaimed that students and teachers were not to discuss these books in class. The U.S. District Court found for the school board, but on appeal to the U.S. Circuit Court of Appeals, the three-member panel reversed the lower court. Judge Edwards focused on the main issues of the case in eloquent words widely quoted and much admired by school librarians:

> A library is a storehouse of knowledge. When created for a public school it is an important privilege created by the state for the benefit of the students in the school. That privilege is not subject to being withdrawn by succeeding school boards whose members might desire to "winnow" the library for books the content of which occasioned their displeasure or disapproval. Of course, a copy of a book may wear out. Some books may become obsolete. Shelf space alone may at some point require some selection of books to be retained and books to be disposed of. No such rationale is involved in this case.

The opinion of the Court that library books gained a tenure of sorts and could not easily be culled by a school board was at odds with the parallel U.S. Circuit Court in *Presidents Council*, but again, the Ohio decision served as precedent only if judges in other federal district courts (or federal appeals courts) wished to so use it.

A year later in *Right to Read Defense Committee of Chelsea (Massachusetts) v. School Committee of the City of Chelsea* (454 F. Supp. 703) in the U.S. District Court for Massachusetts, another decision supported the rights of students and libraries. The librarian of Chelsea High School ordered and made available a paperback anthology, *Male and Female under Eighteen*, containing a poem by a student, "The City to the Young Girl," which had, as the judge wrote, "street language." A parent felt the language was "offensive" and called the board chairman, who was also the editor of the local paper. The chair-editor concluded that the poem was "filthy" and contained "offensive" language and should be removed from the library. He scheduled an emergency meeting of the school committee to consider the subject of "objectionable, salacious and obscene material being made available in books in the High School Library" and wrote an article for his newspaper about the matter, concluding with these words:

> Quite frankly, I want a complete review of how it was possible for such garbage to even get on bookshelves where 14-year-old high school ninth graders could obtain them.

The superintendent urged caution and noted that the book could not be removed from the library without a formal review, but the chair was adamant. When the librarian argued that the poem was not obscene, the chair-editor wrote in his newspaper:

> [I am] shocked and extremely disappointed to have our high school librarian claim there is nothing lewd, lascivious, filthy, suggestive, licentious, pornographic or obscene about this particular poem in this book of many poems.

The school committee claimed "an unconstrained authority to remove books from the shelves of the school library." Although the judge agreed that "local authorities are, and must continue to be, the principal policymakers in the public schools," he was more swayed by the reasoning in *Minarcini* than in *Presidents Council*. He wrote:

> The Committee was under no obligation to purchase *Male and Female* for the High School Library, but it did. . . . The Committee claims an absolute right to remove *City* from the shelves of the school library. It has no such right, and compelling policy considerations argue against any public authority having such an unreviewable power of censorship. There is more at issue here than the poem *City*. If this work may be removed by a committee hostile to its language and theme, then the precedent is set for removal of any other work. The prospect of successive school committees "sanitizing" the school library of views divergent from its own is alarming, whether they do it book by book or one page at a time.
>
> What is at stake here is the right to read and be exposed to controversial thoughts and language—a valuable right subject to First Amendment protection.

What proved to be a most significant decision about school libraries began in September 1975 when three members of the Island Trees (New York) School Board attended a conference sponsored by the conservative Parents of New York—United (PONY-U). After examining lists of books deemed "objectionable" by PONY-U, the three returned home, checked their district's school libraries, and found several suspect works—Bernard Malamud's *The Fixer*, Kurt Vonnegut's *Slaughterhouse-Five*, Desmond Morris's *The Naked Ape*, Piri Thomas's *Down These Mean Streets*, Langston Hughes's edition of *Best Short Stories of Negro Writers*, Oliver LaFarge's *Laughing Boy*, Richard Wright's *Black Boy*, Alice Childress's *A Hero Ain't Nothin' but a Sandwich*, Eldridge Cleaver's *Soul on Ice*, and the anonymous *Go Ask Alice*. In February 1976, the board gave "unofficial direction" that the books be removed from the library and delivered to the board for their reading.

Once the word was out, the board issued a press release attempting to justify its actions, calling the books "anti-American, anti-Christian, anti-Semitic, and just plain filthy" and argued:

> It is our duty, our moral obligation, to protect the children in our schools from this moral danger as surely as from physical or medical dangers.

When the board appointed a review committee—four members of the school staff and four parents—the board politely listened to the report suggesting that five books should be returned to the shelves and that two should be removed

(*The Naked Ape* and *Down These Mean Streets*) and then ignored their own chosen committee. (The board did return one book to the shelves, *Laughing Boy*, and placed *Black Boy* on a restricted shelf available only with parental permission.) Stephen Pico, a student, and others brought suit against the board, claiming that their rights under the First Amendment had been denied by the board.

The U.S. District Court heard the case in 1979 and granted a summary judgment to the board. The court held that the state had vested school boards with broad discretion to formulate educational policy, and the selection or rejection of books was clearly within their power. The court found no merit in the First Amendment claims of Pico, et al. A three-judge panel of the U.S. Court of Appeals for the Second Circuit (638 F. 2d 404) reversed the District Court's decision 2–1 and remanded the case for trial. The case then, although not directly, wended its way to the U.S. Supreme Court, the first such case ever to be heard at that level.

In a strange and badly fragmented decision—and for that reason it is unclear how certainly it will serve as precedent—Justice Brennan delivered the plurality (*not* majority) opinion in *Board of Education, Island Trees Union Free School District v. Pico* (102 S. Ct. 2799). He immediately emphasized the "limited nature" of the question before the court, for "precedents have long recognized certain constitutional limits upon the power of the State to control even the curriculum and classroom," and he further noted that *Island Trees* did not involve textbooks "or indeed any books that Island Trees students would be required to read." The case concerned only the removal, not the acquisition, of library books. He concluded the first section of his opinion by pointing out that the case concerned two questions:

> First, does the First Amendment impose *any* limitations upon the discretion of petitioners to remove library books from the Island Trees High School and Junior High School? Second, if so, do the affidavits and other evidential materials before the District Court, construed most favorably to respondents, raise a genuine issue of fact whether petitioners might have exceeded those limitations?

Brennan proceeded to find for *Pico* (and ultimately for the library and the books):

> . . . we think that the First Amendment rights of students may be directly and sharply implicated by the removal of books from the shelves of a school library.
>
> Petitioners emphasized the inculcative function of secondary education, and argue that they must be allowed *unfettered* discretion "to transmit community values" through the Island Trees schools. But that sweeping claim overlooks the unique role of the school library. . . . Petitioners might well defend their claim of absolute discretion in matters of *curriculum* by reliance upon their duty to inculcate community values. But we think that petitioners' reliance upon that duty is misplaced where, as here, they attempt to extend their claim of absolute discretion beyond the compulsory environment of the classroom, into the school library and the regime of voluntary inquiry that there holds sway.
>
> Petitioners rightly possess significant discretion to determine the content of their school libraries. But that discretion may not be exercised in a narrowly partisan or political manner. . . . Our Constitution does not permit the official suppression of ideas. Thus whether petitioners' removal of books from their school

libraries denied respondents their First Amendment rights depends upon the motivation behind petitioners' actions. If petitioners *intended* by their removal decision to deny respondents access to ideas with which petitioners disagreed, and if this intent was the decisive factor in petitioners' decision, then petitioners have exercised their discretion in violation of the Constitution.

Four pages follow before Justice Blackmun's generally concurring opinion and Justices Burger, Rehnquist, Powell, and O'Connor offered their stinging dissents, but it is clear that school librarians won something, although precisely what and how much is still being resolved by other court decisions.

It is equally clear that secondary teachers lost something in *Island Trees*. In an understandable ploy, the American Library Association, the New York Library Association, and the Freedom to Read Foundation submitted an *Amicus Curiae* brief, which sought to distinguish between the functions of the school classroom and the school library, a distinction that worked to the advantage of the school librarian but certainly not to that of the classroom teacher. Apparently, Brennan bought the argument as readers can see, comparing Brennan's words with those from the following brief:

> This case, however, is about a library, not a school's curriculum. This is an extremely important distinction for the evaluation of the First Amendment interests at stake here.
>
> The school board below banned books from a library. Thus, this case does not present an issue concerning the board's control of curriculum, i.e., what is taught in the classroom. We freely concede that the school board has the right and duty to supervise the general content of the school's course of study.

These words caused serious disagreements between teachers and librarians. The phrase "we freely concede," has rankled a number of English teachers who recognized that *Island Trees* was a serious setback for intellectual freedom in the classroom, a point that was taken up in *Hazelwood* (108 S. Ct. 562, 1988) and later in *Virgil* (862 F. 2d 1517, 11th Cir., 1989).

Anyone who assumed that *Pico* quieted the waters of school censorship must have been surprised by five court decisions from 1986 through 1989. These decisions might have been expected to clear up the censorial waters; instead, they made the waters murkier.

On July 7, 1986, the U.S. Supreme Court announced its decision in *Bethel School District v. Fraser* (106 S. Ct. 3159, 1986) upholding school officials in Spanaway, Washington, who had suspended a student for using sexual metaphors in describing the political potency of a candidate for student government. Writing the majority opinion in the 7–2 decision, Chief Justice Burger said, "Surely it is a highly appropriate function of public school education to prohibit the use of vulgar and offensive terms in public discourse. . . . schools must teach by example the shared values of a civilized social order." To some people's surprise, Justice Brennan agreed with Justice Burger that the student's speech had been disruptive, although Brennan refused to label the speech indecent or obscene.

That decision worried many educators, but a lower court decision on October 24, 1986, frightened more teachers. *Mozert v. Hawkins County (Tennessee)*

Public Schools (579 F. Supp. 1051, 1984) began in September 1983 when the school board of Hawkins County refused a request by parents to remove three books in the Holt, Rinehart and Winston reading series from the sixth-, seventh-, and eighth-grade program. The parents formed Citizens Organized for Better Schools and ultimately brought suit against the school board. U.S. District Judge Thomas Hull dismissed the lawsuit, but on appeal before the Sixth Circuit of the Court of Appeals, a panel of three judges remanded the case back to Judge Hull.

Not all the testimony in the trial during the summer of 1986 concerned humanism, particularly secular humanism, but so it seemed at times. Vicki Frost, one of the parents who initiated the suit, said that the Holt series taught "satanism, feminism, evolution, telepathy, internationalism, and other beliefs that come under the heading of secular humanism." Later she explained why parents objected to any mention of the Renaissance by saying that "a central idea of the Renaissance was a belief in the dignity and worth of human beings," presumably establishing that teaching the Renaissance was little more than teaching secular humanism.

Judge Hull ruled in favor of the parents on October 24, 1986, but the U.S. Sixth Circuit Court of Appeals overturned Hull's decision. Worse yet for the fundamentalist parents, the U.S. Supreme Court refused to hear an appeal of the Court of Appeals' ruling in February 1988. Beverly LaHaye, leader of the Concerned Women for America, who had filed the original suit in 1983 and whose group had helped finance the legal fees for the parents, said, "School boards now have the authority to trample the religious freedom of all children." Other people, notably educators, were grateful to the court for giving them the right to teach.

While *Mozert* worked its way through the courts, an even more troublesome and considerably louder suit was heard in Alabama. Judge Brevard W. Hand had earlier helped devise a suit defending the right of Alabama to permit a moment of silence for prayer in the public schools. The U.S. Supreme Court overturned Judge Hand's decision, so he devised another suit, *Smith v. School Commissioners of Mobile County, Alabama* (655 F. Supp. 939, 1987), alleging that social studies, history, and home economics textbooks in the Mobile public schools unconstitutionally promoted the "religious belief system" of secular humanism, as Judge Hand wrote in his March 4, 1987, decision maintaining that forty-four texts violated the rights of parents.

The decision was both silly and certain, but those who feared the bogeyman of secular humanism celebrated for a few weeks. Then, late in August 1987, the Eleventh U.S. Circuit Court of Appeals reversed Judge Hand's decision. The Court of Appeals did not address the question of whether secular humanism was a religion, but it did agree that the forty-four texts did not promote secular humanism. Phyllis Schlafly said she was not surprised by the ruling, but it mattered little because the decision would be appealed to the U.S. Supreme Court. Oddly enough for a case that began so loudly, the plaintiffs were mute, the date for the appeal quietly passed, and all was silence.

The fourth case, *Hazelwood School District v. Kuhlmeier* (108 S. Ct. 562, 1988), will trouble many educators, although nominally the case was concerned with school journalism and the publication of a school newspaper. The case began in 1983 when the principal of a high school in Hazelwood, Missouri, objected to two stories in the school newspaper dealing with teenage pregnancy and divorce's effects on young people.

Associate Justice Byron White wrote the majority opinion in the 5–3 decision announcing that educators (i.e., administrators) are entitled to exercise great control over student expression. Although the case presumably dealt only with a school newspaper, White's words—inadvertently or not—went further. White wrote:

> The policy of school officials toward [the school newspaper] was reflected in Hazelwood School Board Policy 348.51 and the Hazelwood East Curriculum Guide. Board Policy 348.51 provided that "school-sponsored publications are developed within the adopted curriculum and its educational activities."

After commenting on needed school standards and the right of administrators to set standards, White added:

> This standard is consistent with our oft-expressed view that the education of the nation's youth is primarily the responsibility of parents, teachers, and state and local school officials, and not of federal judges.

The three court decisions, which came less than a week apart, supported a Florida school board's banning of a humanities textbook, a California principal's seizure of an "April Fool's" edition of a school newspaper, and a Nebraska school district's decision not to provide meeting space to a student Bible Club.

The Florida decision was particularly troubling and hinted that parallel decisions citing *Hazelwood* as precedent might be on the way. *Virgil v. School Board of Columbia County, Florida* (862 F. 2d 1517, 11th Cir., 1989) concerned a challenge to a school board's decision to stop using a humanities text in a high school class because it contained Chaucer's "The Miller's Tale" and Aristophanes's *Lysistrata*, two works to which parents had objected. After a formal complaint had been filed in April 1986, the school board appointed an advisory committee and then ignored that committee when it recommended keeping the text. Parents filed an action against the school board.

In the district court decision in January 1988, Judge Black agreed with the parents that the school board had overestimated the potential harm to students of Chaucer or Aristophanes, but she concluded that the board had the power as announced in *Hazelwood* to decide as it had.

The parents appealed to the Eleventh Circuit Court of Appeals, which, as in the district court, fell back on *Hazelwood* for precedent for curricular decisions, not merely those concerned with school newspapers. As Judge Anderson wrote in his decision of January 1989:

> In applying the *Hazelwood* standard to the instant case, two considerations are particularly significant. First, we conclude that the Board decisions at issue were curricular decisions. The materials removed were part of the textbook used in a regularly scheduled course of study in the school. . . . The second consideration that is significant in applying the *Hazelwood* standard to this case is that the motivation for the Board's removal of the readings has been stipulated to be related to

the explicit sexuality and excessively vulgar language in the selections. It is clear from *Hazelwood* and other cases that this is a legitimate concern.

Judge Anderson found that the school board had acted appropriately, although in the last paragraph he and the court distanced themselves from the folly of the board's decision to ban two classics.

We decide today only that the Board's removal of these works from the curriculum did not violate the Constitution. Of course, we do not endorse the Board's decision. Like the district court, we seriously question how young persons just below the age of majority can be harmed by these masterpieces of Western literature. However, having concluded that there is no constitutional violation, our role is not to second-guess the wisdom of the Board's action.

Florida teachers must have been touched by those words.

Joan DelFattore's *What Johnny Shouldn't Read: Textbook Censorship in America* is a recent scholarly and readable work that admirably covers major court decisions involving teachers and librarians.

For a more personal view of what it means to an author to be involved in a court case, read the write-up on Margaret A. Edwards Award winner, Nancy Garden, who was called to be a court witness when her *Annie on My Mind* was "tried" in a Kansas state court in 1995.

Two recent decisions deserve our attention. In October 1989, the U.S. Court of Appeals of the Ninth Circuit ejected a mother's request to remove Mark Twain's *Huckleberry Finn* and William Faulkner's short story "A Rose for Emily" from the required reading list of the Tempe Union High School in Arizona. Kathy Monteiro asked that the two literary works in effect constituted harassment of African American students. In *Monterio v. Tempe Union High School District*, a three-judge panel acknowledged that "books can hurt, and words can hurt," but Judge Stephan Reinhardt added that "we reject the notion that putting books on trial in our courts is the proper way to determine the appropriateness of their use in the classroom." He also suggested that students may benefit from reading books that offend. "A necessary component of any education is learning to think critically about offensive ideas—without that ability one can do little to respond to them. . . . [It is] also important for young people to discover both the good and the bad in our history."[30]

In *Counts v. Cedarville*, decided in 2003 for the Western District of Arkansas, parents alleged that their school had restricted access for students to J. K. Rowling's *Harry Potter and the Sorcerer's Stone*. A parent filed a Reconsideration Request Form, and a committee voted to keep the book on the open shelf without any restriction. The board of education overruled the committee's recommendation and voted to restrict students' access to the Harry Potter series. The court determined restrictions on checking out the books infringed on students' legally protected interests to receive information. Though the board argued that the book would promote student disobedience or disrespect to authority, the court found no evidence to support their argument. The court also found nothing to support the board's contention that the book promoted the religion of witchcraft. The court found that "The conclusion is inevitable that the defendant

Margaret A. Edwards Award (2003)

Nancy Garden, Stretching Our Minds on Sexuality

Garden was honored for her 1982 *Annie on My Mind*, but other well-written books include her 1984 *Prisoner of Vampires*, 1991 *Lark in the Morning*, 1996 *Good Moon Rising*, and 1999 *The Year They Burned the Books. Endgame*, a powerful story about the rippling effects of school bullying, was published in 2006. The book starts with fifteen-year-old Gray Wilson waiting in juvenile detention for his trial as a murderer. The heart of the story is what leads up to the day that Gray, who has been bullied in increasingly mean ways at two different high schools, takes a gun to school and starts shooting.

Nancy Garden has two worlds: one the world of her books, the other the world of censorship and defending her books. In *Annie on My Mind*, *Lark in the Morning*, and *Good Moon Rising*, Garden has dealt honestly with what it is like to be a gay young adult in our world. The protagonists speedily learn that prejudice is a given and ignorance is rampant. Garden has confessed that she finds it hard to avoid using her characters as "mouthpieces" for her own views. It would be all too easy to stand them up on soapboxes and have them shout "Hey, we're decent people, most of us; like every other group, we're not all good or all bad—and it's wrong that we're often treated unfairly, or harassed, or beaten up."

Unquestionably, Garden's best-known book is *Annie on My Mind*. Earlier books concerned with same-sex love ended unhappily, presumably proving that was the way such loves should expect to end. In the beginning, Garden's *Annie* appears on its way to a similar ending, but Liza and Annie eventually handle their problems and accept their love for each other. It's a problem novel marvelously well handled and touching.

Lark in the Morning may be a better book than *Annie*. The protagonist is gay but her sexuality is not the central concern of the book. Rather, two runaways that Gillian discovered hiding near her summer home take up her attention and make her lesbian character less than the major issue of *Lark*.

Garden told Christine A. Jenkins, who interviewed her for the June 2003 *School Library Journal*, that she was at a writers' conference when someone asked her if she'd had any troubles with *Annie on My Mind*. She responded that she had not. Two days later a phone call notified her that *Annie* had been burned in Olathe, Kansas.

The event soon made her a controversial young adult author. YA novels don't come to trial very often, and even less often are authors asked to participate. But her visit to the scene was not altogether unpleasant. Garden said,

> When I was in Kansas, people would come up to me even before the case was filed saying that they were embarrassed that this had happened where they lived. There were a lot of people who didn't believe in the First Amendment, and a lot of people who were pretty homophobic. But there were a lot of very good people also, and that was a very good thing to learn.

The trial also gave her strong opinions about censorship, some of which she put into *The Year They Burned the Book*. "It's important to remember that censorship is a two-way street," she says. "If you can ban a book you don't like, I can ban one you do like! If everyone could remove books they disagree with, I'm not sure there'd be a lot of books in the library any more." At the trial, Garden braced herself for hostile questions, but after her lawyer finished asking her questions, the other side chose not to cross-examine, which she assumes means that they didn't think she would help their case.

Much of the language in District Court Judge G. T. Bebber's November 29, 1995, opinion in the case, *Stevana Case et al. v. United School District No. 233* comes from the Supreme Court's language in *Pico v. Board of Education, Island Trees (NY) Union Free School District.* The lawyer representing the Olathe students said, "I think it's a clear message to schools and school libraries that they can't remove books simply because they disagree with the views expressed in a book. That's what the rule of the *Pico* case is. This decision very strongly reaffirms that principle." ●

removed the books from its library shelves for reasons not authorized by the Constitution."[31]

Extralegal Decisions

Most censorship episodes do not result in legal hearings and court decisions. Teachers or librarians come under attack and unofficial rumor-mongering charges are lodged because someone objects and labels the offending work "obscene" or "filthy" or "pornographic." The case is heard in the court of public opinion, sometimes before the school board, with few legal niceties prevailing. The censors (and too often the school board) almost never operate under any definitions of obscenity that a court would recognize, but their interpretations of the issues are operationally effective for their purposes. The book may not always be judged as a whole book (although individual parts may be juicily analyzed), and the entire procedure may be arbitrary and capricious. The decision, once announced, rapidly disposes of the offending book and frequently the teacher or librarian to boot, a variation of old-fashioned Western justice at work. Extralegal trials need not be cluttered with trivia such as accuracy or reasoning or fairness or justice. Many of the eighteen censorship incidents described earlier in this chapter were handled extralegally.

Why would librarians or teachers allow their books and teaching materials to be so treated? Court cases cost a great deal of money, and unless a particular case is likely to create precedent, many lawyers discourage educators from going to the courts. Court cases, even more important, cause friction within the community and—surprising to many neophyte teachers and librarians—cause almost equal friction among a school's faculty. A teacher or librarian who assumes that all fellow teachers will automatically support a case for academic freedom or intellectual freedom is a fool. Many educators, to misuse the word, have little sympathy for troublemakers or their causes. Others are frightened at the prospect of possibly antagonizing their superiors. Others "know their place" in the universe. Others are morally offended by anything stronger than *darn* and may regard most of modern literature (and old literature) as inherently immoral and therefore objectionable to high school students' use. Others find additional or different reasons aplenty for staying out of the fray. And that, more likely than not, is the reason most censorship episodes do not turn into court cases.

A New Kind of Censorship

N. R. Kleinfield's article, "The Elderly Man and the Sea? Test Sanitizes Literary Texts," in the June 2, 2002, *New York Times* revealed a certain kind of censorship and hinted at one far more important and pervasive. He told how Jeanne Heifetz was skimming through a familiar quotation on the New York State Regents Examination in English and discovered that words were missing. She checked and indeed the missing words were missing. And there were several quotations that were cut or rewritten.

For example, a quotation from a speech by the United Nations Secretary General was given thus:

Polls show strong American support for the organization at the grass-roots level.

But the original quotation was this:

Polls show strong American support for the organization at the grass-roots level regardless of what is said and done on Capitol Hill.

Surely a major change in meaning took place between quotations one and two. But another alteration in the speech by the United Nations Secretary General was even more puzzling. At one point, he praised "the fine California wine and seafood," but that was altered so that he praised only "the fine California seafood." Presumably, the mere mention of wine on a test might prove offensive or disturbing to a student.

When the Education Department's Assistant Commissioner for Curriculum, Instruction, and Assessment was asked about the alterations in various passages, she responded, "We do shorten the passages and alter the passages to make them suitable for testing situations." She extended her remarks by explaining that the changes were made to satisfy the sensitivity guidelines used by the department so no student will be "uncomfortable in a testing situation."[32] If the meaning of all those words remained unclear or ambiguous, one thing was clear—passages were rewritten or cut to ensure that no student would be "uncomfortable" while taking a test. It turned out that students could be made "uncomfortable" because of race or ethnic background or place of origin (or where a student may now live). As John Leo wrote in his "Heck Hath No Fury" column in the June 17, 2002, *U.S. News & World Report*:

The New York sensitivity review guidelines ban "language, content, or context that is not accessible to one or more racial or ethnic groups."
Translation: Keep everything bland and down the middle.[33]

Leo also noted that New York University professor Diane Ravitch was preparing a book on the subject, and several months later *The Language Police: How Pressure Groups Restrict What Students Learn* appeared.[34]

Ravitch's book is a detailed commentary and analysis of this new censorship, which is practiced by textbook publishers, school boards, and bias and sensitivity committees. Committee members go through texts to weed out anything that might somehow or somewhere offend or disturb someone for some reason. Text publishers, or any sort of publisher dealing with public schools, have no wish to offend anyone, and "publishers found that the best way to avoid controversy is to eliminate anything that might cause controversy."[35] In many ways, the guidelines of the sensitivity and bias committees are censorship guidelines.

But this is a different sort of censorship than teachers or librarians usually encounter. Censors—as we usually know them—object to the rude, the violent, the disturbing, the offensive, and they want it removed. In this case, people we would expect to be on the side of teachers and librarians already censor what is offensive or violent or rude. As Ravitch noted, "This language censorship and thought control should be repugnant to those who care about freedom of thought,"[36] but clearly the language police do not care about freedom of thought. Protection and condescension are the aim of their notion of education.

What does Ravitch advocate?

> We can stop censorship. We must recognize that the censorship that is now so widespread in education represents a systemic breakdown of our ability to educate the next generation and to transmit to them a full and open range of ideas about important issues in the world. By avoiding controversy, we teach them to avoid dealing with reality. By expurgating literature, we teach them that words are meaningless and fungible.[37]

At the very least, teachers and librarians ought to know Ravitch's Appendix 1, "A Glossary of Banned Words, Usages, Stereotypes, and Topics." Ravitch lists words and expressions that have offended the bias and sensitivity of people, beginning with "able-bodied," which has been "banned as offensive, replace with *person who is non-disabled.*" *Birth defect* is apparently offensive and should be replaced with *people with congenital disabilities. Courageous* is banned as patronizing when referring to a person with disabilities. *Fairy* is banned because it suggests homosexuality and should be replaced with *elf.*

And so it goes.

What to Do before and after the Censors Arrive

Certain steps should be taken by librarians and teachers, preferably acting in concert, to prepare for censorship.

Before the Censors Arrive

Teachers and librarians should have some knowledge about the history of censorship and why citizens would wish to censor (see the books and articles listed in the Starter Bibliography on Censorship). They should keep up-to-date with censorship problems and court decisions and what books are coming under attack for what reason. That means they should read the *Newsletter on Intellectual Freedom, School Library Journal, English Journal,* and *Voice of Youth Advocates,* along with other articles cited in the bibliography that concludes each issue of the *Newsletter.* A lot of work? Of course, but better than facing a censor totally ignorant of the world of censorship.

They should develop clear and succinct statements, devoid of any educational or library or literary jargon, on why they teach literature or stock books. These statements ought to be made easily available to the public, partly to demonstrate educators' literacy—always an impressive beginning for an argument— and to make parents feel that someone intelligent works in the school, partly because teachers and librarians have a duty to communicate to the public what is going on and why it goes on.

They need to develop and publicize procedures for book selection in the library or the classroom. Most parents have not the foggiest notion of how educators go about selecting books, more or less assuming it comes about through sticking pins in a book catalogue. It might be wise to consider asking some parents to assist teachers and librarians in selection, partly to let parents learn how difficult the matter is, partly to use their ideas (which might prove surprisingly helpful).

They need to develop procedures for handling censorship, should it occur. The National Council of Teachers of English monographs *The Students' Right to Read* and *The Students' Right to Know* should prove helpful, as should the American Library Association's *Intellectual Freedom Manual,* both for general principles and for specific suggestions. Whether adopted from any of these sources or created afresh, the procedure should include a form to be completed by anyone who objects to any teaching material or library book and a clearly defined way in which the matter will be handled after completion of the form. (Will it go to a committee? How many are on the committee? Are people outside the school on the committee? How many teachers? How many administrators?) The procedural rules must be openly available for anyone to consult, the procedures must apply to everyone (no exceptions should be allowed, no matter whether the complainant is the local drunk or the school board president), every complainant must be treated courteously and promptly, and the procedures must be approved by the school board. If the board does not approve the document, it has no legal standing. If the school board is not periodically reminded of the procedures—say, every couple of years—it may forget its obligation. Given the fact that many school boards change membership slightly each year and may change their entire composition within five or six years, teachers and librarians should take it upon themselves to remind the board. Otherwise, an entirely new board may wonder why it should support something it neither created nor particularly approves of.

Teachers who assign long works (other than texts) for common reading should write rationales—statements aimed at parents but open to anyone— explaining why the teacher chose *1984,* or *Silas Marner, Manchild in the Promised Land,* or *Hamlet* for class reading and discussion. Rationales should answer the following, although they should be written as informal essays, devoid of any educational jargon, not answers to essay tests: (1) Why would the teacher use this book with this class at this time? (2) What specific objectives—not couched in behavioral terms unless the teachers are anxious to alienate parents— literary or pedagogical, is the teacher aiming at? (3) How will this book meet those objectives? (4) What problems of style, tone, theme, or subject matter exist, and how will the teacher face them? Answering those questions should force teachers to take a fresh look at the book and think more carefully about the possibilities and problems inherent in the book. Rationales are *not* designed to protect the teacher by showing careful advance preparation before teaching, although clearly such rationales would be valuable should censorship strike. Rather, rationales should be written for public information, easily available to anyone interested as part of the professional responsibility of teachers. Diane Shugert offers a number of sample rationales in the fall 1983 *Connecticut English Journal* and in "How to Write a Rationale in Defense of a Book" in James Davis's *Dealing with Censorship*.

The following three books have rationales for many books often under attack. None will replace rationales written by the local teachers or librarians who recommended or purchased the offending literature; who else would better know why the book was selected (or bought) for these kids at this time for these specific reasons? But the rationales listed here will serve in an emergency, and they should provide ideas or details for local teachers or librarians in writing their own rationales.

> *Censored Books: Critical Viewpoints*, edited by Nicholas J. Karolides, Lee Burress, and John M. Kean (Scarecrow, 1993). Among the 56 rationales for both YA and adult books are ones for *Annie on My Mind*, *Brave New World*, *The Chocolate War*, *The Crucible*, *Forever*, *If Beale Street Could Talk*, *The Outsiders*, and *Then Again, Maybe I Won't*.
>
> *Censored Books II: Critical Viewpoints, 1985–2002* edited by Nicholas Karolides (Scarecrow, 2002). Defenses are written for sixty-four popular books including *The Bluest Eye*, *Bridge to Terabithia*, *A Day No Pigs Would Die*, *Fade*, *Fallen Angels*, *The Giver*, *I Am the Cheese*, *Killing Mr. Griffin*, *The Last Mission*, and *Tiger Eyes*.
>
> *Rationales for Teaching Young Adult Literature* edited by Louann Reid with Jamie Hayes Neufeld (Heinemann, 1999). Among the twenty-two rationales in Reid and Neufeld's book are ones for *Weetzie Bat*, *Ironman*, *Annie on My Mind*, *Jack*, *In Country*, *Fallen Angels*, and *When She Hollers*.

Educators should woo the public to gain support for intellectual and academic freedom. Any community has its readers and former teachers interested in students' freedom to read. Finding them ahead of time is part of teachers' and librarians' jobs. Waiting until censorship strikes is too late. Pat Scales's ideas about working with parents in the November 1983 *Calendar* (distributed by the Children's Book Council) are most helpful. Scales was talking to a parent who helped in Scales's school library and who had picked up copies of Maureen Daly's *Seventeenth Summer* and Ann Head's *Mr. and Mrs. Bo Jo Jones* and wondered about students reading books with such provocative covers. Scales asked the mother to read the books before forming an opinion. From that experience came a program called "Communicate Through Literature," with monthly meetings to discuss with parents the reading that young adults do.

Also we should not forget about discussing the topic of censorship with our current students. See Focus Box 12.1, Censorship and Free Speech in Books for Young Readers. Of course, authors are more likely to think about the complications of censorship than are people whose life work is not so closely connected to the matter. When we talk with young people and with their parents, we would do well to bring in some of their comments as with Laurie Halse Anderson's thoughtful statement on p. 421. To lead off discussions and writing assignments, teachers can also use some of the quotes on p. 425 that we selected from the three Banned Books Week posters distributed by the American Library Association for their 2005 Banned Books Week. The idea behind Banned Books Week, which is

The Day They Came to Arrest the Book by Nat Hentoff. Delacorte, 1982. Parents object to *Adventures of Huckleberry Finn* because the book is, according to them, racist and sexist. Hentoff advances the cases for both sides.

Fahrenheit 451 by Ray Bradbury. Ballantine, 1953. Although Bradbury's classic story of book burning was published as an adult novel, it is now read by more teenagers than adults. Ironically, a recent "school edition" was published minus the swear words.

The Last Safe Place on Earth by Richard Peck. Delacorte, 1995. Walden Woods seems like the perfect place to live until a group dedicated to protecting young people from evil books decides to raid libraries.

Lemony Snicket: The Unauthorized Autobiography. HarperCollins, 2002. As part of the madcap adventures in this best-selling children's book, three pages are devoted to a letter from Vice Principal Nero thanking Mr. and Mrs. Spats for sending him the article from *The Daily Punctilio*, which explained "the danger of allowing young people to read certain books." He fired Ms. K. thus saving the children from reading such books as *Ramona Quimby, Age 8; Matilda;* and *Ivan Lachrymose: Lake Explorer.*

Maudie and Me and the Dirty Book by Betty Miles. Knopf, 1980. Eleven-year-old Kate chooses to read a book to first graders that describes a dog giving birth to puppies. Someone objects on the opinion page of the local newspaper and the project of older children reading to first graders almost gets cancelled.

Memoirs of a Bookbat by Kathryn Lasky. Harcourt, 1994. Lasky's book does a good job of showing how censorship can cause dissension within families. Fourteen-year-old Harper runs away to live with her grandmother because she does not agree with her parents' campaign against books and schools that do not espouse their "brand" of traditional values.

Nothing but the Truth: A Documentary Novel by Avi. Orchard, 1991; Scholastic, 2003. No one dreams that what starts out as a fairly simple teacher/student confrontation over free speech will give both Miss Narwin and ninth-grader Philip Malloy their fifteen minutes of fame.

The Sledding Hill by Chris Crutcher. HarperCollins/Greenwillow, 2005. Crutcher puts himself and a pretend novel entitled *Warren Peece* in this postmodern attack on censors. Rather than sounding angry and resentful, Crutcher turns the story into a playful fantasy about fourteen-year-old Eddie Proffit, whose best friend was killed in an accident, but nevertheless decides to hang around and watch out for Eddie.

A Small Civil War by John Neufeld. Fawcett/Ballantine, 1982; Revised edition, Atheneum, 1996. Neufeld's book is set in a small Iowa town where controversy rages over the appropriateness of teaching John Steinbeck's *The Grapes of Wrath.* People on both sides of the issue become so outraged that hostilities expand far beyond the original quarrel.

Strike by Barbara Corcoran. Atheneum, 1983. Corcoran adds two countermelodies to the basic tune of a father-son debate about the boy's life and plans—a strike by teachers and a group anxious to go through libraries looking for filth.

Tinker vs. Des Moines: Student Rights on Trial by Doreen Rappaport. Be the Judge—Be the Jury series. HarperCollins, 1993. This trial is probably the single most influential U.S. Supreme Court decision on students' First Amendment rights.

The Trials of Molly Sheldon by Julian F. Thompson. Holt, 1995. The family store where Molly works becomes the site of protests by a group objecting to rental films, as well as books and magazines. Thompson relies on irony as he develops a comparison to the Salem witch trials and what Molly goes through.

The Year They Burned the Book by Nancy Garden. Farrar, Straus and Girouox, 1999. Jamie is editor of the school newspaper and a supporter of sex education in schools. Her editorial touches some raw nerves and the fight is on.

Young Adult Authors Speak Out

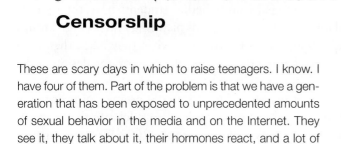

Laurie Halse Anderson **on Censorship**

These are scary days in which to raise teenagers. I know. I have four of them. Part of the problem is that we have a generation that has been exposed to unprecedented amounts of sexual behavior in the media and on the Internet. They see it, they talk about it, their hormones react, and a lot of kids wind up in painful situations.

Literature is the safe and traditional vehicle through which we learn about the world and pass on values from one generation to the next. Books save lives. Contemporary young adult literature surprises some people, because it is an accurate reflection of the way today's teenagers talk, think, and behave. But these books must be honest in order to connect to the teen reader. America's teens are desperate for responsible, trustworthy adults to create situations in which they can discuss the issues that are of the highest concern for them. Reading and discussing books is one of

the most effective ways to get teens to think through and learn about the challenges of adolescence.

Most of the censorship I see is fear driven. I respect that. The world is a very scary place. It is a terrifying place in which to raise children, and in particular, teenagers. It is human nature to nurture and protect children as they grow into adulthood. But censoring books that deal with difficult, adolescent issues does not protect anybody. Quite the opposite. It leaves kids in darkness and makes them vulnerable.

Censorship is the child of fear and the father of ignorance. Our children cannot afford to have the truth of the world withheld from them. They need us to be brave enough to give them great books so they can learn how to grow up into the men and women we want them to be.

● Laurie Halse Anderson first wrote this as an add-on to her 1999 *Speak*. We liked it so much that we asked to include it here. Anderson's other books include *Twisted* (2007), *Prom* (2005), and *Catalyst* (2002), all from Viking.

celebrated the last full week of every September, is to encourage both young and old readers to think about the issue of censorship before they get involved in the emotions of a particular case.

Questions about Free Speech

In writing about such books as those listed in Focus Box 12.1, Suzann Holland predicted that we will begin to see more variety in such books as authors begin to tackle "the censorship of music and movies, freedom of assembly, or Internet filters." While acknowledging the possibilities for censorship in virtually all communities, she observed that "the fuse won't always be found in the local Bible study group." Nor will the censors be fundamentalists who act without plans. She was disappointed that in so many books, "the censors stumble badly in their arguments and appear far less intelligent than those trying to prevent such instances of *protection*."[38]

Judging from recent news clippings, the topic of young people's rights to free speech is on its way to receiving increased attention. While Charles C. Haynes, Sam Chaltain, and Susan M. Glisson's 2006 *First Freedoms: A Documentary History of the First Amendment Rights in America* is written for adults, teachers and librarians can bring many of the concepts to students. One of the truths emerging from the book is that while the concept of "free speech" sounds like a clearly defined privilege, it is not as easy to figure out as we would like it to be. Recent cases in the news have ranged from whether students have the right to protest mandatory school uniforms by wearing pins picturing Hitler youth groups to whether the gifted students at a school played fair when they made their own "Giftie" T-shirts to protest not getting to make the decision on the design of the official school T-shirt.

A case that made it all the way to the United States Supreme Court began in Juneau, Alaska, when students were let out of school to celebrate the Olympic torch being carried through the streets on its way to the 2002 Winter Games in Salt Lake City. Student Joseph Frederick had something else that he planned to celebrate as he and some friends unfurled a fourteen-foot-long banner emblazoned with, "Bong Hits 4 Jesus." Later, Frederick testified that he designed the banner "to be meaningless and funny, in order to get on television." The high school's principal Deborah Morse was not amused, but she did recognize "bong hits" as slang for using marijuana. She demanded that Frederick take down the banner. He refused and she ordered him to her office and gave him a ten-day suspension.

The resulting lawsuit (*Morse v. Frederick*) was the first Supreme Court case to ask questions about students' free speech since 1988. The result was nine justices hesitating on precisely how the tension between students and administration could be resolved. After the decision in *Morse v. Frederick*, Alex Kreit noted that student free-speech rights are now less clear-cut than they once seemed.

> Prior to *Morse*, there was a reasonably clear bright-line test: Student speech that was disruptive or lewd could be punished, while other speech could not. Now, even First Amendment scholars are unsure how courts will treat the great majority of student speech that mentions drugs or alcohol.[39]

The ambiguity in the June 25, 2007, decision did not arise from Chief Justice Roberts's opinion in the 6–3 decision that school officials may reasonably punish speech that "promotes illegal drug use." Rather the problem arose with the concurring opinion of Justices Samuel A. Alito, Jr., and Anthony M. Kennedy, who wrote that "speech that can plausibly be interpreted as commenting on any political or social issue," including "the wisdom of the war on drugs or of legalizing marijuana for medicinal use" is constitutionally protected.

Since Alito and Kennedy's votes were needed for the 6–3 majority, their reasoning became the controlling legal rule, one not likely to make school officials overjoyed with the decision in *Morse v. Frederick*. The decision as it now stands is limited to speech advocating the use of illegal drugs. It does not apply to student speech on political or social issues.

Educators should be prepared to take on the usual arguments of censors—for example, that educators are playing word games when we insist that we select and some parents try to censor. There is a distinction between *selection* and *censorship,* no matter how many people deliberately or inadvertently misuse or confuse the two. The classic distinction was drawn by Lester Asheim in 1952:

> Selection begins with a presumption in favor of liberty of thought; censorship with a presumption in favor of thought control. Selection's approach to the book is positive, seeking its values in the book as a book, and in the book as a whole. Censorship's approach is negative, seeking for vulnerable characteristics wherever they can be found anywhere in the book, or even outside it. Selection seeks to promote the right of the reader to read; censorship seeks to protect not the right—but the reader himself from the fancied effects of his reading. The selector has faith in the intelligence of the reader; the censor has faith only in his own.
>
> In other words, selection is democratic while censorship is authoritarian, and in our democracy we have traditionally tended to put our trust in the selector rather than in the censor.[40]

Finally, teachers and librarians should know the organizations that are most helpful if censorship does strike. Diane Shugert's "A Body of Well-Instructed Men and Women: Organizations Active for Intellectual Freedom," in James Davis's *Dealing with Censorship,* has a long list of such groups. Following are six national groups every educator ought to know:

The American Civil Liberties Union, 132 W. 43rd St., New York, NY 10036

The Freedom to Read Foundation, 50 E. Huron St., Chicago, IL 60611

The National Coalition Against Censorship, 2 W. 64th St., New York, NY 10023

People for the American Way, 2000 M St., N.W., Washington, DC 20036

SLATE (Support for the Learning and Teaching of English), National Council of Teachers of English, 1111 Kenyon Road, Urbana, IL 61801

The Standing Committee on Censorship, c/o National Council of Teachers of English, 1111 Kenyon Road, Urbana, IL 61801

After the Censors Arrive

Teachers and librarians should begin by refusing to panic—easier said than done, but essential. Censors always have one advantage. They can determine the time and the place for the attack. No matter how well prepared the teacher or the librarian, only the censor can say *when.*

Educators should not be too surprised or appalled to discover that not all their fellow teachers or librarians rush in with immediate support. If teachers and librarians assume they represent the entire cause by themselves, they are far better off and considerably less likely to be instantly disillusioned.

Educators ought to urge (or even require that) potential censors talk first to the teacher or librarian in question before completing the complaint form, not to stall the objectors but to assure everyone of fair play all around. Teachers or

ALA's Banned Books Week

www.ala.org/bbooks: Each September, the American Library Association sponsors Banned Books Week to highlight intellectual freedom issues. This site provides information, publicity materials available for purchase, and lists of the most frequently challenged books in America.

ALA's Censorship in the Schools

www.ala.org/alaorg/oif/censorshipintheschools.html: A long-time advocate of intellectual freedom, the American Library Association's Office of Intellectual Freedom offers advice about how to cope with book challenges in the school setting.

ALA's Freedom to Read Foundation

www.ftrf.org: Founded in 1969, the Freedom to Read Foundation defends "the public's right of access to information and materials stored in the nation's libraries." The FTRF will assist librarians and teachers in securing legal counsel if needed to defeat a book challenge.

Free Expression Clearinghouse—A Guide to Free Speech and the First Amendment

www.freeexpression.org: Headlines from current controversies are given on the opening pages with the complete news stories being just a click away. News items range from the awarding of the Jefferson "Muzzles" awards to the year's top censors, to homeowners' rights to display artwork on their front lawns, and to school bans on the Harry Potter books.

KidSpeak!

www.kidspeakonline.org/: Inspired by the 1999 banning of Harry Potter books in the Zeeland, Michigan, school system, KidSpeak! offers advice, support, and a place for young people to comment on book censorship.

National Coalition Against Censorship

www.ncac.org/index.html: A somewhat broader resource, the NCAC can assist teachers and librarians when dealing with a book challenge.

NCTE's Anti-Censorship Page

www.ncte.org/censorship/: This site, from the National Council of Teachers of English, offers advice about dealing with censorship in teaching YA and children's literature. Of particular interest is a CD-ROM available for purchase, containing rationales for teaching over 170 challenged books.

librarians may discover what others have before, that objectors sometimes simply want to be heard and their complaints treated with dignity and dispatch. Sometimes, teachers and librarians may even be able to talk calmly—once the need to battle has died down—with the objectors and to reason with them, which is not exactly the same as convincing them that the teachers or librarians are necessarily right. The objectors may even see why the offending work was assigned or recommended, sometimes even seeing the difficulty in choosing a book for a class or an individual. Many teachers and librarians, although by no means all, agree that if parents ask that their child not be required to read a certain book, educators must agree to find a substitute book. If a substitute book is to be found and if it is to meet a different fate than the first book, parents must help in selecting the new book. Most objectors deeply care about their children's education, and they understand why the substitute book should not be easier or shorter (thus rewarding the student) or harder and longer (thus unduly punishing the student). Finding another book approximately as long and as difficult as the orig-

Quotations Taken from ALA's Banned Books Week Posters 2005

"Censorship, like charity, should begin at home, but unlike charity, it should end there."
> —Clare Boothe Luce

"If there is a bedrock principle underlying the First Amendment, it is that the government may not prohibit the expression of an idea simply because society finds the idea itself offensive or disagreeable."
> —William J. Brennan, Jr.

"If we don't believe in freedom of expression for people we despise, we don't believe in it at all."
> —Noam Chomsky

"You don't have to burn books to destroy a culture, just get people to stop reading them."
> —Ray Bradbury

"All the secrets of the world are contained in books. Read at your own risk."
> —Lemony Snicket

"Books and ideas are the most effective weapons against intolerance and ignorance."
> —Lyndon Johnson

"A censor is a man who knows more than he thinks you ought to."
> —Granville Hicks

"Did you ever hear anyone say, 'That work had better be banned because I might read it and it would be very damaging to me'?"
> —Joseph Henry Jackson

"If she could have done one thing to make absolutely sure that every single person in this school will read your interview, it was banning it!"
> —Hermione to Harry in *Harry Potter and the Order of the Phoenix* by J. K. Rowling

"I have met thousands of children now, and not even one time has a child come up to me and said, 'Ms. Rowling, I'm so glad I've read these books because now I want to be a witch.'"
> —J. K. Rowling

"If [the] book be false in its facts, disprove them; if false in its reasoning, refute it. But, for God's sake, let us freely hear both sides, if we choose."
> —Thomas Jefferson

"Censorship is crippling, negating, stifling. It should be unthinkable in a country like ours."
> —Norma Fox Mazer

"Restriction of free thought and free speech is the most dangerous of all subversions. It is the one un-American act that could most easily defeat us."
> —William O. Douglas

"They that can give up essential liberty to obtain a little temporary safety deserve neither liberty nor safety."
> —Benjamin Franklin

"I'm not a rebel, trying to stir things up just to be provocative. I'm doing it because I feel like writing about real life. I still can't believe there's anything objectionable about telling it like it is."
> — Norma Klein

inal choice is no easy matter, but parents who demand substitutes must help, lest the teacher offend once more.

Librarians and teachers must treat objectors with every possible courtesy. Objectors should be expected to complete the school's forms detailing the objection, but the forms should be easily accessible and politely distributed. The complaint form should *never* be used to stall objectors. If it is so long that objectors get discouraged, the school may win one battle, but it will have produced one more disgruntled citizen, and at school bond time one irritated citizen and friends are quite enough to harm the cause of education.

Last, a committee (spelled out in detail before the censorship) meets to look at and discuss the complaint. After considering the problem but before arriving at a decision, the committee must meet with the teacher or librarian in question *and* the objectors to hear their cases. The committee then makes its decision and forwards it to the highest administrator in the school, who forwards it to the superintendent, who then forwards it to the school board. That body, already aware of the policy and procedures much earlier adopted to handle such matters, considers this objection and makes its decision, probably after at least one open meeting.

In no case and at no level should the actions of the educators or administrators or the school be viewed as pro forma. They should be considered as thoughtful actions to resolve a problem, not as an attempt to create newer and bigger ones. Objectors should feel that they have been listened to and courtesy has been extended them at all levels and all stages.

Concluding Comments

We believe that the school—classroom or library—must be a center of intellectual ferment in the community. This implies not that schools should be radical, but that they should be one place where freedom to think and inquire is protected, where ideas of all sorts can be considered, analyzed, investigated, and discussed, and their consequences thought through. We believe librarians and English teachers must protect these freedoms, not merely in the abstract but in the practical, day-by-day world of the school and library. To protect those freedoms, we must fight censorship, for without them no education worthy of the name is possible.

Notes

1. Colin Campbell, "Book Banning in America," *New York Times Book Review,* December 20, 1981, p. 1.
2. *ALAN Review* 31 (Fall 2003): 48–49.
3. Kelly Pearce, "Twain's Sawyer Is Wrong for Mesa," *Arizona Republic,* September 3, 1999, pp. 5-1, 4.
4. Alison Leigh Cowan, "Canceled by Principal, Student Play Heads Off-Broadway," *New York Times,* April 12, 2007, p. A-19.
5. *Newsletter on Intellectual Freedom* 55 (September 2006): 231.
6. *Newsletter on Intellectual Freedom* 53 (July 2004): 138–139.
7. *Newsletter on Intellectual Freedom* 46 (July 1997): 98.
8. *Newsletter on Intellectual Freedom* 45 (November 1996): 198.

9. *Newsletter on Intellectual Freedom* 42 (July 1993): 105–106.
10. Reprinted in *The New England Quarterly Magazine* 1 (April-May-June 1802): 172–173.
11. Comstock's life and work have been the subject of numerous books and articles. Heywood Broun and Margaret Leech's *Anthony Comstock: Roundsman of the Lord* (Boni, 1927) is amusing and nasty and still worth reading. A brief overview of Comstock's life can be found in Robert Brenner's introduction to a reprinting of *Traps for the Young* (Harvard University Press, 1967), pp. vii–xxxi. See also Paul Boyer's *Purity in Print: The Vice-Society Movement and Book Censorship in America* (Scribner, 1968) and Robert W. Haney's *Comstockery in America: Patterns of Censorship and Control* (Beacon, 1960).
12. "Fiction in Public Libraries," *American Library Journal* 1 (March 1877): 278.
13. *Library Journal* 21 (December 1896): 144.
14. James Buckham, "Objectionable Reading for Children," *The Teachers' Institute* 20 (November 1897): 89.
15. W. M. Stevenson, "Weeding Out Fiction in the Carnegie Free Library of Allegheny, Pa," *Library Journal* 22 (March 1897): 135.
16. *Public Libraries* 8 (March 1903): 114–115.
17. Evaline Harrington, "Why Treasure Island?" *English Journal* 9 (May 1920): 267–268.
18. "Standards in Selecting Fiction," *Library Journal* 67 (March 1932): 243.
19. Newsletter on Intellectual Freedom (November, 2002): 253, 292.
20. Louise Kingsbury and Lance Gurwell, "The Sin Fighters: Grappling with Gomorrah at the Grass Roots," *Utah Holiday* 12 (April 1983): 46.
21. Lee Gant, "Shoot-Out in Texas," Calendar section, *Los Angeles Times*, December 25, 1983, p. 23.
22. *Phoenix Gazette*, June 10, 1981, p. SE-6.
23. *Arizona English Bulletin* 11 (February 1969): 37.
24. *Connecticut English Journal* 9 (Spring 1978): 59–61.
25. Kathleen Beck, "Censorship and Celluloid," *Voice of Youth Advocates* 18 (June 1995): 73–76.
26. Ken Donelson, "Censorship in the 1970s: Some Ways to Handle It When It Comes (And It Will)," *English Journal* 63 (February 1974): 47–51.
27. "Protest Groups Exert Strong Impact," *Publishers Weekly* 216 (October 29, 1979): 42–44.
28. "Sixty-Seven Targets of the Textbook Protesters," *Missouri English Bulletin* 38 (May 1980): 27–32.
29. M. E. Kerr, "On Gay Books," *Literature for Today's Young Adults* by Alleen Pace Nilsen and Ken Donelson (Longman, 2001), p. 293.
30. *Newsletter on Intellectual Freedom* 48 (January 1999): 14.
31. Todd A. DeMitchell and John J. Carney, "Harry Potter and the Public School Library," *Phi Delta Kappan* 87 (October 2005).
32. *New York Times*, June 2, 2002, p. 30.
33. *U.S. News & World Report*, p. 53.
34. Knopf, 2003.
35. Ravitch, p. 24.
36. Ravitch, p. 48.
37. Ravitch, p. 165.
38. Suzann Holland, "Censorship in Young Adult Fiction: What's Out There and What Should Be," *VOYA* 25.3 (August 2000): 176–177.
39. Alex Kreit, "'Bong Hits' for Student Speech," *Education Week*, August 29, 2007.
40. Lester Asheim, "Not Censorship but Selection," *Wilson Library Bulletin* 28 (September 1953): 67. See also Asheim's later article, "Selection and Censorship: A Reappraisal," *Wilson Library Bulletin* 58 (November 1983): 180–184. Julia Turnquist Bradley's "Censoring the School Library: Do Students Have the Right to Read," *Connecticut Law Review* 10 (Spring 1978): 747–755, also draws a distinction between selection and censorship.

A Starter Bibliography on Censorship

Bibliographical Source

Newsletter on Intellectual Freedom. A bimonthly newsletter edited by Judith Krug with a sizeable bibliography concluding each issue. Available from the American Library Association (ALA), 50 Huron St., Chicago, IL 60611.

Three Basic Policy Statements and Recommended Procedures

Burress, Lee, and Edward B. Jenkinson. *The Students' Right to Know.* National Council of Teachers of English (NCTE), 1982.

Burress, Lee, and Edward B. Jenkinson. *The Students' Right to Read*, 3rd ed. NCTE, 1982. NCTE's official policy on censorship.

Intellectual Freedom Manual, 7th ed. ALA, 2006. ALA's official policy on censorship along with a mass of helpful material.

Some General Books on Censorship

Atkins, Robert, and Svetlana Mintcheva, eds. *Censoring Culture: Contemporary Threats to Free Expression.* New Press, 2006.

Blanshard, Paul. *The Right to Read: The Battle against Censorship.* Beacon, 1955.

Cline, Victor B., ed. *Where Do You Draw the Line?* Brigham Young University Press, 1974.

Donnerstein, Edward, Daniel Linz, and Steven Penrod. *The Question of Pornography; Research Findings and Policy Implications.* Free Press, 1987.

Downs, Robert B., and Ralph E. McCoy, eds. *The First Freedom Today: Critical Issues Relating to Censorship and to Intellectual Freedom.* ALA, 1984.

Foerstel, Herbert N. *Banned in the U.S.A.: A Reference Guide to Book Censorship in Schools and Public Libraries.* Greenwood, 2002.

Foerstel, Herbert N. *Free Expression and Censorship in America: An Encyclopedia.* Greenwood, 1997.

Green, Jonathon. *The Encyclopedia of Censorship.* Facts on File, 2005.

Haynes, Charles C., Sam Chaltain, and Susan M. Gilsson. *First Freedoms: A Documentary History of the First Amendment Rights in America.* Oxford University Press, 2006.

Heins, Marjorie. *Not in Front of the Children: "Indecency," Censorship, and the Innocence of Youth.* Hill and Wang, 2001.

Heins, Marjorie. *Sex, Sin, and Blasphemy: A Guide to America's Censorship Wars.* Norton, 1993.

Hentoff, Nat. *The First Freedom: The Tumultuous History of Free Speech in America.* Delacorte, 1980.

Hentoff, Nat. *Free Speech for Me—But Not for Thee: How the American Left and Right Relentlessly Censor Each Other.* Harper, 1992.

Hentoff, Nat. *The War on the Bill of Rights: And the Gathering Resistance.* Seven Stories, 2003.

Hoffer, Eric. *The True Believer: Thoughts on the Nature of Mass Movements.* New American Library, 1958.

Hofstadter, Richard. *Anti-intellectualism in America.* Knopf, 1963.

Hull, Mary. *Censorship in America: A Reference Handbook.* ABC-CLIO, 1999.

Karolides, Nicholas J., Margaret Bald, and Dawn B. Sova, eds. *120 Banned Books: Censorship Histories of World Literature.* Checkmark, 2005.

Levine, Judith. *Harmful to Minors: The Perils of Protecting Children from Sex.* University of Minnesota, 2002.

Marsh, Dave. *50 Ways to Fight Censorship: And Important Facts to Know about the Censors.* Thunder's Mouth, 1991.

Mill, John Stuart. *On Liberty.* 1859. With John Milton's *Areopagitica*, two of the basic sources in facing censorship.

Milton, John. *Areopagitica.* 1644. The title comes from the Areopagus hills near the Acropolis in Athens where the Upper Council met.

Nakaya, Andrea, ed. *Censorship* (in the Opposing Viewpoints series). Greenhaven, 2005.

Noble, William. *Bookbanning in America: Who Bans Books?—and Why?* Eriksson, 1990.

Oboler, Eli M. *The Fear of the Word: Censorship and Sex.* Scarecrow, 1974.

Oboler, Eli M., ed. *Censorship and Education.* Wilson, 1981.

Shinder, Jason, ed. *The Poem That Changed America: "How" Fifty Years Later.* Farrar, Straus and Giroux, 2006.

The History of Censorship

Boyer, Paul S. *Purity in Print: The Vice-Society Movement and Book Censorship in America.* Scribner, 1978.

Cohen, Mark. *Censorship in Canadian Literature.* McGill-Queens University Press, 2001.

Comstock, Anthony. *Frauds Exposed, or How the People Are Deceived and Robbed, and Youth Corrupted.* J. Howard Brown, 1880.

Comstock, Anthony. *Morals versus Art.* Ogilvie, 1888.

Eldridge, Larry D. *A Distant Heritage: The Growth of Free Speech in Early America.* New York University Press, 1993.

Fryer, Peter. *Mrs. Grundy: Studies in English Prudery.* London House, 1964.

Haight, Anne Lyon. *Banned Books: Informal Notes on Some Books Banned for Various Reasons at Various Times and in Various Places,* 4th ed. Bowker, 1978.

Haney, Robert W. *Comstockery in America: Patterns of Censorship and Control.* Beacon, 1960.

Ingelhart, Louise Edward. *Press and Speech Freedom in the World: from Antiquity until 1998.* Greenwood, 1998.

Knuth, Rebecca. *Libricide: The Regime-Sponsored Destruction of Books and Libraries in the Twentieth Century.* Praeger, 2003.

McCoy, Ralph E. *Banned in Boston: The Development of Literary Censorship in Massachusetts.* University of Illinois Press, 1956.

Neier, Aryeh. *Taking Liberties: Four Decades in the Struggle for Rights.* Public Affairs, 2003.

Nicholson, Steve. *The Censorship of British Drama, 1900–1968.* University of Exeter Press, 2003.

Perrin, Noel. *Dr. Bowdler's Legacy: A History of Expurgated Books in England and America.* Atheneum, 1959. Brilliant, as is anything by Perrin.

Plato. *The Republic,* especially Book 2.

Sova, Dawn B. *Banned Plays: Censorship Histories of 125 Stage Dramas.* Facts on File, 2004.

Stone, Geoffrey R. *Perilous Times: Free Speech in Wartime, from the Sedition Act of 1798 to the War on Terrorism.* Norton, 2004.

Taylor, Jon Tinnon. *Early Opposition to the English Novel: The Popular Reaction from 1760 to 1830.* King's Crown, 1943.

Thomas, Donald S. *A Long Time Burning: The History of Literary Censorship in England.* Praeger, 1969.

Zeisler, William, ed. *Censorship: 500 Years of Conflict.* Oxford University Press, 1984.

Censorship and the Courts

Abrams, Floyd. *Speaking Freely: Trials of the First Amendment.* Viking, 2005.

Books on Trial: A Survey of Recent Cases; A Report from the Clearinghouse School Book-Banning Litigation, rev. ed. National Coalition Against Censorship, 1985.

Bosmajian, Haig A., ed. *Censorship: Libraries and the Law.* Scribner, 1983.

Boismajian, Haig A., ed., *The First Amendment in the Classroom,* 5 Volumes. Neal-Schuman.
Vol. 1. *The Freedom to Read,* 1987.
Vol. 2. *Freedom of Religion,* 1987.
Vol. 3. *Freedom of Expression,* 1988.

Vol. 4. *Academic Freedom*, 1989.

Vol. 5. *The Freedom to Publish*, 1989.

De Grazia, Edward. *Censorship Landmarks*. Bowker, 1969.

Lewis, Anthony. *Freedom for the Thought You Hate: A Biography of the First Amendment*. Basic Books, 2008.

Lewis, Felice Flanery. *Literature, Obscenity and Law*. Southern Illinois University Press, 1976.

Moffett, James. *Storm in the Mountains: A Case Study of Censorship, Conflict, and Consciousness*. Southern Illinois University Press, 1988.

Rembar, Charles. *The End of Obscenity: The Trials of Lady Chatterley, Tropic of Cancer, and Fanny Hill*. Random House, 1968.

Tobin, Jeffrey. *The Nine: Inside the Secret World of the Supreme Court*. Doubleday, 2007.

Censorship and Libraries

Bielefield, Arlene. *Library Patrons and the Law*. Neal-Schuman, 1995.

Bryson, Joseph E., and Elizabeth W. Detty. *The Legal Aspects of Censorship of Public School Library and Instructional Materials*. Michie, 1982.

Carrier, Esther Jane. *Fiction in Public Libraries: 1876–1900*. Scarecrow, 1965.

Carrier, Esther Jane. *Fiction in Public Libraries: 1900–1956*. Libraries Unlimited, 1985.

Curry, Ann. *The Limits of Tolerance: Censorship and Intellectual Freedom in Public Libraries*. Scarecrow, 1997.

Fiske, Marjorie. *Book Selection and Censorship: A Study of School and Public Libraries in California*. University of California Press, 1959.

Geller, Evelyn. *Forbidden Books in American Public Libraries, 1876–1939: A Study in Cultural Change*. Greenwood, 1984. Geller and Robbins (see Robbins) give readers a history of the ALA's role in censorship problems from 1876 to 1969.

Jones, Barbara M. *Libraries, Access, and Intellectual Freedom Developing Policies for Public and Academic Libraries*. ALA, 1999.

Kravitz, Nancy. *Censorship and the School Library Media Center*. Libraries Unlimited, 2002.

McDonald, Frances Beck. *Censorship and Intellectual Freedom: A Survey of School Librarians' Attitudes and Moral Reasoning*. Scarecrow, 1993.

Peck, Robert S. *Libraries, the First Amendment, and Cyberspace: What You Need to Know*. ALA, 2000.

Pope, Michael. *Sex and the Undecided Librarian: A Study of Librarians' Opinions Sexually Oriented Literature*. Scarecrow, 1974.

Robbins, Louise S. *Censorship and the American Library: The American Library Association's Response to Threats to Intellectual Freedom, 1939–1969*. Greenwood, 1996.

Robbins, Louise S. *The Dismissal of Miss Ruth Brown: Civil Rights, Censorship, and the American Library*. University of Oklahoma Press, 2000.

West, Mark I. *Trust Your Children: Voices against Censorship in Children's Literature*. Neal-Schuman, 1997.

Wiegand, Wayne A., ed. "The Library Bill of Rights," the entire Summer 1996 Issue of *Library Trends*.

Censorship and Schools

Ahrens, Nyla Herber. "Censorship and the Teacher of English: A Questionnaire Survey of a Selected Sample of Secondary Teachers of English." Dissertation, Columbia University, 1965.

Beale, Howard K. *Are American Teachers Free? An Analysis of the Restraints upon the Freedom of Teaching in American Schools*. Scribner, 1936.

Beale, Howard K. *A History of Freedom of Teaching in American Schools*. Scribner, 1941.

Brinkley, Ellen Henson. *Caught Off Guard: Teachers Rethinking Censorship and Controversy*. Allyn and Bacon, 1999.

Brown, Jean E., ed. *Preserving Intellectual Freedom: Fighting Censorship in Our Schools*. NCTE, 1994.

Burress, Lee. *Battle of the Books: Literary Censorship in the Public Schools, 1950–1985*. Scarecrow, 1989.

Davis, James E., ed. *Dealing with Censorship*. NCTE, 1979.

DelFattore, Joan. *What Johnny Shouldn't Read: Textbook Censorship in America*. Yale University Press, 1992.

DelFattore, Joan. *The Fourth R: Conflicts over Religion in America's Public Schools*. Yale University Press, 2004.

Edwards, June. *Opposing Censorship in the Public Schools: Religion, Morality, and Literature*. Erlbaum, 1998.

Homstad, Wayne. *Anatomy of a Book Controversy*. Phi Delta Kappa Educational Foundation, 1995.

Jenkins, Edward B. *Censors in the Classroom: The Mind Benders*. Southern Illinois University Press, 1979.

Ochoa, Anna S., ed. *Academic Freedom to Teach and to Learn: Every Teacher's Issue*. NEA, 1990.

O'Neil, Robert M. *Classrooms in the Crossfire: The Rights and Interests of Students, Parents, Teachers, Administrators, Librarians, and the Community*. Indiana University Press, 1981.

Pipkin, Gloria. *At the Schoolhouse Gate: Lessons in Intellectual Freedom*. Heinemann, 2002.

Ravitch, Diana. *The Language Police: How Pressure Groups Restrict What Students Learn*. Random House, 2003.

Scale, Pat. *Teaching Banned Books: 12 Guides for Young Readers*. ALA, 2001.

Simmons, John S., ed. *Censorship: A Threat to Reading, Learning, and Thinking*. IRA, 1994.

Steinle, Pamela Hunt. *In Cold Fear: The Catcher in the Rye Censorship Controversies and Postwar American Character*. Ohio State University Press, 2000.

Rationales for Defending Books

Karolides, Nicholas J., ed. *Censored Books: II: Critical Viewpoints, 1985–2000*. Scarecrow, 2002.

Karolides, Nicholas J., Lee Burress, and John M. Kean, eds. *Censored Books: Critical Viewpoints*. Scarecrow, 1993.

Rationales for Challenged Books. NCTE and IRA, 1998. Compact disc for all CD players.

Rationales for Challenged Books, vol. 2. NCTE and IRA, 2005. Compact disc for all CD players.

Reid, Louanne, ed. *Rationales for Teaching Young Adult Literature*. Heinemann, 1999.

Shugert, Diane, ed. *Rationales for Commonly Challenged Books*. Connecticut Council of Teachers of English, 1983.

Censorship and Movies

Carmen, Ira H. *Movies, Censorship, and the Law*. University of Michigan Press, 1966.

DeGrazia, Edward. *Girls Lean Backward Everywhere: The Law of Obscenity and the Assault on Genius*. Random House, 1992.

DeGrazia, Edward, and Roger K. Newman. *Banned Films: Movies, Censors, and the First Amendment*. Bowker, 1982.

Gardner, Gerald C. *The Censorship Papers: Movie Censorship Letters from the Hays Office, 1934–1968*. Dodd, 1987.

Martin, Olga J. *Hollywood's Movie Commandments: A Handbook for Motion Pictures and Reviewers*. Wilson, 1937.

Randall, Richard C. *Censorship of the Movies: The Social and Political Control of a Mass Medium*. University of Wisconsin Press, 1968.

Schumach, Murray. *The Face on the Cutting Room Floor: The Story of Movie and Television Censorship*. Morrow, 1964.

Skinner, James M. *The Cross and the Cinema: The Legion of Decency and the National Catholic Office for Motion Pictures, 1933–1970*. Praeger, 1993.

Walsh, Frank. *Sin and Censorship: The Catholic Church and the Motion Picture Industry*. Yale University Press, 1996.

Westin, Alan F. *The Miracle Case: The Supreme Court and the Movies*. University of Alabama Press, 1961.

Selected Articles about Censorship

"A Brief Chronology on the West Virginia Textbook Crisis." *Arizona English Bulletin* 17 (February 1975): 203–212.

"Academic Freedom and the Social Studies Teacher." *Social Education* 55 (January 1991): 13–15.

Agee, Jane. "'There It Was, That One Sex Scene': English Teachers on Censorship." *English Journal* 89 (November 1999): 61–69.

"Are Libraries Fair? Pre-Selection Censorship in a Time of Resurgent Conservatism." *Newsletter on Intellectual Freedom* 31 (September 1982): 151, 181–188. Comments by Cal Thomas and Nat Hentoff. Twenty-five-plus years old and still worth reading.

Asheim, Lester. "Not Censorship, but Selection." *Wilson Library Bulletin* 28 (September 1953): 63–75. The most-often cited article on the subject.

Asheim, Lester. "Selection and Censorship: A Reappraisal." *Wilson Library Bulletin* 58 (November 1983): 180–184.

Baker, Mary Godron. "A Teacher's Right to Know Versus a Student's Right to Privacy." *Journal of Law and Education* 16 (Winter 1987): 71–91.

Bernays, Anne. "I Don't Want to Read a Novel Passed by a Board of Good Taste." *Chronicle of Higher Education* 37 (March 6, 1991): B-l, 3.

Berninghausen, David K. "The Librarians' Commitment to the Library Bill of Rights." *Library Trends* 14 (July 1970): 19–38.

Berninghausen, David K. "Social Responsibilities vs. the Library Bill of Rights." *Library Journal* 97 (November 15, 1972): 3675–3682.

Blumenthal, Walter Hart. "American Book Burnings." *American Book Collector* 6 (Summer 1956): 13–19.

Booth, Wayne. "Censorship and the Values of Fiction." *English Journal* 53 (March 1964): 155–164. Likely the best article on the subject.

Bradley, Julia Turnquist. "Censoring the School Library: Do Students Have a Right to Read?" *Connecticut Law Review* 10 (Spring 1978): 747–775.

Broderick, Dorothy. "Moral Conflict and the Survival of the Public Library." *American Libraries* 24 (May 1993): 447–448.

Broderick, Dorothy. "Serendipity at Work." *Show-Me Library* 35 (February 1984): 14.

Brown, Jean. E. "Creating a Censorship Simulation." *ALAN Review* 27 (Spring/Summer 2000): 27–30.

Broz, William J. "Hope and Irony; Annie on My Mind." *English Journal* 40 (July 2001): 47–53.

Burger, Robert H. "The Kanawha County Textbook Controversies: A Study of Communication and Power." *Library Quarterly* 48 (April 1982): 584–589.

Carter, Betty, and Chris Heckman. "They Just Can't Do This: Parents Respond to Censorship." *ALAN Review* 23 (Fall 1995): 56–59.

Chaltain, Sam. "Does the First Amendment Have a Future?" *Social Education* 69 (April 2005): 126–130.

Clark, Todd, ed. "The Question of Academic Freedom." *Social Education* 39 (April l975): 202–252.

Davis, James E. "What Principals and Other Administrators Have Done and Can Do in Defending Intellectual Freedom." *ALAN Review* 20 (Winter 1993): 11–13.

Delp, Vaughn N. "The Far Right and Me: It's Not So Far Away and It's Not So Right." *Arizona English Bulletin* 37 (Fall l994): 71–76.

Donelson, Ken. "A Rationale for Writing Rationales: Advice to (and Comments on) Teachers Who Don't See Any Point in Writing Rationales." *Contemporary Education* 54 (Fall 1982): 9–12.

Donelson, Ken. "Censorship and the Teaching of English: A Few Problems and Fewer Solutions." *Statement* 4 (October 1968): 5–15, 18–20.

Farrell, Edmund, "Literature in Crisis." *English Journal* 70 (January 1981): 13–18.

Fitzgerald, Frances. "A Disagreement in Baileyville." *New Yorker* 59 (January 16, 1984): 47–90.

Freedman, Lauren, and Holly Johnson. "Who's Protecting Whom? *I Hadn't to Tell You This*: A Case in Point in Confronting Self-Censorship in the Choice of Young Adult Literature." *Journal of Adolescent and Adult Literacy* 44 (December 2000/January 2001): 356–369.

Garden, Nancy. "Annie on Trial: How It Feels to Be Author of a Challenged Work." *Voice of Youth Advocates* 19 (June 1996): 79–82, 84.

Geller, Evelyn. "Intellectual Freedom: Eternal Principle or Unintended Consequence." *Library Journal* 99 (May 15, 1974): 364–367.

Geller, Evelyn. "The Librarian as Censor." *Library Journal* 101 (June 1, 1976): 1255–1258.

Glatthorn, Allan A. "Censorship and the Classroom Teacher." *English Journal* 66 (February 1977): 12–15.

Groves, Cy. "Book Censorship: Six Misunderstandings." *Alberta English* 71:11 (Fall 1971): 5–7. Reprinted in *Arizona English Bulletin* 57 (Fall 1994): 19–20.

Hentoff, Nat. "Any Writer Who Follows Anyone Else's Guidelines Ought to Be in Advertising." *School Library Journal* 24 (November 1977): 27–29.

Hentoff, Nat. "When Nice People Burn Books." *Progressive* 47 (February 1985): 42–44.

Hess, Diana, and Lee Arbetman. "Cases, Controversy, and the Court: Teaching about the Supreme Court." *Social Education* 66 (January/February 2002): 29, 40–41, 53–62.

Hipple, Ted. "Somnolent Bulls, Red Flags, Dirty Books, and Censorship Pedagogy." *English Journal* 90 (January 2001): 18–19.

Holland, Suzann. "Censorship in Young Adult Fiction: What's Out There and What Should Be." *Voice of Youth Advocates* 25 (August 2002): 176–177.

Janeczko, Paul. "How Students Can Help Educate the Censors." *Arizona English Bulletin* 17 (February 1975): 78–80.

Kingsbury, Louise, and Lance Gurwell. "The Sin Fighters: Grappling with Gomorrah at the Grass Roots." *Utah Holiday* 12 (April 1983): 41–61.

Krug, Judith. "Intellectual Freedom: A History of the Bill of Rights." *American Libraries* 3 (February 1973): 183–184.

Lacks, Cissy. "The Teacher's Nightmare: Getting Fired for Good Teaching." *English Journal* 86 (February 1997): 29–33.

Lent, ReLeah and Gloria Popkin. "We Keep Pedaling." *ALAN Review* 28 (Winter 2001): 9–11.

Marking, Stacy. "The House of Burned Books." *Index on Censorship* 31 (October 2002): 63–68.

Martin, William. "The Guardians Who Slumbereth Not." *Texas Monthly* 10 (November 1982): 145–150.

Meyer, Randy. "Annie's Day in Court: The Decision from the Bench." *School Library Journal* 42 (April 1995): 22–25.

Moffett, James. "Hidden Impediments in Improving English Teaching." *Phi Delta Kappan* 67 (September 1985): 50–56.

Peck, Richard. "The Genteel Un–shelving of a Book." *School Library Journal* 32 (May 1986): 37–39.

Peck, Richard. "The Great Library-Shelf Witch Hunt." *Booklist* 88 (January 1, 1992): 816–817.

Pipkin, Gloria. "Challenging the Conventional Wisdom of Censorship." *ALAN Review* 20 (Winter 1993): 35–37.

Russo, Elaine M. "Prior Restraint and the High School 'Free Press': The Implications of *Hazelwood v. Kuhlmeir*." *Journal of Law and Education* 18 (Winter 1989): 1–21.

Shafer, Robert E. "Censorship in Tucson's Flowing Wells School District Makes a Nationally Publicized Non-Event." *Arizona English Bulletin* 37 (Fall l994): 51–57.

Shugert, Diane. "How to Write a Rationale in Defense of a Book," in *Dealing with Censorship*, James E. Davis. NCTE, 1979, pp. 187–201.

Simmons, John S. "What Teachers under Fire Need from Their Principals." *ALAN Review* 20 (Winter 1993): 22–25.

Small, Robert C., Jr. "Censorship as We Enter 2000, or the Millennium, or Just Next Year: A Personal Look at Who We Are." *Journal of Youth Services Libraries* 13 (Winter 2000): 19–23.

Stieluw, Frederick J. "Censorship in the Early Professionalization of American Libraries, 1876 to 1929." *Journal of Library History* 18 (Winter 1983): 37–54.

Strike, Kenneth A. "A Field Guide of Censors: Toward a Concept of Censorship in Public Schools." *Teachers College Record* 87 (Winter 1985): 37–54.

Trillin, Calvin. "U. S. Journal: Kanawha County, West Virginia." *New Yorker* 50 (September 30, 1974): 119–122, 126–127.

Tyack, David B., and Thomas James. "Moral Majorities and the School Curriculum: Historical Perspectives and the Legalization of Virtues." *Teachers College Record* 86 (Summer 1985): 513–537.

Vonnegut, Kurt. "Why Are You Banning My Book?" *American School Journal* 168 (October 1981): 35.

Watson, Jerry, and Bill C. Snider. "Educating the Potential Self-Censor." *School Media Quarterly* 9 (Summer 1981): 272–276.

Weiss, M. Jerry. "Rumbles! Bangs! Crashes! The Roar of Censorship." *ALAN Review* 29 (Spring/Summer 2002): 54–57.

Winkler, Lisa K. "Celebrate Democracy! Teach about Censorship." *English Journal* 94 (May 2005): 48–51.

Zeeman, Kenneth L. "Grappling with Grendel or What We Did When the Censors Came." *English Journal* 86 (February 1997): 46–49.

Glossary of Literary Terms Illustrated by YA Literature

Allegory: An extended metaphor or comparison in which characters, events, or objects are equated with meaning outside of the story. Allegorical stories can be enjoyed on a surface level as well as on a second or deeper level. For example, William Golding's *Lord of the Flies* is on the surface an adventure story, while on the allegorical level it is a warning against lawlessness and how easy it is for people to be corrupted by power.

Allusion: A figure of speech that refers to something likely to be familiar to readers because of their knowledge of history, literature, or popular culture. Allusions are efficient communication because good readers can turn a single reference into an extended idea. For example, Robert Cormier's title *I Am the Cheese* might remind a reader of the old nursery song and game, "The Farmer in the Dell." This alludes to the family's newly given surname of *Farmer* and to the closing lines of the song: "The cheese stands alone" and "The rat takes the cheese."

Antagonist: The character (or sometimes event) that opposes the protagonist.

Archetypes: Images, patterns, or symbols that are part of the collective unconscious. Archetypal images are stronger and more durable than stereotypes. The Innocent setting out on a journey is an archetype especially common in YA literature, and so are generational conflicts in which young people struggle to gain their independence from adults.

Backdrop setting: A context of time and place that is like a stage setting in that it does not play an essential or unique part in the plot. The most common backdrop setting is that of a high school because school is the everyday business of teenagers. The fact that there are only so many ways to describe stairways, restrooms, lockers, cafeterias, classrooms, and parking lots gives a sameness to books for this age group.

Characterization: Whatever an author does to help readers know and identify with the characters in a story. Common techniques include providing physical descriptions, letting readers know what the characters say and what others say to and about them, showing the characters in action, showing how others relate to them, and revealing what they are thinking. See also **dynamic** and **static characters.**

Deconstruction: The idea that literature is constructed from words, which only approximately represent thoughts or actions. Once we realize this about a piece of literature, then we are able to undo the construct, that is, to examine and pull out different possible meanings. Deconstructing a piece of literature is taking it apart in different ways. Writers can also deconstruct events before they put them in their novels; for example, Virginia Euwer Wolff's *Bat 6* and Karen Hesse's *Witnesses* are told and retold by various characters who each have a unique point of view.

Dénouement: Literally, the untying of the knots at the end of a story. The purpose of the dénouement is to let the reader down after the excitement of the climax. Orson Scott Card softens the ending of *The Lost Boys: A Novel* by alluding to an afterlife when he writes that on the Christmas Eve when Stevie was abducted and murdered, they lost one other thing: their nicknames. No one made a conscious decision, it was just that they were part of a set, and it didn't seem right to use only some of them. "But someday they would use all those names when *Doorman* [Stevie] met them on the other side."

Dialect: Using characters' individual speech patterns to set them apart from mainstream speakers. A dialect might be illustrated through wording as when Hal Borland wrote in *When the Legends Die,* "The Ute people have lived many generations, many grandmothers, in that land," or it might be through "different" grammar and pronunciation as when such African American writers as Ntozake Shange, Maya Angelou, Virginia Hamilton, Toni Morrison, and Walter Dean Myers use black dialect for a variety of purposes, including the communication of pride in ethnic heritage. For the most part, difficulties in spelling and reading make authors rely sparingly on dialect.

Didacticism: Preachiness, as when an obvious moral or a lesson is tacked onto a story. Actually, most people who write for young readers want to teach lessons or impart some kind of wisdom or understanding. When something is described as didactic, it is being criticized for having a lesson so obvious that it detracts from the story.

Dynamic character: One who undergoes some change during the story. A dynamic character usually plays a major role in a story because an author needs considerable space in which to show how the character changes.

Escape literature: That which requires a minimum of intellectual energy so that readers can relax and enjoy the story with little or no intention of gaining insights or learning new information.

Euphemism: The use of circumlocution or an indirect kind of speech, usually to avoid giving offense. The word is cognate with *euphonious* meaning "pleasing to the ear." Modern writers usually prefer direct speech, but Margaret Craven's title *I Heard the Owl Call My Name* is more intriguing than a bald statement such as "I knew I was going to die," while Hemingway's title *For Whom the Bell Tolls* is both more euphemistic and euphonious than "the one who has died."

Figurative language: Intentional use of language in such a way that additional meanings are given to what would be expected in standard usage. Metaphors, symbolism, and allusions are figures of speech based on semantics or meaning. Other figurative speech is based on such phonological aspects as alliteration (the repetition of consonants), assonance (the repetition of vowels), rhyme (the repeating of sounds), and rhythm and cadence (the patterning of sounds).

Foreshadowing: The dropping of hints to prepare readers for what is ahead. The purpose is not to give away the ending but to increase excitement and suspense and to keep readers from feeling manipulated. For example, readers would feel cheated if the problems in a realistic novel are suddenly solved by a group of aliens when there had been no foreshadowing that the story was science fiction.

Formula literature: That which is almost entirely predictable because it consists of variations on a limited number of plots and themes. To some extent, this description fits most literature; the difference is a matter of degree. Many of the situation comedies, crime shows, and adventure shows on television are formula pieces, as are many of the mysteries, romances, and even horror stories that young people—and adults—enjoy reading.

***In medias res*:** Latin for "in the midst of things." This device of bringing the reader directly into the middle of a story is usually followed by flashbacks to fill in the missing details.

Integral setting: The time and place that an author has created so that it will play an important part in the story. In protagonist-against-nature stories, historical fiction pieces, and regional stories, the settings are often integrated into the plots.

Intertextuality: A term created by Julia Kristeva, who pointed out that writers build their new texts on all that they have absorbed and transformed from their life's reading. When readers compare the similarities among the styles or the topics of various writers, they are doing intertextual analysis. Sharon Creech did intertextual writing in *Love That Dog* when she had her young protagonist become so enchanted with the poetry written by Walter Dean Myers that he begins writing poetry himself.

Literature with a Capital L: That which has a degree of excellence not found in the mass of material that is printed every day. Such literature rewards study not only because of its content but also because of its style, universality, permanence, and the congeniality of the ideas expressed.

Magical realism: A kind of magic that happens without genies or good fairies to grant the protagonist's wishes. The magic is all the more startling because of the way it creeps up on the reader as part of what is being read as a realistic story. Francesca Lia Block is usually praised for the way she brings magical elements into her stories. However, some critics suggested it was too jarring when in *Missing Angel Juan,* Witch Baby found herself in a diner filled with the kind of humanoids usually reserved for science fiction.

Metaphor: Figurative language in which basically dissimilar things are likened to each other. A metaphor can consist of only a word or a phrase (a *head* of lettuce or the *outskirts* of a city), or it can be a series of interwoven ideas running through an entire book as when Walter Dean Myers in *Fallen Angels* compares the Vietnam war to various aspects of movies or television.

Mode: A broad term describing the way authors treat their material as comedy, romance, irony, satire, and tragedy. Together these modes make up the story of everyone's life, and in literature as in life, they are interrelated, flowing one into the other.

Narrative hook: A device that authors use to entice readers into a story; for example, a catchy title as in Douglas Adams's *The Hitchhiker's Guide to the Galaxy,* a question as in Richard Peck's *Are You in the House Alone?,* or an intriguing first few sentences as in Paul Zindel's *The Pigman,* when John says, "Now Lorraine can blame all the other things on me, but she was the one who picked out the Pigman's phone number. If you ask me, I think he would have died anyway. Maybe we speeded things up a little, but you really can't say we murdered him . . . Not murdered him."

Open endings: Those that leave readers not knowing what happens to the characters. Alice Childress in *A Hero Ain't Nothin' but a Sandwich* did not want to predict either that Benjie would become a confirmed drug addict or that he would go straight because she wanted readers to think about the fact that boys in his situation turn both ways. Books with open endings are good for group discussions because they inspire involved readers to consider the options.

Personification: The giving of human characteristics to something that is not human. For example, Maya Angelou in *All God's Children Need Traveling Shoes* writes, "July and August of 1962 stretched out like fat men yawning after a sumptuous dinner. They had every right to gloat, for they had eaten me up. Gobbled me down. Consumed my spirit, not in a wild rush, but slowly, with the obscene patience of certain victors."

Plot: The skeleton on which the other aspects of a story hang. Plots are made from the challenges, conflicts, and problems faced by the main characters. The most exciting plots are the ones in which the action is continually rising, building suspense, and finally leading to some sort of a climax. Episodic plots are accounts of a series of events as with such memoirs as James Herriot's *All Creatures Great and Small* and Anita Lobel's *No Pretty Pictures.*

Point of view: The vantage point and the distance from which the author decides to tell the story. The point of view that gives the author the most freedom is the one called omniscient or "all knowing," in which authors can plant themselves anywhere in the story, including inside characters' minds. With first-person point of view, the author speaks through the voice of a particular character. While this has the advantage of sounding authentic and personal, only one character's thoughts and observations can be given. Some authors get around this limitation by writing different chapters through the voices of different characters. Third-person point of view is more objective and is used for nonfiction as well as for many fictional stories. In YA books, the third-person narrator is often a character in the story who is writing about another "more interesting" or "more extreme" character.

Protagonists: The main characters in stories, the ones with which readers identify. Novels for young readers usually include only one or two protagonists because the stories are shorter and less complex than something like Leo Tolstoy's *War and Peace*. Protagonist-against-another is the kind of plot in which two people are in conflict with each other as are Louise and Caroline in Katherine Paterson's *Jacob Have I Loved* and Rambo and the sheriff in David Morrell's *First Blood*. Protagonist-against-nature stories are often accounts of true adventures such as Piers Paul Read's *Alive: The Story of the Andes Survivors*, Thor Heyerdahl's *The "RA" Expeditions*, and Steve Callahan's *Adrift: Seventy-Six Days Lost at Sea*. Protagonist-against-self is a common plot in young adult literature because so many stories recount rites of passage in which the protagonist comes to a new understanding or level of maturity. In Paula Fox's *One-Eyed Cat*, the conflict takes place inside the mind and heart of 11-year-old Ned, who has to come to terms with the fact that when he tried out his new gun, he partially blinded his neighbor's cat. Protagonist-against-society stories often feature members of minority groups whose personal struggles relate to tensions between their ethnic groups and the larger society. Examples include Chaim Potok's *My Name Is Asher Lev* and *The Chosen*, Gary Soto's *Baseball in April* and *Jesse*, Louise Erdrich's *Love Medicine*, and Marie Lee's *Finding My Voice*.

Setting: The context of time and place. Setting is more important in some genres than in others. Fantasies are usually set in the far past or in some place where people have never been, while most science fiction stories are set in the future or in outer space. See also **Backdrop** and **Integral Settings**.

Static character: One whose personality and actions stay basically the same throughout the story. Because in young adult literature the focus is on the young protagonist, most adult characters (parents, teachers, friends, etc.) are portrayed as static.

Stereotype: Literally a printing process through which an image is created over and over again. When reviewers say that an author's characters are stereotypes, they are probably making a negative criticism. However, at least some characters must be stereotyped because stories would fall under their own weight if authors had to start from scratch in developing each character. For the sake of efficiency, many background characters are stereotypes. To solve the problem of always having the same people stereotyped, contemporary authors are making an effort to feature as main characters many of those who have previously been ignored or relegated to stereotypes.

Stock characters: Stereotyped characters that authors can use in the way that shoppers pluck items from the well-stocked shelves of grocery stores. While a laughingstock is an object of ridicule, other stock characters include villains, tramps, bad boys, and little princesses.

Style: The way a story is written in contrast to what it is about. No two authors have exactly the same style because with writing, just as with appearance, behavior, and personal belongings, style consists of the unique blending of all the choices each individual makes. From situation to situation, these choices may differ, but they are enough alike that the styles of particular authors, such as Kurt Vonnegut, Jr., Richard Brautigan, and E. L. Doctorow are recognizable from book to book. Style is also influenced by the nature of the story being told. For example, Ursula K. Le Guin used a different style when she wrote the realistic *Very Far Away From Anywhere Else* from the one she used when she wrote her fantasy *A Wizard of Earthsea*. Nevertheless, in both books she relied on the particular writing techniques that she likes and is skilled at using. J. D. Salinger's *The Catcher in the Rye* has had such an influence on the style of writing about young protagonists that every year promotional materials or reviews compare two or three new books to *Catcher*.

Symbol: An item that is itself but also stands for something else. An example is the title of Linda Sue Parks's *A Single Shard*, in which the one piece of the master's pottery that Tree-Ear manages to deliver to the emperor symbolizes the great challenge that the boy faced on his journey.

Theme: A central idea that ties a story together and answers such questions as what the story means and what there is to think about when it is all over. Some authors are explicit in developing a theme, even expressing part of it in the title as did Maya Angelou with *All God's Children Need Traveling Shoes* and Virginia Euwer Wolff with *Make Lemonade*. Books may have more than one theme, but usually the secondary themes are less important to the story.

Tone: The author's attitude toward the subject and the readers. Biblical language may lend weight and dignity to a book as with James Herriot's title *All Creatures Great and Small* or Claude Brown's *Manchild in the Promised Land*. Exaggeration or hyperbole may communicate a flip tone as in Ellen Conford's title *If This Is Love, I'll Take Spaghetti* and Ron Koertge's *Where the Kissing Never Stops*.

Book Selection Guides

The following sources are designed to aid professionals in the selection and evaluation of books and other materials for young adults. We attempted to include sources with widely varying emphases, but, in addition to these sources—most of which appear at regular intervals—many specialized lists are prepared by committees and individuals in response to current and/or local needs. Readers are advised to check on the availability of such lists with librarians and teachers. Also, publications for adults such as *The New York Times Book Review* and *Smithsonian* magazine give attention to books for children and teenagers, especially in the weeks prior to Christmas when people are looking for gift ideas.

Simply by typing the names into a search engine, we checked the websites for all of these publications (August 1, 2007) and were happy to see how much information they each provide online. Some require an online subscription to read the full journal, but many provide a surprising amount of information simply for the looking.

The ALAN Review (Assembly on Literature for Adolescents). National Council of Teachers of English. Order from NCTE, 1111 W. Kenyon Road, Urbana, IL 61801. Subscribers need not be members of NCTE.

Since 1973, this publication, which is devoted entirely to adolescent literature, has appeared three times a year. Current editors are James Blasingame, Jr., from Arizona State University, and Lori Atkins Goodson from Manhattan, Kansas. Each issue contains approximately fifty "Clip and File" reviews written by ALAN members who are mostly secondary school teachers or librarians. Also included are feature articles, news announcements, and occasional reviews of professional books.

Booklist. American Library Association, 50 E. Huron Street, Chicago, IL 60611. Website: www.ala.org.

Reviews, which constitute a recommendation for library purchase, are written by professional staff members, who also attach a YA designation to selected adult titles. Stephanie Zviran is the current YA editor, with Hazel Rochman being a contributing editor. The "Books for Youth" section is divided for older, middle, and young readers. Exceptional books are given starred reviews and sometimes special features on related books. The end-of-the-year "Editors' Choice" issue is especially useful as are the lists of "Best Books" compiled by various committees affiliated with the American Library Association. Check the website for several lists related to young adults.

Books for the Teen Age. Published annually by Office of Young Adult Services, New York Public Library. Order from Office of Branch Libraries: New York Public Library, 455 Fifth Avenue, New York, NY 10016.

The over 1,000 recommendations in this booklet come from the young adult librarians in the eighty branches of the New York Public Library. Annotations are minimal, grouping is by subject with titles and authors indexed. Young adults are invited to enter an art contest for each year's cover.

Books for You: An Annotated Booklist for Senior High, Your Reading: An Annotated Booklist for Middle School/Junior High, and *High Interest—Easy Reading: An Annotated Booklist for Middle School* and *Senior High School*. National Council of Teachers of English, 1111 Kenyon Road, Urbana, IL 61801.

Committees of English teachers put these books together every few years. They are written for direct use by students and contain concise annotations for between 200 and 1,000 recommended books organized under such categories as "Growing Up," "Issues of Our Time," and "Sports." Kylene Beers and Teri Lesesne have been among the recent editors.

Bulletin of the Center for Children's Books. Johns Hopkins University Press, 2715 N. Charles Street, Baltimore, Maryland 21218-4363. Website: http://bccb.lis.uiuc.edu/

This is the journal founded by Zena Sutherland and published by the University of Chicago Press. When Chicago's Graduate Library School closed, the *Bulletin* moved to the University of Illinois in Urbana-Champaign but is officially published by Johns Hopkins University Press for the Graduate School of Library and Information Science at the University of Illinois. In each issue staff members review approximately sixty new books, with approximately twenty being identified as appropriate for grades nine through twelve. Reviews are coded with *R* standing for "recommended," *Ad* for "additional title if topic is needed," *M* for "marginal," and *NR* for "not recommended." The website reprints starred reviews and each month features a theme-based list of a dozen recommended titles.

Children's Literature in Education: An International Quarterly. Kluwer Academic/Human Sciences Press, 233 Spring Street, New York, NY 10013-1578.

In this British/American cooperative effort, the editors show a preference for substantive analysis rather than pedagogical advice or quick once-overs. A good proportion of the articles are about YA authors and their works. The table of contents is printed online and access is given to selected articles.

English Journal. National Council of Teachers of English, 1111 Kenyon Road, Urbana, IL 61801.

This is the largest journal published by NCTE with its audience being mainly high school English teachers. It appears six times a year and frequently has articles about young adult literature, plus a regular column on young adult books.

Horn Book Magazine. Horn Book, Inc., 11 Beacon Street, Suite 1000, Boston, MA 02108. Website: http://www.hbook.com

Since 1924, the *Horn Book Magazine* has been devoted to the critical analysis of children's literature. Many of the articles are written by noted authors, while the book reviews are staff written. Since Roger Sutton, a former YA librarian, became editor, more attention has been given to young adult literature. Big names in YA literature who are either regular contributors or reviewers include Betty Carter, Tim Wynne-Jones, and Patty Campbell. *Horn Book* cosponsors the Boston Globe Horn Book Awards and also prints a yearly "Fanfare" list of best books.

JAAL (Journal of Adolescent and Adult Literacy). International Reading Association, 800 Barksdale Road, Box 8139, Newark, DE 19711-8139.

The audience is high school reading teachers. Although most of the articles are reports on research in the teaching of reading, some articles focus on reading interests and literature. James Blasingame edits a regular review column on young adult literature.

Kirkus Reviews. Kirkus Service, Inc., 200 Park Avenue South, New York, NY 10003.

Kirkus reviews are approximately two hundred words long and are relied on throughout the publishing industry. The big advantage is timeliness and completeness made possible by twice-a-month issues.

Publishers Weekly. 245 W. 17th Street, New York, NY 10011. Website: http://www.publishersweekly.com.

While the focus is on the general world of adult book publishing, much of the information is relevant to anyone working with books; for example, what will company mergers mean to readers, what are the current best sellers, and who are the prize winners. Staff members write the reviews, which include some for children ages twelve and up.

School Library Journal. Editorial correspondence to *SLJ* Editor Brian Kenney, 360 Park Avenue South, New York, NY 10011; subscription correspondence to P.O. Box 5670, Harlan, Iowa 51995-1170. Website: http://www.slj.com.

SLJ is the most comprehensive of the review media. In monthly installments, it used to try to review all books published for young people, but as the numbers have increased it has begun to group books that are published in series or sets. Still, it publishes more than 4,000 reviews per year with about one-third of them being for readers twelve and older. Advertisements and feature articles provide good information along with the reviews, which are written by a panel of four hundred librarians. A starred review or inclusion on the December best books list, or both, signifies an exceptional book.

Teacher Librarian: The Journal for School Library Professionals. Published by Scarecrow Press. 4501 Forbes Blvd., Suite 200, Lanham, MD 20706. Website: www.teacherlibrarian.com.

For over thirty years, *TL* has published both feature articles and regular columns about issues, concerns, and materials for K–12 school librarians. It just started a new Wiki for online reviewing www.seedwiki.com/wiki/lmc_reviews.

Voices from the Middle. National Council of Teachers of English. Order from NCTE, 1111 W. Kenyon Road, Urbana, IL 61801.

This relatively new quarterly is sponsored by the National Council of Teachers of English for teachers in middle and junior high schools. It regularly includes information about YA lit appropriate for tweeners.

VOYA (Voice of Youth Advocates). Scarecrow Press, Inc. 4720A Boston Way, Lanham, MD 20706.

Published every other month, this is a journal prepared mainly for librarians who work with teenagers. It was founded in 1978 by Mary K. Chelton and Dorothy Broderick. VOYA consistently has good articles on current trends in literature and youth services in libraries. The editors and contributors do an especially good job with fantasy and science fiction.

YALS (Young Adult Library Services) is sponsored by the American Library Association, 50 E. Huron Street, Chicago, IL 60611. Website: http://www.ala.org.

In its history, this journal has been called *Top of the News* (before 1987) and *JOYS: Journal of Youth Services* (between 1987 and 2002). In its earlier forms, it covered both children's and YA literature as well as research and developments of interest to librarians. *YALS* now appears biannually and is sent to all YA librarians who belong to ALA. Its focus is strictly YA. A recent issue, for example, had as its theme, Go Graphic!

Some Outstanding Books and Articles about Young Adult Literature

Books

History and Young Adult Literature

Avery, Gillian. *Behold the Child: American Children and Their Books, 1621–1922.* Bodley House, 1994.

Avery, Gillian. *Childhood's Pattern: A Study of the Heroes and Heroines of Childhood's Fiction.* Hodder and Stoughton, 1975.

Barnhouse, Rebecca. *The Middle Ages in Literature for Youth: A Guide and Resource Book.* Scarecrow, 2004.

Berg, Rebecca L. *The Great Depression in Literature for Youth, A Geographical Study of Families and Young Lives: A Guide and Resource Book.* Scarecrow, 2004.

Billman, Carol. *The Secret of the Stratemeyer Syndicate: Nancy Drew, the Hardy Boys, and the Million Dollar Fiction Factory.* Ungar, 1986.

Blanck, Jacob. *Peter Parley to Penrod: A Bibliographical Description of the Best-Loved American Juvenile Books.* Bowker, 1956.

Cadogan, Mary, and Patricia Craig. *You're a Brick, Angela! A New Look at Girls' Fiction from 1839 to 1975.* Gollancz, 1976. Delightful funny and rich.

Campbell, Patricia. *Sex Education Books for Young Adults, 1892–1979.* Bowker, 1979. Accurate and funny. Most of us can only envy Campbell's prose.

Campbell, Patricia. *Two Pioneers of Young Adult Library Service.* Scarecrow, 1999. On Mabel Williams and Margaret A. Edwards.

Carrier, Esther Jane. *Fiction in Public Libraries, 1876–1900.* Scarecrow, 1965.

Carrier, Esther Jane. *Fiction in Public Libraries, 1900–1950.* Libraries Unlimited, 1985.

Cart, Michael. *From Romance to Realism: 50 Years of Growth and Change in Young Adult Literature.* Harper, 1996.

Cech, John, ed. *American Writers for Children, 1900–1960. Dictionary of American Biography,* Vol. 22. Gale Research, 1983.

Children's Fiction, 1876–1984. 2 Vols. Bowker, 1984.

Collins, Max Allan. *The History of Mystery.* Collector's Press, 2001.

Crouch, Marcus. *The Nesbit Tradition: The Children's Novel in England, 1945–1970.* Ernest Benn, 1972.

Crouch, Marcus. *Treasure Seekers and Borrowers: Children's Books in Britain, 1900–1960.* Library Association, 1962.

Crowe, Chris. *More Than a Game: Sports Literature for Young Adults.* Scarecrow, 2004.

Darling, Richard. *The Rise of Children's Book Reviewing in America: 1865–1881.* Bowker 1968. A seminal book.

Darton, F. J. Harvey. *Children's Books in England: Five Centuries of Social Use.* 2nd ed. Cambridge University Press, 1958. First published in 1932. Helpful, though a bit stuffy.

Deane, Paul. *Mirrors of American Culture: Children's Fiction Series in the Twentieth Century.* Scarecrow, 1991.

Demers, Patricia. *A Garland from the Golden Age: An Anthology of Children's Literature from 1850 to 1900.* Toronto: Oxford University Press, 1983.

Dyer, Carolyn Stewart, and Nancy Tillman Romalov, eds. *Rediscovering Nancy Drew*. University of Iowa Press, 1995. Papers from the 1993 Nancy Drew Conference.

Egoff, Sheila. *The Republic of Childhood: A Critical Guide to Canadian Children's Literature*, 2nd ed. Oxford University Press, 1975.

Egoff, Sheila. *Worlds Within: Children's Fantasy from the Middle Ages*. ALA, 1988.

Erisman, Fred. *Boys' Books, Boys' Dreams, and the Mystique of Flight*. Texas Christian Press, 2006.

Estes, Glenn E., ed. *American Writers for Children before 1900*. Dictionary of Literary Biography, Vol. 42. Gale Research, 1985.

Foster, Shirley, and Judy Simmons, eds. *What Katy Read: Feminist Re-Readings of "Classic" Stories for Girls*. University of Iowa Press, 1995.

Girls' Series Books: A Checklist of Hardback Books Published 1900–1975. Children's Literature Research Collection, University of Minnesota Library, 1978. Basic for any study of early girls' books. Much like Hudson's work (see Hudson).

Gorham, Deborah. *The Victorian Girl and the Feminine Ideal*. Indiana University Press, 1982.

Griswold, Jerry. *Audacious Kids: Coming of Age in America's Classic Children's Books*. Oxford University Press, 1992.

Helbig, Althea K., and Agnes Perkins. *Dictionary of American Children's Fiction, 1859–1959*. Greenwood, 1985.

Howarth, Patrick. *Play Up and Play the Game: The Heroes of Popular Fiction*. Eyre Methuen, 1973.

Hudson, Harry K. *A Bibliography of Hard-Cover Boys' Books*, rev. ed. Data Print, 1977. Basic for any study of early boys' books—and great fun to skim through.

Inness, Sherrie A., ed. *Nancy Drew and Company: Culture, Gender, and Girls' Series*. Bowling Green State University Popular Press, 1999.

Jackson, Mary V. *Engines of Instruction, Mischief, and Magic: Children's Literature in England from Its Beginnings to 1839*. University of Nebraska Press, 1989.

Johannssen, Albert. *The House of Beadle and Adams and Its Dime and Nickel Novels: The Story of a Vanished Literature*, 3 Vols. University of Oklahoma Press, 1950–1952.

Johnson, Deidre. *Edward Stratemeyer and the Stratemeyer Syndicate*. Twayne, 1993. Anyone working on early young adult literature owes a debt to Johnson.

Johnson, Deidre, ed. *Stratemeyer Pseudonyms and Series Books: An Annotated Checklist of Stratemeyer and Stratemeyer Syndicate Publications*. Greenwood, 1982.

Jones, Daryl. *The Dime Novel Western*. Bowling Green State University Popular Press, 1978.

Kensinger, Faye Riter. *Children of the Series and How They Grew*. Bowling Green State University Popular Press, 1987.

Kiefer, Monica. *American Children through Their Books, 1700–1835*. University of Pennsylvania Press, 1948.

Kilgour, Raymond L. *Lee and Shepard: Publishers for the People*. Shoe String, 1965.

Kloes, Christine A. *After Alice: A Hundred Years of Children's Reading in Britain*. Library Association, 1977.

MacLeod, Anne Scott. *American Childhood: Essays on Children's Literature of the Nineteenth and Twentieth Centuries*. University of Georgia Press, 1994.

MacLeod, Anne Scott. *A Moral Tale: Children's Fiction and American Culture, 1820–1860*. Archon, 1975.

McFarlane, Leslie. *Ghost of the Hardy Boys: An Autobiography of Leslie McFarlane*. Two Continents, 1976.

Mason, Bobbie Ann. *The Girl Sleuth: A Feminist Guide*. Feminist Press, 1975. Delightful and perceptive.

Meigs, Cornelia, H.S. Commager, A. Eaton, E. Nesbitt, and R. H. Viguers. *A Critical History of Children's Literature*, rev. ed. Macmillan, 1969. Encyclopedic and often most helpful.

Mott, Frank Luther. *Golden Multitudes: The Story of Best Sellers in the United States*. Macmillan, 1947.

Nilolajeva, Neva, ed. *Aspects and Issues in the History of Children's Literature*. Greenwood, 1995.

Nye, Russel. *The Unembarrassed Muse: The Popular Arts in America*. Dial, 1970.

Oriad, Michael. *Dreaming of Heroes: American Sports Fiction 1868–1980*. Nelson-Hall, 1982.

Papashvily, Helen Waite. *All the Happy Endings*. Harper, 1956.

Pattee, Fred Lewis. *The Feminist Fifties*. Appleton, 1940.

Perry, Phyllis J. *Teaching Fantasy Novels: From* The Hobbit *to* Harry Potter and the Goblet of Fire. Teachers Ideas Press, 2003.

Reynolds, Kimberley. *Girls Only? Gender and Popular Children's Fiction in Britain, 1880–1910*. Temple University Press, 1990.

Richardson, Selma K., ed. *Research about Nineteenth-Century Children and Books*. University of Illinois Graduate School of Library Science, 1980.

Salmon, Edward. *Juvenile Literature as It Is*. Drane, 1888. Old and significant.

Sloane, William. *Children's Books in England and America in the Seventeenth Century*. Columbia University Press, 1955.

Stonely, Peter. *Consumerism and American Girls' Fiction, 1860–1940*. Cambridge University Press, 2003.

Sullivan, C. W. III. *Welsh Myth in Modern Fiction*. Greenwood, 1989.

Thwaite, Mary F. *From Primer to Pleasure in Reading: An Introduction to the History of Children's Books in England from the Invention of Printing to 1914*. Horn Book, 1972.

Townsend, John Rowe. *25 Years of British Children's Books*. National Book League, 1977. A sixty-page pamphlet worth searching for.

Wishy, Bernard. *The Child and the Republic: The Dawning of Modern American Child Nurture*. University of Pennsylvania Press, 1968.

Commentary and Criticism on Young Adult Literature

Aronson, Marc. *Beyond the Pale: New Essays for a New Era*. Scarecrow, 2003.

Barron, Neal, ed. *Fantasy and Horror: A Critical and Historical Guide to Literature, Illustration, Film, TV, Radio and the Internet*. Scarecrow, 1999.

Bauer, Marion Dane. *What's Your Story? A Young Person's Guide to Writing Fiction.* Clarion, 1992.

Bilz, Rachelle Lasky. *Life Is Tough: Guys, Growing Up, and Young Adult Literature.* Scarecrow, 2004.

Broderick, Dorothy. *Images of the Black in Children's Fiction.* Bowker, 1973.

Cameron, Eleanor. *The Green and Burning Tree: On the Writing and Enjoyment of Children's Books.* Dutton, 1993.

Cart, Michael, and Christine A. Jenkins. *The Heart Has Its Reasons: Young Adult Literature with Gay/Lesbian/Queer Context, 1969–2004.* Scarecrow, 2006.

Carter, Betty, and Richard Abrahamson. *Nonfiction for Young Adults: From Delight to Wisdom.* Oryx, 1990.

Chambers, Aidan. *Introducing Books to Children,* 2nd ed. Horn Book, 1983.

Chambers, Aidan. *The Reluctant Reader.* Pergamon, 1969. This reads better the older it gets (or the older we get). Practical ideas about hard-to-reach students.

Children's Literature Review. Gale Research, 1973.

Christian-Smith, Linda K. *Becoming a Woman through Romance.* Rutledge, 1990.

Dixon, Bob. *Catching Them Young: Political Ideas in Children's Fiction.* Pluto, 1977.

Dixon, Bob. *Catching Them Young: Sex, Race, and Class in Children's Fiction.* Pluto, 1977.

Egoff, Sheila A. *Thursday's Child: Trends and Patterns in Contemporary Children's Literature.* ALA, 1981.

Ettinger, John R., and Diana L. Spirit, eds. *Choosing Books for Young People, Vol. 2: A Guide to Criticism and Bibliography, 1976–1984.* ALA, 1982.

Eyre, Frank. *British Children's Books in the Twentieth Century.* Dutton, 1971.

Fisher, Margery. *The Bright Face of Danger.* Hodder and Hodder, 1986.

Fox, Geoff, Graham Hammond, Terry Jones, Frederick Smith, and Kenneth Sterck, eds. *Writers, Critics, and Children: Articles from Children's Literature Education.* Agathon, 1976.

Harrison, Barbara, and Gregory Maguire, eds. *Innocence and Experience: Essays and Conversations on Children's Literature.* Lothrop, 1987.

Hazard, Paul. *Books, Children and Men.* Trans. Marguerite Mitchell. Horn Book, 1944.

Hearne, Betsy, ed. *The Zena Sutherland Lectures.* Clarion, 1993.

Hearne, Betsy, and Marilyn Kaye, eds. *Celebrating Children's Books: Essays on Children's Literature in Honor of Zena Sutherland.* Lothrop, 1981.

Hendrickson, Linnae. *Children's Literature: A Guide to the Criticism.* Hall, 1987.

Hogan, Walter. *Humor in Young Adult Literature: A Time for Laughs.* Scarecrow, 2005.

Horning, Kathleen. *From Cover to Cover: Evaluating and Reviewing Children's Books.* Harper, 1997.

Howard, Elizabeth F. *America as Story: Historical Fiction for the Secondary Schools.* ALA, 1988.

Hunt, Peter. *Criticism, Theory, and Children's Literature.* Basil Blackwell, 1991.

Hunt, Peter. *An Introduction to Children's Literature.* Oxford University Press, 1994.

Hunter, Mollie. *The Pied Piper Syndrome and Other Essays.* Harper, 1992.

Hunter, Mollie. *Talent Is Not Enough: Mollie Hunter on Writing for Children.* Harper, 1976.

Inglis, Fred. *The Promise of Happiness: Value and Meaning in Children's Fiction.* Cambridge University Press, 1981.

Kelly, Patricia P., and Robert C. Small, eds. *Two Decades of the ALAN Review.* NCTE, 1999.

Kohn, Rita, comp. *Once Upon . . . a Time for Young People and Their Books: An Annotated Resource Guide.* Scarecrow, 1986.

Lentz, Millicent, and Ramona M. Mahood, eds. *Young Adult Literature: Background and Criticism.* ALA, 1980.

Lesnick-Oberstein, Karin. *Children's Literature: Criticism and the Fictional Child.* Clarendon, 1994.

Lukens, Rebecca. J. *A Critical Handbook of Children's Literature.* Scott, Foresman, 1976.

Lynn, Ruth Nadelman. *Fantasy Literature for Children and Young Adults.* Bowker, 1989.

MacCann, Donnarae, and Gloria Woodward, eds. *The Black American in Books for Children: Readings on Racism.* Scarecrow, 1972.

MacCann, Donnarae. *White Supremacy in Children's Literature: Characteristics of African-Americans, 1830–1900.* Garland, 1998.

McCallum, Robyn. *Ideologies of Identities in Adolescent Fiction: The Dialogic Construction of Subjectivity.* Garland, 1999.

Moore, John Noell. *Interpreting Young Adult Literature: Literary Theory in the Secondary Classroom.* Boynton/Cook, 1997.

Nikolajeva, Maria. *Aspects and Issues in the History of Children's Literature.* Greenwood, 1995.

Nikolajeva, Maria. *Children's Literature Coming of Age: Towards a New Aesthetic.* Garland, 1996.

Nikolajeva, Maria. *From Mythic to Linear: Time in Children's Literature.* Scarecrow, 2000.

Nikolajeva, Maria. *The Rhetoric of Character in Children's Literature.* Scarecrow, 2002.

Rochman, Hazel. *Against Borders: Promoting Books for a Multiracial World.* ALA, 1993.

Rohn, Suzanne. *Children's Literature: An Annotated Bibliography of the History and Criticism.* Garland, 1981.

Shields, Nancy E. *Index to Literary Criticism for Young Adults.* Scarecrow, 1988.

Silvey, Anita. *500 Great Books for Teens.* Houghton Mifflin, 2006.

Sloan, Glenda. *The Child as Critic.* Teachers College Press, 1975. Northrop Frye's theories applied to YA literature.

Soter, Anna. *Young Adult Literature and New Literary Theory.* Teachers College Press, 1999.

Spencer, Pam. *What Do Young Adults Read Next? A Reader's Guide to Fiction for Young Adults,* 2 Vols. Gale Research, 1997.

Stensland, Anna Lee. *Literature by and about American Indians: An Annotated Bibliography,* 2nd ed. NCTE, 1970.

Street, Douglas, ed. *Children's Novels and the Movies.* Ungar, 1984.

Stringer, Sharon. *Conflict and Connection: The Psychology of Young Adult Literature*. Heinmann, 1997.

Sullivan, C. W. *Science Fiction for Young Readers*. Greenwood, 1993.

Sullivan, Edward T. *The Holocaust in Literature for Youth: A Guide and Resource Book*. Scarecrow, 1999.

Sutherland, Zena, ed. *The Arbuthnot Lecture, 1970–1979*. ALA, 1980.

Townsend, John Rowe. *Written for Children: An Outline of English-Language Children's Literature*, 3rd ed. Lippincott, 1988. Townsend's finest work.

Tucker, Nicholas, ed. *Suitable for Children? Controversies in Children's Literature*. University of California Press, 1976.

Yolen, Jane. *Touch Magic: Fantasy, Faerie, and Folklore in the Literature of Childhood*. Philomel, 1981.

Zipes, Jack, ed. *The Oxford Encyclopedia of Children's Literature*, 4 Vols. Oxford University Press, 2006.

Zitlow, Connie. *Lost Masterworks of Young Adult Literature*. Scarecrow, 2002.

Using Young Adult Literature in Libraries and Classrooms

Applebee, Arthur N. *Literature in the Secondary School: Studies in Curriculum and Instruction in the United States*. NCTE, 1993.

Applebee, Arthur N. *Tradition and Reform in the Teaching of English*. NCTE, 1974.

Appleman, Deborah. *Critical Encounters in High School English: Teaching Literary Theory to Adolescents*. Teachers College Press, 2000.

Beach, Richard. *A Teacher's Introduction to Reader-Response Theories*. NCTE, 1993.

Blasingame, James. *Books That Don't Bore 'em: Young Adult Books That Speak to This Generation*. Scholastic, 2007.

Bodart, Joni. *Booktalking and School Visiting for Young Adult Audiences*. Wilson, 1980.

Bodart, Joni. *Booktalk 2: Booktalking for All Ages and Audiences*. Wilson, 1985.

Books for the Teen Age. New York Public Library, published annually.

Brown, Jean A., and Elaine C. Stephens. *Teaching Young Adult Literature: Sharing the Connection*. Wadsworth, 1995.

Burton, Dwight. *Literature Study in the High Schools*, 3rd ed. Holt, 1970. For many teachers and librarians this was THE book that introduced them to young adult literature.

Carlsen, G. Robert. *Books and the Teen-Age Reader*, 2nd ed. Harper, 1980.

Carr, Jo, ed. *Beyond Fact: Nonfiction for Children and Young People*. ALA, 1982.

Cawelti, John G. *Adventure, Mystery, and Romance: Formula Stories as Art and Popular Culture*. University of Chicago Press, 1976.

Chambers, Aidan. *Introducing Books to Children*. Heinemann, 1973.

Dunning, A. Stephen. "A Definition of the Role of the Junior Novel Based on Analyses of Thirty Selected Novels." Ph.D. dissertation, Florida State University, 1959.

Edwards, Margaret A. *The Fair Garden and the Swarm of Beasts: The Library and the Young Adult*, rev. ed. Hawthorn, 1974. The problems but mostly the joys of working in a library with young people.

Eiss, Harry, ed. *Literature for Young People on War and Peace: An Annotated Bibliography*. Greenwood, 1989.

Elliott, Joan B., ed. *Young Adult Literature in the Classroom: Reading It, Teaching It, Loving It*. IRA, 2002.

Fader, Daniel N., and Elton B. McNeil. *Hooked on Books: Program and Proof*. Berkeley, 1968.

Farrell, Edmund, and James R. Squire, eds. *Transactions with Literature: A Fifty-Year Perspective*. NCTE, 1990.

Field, Carolyn W., ed. *Special Collections in Children's Literature*. ALA, 1982.

Gillespie, John. *More Juniorplots: A Guide for Teachers and Librarians*. Bowker, 1977.

Gillespie, John T., and Catherine Barr. *Best Books for Middle School and Junior High Readers, Grades 6–9*. Libraries Unlimited, 2004.

Gillespie, John T., and Diana L. Lembo. *Juniorplots: A Book Talk Manual for Teachers and Librarians*. Bowker, 1967.

Gillespie, John T., and Corinne Naden. *Juniorplots 3: A Book Talk Guide for Use with Readers Ages 12–16*. Bowker, 1987.

Gillespie, John T., and Corrine Naden. *The Newbery Companion: Booktalk and Related Materials for Newbery Medal and Honor Books*. Libraries Unlimited, 1996.

Gillespie, John T., and Corinne Naden. *Seniorplots: A Book Talk Guide for Use with Readers Ages 15–18*. Bowker, 1989.

Gilmore, Barry. *Speaking Volumes: How to Get Students Discussing Books—And Much More*. Heinemann, 2006.

Goebel, Bruce A. *Reading Native American Literature: A Teacher's Guide*. NCTE, 2004.

Heller, Frieda M., and Lou LaBrant. *The Librarian and the Teacher of English*. ALA, 1938.

Hertz, Sarah, and Donald Gallo. *From Hamlet to Hinton: Building Bridges between Young Adult Literature and the Classics*, 2nd ed. Greenwood, 2005.

Isaac, Megar Lynn. *Heirs to Shakespeare: Reinventing the Bard in Young Adult Literature*. Heinemann, 2000.

Kaywell, Joan F., ed. *Adolescent Literature as a Complement to the Classics*. Christopher-Gordon, 1993.

Lesesne, Teri. *Making the Match: The Right Book for the Right Reader at the Right Time, Grades 4–12*. Stenhouse, 2003.

Lesesne, Teri. *Naked Reading: Uncovering What Tweens Need to Become Lifelong Readers*. Stenhouse, 2006.

Marshall, Margaret R. *Libraries and Literature for Teenagers*. Deutsch, 1975.

McCann, Thomas M. *Reflective Teaching, Reflective Learning: How to Develop Critically Engaged Reading, Writing, and Speaking*. Heinemann, 2005.

Monseau, Virginia, and Gary M. Salvner, eds. *Reading Their World: The Young Adult Novel In the Classroom*. Boynton/Cook, 1992.

Moore, John Noell. *Interpreting Young Adult Literature: Literary Theory in the Secondary Classroom*. Boynton/Cook, 1997.

Peck, David, *Novels of Initiation: A Guidebook for Teaching Literature to Adolescents*. Teachers College Press, 1989.

Peck, Richard. *Love and Death at the Mall: Teaching and Writing for the Literate Young*. Delacorte, 1994.

Petitt, Dorothy. "A Study of the Qualities of Literary Excellence which Characterize Selected Fiction for Younger Adolescents." Ph.D. dissertation, University of Minnesota, 1961.

Probst, Robert. *Adolescent Literature: Response and Analysis*. Merrill, 1984.

Purves, Alan C., and Richard Beach. *Literature and the Reader*. NCTE, 1972.

Purves, Alan C., Theresa Rogers, and Anna O. Soter. *How Porcupines Make Love II: Teaching a Response-Centered Curriculum*. Longman, 1990.

Rochman, Hazel. *Tales of Love and Terror: Booktalking the Classics, Old and New*. ALA, 1987.

Rosenberg, Betty. *Genreflecting: A Guide to Reading Interests in Genre Fiction*, 2nd ed., Libraries Unlimited, 1987.

Rosenblatt, Louise. *Literature as Exploration*, 4th ed., MLA, 1983.

Rosenblatt, Louise. *The Reader, the Text, and the Poem: The Transactional Theory of the Literary Work*. Southern Illinois University Press, 1978.

Scholes, Robert. *Textual Power: Literary Theory and the Teaching of English*. Yale University Press, 1985.

Spencer, Pam. *What Do Young Adults Read Next? A Reader's Guide to Fiction for Young Adults*. Gale Research, 1994.

Trupe, Alice. *Thematic Guide to Young Adult Literature*. Greenwood, 2006.

Books about Literary Genres

Aldiss, Brian, and David Wingrove. *Trillion Year Spree: The History of Science Fiction*. Atheneum, 1986.

Attebury, Brian. *The Fantasy Tradition in American Literature: From Irving to Le Guin*. Indiana University Press, 1980.

Barnhouse, Rebecca. *Recasting the Past: The Middle Ages in Young Adult Literature*. Heinemann, 2000.

Barron, Neil. *Anatomy of Wonder: A Critical Guide to Science Fiction*, 5th ed. Libraries Unlimited, 2004.

Burgess, Michael, and Jill H. Vassilakos, eds. *Murder in Retrospect: A Selective Guide to Historical Mystery Fiction*. Libraries Unlimited, 2005.

Brown, Joanne, and Nancy St. Clair. *The Distant Mirror: Reflections on Young Adult Historical Fiction*. Scarecrow, 2006.

Eiss, Harry, ed. *Literature for Young People on War and Peace: An Annotated Bibliography*. Greenwood, 1989.

Gannon, Michael B. *Blood, Bedlam, Bullets, and Bad Guys: A Reader's Guide to Adventure/Suspense Fiction*. Libraries Unlimited, 2004.

Gates, Pamela S., Susan B. Steffel, and Francis J. Molson, eds. *Fantasy Literature for Children and Young Adults*. Scarecrow, 2003.

Herald, Diana Tixier. *Fluent in Fantasy: A Guide to Reading Interests*. Libraries Unlimited, 2000.

Herald, Diana Tixier. *Strictly Science Fiction*. Libraries Unlimited, 2002.

Hintz, Carrie, and Elaine Ostry, eds. *Utopian and Dystopian Writing for Children and Young Adults*, Routledge, 2003.

Johannessen, Larry R. *Illumination Rounds: Teaching the Literature of the Vietnam War*. NCTE, 1992

Johnson, Sarah L. *Historical Fiction: A Guide to the Genre*. Libraries Unlimited, 2005.

Jones, Diana Wynne. *The Tough Guide to Fantasyland*, rev. ed. Penguin, 2006.

MacRae, Cathi Dunn. *Presenting Young Adult Fantasy Fiction*. Twayne, 1998.

Marcus, Leonard, ed. *The Wind in the Word: Conversations with Writers of Fantasy*. Candlewick, 2006.

Reid, Suzanne Elizabeth. *Presenting Young Adult Science Fiction*. Twayne, 1998.

Sandoz, Joli, and Joby Winans, eds. *Whatever It Takes: Women on Women's Sports*. Farrar, 1999.

Stableford, Brian. *The A to Z of Science Fiction Literature*. Scarecrow, 2005.

Stableford, Brian, *Historical Dictionary of Fantasy Literature*. Scarecrow, 2005.

Sullivan, C. W. III, ed. *Science Fiction for Young Readers*. Greenwood, 1993.

Sullivan, C. W. III, ed. *Young Adult Science Fiction*. Greenwood, 1999.

Taylor, Beverly, and Elizabeth Brewer. *The Return of King Arthur: British and American Literature Since 1900*. Barnes and Noble, 1983.

Taylor, Desmond. *The Juvenile Novel of World War II: An Annotated Bibliography*. Greenwood, 1994.

Thompson, Raymond H. *The Return from Avalon: A Study of the Arthurian Legend in Modern Fiction*. Greenwood, 1985.

Wee, Patricia Hachter, and Robert James Wee. *World War II in Literature for Youth: A Guide and Reference Book*. Scarecrow, 2004.

Authors of Young Adult Literature

Bondart, Joni Richards. *100 World-Class Thin Books, or What to Read When Your Book Report Is Due Tomorrow*. Libraries Unlimited, 1993.

Chevalier, Tracy. *Twentieth-Century Children's Writers*, 3rd ed. St. James Press, 1989.

Commire, Anne, ed. *Something about the Author*. Gale Research, 1971.

Commire, Anne, ed. *Yesterday's Authors of Books for Children*. Gale Research, 1977. Lives of authors who died before 1961.

de Montreville, Doris, and Elizabeth D. Crawford, eds. *Fourth Book for Junior Authors and Illustrators*. Wilson, 1978.

de Montreville, Doris, and Donna Hill, eds. *Third Book of Junior Authors*. Wilson, 1972.

Drew, Bernard A. *The 100 Most Popular Young Adult Authors: Biographical Sketches and Bibliographies*. Libraries Unlimited, 1996.

Estes, Glenn E., ed. *American Writers for Children Since 1960: Fiction. Dictionary of Literary Biography*, Vol. 52. Gale Research, 1986.

Estes, Glenn E., ed. *American Writers for Children Since 1960: Poets, Illustrators, and Nonfiction Authors. Dictionary of Literary Biography*, vol. 61. Gale Research, 1987.

Fuller, Muriel, ed. *More Junior Authors*. Wilson, 1963.

Gallo, Donald R., ed. *Authors Insights: Turning Teenagers into Readers and Writers*. Boynton/Cook, 1992.

Gallo, Donald R., ed., *Speaking for Ourselves: Autobiographical Sketches by Notable Authors of Books for Young Adults*. NCTE, 1990. In this and a 1993 sequel, nearly two hundred YA authors introduce themselves.

Helbig, Alethea K., and Agnes Regan Perkins, eds. *Dictionary of American Children's Fiction. 1960–1984*. Greenwood, 1986.

Helbig, Alethea K., and Agnes Regan Perkins, eds. *Dictionary of British Children's Fiction*. Greenwood, 1989.

Hipple, Ted, ed. *Writers for Young Adults*. 3 Vols. Scribner, 1997. Vol. 4, 2000.

Holtze, Sally Holmes, ed. *Fifth Book of Junior Authors and Illustrators*. Wilson, 1987.

Kirkpatrick, D. L., ed. *Twentieth-Century Children's Writers*, 3rd ed. Macmillan, 1990.

Kunitz, Stanley J., and Howard Haycraft, eds. *The Junior Book of Authors*, 2nd rev. ed. Wilson, 1951.

Pendergast, Tom, and Sara Pendergast, eds. *The St. James Guide to Young Adult Writers*. St. James, 1999.

Rees, David. *The Marble in the Water: Essays on Contemporary Writers of Fiction for Children and Young Adults*. Horn Book, 1980.

Rees, David. *Painted Desert, Green Shade: Essays on Contemporary Writers of Fiction for Children and Young Adults*. Horn Book, 1984.

Rees, David. *What Do Draculas Do? Essays on Contemporary Writers of Fiction for Children and Young Adults*. Scarecrow, 1990.

Rockman, Connie C., ed. *Eighth Book of Junior Authors and Illustrators*. Wilson, 2000.

Roginski, Jim. *Behind the Covers: Interviews with Authors and Illustrators of Books for Children and Young Adults*. Libraries Unlimited, 1985. Vol. 2, 1989.

Sarkissian, Adele, ed. *Writers for Young Adults: Biographies Master Index*. Gale Research, 1984.

Townsend, John Rowe. *A Sense of Story: Essays on Contemporary Writers for Children*. Lippincott, 1971.

Weiss, M. Jerry, ed. *From Writers to Students: The Pleasures and Pains of Writing*. IRA, 1979.

Wintle, Justin, and Emma Fisher, eds. *The Pied Pipers: Interviews with the Influential Creators of Children's Literature*. Paddington, 1974.

Books of Readings about Young Adult Literature

Broderick, Dorothy M., ed. *The VOYA Reader*. Scarecrow, 1990.

Egoff, Sheila, G. T. Stubbs, and L. F. Ashley, eds. *Only Connect: Readings in Children's Literature*, 2nd ed. Oxford University Press, 1980.

Salway, Lance, ed. *A Peculiar Gift: Nineteenth Century Writings on Books for Children*. Kestrel, 1976.

Varlejs, Jana, ed. *Young Adult Literature in the Seventies: A Selection of Readings*. Scarecrow, 1978.

Articles

History and Young Adult Literature

Alm, Richard S. "The Development of Literature for Adolescents." *School Review* 64 (April 1956): 172–177.

Cantwell, Robert. "A Sneering Laugh with the Bases Loaded." *Sports Illustrated* 16 (April 23, 1962): 73–75.

Carlsen, G. Robert. "Forty Years with Books and Teen-Age Readers." *Arizona English Bulletin* 18 (April 1976): 1–5.

Crandall, John C. "Patriotism and Humanitarian Reform in Children's Literature: 1825–1860." *American Quarterly* 21 (Spring 1969): 1–22.

Edwards, Margaret A. "The Rise of Teen-Age Reading." *Saturday Review of Literature* 37 (November 13, 1954): 88–89, 95.

Evans, Walter. "The All-American Boys: A Study of Boys' Sports Fiction." *Journal of Popular Culture* 6 (Summer 1972): 104–121.

"For It Was Indeed He." *Fortune* 9 (April 1934): 86–89, 193–194, 204, 206, 208–209. An important, influential, and biased article on Stratemeyer's Literary Syndicate.

Geller, Evelyn. "The Librarian as Censor." *Library Journal* 101 (June 1, 1976): 1255–1258.

Geller, Evelyn. "Tom Sawyer, Tom Bailey, and the Bad-Boy Genre." *Wilson Library Bulletin* 52 (November 1976): 245–250.

Green, Samuel S. "Sensational Fiction in Public Libraries." *Library Journal* 4 (September/October 1879): 345–355. Extraordinarily intelligent comments about young adults and their books. The entire issue is worth reading, particularly papers by T. W. Higginson (pp. 357–359), William Atkinson (pp. 359–362), and Mellen Chamberlain (pp. 362–366).

Hutchinson, Margaret, "Fifty Years of Young Adult Reading, 1921–1971." *Top of the News* 29 (November 1973): 24–53.

Kelly, R. Gordon. "American Children's Literature: An Historiographical Review." *American Literary Realism, 1870–1910* 5 (Spring 1973): 89–107.

LaBrant, Lou. "Diversifying the Matter." *English Journal* 40 (March 1951): 134–139.

Lapides, Linda F. "A Decade of Teen-Age Reading in Baltimore, 1960–1970." *Top of the News* 27 (Spring 1971): 278–291.

MacLeod, Anne. "For the Good of the Country: Cultural Values in American Juvenile Fiction, 1825–1860." *Children's Literature in Education* 5 (1976): 40–51.

McCue, Andy. "From Frank Merriwell to Henry Wiggen: A Modest History of Baseball Fiction." *SABR* (Society for American Baseball Research) *Review* 5 (1990): 54–71.

McEntegart, Pete, et al. "The Top 100 Sports Books of All Time." *Sports Illustrated* 97 (December 16, 2002): 126–248.

Messenger, Christian K. "Sport in the Dime Novel." *Journal of American Culture* 3 (Fall 1978): 494–505.

Phelps, William Lyon. "The Virtue of the Second-Rate." *English Journal* 16 (January 1927): 10–14. A marvelous article.

Popkin, Zelda F. "The Finer Things in Life." *Harpers* 164 (April 1932): 606–611. Contrasts between what young adults like to read and what parents and other adults want kids to read.

Radnor, Rebecca. "You're Being Paged Loudly in the Kitchen: Teen-Age Literature of the Forties and Fifties." *Journal of Popular Culture* 11 (Spring 1978): 289–299.

Repplier, Agnes. "Little Pharisees in Fiction." *Scribner's Magazine* 20 (December 1896): 718–724. The didactic and joyless goody-goody school of YA fiction in the last half of the nineteenth century.

Scroggins, Margaret C. "Do Young People Want Books?" *Wilson Library Bulletin for Librarians* 11 (September 1936): 17–20, 24.

Shadiow, Linda K. "The Development of the Young Adult Novel: A Progression of Lessons and Lives," in *Reading Their World: The Young Adult Novel in the Classroom*, ed. Virginia R. Monseau and Gary N. Salvner, Boynton/Cook Heinemann, 1992, pp. 48–62. A fine summary of who and what.

Small, Dora V. "Extensive Reading in Junior High School: A Survey of Teacher Preparation." *English Journal* 19 (June 1930): 449–462.

Trensky, Anne. "The Bad Boy in Nineteenth-Century American Fiction." *Georgia Review* 27 (Winter 1973): 503–517.

Thurber, Samuel. "Voluntary Reading in the Classical High School: From the Pupil's Point of View." *School Review* 13 (February 1905): 168–179. Thurber was a leader of English Education long before NCTE, and his many articles are worth any teacher's time.

Commentary and Criticism on Young Adult Literature

Abrahamson, Jane. "Still Playing It Safe: Restricted Realism in Teen Novels." *School Library Journal* 22 (May 1976): 38–39.

Abrahamson, Richard F. "Collected Wisdom: The Best Articles Ever Written on Young Adult Literature and Teen Reading." *English Journal* 86 (March 1997): 50–54.

"Adolescent Literature, Adolescent Reading, and the English Class." *Arizona English Bulletin* 14 (April 1972): entire issue.

"Adolescent Literature Revisited after Four Years." *Arizona English Bulletin* 18 (April 1976): entire issue.

Alexander, Lloyd. "Fools, Heroes, and Jackasses." *School Library Journal* 42 (March 1996): 114–116.

Alm, Richard C. "Goose Flesh, and Glimpses of Glory." *English Journal* (42 April 1963): 262–268.

Anderson, Philip M., and Mitchell Katcher. "YA Literature as Cannon Fodder." *ALAN Review* 20 (Fall 1992): 35–38.

Angel, Ann. "The Voices of Cultural Assimilation in Current Young Adult Novels." *ALAN Review* 30 (Winter 2003): 52–55.

Aronson, Marc. "The Betrayal of Teenagers: How Book Awards Fail America's Most Important Readers." *School Library Journal* 42 (March 1996): 23–25.

Aronson, Marc. "The Myths of Teenage Readers." *Publishing Research Quarterly* 16 (Fall 2000): 4–9.

Breen, Karen, Ellen Fader, Kathleen Odean, and Zena Sutherland. "One Hundred Books That Shaped the Century." *School Library Journal* 46 (January 2000): 50–58.

Broderick, Dorothy. "How to Write a Fiction Annotation." *Voice of Youth Advocates* 15 (February 1993): 333.

Broderick, Dorothy. "Reviewing Young Adult Books: The VOYA Editor Speaks Out." *Publishing Research Quarterly* 8 (Spring 1882): 35–40.

Brubaker, James M. "'Are You There, Margaret? It's Me, God.' Religious Contexts in Recent Adolescent Fiction." *English Journal* 72 (September 1983): 82–86.

Burton, Dwight L. "Trailing Clouds of Boredom Do They Come." *English Journal* 51 (April 1962): 259–263.

Campbell, Patricia. "Perplexing Young Adult Books: A Retrospective." *Wilson Library Bulletin* 62 (April 1988): 20, 22, 24, 26. Campbell looks back on ten years of her YA column.

Campbell, Patricia. "The Sand in the Oyster: YA and OP." *Horn Book Magazine* 73 (September/October 1997): 543–548.

Carlsen, G. Robert. "Conflicting Assumptions in the Teaching of English." *English Journal* 49 (September 1960): 377–386.

Carlsen, G. Robert. "For Everything There Is a Season." *Top of the News* 21 (January 1965): 103–110. Stages in reading growth.

Carlsen, G. Robert. "Literature Is." *English Journal* 63 (February 1974): 23–27.

Carlsen, G. Robert. "Teaching Literature for the Adolescent: A Historical Perspective." *English Journal* 73 (November 1984): 28–30.

Cart, Michael. "Of Risk and Revelation: The Current State of Young Adult Literature." *Journal of Youth Services in Libraries* 8 (Winter 1995): 151–164.

Chambers, Aidan. "All of a Tremble to See His Danger." *Top of the News* 42 (Summer 1986): 405–422. The brilliant 1986 May Hill Arbuthnot lecture.

Chelton, Mary K. "Unrestricted Body Parts and Predictable Bliss." *Library Journal* 116 (July 1991): 44–49.

Corbett, Linda. "Not Wise the Thought—A Grave for Arthur." *ALAN Review* 21 (Fall 1993): 45–48.

Crowe, Chris. "The Problems with YA Literature." *English Journal* 90 (January 2001): 146–150.

Daniels, Cindy Lou. "Literary Theory and Young Adult Literature: The Open Frontier in Critical Studies." *ALAN Review* 33 (Winter 2006): 78–82.

Early, Margaret J. "Stages of Growth in Literature Appreciation." *English Journal* 49 (March 1960): 161–167. A major article.

Edwards, Margaret A. "A Time When It's Best to Read and Let Read." *Wilson Library Bulletin* 35 (September

1960): 43–47. Myths on buying books for young adults demolished.

Engdahl, Sylvia. "Do Teenage Novels Fill a Need?" *English Journal* 64 (February 1975): 48–52.

Ewers, Hans-Heins. "The Limits of Literary Criticism of Children's and Young Adult Literature." *Lion and the Unicorn* 19 (1995): 77–94.

Fitzgerald, Frances. "The Influence of Anxiety: What's the Problem with Young Adult Novels?" *Harpers* 307 (September 2004): 62–63, 66–70.

Freedom, Russell. "Bring 'em Back Alive. Writing History and Biography for Young Adults." *School Library Journal* 40 (March 1994): 139–141.

Gale, David. "The Business of Books." *School Library Journal* 42 (July 1996): 18–21. How publishers take a YA manuscript and turn it into a book.

Garfield, Leon. "Historical Fiction for Our Global Times." *Horn Book Magazine* 64 (November/December 1988): 736–742.

Gauch, Patricia. "Good Stuff in Adolescent Fiction." *Top of the News* 40 (Winter 1984): 125–129.

Glasgow, Jacqueline N. "Reconciling Memories of Internment Camp Experiences During WWII I in Children's and Young Adult Literature." *ALAN Review* 29 (Fall 2002): 41–45.

Hamilton, Virginia. "Everything of Value: Moral Realism in the Literature of Children." *Journal of Youth Services in Libraries* 6 (Summer 1993): 363–367.

Hentoff, Nat. "Fiction for Teen-Agers." *Wilson Library Bulletin* 43 (November 1968): 261–264. On the shortcomings of YA fiction.

Hentoff, Nat. "Tell It as It Is." *New York Times Book Review*, May 7, 1967, pp. 3, 51.

Hinton, S. E. "Teen-Agers Are for Real." *New York Times Book Review*, August 27, 1967, pp. 28–29. Brief and excellent.

Hipple, Ted, and Amy B. Maupin. "What's Good about the Best?" *English Journal* 90 (January 2001): 40–42.

Hipps, G. Melvin. "Adolescent Literature: Once More to the Defense." *Virginia English Bulletin* 23 (Spring 1973): 44–50. Thirty-plus years old and still one of the best rationales for adolescent literature.

Holindale, Peter. "The Adolescent Literature of Ideas." *Children's Literature in Education* 26 (March 1995): 83–95.

Hunt, Caroline. "Young Adult Literature Evades the Theorists." *Children's Literature Association Quarterly* 21 (Spring 1996): 4–11.

"Is Adolescent Literature Worth Studying?" *Connecticut English Journal* 10 (Fall 1978). Two opposing positions— Robert P. Scaramella, "Con: At the Risk of Seeming Stuffy," pp. 57–58 and Robert C. Small, Jr., "Pro Means and Ends," pp. 59–63.

Janeczko, Paul. "Seven Myths about Adolescent Literature." *Arizona English Bulletin* 18 (April 1976): 11–12.

Kaye, Marilyn. "In Defense of Formula Fiction, Or, They Don't Write Schlock the Way They Used To." *Top of the News* 37 (Fall 1980): 87–90.

Knickerbocker, Joan L., and James Rycik, "Growing into Literature: Adolescents' Literary Interpretation and Appreciation." *Journal of Adolescent and Adult Literacy* 46 (November 2002): 196–208.

Kraus, W. Keith. "Cinderella in Trouble: Still Dreaming and Losing." *School Library Journal* 21 (January 1975): 18–22. Pregnancy in YA novels, from Felsen's *Two and the Town* (1952) to Neufeld's *For All the Wrong Reasons* (1973).

Lenz, Millicent. "Varieties of Loneliness: Alienation in Contemporary Young People's Fiction." *Journal of Popular Culture* 13 (Spring 1980): 672–688.

"Living with Adolescent Literature." *Connecticut English Journal* 12 (Fall 1980): entire issue.

McLeod, Anne Scott. "Writing Backward: Modern Novels in Historical Fiction." *Horn Book Magazine* 74 (January/February 1998): 26–33.

Martinec, Barbara. "Popular—But Not Just a Part of the Crowd: Implications of Formula Fiction for Teenagers." *English Journal* 60 (March 1971): 339–344.

Matthews, Dorothy. "Writing about Adolescent Literature: Current Approaches and Future Directions." *Arizona English Bulletin* 18 (April 1976): 216–219.

McDowell, Myles. "Fiction for Children and Adults: Some Essential Differences." *Children's Literature in Education* 4 (March 1973): 48–63.

Meek, Margaret. "Prologomena for a Study of Children's Literature, or Guess What's in My Head," in *Approaches to Research in Children's Literature*, ed. Michael Benton. University of Southampton, 1980, pp. 29–39.

Meltzer, Milton. "Where Do All the Prizes Go? The Case for Nonfiction." *Horn Book Magazine* 52 (February 1976): 17–23.

Merla, Patrick. "'What Is Real?' Asked the Rabbit One Day." *Saturday Review* 55 (November 4, 1972): 43–49. The rise of YA realism and adult fantasy.

Mertz, Maia Pank, and David A. England. "The Legitimacy of American Adolescent Fiction." *School Library Journal* 30 (October 1983): 119–123,

Myracle, Lauren. "Molding the Minds of the Young: The History of Bibliotherapy as Applied to Children and Adolescents." *ALAN Review* 22 (Winter 1995): 36–40.

Nicholson, George. "The Young Adult Novel: History and Development." *CBC Features* 47 (Fall Winter 1994). Worth the search.

Nixon, Julia H., and Robert C. Small, Jr. "Christianity in American Adolescent Realistic Fiction from 1845 to 1981," *ALAN Review* 12 (Spring 1985): 9–12, 53.

Noble, Susanne. "'Why Don't We Ever Read Anything Happy?' YA Literature and the Optimistic Ending." *ALAN Review* 26 (Fall 1998): 46–50.

Patterson, Emma L. "The Junior Novels and How They Grew." *English Journal* 45 (October 1956): 381–387, 405.

Peck, Richard. "Huck Finns of Both Sexes: Protagonists and Peer Leaders in Young Adult Books." *Horn Book Magazine* 69 (September/October 1993): 554–558.

Peck, Richard. "In the Country of Teenage Fiction." *American Libraries* 4 (April 1973): 204–207.

Peck, Richard. "Some Thoughts on Adolescent Literature." *News from ALAN* 3 (September/October 1975): 4–7.

Petitt, Dorothy. "The Junior Novel in the Classroom." *English Journal* 52 (October 1963): 512–520.

Pierce, Tamora. "Fantasy: Why Kids Read It, Why Kids Need It." *School Library Journal* 39 (October 1993): 10–14.

Poe, Elizabeth Ann, Barbara G. Samuels, and Betty Carter. "Twenty-Five Years of Research in Young Adult Literature: Past Perspectives and Future Directives." *Journal of Youth Services in Libraries* 28 (November 1981): 25–28.

Probst, Robert. "Reader Response Theory and the Problem of Meaning." *Publishing Research Quarterly* 8 (Spring 1992): 64–73.

Reed, W. Michael, and Jeanne M. Gerlach. "Literary Merit and the Adolescent Novel." *ALAN Review* 21 (Fall 1993): 51–56.

Reid, Suzanne, and Sharon Stringer. "Ethical Dilemmas in Teaching Problem Novels: The Psychological Impact of Troubling YA Literature on Adolescent Readers in the Classroom." *ALAN Review* 24 (Winter 1997): 16–18.

Root, Sheldon L. "The New Realism—Some Personal Reflections." *Language Arts* 54 (January 1977): 19–24.

Ross, Catherine Sheldrick. "Young Adult Realism: Conventions, Narrators, and Readers." *Library Quarterly* 55 (April 1985): 174–191.

Roxburgh, Stephen. "The Art of the Young Adult Novel." *ALAN Review* 32 (Winter 2005): 4–10.

Salvner, Gary M. "Lessons and Lives: Why Young Adult Literature Matters." *ALAN Review* 28 (Spring/Summer 2001): 9–13.

Silver, Linda R. "Criticism, Reviewing, and the Library Review Media." *Top of the News* 35 (Winter 1979): 123–130. The entire issue on reviewing YA books is fine, particularly "What Makes a Good Review? Ten Experts Speak" (pp. 146–152) and Patty Campbell's "Only Puddings Like the Kiss of Death" (pp. 161–162).

Small, Robert C., Jr. "The Literary Value of the Young Adult Novel." *Journal of Youth Services in Libraries* 5 (Spring 1992): 277–285.

Sutton, Roger. "The Critical Myth: Realistic YA Novels." *School Library Journal* 29 (November 1982): 33–35.

Thacker, Deborah. "Disdain or Ignorance? Literary Theory and the Absence of Children's Literature." *Lion and the Unicorn* 24 (January 2000): 1–17.

Townsend, John Rowe. "Didacticism in Modern Dress." *Horn Book Magazine* 43 (April 1967): 159–164. Townsend argues that nineteenth-century didacticism is remarkably like didacticism in modern YA novels.

Townsend, John Rowe. "Standards of Criticism for Children's Literature." *Top of the News* 27 (June 1971): 383–387.

Wilson, David E. "The Open Library: YA Books for Gay Teens." *English Journal* 73 (November 1984): 60–63.

Using Young Adult Literature in Libraries and Classrooms

Abrahamson, Richard, and Eleanor Tyson. "What Every English Teacher Should Know about Free Reading." *ALAN Review* 14 (Fall 1986): 54–58, 69.

Adams, Lauren. "Disorderly Fiction." *Horn Book Magazine* 78 (September/October 2002): 521–528.

Alexander, Lloyd. "Seeing with the Third Eye." *English Journal* 63 (May 1974): 35–40.

Anderson, Laurie Halse. "Loving the Young Adult Reader Even When You Want to Strangle Him (or Her)!" *ALAN Review* 32 (Winter 2005): 53–58.

Appleby, Bruce C., and John W. Conner. "Well, What Did You Think of It?" *English Journal* 54 (October 1965): 606–612.

Barker, Clive. "Fearful Symmetry: The Art of Fantasy." *ALAN Review* 32 (Winter 2005): 26–31.

Broderick, Dorothy. "Serving Young Adults: Why Do We Do What We Do?" *Voice of Youth Advocates* 12 (October 1989): 203–206.

Bushman, John. "The Reading/Writing Connection: The Role of Young Adult Literature." *ALAN Review* 20 (Fall 1992): 412–46.

Bushman, John. "Young Adult Literature in the Classroom— Or Is It?" *English Journal* 86 (March 1997): 35–40.

Bushman, John, and Shelley McNerny. "Moral Choices: Building a Bridge between YA Literature and Life." *ALAN Review* 32 (Fall 2004): 61–67.

Campbell, Patricia. "Prizes and Paradoxes." *Horn Book Magazine* 79 (July/August 2003): 501–505.

Carico, Kathleen M. "Professional Journal Articles and the Novels They Illuminate: A Resource for YA Courses." *ALAN Review* 29 (Fall 2002): 62–66.

Carroll, Pamela Sissi. "Today's Teens, Their Problems, and Their Literature: Revisiting G. Robert Carlsen's *Books and the Teenage Reader* Thirty Years Later." *English Journal* 86 (March 1997): 25–34.

Carter, Betty. "Adult Books for Young Adults." *English Journal* 86 (March 1997): 63–68.

Carter, Linda Purdy. "Addressing the Needs of Reluctant Readers through Sports Literature." *Clearing House* 71 (May/June 1998): 309–311.

Chelton, Mary K. "Booktalking: You Can Do It." *School Library Journal* 22 (April 1976): 39–43.

Donelson, Ken. "Free Reading: Another View." *Journal of Reading* 12 (April 1969): 454–458, 606, 611.

Donelson, Ken, and Beverly Haley. "Adolescent Literature: You Mean That Garbage Written for Kids Who Can't Read?" *Clearing House* 47 (March 1973): 440–443.

Franzak, Judith, and Elizabeth Noll. "Monstrous Acts: Problematizing Violence in Young Adult Literature." *Journal of Adolescent and Adult Literacy* 49 (May 2006): 662–672.

George, Marshall A. "Furthering the Cause: The Study and Teaching of Young Adult Literature." *English Education* 37 (October 2004): 80–84.

Gibbons, Laurel, Jennifer S. Dail, and B. Joyce Stallworth. "Young Adult Literature in the English Curriculum Today: Classroom Teachers Speak Out." *ALAN Review* 33 (Summer 2006): 53–61.

Glenn, Wendy. "True Confessions of a Hypocrite: Failing to Make the Most of Young Adult Literature." *California English* 8 (September 2002): 8–10.

Goodson, F. Todd. "A Pinch of Tobacco and a Drop of Urine: Using YA Literature to Examine Local Culture." *ALAN Review* 32 (Fall 2004): 50–58.

Hale, Lisa A., and Chris Crowe. "'I Hate Reading If I Don't Have To': Results from a Longitudinal Study of High

School Students' Reading Interests." *ALAN Review* 28 (Spring/Summer 2001): 49–58.

Harmon, Janis M., and Monica C. Gonzales. "Are These Parents for Real? Students' Views of Parents in Realistic and Historical Fiction." *ALAN Review* 30 (Winter 2003): 57–62.

Hautman, Pete. "How to Win a National Book Award: A Primer." *ALAN Review* 32 (Summer 2005): 24–28.

Hipple, Ted, Lisa Scherff, Jennifer Claiborne, Amy Cirici Sullins. "Teaching the Mock Printz Novels." *English Journal* 93 (January 2004): 69–74.

Hopper, Rosemary. "The Good, the Bad, and the Ugly: Teachers' Perceptions of Quality in Fiction for Adolescent Readers." *English in Education* 40 (Summer 2006): 55–70.

Janeczko, Paul. "Seven Myths about Teaching Poetry, Or, How I Stopped Chasing Foul Balls." *ALAN Review* 14 (Spring 1987): 13–16.

Johannessen, Larry. "Young Adult Literature and the Vietnam War." *English Journal* 82 (September 1993): 43–49.

LaFaye, Alexandria. "It's a Teen Thing: The Importance of Young Adult Literature in Helping Young Adults to Become Lifelong Readers." *California English* 8 (September 2002): 24–26.

Lesesne, Teri S. "Developing Lifetime Readers: Suggestions from Fifty Years of Research." *English Journal* 80 (October 1991): 61–64.

Ley, Terry C. "Getting Kids into Books: The Importance of Individualized Reading." *Media and Methods* 15 (July 1979): 22–26.

Nelms, Ben F. "Reading for Pleasure in Junior High School." *English Journal* 55 (September 1966): 676–681.

Oriard, Michael. "From Jane Allen to Water Dance: A Brief History of the Feminist Sports Novel." *Modern Fiction Studies* 32 (Spring 1987): 9–20.

Pace, Barbara G. "Resistance and Response: Deconstructing Community Standards in a Literature Class." *Journal of Adolescent and Adult Literacy* 46 (February 2003): 408–412.

Peck, Richard. "In the Beginning." *Horn Book Magazine* 82 (September/October 2006): 505–508.

Peck, Richard. "Ten Questions to Ask about a Novel." *ALAN Newsletter* 5 (Spring 1978): 1.

Proukou, Katherine Kim. "Young Adult Literature: Rite of Passage or Rite of Its Own." *ALAN Review* 32 (Summer 2005): 62–68.

Ritter, John H. "Are YA Novelists Morally Obligated to Offer Their Readers Hope?" *ALAN Review* 30 (Spring 2003): 8–13.

Ross, Catherine Sheldrick. "If They Read Nancy Drew, So What? Series Books Readers Talk Back." *Libraries and Information Science Research* 17 (Summer 1995): 201–236.

Santoli, Susan P., and Mary Elaine Wagner. "Promoting Young Adult Literature: The Other 'Real' Literature." *American Secondary Education* 33 (Fall 2004): 65–75.

Scharf, Peter, "Moral Development and Literature for Adolescents." *Top of the News* 33 (Winter 1997): 131–136. Kohlberg's six stages of moral judgment applied to YA books.

Seely, Debra. "You Can't Change History, Can You?" *ALAN Review* 31 (Summer 2004): 20–24.

Sprague, Marsha M., and Lori Risher. "Using Fantasy Literature to Explore Gender Issues." *ALAN Review* 29 (Winter 2002): 39–42.

Stotsky, Sandra. "Is the Holocaust the Chief Contribution of the Jewish People to World Civilization and History? A Survey of Leading Literature Anthologies and Reading Instructional Textbooks." *English Journal* 85 (February 1996): 52–59.

Sullivan, Ed. "Going All the Way: First-Time Sexual Experiences of Teens in Fiction." *Voice of Youth Advocates* 26 (February 2004): 461–463.

Thomas, Melissa. "Teaching Fantasy: Overcoming the Stigma of Fluff." *English Journal* 92 (May 2003): 60–66.

Tuccillo, Diane P. "Leading Them to Books—for Life." *Publishing Research Quarterly* 8 (Spring 1992): 14–22.

Acknowledgments

(p. 3) Photo by A. P. Nilsen, courtesy of Elaine Meyers, Phoenix Public Library.

(p. 5) Photo by A. P. Nilsen. Statement courtesy of Michael Cart.

(p. 6) From THE ABSOLUTELY TRUE DIARY OF A PART-TIME INDIAN by Sherman Alexie. Copyright © 2007 by Sherman Alexie. Illustrations copyright © by Ellen Forney. By permission of LITTLE, BROWN & COMPANY.

(p. 8) Courtesy of Penguin Group.

(p. 15) Courtesy of permission of Farrar, Straus and Giroux.

(p. 33) Photo by A. P. Nilsen.

(p. 46) Photo by A. P. Nilsen.

(p. 48) Photo by A. P. Nilsen, courtesy of Ken Donelson.

(p. 53) Photo courtesy of the Tempe Historical Museum.

(p. 64) Photo courtesy of A. P. Nilsen.

(p. 68) Photo by A. P. Nilsen, courtesy of VOYA.

(p. 72) Photo by James Patrick Langlands, courtesy of Random House Children's Books.

(p. 74) Photo by Sigrid Estrada, courtesy of Judy Blume.

(p. 82) Photo by Luiz Calado.

(p. 86) Photo by A. P. Nilsen.

(p. 91) Photo by A. P. Nilsen.

(p. 98) Photo by A. P. Nilsen.

(pp. 98–99) Statement courtesy of Cynthia and Greg Leitich Smith.

(p. 112) Photo by Kevin Hearne, Desert Ridge High School.

(p. 123) Photo by A. P. Nilsen; artwork by ASU students.

(p. 137) Photo by Tillman Crane.

(p. 142) Photo by A. P. Nilsen.

(p. 143) Photo by A. P. Nilsen.

(p. 144) Photo by Bob Henderson, Henderson Photography, Inc.

(p. 151) Photo by A. P. Nilsen, courtesy of ASU young adult literature students.

(p. 153) Photo by Michael Nye; photo and statement courtesy of Naomi Shihab Nye.

(p. 158) Photo and statement courtesy of Aaron Levy.

(p. 164) Photo courtesy of Paul Zindel.

(p. 165) Photo by A. P. Nilsen.

(p. 176) Photo by A. P. Nilsen. Statement courtesy of Stefanie Craig.

(p. 178) Photo by A. P. Nilsen.

(p. 187) Photo by Tim Keating, courtesy of Random House.

(p. 191) Printed with the permission of the American Library Association.

(p. 195) Photo by A. P. Nilsen.

(p. 197) Photo by Sandy Geis.

(p. 207) Photo by Michael Moucette, courtesy of Random House Children's Books.

(p. 222) Photo by Marian Wood Kolisch.

(p. 224) Photo by Kelvin Nilsen, courtesy of Kami Nilsen.

(p. 225) Photo by Irene Graham.

(p. 227) Photo by A. P. Nilsen.

(p. 228) Photo by A. P. Nilsen.

(p. 239) Photo by Andrew Brilliant, courtesy of Clarion Books.

(p. 251) Photo by A. P. Nilsen.

(p. 257) Photo by Constance Myers.

(p. 269) Photo by A. P. Nilsen.

(p. 275) Courtesy of Penguin Group.

(p. 279) Photo by A. P. Nilsen.

(p. 281) Photo by A. P. Nilsen; photo and statement courtesy of James Cross Giblin.

(p. 282) Photo by A. P. Nilsen.

(p. 303) Photo by A. P. Nilsen.

(p. 309) Photo by A. P. Nilsen.

(p. 331) Photo by Zoe Kamitses, courtesy of M. E. Kerr.

(p. 335) Photo by A. P. Nilsen.

(p. 341) Photos by A. P. Nilsen.

(p. 342) Photo by A. P. Nilsen, courtesy of Mary J. Wong.

(p. 346) Photo by Cheron Bayna. Statement copyright © 2007 by Pat Mora. All rights reserved. Reprinted by permission of Curtis Brown, Ltd.

(p. 360) Photos by A. P. Nilsen.

(pp. 368–369) "Ten Questions" courtesy of Richard Peck.

(p. 371) Courtesy of Young Adult Library Services Association.

(p. 375) Courtesy of Vivian Vande Velde.

(p. 376) Photo by A. P. Nilsen.

(p. 377) Photo by A. P. Nilsen. Statement courtesy of Kimberly Willis Holt.

(p. 393) Photo by A. P. Nilsen.

(p. 414) Photograph of Nancy Garden © Sandra Scott. Used with permission of Farrar, Straus and Giroux.

(p. 421) Photo by Joyce Tenneson, courtesy of Penguin. Statement courtesy of Laurie Halse Anderson.

(p. 425) Photo by A. P. Nilsen, courtesy of Erika Watt and American Library Association.

Authors, Critics, and Commentators Index

Bott, C.J., 93, 94
Box, Edgar (né Gore Vidal), 201
Boyd, Herb, 255
Boylston, Helen, 43, 59
Boyne, John, 271
Brackett, Leigh, 236
Bradbury, Ray, 155, 216, 236, 237,
    420, 425
Braddy, Nella, 160
Bradford, Richard, 66
Bradley, Kimberly Brubaker, 125
Bradley, Marion Zimmer, 230, 232
Branagh, Kenneth, 269
Brancato, Robin, 380
Branch, E. Douglas, 47
Brandt, Anthony, 184
Brashares, Ann, 22, 40, 142, 143,
    328, 343
Brashler, William, 199
Breck, Vivian, 62
Bredesen, Phil, 87
Bredsdorff, Bodil, 100
Brennan, William J., Jr., 404, 406,
    409, 410, 425
Brenner, Robin, 172
Bridgers, Sue Ellen, 26, 67, 134
Brimmer, Larry Dane, 255
Broderick, Dorothy, 73, 112, 336
Brokaw, Tom, 297
Brontë, Emily, 166
Brooks, Bruce, 24, 25, 29, 135, 136
Brooks, Charles, 172
Brooks, Hindi, 156
Brooks, Kevin, 80, 170, 206
Brooks, Laurie, 165
Brooks, Martha, 22, 138
Brooks, Mel, 233
Brooks, Noah, 42
Brown, Claude, 66, 282, 399
Brown, Dan, 97, 314
Brown, Dee, 280
Brown, Jeffrey, 74
Browne, Des, 265
Browning, Robert, 152
Bruchac, Joseph, 209, 256, 309
Brunvand, Jan Harold, 166
Brynie, Faith Hickman, 301
Bugbee, Emma, 43
Bugliosi, Vincent, 299
Buck, Pearl, 61
Bunting, Eve, 209
Bunyan, John, 41, 326
Burciaga, José Antonio, 148
Burger, Warren E., 405, 410
Burke, Jim, 108, 109
Burnett, Frances Hodgson, 132
Burns, Charles, 232
Burns, Loree Griffin, 280
Burns, Olive Ann, 25, 27, 31, 141

Burns, Tyrrell, 118
Burress, Lee, 392, 393, 419
Burroughs, Edgar Rice., 51
Burton, Dwight L., 63, 64, 363
Butcher, Nancy, 232
Butler, Francelia, 71
Byars, Betsy, 327
Byatt, A.S., 221

Cabot, Meg, 143
Cadier, Florence, 302
Cadnum, Michael, 247
Calabro, Marian, 259
Caletti, Deb, 117, 127
Callahan, John, 298
Callahan, Stephen, 293
Cameron, Ann, 350
Cameron, Steve, 301
Campanella, Roy, 63
Campbell, Colin, 360, 387
Campbell, Joseph, 98, 135, 324
Campbell, Patty, 4, 72, 73, 111, 133,
    301, 332
Canby, Henry Seidel, 188
Caney, Steven, 280
Canfield, Jack, 301
Caniff, Milton, 176
Capote, Truman, 283
Card, Orson Scott, 19, 25, 27, 144,
    211, 231, 332, 367
Carle, Eric, 290
Carlsen, G. Robert, 60, 70, 113
Carlson, Lori M., 148, 157
Carlyle, Thomas, 84
Carnegie, Andrew, 49
Carr, John Dickson, 204
Carroll, Pamela S., 71, 358
Carroll, Rebecca, 295
Carson, John F., 43, 193
Cart, Michael, 4, 5, 82, 124, 126,
    225, 232, 358, 383
Carter, Alden R., 194
Carter, Betty, 278
Carter, James Bucky, 78
Carter, Julia, 51
Carter, Peter, 260
Carus, Marianne, 383
Carvel, Marlene, 150
Carver, Raymond, 356, 365
Casals, Pablo, 109
Cassidy, Anne, 127
Castellucci, Cecil, 141
Castlemon, Harry (né Charles Austin
    Fosdick), 42
Cather, Willa, 260, 297, 326
Cavanna, Betty, 59, 63
Cayrol, Jean, 268
Certain, C.C., 56
Chabon, Michael, 177, 220

Chaiet, Donna, 301
Chaltain, Sam, 422
Chamberlain, Wilt, 299
Chambers, Aidan, 22, 134, 140, 264
Chan, Gillian, 220
Chang, Ina, 297
Chandler, Raymond, 201
Charney, Maurice, 172
Chatwin, Bruce, 293
Chelton, Mary K., 73, 336, 339
Chen, Steve, 84
Cheripko, Jan, 125
Chesler, Ellen, 297
Chevalier, Tracy, 249
Childress, Alice, 26, 29, 67, 128, 134,
    383, 408
Chin, Frank, 106
Chomsky, Noam, 425
Christenbury, Leila, 71
Christie, Agatha, 201, 202, 315
Chute, Marchette, 43
Cisneros, Sandra, 19, 25, 27, 108,
    191, 332
Citrin, Michael, 205
Clarke, Arthur C., 237, 238
Clayton, John Bell, 364
Cleary, Beverly, 13, 328
Cleaver, Eldridge, 67, 128, 282, 408
Clement-Davies, David, 229
Clements, Bruce, 66, 249, 259
Clifton, Lucille, 157
Cline, Ruth, 70
Clinton, Catherine, 156
Cluley, Graham, 87
Cofer, Judith Ortiz, 333
Cohn, Rachel, 138
Cole, Brock, 16, 23–25
Colfer, Eoin, 220
Collier, Christopher, 244, 245, 250
Collier, James Lincoln, 250
Collins, Billy, 148
Coman, Carolyn, 22, 126, 138
Commire, Anne, 130
Comstock, Anthony, 391, 396
Conford, Ellen, 328
Cook, Daniel, 84
Cook, Luella, 153, 155
Coolidge, Susan (née Sarah Chauncey
    Woolsey), 40, 42
Cooney, Caroline, 23, 315
Cooper, Michael L., 282, 297
Coover, Robert, 241
Coppola, Francis Ford, 8, 374
Corcoran, Barbara, 420
Cormier, Robert, 16, 22, 24, 25, 27,
    31, 37, 65, 70, 72, 94, 103, 116,
    124, 134, 135, 144, 164, 205, 209,
    289, 327, 332, 341, 367, 381, 383,
    387, 389, 399, 400

Hillerman, Tony, 201, 203
Hillesum, Etty, 267
Hilton, Paris, 90
Hinds, Gareth, 209
Hinton, Kaa Vonia, 108
Hinton, S.E., 5, 8, 32, 70, 72, 111, 315, 316, 348, 372, 374, 400
Hirschfelder, Arlene, 290
Hirth, Paul, 277, 278
Hiscock, Susan, 184
Hitchcock, Alfred, 210
Hobbs, Valerie, 272
Hobbs, Will, 16, 164, 186, 316
Hockensmith, Steve, 204
Hoffman, Alice, 120, 247
Holbrook, Sara, 150
Holland, Isabelle, 67
Holland, Suzann, 421
Hollyer, Belinda, 383
Holt, Kimberly Willis, 23, 123, 141, 376, 377
Homer, 326
Hopper, Rosemary, 17
Hornby, Nick, 117, 194
Hornig, Doug, 199
Horowitz, Anthony, 209
Horvath, Polly, 21, 142, 171, 332
Hosic, James Fleming, 54
Hosseini, Khaled, 130
Houston, James D., 270
Houston, Jeanne Wakatsuki, 270
Houston, Julian, 255
Howe, Neil, 36
Howe, Norma, 133
Hubert, Jennifer, 380
Hudson, Lane, 84
Hughes, Dean, 133
Hughes, Jacque, 168
Hughes, Langston, 408
Hughes, Monica, 382
Hunt, Clara Whitehill, 51
Hunt, Irene, 66, 246
Hunt, Lenore, 189
Hunter, Erin, 229
Hurley, Chad, 84
Huxley, Aldous, 241, 381, 389, 396, 400
Hwang, David Henry, 106
Hylton, Jaime, 137

Ibsen, Henrik, 381, 388
Immell, Myra H., 301
Inge, M. Thomas, 290
Ireland, G.O., 60
Irving, Washington, 53
Itkin, Jason A., 85

Jackson, Brooks, 79
Jackson, Donna M., 288

Jackson, Joseph Henry, 425
Jackson, Shirley, 400
Jackson, Helen Hunt, 54
Jackson, Richard, 361
James, Betsy, 220
James, P.D., 201, 233
Jamieson, Kathleen Hall, 79
Janeczko, Paul B., 152, 155, 379
Jansen, Hanna, 100
Jefferson, Thomas, 425
Jenkins, A.M., 22, 122
Jenkins, Christine A., 358, 414
Jenkinson, David, 394
Jenkinson, Edward B., 392, 401, 402
Jenks, Tom, 365
Jennings, Frank G., 64
Jens, Inge, 264
Jimenez, Francisco, 129
Jinks, Catherine, 80
Jocelyn, Marthe, 246
Johannessen, Larry R., 273
Johnson, A.E., 66
Johnson, Angela, 21, 28
Johnson, Dolores, 296
Johnson, Lyndon, 425
Johnson, Nancy J., 374
Johnson, Scott, 23
Johnson, Steven, 78
Johnston, Julie, 127
Johnston, Mary, 54
Johnson, Maureen, 121
Johnston, Tony, 129
Jones, Diana Wynne, 24, 211, 219, 221, 226, 230, 233
Jones, G.M., 391
Jones, Lloyd, 129
Jones, Tim, 199
Jordan, Alice M., 51
Jordan, Jennifer, 192
Joyce, James, 63, 403
Jung, Carl, 324
Juster, Norton, 219

Kadohata, Cynthia, 128, 272, 282, 332, 333, 360
Kahn, Roger, 199
Kakutani, Michiko, 298
Kaminsky, Stuart, 201
Karim, Jawed, 84
Karolides, Nicholas J., 419
Karr, Kathleen, 138, 194
Karres, Erika V. Shearin, 302
Kean, John M., 419
Keats, Ezra Jack, 326
Keehn, Sally M., 219
Kegler, Stanley B., 62
Keillor, Garrison, 156, 169
Keller, Michelle, 96
Kellerman, Faye, 201

Kelley, Kitty, 297
Kelly, David, 299
Kelly, Patricia, 71
Kelly, Tim, 160
Kelly, Walt, 177
Kemprecos, Paul, 40
Keneally, Thomas, 268
Kennedy, Anthony M., 422
Kennedy, Bobby, 305
Kephart, Beth, 45
Keresey, Gayle, 399
Kerley, Barbara, 157
Kerr, M.E., 16, 23, 37, 70, 71, 133, 134, 135, 141, 142, 164, 323, 331, 332, 379, 381, 402
Ketchum, Liza, 256
Key, Joshua, 266
Khurshid, Ali, 84
Kindl, Patrice, 219
King, Larry, 113
King, Laurie R., 204
King, Stephen, 213, 221, 314
Kingston, Maxine Hong, 106
Kipling, Rudyard, 54
Kirchner, Ann, 271
Kishimoto, Masashi, 179
Kisilinsky, Harriet, 96
Kite, William, 365, 391
Klass, David, 194, 232, 240
Klause, Annette Curtis, 23, 24, 30, 31, 144, 211, 212
Klausner, Harriet, 84
Klein, Norma, 425
Kleinfield, N.R., 415
Knowles, John, 66, 328
Knox, Elizabeth, 21, 240
Koertge, Ron, 24, 121, 125, 149
Koja, Kathe, 125, 132
Koontz, Dean, 314
Koop, C. Everett, 292
Korman, Gordon, 132, 141, 171, 379
Kostick, Conor, 182, 220
Krakauer, Jon, 190, 191
Kratzke, Peter, K., 365
Kreit, Alex, 422
Kress, Nancy, 232
Krisher, Trudy, 83, 246
Krishnaswami, Uma, 333
Kunzel, Bonnie, 358
Kuralt, Charles, 293

L'Amour, Louis, 258
L'Engle, Madeleine, 15, 63, 134, 236
LaBrant, Lou, 55, 60
LaFarge, Oliver, 408
LaHaye, Beverly, 411
Lamb, Chris, 172
Landy, Derek, 210
Lane, Dakota, 138

Subject Index

Title Index

Abbreviations for publishers have been used in this index, as follows: American Library Association = ALA; Coward McCann = Coward; Farrar, Straus and Giroux = Farrar; Harcourt Brace, Jovanovich = Harcourt; HarperCollins = Harper; Houghton Mifflin = Houghton; International Reading Association = IRA; Little, Brown = Little; Lothrop, Lee, and Shepard = Lothrop; National Council of Teachers of English = NCTE; Penguin/Putnam = Penguin; Random House = Random; and Simon & Schuster = S&S. Nat. has also been used for National and U. for University.

Changeover, A Supernatural Romance, The by Margaret Mahy (Macmillan, 1984), 25

Chapters: My Growth as a Writer by Lois Duncan (Little, 1982), 207

Charles A. Lindbergh, A Human Hero by James Cross Giblin (Clarion, 1997), 281, 306

Charlotte's Web by E. B. White (Harper, 1951), 13, 34, 327

Charmed Life, A by Diana Wynne Jones (Greenwillow, 1977), 226

Chasing Redbird by Sharon Creech (Harper, 1997), 138

Chemical and Biological Warfare: The Cruelest Weapons by Lawrence Pringle (Enslow, 1993), 308

Cherokee Bat and the Goat Guys by Francesca Lia Block (Harper, 1992), 82

Chew on This: Everything You Don't Want to Know about Fast Food by Eric Schlosser and Charles Wilson (Houghton, 2006), 280

Chicken Soup for the Pet Lover's Soul: Stories about Pets as Teachers, Healers Heroes, and Friends by Jack Canfield (Health Communications, 1998), 301

Chicken Soup for the Teenage Soul: 101 Stories of Life, Love, and Learning, I and II by Jack Canfield (Health Communications, 1997, 1998), 301

Chicken Soup for the Woman's Soul: 101 Stories to Open the Hearts and Rekindle the Spirits of Women by Jack Canfield (Health Communications, 1996), 301

Chief, The by Robert Lipsyte (Harper, 1993), 197

Child Called It, A by Dave Pelzer (Tandem, 1999), 316

Child's War: World War II through the Eyes of Children, A by Kati David (Four Walls Eight Windows, 1990), 267

Childhood in America: An Eyewitness History by Catherine Reef (Facts on File, 2002), 309

Childhood's End by Arthur C. Clarke (Houghton, 1953), 237

Children of a Lesser God by Mark Medoff (Dramatists, 1980), 160

Children of Hurin, The by J. R. R. Tolkien, edited by Christopher Tolkien (Houghton, 2007), 229

Children of Llyr, The by Evangeline Walton (Ballantine, 1971), 230

Children of the Great Depression by Russell Freedman (Clarion, 2005), 305

Children of the River by Linda Crew (Delacorte, 1989), 129

Children of War by Roger Rosenblatt (Doubleday, 1983), 265

Children We Remember, The by Chana Byers Abells (Greenwillow, 1987), 268

Chinese Handcuffs by Chris Crutcher (Harper, 1989), 195

Chocolate War, The by Robert Cormier (Pantheon, 1974), 72, 94, 112, 113, 124, 134, 341, 359, 367, 368, 387, 399, 400, 419

Chosen, The by Chaim Potok (S&S, 1967), 66, 134, 349

Christmas Killer, The by Patricia Windsor (Scholastic, 1991), 206

Chronicles of Narnia, The by C. S. Lewis (Macmillan, 1950–1956), 97, 314, 316

Chronicles of Prydain (*The Book of Three, The Black Cauldron, The Castle of Llyr, Taran Wanderer,* and *The High King*) by Lloyd Alexander (Holt, 1964–1969), 223–224

Cinderellis and the Glass Hill by Gail Carson Levine (Harper, 2000), 44

Circuit, The: Stories from the Life of a Migrant Child by Francisco Jimenez (U. of New Mexico Press, 1997), 129

Circular Staircase, The by Mary Roberts Rinehart (Bobbs-Merrill, 1908), 201

City of the Beasts by Isabel Allende (Harper, 2002), 350

Clan of the Cave Bear by Jean M. Auel (Crown, 2001), 276

Claws by Will Weaver (Harper, 2003), 126

Clem's Chances by Sonia Levitin (Orchard, 2001), 260

Climb to Conquer: The Untold Story of World War II's 10th Mountain Division Ski Troops by Peter Shelton (Scribner, 2003), 266

Clockwork—Or All Wound Up by Philip Pullman (Scholastic, 1998), 23

Clouds from Both Sides by Julie Tullis (Sierra Club Books, 1987), 192

Cold Sassy Tree by Olive Ann Burns (Ticknor & Fields, 1984), 25, 27, 31, 141

Colibri by Ann Cameron (Farrar, 2003), 350

Color Purple, The by Alice Walker (Harcourt, 1982), 155, 399

Come a Stranger by Cynthia Voigt (Atheneum, 1986), 137

Comedy: A Geographic and Historical Guide, 2 Volumes edited by Maurice Charney (Praeger, 2005), 172

Comfort by Carolee Dean (Houghton, 2002), 127

Coming of Age: The Story of Our Century by Those Who've Lived It by Studs Terkel (New Press, 1995), 297

Companions of the Night by Vivian Vande Velde (Magic Carpet, 2002), 211

Confucius: The Golden Rule by Russell Freedman (Scholastic, 2002), 305

Connections edited by Donald R. Gallo (Delacorte, 1989), 365

Conscience and Courage: Rescuers of Jews in the Holocaust by Eva Fogelman (Anchor, 1994), 268

Contender, The by Robert Lipsyte (Harper, 1967), 5, 19, 70, 111, 136, 196, 197, 400

Convicts, The by Iain Lawrence (Delacorte, 2005), 190

Cool Salsa: Bilingual Poems on Growing Up Latino in the United States by Lori Carlson (Holt, 1994), 148

Copper Sun by Sharon Draper (S&S, 2006), 246

Coraline by Neil Gaiman (Harper, 2002), 211, 219

Corner of the Universe, A by Ann Martin (Scholastic, 2002), 116

Count on Us: American Women in the Military by Amy Nathan (Nat. Geographic, 2004), 288

Counterfeit Son by Elaine Marie Alphin (S&S, 2000), 206

Counting on Grace by Elizabeth Winthrop (Random, 2006), 246

Counting Stars by David Almond (Delacorte, 2002), 37

Coyote by Allen M. Steele (Ace, 2003), 232

Crackback by John Coy (Scholastic, 2005) 194

Cranes at Dusk by Hisako Matsubara (Doubleday, 1985), 328

Crash Club by Henry Gregor Felsen (1958), 43

Crazy '08: How a Cast of Crooks, Rogues, Boneheads, and Magnates Created the Greatest Year in Baseball History by Cait Murphy (Smithsonian, 2007), 199

Crazy Horse Electric Game, The by Chris Crutcher (Greenwillow, 1987), 2, 24, 31, 139, 195

Crazy Weather by Charles L. McNichols (1944), 258

Spike Lee: By Any Means Necessary by James Haskins (Walker, 1997), 306

Spirit Seeker by Joan Lowery Nixon (Delacorte, 1995), 206

Split Image by Mel Glenn (Harper, 2000), 150

Spoken Word Revolution (Slam, Hip Hop & the Poetry of a New Generation), The by Marc Smith and Mark Eleveld (Sourcebooks Trade, 2003), 151

Squared Circle, The by James Bennett (Scholastic, 1995), 196

Squashed by Joan Bauer (Delacorte, 1992), 102

Squire, His Knight, and His Lady, The by Gerald Morris (Houghton, 1999), 247

St. Elmo by Augusta Jane Evans Wilson (1867), 47

Stand Tall by Joan Bauer (Putnam, 2002), 327

Stay Strong: Simple Life Lessons for Teens by Terrie Williams (Scholastic, 2001), 301

Staying Fat for Sarah Byrnes by Chris Crutcher (Harper, 1993), 195

Staying Safe on Dates by Donna Chalet (Rosen, 1996), 301

Step from Heaven, A by An Na (Front Street, 2001), 22

Stepping Out with Grandma Mac by Nikki Grimes (Scholastic, 2001), 162

Steven Caney's Ultimate Building Book by Steven Caney (Running Press, 2006), 280

Stop the Train by Geraldine McCaughrean (Harper, 2001), 260

Storm in Summer, A by Rod Serling in *Great Television Plays*, Vol. 2, edited by Ned E. Hoopes and Patricia Neale Gordon (Dell, 1975), 160

Story of a Bad Boy, The by Thomas Bailey Aldrich (1870), 42

Story of a Girl by Sara Zarr (Little, 2007), 117

Story of Negro League Baseball, The by William Brashler (Ticknor & Fields, 1994), 199

Stotan by Chris Crutcher (Greenwillow, 1986), 195

Strange Affair of Adelaide Harris by Leon Garfield (Pantheon, 1971), 67, 252

Stranger in a Strange Land by Robert Heinlein (Putnam, 1961), 237

Stranger with My Face by Lois Duncan (Little, 1981), 25, 214

Straydog by Kathe Koja (Farrar, 2002), 132

Strays by Ron Koertge (Candlewick, 2007), 121

Strike by Barbara Corcoran (Atheneum, 1983), 420

Strike Three, You're Dead by R. D. Rosen (Walker, 1984), 201

String in the Harp, A by Nancy Bond (Atheneum, 1976), 67

String of Chances, A by Phyllis Reynolds Naylor (Atheneum, 1992), 134

Stuck in Neutral by Terry Trueman (Harper, 2000), 22, 117

Students' Right to Know, The by Lee Burress and Edward B. Jenkinson (NCTE, 1982), 392

Subtle Knife, The by Philip Pullman (Knopf, 1997), 16, 228

Suite Française by Irène Némirovsky (Knopf, 2007), 271

Summer of Fear by Lois Duncan (Little, 1976), 207, 213, 214

Summer of Kings, A by Han Nolan (Harcourt, 2006), 255

Summer to Die, A by Lois Lowry (Houghton, 1977), 121, 239

Summerland by Michael Chabon (Hyperion, 2002), 220

Sunburned Prayer, A by Marc Talbert (S&S, 1995), 134

Surrender by Sonya Hartnett (Candlewick, 2006), 21, 101, 117, 381

Surviving Hitler; A Boy in the Nazi Death Camps by Andrea Warren (Harper, 2001), 271

Surviving the Applewhites by Stephanie S. Tolan (Harper, 2002), 171

Survivor by Chuck Palahniuk (Norton, 1999), 316

Sweet Whispers, Brother Rush by Virginia Hamilton (Philomel, 1982), 25, 29

Sweet, Terrible, Glorious Year I Truly, Completely Lost It, The by Lisa Shanahan (Delacorte, 2007), 350

Swiftly Tilting Planet, A by Madeleine L'Engle (Farrar, 1978), 15

Swiftwater by Paul Annixter (né Howard A. Sturzel) (1950), 43, 69

"T" Is for Trespass by Sue Grafton (Putnam, 2007), 202

Tadpole by Ruth White (Farrar, 2003), 123

Taking of Room 114: A Hostage Drama in Poems, The by Mel Glenn (Dutton 1997), 150

Tales from Earthsea by Ursula K. Le Guin (Harcourt, 2001), 222

Talkin' about Bessie: The Story of Aviator Elizabeth Coleman by Nikki Grimes (Scholastic, 2002), 162

Talking to Dragons by Patricia C. Wrede (Tempo, 1985), 230

Tamar: A Novel of Espionage, Passion, and Betrayal by Mel Peet (Candlewick, 2007), 21

Tangerine by Edward Bloor (Harcourt, 1997), 315

Tangled Waters by Florence Crannell Means (1936), 42

Tantalyze by Cynthia Leitich Smith (Candlewick, 2007), 99, 212

Tarantula Scientist, The by Sy Montgomery (Houghton, 2004), 288

Tarzan of the Apes by Edgar Rice Burroughs (1914), 51

Taste of Salt: A Story of Modern Haiti by Frances Temple (Orchard, 1992), 350

Tasting the Sky: A Palestinian Childhood by Ibtisam Barakat (Farrar, 2007), 129, 269, 350

Teaching and Learning about Multicultural Literature: Students Reading Outside Their Culture in a Middle School Classroom by Janice Hartwick Dressel (IRA, 2003), 358

Teaching as a Subversive Activity by Neil Postman and Charles Weingartner (Delacorte, 1969), 70

Teaching Literature to Adolescents: Poetry by Stephen Dunning (Scott, Foresman, 1966), 154

Teacup Full of Roses by Sharon Bell Mathis (Viking, 1975), 128

Teahouse of the August Moon, The by John Patrick (Dramatists, 1953), 160

Teammates: A Portrait of a Friendship, The by David Halberstam (Hyperion, 2003), 196

Technically, It's Not My Fault: Concrete Poems by John Grandits (Clarion, 2004), 379

Teen Fathers Today by Ted Gottfried (Twenty-first Century, 2001), 301

Teen Pregnancy edited by Myra H. Immell (Gale, 2001), 301

Teen Reads Series edited by James Blasingame, Jr. (Greenwood, 2007), 358

Teen's Guide to Getting Published: Publishing for Profit, Recognition, and Academic Success, 2nd edition by Jessica Dunn and Danielle Dunn (Prufrock, 2006), 379